BASIC TEXTS IN COUNSELLING AND PSYCHOTHERAPY

Series editors: Arlene Vetere and Rudi Dallos

This series introduces readers to the theory and practice of counselling and psychotherapy across a wide range of topic areas. The books appeal to anyone wishing to use counselling and psychotherapeutic skills and are particularly relevant to workers in health, education, social work and related settings. The books are unusual in being rooted in psychodynamic and systemic ideas, yet being written at an accessible, readable and introductory level. Each text offers theoretical background and guidance for practice, with creative use of clinical examples.

Published

Jenny Altschuler
COUNSELLING AND PSYCHOTHERAPY FOR FAMILIES IN TIMES OF ILLNESS AND DEATH 2nd Edition

Jenny Altschuler
WORKING WITH CHRONIC ILLNESS

Bill Barnes, Sheila Ernst and Keith Hyde
AN INTRODUCTION TO GROUPWORK

Stephen Briggs
WORKING WITH ADOLESCENTS AND YOUNG ADULTS 2nd Edition

Alex Coren
SHORT-TERM PSYCHOTHERAPY

Jim Crawley and Jan Grant
COUPLE THERAPY

Emilia Dowling and Gill Gorell Barnes
WORKING WITH CHILDREN AND PARENTS THROUGH SEPARATION AND DIVORCE

Loretta Franklin
AN INTRODUCTION TO WORKPLACE COUNSELLING

Gill Gorell Barnes
FAMILY THERAPY IN CHANGING TIMES 2nd Edition

Fran Hedges
AN INTRODUCTION TO SYSTEMIC THERAPY WITH INDIVIDUALS

Fran Hedges
REFLEXIVITY IN THERAPEUTIC PRACTICE

John Hills
INTRODUCTION TO SYSTEMIC AND FAMILY THERAPY

Margaret Henning
POSITIVE DYNAMICS: A SYSTEMIC NARRATIVE APPROACH TO FACILITATING GROUPS

Sally Hodges
COUNSELLING ADULTS WITH LEARNING DISABILITIES

Linda Hopper
COUNSELLING AND PSYCHOTHERAPY WITH CHILDREN AND ADOLESCENTS

Sue Kegerreis
PSYCHODYNAMIC COUNSELLING WITH CHILDREN AND YOUNG PEOPLE

continued overleaf...

Desa Markovic
WORKING WITH SEXUAL ISSUES IN PSYCHOTHERAPY

A McFayden
WORKING WITH CHILDREN WITH LEARNING DIFFICULTIES

Liz Ormand
SUPERVISION IN COUNSELLING AND PSYCHOTHERAPY

Ravi Rana
COUNSELLING STUDENTS

Peter Rober
IN THERAPY TOGETHER: FAMILY THERAPY AS A DIALOGUE

Tricia Scott
INTEGRATIVE PSYCHOTHERAPY IN HEALTHCARE

Geraldine Shipton
WORKING WITH EATING DISORDERS

Gerrilyn Smith
WORKING WITH TRAUMA

Laurence Spurling
AN INTRODUCTION TO PSYCHODYNAMIC COUNSELLING 3rd Edition

Laurence Spurling
THE PSYCHOANALYTIC CRAFT: HOW TO DEVELOP AS A PSYCHOANALYTIC PRACTITIONER

Paul Terry
COUNSELLING AND PSYCHOTHERAPY WITH OLDER PEOPLE 2nd Edition

Jan Wiener and Mannie Sher
COUNSELLING AND PSYCHOTHERAPY IN PRIMARY HEALTH CARE

Shula Wilson
DISABILITY, COUNSELLING AND PSYCHOTHERAPY

Steven Walker
CULTURALLY COMPETENT THERAPY

Jenny Walters
WORKING WITH FATHERS

Jessica Yakeley
WORKING WITH VIOLENCE

Invitation to authors

The series editors welcome proposals for new books with the Basic Texts in Counselling and Psychotherapy series. They should be sent to Arlene Vetere at the University of Surrey (email drarlenevetere@hotmail.com) or Rudi Dallos at Plymouth University (email R.Dallos@plymouth.ac.uk).

Basic Texts in Counselling and Psychotherapy
Series Standing Order ISBN 0–333–69330–2
(outside North America only)

You can receive future titles in this series as they are published by placing a standing order. Please contact your bookseller or, in the case of difficulty, write to us at the address below with your name and address, the title of the series and the ISBN quoted above.
Customer Services Department, Macmillan Distribution Ltd
Houndmills, Basingstoke, Hampshire RG21 6XS, England

WORKING WITH SEXUAL ISSUES IN PSYCHOTHERAPY

A Practical Guide Using a Systemic Social Constructionist Framework

DESA MARKOVIC

First published 2017 by
PALGRAVE

Palgrave in the UK is an imprint of Macmillan Publishers Limited, registered in England, company number 785998, of 4 Crinan Street, London, N1 9XW.

ISBN 978–1–137–58222–5 paperback

This book is printed on paper suitable for recycling and made from fully managed and sustained forest sources. Logging, pulping and manufacturing processes are expected to conform to the environmental regulations of the country of origin.

A catalogue record for this book is available from the British Library.

A catalog record for this book is available from the Library of Congress.

CONTENTS

List of figures viii
List of tables x
Acknowledgements xi
Introduction xii

1 Multidimensional open-minded sex therapy (MOST) 1
Multidimensional open-minded sex therapy (MOST) resources and restraints 3
The emotional dimension 4
The cognitive dimension 9
The physical dimension 14
The behavioural dimension 16
The relational dimension 19
The cultural dimension 27

2 Definitions of sex and sexual response 37
Human sexual response models 37
A spectrum of sex 42
Sexual minorities 55

3 Sexual misconceptions and prejudice 78
Sex as a cultural taboo 78
Professional sexual myths 86

4 Classification and assessment of sexual disorders 91
Introduction 91
MOST dimensions: assessment guide 96
Discussion and conclusions 106
Delayed ejaculation (DE) 107

Erectile disorder (ED) 114
Female orgasmic disorder (FOD) 124
Female sexual interest/arousal disorder (FSI/AD) 133
Genito-pelvic pain/penetration disorder (GPPPD) 143
Male hypoactive sexual desire disorder (MHSDD) 152
Premature/early ejaculation (PE) 164
Persistent genital arousal disorder (PGAD) 173
Sexual aversion disorder (SAD) 176
Sexual compulsivity, addiction or hypersexuality 183
Dyspareunia in men 196
Assessment: discussion and conclusions 203
Formulation in systemic psychosexual therapy 207

5 Treatment options for sexual dysfunctions 212
Introduction 212
Delayed ejaculation (DE) treatment options 233
Erectile disorder (ED): treatment options 240
Female orgasmic disorder (FOD): treatment options 249
Female sexual interest/arousal disorder (FSI/AD): treatment options 257
Genito-pelvic pain/penetration disorder (GPPPD): treatment options 267
Male hypoactive sexual desire disorder (MHSDD): treatment options 274
Premature/early ejaculation (PE): treatment options 282
Persistent genital arousal disorder (PGAD): treatment options 288
Sexual aversion disorder (SAD): treatment options 291
Sexual compulsivity, addiction or hypersexuality: treatment options 295
Dyspareunia in men: treatment options 304

6 Client vignettes 309
Introduction 309
Melanie: 'anorgasmia' 309
Formulation session with Melanie 316
David and Janet: presenting problem of male hypoactive sexual desire disorder 326
Supervision session with Emily 336

Dan and Eric: obsession with visiting sex workers 344
Ben and Roy; Alma and Jay: use of sensate focus 348
Karl and Dalia: presenting problem of delayed ejaculation 353
Gary: presenting problem of erectile disorder 360

References 368
Author index 411
Subject index 415

LIST OF FIGURES

1.1 Multidimensional open-minded sex therapy (MOST) resources and restraints 3

2.1 A spectrum of sex 43
2.2 Theoretical perspectives on paraphilias 73

4.1 Relationship map: the case that went wrong 103
4.2 Relationship map: Dan and Tina 104
4.3 Delayed ejaculation: contributing factors 111
4.4 Erectile disorder: contributing factors 118
4.5 Female orgasmic disorder: contributing factors 129
4.6 Female sexual interest/arousal disorder: contributing factors 138
4.7 Female sexual interest/arousal: enhancing factors 142
4.8 Genito-pelvic pain/penetration disorder: contributing factors 147
4.9 Male sexual desire: enhancing factors 156
4.10 Male hypoactive sexual desire disorder: contributing factors 158
4.11 Premature/early ejaculation: contributing factors 168
4.12 Persistent genital arousal disorder: contributing factors 175
4.13 Sexual aversion disorder: contributing factors 180
4.14 'Hypersexuality': theoretical perspectives 189
4.15 Sexual compulsivity, addiction or hypersexuality: contributing factors 194
4.16 Dyspareunia in men: contributing factors 199

5.1 Delayed ejaculation: treatment options 235
5.2 Erectile disorder: treatment options 241
5.3 Female orgasmic disorder: treatment options 251
5.4 Female sexual interest/arousal disorder: treatment options 258
5.5 Genito-pelvic pain/penetration disorder: treatment options 270
5.6 Male hypoactive sexual desire disorder: treatment options 277
5.7 Premature/early ejaculation: treatment options 284

5.8 Persistent genital arousal disorder: treatment options 289
5.9 Sexual aversion disorder: treatment options 292
5.10 Sexual compulsivity, addiction or hypersexuality: treatment options 300
5.11 Dyspareunia in men: treatment options 305

6.1 Melanie: resources 317

LIST OF TABLES

6.1 Formulation: from 'anorgasmia' to 'lack of sexual confidence' 313
6.2 Premature/early ejaculation: MOST and CBT factors combined 350
6.3 Delayed ejaculation: couple resources 358
6.4 Acquired and situational delayed ejaculation: restraints 359
6.5 Erectile disorder: an integrated analysis using MOST and CBT factors 365

ACKNOWLEDGEMENTS

This book would not have been possible without the support, patience and encouragement of many people.

My deepest gratitude goes to my husband, my best friend and most inspirational colleague, Simon Cutteridge, whose systemic wisdom has been a vital source of strength and endurance in completing this volume.

The intelligence and incredible creativity of my daughters, Anna Cutteridge and Dasha Radovanovic, along with their love and belief in me, sparked my ideas and enlightened my thoughts.

I am hugely grateful to my dearest friend Teresa Wilson, an amazing systemic therapist, for her most uplifting comments, her warmth, her laughter and unconditional appreciation of my work.

Among many wonderful teachers, the insight, wit and prudence of systemic therapist John Burnham and sexologist Professor Kevan Wylie have been an ongoing source of inspiration in my thinking and my practice.

I am indebted to Professor Stephen Frosh, whose most impressive mind and gentle nudging opened up the possibility for me to begin writing this book.

INTRODUCTION

Sexual issues have been consistently under-addressed in psychotherapy training, literature, research and clinical practice. Several prominent systemic and couple psychotherapists have, over time, drawn attention to the exclusion of sexual topics from psychotherapy training courses and supervision, e.g. Sanders (1988), Kantor and Okun (1989), Madanes (1990), Mason (1991), Pascoe (1994a, 1994b), Gorrell-Barnes, Down and McCann (2000), Weeks (2005) and Iasenza (2010). However, this situation has not changed much over recent decades and, as a result, sexual issues remain overlooked. While many therapists work with the topic of sex in skilful and creative ways, they are mainly left to their own devices due to the lack of professional support systems. The topic is often wrapped in silence and treated as a taboo in psychotherapy practice, training, research and supervision, reflecting the social and cultural constraints that typically surround it.

This secretive and taboo treatment of sex may serve to increase clients' anxieties and feelings of shame and embarrassment about the subject, mirroring and feeding into societal pathologising and confusing views on sexuality. Ironically, these very factors tend to lead to the onset, development and persistence of sexual dysfunctions. Directly addressing sexual concerns through open and meaningful conversations, substantiated by well-thought-through theoretical and practical frameworks, is a pre-requisite for successful treatment. This book constitutes guidance in that direction, filling a gap in psychotherapy literature and training by opening up avenues for the inclusion of sexual issues and offering an open-minded approach to appreciating the complexity of human sexuality. The aim is to encourage psychotherapists to use their existing knowledge and skills while expanding their repertoire of theories and practical applications so as to include the issues of sex and sexual relationships as an integrated component of their practice. To this end, this book seeks to provide both trainee and qualified therapists, practising within different therapeutic modalities, a theoretical framework to address and treat sexual difficulties, which considers sex and sexual relationships integral parts of the human condition. Furthermore, it describes relevant therapeutic interventions using clinical examples to illustrate ways of working with a variety of sexual problems. References to recent research studies and other literature are provided to enhance therapists' expertise and confidence in approaching this topic effectively. Each chapter contains a series of proposed exercises to facilitate readers' reflections on their own practice, including in a supervisory context.

The approach proposed in the book brings together the medical perspective of sexology and systemic psychotherapy from a social constructionist perspective. The value and effectiveness of this approach and the usefulness of its application to the topic of sex is based on the author's extensive clinical experience, both as a systemic and a psychosexual therapist. The emphasis moves between a 'pure' systemic and a 'pure' sexology perspective; at times it is more systemically, and at others more sexologically informed; sometimes it is both, integrating the two in a single, combined intervention.

Qualification as a psychosexual therapist requires completion of an accredited training programme. This book, as comprehensive as it is, does not replace further reading, conversations, training courses and supervision as additional learning sources. In some cases, referral to a psychosexual specialist may still be the best option for the client.

The 'systemic approach' as described in this book refers to a relational psychotherapy that originated from family therapy in the 1950s resulting in a variety of different family therapy schools of thought worldwide; through the continual evolution of the approach over the second part of the 20th century, enriched by the Milan systemic family therapy school (Selvini-Palazzoli et al., 1980), and subsequent postmodern philosophies of constructivism (Maturana & Varela, 1980) and social constructionism (Pearce, 1989; McNamee & Gergen, 1992). Fundamental notions of systemic philosophy, such as the Milan team's concepts of hypothesising, circularity and neutrality are explained later in the text. The social constructionist premise that realities are multiple, relative and constructed through communication and language (Pearce, 1994) serves as an overarching theoretical frame.

The term 'sexology' is used in the text to signify a medical approach to sexual health based on scientific evidence informed by large-scale research findings and the diagnostic categorisation of sexual dysfunctions (Wylie, DeColomby & Giami, 2004). Sexology clinicians provide medical treatment of medically based sexual problems. 'Sex therapy' and 'psychosexual therapy', terms that will be used interchangeably, signify a specialised form of psychotherapy provided by mental health professionals specifically trained to work with sexual problems. Psychosexual/sex therapists are usually qualified counsellors, psychotherapists or medical healthcare professionals such as nurses, general practitioners (GPs), psychiatrists, gynaecologists and obstetricians who have completed additional specialised training in psychosexual therapy (Whiteley, 2006).

Chapter 1: Multidimensional open-minded sex therapy (MOST)

Chapter 1 presents Multidimensional open-minded sex therapy (MOST), a model that the author has developed during her career practising both as a systemic and a psychosexual therapist (Markovic, 2013). The model is proposed as a working framework, integrating sexology and systemic social constructionist psychotherapy. It focuses on the six dimensions of human lived experience: emotional, cognitive, physical, behavioural, relational and cultural. These dimensions are interconnected and are seen as mutually influencing each other. For clarity, they are presented individually: each dimension is described in relation to its relevance to understanding and working with sexual issues in psychotherapy.

Chapter 2: Definitions of sex and sexual response

Chapter 2 outlines the evolution of the most prevalent models of human sexual response through the history of sexology. It then discusses the meaning of sex and proposes a representation of sex as a spectrum of experiences, thoughts, actions and fantasies that include many layers of communication, sensuality, sexuality and desire, to encompass a comprehensive, multidimensional view on human sexuality. It stresses the importance of appreciating the multidimensional nature of sex and a wide variety of its possible definitions. The reader is guided in ways of using different elements of the spectrum and encouraged to recognise the importance of shifting the focus between the narrow meanings of sex to the inclusion of wider social and cultural contexts. The ways of applying the spectrum of sex model in clinical practice are illustrated with a number of case examples as well as descriptions of specific therapeutic and supervisory interventions.

This chapter underlines the significance of sexual diversity and discusses the concept of sexual minorities in the context of social and cultural oppression. The section on sexual minorities relates to lesbian, gay, bisexual, transgender, asexual, non-monogamous and polyamorous communities.

Diversity of sexual practices or 'sexual preferences' includes 'unusual sexual practices', 'kinky', 'queer' and 'BDSM' activities (bondage/domination/sadism/masochism). Paraphilias are distinguished from paraphilic disorders as suggested in the most recent *Diagnostic and Statistical Manual of Psychiatric Disorders* (DSM-5, APA, 2013). 'Sexual preferences' is used as an affirmative concept, appreciative of sexual diversity, aimed at embracing a wide scope of chosen sexual activities representing the richness, divergence and idiosyncrasies of sexual possibilities. The importance of the therapist's ability to offer non-judgemental listening support and engagement with the specific detail of clients' experiences is emphasised for building an effective therapeutic relationship by demonstrating respect for clients' integrity and freedom of choice in adult consenting sexual interactions. Theories explaining paraphilic sexual interest and practices are summarised to highlight the current state of debate in the fields of sexology, psychosexual therapy and psychotherapy.

Chapter 3: Sexual misconceptions and prejudice

This chapter focuses on the concept of sexual myths and misconceptions, widely used in sexology, representing a set of beliefs, judgements and values about sex that have the potential to restrict the experience of sex and adversely impact sexual relationships. Sexual myths typically encountered in clinical practice that contribute to distorted, often punitive views on sex are described, suggesting systemic and sexology interventions for deconstructing and dispelling them. The concept of 'professional sexual myths' is introduced, drawing attention to the importance of examining therapists' own stories and myths about sex and of employing self-reflexivity and relational reflexivity in clinical practice when working with sensitive topics such as sex.

Chapter 4: Classification and assessment of sexual disorders

Using sexology resources, a range of sexual difficulties and disorders are discussed. The chapter contains a chart of each of the most frequently presented sexual dysfunctions, using the MOST model framework as a succinct and informative resource for grasping the typical factors contributing to the onset, development and ongoing persistence of sexual concerns. Each dysfunction is presented separately, referring to definitions from literature. In addition to the diagnostic manuals and sexology textbooks, the chapter cites the most recent international research studies supporting current professional views. Guideline questions for conducting assessment of presenting sexual difficulties are offered as a means of determining a diagnosis and establishing a clear focus for treatment. The relevance of forming an appropriate diagnosis is explained as a means of helping clients and therapists to understand the nature and characteristics of the presenting difficulties. At the same time, the importance of having a 'systemic mind' is emphasised in terms of considering diagnoses as social constructions, therefore relative, often approximate, and potentially stigmatising. The advantages and disadvantages of using diagnostic categories and the label of 'sexual dysfunction' are discussed.

Chapter 5: Treatment options for sexual dysfunctions

This chapter follows the format of Chapter 4 in that sexual disorders are presented in terms of their origin and contributing factors and are mapped out in relation to relevant treatment options. Resources within both sexology and systemic psychotherapy are combined for determining specific therapeutic interventions indicated for particular sexual dysfunctions. A range of interventions is described, bringing together sexology and systemic psychotherapy resources in a way that constructively integrates them, illustrated by examples from clinical practice. The therapeutic relationship in systemic psychosexual therapy is considered, with emphasis on the balance of power between therapist and client, forming a collaborative alliance whereby both the therapist and the client are the experts, sharing responsibility for the therapeutic process and outcomes.

Chapter 6: Client vignettes

The final chapter provides several clinical vignettes incorporating examples of assessment, formulation, treatment and supervision. A synthesis of sexology and systemic psychotherapy interventions is demonstrated to show their application at various stages of work. Examples encompass a variety of presenting sexual concerns, including delayed ejaculation; loss of desire; erectile dysfunction; premature ejaculation, and others. The chapter contains a transcript from a supervision session, illustrating possible supervisory approaches with therapists who are not used to working with sexual issues and includes the supervisor's reflections on the session. The reader is invited to reflect on their learning from the practice examples. Clients' and therapists' confidentiality is protected by anonymising their identities and altering their specific background details. In addition, some cases are composites of different client situations and some aspects are fictionalised. This chapter further illustrates the complexity of sexuality and the need for a multidimensional, open-minded approach.

1

MULTIDIMENSIONAL OPEN-MINDED SEX THERAPY (MOST)

The Multidimensional open minded sex therapy model is proposed as a working framework that integrates systemic social constructionist therapy and sexology. In many ways, integration of these two approaches, the medical approach of the sexual science and a social constructionist systemic psychotherapy, is a synthesis of opposites. For example, sexology bases its assessment and treatment on categorisation of sexual disorders as classified in diagnostic and statistical manuals (WHO, 2010; APA, 2013). Conversely, a social constructionist approach sharply critiques normative perspectives and sees categorisation as reductionist and pathologising (White, 2007). While the medical approach to sexology bases its definition of the problems on generalised quantitative research data, the systemic approach focuses on the process of meaning-making of clients' experiences brought to therapy. These may seem diametrically opposed; however, within the integrated framework proposed by the MOST model, both perspectives are important and, when applied in combination, can provide a broader understanding from a wide range of perspectives leading to more fully informed treatment options and higher level of treatment success. Both the clarity of the presenting problem enabled by the diagnostic criteria derived from sexology, and the systemic questioning and the exploration of the meaning of the concerns, are constitutive parts of this integrated practice. Sexology provides useful 'linear' information towards building a clear description, definition and diagnosis of presenting concerns, enabling both clients and professionals to reach a detailed understanding of the origins, specific nature and manifestations of the problem. A systemic enquiry provides a 'circular' and 'reflexive' framework to explore these issues contextually and relationally: 'How did it become a problem in the first place?'; 'Who is it a problem for?';

'Who is most concerned?'; 'What worries you most?', engaging the client in reflecting and making new connections. Using the concept of 'both-and' (Bateson, 1972), a fundamental principle of the systemic approach, these two different perspectives can be incorporated when working with sexual concerns; a perspective that appreciates the scientific, factual and somatic, as well as one that appreciates the philosophical, psychological, relational and subjective spheres of human existence.

Furthermore, sexology proposes sophisticated procedures for identifying problems, their extent and specific characteristics; while systemic therapy has refined methods for detecting hidden strengths in clients and bringing forth their underused resources and forgotten, sometimes dormant skills. Using these in conjunction contributes to comprehensive and constructive assessment and treatment.

The stance of the professional differs in some aspects between these two approaches: in sexology there is more emphasis on the professional as the expert, who takes charge of the planning, structure of sessions, assessment, formulation and treatment options and leads the sessions in particular directions, all determined by scientific guidelines (Bancroft, 2009). By contrast, within the systemic approach the client is the expert and the therapist tunes into clients' grammar through a stance of curiosity using open questioning and tentative suggestions (Anderson, 2000). Within the proposed 'MOST' model, a combination of these two stances works well in that both client and therapist are experts (Markovic, 2010). This framework could be described as 'non-impositional taking charge' (Markovic, 2013, p.317), allowing clients to benefit from a wide scope of therapeutic interventions. These may include: educative input, giving advice and clarifying information, bibliotherapy, behavioural tasks, and using open, exploratory questioning. A creative synthesis of these two approaches enriches both fields providing a wide pool of options for clients.

The MOST model is informed by existing models of integration between psychotherapy and sexology, e.g. 'multiple domains of intervention' (Sanders, 1986), 'sexual crucible' (Schnarch, 1991), feminist perspectives on power and relationships (Dallos & Dallos, 1997), Leiblum and Rosen's 'principles and practice of sex therapy' (2000), 'psycho-biosocial sex therapy model' (McCarthy & Thestrup, 2008), the 'intersystem model' (Weeks, 2005) and the 'behavioural-systems model' (Crowe & Ridley, 1990). MOST is proposed as an additional and updated model, incorporating systemic and social constructionist perspectives, including therapists' self-reflexivity and relational reflexivity, thus expanding the framework of viewing sexuality as a phenomenon including multiple dimensions. Psychotherapy theories tend to emphasise a single or a limited scope of dimensions creating separate approaches, such as behavioural therapy; cognitive therapy; rational-emotive therapy, and so on; the comprehensiveness and inclusiveness of MOST embraces the multidimensional nature of sexuality incorporating six dimensions of human lived experience: emotional, cognitive, behavioural, physical, relational and cultural (see Figure 1.1). These dimensions are interconnected, but will be presented individually in the text that follows in the interests of clarity.

Multidimensional open-minded sex therapy (MOST) resources and restraints

'Open' in the title relates to being unbiased, flexible and tolerant when working with sexual issues, acknowledging the multiplicity of sexual practices and experiences, encompassing sexual diversity in its varied forms. The concept of 'therapeutic stories co-constructed', at the centre of the diagram, implies that the dimensions are constructed through interpersonal communication, rather than existing as an objective truth in a separate reality. This signifies that knowledge about clients and their situation is

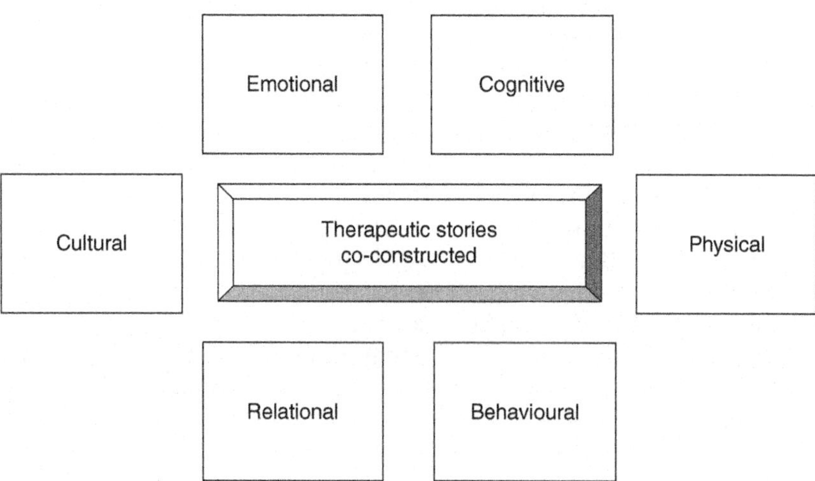

Figure 1.1 Multidimensional open-minded sex therapy (MOST) resources and restraints

derived from the therapeutic relational context: interaction with the clients, the context of supervision, the therapeutic professional communications and the cultural discourses. 'Resources and restraints' in the diagram title refers to working both with areas of strengths and resiliencies, as well as areas of difficulty and weakness. Each of the dimensions will be elaborated on, and this will include examples to illustrate the use of the model in psychotherapy practice.

The emotional dimension

Emotional factors in sexual experiences

Working with sexual issues in psychotherapy involves addressing a wide range of clients' emotions and often complex emotional experiences. Frequently encountered emotions include: fear of sex; performance anxiety; shame of own sexuality, fantasy, desire or sexual behaviour and worry or guilt about being sexual. Disappointment, anger and resentment within the relationship can present barriers to sex, compounding, and sometimes even superseding, the original sexual problem.

Research within sexology has shown that emotions such as anxiety, particularly performance anxiety, guilt, fear and shame typically underlie the most frequently presented sexual dysfunctions (Leiblum & Rosen, 2000). Fear of intimacy, low self-esteem, stress and depression can be closely connected to sexual concerns (Bancroft, 2009). Emotional factors are both a cause and effect of sexual dysfunctions, contributing to their development as well as their persistence (Wincze & Carey, 2001).

Systemic and social constructionist perspectives, including connections with attachment theory (Vetere & Dallos, 2008), highlight the magnitude of childhood emotions and events, and particularly the effects of loss and trauma on adult sexuality and relationships. Reflecting on these emotions can reveal their impact on sexual experience. Tracking the origin of emotional experiences might lead back to early family messages, or, equally, they could relate to more recent episodes, reactions to emotional display by others, the manifestation of one's femininity/masculinity, and expression of sexuality. Allowing for these emotions to be communicated, thought about, discussed and reflected upon can bring about healing effects.

The subject of sex can be emotionally provocative for both clients and therapists. The therapist should create a context for clients' reflection on any repressed emotions or intense emotional reactions. Equally, therapists' own emotional awareness and monitoring of their own emotional responses form an integral and vital part of a responsible and ethical professional stance.

Therapeutic interventions addressing emotions

A range of therapeutic interventions can be helpful in addressing, exploring and providing a context for change in relation to the emotional dimension. Systemic techniques such as normalisation, constructive and supportive challenge, reflexive questions, reframing and various other interventions referred to later in the text are aimed at strengthening clients' emotional resilience and empowering their sense of agency.

Sometimes clients' expectation of therapy is to cure their 'abnormality', a perception they hold of themselves stemming from an episode from their distant past, or from a fantasy they have had which has caused them strong feelings of guilt and shame. Therapeutic interventions in these situations may focus on normalisation, challenging a client's tendency towards disproportionate self-blame. Clients who have experienced criticism of their sexual performance often bring to therapy feelings of their sexual inadequacy, apprehension and anxiety related to sex. Normalisation of such feelings often provides a context for thinking of these experiences differently and redefining the problem from inadequacy to criticism-induced performance anxiety.

Future hypothetical questions (Penn, 1985), an important systemic resource, encourage imagining of alternative possibilities allowing for different meanings to emerge, such as:

- If you decided to believe that your sexual performance is as good as anyone else's, how might you approach your next sexual encounter?
- If you imagine a sexual encounter, with your partner being positively responsive to you, how might you be thinking of your sexual competence?

In this way, therapeutic interventions provide normalisation of feelings of sexual inadequacy by putting them in the context of the experiences of partners' criticism and sexual rejection.

In addition, past hypothetical questions can have rich therapeutic potential, offering the possibility for reconsidering meanings such as:

- If you imagine this never happened...

or hypothetical questions offering the possibility of a different emotional response to the situation:

- If you decide not to be affected by the critical comments...

or offering a different meaning:

- If you consider the possibility that underneath your partner's criticism lies their deep sexual insecurity...

are further examples of the use of a variety of hypothetical questions in systemic psychotherapy. Hypothetically altering the context of the events, experiences and interpersonal exchanges has the potential to constructively challenge the meanings attributed to them, opening up space for different feelings and alternative options for responding.

Sexology and psychosexual therapy interventions addressing the emotional dimension are typically: behavioural, cognitive-behavioural and psycho-educational. Engaging clients in relaxation techniques, which are particularly effective in behavioural treatments of anxiety, including the possible use of tapes or exercises, as also described in hypnotherapy and mindfulness literature (Brotto & Barker, 2014), can be added to the list of helpful resources addressing sexual anxieties. In addition, advocating a healthy lifestyle can significantly improve emotional experiences. More of this will be discussed within 'The physical dimension' later in the chapter. The psycho-educational approach, based on sexology research and practice, is an invaluable resource in psychosexual therapy to effectively address the emotional dimension. Cognitive behavioural therapy (CBT) techniques, regularly applied in psychosexual therapy and coherent with some aspects of the systemic theoretical and practical framework, can be effective with frequently presented emotional difficulties such as fear of failure, performance anxiety, guilt and shame. CBT is based on the premise that negative feelings arise from negative thoughts leading to negative conclusions and maladaptive behaviours (Greenberger & Padesky, 2014). It provides a set of techniques to assist in identifying and challenging such thoughts. These include: conducting experiments, weighing the pros and cons of avoiding the feared situations, and replacing irrational negative thoughts with more realistic ones. Homework tasks might be offered such as: 'noting things you appreciate about your partner'; 'practising ways in which you can show your appreciation'; 'considering observations that your partner might be making if they were in the session', and so on. The material from completed tasks, that is then brought back to the therapy session, allows for the possibility of changing irrational negative thought patterns and unwanted behaviours and provides a challenge one's own conclusions through the exploration of different interpretations.

During the course of treatment which combines interventions from psychosexual and systemic therapy, emotional responses frequently shift in that what used to be a source of guilt, shame and anxiety becomes integrated as part of the person's repertoire of relating and is regarded as their valid choice within the spectrum of sexuality. For example, masturbation habits are a typical source of guilt and shame. Bondage, domination, sadism, masochism (BDSM) is often practised in secrecy because of the possibility of shame due to social stigma and the risks of potentially serious interpersonal and/or career consequences. Recently, another layer of shame has begun to emerge in relation to so-called 'ordinary', 'narrow', or 'vanilla' sex, gradually evolving in parallel with the growing trend of sexual liberation. A client was almost apologising for liking 'vanilla sex': 'I am quite boring when it comes to sex...' A woman reported shyly: 'I quite like penetration, in a missionary position. I know it's not the most exotic...' This double face of shame reflects the cultural paradox of promoting the typical and normative and condemning the unusual, while simultaneously valuing taking risks and engaging in adventurous and 'brave' sexual practices, unconstrained by social norms. Therapy becomes a place for normalisation, reflection on this culturally induced shame, supporting self-acceptance and, moreover, the individual's self-appreciation through encouraging awareness of their sexual rights (WAS, 2014) and the ability to think through the possibilities, including both advantages and disadvantages of making certain sexual choices.

Techniques from different psychotherapy approaches can be effectively integrated as part of this multidimensional framework. For example, the 'empty chair' technique from gestalt psychotherapy (Nevis, 2000) and emotionally focused therapy (Johnson, 2008) encourages clients to enact an imaginary dialogue with their partner or other significant people from their lives who seem to have impacted in a powerful way on their sexual feelings. This technique has the potential to release an active energy in clients who feel stuck and locked in the same circle of thinking and feeling, and to strengthen their ability to act in constructive ways.

Emotional resources and resiliencies

In parallel with emotional frustrations and difficulties, systemic psychosexual therapy explores emotional fulfilments and the capacity for emotional gratification. Solution-focused (deShazer, 1991) and narrative therapy (White & Epston, 1990), and the widely used systemic technique of reframing can be effectively applied to drawing on clients' existing and future desires, sexual hopes, dreams, pride and pleasures and using them as resources to strengthen their sense of agency and increase their options for sexual growth.

The narrative approach, based on social constructionist philosophy, posits that language influences thinking and that the way we story our experiences impacts on our lived emotions; in other words, language creates reality (Pearce, 2007). The aim of narrative methods and techniques is to elevate the person, to help them come to terms with problems through recognising their strengths and capabilities, leading to 're-storying' of their problem-saturated and self-pathologising narratives. Stories seem to become imprinted on the mind in a way that can be powerful in determining feelings, including feelings about oneself and one's capabilities (White, 2007). On listening to a client's self-deprecating account of an intimate interpersonal episode interspersed with listing her inadequacies and placing the whole responsibility for the situation onto herself: 'I was unable to...', 'I couldn't...', 'I didn't know what else to do so I just...', 'I don't know why I react this way, I am so stupid...' , the therapist invited her to re-tell the episode from a position of strength, her right to her sexual choices and her competent decision making: 'If you describe the same situation in the way that reflects your respect for yourself and your belief that you did the best you could, based on your knowledge, giving a fair assessment of the situation and applying the best qualities of yourself as a person, how would you then start telling me about it?' This kind of intervention illustrates the narrative method of bringing forth a sense of agency, choice and strength from the client whose self-pathologising stories might be at the root of their sexual problems.

The systemic technique of 'reframing' (Watzlawick, Weakland & Fisch, 1974), based on the premise that language creates meaning and in that way influences behaviour, feelings and relationships, offers a different perspective on presenting problems. Reframing can help to create a different way of looking at a situation, perhaps changing its meaning, for example suggesting that a person is 'appreciative of others' views' rather than 'easily led'; or 'generous and kind' as opposed to 'too soft'; 'flexible' rather than 'indecisive', and so on, has the potential to create a different perception for the client and different feelings about themselves and others. When the frame is shifted, such as in the examples above, things are seen in a new light, which can support more positive feelings about oneself, the partner, and the relationship, and facilitate effective ways of acting. Applying the technique of reframing requires prior therapeutic rapport so that feelings and experiences are fully appreciated and the client feels heard. More about reframing will be included in Chapter 5.

The cognitive dimension

Cognitive factors in sexual experiences

The cognitive dimension relates to beliefs and stories about sex, intimacy, relationships and oneself as a sexual person, constructed over time. It encompasses liberating, encouraging and stimulating stories, as well as restrictive misconceptions and myths. Discourses about sex can be burdened with prejudice, strong ideas about what is permissible and what is to be prohibited; what is abnormal and what is open to personal choice; what is idiosyncratic; and what we should call a disorder. In many cases psychosexual therapy is about revisioning ideas about sex. Sex therapy literature stresses the relevance of education, recognising that insufficient sexual knowledge contributes to the majority of sexual problems. Weeks and Gambescia (2000) write: 'The most common mistake any therapist can make is to assume that couples know everything about sex or can talk comfortably about what is desired during lovemaking' (p.119). Clients often construct their scope of choice on the basis of oppressive beliefs such as: *'Given that I'm a woman, sex is not to be enjoyed'*; or: *'Given my penis size, I will never be able to satisfy a partner.'* The concept of a 'sexual self-schema', or one's self-perception of one's sexuality, described in the sex therapy literature as: 'cognitive generalisations about sexual aspects of oneself that are derived from past experiences, manifest in current experiences, influential in the processing of sexually relevant social information, that guide sexual behavior' (Anderson & Cyranowski, 1994, p.1079) is considered to be a highly influential factor in sexual functioning. Large-scale cross-cultural sexology studies suggest that dysfunctional sexual beliefs and negative sexual self-schema are vulnerability factors for sexual dysfunction (Nobre & Pinto-Gouveia, 2009). Their results showed that people diagnosed with a sexual dysfunction are more likely to interpret unsatisfactory sexual experiences according to an 'incompetence sexual self-schema'.

Therapeutic interventions addressing the cognitive dimension

A range of systemic and sex therapy interventions can usefully address sexual mythology, as illustrated below.

Through systemic questioning clients' restrictive stories can be challenged; for example, a therapist asked a client who attributed her sexual unhappiness to her own inadequacies: 'How come you seem to believe that you have no right to your sexual choices?', intending to facilitate reflection and encourage appreciation and ownership of her sexual rights. Numerous types of systemic reflexive questioning, which intend to facilitate clients' self-reflexivity and examine pre-existing belief systems, can enable them to generate more constructive patterns of cognition and behaviours, for example:

'Questions that discourage generalisations and challenge assumptions' (Scaife, 2010, p.102):

- At what times do you most notice your partner's aggression?
- What have you noticed are the limits of your kindness?
- What might be her motivation in shouting?

'Normative comparison questions' (Tomm, 1987), aiming at normalising the client's situation:

- Many people's sexual lives are affected by pregnancy and childbirth. How do you think you are managing that transition in your emotional and sexual lives?

'Contextual perspective questions' (Hornstrup, Tomm & Johansen, 2009), aiming to generate new ways of understanding the subject in focus by inviting other relevant voices into the conversation:

- How might other people react in the same situation?
- What might other people tell you about how they feel when they are stressed and tired?
- How frequently do you think other people of your age have sex?

Reframing offers a constructive challenge to fixed ideas and interpretations through 'embedded suggestion reflexive questions' (Tomm, 1987) such as:

- If you understood her persistent questioning rather than as an exercise of control over you, as a sign of deep interest in you and the wish to get closer, how might you react differently then?
- If you thought of your lack in confidence as a sign of your sensitivity to your partner's sexual needs, would you consider it a helpful ingredient in sexual interaction that may give you useful clues...?

In this way, clients are invited to think through different meanings by engaging in alternative hypothetical possibilities. Systemic questions are phrased in a way that emphasises clients' choice with regards to the content and process of sessions. This type of consenting relates to the concepts of collaboration and co-construction (Hoffman, 2007) embedded in social constructionist practice, whereby clients are encouraged to be active participants in all aspects of their therapy. Therapists must offer different possibilities tentatively, without implying that their suggestions are necessarily more valid. Sometimes it is worth checking with clients explicitly: What are the beliefs you want to change? What are the ones you don't wish to change? What should we pay attention to in working with you? It is important to establish with clients where therapeutic interventions should focus, to avoid the possibility of creating a symmetrical interactional pattern (Pearce, 2007). A male client once said to the therapy team: You sex therapists, you just want people to have sex and have it regularly and to want to have sex...! The couple's presenting problem was the male client's lack of sexual interest causing distress to his wife with consequent strain on the relationship. The assumption of the therapy team, not sufficiently checked with the clients, was that the couple both wanted to rekindle their sexual lives. The treatment options were all based on the couple becoming sexual again and failed to consider other possibilities.

Even when the terms of treatment are carefully negotiated, it may still be important to employ therapeutic transparency (White, 2007), explaining the reasons for asking a certain question, for making a particular suggestion or exploring specific issues. Clients' responses often relate to their interpretation of the therapists' intentions which may or may not be accurate. The skill of self-reflexivity as defined by Fruggeri (1989) 'How is what I am saying being heard?' is systemically crucial in the process of conducting therapy within a collaborative framework.

Sometimes the straightforward educational input of sexology can dispel constraining myths. For example, one client, who had self-referred to a psychosexual therapy practice, expressed her distress about her boyfriend's comment that 'her clitoris was too small'. The main therapeutic intervention was for her to read the book *The Clitoral Truth* (Chalker, 2000) which, together with the therapist's explanation of how the clitoris externally appears small while being connected to a vast amount of nerve endings, thus simply communicating some relevant biological facts, provided sufficient encouragement which served to lessen her anxiety.

Apart from the materials already available in their practice such as books, DVDs and handouts, therapists can direct clients to the plethora of publicly available texts on sexual topics. Sex therapists often encourage couples to discuss reading materials to enhance their understanding of their own and their partner's sexuality and also as a way of facilitating their sexual communication. 'The goal of reading is more than acquisition of knowledge' (Weeks & Gambescia, 2000, p.120).

For clients worrying about the size, shape or any other characteristics of their genitals, it can be helpful to use photos, diagrams or drawings of genital organs to illustrate their variety. Referring to the personal experience of Betty Dodson, a sex therapist, who wrote about how as a young person she thought that her vagina was 'deformed' due to her extended inner lips (Dodson, 2010), can serve as an educational, normalising intervention. Such uninformed beliefs about one's own genital abnormality can be profoundly distressing, causing anxiety, depression and even suicidal tendencies. The tragic story of the 14-year-old girl who committed suicide after having her first period, having had no sexual education and no one to talk to, the trigger for Chad Varah to form the Samaritans charity to befriend and support the depressed and suicidal (Varah, 1973), highlights the necessity for education in this field and the potential catastrophic consequences of treating sex as a taboo subject.

The CBT approach addresses what it classifies as 'cognitive distortions' (Beck, Emery & Greenberg, 2005), or irrational, automatic, habitual thoughts, namely over-generalisations, catastrophising, discounting the positive, anticipating the negative and excessive self-criticism. These can have a powerful negative impact on a person's perceptions, feelings and mental wellbeing. Classical CBT goal-oriented techniques in sex therapy aim to build on clients' existing strengths through challenging cognitive distortions such as 'testing the validity of thoughts'; or writing a journal to record different situations and reviewing their interpretations with the therapist in order to identify maladaptive thought patterns. For example, if clients claim they never receive appreciation from their sexual partners, this may be an unhelpful over-generalisation. In such cases, the therapist's suggestion to keep a diary of any verbal and non-verbal appreciation shown to them, however modest, has the potential to encourage the client to notice positive reactions of others. At the same time, this can contribute to a different co-construction of interpersonal interactions. One client was pleasantly surprised by the effect such a task had, making the connection between his strong beliefs and their impact on the creation of his revised interpersonal reality: 'I don't know if it was because I was set to notice good things, my mind was released of this propelling negativity and it made me look friendlier, so people reacted more positively to me.'

Cognitive resources and resiliencies

Systemic reflexive questioning can be applied to open up new awareness for thinking and behaving, through strengthening already existing resiliencies and positive stories, for example:

Questions that aim to encourage a sense of agency by introducing thinking of situations that contradict the principal negative belief (Hornstrup, Tomm & Johansen, 2009):

- Can you think of a time when you felt in tune with your sexual partner?
- Can you recall a sexual encounter that felt mutually pleasurable and satisfying?

Questions based on unexpected context change to support developing preferred narratives about self (self-concept), as opposed to self-pathologising and problem saturated and to build upon past resources and encourage agency (Tomm, 1987):

- When was the last time you had good sex?
- What skills and capabilities did you use then to bring about such a positive experience? What does it tell you about your sexual abilities...?

Questions that encourage the making of connections (Hornstrup, Tomm & Johansen, 2009), drawing attention to contextual factors and focusing on existing strengths, potentially reducing self-blame:

- What other circumstances could have influenced how you have been feeling sexually lately?
- In the absence of these difficult circumstances, how might you have reacted differently?

Since the early days of family therapy the concept of 'utilisation', developed in 1954 by Milton Erickson, has served as a guiding principle for strengthening clients' resilience by utilising their existing traits as the core of therapeutic interventions (Erickson, 2009). It relates to the therapist's ability to accept, without judgement, clients' thoughts, behaviours and feelings, including the ones that can be seen as problematic, as their legitimate characteristics and to use them as a resource in therapy. In this context, utilisation means using whatever it is the person is already doing or capable of (Lankton & Lankton, 2007). For example, a couple who struggled with discrepancy of sexual desire in an otherwise committed and loving relationship engaged in frequent conflict resulting from their respective sexual frustrations. The therapist devised an exercise linking with the clients' language which included frequent use of 'shoulds', suggesting that they write down separately at first, three things they should be doing and three things they should not be doing prior to the following session; and to then discuss and decide together on the three joint things from their respective lists. Rather than attempting to challenge these seemingly strongly embedded and potentially restraining 'shoulds', the therapist 'befriended' them by utilising them as a foundation upon which to create an intervention. This had a strong impact on the couple; they managed to turn a conflictual conversation into a co-operative discussion and were able to agree on their joint lists, including 'to smile'; 'to kiss more'; 'not to shout'. They came back to the next session saying: 'we turned the corner'; 'we love the shoulds'; 'we put them on the fridge…'.

The physical dimension

Physical factors in sexual experiences

The physical dimension comprising: body image, physical health and fitness, the use of medication, medical treatments and the conduciveness of the physical environment to intimacy, is typically marginalised in psychotherapy. The evolution of body psychotherapy (Staunton, 2002) drew attention to the importance of this undervalued dimension and pointed to mind/body separateness in psychotherapy. The MOST model considers the physical dimension to be as relevant as the others. Body image can have a major impact on one's sexual experiences and on one's sense of self as a sexual being. Various behavioural exercises have been developed within sex therapy for improving body image, aimed at developing a kinder, friendlier and more accepting relationship with one's body in order to reduce the tendency to negatively focus on and search for imperfections in one's appearance.

Therapeutic explorations engaging clients to reflect upon when and where they started feeling and thinking negatively about their bodies can create meaningful therapeutic conversations. Sometimes connections are made between negative body image and past experiences of bullying, abuse and severe criticism. Media promotion of certain body images can create a powerful negative impact on an already vulnerable sense of bodily self. Rejection of one's own body can also be a manifestation of self-loathing and, in such cases, psychological therapeutic interventions aim to empower enhanced self-image.

Therapeutic interventions addressing the physical dimension

Physical examination should be routinely recommended to clients presenting sexual difficulties, as this can be a means for detecting underlying physical problems that may be easily treatable, thereby eliminating potentially redundant psychological interventions. On one occasion, a woman presented for sexual and relationship treatment with symptoms of low sexual desire; a routine blood test revealed that a major cause of her lack of sexual interest was extreme anaemia. Her situation drastically improved following medical treatment, rendering psychotherapy unnecessary. Poor physical health can in itself impact sexual experience. For example, high cholesterol, hormonal imbalance, iron deficiency and low vitamin D can all have serious impact on sexual functioning. Equally, certain medical conditions such as diabetes, cardiovascular diseases, neurological problems, cancer, various infections and inflammations and other serious illnesses can each be a sole factor in bringing forth a sexual problem. Medical treatment of these illnesses can improve the health condition; however, often the medication and medical procedures involved in treating these problems produce side effects which may also impair sexual functioning. Unfortunately, patients subjected to medical treatments are not always informed about such side effects, leaving them to their own conclusions and sometimes misleading them to believe in the hopelessness of their case. The movement 'What Doctors Don't Tell You' (McTaggart, 2005) offers some important revelations, warning patients undergoing medical treatments of the need to carefully check and proactively seek as much information as possible, in order to fully understand the available medical and alternative treatment options.

Physical treatment of sexual difficulties, whether brought about by any physical factors or not, can contribute to effective outcomes at physical, cognitive, emotional and relational levels. For example, temporary medication, hormonal replacement, vacuum devices for erectile dysfunction, penile rings, vibrators, vaginal dilators, lubricants and oils, are amongst the many physical and medical devices supporting effective sexual functioning, which in turn can contribute to not only overcoming the original difficulty but also enhancing sexual confidence, improving body image and creating positive relational experiences. Body image can also significantly improve through maintaining a healthy diet and enhancing fitness through exercise; these activities are typically encouraged in psychosexual therapy.

Paradoxically, a medical diagnosis can bring forth normalisation of an undesired sexual response. When a physical cause of a sexual difficulty is detected, clients are sometimes relieved and empowered that 'it is not all in their mind'. On one occasion, a female client expressed her upset with her husband who seemed angry about her lack of sexual desire: 'I wish you could be in my skin for five minutes, to see how it feels... I want to be close, to be intimate with you but my body is letting me down, do you know how upsetting it is for *me*?' On receiving the laboratory results showing extremely low testosterone levels, she explained: 'for the first time I feel there is a reason. I was thinking, was I mad? Was I crazy? What is wrong with me? I have everything I need and want in this relationship...'. Equally, the reverse often happens, as body and mind have a mutually recursive relationship. For example, a male gay couple attended psychosexual therapy for a period of six months while waiting for testosterone replacement therapy for the client whose testosterone levels were chronically extremely low. In couple therapy many relationship issues were addressed and their communication and emotional intimacy significantly improved. By the time they reached the top of the waiting list, his updated testosterone test revealed normal results for the first time in several years.

Physical resources and resiliencies

Clients experiencing sexual difficulties sometimes do not perceive the body and mind as connected in this context and seek exclusively physical or exclusively psychological treatment. The 'medicalisation of sex' (Tiefer, 2001) contributes to the narrowing down of the meaning of sex as primarily performance related and emphasises bodily functioning as the single most important component. At the same time, undermining the physical aspects can be similarly misleading. Adopting the framework of the MOST model, clients are encouraged to make a range of connections amongst its various dimensions, gaining a more comprehensive understanding of their sexual experiences. A client's questioning, based on a self-pathologising premise: 'Why does my body shut down? What's wrong with my body?' shifts to a different perspective through making the following connection: 'When my partner is angry and I feel attacked when we have a conflict, my body adjusts to these circumstances by switching off from sexual desire'.

The behavioural dimension

Behavioural factors in sexual experiences

Behavioural therapy has long been used as a resource within sex therapy and sexology. A wide spectrum of behavioural techniques has proven therapeutically effective with a range of sexual dysfunctions. Knowing and being in tune with one's body is seen in sexology and psychosexual therapy as an important aspect of improving sexual experience. Various behavioural tasks are prescribed for learning about one's own and one's partner's body and for improving self-image, such as bodily exploration including genitalia, masturbatory exercises, and sensate focus (described in Chapter 5).

Specific sexual activities, skills and techniques are regularly explored in psychosexual therapy in order to establish whether a sexual problem may be the result of unsatisfactory sexual stimulation. In redefining female sexual response, Basson (2000) reinforced the importance of the 'adequacy of the sexual stimulus', drawing attention to this crucial contextual factor. This is well illustrated in Woody Allen's movie *Everything You Always Wanted to Know About Sex*... Mia Farrow plays the role of a woman who remains unmoved by her husband's various attempts to get a response from her in the bedroom. One day, as they visited a rather crowded exhibition, she initiates a passionate sexual exchange away from the crowd, but with the clear possibility of being seen. This example illustrates one of the fundamental premises of the systemic approach, the connection between meaning and context (Bateson, 1972), further elaborated within co-ordinated management of meaning theory (CMM) (Pearce & Cronen, 1980) as connectedness between meaning, context and action. So, in the language of this theory, in the context of any of the bedroom scenes, she could have been diagnosed with a sexual dysfunction; her behaviour would have been given the meaning of severe lack of interest in sex and difficulty with sexual arousal. However, on receiving the right type of a stimulus, i.e. in the context of the physical environment that sparks her imagination, she acts eagerly, is highly aroused and sexually expressive. A completely different conclusion would then be drawn from such an action, that of a lavishly sexual person freely expressing her sexual desires. CMM theory proposes two sets of rules that co-ordinate decision-making and interpersonal relationships: constitutive rules, governing the meaning attribution, such as: 'If my partner refuses to have sex with me, it means they don't love me', and regulative rules, governing the action, such as: 'When my partner is too tired, I should not initiate sexual contact'. The process of meaning-making is often explored in systemic therapy and sometimes reveals that the meaning given to a problem can reinforce the problem, leading to further complications. The resulting action, based on the meaning assigned to a situation, is deconstructed (White, 1991) in therapy, through exploring the links between the event and the significance attached to it.

Therapeutic interventions addressing the behavioural dimension

Exploration of the body and genitalia is typically referred to in sex therapy as 'self focus', 'individual sexual growth' (Heiman, & LoPiccolo, 1988) or 'self-exploration' (McCarthy & McCarthy, 2012). These exercises consist of firstly observing one's body before progressing to gentle touching and developing a physical and sensual feel of it. This graduated exercise involves several steps, aimed at increasing a sense of ownership and acceptance of one's body, as well as tuning into bodily sensations based on sensual and sexual feelings. One element of this exercise involves using a mirror to explore and familiarise oneself with one's own genital organs. Depending on the specific purpose of the exercise, variations may include the use of vaginal dilators, in the case of vaginismus, or sensual and sexual self-stimulation in cases of arousal and orgasm difficulties for both women and men. These exercises also aim to encourage mind/body connection and ownership of one's sexual embodiment, through learning about one's sensual and sexual responsiveness and integrating the frequently disowned genital area within the whole body. Behavioural exercises devised within sex therapy will be referred to in more detail in Chapter 5 when discussing treatment options for specific sexual dysfunctions.

Behavioural resources and resiliencies

Systemic exploration of sexual interactions involves identifying skills and strengths in sexually relating, highlighting the points where different courses of action could be taken. Deconstruction of a sexual episode focusing on positive experiences and preferred possibilities could be guided by questions to encourage self-reflection:

- What are typically the most exciting sexual moments between you and your partner?
- When do you feel your arousal is at its highest?
- If instead of going along with your partner's leads, you introduced a different element, what would it be? How might you go about it?
- What part of the sexual activity do you most look forward to?
- What do you think your partner thinks you enjoy most?
- What do you believe your partner thinks you enjoy most?
- If you showed your partner how much you enjoy specific aspects of what they do, how would you do it?
- If you decided to guide your partner's hands towards the parts of your body where you most want them to touch at certain points in time during sex, how would you do it? How do you think they might respond?

Systemic questions can facilitate clients' understanding and expression of their sexual preferences, such as:

- How would you like to be seduced?
- What would need to happen so you look forward to sex?

- What kind of a sexual invitation would you find most appealing?
- Do you prefer an agreed time/knowing when sex is going to happen or to be surprised/knowing in advance what will happen sexually or improvise and be inventive as you go along?

Such questions are aimed to encourage and inspire behavioural change in sexual communication. A female client who reported a lack of desire and arousal during partnered sex described enjoyable self-pleasuring; she held strong negative stories about her 'sexual inadequacy'. Different behavioural possibilities were brought forth through therapeutic questions drawing attention to the relevance of the sexual stimulus: 'If the partner was doing what you are doing when you give yourself pleasure, how do you think you would react differently when being sexual with them?' A typical psychosexual therapy question for clients to describe their 'ideal sexual scenario' often identifies specific needs and preferences, giving cues as to the desired sexual stimulus, be it in the form of words, sounds, smells, the physical environment, specific sexual behaviours, the atmosphere of the sexual encounter, or a combination of these.

The relational dimension

Relational factors in sexual experiences

Psychosexual therapy aims to encourage the development of communication skills, as communicational problems are amongst the major contributing factors to the development and persistence of sexual concerns in relationships. Being able to listen non-defensively to criticism and anger is one of the most typical relationship challenges encountered in therapy and one of the most important interpersonal skills. Many research studies have confirmed the primary importance of being listened to and feeling understood as factors leading to relationship satisfaction. For example, a UK study using 4,494 participants, recruited by academics in sociology and psychology, investigated factors that make adult relationships endure and flourish in the sociocultural context of shifting discourses on love, intimacy, relationships and commitment. The study identified that good communication was important for all: 'Talking and listening were appreciated as one of the most effective means by which couples came to understand, reassure and comfort each other' (Gabb et al., 2013, p.7).

Systemically thinking, there is no such thing as 'no communication'; all interpersonal situations, including silence, distance and withdrawal, are a form of communication. Within such understanding, the question is not: 'Why is it that we don't communicate?', but rather: 'How do we communicate?' Therapeutic conversations can helpfully identify 'unwanted repetitive interpersonal patterns' (Pearce, 2007), described within social constructionist CMM theory, which can be altered through a variety of therapeutic interventions.

Therapeutic interventions addressing the relational dimension

A frequent unwanted repetitive pattern is encountered in psychosexual therapy, whereby the consequence becomes the cause; for example, when one partner loses interest in sex, the other feels rejected and angry, and conflict takes over, blocking sexual interest. Contrary to the widespread belief that anger fosters passion and fuels excitement, psychosexual therapy practice and research results suggest that anger is one of the most common barriers to sexual desire (Weeks & Hof, 1995). Over many years, clients presenting low sexual desire have reported situations whereby their partners would respond to their sexual withdrawal with frustration and anger. It can be difficult for partners to step outside and recognise the circle whereby their conflictual communication about the sexual problem maintains and reinforces the problem. The circular pattern connecting anger and withdrawal, however apparent it may seem to the therapist, may be almost invisible to the clients as their strong emotions overwhelm and overshadow their rationality and their ability to take a wider perspective. Therapists might take the clients through an interactive step-by-step sequence of anger and withdrawal in slow motion mode, possibly demonstrating diagrammatically on paper how one influences the other in a mutually reinforcing manner.

Sometimes clients withhold communicating their needs because they fear that it will come out in the 'wrong way' or be heard as too negative or critical by the partner. In these situations, therapists can suggest to them to enact their worst fear by saying things in the 'wrong way' in their individual session; this can result in the recognition that their fear exaggerated the possible outcomes. Enacting different scenarios could be used in a variety of ways to increase a range of alternative options. This technique has commonalities with aspects of structural family therapy (Minuchin & Fishman, 1981) where the therapist guides clients to enact certain interpersonal situations in a desired way.

One client expressed the importance of the 'moment' and the ways of opening up a topic of conversation. She said, 'If I approach my husband in a way that appears to be complaining about our relationship, he will be defensive and upset which usually worsens the situation. I learned that a more effective way of communicating is to be very specific and make positive suggestions.' In this example, the client thoughtfully and considerately took responsibility for her own change. Therapists can reinforce this with clients who present with the problem that others are 'not listening' and the impact of being unheard by asking: 'How do you make yourself heard?'; 'How can you create a context for listening?' The aim is not to critically appraise the client's behaviour, but rather to draw their attention to power to create a desired context. The therapist subsequently introduced this idea to other clients (an intervention that can be highly productive, to offer one client's insights as learning for others in similar situations). While some embraced this idea, others disapproved, expressing that they felt that such an approach would constitute strategic manipulation, a dishonest and almost exploitative tactic. Therapeutically speaking, however, the 'myth of honesty' (Markovic, 2013) can create further communicational problems. Clinical experience suggests that communicating uncensored and unprocessed feelings can create misunderstandings and escalate the communication problem. Partners may get trapped in the belief that they have to express their thoughts and feelings about their partner in a 'true' and 'exact' way, sharing every detail of how the other's behaviour, characteristics and habits affect them. Following this belief that a 'true representation' of feelings is the only 'honest' way of relating can adversely impact relationships, leading to increased conflict and upset.

Negotiating closeness and distance is another interpersonal dimension that needs attention in psychosexual therapy. One partner's fear of intimacy coupled with the other's fear of abandonment often plays a part in perpetuating conflict, causing marked distress to both. The therapeutic environment creates a relational context that allows for their respective feelings to be acknowledged. A key to bringing about significant changes in a couple's patterns of interaction is a therapeutic relationship whereby both partners are listened to attentively, are respectfully and supportively challenged and encouraged to take risks in creating interpersonal change (Flaskas & Perlez, 1996).

Systemic observer perspective questions (Tomm, 1987), aiming to enhance empathy between the partners, can encourage new interpersonal awareness, for example:

- What do you think your partner is worried about?
- How did you understand your partner's response to your sexual invitation?
- When you responded the way you did, how did you feel about your reaction?
- What else could you have done?
- If you had the chance, what would you have done differently?
- What do you think your partner would think of it?

Couples sometimes come to therapy at a stage where their mutual criticism reaches such a point that neither one of them can do almost anything without feeling they are criticised by the other. This pattern is usually accompanied by a sense of powerlessness. Externalisation (White, 1995) of the problem is indicated in these situations, a method that aims to unite the couple against the 'joint enemy' of criticism. Typical externalising interventions could be used such as:

- It seems that criticism comes into your space like an uninvited guest, an intruder; ... who robs you of joy and burdens your relationship
- When was the last time you resisted the invitation of this intruder to come between you?
- What would it take you to decide to close the door and not let them in..., to turn away and ignore their interference?

A repetitive pattern of negative anticipation often features in couples' interaction. In one clinical case involving a heterosexual married couple, such a pattern was identified over the course of several sessions. On his return from work, the husband would start imagining coming home hearing the children screaming and seeing his wife exhausted, angry and unfriendly; as a result, he already felt resentful about being so unwelcome before opening the door. The wife's sequence of thoughts mirrored his; she negatively anticipated his entry, preparing herself automatically for a tirade of unhappiness as soon as he would come in. The structure of their busy lives, tiredness and their high expectations of both their parental and professional roles, had buried affection towards each other under this habitual interpersonal pattern. After allowing space for frustrations and irritations to be heard, the sessions moved onto desired future possibilities; the couple were asked to re-write a more amicable version of their joining together at the end of the day, guided by such questions as:

- How would you like to be greeted?
- What would you like to say to your wife when you come home that reflects the warmth you feel for her?
- If she smiled and kissed you "Hello", how would you show your appreciation?
- How could you explain you felt tired in a gentle and loving way?
- What are the five different ways of saying "Hello" that convey care for each other and the family?
- How can you show him that you missed him during the day?

Issues of perceived power difference tend to create a barrier to a satisfactory sexual relationship. A couple who outwardly had a fully functioning relationship came to therapy at the instigation of the woman who had sexually withdrawn from her husband. In therapy, she spoke of having 'lost herself in this perfect relationship', which she very much saw as dominated by her husband. 'Many women would think he's a prince on a white horse... perfect looking, perfect cook, perfect husband, so competent in everything'. The more he wanted to please her and do things for her, however, the more she felt she was sinking into his shadow. Unfortunately, the couple came to therapy when her emotional separation from him reached the point of irretrievable distance and she was undertaking divorce proceedings. She experienced a different sense of self when she met someone else with whom she felt equal. 'I forgot what it is I wanted', she said, 'until I met this man who was interested in me, wanted to know my thoughts and listened without trying to make it all immediately better. He let me be...'. Her sense of her own power and strength in this new relationship made her feel sexually attracted to her new partner and awoke her desires. This example reveals a pattern where one person feels overcome by a 'positive power', the power of a generous giving which can be contrasted with a 'negative power', the power of violence, abuse or undermining the other. Both kinds of power, however, can be silencing and have the potential to destroy a partner's sense of self-worth, which can lead to detachment from one's own desires. The above example reflects gender differences in terms of shifting inequalities of power between women and men, as described by systemic therapists Dallos and Draper (2000):

> Many women who have described their relationships as egalitarian are shocked to realize the extent of their inequality and dependence when that relationship disintegrates. At this point they may become painfully aware that much of their power was contingent on the wishes of their partner, and the particular nature of their relationship (Dallos & Draper, 2000, p.53).

Self-reflexivity of the therapist is particularly important in systemic psychosexual therapy, and in that context assumptions about what constitutes a good relationship need ongoing consideration and reflection; to this end, questions that can usefully be asked are, for example:

- How do we as therapists relate to issues such as: couples who have no sex; have no desire for sex; do not want to talk about sex; engage in unusual and peculiar sexual practices?
- How much conflict is desirable/acceptable for a good relationship?
- If clients' and therapists' views differ, who is to decide which one is right, and how should this be addressed?
- How do we as therapists relate to relationship constellations which involve more than two people in a committed and intimate sexual partnership?

Various sexology, sex therapy and CBT techniques offer specific advice to partners for conflict resolution and effective listening, such as being conciliatory, asking open and clarifying questions, showing understanding, agreeing, acknowledging the problem as opposed to denying it and taking the opposite position and trying to empathise with the partner's perspective. Sex therapists might sometimes take more of a directive approach, providing clients with tasks and exercises aimed at teaching them techniques of effective communication. One such technique, 'reflective listening', an intervention which combines behavioural with systemic ideas, stems from a 'behavioural–systems approach' to the treatment of sexual and relationship problems (Crowe & Ridley, 1990). It consists of a suggestion to the couple to take clearly divided roles; one being in the position of the 'talker', the other one the 'listener'. The first chooses to talk for ten to fifteen minutes, (pausing regularly), about something that is important to them in relationship terms. The task of the 'talker' is to help the 'listener' understand, and to this end, they put their view across as clearly as possible. The task of the 'listener' is to understand without commenting or giving their perspective. The 'listener' simply summarises, after each pause, the essence of what they heard during this exercise by the 'talker'. The conversation only proceeds once the 'talker' is satisfied that he/she has been understood. The same pattern is then repeated with roles reversed in the same or in the subsequent session. It is generally recommended that this second part should relate to a separate topic to avoid it becoming merely a riposte to the first part. If the couple appears to benefit from the exercise, it can be suggested as homework between therapy sessions. This regular practice can enhance the couple's communication skills with real potential to improve general relationship satisfaction.

Zilbergeld (1999), an American sexologist, offers a wealth of useful tools for dealing with relationship conflict:

- keeping agreements and promises
- understanding that not everything can be resolved
- ensuring regular times to discuss the feelings about the relationship
- understanding that conflict is a part of relationships
- calling time out to stop escalation of a conflict
- expressing agreement
- offering apology
- being conciliatory
- showing an ability to understand and forgive the partner
- expressing compliments and appreciation
- considering writing a note.

Wincze and Weisberg (2015, p.144) have developed a ten-page handout for clients that describes couples' common communication problems, such as: 'off beam', when partners start discussing one problem and drift into another; 'mind reading', when partners interpret each other's meanings without checking; 'yes, but', when each partner listens but continues to think that the other one is wrong; 'cross – complaining', when each exchange brings a new complaint; 'standoff', when the same problems are discussed repeatedly in circles. The similarity between the communication patterns described above and transactional analysis illustrated in *Games People Play* (Berne, 1964) is striking both in terms of the pertinence of the described patterns and in the use of playful language likely to facilitate the engagement and enthusiasm of the clients. This handout can be given to clients with the task of identifying which patterns apply to them. Effective communication is then facilitated by encouraging skills of listening, compromising and maintaining a respectful stance with regard to one another.

Handouts and standardised procedures are typically used in sex therapy, in this respect being similar to CBT and behavioural therapeutic approaches. Systemically, interventions are usually more tailored to the individualities and idiosyncrasies of clients, encouraging them to devise their own exercises. Both types of interventions can be applied, either separately or in combination, providing a wide range of treatment possibilities.

Relational resources and resiliencies

The social constructionist method of appreciative inquiry, developed by Cooperrider and Srivastva (1987), can be applied in systemic psychosexual therapy with the purpose of eliciting positive change through focusing on strengths and preferred choices, as opposed to deficiencies, difficulties and problems. The 'unconditional positive questions' of appreciative inquiry are aimed to trigger transformational dialogue and action (Ludema, Cooperrider & Barrett, 2000, p.194), searching for, highlighting and illuminating what is best in the relationship:

- What examples illustrate your best ways of communicating and relating?
- What are the unique aspects of each one of you that most positively affect the spirit, vitality and values of your relationship?
- Think of a time during the entire experience of your relationship when you felt most excited, engaged and alive. What were the factors,

behaviours, and ways of relating and communicating that made it such a good experience?
- What was it about you, your partner and others, that made it such a good experience for you?

Desired possibilities are then elicited through questions encouraging the positive construction of future interpersonal experiences:

- What are the possibilities, latent or expressed, that provide opportunities for even better and more effective ways of functioning?
- What are the most important hopes you have to increase mutual satisfaction within your relationship?

These questions are seen as keys for unlocking existing deficit constructions, creating space for new voices and languages, promoting 'collaborative competence' (Barrett & Fry, 2005). Employing the vocabulary of possibility and hope can provide a path to relationship strengthening through tapping into the clients' hidden reservoir of strengths, capacities and achievements. One of the main premises of this approach is that partnerships between people are co-constructed through the language and discourse of day-to-day interactions. It posits that words have an impact far beyond just words themselves; language assigns interpretations, evaluations and conclusions, influencing reasoning, judgement and feeling. 'Words create worlds', a phrase attributed to philosophers Heschel (1996) and Wittgenstein (2009), summarises this standpoint. Within this reasoning, when conversations focus on problems and conflicts, the number and severity of these problems grow; in the same manner, when attention is paid to high human ideals and achievements, such as peak experiences, best practices and noble accomplishments, these phenomena, too, tend to flourish (Ludema, Cooperrider & Barrett, 2000, p.192).

Relational resiliencies could be drawn out through systemic observer perspective questions (Tomm, 1987), such as:

- If your relationship improved, who would notice it first?
- Who would be most pleased?
- How would you show it?
- How would you celebrate it?

or unexpected context change questions (Tomm, 1987):

- How come you stayed together in spite of these difficulties?
- What are the best aspects of your sexual relationship?

Management of differences is a frequently presented issue in psychosexual therapy, including discrepancy of desire and incompatibility of sexual preferences. A lesbian couple came to therapy early on in their relationship, disappointed and worried about the differences in their sexual preferences. One partner was saying: 'I can't have this vanilla sex, it is boring'; and the other was expressing her wish for tender and loving sex: 'I can't hurt you, I love you!' As their negotiation skills evolved throughout therapy, they came up with imaginative solutions. For example, they filmed a 'vanilla sex scene' between them; and on another occasion used rubber clothing while engaging in tender sex. Utilising (Erickson, 2009) their pre-existing preferences, previously seen as clashing, allowed them both to experience joint pleasure by bringing them together in a constructively combined way.

Weeks & Gambescia (2000, p.128) suggest a couple exercise, 'creating a positive anticipation', analogous to planning a special vacation together. The couple are asked to imagine their next sexual encounter guided by the therapist's questions:

- What would you like to happen?
- What would you like to do for your partner?
- What would you like the partner to do for you?

The couple are then encouraged to share these thoughts with one another and eventually put them into practice in a relaxing private environment.

The cultural dimension

Cultural factors in sexual experiences

The cultural dimension permeates all other dimensions of the model in that cultural stories and practices contextualise personal and interpersonal meanings and the experience of sex. The MOST model places significance on exploring both constraining and liberating cultural stories about sex, religious and cultural loyalties that people adhere to and their impact on sexual behaviour. This dimension emphasises 'the importance of assessing community and societal influences on the sexual experience of individuals and couples, making it possible to identify and diminish the effects of homophobia and sexism' (Iasenza, 2004, p.24).

Within a social constructionist framework, phenomena such as sexual functioning and dysfunctions, intimacy, pleasure, privacy, desire, arousal and satisfaction are understood as social constructions whose meaning, significance and impact varies across different cultural contexts. Social constructionists emphasise gender, power and cultural discourses on sex and intimacy (Hare-Mustin, 1991, 1994; Foreman & Dallos, 1992; Dallos, 1997; Dallos & Dallos, 1997). Gavey's (1989, in Mustin, 1991) definition of discourse as used by Hare-Mustin (1991) is helpful, describing it as 'a system of statements and practices that share common values' (p.64). The importance of therapeutic explorations of culturally embedded discourses when working with sex and sexual relationships is illustrated by a male client's response to a therapeutic suggestion involving a romantic and sensual couple exercise: 'I can't do that, I'm a Yorkshireman!' The construction of what is right and wrong for a man of his age, in terms of intimately relating to his wife, was determined most powerfully by his interpretation of his cultural and gender belonging which he held as the highest context (Pearce & Cronen, 1980) influencing his sexual being. This corresponds with the social constructionist position (Rorty, 1979; Foucault, 1980; Lyotard, 1984), which holds that we are constrained by cultural meanings and that we construct the world from within the meaning community to which we belong. Hare-Mustin (1994) suggested that it was essential that therapists recognised how embedded communication was in cultural belief systems and how influenced it was by the discourses that created male and female identities of power. Her research on discourses concerning sexuality uncovered the layers that define what is expected of men and women in relation to each other, disguising gender inequality. Hare-Mustin's (1994) discourse analysis found dominant stories about the forceful and uncontrollable nature of the male sexual drive. This particular discourse has impacted widely on sexual relationships of all genders. Feminism in family and systemic therapy has pointed to gender inequality and the oppression of patriarchy, and the anxieties that all genders feel in trying to fulfil socially expected roles. The position of social constructionism inspired by feminist writers emphasised that there are fundamental inequalities of power between men and women and that they are embedded in wider social, cultural and political discourses (Hollway, 1983, 1989; Foreman & Dallos, 1992; Dallos & Dallos, 1997; Goldner, 2004). They suggested that it was crucial for systemic therapists to understand major societal discourses and their impact on individuals and couples, particularly when working in areas such as marital violence and sexual problems. Foreman and Dallos' (1992) research, revealing some influential discourses specifically concerning sexuality and gender, described the influences of these discourses in the interplay of power and relationship dynamics in the area of couple sexuality:

- gender dichotomy discourse, emphasising differences between men and women and constructing the differences as natural, functional and largely unchangeable
- sexual drive discourse, based on the assumption that people are driven by a biological sexual 'impulse' or 'instinct'
- sexual initiative discourse, concerning the division of gender roles in terms of who suggests sex and who should take responsibility for their own and their partner's sexual satisfaction
- mutuality discourse, which minimises differences between women and men and holds that both equally enjoy and desire sex and have equal rights in sex (this discourse is described by the authors as idealistic and minimising of differences of power and the influential forces of social conditioning and attitudes), and
- female sexuality as a commodity discourse, conceptualising female and male sexuality as something that one can buy and exchange.

Culturally, communication about sex seems to be divided between two extremes: on the one hand, it is overdosed, exaggerated and overstated, particularly in social media in the UK, which portrays a commercialised outlook on sex; on the other hand, meaningful conversations about sex are narrowed down and suppressed. This suppression is supported by political, educational and religious systems falling back on 'traditional values'. Cultural ambiguity, with two opposite extremes and no middle ground, produces anxiety and distress in people caught in mixed messages fearing that whichever way they go, they cannot win. Furthermore, different cultural norms and expectations bring additional layers of confusion in cross-cultural encounters.

Therapeutic interventions addressing the cultural dimension

Various therapeutic options for addressing the cultural dimension can be applied in systemic psychosexual therapy. The educational input of sexology that normalises clients' situations within a wider context, combined with exploratory reflexive systemic questions, provides a therapeutic space for addressing gender inequality and the oppression of patriarchy. It is not unusual to come across the female faking an orgasm with their male partners, for example, as a means of covering up what they thought were their own sexual inadequacies, feeling inhibited to express their sexual needs and preferences and fearing rejection. This is often a result of women not knowing their own bodies and not being in tune with their sexual needs, to the point of being detached from the sexual experience altogether. This cultural oppression in the form of sexism and heterosexism could be addressed and explored via systemic questions such as 'contextual situation questions' (Tomm, 2011):

- In many societies, female sexuality is suppressed. How did you learn to keep your sexual needs hidden?
- What is it like to live as a gay couple in a predominantly heterosexual environment?
- How have you managed to pursue your bisexual interests in spite of many external obstacles and judgements?
- What assumptions from the cultural environment could be limiting your movements, or holding you back?

'Audience questions' (Hornstrup, Tomm & Johansen, 2009) aim to create an expansive contextual awareness by seeing one's presenting difficulties in a larger frame of cultural experiences, practices and discourses such as:

- If you imagine this session were taking place on a stage and hundreds of gay women were sitting and listening to your experiences that you just shared with me, how many do you think would stand up and say: "I feel exactly the same" How many might add another angle to your story... what might that be?

A 'two rooms question' (Markovic, 2011) can provide another perspective in situations where clients bring dilemmas to therapy regarding their relationship choices. Clients can be invited to engage with this hypothetical scenario:

> Imagine people who have known you well in different situations over time had to vote whether you stay in this relationship or not by entering one of the two rooms: Room A would mean 'Yes' and Room B would mean 'No'. Which room would be fuller? Would there be more family or more friends in one of the rooms? Would either of the rooms be filled more by people from your past or more from your present? Imagine entering Room A now... what kind of noise would you be hearing, more cheerful or more serious voices? Who do you recognise first? If you start talking to these people individually, what reasons would they give for choosing to enter this room? Would there be more men or more women in this room?

This scenario can be developed further through a co-constructed exploration between the therapist and clients.

A useful reminder of the cultural diversity and relativity of perspectives is offered through the systemic concept of 'multiple realities' whereby social worlds are understood as subjective, plural and created in interpersonal communication through language and are subject to a variety of meaning attributions (Pearce, 2007). Thinking systemically, particularly influenced by social constructionist philosophy, people's choices would be regarded as inseparable from their prediction of the impact of those choices on their cultural and social systems. Decisions and options are considered within the wider contexts of relationships and culturally established practices, even though it often seems as if they are only focused on immediate personal and relationship issues. Expanding therapeutic explorations so as to include wider contexts and enlighten clients' contextual understanding of their issues is often a major therapeutic task and can be a potentially effective intervention.

Therapists' self-reflexivity and relational reflexivity

Systemically, it is stressed that therapists should monitor their own prejudices (Cecchin, Lane & Ray, 1992), acknowledging that these can comprise both a resource and a hindrance in their work with clients. The therapists' awareness in terms of understanding cultural variety, such as appreciating that there are typical cultural patterns and norms that determine what is acceptable, what is prohibited, what is a matter of pride and what constitutes cultural shame and betrayal, is crucial in systemic psychosexual therapy. It is also important that therapists are aware of cultural differences between themselves and their clients and to monitor their assumptions and prejudices (Cecchin, Lane & Ray, 1994) to avoid possible misinterpretations and pathologising of clients. The 'cure' for therapists' immersion in the dominant discourses (White, 1991) and the tool for allowing themselves to challenge their own prejudices and the cultural origins of their assumptions is seen as mastering the skill of self-reflexivity (Morawski, 1990; Gergen, 1999), questioning their own views (Madigan, 1993) or, as Tomm (1991) wisely put it: 'Think of your thinking, listen to your listening, question your questioning...'. Clifton, Doan and Mitchell (1990) provide guidance for therapists' self-reflexivity in the style of the narrative approach. Adjusted to this context, their mode of questioning could be applied in the following ways:

- If I perceived this client as stronger and more sexually liberated than I have previously thought, what would I be saying to them?
- How did I get to believe that particular clients have been oppressed by their cultural mythology?

- How does that relate to my cultural stories and loyalties?
- Am I approaching clients too cautiously?
- If I decided to take a more challenging approach, what would I be doing?
- If I decided to address gender inequality in their relationship, how might I do that?
- If, instead of typically inviting clients to participate in joint decision-making, I decided in this instance to just tell them that this is the best way forward, how would I justify that intervention to my supervisor?
- How is the client's compliance and tendency to leave the final decision to her husband, believing he has better ideas and should lead her as a man, influencing my ways of relating to her and how is my eagerness for asserting her female voice and my disappointment in her failings to do so affecting my emotional responses to her?

Burnham (2005) defines self-reflexivity as 'a process in which a therapist makes, takes or grasps an opportunity to observe, listen to, and question the effects of their practice, then use their responses to their observation/listening to decide "how to go on" in the particular episode or the work in general' (p.3). The process of self-reflexivity is an internal dialogue a therapist has while listening to clients in the session. For example, they may ask themselves questions and express thoughts such as:

- Where is the session going?
- Are we on the right track?
- Does the client seem reflectively engaged with the issues?
- What could I do differently?
- I must be more sensitive to gender and culture,

and so on. In this way, the therapist searches for their own resources in conducting the therapy session in the best interests of their clients.

Relational reflexivity (Burnham, 2005) extends this mode of thought by putting self-reflexive questioning in the conversational context with clients. The therapist uses their self-reflective internal dialogue as a prompt to initiate questions for the client. The therapeutic intention is to open a relationally reflexive space for clients to experience empowerment in co-constructing with the therapist a relationship with positive therapeutic potential. For example, relationally reflexive questions could be:

- Have I challenged you too much, too little, or just right?
- Do you prefer questions or statements?

- What kinds of statements/questions?
- What question was most interesting/useful/difficult?
- Would you like to proceed in the same way or would you like to make any changes in the way we have been talking today?
- Have I shown sensitivity to your gender and culture in our conversations?

This corresponds with Tomm's (2011) reflexive questions, which could be equally applied in co-constructing this kind of a collaborative conversation in therapy, such as:

- What else could I be asking you about that would help me understand your situation more fully? ('meta-situation questions')
- What else could I be enquiring about that would help you create new understanding and possibilities? ('meta-possibilities questions')
- Whose perspective could I be asking you about that would help you see another angle in your situation? ('meta-perspective questions').

Cultural resources and resiliencies

Social and cultural contexts constitute restraints of pressure, as well as resources for individuals and relationships. Both of these are important to explore in therapy to empower (Tomm, 1991) effective, proactive practices. Opening up conversations about sex, a largely taboo subject, and supporting clients in talking about it with others demystifies the topic, providing normalisation and a better understanding of their sexual issues, peeling away layers of anxiety and shame attached to the subject.

Deconstructing (White, 1991) gender and cultural discourses is an intrinsic part of the therapeutic process in systemic psychosexual therapy. Personal cultural scripts are often highly emotionally charged and may relate to intense feelings of pride or shame. An adult man presented with the issue of sexual anxiety. Most of his adolescence was emotionally difficult as he was ostracised by his peers and labelled as 'depressed' by the psychiatrist to whom his worried parents sent him because he was not socialising, partying and clubbing. His preferred ways of spending his time were having quiet chats with friends, reading books, listening to classical music and playing the piano. Now in his early 30s, suffering from sexual anxiety, he reflected on that time in his life and how difficult the experience of being treated as abnormal had been for him. During conversations in therapy, he started developing an idea that this may not have been his pathology and that he suffered from social exclusion. 'I wasn't crazy', he said, 'I was different... but I was being me...'. This reflection and the development of a different perception of his adolescent experiences were connected with the theme of his current sexual concerns and encouraged focus on his sexual choices regardless of his construction of how he might be fitting into the cultural expectations of 'normal sexual behaviour'.

It is important for therapists to recognise when social and cultural contexts may pose restraint and pressure and when they may provide resources for individuals and relationships. Clients' relevant wider systems are referred to in the systemic approach as the 'network of support' and the 'network of concern' (McAdam, 1995), and therapists aim to enhance clients' resourcefulness in making stronger and more effective use of these. Clients' choices are often determined by their prediction of the impact of their actions on their social and cultural systems. Decisions related to emotional, relational, sexual and physical spheres are often considered within the wider contexts of relationships and culturally established practices. For example, a particular body image is promoted in most cultures, and a culturally desirable appearance is communicated via a variety of channels including social media. Zilbergeld (1999) writes about 'the fantasy model of sex', which is disseminated through popular films, literature and magazines, presenting a limited and prescriptive template of sex based on narrow, sexist and heterosexist perspectives, idealising the extremes of passion and imposing the idea of 'perfect functioning'. Sharing sexology research results, including the DSM-5 (APA, 2013) findings about the prevalence of various sexual dysfunctions, can provide a contextual normalisation of certain sexual constraints. For instance, in some cultures that strictly forbid masturbation and see it as a sin and betrayal of religious values, it is practised secretly in a great rush with the constant fear of being discovered, setting a pattern for premature ejaculation in adult sexual relationships. Vaginismus is frequently linked with cultural oppression of female sexual expressiveness, leading to sexual anxiety and both psychological and physical tension. Sharing such information with clients can offer an additional layer of understanding to their difficulties and a cultural normalisation of the experienced constraints. Various systemic contextual questions (Tomm, 2011) could also be used to this end, such as:

- What kind of conversation would you choose to have with your family member/partner/friend in order to open up possibilities for moving forward in this situation?
- How might you go about setting this meeting up?
- What would be your main points of emphasis?

Concluding summary: the MOST model

The MOST model is applicable to a wide variety of sexual issues and can be used in all stages of work, from assessment, through formulation, to deciding on treatment options for conducting therapy, including follow-up and feedback, and is focused on problems and pathology, as well as resources and strengths within each dimension. It integrates sexology and systemic therapy, providing a broad scope of treatment options, combining the medical and the scientific with social constructionist and relational perspectives while allowing space for the integration and application of a variety of other psychotherapeutic approaches. These include CBT, gestalt therapy, behavioural therapy, attachment therapy, and emotionally focused therapy. Psychotherapists of different theoretical orientations could utilise the model as a working framework for their specific practices. The self of the therapist, self-reflexivity and relational reflexivity are concepts deeply embedded in the model highlighting on the one hand the importance of therapists examining their own sexual stories, prejudices and subjectivity when working with the delicate topic of sex and, on the other, privileging social constructionist awareness of the relational meaning-making of reality.

The six dimensions of the MOST model are not as separate as represented in the diagram; they are interconnected and sometimes overlap to the extent of being inseparable. All dimensions have some degree of impact on every issue. Even if the origin of a sexual problem may be purely and narrowly biological, the impact of the problem will be multidimensional, in terms of how one feels about the problem and the biological situation; what the person thinks is the best way forward; their beliefs about medication; and their beliefs about therapy. Furthermore, their self-image and relationships may be affected by and affecting the problem. It is always useful to consider all dimensions, and sometimes the emphasis may be more on certain ones than others while bearing in mind that the processes in one dimension would affect the processes in others in an ongoing, active and fluid way. Some therapeutic interventions affect more than one dimension, or may affect all spheres. Comprehensive treatment, combining a variety of methods and techniques from sexology and systemic therapy, focused both on problems and resources within each dimension, is likely to bring about the most effective outcomes, aimed at building on clients' existing resiliencies.

Finally, the construct of the six dimensions can be used as a clinical tool in itself, being communicated directly to clients in either verbal or written form. Offering ideas about the factors that are likely to have contributed to the onset, development and maintenance of clients' presenting issues and on the ways of addressing and making changes within each set of contributing aspects, through use of diagrammatic representation, has the potential to engage clients in thoughtful reflections. This can enrich their understanding of their experiences and strengthen their sense of control and confidence by bringing clarity to a complex and multifaceted picture. Sometimes, mapping out the factors makes a stronger impact on clients than verbally describing them through therapeutic conversations. It can be particularly useful as a means of broadening the meaning of sex, as well as developing more connections by seeing the factors as interrelated across different dimensions and mutually influencing each other.

EXERCISES

- Reflect on a recent case example using the diagrammatic representation of the MOST model by completing its sections. Which sections are fullest? Where could you focus your work further? How could that be relevant for clients?
- Imagine working with the presenting problem of low sexual desire. Create therapeutic questions within each dimension as possible therapeutic interventions.
- Trainee groups: practise the use of these questions in a role-play therapy session, with observers to the role-play making notes of which questions are more useful as assessment/diagnostic ones and which are potentially useful as more healing/therapeutic ones.

2

DEFINITIONS OF SEX AND SEXUAL RESPONSE

When working with sexual issues, it is important to be clear as professionals which beliefs we uphold about sex and what model of human sexual response we regard as our practice framework before going on to explore the meaning of sex for clients. However, this most basic task of defining sexuality seems most difficult and has presented immense dilemmas for researchers and clinicians over time. Without an expectation that 'the' definition of sex is sought, the following pages will first address the historical context by summarising the most influential models of human sexual response developed within sexology, starting from Masters and Johnson, the first practitioners of sex therapy, to the current definitions embraced by social constructionist views.

Human sexual response models

Masters and Johnson, a four-stage model (1966)

This first model was developed by Masters and Johnson (1966) who proposed that human sexual response evolves through four distinct stages:

- *Excitement stage*: the stage of initial arousal, where a series of physiological changes happen including: increased muscle tension, heart rate, and blood pressure; increased blood flow to the genitals; men experience erection, swelling of the testicles and the scrotum, and women swelling and lubrication of the vaginal walls and inner lips, and clitoral enlargement.

- *Plateau*: as stimulation continues, during the plateau phase the high physiological sensitivity as described above continues and arousal is maintained and intensified; this phase can last between a few seconds and several minutes.
- *Orgasm*: manifests itself in involuntary contractions of the muscles around the body and the genitals, a peak in heart and breathing rate and ejaculation for men and sometimes women.
- *Resolution*: ends the cycle, where the muscles relax and the genital areas slowly return to their normal state.

'Only one sexual response pattern has been diagrammed for the human male', write Masters and Johnson (1966, p.4). The only variation they saw in the male sexual response relates to duration rather than intensity or any other characteristics of the sexual response. Variations relate to the duration of the plateau phase thus allowing for a shorter or longer period of sexual activity before reaching orgasm.

The female cycle, on the other hand, shows variations both in the duration and intensity of the response. A woman can have a smooth transition from excitement and plateau to resolution. Woman 'A' in Masters and Johnson's model has multiple orgasms. Woman 'B' proceeds to the plateau phase but does not experience orgasm; this is not a problem if it is an occasional occurrence, however regular occurrence might lead to the diagnosis of female orgasmic disorder. Woman 'C''s cycle is shorter and more intense; she reaches orgasm more quickly and proceeds to resolution faster. These three different patterns may also relate to the same woman at different times. Masters and Johnson emphasise that there is an infinite variety in female sexual response. However, they all seem to be evolving around the same basic template of the four stages and all varieties simply relate to the duration and intensity of response within this narrow framework.

Masters and Johnson's model: critique

The Masters and Johnson model dominated the fields of sexology and sex therapy for many decades and, despite being criticised and superseded by the creation of different models that have been widely accepted as improved versions based on updated knowledge and expanded paradigms, it is still used by many practitioners in educating clients, students and the general public about 'normal' sexuality. The major points of critique (Hite, 2004; Lloyd, 2009) have been that it is:

- gender insensitive, as it does not sufficiently consider the differences between male and female sexuality
- exclusively biologically based, ignoring psychological and relational aspects
- a linear model, mistakenly implying that a sexual response evolves in a linear progression
- normative, suggesting how humans 'should' operate sexually and therefore pathologising for those who do not function in this way.

Tiefer, a social constructionist, feminist, sex educator, a proponent of the 'new view on women's sexual problems' (Kaschak & Tiefer, 2014) and a leading figure in challenging the medicalisation of sexology, critiqued Masters and Johnson's model particularly sharply. Viewing it as a major paradigm still underpinning the foundations of sexology and the *Diagnostic and Statistical Manual of Psychiatric Disorders* (DSM), she saw significant problems with this model in privileging biology and, in particular, genital physiology over other aspects of bodily experience in sex, and in ignoring sociocultural contexts and gender differences (Tiefer, 2004).

Following Tiefer's critique, rigidly adopting this model could dangerously imply that:

- there is universality in sex
- all people should respond sexually in the same way
- sex is acontextual; detached from sociocultural and relational contexts
- there is no relevance of choice and personal or relational preference in sex
- sex is monolithic, monochrome, a single-meaning category
- there is no variety in sex in terms of how it is experienced, desired, felt, imagined, described, interpreted or remembered
- sex is mechanistic, mechanical and functionalistic
- sex is unidirectional; it has a starting-point, a mid-point and an end-point, leading to a (externally defined by experts) single eternal goal
- sex is a universal, absolute category
- sex is objective, objectifiable and quantifiable
- sex is purely physical, and above all, a genital contact
- mind and body are separate in sex
- there is such a thing as the graph of sex
- sex is general, generic and generalisable
- sex is the same for everyone (who is normal).

Kaplan: three-stage model (1979)

Helen Kaplan, an influential, psychoanalytically oriented sex therapist, revised the Masters and Johnson model in the late 1970s reducing it to three stages: desire, arousal and orgasm (Kaplan, 1979). The stage of *desire* was added as a pre-requisite for sexual arousal.

The same points of critique of the Masters and Johnson model have been expressed regarding Kaplan's revision. In addition, considering desire as part of a sexual experience seemed significant; however, it prescribed desire as a necessary condition for the sexual response cycle to be triggered. This is nowadays deemed amongst the most prevalent myths negatively impacting people's sexual experience. Subsequent clinical studies and research findings have overwhelmingly proven that desire can follow arousal and that a pleasurable and satisfying sexual response can begin and evolve without the prior experience of desire.

Circular models: Whipple and Brash-McGreer (1997); Basson (2001)

Two different models were developed in the late 1990s/early 2000s, bringing circularity to the understanding of women's sexual response:

Whipple and Brash-McGreer (1997) built on the model proposed by Reed (Erotic stimulus pathway model; Reed, 1995, in Haffner & Stayton) who merged Masters and Johnson's and Kaplan's models using four stages:

- Seduction (encompassing *desire*; includes everything one might do to entice someone to be sexual with them)
- Sensations (includes *excitement* and *plateau*; this is where senses take over, such as smell, touch and visual sensations)
- Surrender (the phase of *orgasm*) and
- Reflection (*resolution* phase).

The seduction and sensation phases were introduced as psychosocial, appreciating psychological, relational and cultural factors. Whipple and Brash-McGreer revised the model by making it circular. They critiqued the previous models from a female perspective, emphasising that not all women would respond in a linear way. They suggested that circularity develops such that pleasure and satisfaction during one sexual experience feed into desire for the next one. If, on reflection, the sexual experience did not feel satisfactory and pleasurable, there may not be desire to participate in a subsequent sexual encounter.

The main points of an alternative circular model of female sexual response developed by Basson (2000, 2001) are outlined below:

- It incorporates the importance of emotional intimacy, the adequacy of the sexual stimulus and relationship satisfaction.
- If a particular sexual experience did not provide pleasure or satisfaction, the woman may not have the desire to repeat the experience.
- Female sexual functioning proceeds in a more complex and circular manner than it does with men and is significantly affected by numerous psychological issues, e.g. satisfaction with the relationship, self-image and previous sexual experiences.
- Women have many reasons for engaging in sexual activity other than sexual hunger or drive; for example, a desire for increased emotional closeness and intimacy; or overtures from the partner may predispose sexual interest.
- Many women may not experience spontaneous desire and interest; most women do not frequently think of sex or experience spontaneous hunger for sexual activity.
- From the point of sexual neutrality, where a woman is receptive to being sexual but does not initiate sexual activity, the desire for intimacy prompts her to seek ways to be sexually aroused, for example via conversation, music, reading or viewing erotic material, or direct stimulation.
- Once she is aroused, sexual desire emerges and motivates her to continue.
- On the road to satisfaction, there are many points of vulnerability that may derail or distract her from feeling sexually fulfilled.
- The goal of sexual activity for women is not necessarily orgasm but rather personal satisfaction which can manifest as physical and/or emotional.
- Much of women's sexual desire is responsive rather than spontaneous, e.g. the partner's sexual interest.
- It's OK not to always start with desire: 'Sexual arousal in women is more a mental excitement' (Basson, 2000, p.63).

Many aspects of Basson's model rely on concepts that are fundamental to systemic and social constructionist ideas such as: circularity; gender differences; individual differences; importance of the relational context and communication; multicontextual influences impacting an experience; the importance of the meaning given to an experience and appreciation of a diversity of possible meanings.

A social constructionist perspective: Tiefer (2004)

Tiefer believes that many important aspects of sexuality are left out of the earlier sexual response models, including pleasure, emotionality, sensuality, communication, power differences, cultural contexts and female gender oppression. She considers that female sexual problems stem from the internalisation of cultural norms, reinforced by political institutions and the medical establishment. She strongly opposes the medicalisation of sexology, which she sees as a result of the pharmaceutical industry- and politics-controlled sexual education. From her social constructionist perspective, the domination of a biomedical model in sexology is a major obstacle to fully embracing sexuality as a multidimensional, contextually relative phenomenon, open to individual choices and preferences, fluid and changeable, constructed in interaction within particular contexts and open to multiple possibilities.

Tiefer (2004, pp.254–256) proposes a classification of women's sexual problems as follows:

I. *Sexual problems due to sociocultural, political or economic factors,* including: inadequate sex education, perceived inability to meet cultural norms, lack of interest and fatigue due to family or work obligations
II. *Sexual problems relating to partner and relationship,* including: discrepancy of desire, conflict, dislike or fear of partner
III. *Sexual problems due to psychological factors,* such as: depression and anxiety, loss, past sexual traumas, personality problems with attachment and rejection
IV. *Sexual problems due to medical factors*: pregnancy, sexually transmitted diseases, medical conditions, iatrogenic conditions and side effects of medication.

A spectrum of sex

A spectrum of sex is introduced here as an alternative possibility of defining sex, describing its meaning and facilitating conversations about it (see Figure 2.1). The depiction of sex as a spectrum enables appreciation of the complex and multifaceted nature of human sexuality and challenges the widespread narrower definitions, while allowing space for many different variations within it.

Typical definitions of sex tend to narrow it down and reduce its meaning. The spectrum suggests that sex and sexuality could be thought of as a wide range of activities and communicational exchanges that people engage in, including but not limited to the narrow meaning of sex as intercourse and penetration. It expands the possibilities to encompass a variety of sexual and sensual options that do not necessarily involve *penetration* or genital contact, or even any physical contact. The further components of the spectrum include: *sensuality* (physical and non-physical), *emotional*

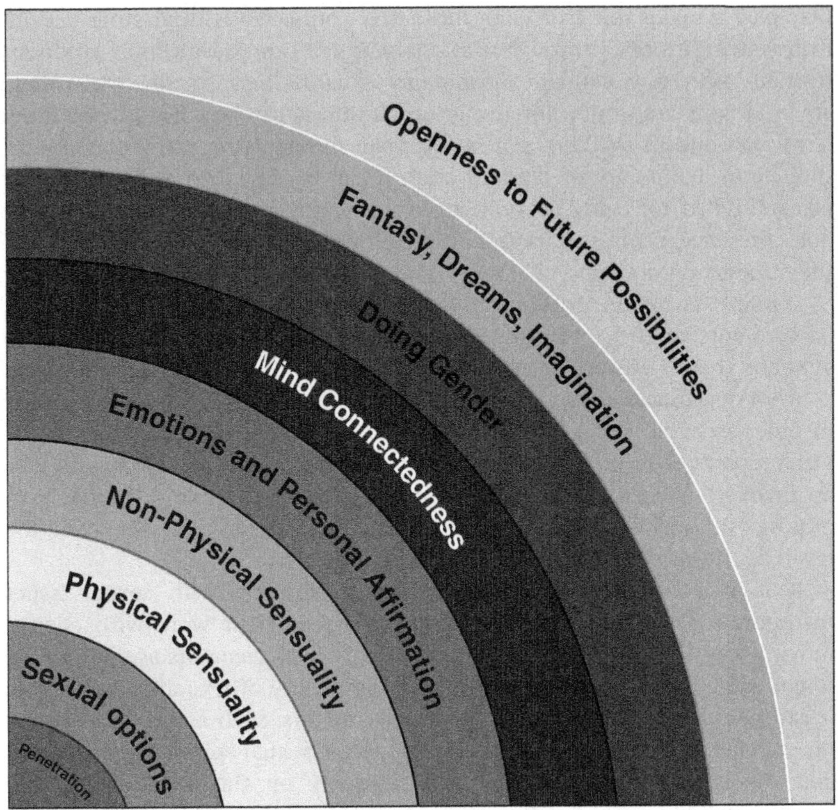

Figure 2.1 A spectrum of sex

intimacy (through which *personal affirmation* can be experienced), *mind connectedness* (conversational or communicational closeness), *doing gender* (ways of expressing own masculinity/femininity), and *fantasy, dreams* and *imagination*. The spectrum of possibilities is not closed and embraces *openness to future possibilities* in evolving one's personal spectrum of sex and appreciating boundless varieties in sexually relating.

Interconnectedness of the spectrum layers

In viewing sex as a spectrum, its many layers are interconnected. Sensuality, intimacy and communicational closeness, for example, connect and intertwine creating mutually influencing patterns. The seductive power of conversation may play a major role in feeling intimately connected with another person. Experiencing intimacy through relational warmth, care and affection, kindness, trust and generosity can all contribute to sexual feelings; equally, when these are lacking, it can inhibit interest in sex. Intimacy can be a feature of a long-term relationship or there can be intimate moments in many encounters, short-term, temporary or random ones; it can be described as listening and being listened to, being acknowledged and being heard, a confirmation of one's presence, having an impact on the other and allowing the experience of their impact on oneself.

While it is helpful to appreciate the interconnectedness of the various components of the spectrum, it can equally be important to be able to separate them. 'Fusion of sex and affection' (Wincze & Carey, 2001), a concept developed within psychosexual therapy, relates to patterns whereby in order to avoid sex a person may avoid expressing physical affection or other aspects of intimacy and sensuality with their partner so as not to give an inadvertent signal of initiation of sex. As such a situation is likely to impoverish people's intimate and emotional connectedness, separating the levels of the spectrum of sex may then be indicated.

It is helpful that therapists working inclusively with sexual issues incorporate all these aspects of sexuality within their work with clients, moving and shifting focus amongst the individual segments as appropriate to embrace the multilayered nature and complexity of sexuality. Sometimes it can be relevant to connect with wider contexts, such as gender, culture, race or class for example; at other times specific sexual episodes are explored and therapeutic conversations focus narrowly on the physical and the behavioural dimensions of the spectrum.

Sex as communication, and communication about sex

Two aspects of sex: sex as a form of communication, and communication about sex, and their recursive connection, can be explored through therapeutic deconstruction of sexual episodes. To explore sex as a form of communication, therapists may be guided by questions such as:

- How adequate is the stimulation received?
- How sufficient is the length and the type of foreplay?
- Are the participants in the sexual activity getting what they need sexually?
- How does what happens sexually fit with their respective sexual preferences?

Sometimes this kind of exploration leads to reformulation of the presenting problem from 'lack of sexual interest' to an 'absence of adequate stimulation', indicating that a behavioural adjustment in sexual technique and/or practice may be sufficient to redress the presenting problem.

To explore communication about sex, therapists may be guided by questions such as:

- How are the participants in the sexual activity asking for what they need sexually?
- How are they expressing their wishes and desires, as well as sexual turn-offs?
- How are they being heard and responded to in their expression of their sexual needs?
- What gets in the way of communicating?
- What needs to happen so that communication about sex is enabled and flows more freely?

Sexual fantasy

When sexual fantasy is, to a lesser or a greater extent, frozen, and clients' knowledge of their sexual self is restricted, then specific therapeutic interventions can defrost the situation. For instance, offering specially developed behavioural exercises for individuals, to explore and learn about their physical interests, or asking therapeutic questions to facilitate building on sexual fantasy. A question such as: 'If you imagine an ideal sexual encounter for you, what would be happening?' is regularly asked in psychosexual therapy and can be broken down into different aspects allowing for a detailed exploration to enlighten the person's understanding of their own sexual preferences, practices and sometimes hidden desires. Questions can be open and general such as:

- What type of a sexual initiation would you find intriguing?
- What do you find most seductive when it comes to sex?
- If I wanted to teach someone to seduce you sexually, what kind of advice would I have to give them? What is most important? What mustn't they do?

A 'worst sexual scenario' equally facilitates clients' reflection and enhances their understanding of the relevant layers in the sexual spectrum that impacts their sexual experiences. Sometimes clients reflect back on their past unsatisfactory sexual experiences or, alternatively, may create undesirable hypothetical scenarios:

- The worst would be if s/he didn't look at me at all
- I really don't like when sex is completely silent, as if there is some unspoken shame underlying it...

- Sometimes s/he is like an animal just wanting sex and I am an object not a person, it's not about me, it could be anyone...

The therapist's ability to create a contemplative, reflective context that enables clients to explore their fantasy world and associated, sometimes deeply hidden, sexual feelings is crucial in this process. Questions can also be specific, offering possibilities and embedded suggestions (Tomm, 1987) in order to tease out more detail to enrich the picture of the client's sexual processes and their understanding of their own psychosexual world. The spectrum can be a useful point of reference in such situations as it can provide a path to broadening the meaning of sex in a way that improves clients' understanding of the connectedness between these different layers and its relevance to their sexual experiences. Sometimes clients feel too shy and inhibited to open up in this way in the therapist's presence, in which case offering some guidance questions for their personal reflection in their own space and time might be indicated, leaving the client to choose whether anything is then brought to therapy.

Sexual options

Exploring individual meanings of sex and sexual preferences does not intend to imply that the aim is to 'discover' a definite and static 'sexual profile'. An individual's sexual preferences may vary over time and depend on many factors, which may not always be possible to determine; in systemic psychosexual therapy sexual behaviour is regarded as a fluid and evolving process rather than a fixed entity. Therapeutic interventions reflect this by introducing the dimension of time, exploring changing preferences in different situations:

- Do you sometimes prefer to be cuddled more than at other times?
- Does kissing generally play an important part in your sexual activity or, in some sexual situations, does it feel less important? What do you believe this depends on?
- Do you sometimes prefer a more gentle, slow and sensual approach and at other times do you wish for brief, rushed and rough genitally focused sex?

Therapists might wish to encourage clients' sexual self-reflexivity by asking:

- How much do your sexual desires and interests vary in different contexts?

- Do you find yourself wishing for a different type of sexual connection in different situations? or different times of day, with different partners and so on.

In order to help clients define their own meaning of sex, therapists may challenge narrow definitions imposed by dominant cultural discourses that limit individual experiences of sex, creating a sense of shame and guilt when people choose to participate in unusual sexual practices. For example, a heterosexual couple in their late 40s said during the first session that they had not had sex for ten years; over the course of the conversation it transpired that their sexual preferences were 'kinky'; they would regularly engage in fully consensual and satisfying bondage, domination, sadism and masochism (BDSM) play. There had been no penetration for ten years and genital contact was rarely practised. Subsequent sessions revealed that the couple were oppressed with strong feelings of guilt; their accounts of their sexual life were tainted with a deficiency discourse which emanated from their assumptions of what was 'normal' in sex, according to the cultural meaning of normality (Tiefer, 2004). When the therapist asked them to describe their subjective experiences of their sexual encounters, however, the descriptions such as: 'fun', 'play', 'connectedness', 'mutuality', 'satisfaction' and 'pleasure' began to emerge. The therapy process brought forth positive stories of the couple's resources, enabling them to appreciate their right to sexual choice and a definition of sex that reflected their consensually negotiated needs.

Different layers of the spectrum of sex reveal diverse meanings for different people and can be the subject of prejudice, stigma, discrimination and feelings of shame. A female client recounted with some distress her recent visit to her general practitioner (GP) regarding abdominal pain. The GP's question: 'Does penetration hurt?' took her by surprise; she and her husband had not been practising penetration for quite some time, initially as a method of contraception, but over time they begun to enjoy various different sensual and sexual options that did not include penetration. The GP's question caused her such embarrassment that she covered up by responding: 'No, it doesn't hurt...' as she felt unable to tell the truth. Her account was shared in therapy through a deep feeling of shame as she had automatically been questioning the appropriateness of her own attitudes and assumptions, rather than that of the medical professional.

A client account cited in sexology literature (Zilbergeld, 1999) illustrates how embracing a personal definition of sex led by a discourse of pleasure and enjoyment, without any of the aspects conventionally considered as mandatory in sex such as penetration or orgasm, for example, can allow for a richer and fuller experience of sex:

> One of the most memorable experiences I had wouldn't even fit most people's definition of sex. My girlfriend and I were in bed one afternoon. Just as she was gliding my penis into her, she came out with phrases she had gotten from a book of pornography she had looked at earlier that day: 'Stick that huge, hard cock into my hot and juicy pussy. I want to feel all twelve inches of you, filling me up, fucking and thrusting as hard as you want, spilling gobs of seed into me.' We both broke up into gales of laughter, and I fell off of her. We laughed and laughed for what seemed like hours. Every time we tried to talk, we started laughing again. There was no intercourse, no other sexual activity, and no orgasm for either of us. But it was an incredibly wonderful experience that I recall vividly and lovingly over twenty years later (p.48).

Similarly, Easton and Hardy's (2009) definition of sex as 'erotic energy' that is 'everywhere' fits with this broad and open definition: 'we have had loving, intense intimate conversations that felt deeply sexual to us. And we have had intercourse that didn't feel terribly sexual' (p.22). Furthermore, they add, the 'best definition of sex' is: 'whatever people engaging in it think it is' (p.22). Within the framework of the spectrum of sex, many sexual and sensual options are included; penetration, orgasm and genital sex, for example, are seen as options within a wider spectrum of sexual and sensual possibilities.

Relational use of the spectrum of sex

The spectrum of sex can be an aid for enhancing mutual understanding between sexual partners. Sexual interest, or lack of it, often has nothing to do with the physical sexual act but more significantly relates to other layers in the spectrum. For example, negative experiences of communication can build on feelings of hurt, disappointment, anger, resentment, feeling unheard, offended, blamed, attacked, exploited, rejected or misunderstood. In such situations it becomes a priority to explore the layers of communication and emotional experiences as these can become strong barriers to sexual intimacy. The prior resolution of difficulties, such as the level of emotional distance or the intensity of interpersonal conflict, is a necessary condition for addressing the sexual issue. Sometimes clients do not connect sexual desire with sensuality, emotions, intimacy and communication and remain confused as to why their sexual feelings have changed over time. This can be due to a disconnect between the bodily sense, sexual interest and the other parts of the sexual spectrum. The clients may experience a loss of desire or even sexual aversion without being able to understand where it may be coming from. By falsely assuming an organic, biological cause, they may seek a medical cure. Sexual withdrawal is typically not a deliberate, calculated or planned behaviour and is often unconscious and incomprehensible both to the person experiencing it and to their partner. On the other hand, sex can become a power game, a means of keeping a sense of control when becoming vulnerable and surrendering to the sexual experience feels unsafe or when sex serves the function of maintaining or gaining power over the partner. The questions for therapy then become: what is the absence of desire communicating? What is the meaning of the so-called 'sexual dysfunction'? For example, partners of clients presenting low levels of sexual interest can unwittingly represent abusive figures from the client's past. The partner's intense emotional responses, such as anger and upset in particular, can trigger immense fear, freezing sexual interest. Power struggles sometimes continue in therapy sessions whereby each partner insists their feelings should be heard, and both bring fear of rejection and abandonment as their primary wounds. Sex can seem unsafe for one or both (or more, depending on how many are involved in a sexual activity), even though the symptomatology may be more obvious for the one withdrawing sexually. This may allow the other/s to appear sexually more confident, stronger and more interested, thus masking their own sexual insecurities. Relationship therapy can be complex in such cases, requiring the patience and sensitivity of all participants in this process. Deconstructing the layers of communication, meanings, affect and cognition can enhance the clients' mutual empathy and both self and relational understanding.

Facilitating clients' reflection

The spectrum diagram can be used to facilitate dialogue with clients, using questions to engage their reflective processes and inspire a wider and enriched understanding of sex, such as:

Questions to affirm existing sexuality:

- Which of these layers do you feel are currently important to you in terms of your sexual experience?
- What aspects of your sexual experience do you enjoy most?
- What aspects of your expressed sensuality do you think your partner enjoys most?

- What are the ways in which you express your feminine/masculine qualities that provoke the most positive response from others?

Questions to support thinking about change and options for future:

- What parts from the spectrum here are perhaps missing from your current sexual relationship?
- What would you most like to work on in order to strengthen that aspect?
- What do you imagine would be different if that aspect became stronger and more prominent as part of your sexual communication?
- How would it look if, for example, non-physical sensuality became more included in your repertoire of behaving and relating as part of intimate communication?
- If you imagine how you would ideally like your sexual life to be in a year's time, where would you put an emphasis in order to feel fulfilled and sexually satisfied?

Questions to reflect on own strengths and positive resources to enable change:

- When was the last time you felt pleased with how you responded to your partner's emotional needs?
- What did you do?
- What is it about you that enabled such a response?

Questions to emphasise connectedness and inter-relatedness amongst the various aspects of the spectrum:

- What part does fantasy play in your sensuality/gender expression/ intimate relationships?
- Which parts of this map feel most important for the creation of an invitational context for physical intimacy?
- How do physical and non-physical intimacy relate in your spectrum of sexual and sensual activities?

Observer perspective questions to enhance self-reflexivity and relational reflexivity:

- Which aspects of the diagram are most important to you now/which ones do you think are most important to your partner?
- If I asked your partner the same questions about you, what do you think they would say?

Questions aiming to expand the meaning of sex:

- Are there any other aspects not mentioned on this map that you would like to add as relevant to you?

The spectrum could be used to enable clients to reflect on a particular relationship, both in individual and in couple sessions, asking questions such as:

- Which aspects are most valuable?
- What is missing?
- What used to be there that does not feature anymore?
- Which ingredients could be added to spice it up?

Sometimes therapeutic exercises serve as a nudge for clients to make the desired relationship changes. One couple took time in the session to construct their individual maps and then presented in turn their ideas to each other by expressing: what they appreciated most in the existing qualities of the relationship, what else could be added and where they would like to see the relationship in the future. The list of ingredients to be added to their relationship to spice it up included uncomplicated and straightforward elements: 'a goodnight kiss', 'a smile', 'an invitation to a surprise destination', 'compliments'... The use of the spectrum facilitated the activation of the client's dormant resources. The couple's habitual patterns, both having busy and stressful lives, created an atmosphere of mutual withholding and competition regarding 'who is most tired', 'who suffers more from various responsibilities', and 'who is most hurt by the lack of attention from the other'. Neither was taking a positive initiative as the space between them felt like a battlefield; however, when the therapist took the role of a facilitator of constructive action, the patterns shifted and the couple united in responding to the therapeutic invitations co-operatively. Allowing individual time for reflection and then space to present their respective spectrum of sex, while the partner attentively listened, enabled a more constructive approach and diffused some of the conflict caused by the clash of their differences and competitive patterns of attempted solutions that had only served to reinforce the communicational problem.

Doing gender

'Doing gender' in this context denotes gender as defined in recent social constructionist literature as a social and cultural construct, created via communication and language, made visible through certain attitudes, actions and behaviours either deemed acceptable or condemned by the prevalent social norms (Curra, 2011). Gender is regarded a psychological, social and cultural category; signifying social and cultural expectations of a person's behaviour, feelings and attitudes, and is fluid, varied, complex and nuanced, a subject of judgement and scrutiny of social norms. 'Gender is not a natural, biological fact' (Moon, 1995, p.496). 'Sex' on the other hand, is defined within this perspective as a biologically given category of male, female or intersex, related to anatomical and physiological features (such as: vagina, penis, testicles, clitoris, ovaries, uterus, prostate, vulva, breasts) and secondary sex characteristics (such as: amount and distribution of body hair and facial hair, and body fat percentage). In addition to the biological definition of 'sex' as a male/female category, the existence of intersex, defined as 'individuals whose anatomy or physiology differ from contemporary cultural stereotypes of what constitute typical male and female' (The UK Intersex Association, www.ukia.co.uk) seems a marginalised category that ought to be acknowledged in the biological continuum of sex, whereby it would not be seen as an anomaly of nature but rather included in the range of sex variance.

Kinsey and colleagues' representation of sexual orientation (Kinsey, Pomeroy & Martin, 1948; Kinsey et al., 1953) on a continuum comprising a scale of seven degrees whereby '7' represented 'exclusively heterosexual' and '6' 'exclusively homosexual' with '3' being 'bisexual' was revised by subsequent researchers (Coleman, 1988). Sanders, for example (1992) created a similar, but non-quantified, continuum placing 'gender/sex neutrality' in the middle. Lev (2004) created a model of sexual and gender identity placing sex on a continuum of 'male' and 'female' on either side; a continuum of gender with 'man' and 'woman' on the opposite sides; a continuum of sex role with 'masculine' and 'feminine'; and a continuum of sexual orientation with 'heterosexual' and 'homosexual' at opposite ends. Anne Fausto-Sterling, a biologist and historian, argues for a redefinition of our two-sex-only world (2000). Curra, a researcher in the area of the social construction of deviance and crime, states:

> Sexologists in the United States in the early 20th century took it for granted that the world was naturally divided into two, mutually exclusive categories of masculine and feminine or male and female, and they did all they could to convince everyone that it was true. This rigid view of sexual differentiation ... gave them control over deciding what was normal and what was not (Curra, 2011, p.240).

Burr (2003) takes an extreme social constructionist perspective that excludes the relevance of any biological facts. A more inclusive perspective, endorsed in this book, encompasses gender as multidimensional; including biological, physical, psychological, social, cultural and relational perspectives. Gender is determined by the idea of the social construction of sexuality (Seidman, 2014) whereby it is seen as 'continually constructed and reconstructed, made and transformed, in the context of our relationship to others' (West & Zimmerman, 2000, p.139; Van Den Wijngaard, 1997).

Seidman, an American social theorist and academic working in the areas of social theory, culture and sexuality, summarises the feminist social constructionist view on gender as a product of social processes. He states that feminists view gender as a social identity and argue that: 'we are not born men or women; we acquire these gender identities through a process of learning and sometimes coercion' (Seidman, 2014, p.18).

Distinguishing biological sex from gender as a socially and culturally constructed concept is crucial in an inclusive psychosexual therapy approach. Clients might bring anxieties, uncertainties and traumas related to their feelings of carrying their gender sexual roles and experiences of gender discrimination. Every culture prescribes a set of explicit and implicit expectations of femininity and masculinity, often imposed in ways that on the one hand celebrate, support, encourage and praise, and on the other direct, limit, oppress, judge and punish. 'Any system of sexual differentiation is almost always coupled with the tendency to prize some characteristics and condemn others' (Curra, 2011, p.241). Many therapists have had clients confessing to having been the subject of emotional, verbal and/or physical gender bullying. Gender stereotypes can creep into language, behaviour and social expectations and intrude on personal and interpersonal space often quietly and unwittingly, yet powerfully. Comfort with one's gender is seen in sexology and psychosexual therapy as a necessary requisite for psychological and sexual health. People who do not fit into the binary sex and gender definitions face all sorts of social and cultural challenges (Wylie et al., 2007).

Incongruence between one's biological sex and one's gender identity, 'a person's innate, deeply felt sense of being male or female, sometimes both or neither' (www.genderdiversity.org) is classified under 'gender dysphoria' in DSM-5. This classification replaces the diagnostic category 'gender identity disorder' from the previous DSM version, and states that a diagnosis of gender dysphoria requires the presence of clinically significant personal distress. The American Psychiatric Association (APA, 2013) justifies the need for keeping the term 'gender dysphoria' within the mental health categorisation in order to facilitate access to insurance coverage and clinical care including counselling, hormonal treatment, gender reassignment surgery and social and legal transition to the desired gender. Gender dysphoria, a subject of debate and discussion in sexology and psychiatry, still occupies a place in the diagnostic psychiatric manuals. It is defined as: 'a profound disconnection between one's felt or experienced gender (most often the gender assigned at birth) and one's biological sex' (Zucker & Brown, 2014, p.234). Although it is not classified as a sexual dysfunction, it has a diagnostic name implying it to be a psychiatric disorder. The debate about whether gender dysphoria should be classified as a mental health category or not, amongst psychiatry, sexology, gender diversity activists, feminists, social constructionists and proponents of the anti-medicalisation of sex movement, continues while the diverse social reality seems to be reflected in an expansion of language definitions as below:

- *Agender or genderblank, genderfree, genderless, non-gendered or null gender:* individuals who find they have no gender identity, or describe themselves as gender neutral.
- *Bigender:* a form of genderfluid identity whereby the person experiences involuntary alternation between female and male states; a person who has two gender identities or some combination of both.
- *Cisgender:* a person whose gender identity, gender expression and biological sex align.
- *Genderqueer:* a gender identity label often used by people who do not identify with the binary of man/woman; or as an umbrella term for many gender non-conforming or non-binary identities (e.g. agender, bigender, genderfluid).
- *Intergender:* A person whose gender identity is between genders or a combination of genders.
- *Pangender:* a person whose gender identity is comprised of many sexual identities and many gender expressions.
- *Pansexual:* a person who experiences sexual, romantic, physical or spiritual attraction for members of all gender identities.
- *Polyamory:* refers to having honest, usually non-possessive relationships with multiple partners and can include: open relationships, polyfidelity (which involves multiple romantic relationships with sexual contact restricted to those), and sub-relationships (which denote distinguishing between a 'primary' relationship or relationships and various 'secondary' relationships).
- *Polygender:* identifying as more than one gender or a combination of genders.
- *Queer:* an umbrella term representative of the vast matrix of identities outside of the gender normative and heterosexual or monogamous majority.
- *Questioning:* an individual who is unsure about, or who is exploring their own sexual orientation or gender identity.

- *Skoliosexual:* a person attracted to genderqueer and transsexual people and expressions.
- *Transsexual:* a person who identifies psychologically with a gender/sex other than the one assigned at birth.
- *Transgender:* a person who lives as a member of gender other than as expected based on anatomical sex.
- *Transitioning:* changing bodily appearance and biological traits to be in harmony with the person's preferred gender expression.
- *Transvestite:* a person who dresses – 'cross-dresses' – as the binary opposite gender expression for any of many reasons, including relaxation, fun and sexual gratification.

(Sources used for the above definitions: www.genderdiversity.org; www.everydayfeminism.com; www.oed.com; https://lgbt.wisc.edu/documents/trans_and_queer_glossary; www.pinktherapy.com; www.lgbt.ucsf.edu/glossaryofterms)

An interesting, all-inclusive definition of 'pansexuality' is provided by Easton and Hardy (2009): 'Pansexual means including everyone as a sexual being: straight, bi, lesbian, gay, transgendered, queer, old, young, disabled, perverts, male, female, questioning, in transition' (p.8).

The list of terminology is much wider than cited here and suggests the need for professionals to familiarise themselves with this diverse web of experiences and practices, as well as to keep their knowledge and the vocabulary updated and keep abreast with the expansion of the meaning of sex and gender and the growing trend towards the liberalisation of sex.

Sexual minorities

The following section on sexual minorities relates to, as part of a spectrum of sex: lesbian, gay, bisexual, transgender, asexual and queer (LGBTQ) communities, unusual sexual preferences including BDSM, non-monogamy, polyamory, paraphilias and paraphilic disorders, and stresses the particular importance of therapists' self-reflexivity and relational reflexivity when working with sexually marginalised groups.

Lesbian, gay, bisexual, transgender and queer (LGBTQ) communities

LGBTQ communities include lesbians, gay men, bisexual men, women and gender non-conforming, transgender, transsexual and queer identified people

(Lev & Nichols, 2015). Historically, the term a 'homosexual couple' has been used interchangeably with a gay/lesbian identity. However, many people in same-sex relationships do not view themselves as homosexuals but identify as bisexual or pansexual. Transgender and transsexual people can identify as a member of any of the categories of sexual orientation (Lev & Nichols, 2015, p.215). The very concept of a sexual orientation can be misleading as it is based on the binary categorisation of sex as 'biological dimorphism' (Lev & Nichols, 2015, p.215) excluding biological sexual variations, i.e. intersex. Feminist, LGBTQ-affirmative and social constructionist perspectives, on the other hand, assume that embodiment, gender identity and eroticism are varied, diverse and fluid categories that can shift and change over time.

Lisa Diamond, a feminist and a professor of developmental psychology at the University of Utah, discussed the concept of 'sexual fluidity' in her study of 100 non-heterosexual women. She followed her participants over 12 years and found that they changed their sexual identity several times during that period (Diamond, 2008). Savin-Williams, a psychologist from Cornell University, concluded in his study of teenagers that more and more young people feel that no sexual identity label captures their experience (Savin-Williams, 2005). While teenagers' non-heterosexuality used to be thought of as an 'identity crisis' or a symptom of a turbulent transitional life stage, today's teenagers proclaim to be less constrained by the normative definitions and feel free to engage with shifting views on sexuality and declare their own fluid sexual identities. Researchers from the University of Minnesota cite one person's self-description which illustrates the concept of the fluid sexual identity: 'first as a guy, then as a gay man, then as a Female to Male, then perhaps ... as a queer Female to Male who still has sex with women (usually butch women of Male to Females) once in a while...' (Bockting, Benner & Coleman, 2009, p.693).

There have been many positive cultural, societal and political changes in relation to the rights, recognition and respect for sexual minorities in many (however, not all) parts of the world, such as the right to domestic partnership, civil unions and marriage, adoption of children, IVF treatments and surrogacy. In spite of these important positive cultural and professional shifts and a trend towards the de-pathologising of gay and lesbian identities, nonetheless LGBTQ communities continue to be affected by discrimination at home, in educational institutions, at the workplace, on the streets and perhaps most unfortunately, in many mental health contexts. Literature describes typical professional myths and prejudices in relation to LGBTQ sexualities (Giammattei & Green, 2012):

- *Homonegativity*, a negative attitude towards homosexuality, anti-homosexual prejudice (Lottes & Grollman, 2010)
- *Homophobia*, irrational fear of homosexuality; an affective response including fear and anxiety, and discomfort when interacting with lesbians and gay men (Lev & Nichols, 2015)
- *Heterosexism*, a bias that heterosexuality is superior to all other sexual orientations, assumes heterosexuality as more natural, dominant and the only viable life option (Perlesz et al., 2006)
- *Heteronormativity*, the uncritical adoption of heterosexuality as an established norm or standard; 'the measuring stick for what is considered normal and healthy for all individuals, couples, and families' (Giammattei & Green, 2012, p.4), or 'the dominant, pervasive, and subtle belief that a viable family consists of a heterosexual mother and father raising heterosexual children together' (Giammattei & Green, 2012, p.4).

An aspect of heterosexism supporting homophobic actions is a system of values about gender roles (the social expectation of how one should perform one's gender and what behaviours are deemed appropriate given the person's biological sex), and gender expression (how they are 'doing their gender'). Beliefs in traditional gender roles and intolerance towards gender non-conformity leads to discrimination and stigmatising of those who, in their behaviour and appearance, differ from the heterosexist norms (Anderson & Holliday, 2007). Oswald, Blume and Marks (2005) warn that clinicians can get caught up in these biases, even if they do not hold such prejudices themselves, because it is a system of privilege often invisible to those who hold it.

Giammattei and Green (2012) list myths and misconceptions held by the professional helping systems, including couple and family therapists:

- *LGBTQ people live in bubbles without partners, spouses, or families* (p.4)
- *The primary issues for which LGBTQ clients enter therapy are their sexual orientation and/or gender identity issues rather than the more universal problems* (p.5)
- *Non-monogamy is detrimental to the maintenance of a healthy relationship* (p.13)
- *Treatment manuals and protocols that work for heterosexual couples translate easily into working with LGBTQ communities* (p.12).

Sexual minorities: clinical implications

Margaret Nichols (2011), an author, activist, postmodern queer theorist and an advocate for LGBTQ rights, warns clinicians not to apply heterosexual standards of normal, ideal or healthy sexuality to sexual minority clients. She places importance on the use of language that may quickly reveal assumptions which could offend LGBTQ clients. She advocates careful use of words and a non-judgemental, neutral and open approach: for example, to avoid questions of 'husband' and 'wife' and use more open expressions such as 'partner' or 'partners'; to avoid the use of the terms 'penetration' and 'intercourse' without previously checking the clients' sexual preferences. In advising clinicians not to make assumptions about clients and their relationships, Ani Ritchie, a researcher and a sociologist from Southampton Solent University cautions: 'Your client may talk about their "husband" but they may also have a girlfriend' (2017). It is important to pay attention to self-definition as not all non-heterosexual persons will identify as gay, lesbian, bisexual or transgender, given their experience of oppression in a heterosexist and homophobic society. Sexual identity labels, however important to consider when exploring sexual experiences and reflecting on one's choices and desires, can also be oppressing and limiting. For example, the label of 'bisexual' can be very complex as it encompasses a great variety of sexual expressions and attractions: 'There are bisexuals who are monogamous, those who consider bisexuality and polyamory as intrinsically linked, individuals with equal attraction to both genders, those with a primary attraction to one gender, and some who feel their desires transcend gender' (Nichols, 2014, p.319). Most existing tools, instruments and manuals in sexology and psychosexual therapy, claims Nichols, focus on heterosexual intercourse as a measure of sexual functioning, so clinicians working with LGBTQ clients need to devise their own questioning, assessment forms and language in order to overcome this bias. The sexual questionnaire used at the Institute of Personal Growth (IPG), a psychotherapy centre in New Jersey which Nichols founded, included questions on a wide variety of sexual practices including BDSM, open and non-monogamous relationships, and other sexual and gender varieties (Nichols, 2014).

McCann and Delmonte (2005) emphasise that there are specific issues and complexities which therapists need to consider when working with lesbian and gay parents, such as: internalised homophobia, anxieties and fears that can contribute to negative ideas about self, even self-loathing, and managing various decisions about how to parent and raise children. Societal pressures and discrimination create situations whereby lesbian and gay parents feel they have to prove themselves to be 'good enough' parents. Such pressures bring additional layers of difficulties in decision making and contribute to the development and escalation of conflict. Managing decisions about when and how to involve families of origin and birth parents, and decisions about the child's surname, religion and education can be very complex, presenting dilemmas and potentially creating additional levels of stress. These authors state some commonly held myths, often shared within the professional healthcare systems (pp.337–338):

- *Children raised in lesbian and gay households will themselves become homosexual*
- *The absence of the opposite gender contact, or appropriate opposite gender role models for children raised in same-sex households creates attachment problems*
- *Children of lesbian and gay parents will be the victims of serious teasing and bullying within the schools and the community at large*
- *Lesbians dislike men and gay men dislike women.*

Literature describes some specific issues that create difficulties for male gay couples. For example, as a result of gender acculturation that socialises men to overvalue emotional autonomy and emotional self-reliance (Gilligan, 1982), the regulation of emotional closeness may be a challenging task for gay men. Young men have often been shamed, particularly by other men, for being 'too emotional'. To protect themselves, they have developed a mechanism of suppressing their emotional worlds. Tunnell (2012) refers to these feelings as 'attachment injuries' that interfere with forming affectional bonds and prevent men from opening up themes of commitment and monogamy with their partners.

Lesbian couples face a 'dual minority status' (Connolly, 2014), being both women and members of a sexual minority. A feminist, multicontextual approach is particularly helpful in working with lesbian couples as it recognises gender roles and inequalities, gender script, race, class and cultural difference and how societal inequalities and related issues of power affect the relationship between partners, their intimacy and views on sexuality. Iasenza (2004) proposes that working with lesbian couples requires viewing their relationship in the context of systemic influences of family, community and society and suggests asking questions such as: 'How do you think living in a homophobic and sexist society has affected your relationship?' (Iasenza, 2004, p.17).

The decision about coming out or not may have nothing to do with the strength of someone's sense of self and identity but rather represent a realistic assessment of the circumstances and potential consequences of such a decision. The 'identity management' (Tunnell, 2012) process is a complex and multilayered task, 'a profoundly personal, political, and spiritual process of knowing self in relation to other' (Halstead, 2003, p.48). The decision to disclose or not requires gay and lesbian individuals and couples to balance their identities amongst different contexts and, as a result, they may experience multiple identities within various relationships and situations which can result in relationship strain and conflict (Slater, 1995).

Research on differences and similarities between heterosexual and same-sex couples

According to numerous research studies, same-sex couples experience many similar issues as heterosexual couples, going through the same relationship stages such as: dating, falling in love, partnering, living together, and planning for children. Lesbian and gay couples describe similarly high levels of satisfaction with relationship quality, stability and their sex lives (Blair & Pukall, 2014). Equally, they struggle with communication, finances, sex, parenting and division of responsibilities (Lev & Nichols, 2015). At the same time, there are important differences. Lesbian and gay couples are less likely to raise children, for example. Research studies have found same-sex couples to be more egalitarian in many aspects of their lives. There seems to be more financial independency, a more equitable division of household chores, more balanced power in decision making, and more equal levels of communication and investment in the nurturing and developing of the relationship. Same-sex couples seem to be free of the power imbalances embedded in the heteronormative and heterosexist culture they are surrounded by. This is not to say that power imbalances do not exist, but they are not based on gender role expectations (Lev & Nichols, 2015). Research shows that 'non-heterosexual participants' seemed more positive about and happier with the quality of their relationship than heterosexual couples (Gabb et al., 2013). Because of the considerable overlap between LGBTQ communities and BDSM and polyamory, same-sex couples are more likely to engage in alternative sexual practices (Barker, 2013). Since many gay men and lesbians have very broad sexual practices, it has been found that they: 'take more time for each other and each other's feelings of pleasure, place less emphasis on rushing towards orgasm, and focus less on simultaneous orgasms' (Sandfort & deKeizer, 2001, p.96). Studies have also found that male couples have the highest frequency of sex, while lesbian couples the lowest, with heterosexual couples in between. Nichols (2011) raised important questions about this: does this imply an inherent biological difference between men and women, or are these studies based on the limited definitions of what 'counts' as sex, such as penetration and genital contact? Iasenza (2002) found that lesbian sex may be less frequent and less genitally focused but is more sensual, with more passion and play. Nichols states that many lesbian couples present in a distinct way: 'They often have high functioning, physically affectionate relationships with minor sexual problems' (Nichols, 2014, p.320). Research suggests that lesbian sex differs from heterosexual sex in many important ways: lesbians seem to take longer with sex, include a larger sexual repertoire, mainly consisting of sensual activities; women seem to be more orgasmic in woman-to-woman than in heterosexual sex, report few sexual pain difficulties, are less likely to agree to sex solely as a result of their partner's expressed desires, report lower incidence of sexually transmitted infections (STIs) and generally lower rates of sexual dysfunction with the most frequently reported complaint being lack of sexual desire (Matthews, Hughes & Tartaro, 2006).

Research on gay male sexuality found that incidences of erectile disorder were higher than with heterosexual men, but difficulties with premature ejaculation, delayed ejaculation and low desire were uncommon (Sandfort & deKeizer, 2001). These differences may be attributed to the relational aspects in gay male sex in that there is less pressure to ejaculate or to prolong the sexual act sufficiently to allow for satisfaction of the sexual partner; there is however, pressure to 'perform' which is proven to be a significant contributing factor in the development of erectile disorder (Nichols, 2014). Studies on male gay sexuality consistently show that gay men are more sexual than women or heterosexual men, that they have more frequent sex, engage more in casual sexual encounters and have greater number of partners (Martin, 2006). Furthermore, nearly half of all male couples are non-monogamous (Parsons et al., 2011). A common form of sexual openness, termed 'monogamish relationships' refers to couples who regularly involve a third male person in their sexual activity. Some research studies indicate that those couples report the highest levels of sexual satisfaction (LaSala, 2004). Gay men's abundant sexuality, both in terms of frequency of sex and number of partners, may provoke therapists to be drawn into judgements, so the therapist should conduct a careful examination of their own prejudices, to avoid pathologisation (Lev & Nichols, 2015).

Working effectively with LGBTQ clients requires more than acceptance of homosexuality; therapists must discard the pathologising views on gender variance, non-monogamy and polyamory being symptoms of a mental disorder, a biological mistake or a consequence of a deficiency in upbringing. Moreover, therapists should be open to learn from their LGBTQ clients about alternative forms of relationships and family and about the range of sexual and gender expression (Nichols, 2014, p.329).

One of the most difficult issues LGBTQ communities struggle with as a result of social discrimination is the lack of a network of support, increasing their level of stress and intensifying social isolation. Some of the differences between heterosexual and LGBTQ communities are due to 'minority stress' issues. 'Minority stress' was described in relation to gay-related stress by Brooks (Brooks, 1977, 1981) and taken up by many authors subsequently, including Meyer (2003) who considered factors such as discrimination, perceived stigma and internalised homophobia to be stressors particularly relevant to the experiences of sexual minorities. Research findings suggest higher incidences of depression, suicidal tendencies, substance abuse and anxiety within sexual minorities compared to the heterosexual population (Lewis et al., 2009). The bisexual population has been found to be particularly vulnerable to depression and self-harming behaviours (Dodge & Sandfort, 2007). People of bisexual orientation suffer added levels of pressure and social stigma including biphobia, a fear and anxiety related to bisexuality. 'Out of all the groups under the umbrella named "queer", bisexuals are probably the most misunderstood and the most invisible' (Cobin & Angello, 2012, p.110). The cultural messages about bisexuality are burdened with assumptions such as that:

- *Bisexuality does not exist*
- *Bisexuals are promiscuous*
- *Bisexuals are carriers of sexually transmitted diseases*
- *Bisexuals are unable to be monogamous*
- *Bisexuals are generally harmful to both the heterosexual and gay and lesbian communities* (Beaber, 2008).

There is a long history of negative attitudes related to bisexuality, based on widespread ignorance and misunderstanding. Bisexuals used to be labelled 'straight' or 'gay' depending on the gender of their partner at the time; lesbians tend to relate bisexual women to the threat of sexually transmitted diseases and many communities unfortunately, including sexologists and sexual therapists, may not recognise the existence of this sexual variance (Nichols, 2014).

Transgender couples' and families' concerns differ significantly from lesbian, gay and bisexual communities, in that they face particular issues of own gender sexual identity. Specific difficulties transgender people present in therapy relate to gender identity and identity in general; feeling misunderstood by others; guilt, shame and loss; suicidal tendencies; and a sense of failure (Zucker & Brown, 2014). As societies continue to support rigid gender prescriptions and fear anything outside the binary norm, transgender people either live an invisible existence (if their appearance does not reveal their sexual minority), or have to deal with ostracism from their communities and families, sometimes suffering violence and discrimination. 'Many sex and gender diverse people, especially transgender and those who practise BDSM (bondage/discipline/dominance/submission/sadism/masochism), are still diagnosed as mentally disturbed even in the most recent edition of the DSM' write Lev and Nichols (2015, p.216). The pathological perspective has historically dominated psychiatry and sexology, but is also currently influencing some sexological research and clinical practices as a result of the label of gender dysphoria. Sexual and relationship therapists emphasise that therapists working with transgender people must recognise that gender non-conformity is not an illness and support them in their struggles to cope with the integration of their changing identities and roles in their lives (Weeks, Gambescia & Hertlein, 2015, p.284).

Asexualities

The following section addresses asexuality as a sexual minority group. Various definitions of asexuality are summarised below, many of which emphasise diversity within this category; thus the plural, 'asexualities', is proposed here, coherent with the views that enlighten the complexity of asexuality and its many diverse forms.

According to AVEN (Asexual Visibility and Education Network), the largest community of asexuals, an asexual individual is a person who 'does not experience sexual attraction' (www.asexuality.org). Hinderliter, a researcher from the University of Illinois-Urbana Champaign, USA, considers AVEN's definition important for the following reasons: firstly, the definition is broad enough to include people who experience non-sexual attraction; secondly, because the definition highlights experience as opposed to behaviour, it delineates an important difference between asexuality and celibacy; furthermore, AVEN's position encourages society to consider asexuality as an identity, calling for acceptance, understanding, respect and a non-pathologising attitude. 'A major goal of the asexual community', writes Hinderliter, 'is for asexuality to be seen as a part of the "normal variation" that exists in the human sexuality rather than a disorder to be cured' (Hinderliter, 2014, p.56).

Different researchers have offered varying definitions of asexuality. Some defined it as a discrete, inborn sexual orientation. For example, Bogaert, a psychologist from Brock University in Canada, defined asexuality as a lifelong lack of sexual attraction towards other people (Bogaert, 2012). However, some researchers, including the ones who embrace a social constructionist perspective on asexuality, have challenged such a definition by emphasising diversity within the asexual community, claiming that it is important to keep the definition fluid. Hinderliter, for example, challenges Bogaert's definition of asexuality being 'lifelong', stressing that one can move 'into and out of the category of asexuality' (Carrigan, Gupta & Morrison, 2014, p.3). Social constructionist perspectives oppose the definition of asexuality based on the binary distinctions of sexual/asexual and propose a continuum which includes varying degrees of sexuality and asexuality. Hinderliter states: 'We should seek to understand the diversity of the life experience of asexuals, gray-As, demisexuals, etc' (Hinderliter, 2014, p.133). Researchers who draw attention to heterogeneity of asexuality stress that asexual communities distinguish between:

- those who experience romantic attraction (romantic asexuals) and those who do not (aromantic asexuals); and within romantic asexuals there are heteroromantic, homoromantic, biromantic and polyromantic asexuals
- those who are indifferent to sex and those who are actively averse to sex to varying degrees (Carrigan, Gupta & Morrison, 2014, p.1).

Gupta (in Bishop, 2014) also reminds us that many asexuals also identify as gay, lesbian, bisexual, transgender and/or queer (Gupta in Bishop, 2014, p.131). Asexual communities include those who engage in sexual activity for non-sexual reasons and those who feel sexual desire but are not motivated to engage in sexual activity with others (Knudson, Brotto & Inskip, 2008). Brotto and Yule (2017) reviewed studies addressing the possibility of asexuality as a: mental disorder; sexual dysfunction; paraphilia; or sexual orientation and concluded that the available evidence suggests that asexuality is best conceptualised as a unique sexual orientation (p.2).

Normalisation of asexuality seems to pose challenging social, cultural and political questions and, above all, brings into question the assumption of sexuality being natural, ever-desirable, almost mandatory; a healthy expression of humanness, a way to be human. Gupta (2014) engages with this perspective by stating that 'asexuality troubles the boundary between the sexual and the nonsexual' and contemplates that asexuality serves as 'a political protest against "compulsory sexuality" and "sex-normativity" to challenge the stigmatization of asexuality and "nonsexuality"' (Gupta in Bishop, 2014, p.129).

Asexual communities experience a pervasive problem of marginalisation and social prejudice. Negativity expressed towards asexual individuals is based on the misconceptions that:

- *Asexual individuals are mentally or physically ill* (Gupta in Bishop, 2014)
- *Asexuality is a problem of low sexual desire disorder* (Gupta in Bishop, 2014)

- *Asexuality is a result of negative childhood experiences* (Brotto et al., 2010)
- *The problem with an asexual person is they haven't found the right sexual partner…All they need is sex with someone to cure them and make them 'normal'* (Bishop, 2014)
- *An asexual person is only a late bloomer* (Carrigan in Bishop, 2014)
- *Asexuality is a hormonal problem* (Carrigan in Bishop, 2014)
- *Asexual men lack vitality* (Gressgard in Bishop, 2014)
- *Asexual individuals are really gays in hiding* (Przybylo in Bishop, 2014)
- *Asexuals are unconsciously repressing their sexual desire* (Gupta in Bishop, 2014).

Unlike many other sexual minorities, asexuals are unlikely to experience harassment and violence because of the lack of visible presence of their sexual identity; however, often they are subject to peer and cultural pressure to have sex to which they sometimes surrender in order to avoid further pressures and obtain social approval (Przybylo, 2014).

Polyamory

Polyamorous individuals are involved in consensual multiple relationships that are emotionally and sexually close and/or romantically intertwined. It is distinguished from swinging and gay open relationships where the focus is on sexual encounters, and may take a range of structural forms and varieties (Ritchie, 2017), for example:

- *Primary/secondary*: a primary couple which sees additional partners as secondary to their own relationship in terms of emotional intensity, connection, commitment, practical and financial matters, or power within the relationship
- *Triad*: a polyamorous relationship involving three people who share romantic and sexual bonds; they may be sexual as a threesome or as couples
- *Poly family*: a family of adults who live together, with or without children, and all identify as part of the same family
- *Quad*: a polyamorous relationship involving four people, each of whom may or may not be sexually and emotionally involved with all the other members; they all live together and often have group sex
- *V* relationship: a relationship involving three people, in which one person is romantically or sexually involved with two partners who are not involved with each other but are aware of the situation.

The above definitions can be found on the website www.morethantwo.com which contains a glossary of 101 polyamory-related terms; defining types of polyamorous relationships in terms of beliefs, feelings and practices, including:

- *Compersion*: a person's feeling of joy when their partner derives pleasure from their sexual or romantic relationship with someone else
- *Emotional fidelity*: a belief or practice that emotional intimacy or love must be kept exclusive to a particular relationship, though sexual activity or other forms of physical intimacy may occur outside the relationship
- *Ethical slut*: a person who openly chooses to have multiple simultaneous sexual relationships in an ethical and responsible way, and who openly revels in that decision. The book *Ethical Slut* (Easton & Liszt, 1997) outlines a framework for responsible non-monogamy and champions taking joy in ethical, safe promiscuity
- *Group marriage*: A relationship in which three or more people consider themselves married to one another.

This dictionary comes from Cherie Ve Ard and Franklin Veaux (morethantwo. org). Veaux, an American author, polyamory and BDSM activist and sex educator, has written an article deconstructing the meaning of polyamory through dispelling myths such as:

- *Polyamory means inability to commit*; Veaux writes that this myth is based on the belief that commitment in a relationship equals exclusivity; while in polyamorous relationships commitment involves building lasting relationships that meet the needs of all people involved
- *Polyamory is about harem-building*; polyamorous relationships' structure, writes Veaux, are egalitarian, allowing both men and women to choose more than one partner
- *Polyamory is about cheating*; cheating is breaking the rules of the polyamory agreement, writes Veaux. Contrary to this myth, polyamorous individuals share core values of honesty and open communication, and define boundaries explicitly
- *Polyamory is a lot of unnecessary hard work*; based on his lifelong experience of being immersed in polyamorous communities, Veaux claims that being polyamorous means working on oneself in building good relationship and communication skills, developing a strong sense of self-confidence and moving through life with courage
- *Being polyamorous means having a higher sex drive than average*; in fact, writes Veaux, it is possible to be polyamorous and asexual, or polyamorous but

in multiple long-distance relationships, or polyamorous but not, for whatever reason, able to have sex. 'To understand why people choose polyamory,' writes Veaux, 'it is necessary to look beyond sex.'

- *One becomes polyamorous if something is lacking in their partner*; Veaux opposes this myth by shifting the focus of polyamory onto self-enhancement through being intimately connected in multiple relationships. He views polyamory as not a reflection of the quality of the partner but rather as self-discovery and self-enrichment
- *Polyamorous people are at higher risk than monogamous people of STIs*; research has in fact shown quite the opposite; this is based on the practice amongst polyamorous individuals to extensively discuss sexual history, sexual health, STI testing and other rules of the relationship before taking on a new lover (Ritchie, 2017).

Sexual and gender preferences: sexual diversity

The notion of 'sexual diversity' is frequently used in literature with respect to sexual orientation and gender identity. In this book, as in some other recent literature (e.g. Barker & Langdridge, 2010) it also applies to a spectrum of preferences related to varied sexual practices. In terms of sexual orientation, the sexual diversity concept is inclusive of gay, lesbian, queer, bisexual, pansexual, asexual and questioning sexualities. Davies (in an interview with Whitaker, 2013) proposes the term 'gender and sexual diversities' (GSD) explaining that LGBT got extended to 'LGBTIQQA' (lesbian, gay, bisexual, transsexual, intersex, queer, questioning, asexual) and still left out plenty of people who were being discriminated against, misunderstood and demonised such as, for example, people involved in BDSM, people in consensually non-monogamous relationships, polyamorous, swingers and so on. 'Sexual preferences' is used here as an affirmative concept appreciative of sexual diversity, encompassing both sexual and gender diversity and embracing a wide range of chosen sexual activities representing the richness, divergence and idiosyncrasy of sexual possibilities.

People in monogamous couple relationships also tend to be stereotyped. Research indicated the diversity of how the parameters of monogamy are constructed amongst consensually monogamous couples, drawing attention to how unproductive it is to homogenise monogamous relationships (Frank & DeLamater, 2010). Monogamous couples set the boundaries of exclusivity in many different ways; what constitutes infidelity encompasses flirting, chatting on the phone, having lunch with a person one feels attracted to, masturbating, having sexual fantasies about other people, using pornography, and so on. However, these boundaries seem to be more often assumed than explicitly discussed. Even though couples seem to have strong ideas as to where exactly limits should lie, the majority responded that they thought it was not necessary to discuss this with their partner. In contrast, non-monogamous couples typically go through a detailed, explicit and sometimes extended process of negotiation. These discussions may include clarification of the specificities of rules defining what kinds of behaviours, emotions, partners and places are acceptable or not, such as: 'not in our bed', 'not in the same place twice', 'no orgasm', 'no penetration', 'no kissing', and so on. Variety amongst non-monogamous partners has prompted the use of the plural, 'non-monogamies' (Barker & Langdridge, 2010, p.6) to emphasise diversity within this group. Many couples contest the definitions that may be attributed to them. Self-definitions should always be carefully checked and clarified; same-sex partners may not accept the self-definition of homosexuality; couples engaging in regular swinging activities may hold the self-description of a monogamous couple; couples who engage with others sexually may not agree with the definition of their relationship as 'open', or accept the description of 'polyamory', and so on. Borders between 'vanilla' and 'kink' can also be questioned as arbitrary and unhelpfully classifying sexual practices within the binary system of distinct categories.

Unusual sexual practices

There exists a great deal of controversy in sexology science and psychosexual therapy theories around what sexual practices to include as part of normal human sexual functioning and what practices constitute sexual pathology, or a mental disorder. Because the definition of 'normal' and 'abnormal' sexuality is currently in the hands of the psychiatry profession and its dominant biomedical model, to avoid being pathologised, condemned or punished, many people worldwide keep any unusual sexual preferences either repressed and inhibited, or enacted in secrecy and cut off from the rest of their lives, thus 'a vast underworld of hidden sexual practices exists that never becomes part of the official world' (Curra, 2011, p.243).

'Unusual sexual preferences', 'atypical sexual interests', 'kink' or 'BDSM', are referred to as paraphilias in sexology literature. DSM-IV-TR (APA, 2000) defined paraphilias as 'recurrent, intense sexually arousing fantasies, sexual urges, or behaviour generally involving i) non-human objects, ii) the suffering or humiliation of oneself or one's partner, or iii) children or other non-consenting persons' (p.566). DSM-IV-TR listed the following paraphilias:

- *exhibitionism*: the recurrent urge or behaviour to expose one's genitals to an unsuspecting person
- *fetishism*: the use of non-sexual or non-living objects or part of a person's body to gain sexual excitement
- *frotteurism*: the recurrent urges or behaviour of touching or rubbing against a non-consenting person
- *masochism*: the recurrent urge or behaviour to be humiliated, beaten, bound, or otherwise made to suffer
- *sadism*: the recurrent urge or behaviour involving acts in which the pain or humiliation of the victim is sexually exciting
- *voyeurism*: a recurrent urge or behaviour to observe an unsuspecting person who is naked, disrobing or engaged in sexual activities or those that may not be of a sexual nature at all
- *chronophilias* such as infantophilia, or paedophilia, sexual attraction to infants
- *other paraphilias*: telephone scatologia (obscene phone calls), necrophilia (sexual attraction to, or sexual acts with corpses), zoophilia (sexual attraction to, or acts with animals), coprophilia (sexual acts involving faeces), klismophilia (sexual excitement involving enemas), urophilia (sexual acts involving urinating on another person or being urinated on).

In order to be classified within the DSM-IV-TR diagnostic categories, paraphilic preferences needed to include personal distress, or social or occupational dysfunction. The DSM-IV-TR definition was strongly opposed by advocates of the removal of adult consenting paraphilias from the DSM (Moser & Kleinplatz, 2005), arguing that personal distress and impaired functioning may be a result of significant others' reaction to such sexual interest rather than a result of the sexual activity per se. Moser and Kleinplatz emphasise that societal discrimination has caused people to lose their jobs, custody of their children, or become victims of assaults due to the association of their sexual behaviour with psychopathology based on normative views on sexuality. They state: 'Judgments should be made on the basis of science rather than morality' (p.107). Moreover, they argue that it is worth considering that unusual sexual interests might enhance one's quality of life rather than diminish it: 'Pro-scribed fantasies, desires, and behaviors may not be pathological; healthy individuals resist giving up life-affirming and enhancing experiences, regardless of social mores' (Moser & Kleinplatz, 2005, p.100). Quincey (2012) suggests that a criterion of 'distress' is not sufficient to distinguish between whether a sexual behaviour belongs to psychopathology or not: 'A behaviour can be illegal, immoral, and undesirable or cause distress, yet not be an expression of an underlying mental disorder' (p.218).

A clinical diagnosis of a paraphilia can be made using either ICD-10 classification codes (WHO, 2010), from F65.0–F65.8, or from the current version of DSM (DSM-5, APA, 2013). However, ICD-10 does not specifically give a definition for paraphilia; therefore, a common definition comes from the DSM-5 which proposes that paraphilia is any powerful and persistent sexual interest other than sexual interest in genital stimulation and/or intercourse (p.685).

DSM-5 introduces separation between paraphilias and paraphilic disorders. A 'paraphilic disorder is a paraphilia that causes distress or impairment to the individual or harm to others' (Kleinplatz, 2014, p.199). The list of paraphilic disorders in DSM-5 is as follows: exhibitionistic disorder, fetishistic disorder, frotteuristic disorder, paedophilic disorder, sexual masochism disorder, sexual sadism disorder, transvestism disorder and voyeuristic disorder. DSM-5 draws a distinction between atypical adult consensual sexual practices that do not cause distress (paraphilia) and the non-consensual ones that cause distress either to the person exhibiting the paraphilic behaviour, or the person subjected to it, or both, making the person a serious threat to the psychological and physical wellbeing of other individuals (paraphilic disorder).

It is a crucial difference that makes it possible for an individual to engage in consensual atypical sexual behaviour without being labelled with a mental disorder. Still, questions remain, both at the levels of theory/conceptualisation and meaning, and practice/implications for treatment about when to make a clinical diagnosis of a paraphilic disorder, and when to embrace paraphilic practices as part of wide diversity and variations of human sexuality. There is no consensus within sexology or psychosexual therapy as to where the exact boundaries between 'normal' and 'abnormal' sexuality lie and how to determine the line between the two. 'Delineating what is normal versus deviant or disordered sexuality is one of the biggest challenges when using the term paraphilia' (McManus et al., 2013, p.5). 'Psychosexual normality/diversity is becoming more complex and difficult to define, because of its changeability, relativity, dependence on partners, morals, laws and cultural bonds' (Popovic, 2006, p.182). Therapists are faced with unanswered questions: how to listen, respond, feel or think about certain sexual practices and where their responsibility lies? Where are the boundaries and how much of the pain and injury inflicted is part of consenting sexual choice and pleasure and how much is unwanted or even abusive? If humiliation games involve use of severely denigrating language; if bondage and restraint are used excessively; if sexual practices involve serious risk of drowning or suffocation, how should therapists position themselves? What constitutes excess? What level of risk is part of play and what indicates violation and lack of self-care? Whose definition of disorder versus sexual rights is to be trusted and according to which criteria? And how would they know?

Psychosexual therapy literature advises that therapists should only focus on resolving BDSM behaviour if asked to by clients themselves and not to assume that unusual sexual practices (however unusual they appear to the therapist) necessarily create a problem for clients or their partners (Hudson-Allez, 2005). A female client in a lesbian relationship commented that only BDSM interests her partner as a sexual activity 'otherwise we wouldn't be having sex'. On enquiring how the client felt about it, she smiled:

> Not what I would necessarily choose if it wasn't for her... but I'm fine honestly, it's not at all a problem for me. We have lots of fun and it is all great. We do things for each other, our relationship is a constant exchange.

The exclusive focus on BDSM in this relationship was mentioned in the session more in passing, not as a topic to focus on and the way the client responded to the therapist's enquiry took away any worry of enforcement or exploitation. She seems to have chosen to engage in a style of sex that was not her natural choice, however, in the context of her enthusiasm for the current relationship she fully embraced it. Therapists need to be able to grasp what may seem a contradiction and allow that in human sexuality not everything always makes sense. On the other hand, it is crucial to check if individuals involved subscribe to such practices voluntarily, or whether there is an exploitative power dynamic in the relationship whereby one partner may be threatened, oppressed or cornered into submission.

Professional literature on paraphilia is limited by the uncertainty as to what constitutes 'unusual' practices and how to define them. Some such activities may be more unusual than others, some may be quite rare although more research is needed to establish the extent to which these practices may exist. Limited studies suggest the possibility of paraphilias being practised more than generally assumed. Going back to Kinsey's research (1948), for example, his report suggested that one in 13 men had had a sexual experience with animals. A more recent internet survey on 114 zoophile men suggests that two thirds of the sample reported having sex with animals before the age of 17 (Williams & Weinberg, 2003). A Swedish national population survey (Langstrom & Seto, 2006) found that 3.9% of women and 11.5% of men reported at least one episode of exhibitionism or voyeurism. A recent German population study found that 62.4% of men reported sexual arousal related to at least one of the DSM-IV-TR paraphilias (Ahlers et al., 2011). Kleinplatz (2014) suggests that one can learn about the astonishingly broad variety of sexual interests via the internet. For example, fetlife.com, a social networking site for the 'kink' world as of May 2016 has almost five million members, who have shared over 24 million pictures and over a quarter of a million videos, and participated in over six million discussions. Anil Aggrawal, a professor of forensic medicine from New Delhi, has compiled a list of 547 terms describing paraphilic sexual interests. He states that:

> not all these paraphilias have been seen in clinical setups. This may not be because they are so innocuous they are never brought to the notice of clinicians or discussed by them. Like allergies, sexual arousal may occur from anything under the sun, including the sun (Aggrawal, 2009, p.369).

A diagram comprising various theoretical views on paraphilias is presented in Figure 2.2 to summarise the range of perspectives operating within the medical and psychotherapy fields. Various theoretical perspectives are presented, showing how paraphilias are thought of from different, mostly pathological angles, whether as a result of neurotic fixations, biological irregularities, character deviance, post-traumatic disorder, cognitive distortions or mental illness. On the other hand, normality theory, the origins of which are largely attributed to Foucault (1980), views paraphilic sexualities as manifestations of normal human sexual interests, or alternative sexual identities which tend to become labelled as 'deviant' or 'abnormal' by social and cultural power structures. Advocates of this perspective remind us that homosexuality was listed as a paraphilia in DSM-I and DSM-II and was only declassified from DSM-III in 1974. Normality theory appreciates the diversity of human sexual interests, and views paraphilias as 'just another facet of the client's life, like their vegetarianism or their hobby of knitting' (Kolmes & Weitzman, 2010, p.2). Similarly, a view conceptualising paraphilias as a 'culturally bound syndrome' (Bhugra, Popelyuk & McMullen, 2010) locates paraphilias within the cultural, religious and societal norms which determine the acceptability of certain sexual behaviours. The pathological label is given 'because it distresses representatives of conventional society' (Curra, 2011, p.243). According to social constructionist views, pathologisation is based on normative views on sexuality. Curra (2016) states:

> Humans are continually finding new sexual turn-ons, using the same old body parts but in new ways, finding new sexual paraphernalia to increase their sensual pleasures, establishing new relationships that provide new

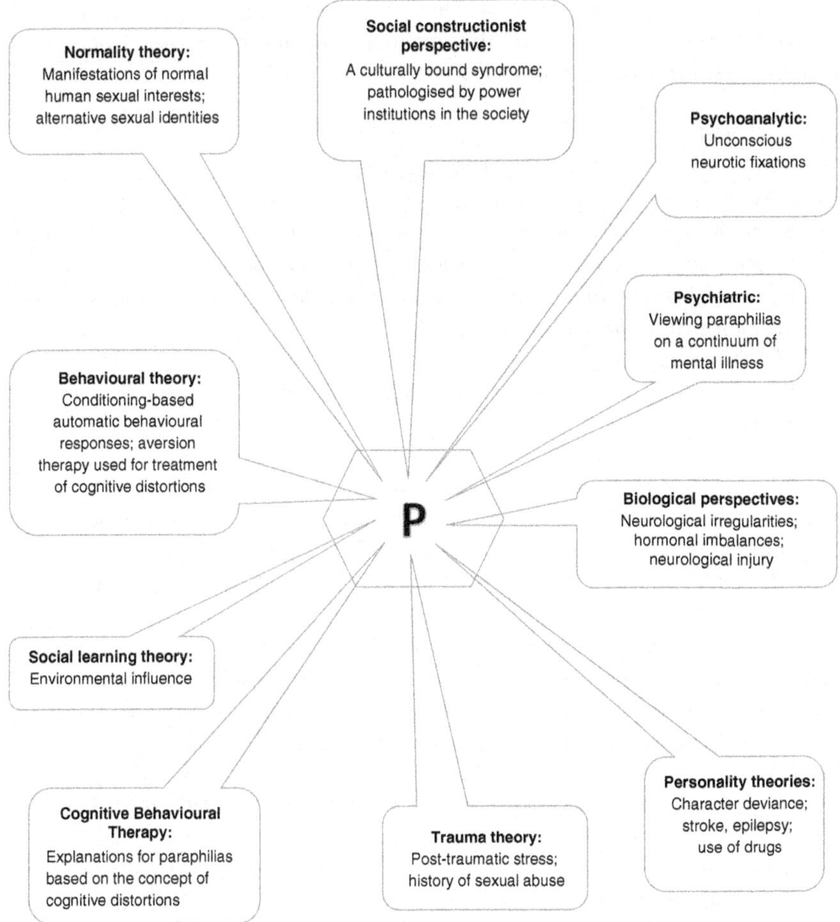

Figure 2.2 Theoretical perspectives on paraphilias

pleasures in the old ways, enjoying solitary sex, or finding comfort in no sex at all (temporarily, or permanently) (p.352).

Therapists' self-reflexivity and relational reflexivity

Barker, Iantaffi and Gupta (2007) write: 'BDSM is one of the most demonized forms of consensual sexuality', 'many counselors still consider it appropriate to make negative comments about BDSM' (p.106). In drawing attention to the importance of therapists' education on these issues and their self-reflexive approach, the authors list widespread misconceptions about BDSM (p.115/116) that:

- *it is all about pain*
- *it always takes place in a couple relationship*
- *BDSMers always assume fixed roles (top or bottom; the top/dom is in control)*
- *people who engage in BDSM have been abused or somehow damaged in their lives (as suggested in the vastly popular 'Fifty Shades of Grey')*
- *BDSM is addictive and the start of a slippery slope into more extreme activities (as indicated in the popular movie '9½ weeks')*
- *BDSM is always about sex*
- *BDSM is always on the same continuum of behaviour as violent sadism or serial murder.*

Iasenza (2010) draws attention to therapists' self-reflexivity: 'therapists need to appreciate how powerful a role their own experiences, values, and biases play in the sexual therapeutic arena. What sexual response cycle does the therapist endorse? What constitutes good enough sex in treatment or in life?' (p.306). Pillai-Friedman, Pollitt and Castaldo (2015) claim it is no longer a choice for sexuality professionals to deal with only 'vanilla sexuality'; equally, it is no longer a choice to describe themselves as 'kink aware' without adequate education and training. Kolmes and Weitzman (2010) distinguish between kink-friendly therapists (those with an open mind in relation to sexual minorities, but lacking in training about the needs of BDSM clients) and kink-aware therapists (those able to distinguish between healthy BDSM and non-consensual abuse, and able to recognise BDSM as a normal part of the sexual spectrum, who have good understanding of the BDSM community and welcome clients who practise BDSM). Therapists may be accepting of a BDSM lifestyle; however, they may not be necessarily able to guide their clients through the numerous kink-specific issues, such as the coming-out process, negotiating boundaries within and outside of the relationship or facilitating the creation of the master-slave contract (Kolmes & Weitzman, 2010). These authors suggest experiential and didactic education and skill development through supervision as necessary pre-requisites for working with BDSM populations on kink-related issues. Iasenza (2010) describes the many roles therapists working with the 'queerness of sex' may include: 'co-creator of safety, interviewer, sex educator, sexual detective, empathic listener, co-meaning maker, hypothesis generator, coach, witness, sex-affirmative parent, and assignment-giving teacher' (p.306).

The therapist's ability to offer non-judgemental listening support and authentic engagement with the specific detail of clients' experiences by demonstrating respect for clients' integrity and freedom of choice in adult, consenting sexual interactions is essential for building an effective therapeutic relationship. To this end, it is imperative that therapists explore, monitor and question their own knowledge, beliefs, prejudices and sexual values when working with sexual issues and particularly so in relation to ideas about sexual 'normalcy' in terms of sex, gender roles and sexual relationships (Cormier-Otaño & Davies, 2012). Therapists need to 'discard most pathology-oriented paradigms of sexuality; adopt new models that allow for neutrality and, at times, celebratory attitudes towards diverse sexuality' (Nichols, 2006, p.299) and to 'remain grounded and maintain a non-judgmental curiosity and openness with therapeutic conversations' when working with kinky clients (Shaw, 2010, p.1). 'Many clients are frustrated', write Barker, Iantaffi and Gupta (2007) 'by having to educate their therapists about BDSM: "that it is not abuse", "that it is not harmful to me", "that I was not self-sabotaging with it", "not acting out past family abuse"' (p.116).

Barker, Iantaffi and Gupta (2007) offer examples of therapeutic questions to illustrate therapists adopting a stance of relational reflexivity in therapy with kinky clients:

- Is this conversation useful for you?
- Are there books/leaflets/websites, which you would like me to read so that I don't need to ask you basic questions about your BDSM practices?
- I notice that you waited five sessions before mentioning BDSM. Was this because it was not relevant until now or was this due to something else? (p.119).

Further examples listed below illustrate relational reflexivity (Burnham, 2005) as 'talking about talking' that could be applied to therapeutic conversations about BDSM practices:

- How did you find talking with me about your BDSM practices?
- How was it different compared to how you might have expected or imagined it?
- If there was anything that didn't feel right to you in our conversations about your BDSM practices, would you tell me?
- What do you think I think of your BDSM practices?
- How would you react if you thought I was judging you negatively based on what you told me about your BDSM practices?

- How would you like our future conversations about your BDSM practices to be different or similar to the conversations we have had about it?

The spectrum of sex can encourage therapists' sexual self-reflexivity and relational reflexivity. Therapists can apply the practice of taking 'doses of own medicine' (Clifton, Doan & Mitchell, 1990), asking themselves reflexive questions in relation to their clinical work such as:

- What aspects of the spectrum do I personally hold most relevant in sex?
- How are my sexual values influencing my approach to clients' issues?
- What would I be doing differently if I held a different value system?
- How is my sexual value system impacting clients' progress?
- What am I paying particular attention to?
- What layers am I undermining?
- Where in the spectrum do I see the greatest potential for clients' change?
- How might I be demonstrating that?

The spectrum of sex is deliberately an imperfect, incomplete map leaving space for additional details, nuances and specificities to be added according to individual context and differences; it is intended to be a conversational tool rather than a template for thinking. It can serve as a tool for broadening the meaning of sex, for increasing understanding of the inter-relatedness of the layers within the spectrum and for understanding the complexity of sex. Nothing is simple when it comes to sex, even what looks, at first sight, like the narrowest level of meaning, 'sex as intercourse', can be very complex, multifaceted and puzzling. Bearing in mind the plethora of ethical, legal, cultural, religious, psychological and social beliefs and boundaries that relate to the subject, there is scope for asking a whole range of open and complex questions related solely to that 'narrowest' level of meaning of sex, i.e. intercourse: What is intercourse? Who should be involved in it? What age, gender, number of people may be involved? What are the right ways of doing it? How much variety, frequency, and deviance is allowed or expected? What should be happening when and where...? The ideas about 'normalcy' pervade all these, as discourses about sex and sexuality are usually loaded with strong ideas about what is permissible, what is prohibited and what is open to individual choice.

EXERCISES

- Draw your own spectrum of sex; include all relevant aspects that are meaningful to you in your present life when thinking about sex and sexual experiences. Interview each other in pairs (training or group supervision context).
- Reflect on how the spectrum of sex can be used in your practice. What could be its relevance for therapy and supervision?
- Think of a case you are currently working with. How could you integrate the spectrum of sex as part of your approach to clients?
- Discuss the theoretical perspectives on unusual sexual preferences. *Experiential exercise*: discuss certain paraphilias, how you feel about them and what it might be like working with clients who practise BDSM.
- Reflect on the theoretical explanations of paraphilias and relate your beliefs to the specific theories. Communicate your theoretical understanding of this phenomenon to a colleague, explaining why your perspective makes sense to you and how you came to believe in it. After this discussion, hypothetically take a position of another perspective and create arguments that would justify it. (The exercise can continue over time so as to include a wide spectrum of theoretical possibilities.)

3

SEXUAL MISCONCEPTIONS AND PREJUDICE

Sex as a cultural taboo

Typically, conversations about sex tend to be polarised; on the one hand, sex is commercialised and used to sell, manipulate and gain power; on the other, it is a suppressed, taboo subject where meaningful, intimate and reflective conversations rarely happen. A family therapist's research on family secrets found that 'sexual secrets are the most common' (Mason, 1993, p.32). This can be illustrated by an example of a client in his 50s, a well-educated, professional, family man who said during his first session: 'I've never talked about sex with anyone, including my wife!' The conclusion drawn from such secrets and taboos is often that the lack of open conversations suggests that the topic is shameful. A postmodern constructivist therapist Winter (1988) highlighted the need to pay attention to the clients' understanding of their sexual problems and to the personal meaning they attribute to sex, sexual experience and their sexual identity. Psychosexual therapy regularly explores these themes, enquiring how clients learned about sex and sexuality, how their sexual curiosity developed, how they searched for answers to their sexual questions, and how they decided which ones to believe in.

Sexual myths frequently encountered in psychosexual therapy include negative and punitive beliefs such as that sex and masturbation are bad and sinful, or that sex should not be enjoyed (Zilbergeld, 1999, p.29). Such attitudes, which can become deeply ingrained, causing distress, conflict and relationship breakdown, are frequently a major factor in sexual dysfunction. Sometimes their influence is more quietly undermining, bringing a sense of shame and embarrassment to people's sexual lives. Mythology, reducing sex to narrow meanings and prescribing rigid rules is cited in sexology literature: '*An erection is necessary in order to have sex*' (Weeks & Gambescia, 2000, p.10); '*Good sex always leads to an orgasm*' (Weeks & Gambescia, 2000, p.13). Sexual misconceptions related to the meaning of sex and what is 'good sex' are summarised in sexology literature, such as: '*In sex, it's performance that counts*'; '*Good sex is spontaneous, with no planning and no talking*' (Zilbergeld, 1999, p.33). Such mythology that relates to what is 'right' in sex, what is 'normal', has rendered many people feeling exposed, worried, feeling sexually inadequate, hiding their own insecurities and looking for a set of prescriptions to follow, in order to achieve a particular 'performance rating'. Many people's lives have been impoverished by the dominant impact of these misconceptions, often limiting their patterns of sexually relating. Therefore, broadening the meaning of sex can often have an important therapeutic effect.

Misconceptions about erections

In the cultural context of over-emphasising sexual performance and functioning, Weeks, a sex therapist and family therapist, and Gambescia, a psychologist and sex therapist, summarised typical misconceptions about erections (Weeks & Gambescia, 2000, pp.10–11), examples of which can be categorised as follows:

Relating to the physical, biological nature of erections and its implications for sex:

- *An erection is necessary in order to ejaculate*
- *An erection during sleep or upon wakening must mean the man was dreaming about something sexual*
- *If the erection is lost during sex, the penis will not regain its tumescence.*

Relating to the man's individual behavioural skills and sexual capabilities:

- *If a man cannot get an erection, it's because he's not trying hard enough*
- *Losing an erection one time must be a sign of impotence.*

Relating to the meaning of erections or their absence:

- *An erection is an indication of sexual desire*
- *When erections are not as firm as they used to be, something must be terribly wrong*
- *Every time a man has erection, he must have sex.*

Relating to the meaning of erections in a relationship:

- *The woman should not initiate sexual contact if a man has an erection problem*
- *Firm erections are essential in a relationship.*

Their book provides helpful educative material that can usefully support therapeutic interventions. For example, their list of misconceptions, together with the explanations that dispel them, can be offered to clients to read and discuss with their partners and/or therapist as a basis for reflecting on the impact of such constraining beliefs on their sexual lives over time, opening up possibilities for the creation of alternative understandings.

Misconceptions about couples' sexual lives

Psychologists and sex therapists McCarthy and McCarthy (2012, p.2) provided a list of false statements about couples' sexual lives, some of which are listed below:

- *Sex is purely natural, not a function of learning and communication*
- *Foreplay is for the woman, intercourse is for the man*
- *Once a couple establishes a good sexual relationship, they do not need to set aside time for intimacy, pleasure, or experimentation*
- *If you love each other and communicate, everything will be fine sexually*
- *Technique is more important than intimacy in achieving sexual satisfaction*
- *If one or both partners become aroused, intercourse must follow or there will be frustration and feelings of failure*
- *Simultaneous orgasms provide the most erotic pleasure*
- *Married people do not masturbate*
- *Using sexual fantasies during intercourse indicates dissatisfaction with your partner.*

Misconceptions about marriage

A marriage and family therapist Larson (2016) identified eight common myths about marriage:

- *If my partner really loves me, he/she should instinctively know what I want and need to be happy*
- *I can change my partner by pointing out his/her inadequacies, errors, and other faults*

- *My partner either loves me or doesn't love me; nothing I do will affect the way he/she feels about me*
- *I must feel better about my partner before I can change my behaviour towards him/her*
- *Marriage is a 50-50 partnership*
- *Marriage can fulfil all of my needs and dreams*
- *The more my spouse discloses positive and negative information to me, the closer I will feel towards them and the greater our marital satisfaction*
- *Couples should keep their problems to themselves and solve them alone.*

Gender-related sexual mythology

Myths related to 'appropriate' gender behaviour and gender-related rules of sexual behaviour are described in various sexology literature:

- *Sex must only ever occur at the instigation of the man* (Hawton, 1985)
- *Any woman who instigates sex is immoral* (Hawton, 1985)
- *Men should not express their feelings* (Hawton, 1985)
- *Good sex can only be enjoyed with bad women* (Zilbergeld, 1999)
- *Good women do not like sex* (Zilbergeld, 1999)
- *A man always wants sex and is always ready* (Zilbergeld, 1999)
- *Having G-spot orgasms and multiple orgasms proves you are a sexually liberated woman* (Metz & McCarthy, 2004)
- *Women use sex to manipulate men* (McCarthy & Metz, 2008).

Sexologists and psychologists Heiman and LoPiccolo cited a list of myths and misconceptions about female sexuality in their classic book '*Becoming Orgasmic*' (1988, pp.37–41):

- *Sex is only for those under thirty*
- *"Normal" (real, feminine, or sexual) women have an orgasm every time they have sex*
- *All women can have multiple orgasms*
- *Pregnancy and delivery reduce women's sexual expansiveness*
- *A woman's sex life ends with menopause*
- *Vaginal orgasms are more feminine and mature than clitoral*
- *A sexually responsive woman can always be "turned on" by her partner*
- *Nice (feminine) women aren't aroused by erotica*
- *You are frigid if you don't like the more exotic forms of sex*
- *If you can't have orgasms quickly and easily, there is something wrong with you*

- *Feminine women don't initiate sex or become wild and unrestrained during sex*
- *Contraception is a woman's responsibility.*

McCarthy and Metz (2008, p.1) identified myths related to men's sexual fitness, such as:

- *Real men are always interested and ready to perform sexually*
- *Penis size is the most important factor in sexually pleasing your partner.*

Such myths can have an extremely negative impact on men's sexual functioning, confidence and satisfaction in sexual relationships.

A sexologist, psychiatrist and systemic therapist Sanders helpfully contextualised sexual myths 'based on power, heterosexism and patriarchy' (Sanders, 1994):

- *All physical contact must lead to sex*
- *Certain feelings should only be felt, or at least expected, by one sex*
- *In sex, it's performance that counts*
- *In sex, as in dancing, the man must take the lead and the woman must follow.*

From a social constructionist position, stories and constructions on sex and intimacy were researched by authors such as Weingarten (1991), Hare-Mustin (1991, 1994), Foreman and Dallos (1992), Dallos (1997), and Dallos and Dallos (1997) highlighting constraining cultural meanings that define what is expected of men and women in relation to each other and those that disguise gender inequality. Dallos and Dallos (1997), for example, suggested it was crucial to understand the major societal discourses and their impact on individuals and couples when working with sexual problems. They provided a critique of some pervasive ideologies, stating: 'some of the dominant explanations of sexuality and problems can be seen to be based in patriarchal discourses...' (Dallos & Dallos, 1997, p.5).

Gender-related sexual mythology has oppressed both men and women limiting their sexual options and creating rigid patterns of sexual interactions, as described in the examples below:

- Women who do not believe they should enjoy sex, feeling guilty if they do, as '*sex is a man's thing*' and is not supposed to be for them
- Women looking for a strong macho man, a hero, who deny their own power and responsibility for sexual pleasure, blaming men for failing to perform this role

- Women relinquishing responsibility for their sexual pleasure to men, rendering themselves constrained and unfulfilled
- Women who blame themselves if anything goes 'wrong' in sex, believing that the man's sexual desire and functioning is 'normal' and that their own perceived lack of desire/pleasure is a sign of their abnormality, leaving them feeling distressed and ashamed by their sexual inadequacy
- Women who surrender to a passive sexual role, expecting no pleasure from sex and not engaging with it in any constructive way, creating a sense of sex being an empty experience, a void
- Women who fake orgasms to prevent being blamed or abandoned by men who expect them to react in a linear progression way, quietly suffering in the fear of being sexually abnormal
- Men who do not trust women and feel underlying hostility and resentment and who, expecting to be sexually exploited, are reluctant to commit
- Men who, fearing intimacy with women, feel inadequate as sexual partners, struggling with performance anxiety, premature ejaculation and erectile difficulties as a result of the pressure of gender role expectations
- Men trying to prove themselves to other men, feeling dishonest about their true feelings and feeling isolated, believing they are the only men who do not perform to the perfect standards of masculinity
- Men taking a superior role in sex trying to assert their masculine power, blaming and pathologising the women who don't respond as a perfect 'sexual machine' going in a linear progression from excitement to arousal, plateau and orgasm in response to vaginal penetration.

The myth of happiness

While exploring what clients enjoy and what makes them happy it is also important to be aware that the language of 'happiness' can be oppressive and constraining (Watzlawick, 1993). A couple presented with the problem of 'not being happy'. They both appeared to be subdued, rather quiet, thoughtful individuals. Over time it emerged they had a strong emotional bond, and a great capacity for understanding and supporting each other. Both had an interest in philosophy, felt strongly about the same political issues and would spend hours discussing such subjects. They cared for animals and volunteered, she with disadvantaged children and he with the Samaritans. They described their sex life as deeply connecting and neither one wished for any changes. 'Why then, are we not happy?' they kept asking. The therapist asked if they were not to use the word 'happiness', what other words would describe the qualities of their relationship. From this it emerged they took great pleasure from their conversations and their various joint activities. They both derived a high level of satisfaction and fulfilment from the relationship, were strongly attracted to each other, and found comfort and contentment in each other's presence but believed something was missing as other couples seemed to be more cheerful and light-hearted. They felt 'different' and wondered if they were 'awkward' in comparison to how they constructed 'everybody else'.

The myth of normality

The widespread 'myth of normality' seems to cause high levels of distress, guilt and anxiety in relation to many aspects of sex. Myths about orgasm, such as that *'it has to be "simultaneous"'*, that *'it has to happen every time there is sex'*, and that *'the purpose of sex is orgasm'*; myths about masturbation such as that *'if people in a relationship masturbate that means they are not sexually satisfied with the partner'*, myths about couple therapy such as that *'if we have to come to couple therapy that means our relationship is seriously flawed'*, myths about sexual frequency such as that *'certain frequency signifies normality or abnormality'*, and the myth that *'sex has or has to have clear universal rules'*, have brought feelings of inadequacy and worries about abnormality to many people's sexual lives. Clients sometimes explicitly ask whether their sexual behaviour and thinking is 'normal', and sometimes the question of normality implicitly underlies the conversation. 'The question is not if it's "normal" but if it's a problem', writes Zilbergeld (1999, p.83), directing thinking towards sexual rights and choices rather than submission to external normative standards. At the heart of every misconception there sits a deeply embedded normative judgement, a moral imperative, dogmatically and exclusively claiming a global truth. Tiefer, a sexologist, feminist and therapist, described 'five meanings of normal' (Tiefer, 2004, p.9):

- *Subjective*: defining 'normal' according to one's own subjective view, i.e.: 'I am normal, and so is anyone who is the same as me'
- *Statistical*: defining 'normal' as the behaviour that is most common; less frequent is 'abnormal'. For example, descriptions such as: 'too much sex'; 'too low sexual desire'; or 'unusual sexual practices' are depictions based on a statistical viewpoint from which persons are pathologised
- *Idealistic*: 'normal means perfect'; this view is likely to produce perfectionistic disappointments and perpetuate negative interpretations
- *Cultural*: defining 'normal' within the culturally acceptable practices: 'Bare breasts or men kissing in public is normal in one place but abnormal in

another', states Tiefer (2004, p.10). From sources like magazines, soap operas, TV dramas and movies, information about sex suggests that:

- Everyone wants a lot of it
- Everyone breaks up relationships, families, and lives to get it
- Everyone's sexual episodes are full of desperately urgent desire
- The best sex is between strangers, especially strangers forbidden or prevented from consummating their desires (Tiefer, 2004, p.13).

The culturally determined norms are often implicit and sometimes difficult to identify as the person becomes immersed in the cultural context in which they live.

- *Clinical*: this meaning of 'normal' uses scientific and medical data when making judgements about health and illness, normality and abnormality. Within this context, clinicians including psychotherapists have enormous assumed power in determining the definition of health and normality. Existence of standards of normality, claims Tiefer (2004, p.11), breeds negative psychological consequences and as such constitutes social control.

Sexuality is a subject of all these discourses and its normality or abnormality is judged based on one or more of the criteria above. When exploring sexual mythology, this may be a useful pointer as to how normative judgements about sex have come into being and have established themselves in clients' value systems and how certain contexts have maintained them. Deconstructing discourses on sex by peeling off successive layers of feelings, thoughts and behaviours often reveals where prejudices lie. This, in turn, opens up opportunities to reconstruct the meaning and implications of certain sexual possibilities. What are the cherished values that are chosen and fully subscribed to? What are clients prepared to reconsider and change? What is the 'cost' of changing a belief? What losses may be involved? Even when it is not possible or not desired by clients to change certain beliefs, therapeutic work can still highlight the impact of their belief system in limiting their sexual options through interventions such as:

- If you are always directed by what you believe a majority of people do sexually, you may not develop your particular individual sexual desires...
- If you continue to believe that your partner's masturbation is your relationship enemy, you may create resentment in them for taking away a healthy sexual option and restricting their sexual choices...
- If orgasm is your only and primary goal in sex, you may be missing out on the richness of other sexual possibilities....

Professional sexual myths

The concept of 'professional sexual myths' (Markovic, 2013) has been created to draw attention to the fact that sexual myths can be and have been created by sexology and psychosexual therapy professionals themselves, indicating that previously existing beliefs held as truths can be inaccurate. It is inevitable and beneficial that these processes happen, as they are a result of advances in the professional field and a sign that knowledge evolves and that understandings can be enriched through discovery of new evidence. However, some constraining historical ideas from sexology continue to operate in the minds and in the lives of people many years after having been superseded, such as the human sexual response model (Masters & Johnson, 1966). Using a constructivist framework, Clement (2002) critiqued the supremacy of normative paradigms in sexology and an emphasis on 'functioning' such as the human response cycle (Masters & Johnson, 1966) (described in Chapter 2), as opposed to approaching each case individually and applying treatment that is suited to a particular person. Many female clients have constructed their sexual responses as abnormal based on the limiting model of Masters and Johnson and for this reason have sought psychosexual therapy.

Schnarch, a clinical psychologist and sex therapist, discussed changes in the sexology field in relation to conceptualisation of sexual desire (Schnarch, 2000) and distinguished two generations: the first generation approach during the 1970s and 1980s, which privileged individual diagnosis, treated sexual desire as a natural, biological and individual function, and as an initial stage in sexual encounters; the second generation approach, which was the current thinking at the time, introduced relational and psychological dimensions, and moved desire from a necessary initial stage of sexual encounters to something that can evolve as a result of sexual activity at any time during the sexual interaction. Treatment is more comprehensive and takes into account multiple contextual factors. By distinguishing these different generations of approach to sexual desire within the sexology field, Schnarch draws attention to the idea of professional mythology and highlights how beliefs and premises held by experts can permeate people's lives, sometimes with long-lasting effects.

Metz and McCarthy (2004, p.5) provide a list of 14 widespread sexual myths, including:

- *Few young men have an unsuccessful first intercourse experience, but if they do, this signals they will have a lifelong sexual problem*
- *Only 5 percent of all men experience an erection problem before the age of forty*

- *If the woman does not perform like the man (that is, have one orgasm during intercourse with no additional stimulation), it means he is an inadequate lover*
- *The larger the man's penis in the flaccid state, the larger it is in the erect state*
- *Penis size is the best measure of virility*
- *Viagra results in firm erections 100 percent of the time*
- *A normal consequence of ageing is the loss of capacity to have an erection.*

The authors state: 'The average man believes six of these myths to be true. For health professionals, the average number true is three. Old myths grew from lack of information and repressive attitudes; new myths arise from commercial exaggeration and unrealistic performance demands' (p.5). Barker (2013, p.150) lists some widespread cultural myths about 'romantic relationships', stressing the importance of sexual and relationship therapists being aware of the constraining and pathologising potential of these:

- *People require a romantic relationship in order to be healthy*
- *Romantic relationships must be sexual*
- *Romantic relationships are more valuable than friendships*
- *Romantic relationships must be monogamous*
- *Relationship 'success' correlates to its longevity.*

Therapists' self-reflexivity and relational reflexivity

A stance of professional self-reflexivity is necessary in order for therapists to separate their own personal and/or professional biases and monitor their own prejudices in relation to sex and reflect on how these may impact their clinical work. The following questions can serve as guidance for supervisors and supervisees in reflecting on how such issues may be addressed in supervision:

- How do you feel talking about sex with clients and colleagues?
- How do you think clients feel talking about it with you?
- What concerns you most when thinking about addressing sexual issues in your clinical work?
- How do you think your value system is affecting your clinical exploration of sexual issues?
- How do you see therapeutic use of self in working with the topic of sex?

- Do you think your personal background and experience is more of a helpful resource or more of a hindrance to you when working with sex and sexual relationships clinically? In what way?
- How has working with sexual relationships in your clinical work affected you personally; what impact has it had on your life?
- What do you think is the level of therapists' personal exposure when addressing sex in therapy; how do you think about this and what are your ways of regulating it?
- What kind of conversation or therapeutic intervention related to sex would be most exposing?
- What risks do you think a therapist undertakes in this area?
- How much are you prepared to take these risks? Which ones would you not take?
- What do you think has influenced you most in the way you think about and talk about sex, both in therapy and in other personal and professional contexts?
- What kind of a development of a therapeutic conversation in your sessions about sex would worry you?
- If you worked with a client/clients whose sexual values are radically different from yours, how do you imagine you would deal with it? Any examples?
- What kind of sexual belief system would present a complex challenge for you?
- Can you give me an example from your practice where you felt most challenged in the area of sex?
- Can you recall the situation where you felt most stuck in your work with clients in relation to sex?
- Can you cite any examples of feeling uncomfortable? How did you deal with that?
- What was the most daring question you have asked of clients within this topic?
- What specific example comes to your mind as a sexual issue that you would not want to deal with in your practice? What would your response be to such referral?

Relational reflexivity, or asking questions of clients to address therapeutic processes and the impact of therapeutic conversations on clients, could be demonstrated through the type of questions offered below (adapted from Burnham, 2005).

Questions about questions:

- Which questions that I asked you did you find most useful?
- Of all the things we have talked about so far, what has been most helpful to you?
- What has been least helpful?
- Which aspects of our sessions have been most interesting?

Evaluating reflexive changes:

- How might you use these aspects that have been interesting and useful to do things differently in your day-to-day life?

Evaluating and co-constructing experience of therapy:

- Are we talking about issues that are important to you, in ways that are useful; or would you rather change the topic and talk about something else?

Co-ordinating resources:

- When you are telling me about your sexual concerns, would it be more important that I understand how difficult it is for you, or would you prefer me to offer you suggestions for doing things differently?
- If I offered you ideas for change, would you be inclined to try them because you like the ideas, or because you believe I have an expertise and you should follow the expert advice?

Deconstructing clients' realities:

- What kind of sexual desire are you talking about that you would like to have: the type that you have seen in the films and read about in the books, or the type that would be something more like your kind of desire?
- We have been talking for a while now and I am wondering what you would hope that I have understood about you as a sexual person?
- If your partner was here in the session with you today, what would you hope they would understand about you sexually from what you have said?

EXERCISES

Guideline questions for therapists' self-reflection (personal context):

- Where did you learn about sex?
- How were issues of sex responded to in your family of origin?
- When did you first become aware of your sexuality?
- What do you regard as the greatest influences on how you think about sex now?

Guideline questions for therapists' self-reflection (professional context):

- What resources do you have/do you lack to work with sexual issues clinically?
- How could you expand your range of resources?
- Randomly choose a question from the last section of this chapter and discuss with a colleague.

Create relational reflexivity questions that you might ask of a client you are working with.

4

CLASSIFICATION AND ASSESSMENT OF SEXUAL DISORDERS

Introduction

This chapter will discuss the sexual disorders as classified in DSM-5 (APA, 2013): delayed ejaculation, erectile disorder, female orgasmic disorder, female sexual interest/arousal disorder, genito-pelvic pain/penetration disorder, male hypoactive sexual desire disorder and premature/early ejaculation. In addition, female persistent genital arousal disorder, sexual aversion disorder, sexual compulsivity, addiction or hypersexuality and dyspareunia in men will be discussed. Each disorder is presented separately, referring both to sexology and systemic social constructionist theory and practice.

Sexology resources such as DSM-5, textbooks and recent international research studies will be drawn upon, from a vast knowledge base within sexology science. Throughout the book, DSM-5 is referred to more than ICD-10. Despite the latter being the most frequently used psychiatric manual, it is far outdated and currently being revised, to be published in May 2018. Such resources are seen in sexology as vital for establishing a correct diagnosis to enable clarity of focus and understanding of the nature and characteristics of presenting sexual difficulties. At the same time, it is relevant to take into consideration that using diagnostic categories and the label of a sexual disorder has its advantages and disadvantages. Having a 'systemic mind' in terms of ongoing awareness that diagnoses are social constructions, i.e. socially constructed meanings put forth by the dominant professional culture (Gergen, Hoffman & Anderson, 1996, p.105) and as such are relative, limiting and potentially stigmatising (White, 1991), is part of this integrated approach whereby the two different epistemologies co-exist.

The MOST model maps serve as a guide to assessment of sexual disorders in this chapter. A comprehensive map of the factors contributing to sexual problems can provide a basis for the therapist's initial assessment explorations. Thinking systemically, such explorations may be linked to the process of 'hypothesising', or generating and examining a working idea which guides the therapist in their work with clients. 'Hypothesising' can be compared to a stance of a 'temporary certainty' (Cecchin, 1987), to distinguish it from having a fixed idea. Therapists should not be too attached to their hypothesis. The Milan team advised: 'don't fall in love with your hypothesis' (Cornwell, 1989, in conversation with Luigi Boscolo); they playfully emphasised the therapists' non-attachment to their own views (Cecchin, Lane & Ray, 1992). To ensure this non-attachment, a therapeutic stance of 'neutrality' was introduced; 'neutrality' was later renamed as 'curiosity', to avoid misinterpretations attributed to neutrality such as aloofness, passivity and coldness of the therapist. Curiosity meant taking a position of appreciation of the multiplicity of possible patterns, plurality of alternatives and 'inventing multiple punctuations' (Cecchin, 1987, p.407). The therapist takes the stance of active, exploratory curiosity, showing tolerance for contradictory perspectives, engages with a variety of hypothetical perspectives, and respects clients' right to make decisions by creating a context in which different meanings can emerge, opening up space for change. The concept of a 'hypothesis' can be helpfully divided into two levels: the level of a 'general hypothesis', and the level of a 'specific hypothesis'. The general hypothesis in this context would then represent the knowledge and ideas derived from extensive quantitative research and clinical studies from sexology and sex therapy. The maps in this chapter, outlining the main factors contributing to sexual dysfunctions, present a certain level of factual, evidence-based knowledge, embedded in the construction of a scientific discourse; such knowledge can be linked to a 'general hypothesis', consisting of data systematically collected through research and accumulated clinical experience. At the same time, clinicians allow for a 'specific hypothesis' to emerge as a result of paying attention to the specificities of different client situations, and opening up space for individualities and idiosyncrasies that each client brings. To this end, therapists listen to both the general and the specific in relation to each individual and each relationship as they get to meet them in the therapeutic space. Therapists develop and discard their hypotheses as new information emerges or is elaborated in subsequent sessions (Vetere & Dallos, 2003). A wide range of contributing factors provides options within which to explore specificities, guided by the map and by the clients simultaneously, navigating through the hypotheses and the possibilities in charting the client's unique territory. Therefore, assessment within this integrated framework contains both routine elements and those tailored to the particular clients, shaped to them and by them as the assessment interview proceeds.

From both sexology and systemic therapy perspectives it can be useful to establish a clear description of the nature and the specificities of the presenting problem. Clients are invited to describe the sexual difficulty they are bringing to therapy in as concrete and detailed terms as possible, in order to obtain a clear picture of how the problem is manifested, how often it presents itself and under which circumstances it occurs. Linked to this, as stated in DSM-5 (APA, 2013) it is helpful to identify the two general dimensions of any sexual problem in terms of:

- whether it is a lifelong (primary) or an acquired (secondary) difficulty, and
- whether it is a generalised or a situational type of difficulty.

These dimensions are relevant in both the medical and the systemic approaches; from a medical point of view, these are the crucial aspects of determining a correct diagnosis. Sexology literature stresses how important it is for clinicians to have a clear understanding of the nature of the problem, including its duration and severity, for most effective treatment (Wincze & Weisberg, 2015). For example, depending on whether the problem is lifelong or acquired, it may lead the clinician in different treatment directions. In case of an acquired dysfunction, it is crucial to explore the length of time the problem has been present for, any variations in its manifestations such as whether there are any situational differences in terms of how it presents itself; and which factors may have contributed to its onset, such as particular events, life transitions, ill health, stresses, and so on. Systemically, exploration of these dimensions provides opportunities for enhancing clients' self-reflexivity through facilitating the making of connections between various contexts and their impact.

To explore whether the difficulty is lifelong or acquired, the therapist traces the onset of the problem. The condition is considered as lifelong if it has been consistently present since the beginning of a person's partnered sexual activity such that they have never experienced successful sexual functioning. These situations are less frequently encountered in clinical practice and are usually more difficult to treat. They may signify more complex situations and sometimes indicate a medical problem at the root of the difficulty. If the problem began some time during the person's life after a period of 'normal sexual activity' (DSM-5, APA, 2013) that would indicate the acquired type of difficulty. Usually at least an approximate timing of the onset of the problem can be given, and can be linked to events in a person's life that might have bearing on their sexual experience. Typical sexology questions in trying to determine the onset of the problem are, for example: How long have you had this problem for? When did you first notice it? In addition, from a systemic perspective, it may be important to ask: Who noticed it first? It may be relevant, perhaps, if the partner noticed the problem first, in that the partner's perception may have affected the person who as a result feels they have a problem. Anderson, Goolishian and Windermand (1986) coined the term 'problem-determined systems' in explaining from a social constructionist perspective how problems get generated in communities through constructing views and values via language and communication. Humberto Maturana, a Chilean biologist whose ideas are attributed to the postmodern movement of constructivism within systemic psychotherapy, created the expression 'bringing forth of pathology' (Mendez, Coddou & Maturana, 1988) to describe socially constructed pathologising processes that often carry a degree of prevailing societal power in determining, defining and naming the phenomena according to the dominant social norms. A systemic social constructionist viewpoint would explore the processes of naming and defining in order to bring a contextual perspective within which to enable a comprehensive understanding of the presenting difficulties. From a CBT perspective, an approach widely used in sex therapy, similar questions could be asked, intended to identify precipitating factors or the factors that may have triggered the development of the problem, such as: What was happening in your life at the time when you noticed the change in your sexual experience? Prompts used in tracking the triggers may be various stresses such as work problems, family illness, financial worries, health worries of the client or of close family and other close relationships, tiredness, extended pressures, losses, bereavement, and so on. Any changes in the nature or circumstances of the clients' relationship at the time may be also significant, such as conflict, communication problems, relationship distance, boredom, anger, resentment, and other difficult emotions and situations. Assessment should explore the clients' routines and the quality of their relationship and any changes that may have occurred at the time to which the onset of the problem may be attributed. This tracking activity is not always straightforward, as people often do not consider the relevance of various life events in terms of their impact on their sexual feelings and/or performance. It is not unusual that sexual lives are thought of as separate from the rest of the person's life. A careful and precise assessment putting the problem in the context of serious and difficult life worries can itself be a treatment intervention by removing the pathologising frame and normalising sexual response as a healthy emotional and physical reaction to adverse circumstances.

To explore whether the difficulty is generalised or situational, the therapist's questions with the intent to facilitate the broadening of the client's description of the problem and its links to any contextual factors, might be: How frequently does the problem happen? In which situations does it manifest itself most? Does it happen each time there is sexual activity? What proportion of the time? Does it happen during masturbation? Responses to these linear, closed questions typically used in sexology assessment can provide information that may significantly assist the treatment plan. For example, if sexual functioning is experienced as normal and satisfactory during masturbation and the problem occurs only or mainly during partnered sex, this is seen as crucial piece of information, indicating that the problem is situational. This depends on the type of the difficulty but if, for example, an erectile problem occurs during masturbation as well as during partnered sex, it may indicate that an organic cause of the problem is likely, or in some exceptional situations that deeply situated individual psychological factors may be operating. If, however, the problem is described as situationally dependent, the therapist's questions would focus more specifically on examination of the specific situations in which the problem occurs. Systemically, this kind of exploration would be seen as guided by the therapist's search for 'patterns that connect' persons, events, actions, beliefs and ideas in interconnected and recursive processes (Bateson, 1972). Relationship patterns have been researched and conceptualised by various systemic therapists including Tomm (1991), who created pathological interpersonal patterns as an alternative to the individualistic approach of psychiatry and the medical model. 'Unwanted repetitive patterns', a concept created within the social constructionist co-ordinated management of meaning (CMM) theory (Pearce, 2007), signifies persistent patterns in interpersonal dynamics that often have a destructive effect on relationships. Therapeutic aims would be to identify and alter these patterns, creating space for different ways of relating. The narrative approach (White, 2007) might use externalising conversations in attempts to alter such pathological patterns and facilitate the development of new, more effective ones. White (2007) writes that patterns have the power to recruit people; through externalising and deconstructing such patterns in therapy, clients can reclaim their own strengths in standing up to unwanted influences, thus creating their desired interpersonal change.

Although the maps included in Chapter 4 relate to sexual 'disorders' as defined in the latest edition of the DSM, the diagnosis of a 'disorder' would not be made in certain situations. For example, if sexual functioning and experience are adversely affected by medication or are a symptom of a medical condition, the diagnosis of a sexual disorder would not be made. Equally, in the absence of adequate stimulus, a sexual difficulty is not considered an individual sexual disorder (APA, 2013). Sexual therapy and psychotherapy can still help an individual to learn about their sexual needs and ways of expressing them, but outside the frame of a diagnosis of a sexual disorder. Sometimes, as Bancroft et al. (2009) pointed out, sexual inhibitory response can be a healthy protective mechanism in situations of perceived danger or threat. Furthermore, sexual response is considered in the context of relational factors; interpersonal conflict, for example, usually inhibits sexual desire and arousal and significantly impacts sexual satisfaction. In these situations, it is highly relevant that the clinician in their assessment, diagnosis and formulation distinguishes between dysfunction and dissatisfaction (Wincze & Carey, 2001).

While DSM-5 acknowledges relevant contextual influences in considering whether a medical diagnosis of sexual disorders should be made, it applies these inconsistently, in that such influences are explicitly stated in relation to some disorders but not to others. DSM-5 lists five factors that must be considered during assessment and diagnosis of sexual disorders: partner factors (e.g. a partner's sexual and general health); relationship (such as poor communication and discrepancies in desire); individual vulnerability (such as poor body image, history of abuse, psychiatric co-morbidity or stresses in life); cultural/religious (such as prohibitions of sexual activity) and medical factors. Only the impact of medical, interpersonal and individual vulnerability factors, such as life stressors on sexual functioning, are considered reasons for not diagnosing a disorder. It is unclear on what basis it has been decided that some contextual influences determine the criteria for applying a diagnostic classification more than some others. Thinking systemically, on the other hand, issues are always contextual; no personal experience, an emotion, thought or a behaviour exists in a vacuum, and so the questions from that point of view would be: What are the indicators warranting a diagnosis? When is a diagnosis viable? Why are contextual factors that bring about impaired sexual functioning unequally considered?

MOST dimensions: assessment guide

The text that follows will address assessment in relation to each of the six dimensions of the MOST model, and offer some typical questions that may be useful for clinicians in exploring the influences of the possible factors contributing to the development and persistence of a sexual concern.

The emotional dimension

This dimension can be explored through listening to clients' emotional expression, observing their emotional reactions and asking direct questions about their emotional experiences, both past and present. Questions such as: 'How do you feel about...?' could be used as a prompt for clients to describe and reflect on the emotional dimension. Clients could also be invited to relate their emotional experiences through semi-open questions, such as regarding their:

- *Current prevalent emotional life*: Are you occupied by any current worries? What are your biggest worries at the moment?
- *Self-perception and others perception in relation to the emotional sense of self*: Do you see yourself more as a relaxed person or more as a tense and worried person? How do you think others see you? What kind of mood do you see yourself in typically?
- *Experience of certain negative feelings*: Do you experience fear and anxiety? When do you most notice it? What brings these feelings about?
- *Feelings about sex*: How do you usually feel about sex? What does it depend on? Is there anything that brings feelings of shame, anger, guilt or shame related to sex?
- *Emotional strengths, resiliencies and preferences*: What makes you happy? When do you feel most satisfied? What gives you pleasure? What makes you proud? How do you show it?

The cognitive dimension

Various questions and prompts could be used to facilitate clients' expression regarding their beliefs, values and stories about sex, relationships, affection and intimacy, such as:

- *About the meaning of sex*: What does sex mean to you? How do you think about sex? What do you like most/least about sex?

Systemic explorations of meanings are seen as crucial to the understanding of clients' experiences and, to this end, mind maps are sometimes used to facilitate self-reflection. Clients can be invited to draw a map of the meaning of sex, having been encouraged to make as many connections as possible, such as, what does it mean emotionally/physically/ relationally? Or, what is the meaning of sex in relation to social and cultural difference, in terms of gender, class, race, ethnicity, ability, education, religion and so on.

- *About views on sex over time, e.g.*: How have you learned about sex? What do you believe were the strongest influences in your learning about sex? What was the most influential source of learning? What was the most positive/most negative meaning of sex you have heard/experienced in your life that has stayed with you?
- *About possible myths and misconceptions*: Have you identified any myths about sex that you used to hold in the past? What were they? How did you realise it was a myth? How has it affected you?

Positive stories, clients' cognitive resiliencies, broad views on sex and good sexual knowledge are considered to be as important as cognitive restraints and mythology. The client's responses to these questions would then guide more specific explorations, which can be introduced during various sessions over time. In addition, clients could be given a list of typical sexual myths in order to identify whether and how they may be pertinent to them.

The physical dimension

From a medical, sexology perspective clinicians should make sure that clients' physical health is thoroughly checked and for this, a medical examination is necessary in most cases.

- *Health status*: the psychotherapist would always make it absolutely clear that, although they are aware that a range of physical factors could be contributing to many sexual difficulties to a lesser or a greater extent, they are not a medical expert and therefore a visit to the GP is typically recommended.
- *Exploring medication*: given that sexual difficulties can be caused by various medications, psychotherapists should enquire if clients are taking any drugs, either prescription or over-the-counter. Contraceptive methods including the pill, the coil, condoms and hormonal injections should be noted, as they may have an effect on one's sexual experience.
- *Fitness and healthy habits*: clients may be healthy with no need for medication; however, a general lack of fitness plus alcohol and nicotine intake could yet be affecting their physical energy, their body image and consequently their sexual feelings. Therapists' assessment therefore enquires about physical exercise, nutritional habits, sleep patterns and intake of potentially harmful substances as part of exploring the

impact of the physical dimension on the clients' sexual life. Both physical vulnerabilities and strengths are explored and noted. A positive body image, for example, good level of fitness, healthy nutrition and so on are noted as important positive factors and resources that can support treatment and be utilised in building on the clients' self-esteem and progress in therapy.

- *The physical environment*: as the physical environment in which sex occurs (or doesn't occur) may be a significant factor, at some point, the therapist would explore its conduciveness to sexual activity from the client's point of view in terms of comfort, privacy and psychological meaning.

The behavioural dimension

A sexual difficulty can be connected with certain behaviours and the purpose of assessment is to establish whether this is the case and which specific behavioural factors may be affecting the sexual problem and in what way. As part of this, assessment explorations may enquire:

- *How sexual activity happens*: how it begins; how it evolves; whether there are any typical patterns; what happens if something 'goes wrong'? The therapist aims to establish whether there are aspects of a sexual technique applied by either the client or their partner/s that might be usefully adjusted; for example, it may be that more 'foreplay' or 'afterplay' are is needed. Or it may be that certain stimulations are more effective than others, or that the partners' sexual preferences are incompatible. Equally, assessment teases out what happens when things work out well: who does what to make it a good experience? Clients' views on future possibilities are also explored: what works for them that they would like more of? What might make it an even better experience? What have they tried in order to introduce positive changes? What else would they like to try?
- *How masturbation is practised*: rigid masturbation patterns frequently create sexual difficulties in partnered sex. Questions related to this area may not always be easy for clients to respond to, or sometimes not easy for therapists to ask. It is possible to obtain equally relevant details through asking 'process' as opposed to 'content' types of questions through inviting clients to describe their masturbatory patterns without necessarily giving an account of what exactly happens. For example, the therapist can say, 'Does your masturbatory activity always go through the same routine?' 'Do you practise it at the same time of day/night; same or different place?' 'Do you have the same fantasy or does it vary?'

The relational dimension

Relationship satisfactions and dissatisfactions should be assessed in a balanced way. Questions could be asked along the following lines: What are the strongest aspects of the relationship? What are the areas of concern? The areas for exploration can be:

- *Relationship difficulties*: The 'contributing factors' maps list the typical relationship difficulties such as conflict, lack of effective communication, distancing, relationship boredom and so on. Conflict, for example, seems a common factor adversely affecting sexual relationships and underlying many sexual dysfunctions. Questions could track: how does conflict start and how does it end? Does it follow a pattern? What typically triggers it? How is it resolved? These are typical methods for exploring if communicational difficulties exist and whether some are of particular concern.
- *Relationship strengths*: assessment should explore relationship strengths and positive qualities of communication patterns. Any good sexual experiences could provide clues as to what partners can create together in terms of the sexual relationship.
- *Hopes, wishes and expectations for future of the relationship*: exploring what hopes for the future partners have and what they are prepared to do differently in order to enable that to happen.
- *The meaning of the sexual concerns and their effects on the relationship*: how is sexual difficulty perceived by each partner and how do they believe it is influencing their relationship? Sometimes the meaning of a sexual concern can be part of the problem, in that partners can construct the idea that the existence of a sexual difficulty in itself signifies that the relationship is seriously flawed.

The cultural dimension

The cultural dimension explores:

- *Early learning about sex and relationships* through questions such as: Where did you learn about sex? How would you describe the environment you grew up in? What particular values may have been of importance to how you viewed sex, intimacy and relationships then and how you view them now? What kinds of conversations have you had in the past that you feel may have significantly impacted your thoughts and feelings about sex, relationships, gender and intimacy? Whose relationships have you

observed as a young person? What do you think you learned about adult intimate relationships?
- *The current network of support and network of concern*: Who in your environment supports you most? Who are the most important people whose opinions matter most to you in relation to what decisions you make in your life? Who do you rely on? Whose views are most precious to you?

To this end, the sexual genogram, a technique developed by Hof and Berman (1989), is particularly helpful for assessing and exploring the impact of intergenerational messages on sexual beliefs and feelings, and is also a useful tool for connecting family therapy and sexology perspectives. In the authors' view, the sexual genogram can uncover both implicit and explicit messages about femininity and masculinity, sex, affection and intimacy, sometimes originating from two or more generations above, which may have an invisible yet powerful impact on sexual relationships. It applies the genogram (or family tree) method that arose out of the practice of family therapy (McGoldrick, Gerson & Shellenberger, 1999) to the area of sexuality. In short, a genogram is a way of presenting in a diagrammatic form, using a set of symbols, signs and codes to signify the basic family structure; household composition; ages, gender and cultural background of various family members; critical life changes, life cycle transitions; and relationship patterns over time. Genograms are useful diagnostic tools that can provide a shared experience for clients often disclosing, for the first time, information that generates a high level of emotional intensity (Dallos & Draper, 2000). The therapeutic benefits of constructing a genogram in the session with clients include:

- organising a large amount of information and sometimes complex family constellations; 'a way to record significant information in formats that are accessible and usable for clients and therapists alike' (Dallos & Draper, 2000, p.58)
- helping both the therapist and the clients to see the bigger picture
- taking away blame; it can shift focus from an individual who is regarded as 'the problematic one' in the family to patterns in the broader family system
- providing information on the values and sensitive and emotionally charged issues in the family context
- enabling the therapist to reframe the individual's behaviour by taking a wider systemic perspective
- joining the clients; creating more closeness, empathy and understanding between the clients when, for example, partners are creating their own genograms and relationship maps in each other's presence in the session

- serving as an important orienting framework for discussion of various formative experiences, providing a vehicle for systemic questioning and as a planning tool for therapists from which they can generate hypotheses for further exploration.

Genograms can provide a route into exploration of issues of power, intimacy, boundaries, beliefs about responsibilities, decision making, duties, obligations and commitments; issues about personal space and privacy; the boundaries of the self versus shared activity in the family; the development of gender-specific roles and sexual and gender identity (Dallos & Draper, 2000). The sexual genogram is a focused version of a genogram that relates to romantic love, attachment, intimacy and other themes associated with sexuality and often reveals sexual secrets in the family such as hidden pregnancies, affairs, abortions, sexual trauma and sexual compulsivity (Gambescia, 2016).

Traditionally, family therapists applied a standard set of symbols for genograms, such as a circle for a woman, and a square for a man, as well as other pre-determined ways of representing various types of relationships in the family. Congruent with the philosophy of co-constructing sessions, clients are encouraged to use their own symbolic representation that allows for great variety. The stereotypical genogram should be questioned in terms of how to signify gender, sexual orientation and family constellations. More recently, sex and couple therapists have extended the application of the sexual genogram to include sexual and gender diversity and proposed a revision of its diagrammatic representation, as well as the use of more open-minded questions, in order to create a more equitable and accepting approach (Belous et al., 2012).

Given that a genogram is limited to the family system, it can be more helpful to use a relationship map instead, with a genogram being a part of it. The main difference is that a relationship map goes beyond the family, and includes other significant relationships and systems such as education, culture and religion, as well as any professional helping systems. The two relationship map examples in Figures 4.1 and 4.2 illustrate inclusion of a genogram into a broader relationship map. These maps were brought to supervision by therapists as a tool for discussion.

The sexual genogram was originally created as a tool combining family therapy and sex therapy in tracking intergenerational stories about sex, masculinity and femininity; sexual secrets; practices of encouragement and discouragement of sexual curiosity and sexual expression, and patterns of communication about sex, intimacy and relationships in the family. It can be expanded into a relationship map including the family and wider

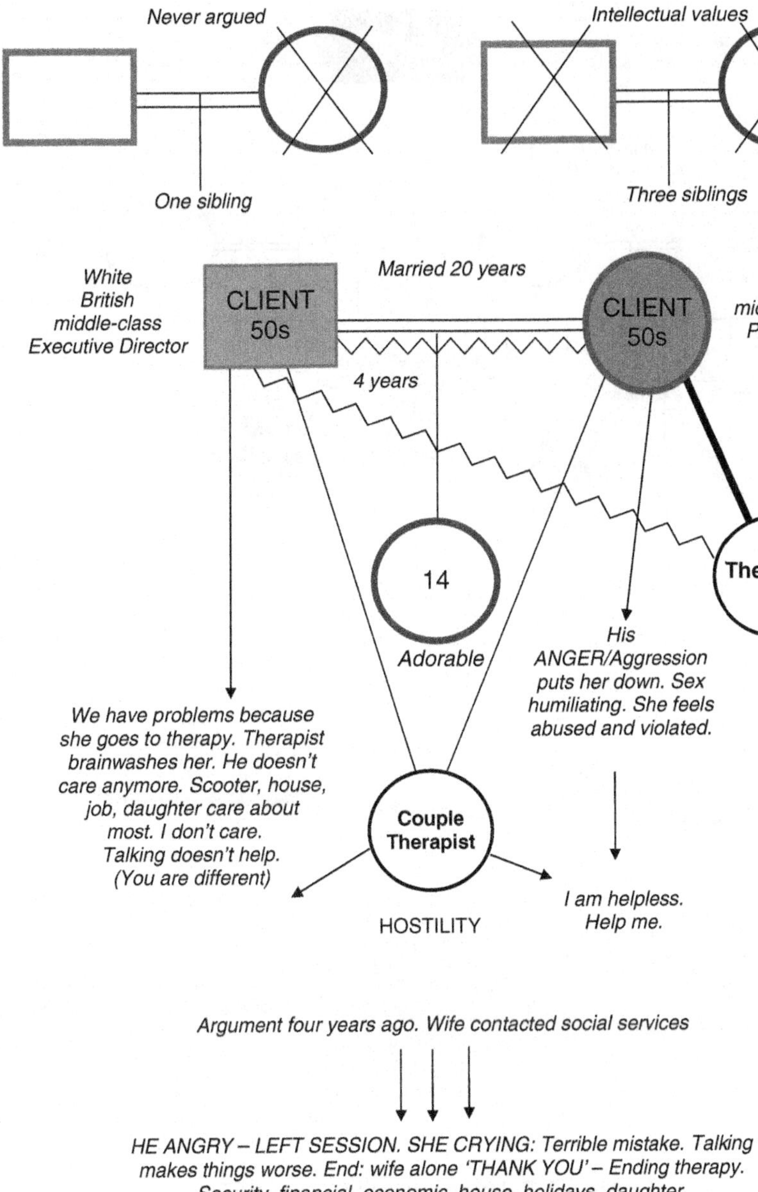

Never argued

Intellectual values

One sibling

Three siblings

White British middle-class Executive Director

CLIENT 50s

Married 20 years

CLIENT 50s

White British middle-class P/T Sales

4 years

14

Adorable

Therapist

His ANGER/Aggression puts her down. Sex humiliating. She feels abused and violated.

We have problems because she goes to therapy. Therapist brainwashes her. He doesn't care anymore. Scooter, house, job, daughter care about most. I don't care. Talking doesn't help. (You are different)

Couple Therapist

HOSTILITY

I am helpless. Help me.

Argument four years ago. Wife contacted social services

HE ANGRY – LEFT SESSION. SHE CRYING: Terrible mistake. Talking makes things worse. End: wife alone 'THANK YOU' – Ending therapy. Security, financial, economic, house, holidays, daughter.

Figure 4.1 Relationship map: the case that went wrong

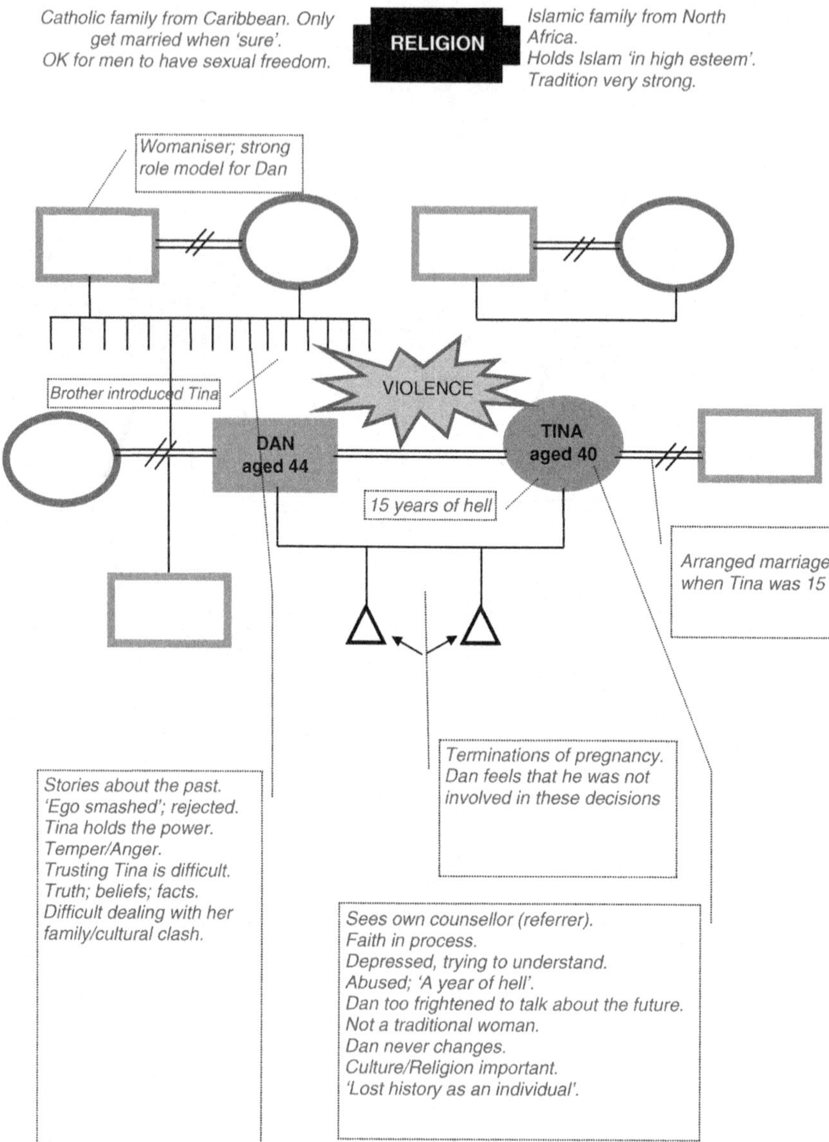

Figure 4.2 Relationship map: Dan and Tina

social, cultural and political systems. Guidelines for exploring a sexual relationship map are presented below:

COMMUNICATION ABOUT SEX

- Who were the significant persons with whom you talked about the subject of sex, sexual behaviour and intimacy?
- Do you recall the overt and covert messages received from a young age about sexual behaviour, masculinity/femininity, intimacy?
- What are the most important messages, ideas and feelings; what stood out?
- How might these have influenced your later sexual choices and experiences?

SEXUAL SECRETS

- Family secrets often relate to issues of shame, e.g. incest, abortion, miscarriage, divorce, children 'out of wedlock', illnesses, sexually transmitted diseases, promiscuity and affairs.
- How have you learned about these and when?

UNPLEASANT SEXUAL EXPERIENCES

- Explore any unpleasant sexual experiences such as abuse, violence, bullying, criticism, inappropriate touch given and received, and other inappropriate sexual non-verbal behaviour.

EMOTIONAL ATMOSPHERE AT HOME

- How were affection and closeness in the household demonstrated?
- Emotional expression (what were you praised for/criticised for/in what ways; who would you go to if upset; what were you scared of, proud of...?)
- How was emotional expression encouraged/discouraged/supported/inhibited?

PARENTS'/CARERS' RELATIONSHIP

- Explore parents' and/or carers' patterns of relating, physical affection, witnessing their sexuality, conflict management, closeness and distance.

EARLY SEXUAL LEARNING

- Where did most significant learning come from (explore contexts such as education, peer culture, religion, cultural customs and beliefs, media)?

- What were your very first ideas about sex?
- Sexual myths and misconceptions/their effect/how were they dispelled?

CURRENT CULTURAL BELIEFS AND LOYALTIES

- Are there any particular religious convictions and faith loyalties that you hold in high regard? How do these relate to your views about sex?

SEXUAL DEVELOPMENT

- How did changes in physical appearance affect you as you were growing up?
- Do you remember the first signs of puberty and your and others' reaction to it?
- Who did you talk to about it?

GENDER ROLE MODELS IN FORMATIVE YEARS

- When did you first become aware of your gender? How did you feel about it?
- Who was particularly significant and how in the 'gender modelling' for you?
- How have parents, school, peers, media, and other social and cultural groups influenced your learning about gender roles?

LIFE TRANSITIONS

- What were the most important events and life cycle changes for you and how could you reflect on the process of going through those?

TIMELINE OF SEXUAL EXPERIENCES

- How could you map your sexual experiences over time?

Discussion and conclusions

Questions and other methods and ideas described as part of the assessment process are offered as a guideline for exploration rather than a prescriptive template. Clients, of course, often volunteer information, in which case, prompts may be unnecessary and the therapist's role becomes to follow the clients' lead in communicating their accounts.

From a medical perspective, assessment may be more structured, comprising a set of pre-formulated questions and led by the clinician. From a systemic social constructionist perspective, the therapist would aim to be led by the clients. Within this integrated framework, a 'both-and' position would be demonstrated through a collaborative, dialogical interaction enacted through the interplay of the expertise of both therapist and clients. For example, the therapist might utilise the following types of questions: 'I'd like to explore with you your past experiences, prior to the current sexual relationship. What would you like to tell me about that? Would it be okay to talk about it in the session today or at any other time? Where would you like to begin?' 'Would you prefer me to ask you questions or would you prefer to start and see how it goes?' Or: 'Usually at the beginning of working together, at the assessment stage, I find it important to explore issues such as your childhood and family history, your previous sexual experiences and your current relationship. Which of these would you prefer to talk about today? Is there anything else you would rather focus on?' 'What else would you like to tell me that feels important from your point of view for me to know so that I can understand you best?' In this way, assessment becomes a co-constructed activity, open to the clients' choice, and attentive to their expertise while making the therapist's role explicit and evident through offering alternatives, suggesting possibilities and exploring certain issues. Therapists are transparent about the relevance of such explorations, while at the same time stressing the clients' right to select, choose and decide when and how they wish to communicate their perspective.

Delayed ejaculation (DE)

Definitions

The terms 'ejaculatory incompetence', 'retarded ejaculation', 'ejaculatory inhibition', and 'coital anorgasmia' are alternative labels for the problem of men experiencing difficulty in ejaculating during partnered sex. DSM-5 (APA, 2013) introduced the term 'delayed ejaculation' to avoid use of pejorative terminology.

Sexologists emphasise the importance of further terminology clarification and of distinguishing between 'orgasm' and 'ejaculation', which are commonly used interchangeably. Ejaculation refers to the expulsion of seminal fluid from the urethra, while orgasm refers to the intense subjective pleasure and genital sensations that are accompanied by rhythmic muscle contractions (Wincze & Weisberg, 2015). 'Nomenclature misunderstanding is in part related to the fact that ejaculation and orgasm usually occur simultaneously, despite being separate physiological phenomena' (Perelman, 2014, p.139).

It is possible to have either ejaculation without the expulsion of the seminal fluid (retrograde ejaculation) or orgasm without ejaculation. For the purposes of this chapter, it is assumed that orgasm and ejaculation occur together. A man who experiences orgasm but no ejaculation would not necessarily report a dysfunction.

Retrograde ejaculation is a medical condition caused by certain medication or health problems, whereby the ejaculatory fluid is expulsed inwardly, into the bladder; this condition requires medical intervention.

A man suffering from delayed ejaculation (DE in further text) typically experiences nocturnal emissions and is able to ejaculate during masturbation.

Diagnosis and assessment

DSM-5 (APA, 2013, p.424) sets the diagnostic criteria for this disorder as involving a minimum duration of six months of experiencing either of the following symptoms on almost all or all occasions of partnered sexual activity:

1. Marked and undesired delay in ejaculation
2. Marked infrequency or absence of ejaculation

The clients must report experiencing a high level of distress for the diagnosis to be made.

The disorder may appear as lifelong (primary), meaning it has been present since the beginning of the man's sexual life with partners; or as acquired (secondary), meaning it began after a period of relatively normal sexual functioning in partnered sex.

The distinction between partnered sex and masturbation here is crucial; men experiencing delayed or inhibited ejaculation during partner sex typically find greater pleasure in masturbating than in partnered sex and have no difficulty ejaculating during the masturbatory activity. Bernard Apfelbaum, a clinical psychologist and sex therapist from Berkeley, California, who researched this disorder referred to it as 'retarded ejaculation – A Much misunderstood syndrome' (Apfelbaum, 2000), and stressed the aspect of 'autosexuality', or autoeroticism, in the condition. Apfelbaum claimed: 'The true retarded ejaculator could never develop masturbatory anorgasmia' (p.208). He attributes a primary contribution to the development of this disorder to rigid masturbatory patterns, whereby an 'idiosyncratic technique' may have been developed such as penile thrusting against the mattress or a pillow, or using excessive pressure producing intense and quick orgasm (Apfelbaum, 2000; Perelman, 2004). Men report the importance of subtleties such as 'strength of grip' around the penis and some acknowledge holding a belief that they are the 'masters of their penis' allowing little scope for others to provide effective stimulation. Apfelbaum proposes 'partner anorgasmia' as an apt term and states that 'men who have difficulty with masturbating to orgasm require quite different treatment than do men who are specifically coitally anorgasmic, but there is yet no discussion on such cases' (Apfelbaum, 2000, p.208), suggesting a crucial diagnostic differentiation between masturbatory and partner anorgasmia. He argues that 'this syndrome is a case of a performance symptom that makes a subtle and specific desire disorder' (p.207).

How is this disorder manifested? The men and their partners report his difficulty or inability to ejaculate despite the presence of what appears as a high state of sexual arousal, as erections are firm and long-lasting, and despite the man's desire to ejaculate. Sexual activity is reported as usually taking a very long time, sometimes in excess of two hours. DE timing is not defined in the literature and is therefore open to subjective and varied interpretations of what constitutes a delay in temporal terms, from whose point of view, who it is a problem for, and how.

Extended intercourse may, on occasions, feel pleasurable for partners; however, it can end with feelings of exhaustion, pain or even injury. Some partners feel rejected and angry, doubting their own attractiveness; in order to avoid conflict or embarrassment, men sometimes resort to faking orgasm (Perelman, 2014).

Apfelbaum believes there is a professional bias of pessimism with regard to the prognosis for DE as a consequence of diagnostic and therapeutic misunderstanding; he summarises that bias as: 'strong erections equal strong arousal', in other words: 'performance implies arousal' (p.209). According to Apfelbaum, paradoxically the fact that erections are sustained far beyond the ordinary range seems to be a consequence of a lack of effective arousal rather than of a high level of arousal. Moreover, he believes that a desire disorder underlies 'partner anorgasmia', which is masked by the long-lasting and firm erections. His argument for this bias, which results in a misunderstanding of the clinical features and treatment prognosis of DE, is that because this disorder is so rare, there has been no opportunity for extensive research as has been with other sexual dysfunctions.

Some authors relate this condition to 'high genital reactivity' whereby the penis reacts with an extreme erectile response that can be compared to priapism (Komisaruk, Beyer-Flores & Whipple, 2006). A precise assessment is necessary so as to distinguish between possible priapism and partner anorgasmia/delayed ejaculation, in order to apply the appropriate treatment. Priapism is often considered a medical emergency and defined as prolonged, unwanted and often painful erections that can last for more than four hours. It is unrelated to sexual stimulation and continues beyond ejaculation, requiring medical intervention (Lue et al., 2004).

Prevalence

While estimates on the prevalence of DE vary, many studies from sexology over the past 50 years consistently indicate that DE is the most rarely presented sexual dysfunction. The prevalence of DE appears higher in older men, which is understandable as ejaculatory function decreases with age (Perelman, 2004). Recent studies suggest that only 3% of men complaining of a sexual dysfunction present DE as a problem (Christensen et al., 2011). DSM-5 states the prevalence of this disorder is unclear due to the lack of a precise definition, but the current state of research findings suggest that less than 1% of men present a complaint of difficulties with reaching ejaculation during intercourse (APA, 2013).

Factors contributing to DE

Because this disorder is so rarely presented, the contributing factors are not as well researched as with other sexual dysfunctions. A recent study suggested a list of typical complaints reported by men with DE problems: high levels of relationship distress, sexual dissatisfaction, low subjective arousal and performance anxiety (Abdel-Hamid & Saleh, 2011). According to therapy and supervision practice and the existing (limited) research, contributory factors are presented on the MOST map in Figure 4.3.

Emotional factors

Shull and Sprenkle's statement from as far back as 1980 is still relevant today: 'If the literature is searched long enough, almost any and every psychological problem can be associated with [male orgasmic disorder]' (p.230). Still, no systematic research has been conducted on emotional or relational factors contributing to this disorder (Wincze & Weisberg, 2015). Some studies have identified fear of castration, fear of being hurt, fear of commitment and performance anxiety as possible factors contributing to the development of DE (Waldinger & Schweitzer, 2005; Perelman & Rowland, 2006). Pregnancy concerns and the related fear of fatherhood have been identified in various sexology studies (Althof, 2012). An earlier study found 'almost distaste of

CONTRIBUTING FACTORS

CULTURAL

- 'FANTASY MODEL OF SEX'; MEN BEING 'POWERFUL IN SEX'; emphasis on performance
- RELIGIOUS PROHIBITIONS AGAINST SEXUAL ACTIVITY
- BEREAVEMENT
- WORK PRESSURES
- PUNITIVE SHAMING IF CAUGHT MASTURBATING OR BEING SEXUALLY CURIOUS
- ANGER WITH THE FATHER; ABSENCE OF FATHER FIGURE OR OVERBEARING AND FEARFUL FATHER'S PRESENCE
- EXPERIENCE OF NOT BEING APPRECIATED BY THE MOTHER
- SIBLING RIVALRY
- HISTORY OF SEXUAL AND EMOTIONAL ABUSE OR TRAUMA

EMOTIONAL

- STRESS, ANXIETY, ANGER
- GUILT AND SHAME RELATED TO SEX
- UNRESOLVED FEELINGS ABOUT PARENTS / SIBLINGS
- FEELING CONFLICTED AND ANXIOUS ABOUT SHOWING AGGRESSION
- NEGATIVE SELF IMAGE
- INSECURITY IN OWN SEXUAL ROLE
- FEELING OF INFERIORITY
- FEAR OF: FATHERHOOD; COMMITMENT; EXPOSURE
- PERFORMANCE ANXIETY
- FEAR OF BEING SELFISH; COMPULSIVE NEED FOR GIVING

COGNITIVE

- PUNISHING / MORALISTIC BELIEFS ABOUT SEX
- STRONG BELIEFS ABOUT MASCULINITY; NEED TO PROVE OWN MASCULINE ROLE
- MYTHS ABOUT SEX BEING A SHAMEFUL ACTIVITY
- NARROW BELIEFS ABOUT SEX: E.G. GENITALLY FOCUSED; ORGASM FOCUSED
- MYTHS THAT 'REAL MEN ALWAYS EJACULATE EASILY' AND 'REAL MEN SHOULD BE EMOTIONALLY DETACHED IN SEX'

RELATIONAL

- POOR COMMUNICATION ABOUT EMOTIONAL & SEXUAL ISSUES
- DISCREPANCY OF SEXUAL DESIRE & PREFERENCES
- UNDERLYING NEGATIVE EMOTIONS ABOUT THE CURRENT OR PAST RELATIONSHIP
- FEELING POWERLESS IN RELATION TO THE PARTNER
- PARTNER'S SEXUAL DYSFUNCTION E.G. DESIRE AND AROUSAL PROBLEMS
- RELATIONSHIP AMBIVALENCE
- UNCONSCIOUS HOSTILITY
- COMPULSION TO SATISFY THE PARTNER
- COMPULSIVE GIVING, INABILITY TO TAKE

BEHAVIOURAL

- 'TRAUMATIC MASTURBATORY SYNDROME'; USING IDIOSYNCRATIC TECHNIQUE
- RIGID MASTURBATION PATTERNS
- DIFFICULTY OF MAINTAINING MASTURBATORY FANTASY IN THE PRESENCE OF A PARTNER
- NOT ENOUGH EROTIC STIMULATION PRIOR TO SEX
- SEXUAL BOREDOM
- COMPULSIVE, GENITALLY FOCUSED SEXUAL STYLE
- AUTOEROTIC FOCUS, AUTOSEXUALITY
- SPECTATORING / SELF DETACHMENT DURING SEX

PHYSICAL

- NEGATIVE BODY IMAGE
- DISSATISFACTION WITH PENIS SIZE (SMALL)
- MEDICATION E.G. SSRIs; TRICYCLIC ANTIDEPRESSANTS;
- ANTIPSYCHOTIC DRUGS
- TESTOSTERONE DEFICIENCY DUE TO AGEING
- TRAUMATIC OR SURGICAL SPINAL INJURIES AFFECTING THE SENSITIVITY OF THE PENILE SKIN
- DIABETES
- PROSTATE CANCER
- HIGH GENITAL REACTIVITY
- LOW PENILE SENSITIVITY

Figure 4.3 Delayed ejaculation: contributing factors

fatherhood' a distinct factor in the development of DE (Lincoln & Thexton, 1983). Anxiety and lack of confidence can distract the man's attention away from erotic cues, interfering with arousal and resulting in insufficient excitement for climax (Perelman, 2004). Feelings of inferiority sometimes related to sibling rivalry; significant psychological distress; and a compulsive need for giving (Apfelbaum, 2000) were also identified as individual psychological factors relevant to this disorder. A history of trauma can create confusion in associating arousal with aggression and shame (Lew, 2004).

Cognitive factors

The man's need to prove his own masculine role and/or his narrow beliefs about sex being genitally and orgasmic focused have been identified as influential factors contributing to DE. Pressure to please the partner can result in the man's experience of sex as 'a continuous demand for performance' (Apfelbaum, 2000, p.217). Misconceptions about male sexuality based on messages received since a young age and supported by media such as that '*real men ejaculate easily and every time they have sex*', and that '*real men should be detached and not intimate*', combined with a lack of sexual education, can have a powerful impact on some men's sexual self-schema and affect their sexual functioning including orgasmic control (Metz & McCarthy, 2007).

Physical factors

A long list of medication that has been proven to contribute to DE include antidepressants, medication for treating high blood pressure and antipsychotic drugs (Segraves, 2010). Acute substance abuse was also found to be a contributing factor to DE (Perelman, 2004).

Various medical conditions including infections of the prostate and the urinary tract, multiple sclerosis, severe diabetes, abdominal surgery and spinal cord injury, for example, have been found to have the potential to alter ejaculatory functioning and orgasm (Preda & Bienenfeld, 2013). Reduction of testosterone due to ageing can significantly affect men's ability to ejaculate (Preda & Bienenfeld, 2013). Negative body image and particularly negative genital perception was found to be a factor in several studies (e.g. Lincoln & Thexton, 1983). Apfelbaum (2000) considers what he calls 'high genital reactivity' one of the major biological factors. He states:

> for reasons yet unknown, some people are highly reactive genitally even when erotic feeling is minimal or absent. Just as there are men who have automatic erections, there are women who lubricate easily, even copiously, when they have hardly begun to experience passion. There are

also those who are bored by orgasms, though they may still have them, and even those who are sexually aversive but still respond with erection or lubrication and orgasm (p.216).

Behavioural factors

Perelman identified three factors highly associated with DE: high frequency of masturbation (more than three times a week); idiosyncratic style of masturbation; and a disparity between the reality of sex with a partner compared with preferred sexual fantasies during masturbation. Idiosyncratic masturbatory style was described above in Apfelbaum's research, a technique he referred to as autoerotic focus that has developed into a rigid habitual pattern, and not easily replicated by a partner's stimulation (Apfelbaum, 2000). Perelman (2005) stated these men fail to communicate their stimulation preferences to their partners because of shame and embarrassment. Shull and Sprenkle (1980) suggested that DE is caused by inadequate stimulation whereby partners are engaged in a sexual activity that does not have a sufficient erotic impact on the man experiencing DE. Wincze and Weisberg (2015) proposed assessment of men's sexual preferences and gave an example of a man who was only able to ejaculate if his female partner was bound in rope (Wincze & Weisberg, 2015, p.38).

Compulsive, genitally focused sexual style, combined with highly arousing fixed masturbatory fantasies and difficulty of maintaining them in the presence of a partner, were amongst the most relevant contributory factors according to Apfelbaum's research (2000).

Relational factors

Apfelbaum criticised early psychodynamic explanations of DE as unconscious unexpressed anger and deep-seated hostility towards the partner resulting in withholding sexual giving (Kaplan, 1974; Gagliardi, 1976). DE is seen as a manifestation of the man's ambivalence about his commitment to the relationship, or his DE may be a way of retaining control in a conflictual relationship (Wincze & Weisberg, 2015). Apfelbaum's findings suggested a directly opposite theory, that a man experiencing DE suffers from a 'compulsion to satisfy the partner' (Apfelbaum, 2000); his concern about being selfish turns into a compulsion to give and to please, causing him to detach from his body sensations through over-focusing on the partner.

Partners of men with DE often feel responsible for the dysfunction and carry a sense of failure for not being attractive enough or not being successful in enabling ejaculation. Both partners' feelings of sexual failure can lead to avoidance of sex, which potentially has an adverse effect on the relationship. Men sometimes fake orgasm to please the partner and prevent deterioration of interpersonal patterns; however, this practice creates further complications by reinforcing the performance aspects of sex, making sex mechanic, devoid of connection, eroticism, mutuality and playfulness (Robbins-Cherry et al., 2011).

Cultural factors

Masters and Johnson (1970) were the first to suggest the link between DE and religious orthodoxy in that certain beliefs can limit sexual knowledge. Guilt and anxiety about 'spilling seed' may result in DE with religiously orthodox/fundamentalist men. Wincze and Weisberg (2015) described cases of DE where men were raised in a sexually condemning religious environment and experienced strong shame and guilt attached to the subject of sex. Experiences of 'punitive shaming if caught masturbating or being sexually curious' as a young person may be a significant contributing factor in developing issues with DE in partnered sex (Foley & Gambescia, 2015, p.113). Some men suffering from DE describe being anxious about showing 'aggression' or 'selfishness' in a sexual encounter; their histories usually reveal either experiences of extreme parents' aggression or strict prohibitions against showing aggression in any form (Hartman & Waldinger, 2007).

Erectile disorder (ED)

Definitions

Problems with erectile functioning were first introduced in DSM in 1954, under the term 'impotence', encompassing difficulties with desire, arousal and orgasm (APA, 1954). The term 'impotence' was replaced by the less pejorative 'inhibited sexual arousal' in DSM-III (APA, 1980). DSM-IV (1994) further revised the terminology introducing the term 'male erectile disorder', defined as 'persistent or recurrent inability to attain or maintain an adequate erection until completion of a sexual activity' (APA, 1994, p.302). In order to meet the criteria for a diagnosis of a sexual disorder, it needs to be accompanied by a significant personal or interpersonal distress, and the difficulty cannot be accounted for by another disorder, i.e. a medical condition or a medical treatment. Lifelong as opposed to acquired erectile disorder (ED in further text), signifying its persistence since the very beginning of first sexual activity, is seen as extremely rare; and generalised, as opposed to situational, signifying its occurrence in all situations, sometimes even including masturbation, is seen as less typical than a situational type, whereby erectile functioning varies according to context.

Diagnosis and assessment

In the 1950s - 1990s most professionals believed that ED was caused by childhood psychological problems. Masters and Johnson (1970) considered that it was primarily a psychological problem, largely due to excessive performance anxiety. Since the availability of Viagra in 1998, medical explanations of ED prevail, both in the medical professions and the minds of the general public. The discovery of Viagra helpfully challenged the secrecy and shame surrounding the dysfunction; however, it misplaced the emphasis on purely physical aspects of the problem (Metz & McCarthy, 2004). The debate on the origins of the problem continues to the present day, with an increasing number of advocates for a combined organic and psychogenic approach, including sexologists and sex therapists who propose integrated assessment and treatment (such as Leiblum & Rosen, 2000; Weeks & Gambescia, 2000; Metz & McCarthy, 2004; Wincze & Weisberg, 2015).

DSM-5 (APA, 2013, p.426) diagnoses this disorder on the basis of at least one of the following symptoms occurring in almost all or all situations of sexual activity and persisting for a minimum of six months:

1. marked difficulty in obtaining an erection
2. marked difficulty in sustaining an erection
3. marked decrease in erectile rigidity.

The third criterion was added to the DSM document for the first time in DSM-5, indicating that erection is not an all-or-nothing phenomenon and that erections can be gained or lost to various degrees.

The problem of ED can manifest itself in various ways: some men report they are completely unable to attain erections (this is the least frequently encountered situation), or that they are able to obtain partial erections, insufficient for penetration (this is the most typical situation); or they are able to achieve erection while subsequently losing it just before or just after penetration; other men can achieve erections only during masturbation but not with a sexual partner (these cases usually signify a strong performance anxiety). Some men are unaware of their bodies and unsure about the pattern of their erectile functioning (Wincze & Carey, 2001). It also happens that some men report a complaint of ED shortly after just one occasion of erectile difficulty (Wincze & Weisberg, 2015).

It is vital that the initial assessment establishes some relevant facts, such as:

- *the onset of the problem*, so as to differentiate between lifelong and acquired dysfunction; this distinction provides pointers between possible organic causes in lifelong or primary types of dysfunctions, and the possible triggers or precipitating factors in case of the acquired or secondary types
- *the context in which it occurs*; distinguishing between generalised and situational, pointing at the possible organic causes if it happens in all situations of sexual activity, with different partners, in different contexts; it is particularly relevant diagnostically if spontaneous morning erections are not occurring, pointing to likely organic causes or severe depression.

Clinical protocols for diagnosis and treatment of ED within medical establishments are rigorous as this dysfunction can be a symptom of a serious health problem, which may or may not have been previously identified or treated. Therefore, medical assessment is a priority in that a psychotherapist has to seek clarity about the exact manifestations of the symptoms as described by clients in as specific terms as possible and refer clients for medical examination as appropriate. Even if the psychotherapeutic assessment indicates a clear psychological problem such as that erectile difficulties only occur with certain partners and never during masturbation and the morning erections are regular and firm, it is still advised to refer clients for a medical investigation as organic factors can underlie the condition and contribute to it to a lesser or a greater degree. When referring clients to a GP or a specialist service, it is important to stress that a thorough physical examination is required (Wylie, Hallam-Jones & Perrett, 1999).

Prevalence

Most recent reviews suggest that ED is the most widely researched sexual dysfunction that has been the focus of intensive scientific and public interest for many decades (Lue et al., 2004; Rosen, Miner & Wincze, 2014). Research studies, however, greatly vary in prevalence estimates of this disorder. This variation is explained by different methods and different definitions used in various studies, and by the fact that research participants varied in age, wellbeing and other risk factors relevant to this disorder. Notwithstanding these discrepancies, research results suggest that this is a widespread disorder affecting a vast population of men around the world (Wincze & Weisberg, 2015). Kaplan, for example, back in 1974, estimated that 50% of all men experience a degree of erectile difficulty at various points in life (Kaplan, 1974). The Massachusetts Male Aging Study (Feldman et al., 1994) found that

10% of men under 35 experience ED; 39% of men aged 40–60; 50% of men aged 60 and 67% of men of 70 years and above. Weeks & Gambescia (2000) estimated that, in the US alone, 30 million men were affected by this disorder. Research suggests comorbidity of ED with other sexual dysfunctions: around 30% of men with ED also report symptoms of premature ejaculation (Rosen et al., 2004).

DSM-5 states that the prevalence of lifelong versus acquired ED is unknown. Increased risk of ED with ageing is acknowledged with an estimate that 2% of men younger than 40–50 years complain of occasional erectile difficulty, whereas 40–50% of men older than 60–70 years may have significant erectile problems. A number of studies have suggested that ED varies across cultures; however, research is yet to confirm any links between cultural specificities and ED (APA, 2013).

Factors contributing to ED

DSM-5 recognises the need for multifactorial assessment and the importance of partner factors, individual vulnerability factors, cultural/religious and medical factors, acknowledging that each of these may contribute differently to the presenting symptoms. The map in Figure 4.4 summarises a range of factors that typically contribute to the development and/or maintenance of this dysfunction within the MOST model. As is the case with other sexual dysfunctions, the factors stated in the map are connected and often influence each other in a sometimes mutually reinforcing way.

Emotional factors

A range of emotional factors may contribute to difficulties in erectile functioning. For example, anxiety, obsessiveness and anger (Metz & McCarthy, 2004), or anxiety disorders, phobias and post-traumatic stress disorder (PTSD) can have a powerful negative impact on men's sexual arousal. Equally, various types of fear seem to be influential factors such as fear of intimacy and commitment; fear of arousal; fear of failure, fear of pregnancy. Weeks & Gambescia (2000) identified 'fear of exposure' as a contributing factor, usually linked to low self-esteem, a belief that one is incompetent, unworthy or unlovable. Fear of expressing feelings may stem from fear of losing emotional control and being overwhelmed by an uncontrollable emotional flow. Fear of commitment and intimacy is usually unconscious and most frequently stems from the family of origin (Weeks & Gambescia, 2000). Performance anxiety was identified by Masters and Johnson (1970), and confirmed in the early work of Kaplan (1974), as well as in many subsequent studies (e.g. Rosen

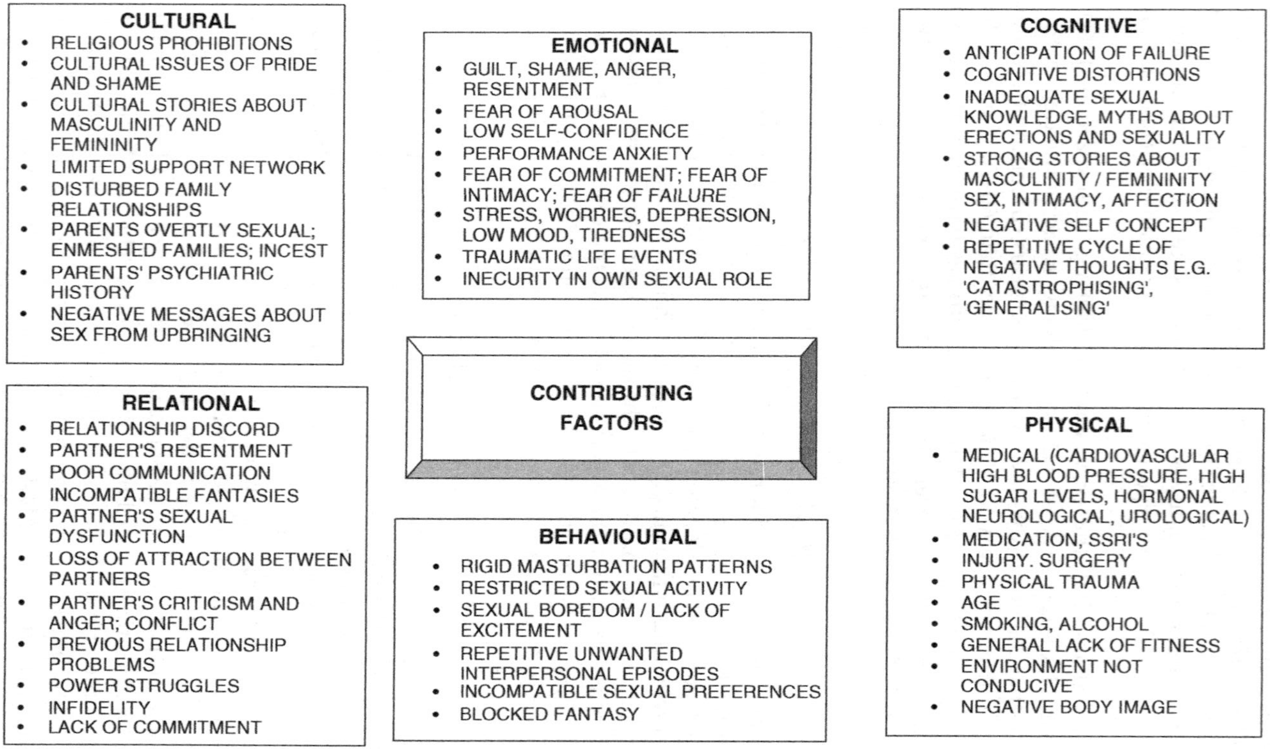

CULTURAL

- RELIGIOUS PROHIBITIONS
- CULTURAL ISSUES OF PRIDE AND SHAME
- CULTURAL STORIES ABOUT MASCULINITY AND FEMININITY
- LIMITED SUPPORT NETWORK
- DISTURBED FAMILY RELATIONSHIPS
- PARENTS OVERTLY SEXUAL; ENMESHED FAMILIES; INCEST
- PARENTS' PSYCHIATRIC HISTORY
- NEGATIVE MESSAGES ABOUT SEX FROM UPBRINGING

EMOTIONAL

- GUILT, SHAME, ANGER, RESENTMENT
- FEAR OF AROUSAL
- LOW SELF-CONFIDENCE
- PERFORMANCE ANXIETY
- FEAR OF COMMITMENT; FEAR OF INTIMACY; FEAR OF FAILURE
- STRESS, WORRIES, DEPRESSION, LOW MOOD, TIREDNESS
- TRAUMATIC LIFE EVENTS
- INECURITY IN OWN SEXUAL ROLE

COGNITIVE

- ANTICIPATION OF FAILURE
- COGNITIVE DISTORTIONS
- INADEQUATE SEXUAL KNOWLEDGE, MYTHS ABOUT ERECTIONS AND SEXUALITY
- STRONG STORIES ABOUT MASCULINITY / FEMININITY SEX, INTIMACY, AFFECTION
- NEGATIVE SELF CONCEPT
- REPETITIVE CYCLE OF NEGATIVE THOUGHTS E.G. 'CATASTROPHISING', 'GENERALISING'

CONTRIBUTING FACTORS

RELATIONAL

- RELATIONSHIP DISCORD
- PARTNER'S RESENTMENT
- POOR COMMUNICATION
- INCOMPATIBLE FANTASIES
- PARTNER'S SEXUAL DYSFUNCTION
- LOSS OF ATTRACTION BETWEEN PARTNERS
- PARTNER'S CRITICISM AND ANGER; CONFLICT
- PREVIOUS RELATIONSHIP PROBLEMS
- POWER STRUGGLES
- INFIDELITY
- LACK OF COMMITMENT

BEHAVIOURAL

- RIGID MASTURBATION PATTERNS
- RESTRICTED SEXUAL ACTIVITY
- SEXUAL BOREDOM / LACK OF EXCITEMENT
- REPETITIVE UNWANTED INTERPERSONAL EPISODES
- INCOMPATIBLE SEXUAL PREFERENCES
- BLOCKED FANTASY

PHYSICAL

- MEDICAL (CARDIOVASCULAR HIGH BLOOD PRESSURE, HIGH SUGAR LEVELS, HORMONAL NEUROLOGICAL, UROLOGICAL)
- MEDICATION, SSRI'S
- INJURY. SURGERY
- PHYSICAL TRAUMA
- AGE
- SMOKING, ALCOHOL
- GENERAL LACK OF FITNESS
- ENVIRONMENT NOT CONDUCIVE
- NEGATIVE BODY IMAGE

Figure 4.4 Erectile disorder: contributing factors

et al., 2014) as the most common factor pertinent to the majority of cases of ED. The pattern of this anxiety starts with worry and anticipation of negative consequences which draws the man's attention away from his partner and the interpersonal sexual context, causing him to obsessively focus on his own performance, thus inhibiting his sexual arousal and pleasure.

Various life stresses, work pressures, financial concerns, often associated with low mood, and sometimes depression, have all been identified as significant factors in erectile functioning. Feelings of inadequacy in one's own sexual role, stemming from low self-esteem, or confusion about one's sexual orientation, can be a factor limiting sexual pleasure and causing ambivalent feelings about sex (Weeks & Gambescia, 2000).

Cognitive factors

'Anticipatory anxiety about ED and other mental distractions about sexual performance are sexual poisons', write Metz & McCarthy (2004, p.12). A repetitive cycle of negative anticipation, anxiety and performance 'failure' sometimes develops into a strong mental pattern. Negative cognitions, or 'cognitive distortions', as named by the CBT approach, attached to this, fuel the cycle of anxious thoughts.

Extensive research has shown that men susceptible to ED are much more likely to endorse myths about male sexuality, e.g. *'a man always wants and is always ready for sex'* (Hawton, 1985, p.61). A helpful list of 'misconceptions about erections' significantly contributing to the development and the maintenance of erectile dysfunction is provided by Weeks and Gambescia (2000), for example: *'An erection is necessary in order to have sex'*; *'An erection is an indication of sexual desire'*; *'The erection should occur almost instantly, regardless of circumstances'*; *'An erection is necessary in order to ejaculate'*; *'If the erection is lost during sex, the penis will not regain tumescence'*, and so on (pp.10–11).

The primary importance given to erections for a satisfactory sexual experience is sometimes a strong contributing factor restraining people's sexual lives. Focus on gaining and sustaining an erection can take away from the possibility of immersion in a sexual experience allowing for a more free-flow sexual activity involving play and imagination. Metz and McCarthy (2004) listed some typical myths about sex, intimacy, masculinity and femininity, which can have tremendous power to interfere with sexual arousal, for example: *'A real man can have an erection with any woman, any time, in any situation'*; *'Successful intercourse is totally the man's responsibility, and intercourse failure is totally his fault'*; *'ED is usually the woman's fault'*; *'A normal consequence of aging is a complete loss of capacity to have an erection'* (pp.4–5).

These authors suggest that male sexual myths are based on a competitive, performance-oriented and fear-based approach to male sexuality.

Negative self-concept has been identified in many research studies with reference to ED, such as men viewing themselves as incompetent and powerless (Nobre & Pinto-Gouveia, 2009), or attaching their self-esteem to sexual performance (Weeks & Gambescia, 2000). Weisberg et al. (2001) explored this phenomenon and identified self-critical attributional style as a typical thought pattern in this context.

Physical factors

Medical conditions that can inhibit erections are: endocrinological, cardiovascular, neurological and pharmacological (Wincze & Weisberg, 2015). Weeks and Gambescia (2000) state that inadequate levels of certain hormones, such as thyroxin, prolactin, steroids, adrenalin and testosterone can influence erectile capability, although the role of hormones in erectile functioning is not precisely determined. Davidson and Rosen (1992) reviewed studies suggesting that testosterone promotes sexual arousal in men; equally, other studies found that low testosterone levels may result in erectile problems (Rakic et al., 1997). Although research indicates that hormonal factors can affect erectile functioning, it appears they are not likely to be a single or a main factor contributing to ED (Weeks & Gambescia, 2000). Cardiovascular problems such as arteriosclerosis, high blood pressure, high cholesterol and diabetes, seem to represent a significant risk to erectile functioning. Central nervous system problems, for example Parkinson's disease; brain tumours; strokes; dementia; multiple sclerosis; spinal cord surgery and injuries, are some of the many conditions that may interfere with erectile capability (Weeks & Gambescia, 2000).

Clients presenting erectile difficulties sometimes report that they have seen a medical practitioner in the recent past, and that a general examination did not detect any health problems. Men experiencing ED should nevertheless request a focused examination of the likely areas of problems. Many types of medications indicate ED as a possible side effect, such as various diuretics, blood pressure drugs, statins, antidepressants, anti-anxiety drugs, anti-epileptic drugs, antihistamines, muscle relaxants, cancer medication and chemotherapy drugs (Crenshaw & Goldberg, 1996). Erectile functioning typically degrades as part of normal biological processes. Although it is something that is potentially lifelong, erections beyond the age of 40 typically start becoming less firm and less consistent over time. Research on ageing and its effects on ED has produced unanimous results. It appears that more than half of all men between 40 and 70 years of age experience a degree of ED, and by the age of 70 over 65% of men experience mild to moderate erectile problems. This is due to normal physiological changes as well as higher incidence of diseases over the lifespan. In addition, as men age, they require higher levels of erotic stimulation in order to achieve and sustain erections (Feldman et al., 1994). Depressants, such as alcohol, and particularly chronic alcohol abuse, have been proven consistently to impair erectile functioning. Other lifestyle factors including smoking, poor diet and lack of exercise leading to general lack of fitness can have an inhibitory effect on erectile functioning (Rosen, Miner & Wincze, 2014). The absence of a conducive physical environment, such as privacy and comfortable conditions for sex have often been noted as factors interfering with erectile functioning. Rosen, Miner and Wincze (2014) alert therapists not to assume that people have sex under favourable circumstances and encourage specific enquiry into the conditions under which sex happens, given that this may be a significant and underestimated contributing factor to the development of ED.

Whether or not the physical assessment detects organic reasons for ED, it can result in high levels of anxiety therefore psychotherapy can be helpful. Occurrences of ED can also cause great relational upset and sometimes couple conflict, thus exacerbating the problem and perpetuating the dysfunction.

Behavioural factors

Rigid masturbation patterns established over time can present difficulties when engaging in sexual activities with a partner; sometimes masturbation practice habitually develops into a firmly set ritual repeated in precise detail every time, creating a strong association between arousal and certain movements, touch, fantasies, place and time of day, making it impossible to experience arousal in a different way. For this reason it may be important to enquire as part of assessment how frequently and in what ways masturbation happens. It may be appropriate to allow for the client's privacy while collecting this information in that the therapist can say: 'You don't have to tell me what exactly you do and think about, but it is relevant if masturbation happens always in the same way as this could be playing a part in your sexual functioning with your partner.' Erectile difficulties may be linked to restrained sexual activity as a result of either strong cultural or religious myths about sex being dirty and sinful, or could be a function of incompatibility of sexual preferences between partners. Sometimes men with erectile difficulties express fear of losing, shocking or hurting the partner by communicating their sexual needs. Openness about sexual preferences can indeed lead to the end of the relationship and this fear is not unrealistic; however, encouraging more open communication about sexual needs and supporting the broadening of a sexual repertoire of sexually relating can lead to effective outcomes in psychosexual therapy:

> Men who approach sex with an awkward narrow repertoire of sexual behaviour may be prone to ED. Some men, for example, may view foreplay as unnecessary or even as a weakness during sexual activity. Comprehensive assessment must explore details about sexual behaviours and attitudes in men experiencing ED to identify any possible inhibiting factors (Rosen, Miner & Wincze, 2014, p.73).

Relational factors

Gottman (1994) summarised many studies demonstrating how communicational problems and conflict mismanagement tend to adversely affect sexual satisfaction and contribute to a broad spectrum of sexual difficulties. Typical relational problems contributing to ED are: conflict, poor communication, ineffective problem solving and relational anger and resentment. Conflict, lack of relationship quality time and blame undermine the interpersonal connection and confidence so necessary for sexual interest and arousal (Metz & McCarthy, 2004). Weeks and Gambescia (2000) describe how partners sometimes develop destructive patterns of relating, which over time evolve into power struggles whereby sex becomes a 'weapon' for punishing the partner. These authors outlined two unhelpful responses of partners exhibiting ED; the most common in their view being a 'motherly', conciliatory attitude, intending to comfort, but actually conveying an 'antierotic message' which may be counterproductive. At the other extreme are partners who react very negatively as a result of feeling unwanted and rejected, often suspecting that the man is interested in someone else, or that the lack of erection is a sign of insufficient effort and care invested in their sexual relationship, leading to anger, demands and pressure resulting in further relationship deterioration.

The partner's own sexual dysfunction can sometimes be hidden behind the man's erectile difficulty; such as, their arousal difficulties, anxiety about sexual performance or their sexual gender role. The partner may be unaware of such problems until such erectile difficulties are overcome through treatment when their own possible dysfunction may begin to surface. Rosen, Miner and Wincze (2014) state: 'It is not at all unusual for a man presenting with ED to mention that his partner has never enjoyed sex, has never initiated sex, or has never been comfortable with sex' (p.75). Equally, a partner's mental health difficulties such as obsessive-compulsive disorder, severe depression or substance abuse can strongly negatively affect sexual desire and performance. In cases where discrepancy of sexual desire and incompatibility of sexual preferences are combined with ineffective communication about sexual needs, resultant anger and resentment may adversely impact the man's sexual functioning. Infidelity, affairs and the resulting lack of trust in the partner are further factors causing distress and relationship discord (Weeks & Gambescia, 2000).

Cultural factors

Religious prohibitions, e.g. what constitutes a sin, and what is unforgivable sexual behaviour or sexual fantasy, can create strong feelings of guilt and shame, leading to fear of commitment and fear of intimacy. Certain sexual practices that are considered religiously or culturally inappropriate can put barriers on the range of permissible sexual activity causing sexual boredom, or, if practised against the cultural and religious expectations, can cause fear of being discovered and punished, leading to sexual performance problems. Homosexual and bisexual preferences, when condemned by wider cultural and religious contexts, can create feelings of inadequacy, a kind of internalised homophobia whereby a person choosing to be open about such sexual preferences still feels guilty, as though committing a sin. Research studies have shown that religious orthodoxy is one of the most compelling guilt-inducing factors impacting sexual functioning. The idea that sex and pleasure are bad and should be punished are part of the Puritan heritage (Weeks & Gambescia, 2000). Some families carry sex-related shameful secrets, such as abortion, incest, infidelities and children born 'out of wedlock'. Men brought up in such families can internalise the family's guilt and develop an anxious response to sexual matters. On the one hand, if sexual messages are suppressed and sex becomes a taboo topic in the family, this can create anxiety and guilt related to sex; on the other hand, a less frequently encountered but equally damaging pattern comes from 'enmeshed families' (Minuchin, 1974) whereby there is a lack of intergenerational boundaries and children are drawn into a pattern of extreme openness about sex to the point of total denial of privacy and the imposition of being exposed to explicit sexual conversations and the sexual behaviour of parents or carers. Weeks and Gambescia (2000) state that men coming from enmeshed families may develop extreme sexual insecurity and shyness.

Men and women brought up to believe in sexual myths related to gender such as that *'a man should lead and the woman should follow'*, or that *'strong erections are a sign of masculinity'* or that *'the lack of erections is shameful'*, are equally oppressed by this sexual mythology. The pressure on men to 'perform' and demonstrate regular, firm and long-lasting erections is exerted by mythology across many different cultures and supported by the media including the tabloid press, popular films and pornography. Clients often speak about feeling different, i.e. less successful sexually from 'others'; comparing themselves with the exaggerated 'sexual supermen' characters portrayed in the media, displaying 'manly' characteristics of: firmness, decisiveness, certainty, often arrogance, superior power and perfect bodies. Such cultural mythology is well explained in the chapter 'The making of anxious performers' (Zilbergeld, 1999) and described in Hare-Mustin's (1994) list of gendered discourses about sex, including the discourse about the '*unstoppable force of the male sexual drive*' which has exerted disempowering effects on generations of men and women in the sphere of sexuality.

Female orgasmic disorder (FOD)

Classifications of orgasmic disorders

Sexology literature has offered various definitions of female orgasm; for example, the following one seems helpful in encompassing the physical, mental and emotional spheres:

> [A] variable, transient, peak sensation of intense pleasure, creating an altered state of consciousness, usually with an initiation accompanied by involuntary rhythmic contractions of the pelvic ... musculature, often with concomitant uterine and anal contractions, ... generally with an induction of well-being and contentment' (Meston et al., 2004, p.173).

Female orgasmic disorder (FOD in further text) was first included in the third edition of DSM (DSM-III, 1980) as 'inhibited female orgasm'. It was renamed as 'female orgasmic disorder' in DSM-IV (1994), when the criterion that the disorder was causing a marked distress was added. FOD was defined in DSM-IV as a 'persistent or recurrent delay in or absence of orgasm following a normal sexual excitement phase' (p.247). The phrase 'following a normal sexual excitement phase' has been omitted from DSM-5 (APA, 2013), given that clinical experience suggested difficulty in establishing whether such a phase has happened or not (Laan & Rellini, 2011). In addition, the phrase suggests a linear, universal and normative approach to female sexual response, which is now considered as incorrect and pathologising of female sexuality (Graham, 2010). In DSM-IV a diagnosis of FOD was to be determined by the 'clinician's judgment that the woman's orgasmic capacity is less than would be reasonable for her age, sexual experience, or sexual stimulation she receives' (APA, 2000, pp.247–248). This phrase became redundant in DSM-5 as the significance of the women's subjective experience of orgasm gained prominence in sexology (Whipple, 2003).

DSM-5 (APA, 2013, p.429) defines FOD as either 'marked delay in, marked infrequency of, absence of orgasm or markedly reduced intensity of orgasmic sensations.' It has brought further change in that FOD is listed as a separate category whereas DSM-IV-TR had 'female orgasmic disorder' and 'male orgasmic disorders' as subcategories of 'orgasmic disorders'. The arguments supporting this emphasis on gender distinction are based on extensive research and clinical evidence, suggesting that female and male sexuality significantly differ in many aspects and therefore need separate diagnostic criteria. As such, assessment and treatment guidelines and procedures need to be sensitive to gender variations in sexual functioning. Furthermore, DSM-5 introduced the criterion of 'reduced intensity of orgasmic sensations' amongst the symptoms defining this disorder. Research has shown that women report reduced orgasmic intensity particularly in some types of neurological conditions and in relation to certain medications (Basson, 2002). The intensity of orgasmic sensation is relevant in acknowledging that orgasm is not an 'all or nothing' phenomenon (Graham, 2014).

Gender differences in orgasm

Research studies have suggested a number of differences between women and men with respect to both the objective signs and the subjective experience of orgasm (Brotto et al., 2010). For example, women, more typically than men, experience multiple orgasms; women may experience an extended orgasm; men and women have different patterns of pelvic rhythmic contractions and a man's orgasm cannot be interrupted once the 'point of inevitability' has been reached, unlike women's. Women can more easily fake orgasms (Wincze & Weisberg, 2015). DSM-5 (APA, 2013) states that women show wide variability in the type and intensity of stimulation that induces orgasm. While orgasms are most commonly induced by genital stimulation, there is research evidence that women can reach orgasm via other types of stimulation, such as non-genital stimulation or even purely mental processes such as thoughts and images (Komisaruk & Whipple, 2011). Research results consistently show that women reach orgasm more easily through masturbation than during partnered sexual activity (Zietsch et al., 2011). Women and men are found to differ in their orgasmic functioning in relation to age in that men are able to experience orgasm independent of age, while for women there appears to be a learning curve with likelihood of experiencing orgasm increasing with age (Wincze & Weisberg, 2015).

Women tend not to express the same level of emotional distress attached to a lack of orgasmic capability as men. Some findings suggest that only half of the women who report being unable to reach orgasm feel distressed about it (King, Holt & Nazareth, 2007). In a US national survey only 3.4% of women who reported orgasmic difficulties reported associated distress. Women who do not achieve orgasm may still experience sexual desire, arousal and sexual satisfaction. This seems coherent with findings suggesting that women differ from men in relation to the importance they attach to orgasm. In a US national sample of heterosexual women, only 29% rated having an orgasm as important to their 'sexual happiness' (Wincze & Weisberg, 2015).

Diagnosis and assessment

DSM-5 diagnoses this disorder on the basis of at least six months' persistence of marked: delay, infrequency or absence of orgasm, or significantly reduced intensity of orgasmic sensations. For a woman to have a diagnosis of orgasmic disorder, it is considered necessary that she is experiencing significant distress as a result of the symptoms as defined by DSM-5. As such, the subjective experience is given prominence and prevails over symptomatology. Whilst the benefits of psychotherapy are not precluded, treatment would not be based on the diagnosis of a 'disorder' as defined in the diagnostic manual.

In psychotherapy, subjective experience of sexual responses has always played a vital part in assessment and approach to treatment, but this has only more recently been the case in sexology. DSM-5 acknowledges that subjective experience of orgasm varies significantly between women and this is supported by a wealth of sexology research. Some women are unsure whether they have experienced orgasm or not, in which case the clinician can usefully facilitate their understanding of their sexual experiences and responses. In the context of supporting their sexual rights, it is important to use women's own terminology and relate to their own way of describing and experiencing their sexual processes. Whipple (2003) emphasised this in her opening plenary speech at the World Association of Sexology (WAS) conference: 'My new definition of female orgasm is, "an orgasm is what the woman says an orgasm is".' Heiman (2007) proposes that a starting point in assessment should be the woman's subjective definition of orgasm.

The 'lifelong' or 'primary' type of this disorder relates to when the symptoms have persisted since the woman became sexually active, whereas 'acquired' or 'secondary' type relates to when the symptoms have developed after a period of relatively normal sexual functioning. DSM-5 does not specify whether becoming 'sexually active' relates to partnered sex only, or whether it includes masturbation, either solitary or otherwise.

If the difficulty is situational rather than generalised, meaning it only happens under certain circumstances, it is crucial to determine the conditions under which it occurs. An understanding of variations according to context will indicate the conditions that enable and the conditions that potentially block orgasmic capability, providing useful guidance for treatment. When assessing the factors that may have contributed to the development and the persistence of acquired orgasmic difficulty, the clinician must consider whether it is an understandable, and even an adaptive response to adverse circumstances in her life and in her relationship. Bancroft et al. (2009) discuss 'an adaptive inhibition of sexual response', calling for caution before a diagnosis of a sexual dysfunction is made, and the need for a contextual understanding of such a response.

Prevalence

Research on the prevalence of female orgasmic difficulties is inconclusive; DSM-5 states that research produced varied results, from 10%–42% of women suffering from FOD (APA, 2013). Researchers acknowledge the lack of conclusive prevalence data, given extremely varied findings, both in terms of subjective experience and the physical manifestations of female orgasm (King et al., 2011). The lack of a consistent statistical estimate of the occurrence of the disorder may be due to the difficulty in identifying positive signs of orgasmic presence; unlike with the male orgasm, which is largely marked by ejaculation, women's orgasm is less obvious (Meston et al., 2004). Furthermore, the problem of defining the disorder creates additional complications in establishing an estimate of its prevalence. Definitions of female orgasm encompass great variability amongst women as well as within an individual woman's experience at various points in time (Graham, 2010). In addition, descriptions of 'adequate sexual stimulus' indicated great variety amongst women (Brotto et al., 2010).

Clinic-based studies have shown that orgasmic difficulties are the second most common presenting female sexual problem, after low sexual desire (Robinson et al., 2011). Large-scale cross-cultural reports have shown inconsistency of results in the prevalence of FOD over time. For example, the National Survey of Sexual Attitudes and Lifestyles (NATSAL) in the UK showed 14.4% of women reporting orgasm problems (Mercer et al., 2003). The Global Survey of Sexual Attitudes and Behaviors in the US (Laumann et al., 2005) showed 17.7% of women in Northern Europe and

41.2% of women in South East Asia reporting 'inability to reach orgasm'. Some researchers critiqued the limitations of large-scale surveys' findings in that such types of studies cannot provide sufficient clinical understanding (Graham & Bancroft, 2006).

The Hite report (1976), a nationwide study on sexuality in the USA, found 4% of women as anorgasmic during masturbation and 70% as anorgasmic during coitus. While this report may be seen as outdated given the time period in which it was conducted, it draws attention to the vast difference in women's orgasmic experience depending on type of stimulation. Further research into female sexuality over the subsequent decades established the importance of clitoral stimulation as a necessary condition for the majority of women's sexual arousal and orgasm. Given that the absence of orgasm during intercourse without direct clitoral stimulation is so common, it is considered as pathologising and heterosexist to suggest that clitoral orgasm is less valid than vaginal orgasm (Chalker, 2000; Wincze & Carey, 2001). A myth about the greater maturity of vaginal orgasm and the inferiority of clitoral orgasm, originating from Freud's early work (Freud, 1953), has also been dispelled in DSM-5, which equalises the validity of both (APA, 2013). Epidemiological surveys showed that 6–15% of women report reaching orgasm 'too quickly' (Richters et al., 2003).

Factors contributing to FOD

The MOST map in Figure 4.5 lists a comprehensive span of possible contributing factors across the six dimensions of human experience.

Emotional factors

A range of emotional factors can potentially contribute to women's experience of sexual activity including orgasm. For example, poor mental health has been associated with orgasmic difficulties (Richters et al., 2003). The need to maintain control and fear of 'letting go' have been identified as a factor in some studies (Nobre & Pinto-Gouveia, 2006). A history of child sexual abuse was found a likely factor, influencing the woman's propensity to avoid relationships for fear of closeness and intimacy (Staples, Rellini & Roberts, 2012).

While there is a wide range of research evidence that psychological factors, particularly anxiety, can potentially impact the woman's ability to achieve orgasm, various findings suggest great individual variability amongst women in relation to these factors (Graham, 2014).

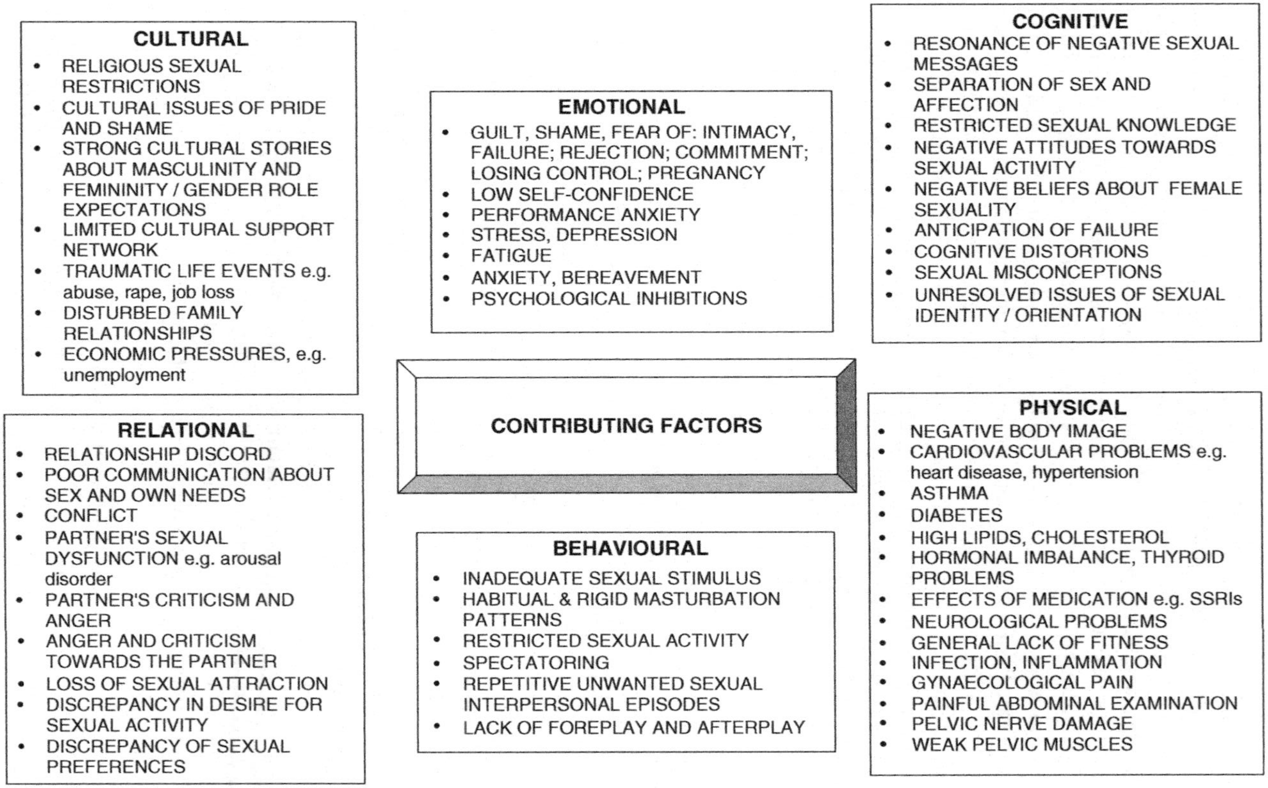

CONTRIBUTING FACTORS

CULTURAL

- RELIGIOUS SEXUAL RESTRICTIONS
- CULTURAL ISSUES OF PRIDE AND SHAME
- STRONG CULTURAL STORIES ABOUT MASCULINITY AND FEMININITY / GENDER ROLE EXPECTATIONS
- LIMITED CULTURAL SUPPORT NETWORK
- TRAUMATIC LIFE EVENTS e.g. abuse, rape, job loss
- DISTURBED FAMILY RELATIONSHIPS
- ECONOMIC PRESSURES, e.g. unemployment

EMOTIONAL

- GUILT, SHAME, FEAR OF: INTIMACY, FAILURE; REJECTION; COMMITMENT; LOSING CONTROL; PREGNANCY
- LOW SELF-CONFIDENCE
- PERFORMANCE ANXIETY
- STRESS, DEPRESSION
- FATIGUE
- ANXIETY, BEREAVEMENT
- PSYCHOLOGICAL INHIBITIONS

COGNITIVE

- RESONANCE OF NEGATIVE SEXUAL MESSAGES
- SEPARATION OF SEX AND AFFECTION
- RESTRICTED SEXUAL KNOWLEDGE
- NEGATIVE ATTITUDES TOWARDS SEXUAL ACTIVITY
- NEGATIVE BELIEFS ABOUT FEMALE SEXUALITY
- ANTICIPATION OF FAILURE
- COGNITIVE DISTORTIONS
- SEXUAL MISCONCEPTIONS
- UNRESOLVED ISSUES OF SEXUAL IDENTITY / ORIENTATION

RELATIONAL

- RELATIONSHIP DISCORD
- POOR COMMUNICATION ABOUT SEX AND OWN NEEDS
- CONFLICT
- PARTNER'S SEXUAL DYSFUNCTION e.g. arousal disorder
- PARTNER'S CRITICISM AND ANGER
- ANGER AND CRITICISM TOWARDS THE PARTNER
- LOSS OF SEXUAL ATTRACTION
- DISCREPANCY IN DESIRE FOR SEXUAL ACTIVITY
- DISCREPANCY OF SEXUAL PREFERENCES

BEHAVIOURAL

- INADEQUATE SEXUAL STIMULUS
- HABITUAL & RIGID MASTURBATION PATTERNS
- RESTRICTED SEXUAL ACTIVITY
- SPECTATORING
- REPETITIVE UNWANTED SEXUAL INTERPERSONAL EPISODES
- LACK OF FOREPLAY AND AFTERPLAY

PHYSICAL

- NEGATIVE BODY IMAGE
- CARDIOVASCULAR PROBLEMS e.g. heart disease, hypertension
- ASTHMA
- DIABETES
- HIGH LIPIDS, CHOLESTEROL
- HORMONAL IMBALANCE, THYROID PROBLEMS
- EFFECTS OF MEDICATION e.g. SSRIs
- NEUROLOGICAL PROBLEMS
- GENERAL LACK OF FITNESS
- INFECTION, INFLAMMATION
- GYNAECOLOGICAL PAIN
- PAINFUL ABDOMINAL EXAMINATION
- PELVIC NERVE DAMAGE
- WEAK PELVIC MUSCLES

Figure 4.5 Female orgasmic disorder: contributing factors

Cognitive factors

Attitudes towards sex, masturbation, female sexuality and pleasure have been evidenced as highly influential factors contributing to women's orgasmic difficulties. Negative attitudes towards sexuality and incorrect sexual knowledge seem extremely relevant. For example, beliefs that women's capacity for sexual pleasure and orgasm decreases over the lifespan can be a contributing factor in women's sexual functioning, including orgasm. Expectations related to female orgasm by the women themselves and by their partners can significantly impact women's sexual functioning and orgasmic capability. Adhering to rigid sexual scripts whereby the woman should reach orgasm before the man, and that it is the man's responsibility to 'bring her to orgasm' has been a limiting factor in the sexual functioning of both women and men (Muehlenhard & Shippee, 2010). Some studies suggest that women's view that sex is for men's pleasure seems a widespread and obstructive belief (Graham, 2014).

Physical factors

A range of physical factors have been found as contributing to FOD. If the causes are purely medical such as: the effect of taking certain medication, e.g. SSRIs (selective serotonin reuptake inhibitors, the most commonly prescribed antidepressants) and oral contraceptives, or medical conditions, then a diagnosis of FOD would not be made. Poor physical health has been associated with orgasmic difficulties in women (Richters et al., 2003). A range of physical neurological and gynaecological illnesses and conditions can adversely affect orgasmic functioning. Multiple sclerosis, thyroid problems, spinal cord injury, and pelvic nerve damage have all been closely linked with FOD (Shifren et al., 2008). Menopause and associated hormonal changes were found to be a direct cause of difficulties related to orgasmic functioning (Avis et al., 2000).

Negative body image is a significant factor in FOD (Nobre & Pinto-Gouveia, 2006). Feeling fit and having a positive attitude towards one's body and being happy about one's weight is a positive factor enhancing female orgasmic functioning; a 'positive genital self-image' was found as being positively associated with the experience of orgasm (Graham, 2014).

Behavioural factors

Some of the factors on the map above could be a single cause of the absence of orgasm such as, for example, inadequate or ineffective sexual stimulation;

in this case, the diagnosis of orgasmic disorder would not be made as the problem lies in the external sphere; however, treatment can still be undertaken such that:

- the woman becomes more aware of what kind of stimulation is more effective, or
- her sexual response is synchronised with the partner's sexual technique so the couple's sexual interaction is adjusted such that their sexual needs are more efficiently fulfilled.

Behavioural factors such as insufficient foreplay or incompatibility of sexual technique between partners were found to be significant contributing factors to female orgasmic functioning in many research studies (Wincze & Weisberg, 2015).

Relational factors

Relationship difficulties were found to be influential factors contributing to orgasmic functioning in women. Poor communication, discrepancy of sexual desire and lack of attraction to the partner were confirmed as significant factors (Graham, 2014). The partner's sexual problems, in particular orgasmic difficulties of the male partners such as premature ejaculation, were found as likely contributing factors (Hobbs et al., 2008).

Equally, sexology studies found high correlation between relationship satisfaction and positive orgasmic experiences in women. Effective communication patterns, such as listening and the partner's understanding of the woman's sexual functioning were positively linked with women's sexual experiences and their experience of orgasm (Purnine & Carey, 1997). More recent research confirmed the importance of relationship satisfaction for women's orgasmic functioning; in a US national sample 83.2% women stated that feeling 'emotionally close to my partner' had direct relevance to their sexual satisfaction and orgasm (Bancroft, Long & McCabe, 2011).

Cultural factors

Larger social influences are highly relevant to women's sexual functioning. Laumann et al. (2005) found that lower socio-economic status and educational levels had higher likelihood of adversely affecting women's sexual experience including orgasm.

There is a growing body of research in sexology, cultural anthropology and social constructionist literature exploring the effects of specific cultural and religious beliefs and practices on female sexual functioning. DSM states survey results indicating the prevalence of FOD in North Europe as 17.7% and 42.2% in South East Asia (APA, 2013, p.432); however, no explanations were given to enable understanding of specific underlying reasons for such cultural variations. Strong media messages about the importance of female orgasm may engender unrealistic expectations and exercise pressure on women to have orgasms (Wincze & Weisberg, 2015).

Sexual misinformation, guilt and shame are key factors in the development and maintenance of women's sexual problems including orgasmic difficulties (Ramage, 2004). The myth of the superiority of the vaginal orgasm (especially if achieved through heterosexual intercourse) has dominated the cultural scene worldwide for over a century. Even though it has been dispelled by a wealth of sexology research and psychological studies, it still pervades and intrudes on many people's sexual lives. 'Most women are taught that the vagina is their primary sexual organ and that it is the greatest source of sexual pleasure', write Heiman & LoPiccolo (1988), whereby the presence of clitoris tends to be ignored. When greater excitement is experienced as a result of clitoral rather than vaginal stimulation, it is often interpreted as 'something strange' and less desirable (p.273). A feminist sex educator, Rebecca Chalker, writes that 'most medical dictionaries and textbooks describe the penis in glorious and meticulous detail, usually with informative illustrations', while the clitoris hardly gets a mention or is described vaguely, within a brief paragraph, and presented as 'a little bump or a squiggly line surrounded by unnamed parts and white space', leaving no clues as to how women can experience sexual pleasure from it (Chalker, 2000, p.16).

In some parts of Africa, South America, South East Asia and the Middle East, the practice of female genital mutilation (FGM) is supported by cultural beliefs that 'terrible consequences will befall a female who does not undergo the procedure'; one belief is that the uncircumcised clitoris will be 'unruly, oversized, unclean, childless, and unmarriageable' (Burstyn, 1997, p.20, cited in Curra, 2016, p.346).

Further cultural mythology is instilled by a lack of universality about where in the genital area women experience most sensitivity and what type of stimulation produces greatest pleasure. Female sexual functioning can be complex, contradictory and confusing as there is no set way in which women experience orgasm and sexual pleasure.

Confusion about female sexuality and FOD is reflected in DSM-5, even though the document implies equal validity of clitoral and vaginal orgasm, stating that 'a woman experiencing orgasm through clitoral stimulation but not during intercourse does not meet the criteria for a clinical diagnosis of FOD' (p.430); still, the diagnosis of a 'secondary' and 'situational' FOD is given if orgasm only occurs with certain types of stimulation, situations and partners (APA, 2013).

Female sexual interest/arousal disorder (FSI/AD)

Definitions and classification

Sexual interest relates to a desire or a drive to engage in sexual activity (Wincze & Weisberg, 2015). The definitions of sexual arousal in women have been changing over time. Disorders of female sexual arousal used to be grouped into the global category of 'frigidity', an imprecise and pejorative term no longer used. Female sexual arousal has been traditionally regarded in sexology as equivalent to and manifesting itself as vaginal lubrication (Bartlik & Goldberg, 2000). DSM-IV defined female sexual arousal disorder (FSAD) as lack of 'an adequate lubrication – swelling response of sexual excitement' (APA, 2000, p.246). A wider span of physical manifestations of arousal has been noted in various research studies over time, acknowledging that this is 'a complex neurovascular phenomenon ... affecting the clitoris, vestibular bulbs, labia minora, and the vagina'; the earliest detectable signs of being 'a significant increase in vaginal wall and clitoral blood flow' (Azadzoi & Siroky, 2006, p.205). Further physical signs of arousal include genital sensations such as tingling, warmth, fullness, swelling and lubrication; and non-genital sensations: '"butterflies" in the stomach; increased heart rate, nipple hardening/deepening in colour, increased skin sensitivity, changes in temperature, shortness of breath, muscle tightness in stomach and legs, flushing in the face and chest' (Graham et al., 2004). Subjective feelings of arousal are not always accompanied by all or any of these signs, including vaginal lubrication.

Komisaruk, Beyer-Flores and Whipple (2006, pp.69–70) distinguish:

- *Subjective sexual arousal disorder,* defined as the absence or reduced feelings of sexual excitement and pleasure from any type of sexual stimulation while vaginal lubrication, genital vasocongestion and other signs of physical arousal are still present
- *Genital sexual arousal disorder,* which manifests itself as reduced or absent physical response to sexual stimuli, such as a lack of vaginal lubrication and minimal vulval swelling. Women reporting such symptoms can still be subjectively aroused by sexual stimulation. This phenomenon has been linked to medical impairment such as autonomic nerve damage or oestrogen deficiency

- *Combined subjective and genital sexual arousal disorder,* which has been identified as both an absence of feelings of sexual arousal and impaired genital response to sexual stimuli
- *Persistent genital arousal disorder,* which manifests as spontaneous, intrusive and unwanted genital arousal, e.g. tingling, throbbing and pulsating, in the absence of a sexual stimuli. It is often temporarily relieved by one or more orgasms but can come back quickly and last for hours or even days.

Research by Meredith Chivers and her colleagues (2010) further stresses gender differences in terms of discrepancy between objective and subjective arousal. In a series of experiments with women, the bodily measurements were registering clear signs of arousal while the woman reported none or minimal; this discrepancy is much less the case with men according to this particular research. This signifies the importance of context to female sexual response drawing attention to the situational factors that impact significantly on the subjective arousal with women.

In the current version of DSM (DSM-5, APA, 2013) FSAD is merged with lack of sexual desire. The previous category of 'hypoactive sexual desire disorder' from DSM-IV disappears from the list of female sexual disorders and merges in DSM-5 with arousal in the category of female sexual interest/ arousal disorder. This is a result of the accumulated clinical experience of sexologists that women typically report both difficulties with sexual desire and sexual arousal as part of the same presenting problem. 'Sexual desire and sexual arousal may even represent different sides of the same sexual coin' (Brotto & Luria 2014, p.21). Sexology clinicians and researchers suggest that treating sexual arousal and desire disorders in women as separate was based on limited understanding of the human sexual response model (Masters & Johnson, 1970) consisting of four stages: arousal, plateau, orgasm and resolution, revised by Kaplan (1974) by adding 'desire' as the initial stage. As a result of further research and academic discussions on female sexuality (e.g. Tiefer, Hall & Tavris, 2002), DSM-5 now combines female desire and arousal disorder into one category.

While acknowledging the importance of recognising specific gender differences in sexual response, the fields of sexology and psychosexual therapy, however, are not fully united on the issue of combining female sexual desire and arousal (Sungur & Gunduz, 2014). Clinicians should keep an open mind regarding both connectedness and separateness while assessing and exploring manifestations of female desire and arousal. Contributing factors in relation to both HSDD (hypoactive sexual desire order, see below) and FSAD may, in many ways, overlap but close attention to the specificities of the woman's experience can provide a fuller differential diagnosis of whether the problem relates to a lack of interest in sex, or to difficulties of achieving and maintaining sexual arousal, or both.

Diagnosis and assessment

According to DSM-5 (p.433), FSI/AD is diagnosed if at least three of the following symptoms have persisted for a minimum of six months: absent or reduced:

- interest in sex
- sexual thoughts and fantasies
- initiation of sexual activity and unresponsiveness to a partner's initiatives
- sexual excitement and pleasure during most sexual encounters
- sexual interest/arousal in response to any erotic cues
- genital or non-genital sensations during the majority of sexual activity.

The advantages of this diagnostic 'polythetic' system, whereby not all of the indicators need to be present in order to diagnose the problem, are that: it addresses the fact that sexual behaviour on its own is an unreliable criterion for measuring sexual desire; it appreciates that sexual response difficulties vary amongst women; it expands the narrow focus on lubrication as the prime indicator of sexual arousal; and it normalises variations in sexual response by requiring a minimal duration of symptoms of six months before a diagnosis can be made (Brotto & Luria, 2014). Further adjustments within DSM-5 criteria include: abandoning reliance on sexual fantasies as an indicator of sexual desire disorder, and accepting that women can experience satisfactory sexual encounters without necessarily engaging in fantasy. Emphasis on the responsive nature of women's sexual desire in DSM-5 is also welcomed (Carvalheira, Brotto & Leal, 2010).

Lifelong FSI/AD type of disorder is defined as being present since the very beginning of the woman's first sexual activity, as opposed to an acquired condition, which began after a period of relatively normal sexual functioning. The generalised type of this disorder means the disorder is persistent notwithstanding the specific circumstances, whereas the situational type is context dependent and varies according to the type of stimuli, situation or partner factors. It is essential that assessment establishes the type of disorder in order to properly determine its causes and the appropriate course of treatment. As with other sexual dysfunctions, a diagnosis would only be made if the symptoms cause significant personal distress to the individual concerned.

Prevalence

DSM-5 states that the prevalence of FSI/AD, as defined in the document itself, is unknown. As DSM first included a diagnosis of FSI/AD in 2013, its prevalence is yet to be researched. Recent research on the prevalence of female sexual desire and sexual arousal difficulties respectively has, however, produced rich and comprehensive data. While there seems to be a lot of variation in the data across different studies, a consistent finding implies that low desire is the most commonly presented female sexual problem in therapy (Brotto & Luria, 2014; Frost & Donovan, 2015). A widely referenced large-scale survey (Laumann, Paik & Rosen, 1999) found that 22% of women in the general US population experience low sexual desire. According to more recent international surveys, prevalence rates of female sexual desire problems are similarly high. For example, in a UK survey 10% of women reported low desire for a period of six months or longer, and 40% reported low sexual desire lasting for up to one month (Mercer et al., 2003). An international study of women in 29 countries suggested a prevalence variance of low desire from 26% to 43% (Laumann et al., 2005). Reviews of various international research studies suggested that reported rates of low sexual desire in women vary from 20% to 40% (e.g. Leiblum et al., 2006; West et al., 2008).

Brotto (2010) draws attention to the fact that many of the research studies have not considered whether women's experience of low desire causes distress. When the distress is taken into account, the results seem quite different. For example, Hayes et al. (2008) found that out of 48% of women who experienced low sexual desire, only 16% felt distressed about it. Similarly, numerous studies showed the same trend of a much reduced prevalence rate of low sexual desire in women when concurrent distress is taken into consideration. For this reason, Frost and Donovan (2015) argue that disorders of female desire may be over-diagnosed. Furthermore, the prevalence rates greatly vary across women of different ages, cultural background, and in relation to interpersonal factors (Brotto, 2010). Studies researching prevalence of low sexual desire across women of different ages indicated decline in desire over the lifespan (McCabe & Goldhammer, 2012). DSM-5 (APA, 2013) suggests that sexual interest may decrease with age and acknowledges great variations in research results according to age, culture, duration of symptoms and presence of distress. The manual points to research findings that lower rates of sexual desire may be more common amongst East Asian women, for example, compared to European and Canadian women, while acknowledging difficulties in measuring the condition. Still, further cultural differences seem worth exploring, given the variance in cultural norms and expectations that impact people's sexual experiences and practices.

Surveys examining women's sexual arousal produced similar results. As with low desire, prevalence rates dramatically drop if the experience of distress is considered. Adequacy of sexual stimulus and interpersonal factors have not always been taken into account when researching women's sexual arousal and desire difficulties, which brings into question the validity of findings about the prevalence of such disorders.

Factors contributing to FSI/AD

Contributing factors are presented in Figure 4.6 within MOST dimensions.

Emotional factors

Emotional factors can be a powerful inhibitor of sexual arousal. As can be seen in Figure 4.6, these factors are numerous and include feelings of guilt, shame, anger, resentment and fear (in particular, fear of intimacy; of arousal; of commitment; of pregnancy), stress and depression. As has been stated, the various dimensions interrelate and overlap, and through therapeutic conversations it is possible to follow their intertwined correlations. For example, feelings of guilt and shame may stem from cultural or familial messages about sex and intimacy that have translated into strong negative beliefs about female sexual expression, and about sex being shameful. This, in turn, can contribute to the woman's negative perception of her own body and its desires thus inhibiting, at the behavioural level, her sexual responsiveness and her sexual engagement, which, over time, can result in restricted patterns of sexual communication.

Guilt about sex linked to sexually conservative views stemming from the family system and wider culture have been associated with female sexual interest and arousal difficulties (Woo, Brotto & Gorzalka, 2012). Correlations between decreased sexual interest, mood instability and low self-esteem have been established in various research studies (Brotto & Luria, 2014). Depression, anxiety and performance anxiety also play a significant part in women's sexual responsiveness (Nobre & Pinto-Gouveia, 2008).

In some cases fear of pregnancy is so intense that it negatively interferes with the sexual experience to the point that it constitutes a single factor in adversely affecting arousal. This can be understood as a natural bodily protective reaction to a perceived threat, rather than a 'disorder'. Equally, traumatic life events, such as losses and bereavement, can have a temporary effect on sexual arousal and the ability to enjoy sex, of a kind that would not be seen as constituting a 'disorder'. Previous sexual abuse, however, may lead to long-term loss of sexual interest and be a major inhibitor of sexual arousal

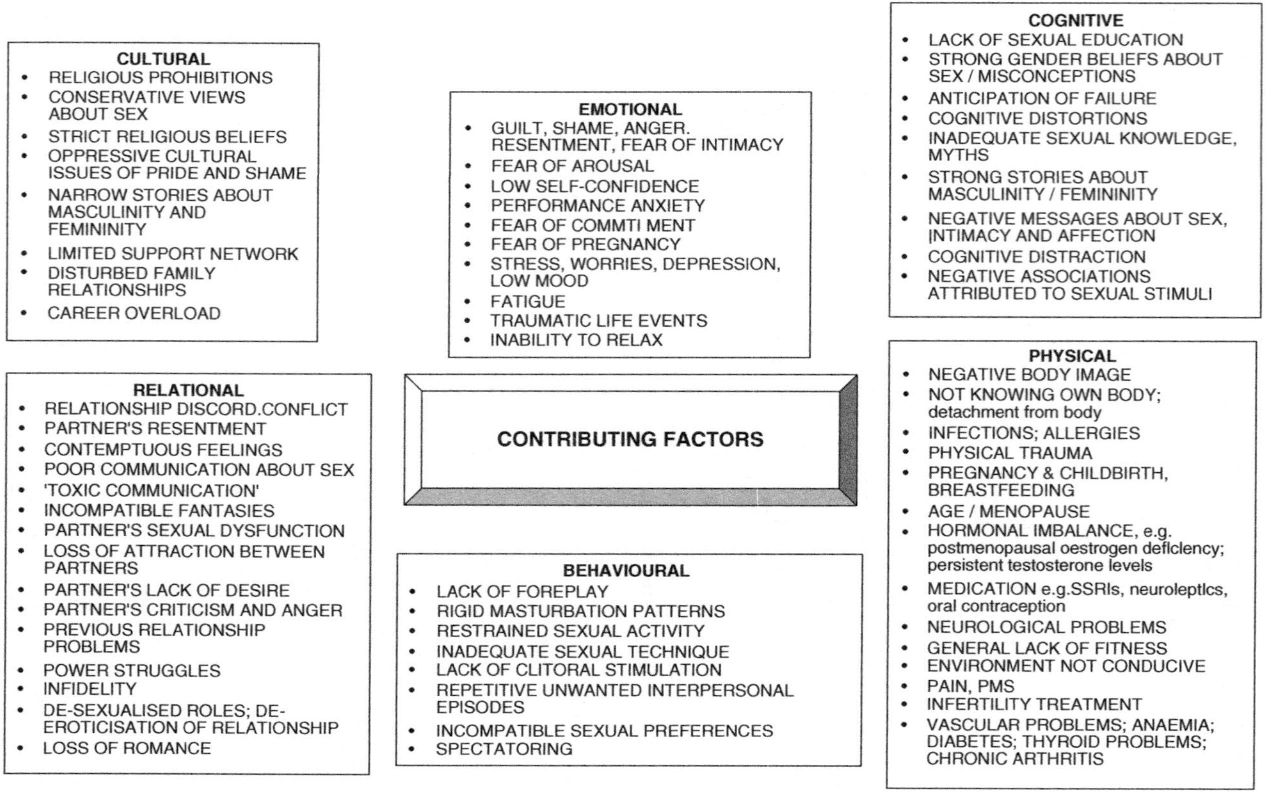

CONTRIBUTING FACTORS

CULTURAL
- RELIGIOUS PROHIBITIONS
- CONSERVATIVE VIEWS ABOUT SEX
- STRICT RELIGIOUS BELIEFS
- OPPRESSIVE CULTURAL ISSUES OF PRIDE AND SHAME
- NARROW STORIES ABOUT MASCULINITY AND FEMININITY
- LIMITED SUPPORT NETWORK
- DISTURBED FAMILY RELATIONSHIPS
- CAREER OVERLOAD

EMOTIONAL
- GUILT, SHAME, ANGER. RESENTMENT, FEAR OF INTIMACY
- FEAR OF AROUSAL
- LOW SELF-CONFIDENCE
- PERFORMANCE ANXIETY
- FEAR OF COMMTI MENT
- FEAR OF PREGNANCY
- STRESS, WORRIES, DEPRESSION, LOW MOOD
- FATIGUE
- TRAUMATIC LIFE EVENTS
- INABILITY TO RELAX

COGNITIVE
- LACK OF SEXUAL EDUCATION
- STRONG GENDER BELIEFS ABOUT SEX / MISCONCEPTIONS
- ANTICIPATION OF FAILURE
- COGNITIVE DISTORTIONS
- INADEQUATE SEXUAL KNOWLEDGE, MYTHS
- STRONG STORIES ABOUT MASCULINITY / FEMININITY
- NEGATIVE MESSAGES ABOUT SEX, INTIMACY AND AFFECTION
- COGNITIVE DISTRACTION
- NEGATIVE ASSOCIATIONS ATTRIBUTED TO SEXUAL STIMULI

RELATIONAL
- RELATIONSHIP DISCORD.CONFLICT
- PARTNER'S RESENTMENT
- CONTEMPTUOUS FEELINGS
- POOR COMMUNICATION ABOUT SEX
- 'TOXIC COMMUNICATION'
- INCOMPATIBLE FANTASIES
- PARTNER'S SEXUAL DYSFUNCTION
- LOSS OF ATTRACTION BETWEEN PARTNERS
- PARTNER'S LACK OF DESIRE
- PARTNER'S CRITICISM AND ANGER
- PREVIOUS RELATIONSHIP PROBLEMS
- POWER STRUGGLES
- INFIDELITY
- DE-SEXUALISED ROLES; DE-EROTICISATION OF RELATIONSHIP
- LOSS OF ROMANCE

BEHAVIOURAL
- LACK OF FOREPLAY
- RIGID MASTURBATION PATTERNS
- RESTRAINED SEXUAL ACTIVITY
- INADEQUATE SEXUAL TECHNIQUE
- LACK OF CLITORAL STIMULATION
- REPETITIVE UNWANTED INTERPERSONAL EPISODES
- INCOMPATIBLE SEXUAL PREFERENCES
- SPECTATORING

PHYSICAL
- NEGATIVE BODY IMAGE
- NOT KNOWING OWN BODY; detachment from body
- INFECTIONS; ALLERGIES
- PHYSICAL TRAUMA
- PREGNANCY & CHILDBIRTH, BREASTFEEDING
- AGE / MENOPAUSE
- HORMONAL IMBALANCE, e.g. postmenopausal oestrogen deficiency; persistent testosterone levels
- MEDICATION e.g.SSRIs, neuroleptics, oral contraception
- NEUROLOGICAL PROBLEMS
- GENERAL LACK OF FITNESS
- ENVIRONMENT NOT CONDUCIVE
- PAIN, PMS
- INFERTILITY TREATMENT
- VASCULAR PROBLEMS; ANAEMIA; DIABETES; THYROID PROBLEMS; CHRONIC ARTHRITIS

Figure 4.6 Female sexual interest/arousal disorder: contributing factors

in women (Oberg, Fugl-Meyer & Fugl-Meyer, 2002). At the same time, it is important to remember that not all women who have been abused, whether as children or as adults, develop sexual difficulties (Greenwald et al., 1990).

Cognitive factors

Anticipation of failure is a typical cognitive mechanism that interferes with arousal. Negative cognitions about the self, partner relationship, sex and intimacy can directly affect sexual desire in both men and women (Geonet, De Sutter & Zech, 2013; Weeks & Gambescia, 2015).

Narrow gender beliefs about sex, masculinity and femininity, and misconceptions about sex as a result of the lack of sexual education and/ or sociocultural beliefs as well as negative messages from upbringing can inhibit sexual desire and limit the ability to enjoy sex. Various beliefs about women and sex have been referred to in sexology and sex therapy literature as typical misconceptions adversely affecting sexual desire and arousal, such as: *'Any woman who initiates sex is immoral'* (Hawton, 1985, p.61); *'In sex, as in dancing, the man must lead and the woman must follow'* (Sanders, 1994); and *'Feminine women don't initiate sex or become wild and unrestrained during sex'* (Heiman & Lopiccolo, 2010, p.40). Therapeutic assessment and explorations focused on learning about sex and its meanings can help to establish the origins of myths and misconceptions as a path to deconstructing these often unconscious beliefs and revealing their constraining effects.

Physical factors

Negative body image can have a powerful negative impact on sexual experience and functioning (Richters et al., 2003). A woman's satisfaction with her appearance, her sense of owning of and feeling good in her body, are important preconditions for satisfactory sexual experience. Negative body image can have a long history and it may be relevant to explore how she came to believe that her body is unattractive, or that her genitals are ugly. This may uncover precipitating factors, such as school bullying, abuse, or other traumatic experiences. Appearance neglect can be a sign of depression or perhaps fear of intimacy, serving as a barrier to protect her from becoming close to another person in an intimate way.

Sexual desire and arousal difficulties could be a symptom of a serious health issue. Vascular and neurological diseases, such as multiple sclerosis and diabetes, may lead to arousal problems. Body pain may bring about decreased sexual interest (Wincze & Weisberg, 2015). There is no consistent evidence of a link between hormonal imbalance and women's sexual functioning. Thyroid dysfunction, PMS (premenstrual syndrome) and menopause have been linked to arousal problems (McCabe & Goldhammer, 2012). On the other hand, some reviews of studies on the potential role of endocrine levels in women's sexual desire and arousal, point at inconclusive results (Santoro et al., 2005).

Prescription drugs, particularly anti-anxiety tablets and antidepressants as well as oral contraceptives, may impair sexual arousal in women (Smith, Jozkowski & Sanders, 2014). Fatigue, stress and generally poor health are frequently linked to women's sexual desire and arousal problems (Laumann et al., 2005; Witting et al., 2008).

A non-conducive environment can be a significant factor impacting sexual feelings, including arousal. It may be a typically more female preoccupation in that many women take time to tune into sexual activity, and so need to be assured of privacy and comfort, and be satisfied with their appearance (Leiblum, 2009).

Behavioural factors

If a woman regularly experiences high levels of arousal when masturbating in contrast to partner sex, it is crucial to explore what exactly happens to enable or stop the development of her arousal and where the differences lie; is it how she feels, what she does, or what she fantasises about? Sometimes spectatoring, not usually a factor during masturbation, gets in the way, signifying that it may be performance anxiety that is interfering with sexual arousal. Victor Frankl, an existential therapist, described the phenomenon of 'hyperreflection' (1985), the term that was labelled as 'spectatoring' by Masters and Johnson (1970). Frankl described how hyperreflection leads to hyperintentionality, i.e. trying to make or even force something to happen; in this context, the process whereby the woman focuses so intensely on getting aroused that for this very reason arousal is impossible as she is disconnected from the pleasurable sensations that create it.

Difficulties with sexual arousal may be a result of incompatibility of sexual needs, fantasies and preferences between the woman and her partner(s). Successful treatment of such situational occurrences of arousal difficulties often depends on the partner's co-operation. Inadequate sexual stimulation, undermining the importance of clitoris in women's sexual response (Chalker, 2000), and lack of foreplay (Wincze & Weisberg, 2015), are frequently stated factors adversely affecting women's sexual arousal.

Relational factors

Research has pointed to the importance of the general quality of the couple relationship with regard to the women's sexual desire. Relationship satisfaction and feelings about the partner are more significant determinants of the woman's desire than hormonal contributions. Negative feelings about the partner were confirmed as the most relevant predictors of sexual distress in women. Relationship conflict and poor communication about sex are significant barriers to women experiencing sexual desire and arousal. Incompatibility of desires and sexual preferences at the relationship level can be a major factor inhibiting a woman's sexual response (Wincze & Weisberg, 2015).

Cultural factors

Family, education, wider cultural and religious messages from early upbringing relating sexual expression of women with moralistic judgements and condemnation can lead to long-term feelings of guilt and shame, blocking sexual desire. Equally, negative messages about female masturbation and views that women should be passive recipients of men's sexual advances can inhibit female sexual interest (Boul, Hallam-Jones & Wylie, 2009). Traditional patriarchal societies have historically regarded sexual desire as a male privilege thus severely restraining women's sexual expression (Weeks & Gambescia, 2002).

Cross cultural studies on female sexual desire are limited; research amongst women of different ethnic and religious backgrounds has revealed the possible impact of different sociocultural influences on female sexual desire (Laumann et al., 2005). Further research into specificities of various cultural norms and their relationship to female sexuality is needed for a fuller understanding of cultural and ethnic influences on female sexual functioning (Brotto & Luria, 2014).

At the beginning of the 21st century a different theoretical framework, the 'new view of women's sexual problems' (Tiefer, 2001; Tiefer, Hall & Tavris, 2002) emerged in response to the medicalisation of sexual issues. This view holds that social and cultural influences are far more relevant to consider in relation to female sexuality than hormonal and biological factors. It posits that in assessing and treating any female sexual difficulties, clinicians must consider factors such as: inadequate sexual education; pressures and often conflicting demands to meet cultural norms regarding sexual attraction and sexual behaviour; and fatigue as a result of numerous and often conflicting responsibilities.

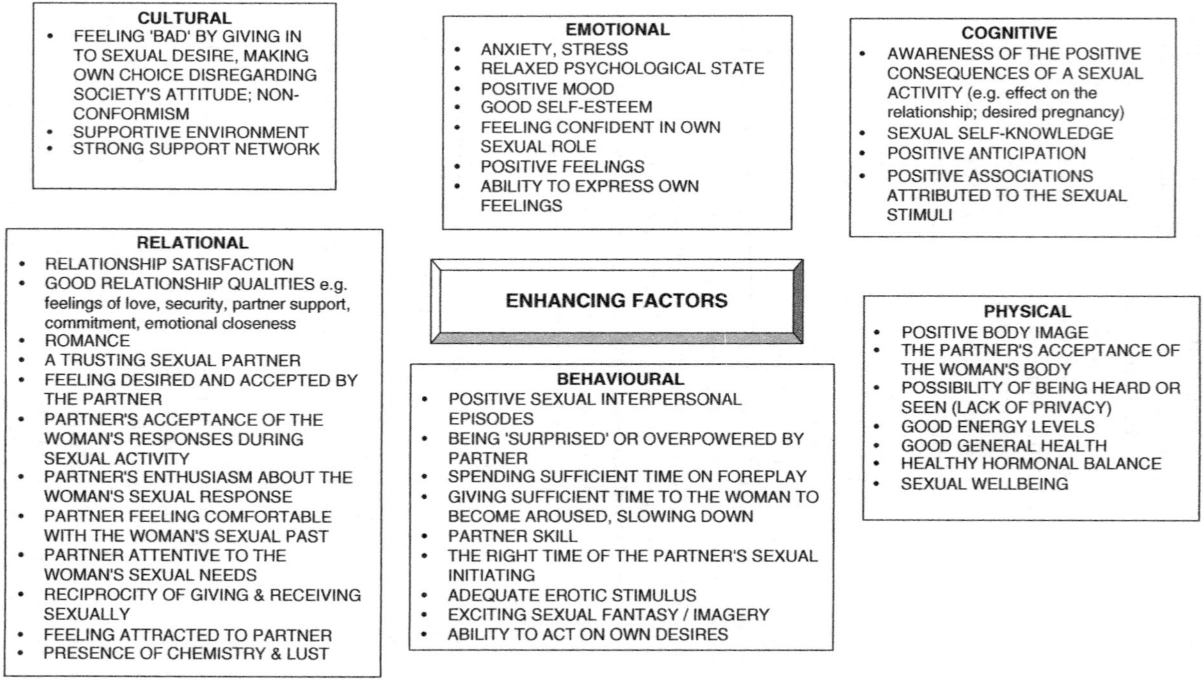

ENHANCING FACTORS

CULTURAL
- FEELING 'BAD' BY GIVING IN TO SEXUAL DESIRE, MAKING OWN CHOICE DISREGARDING SOCIETY'S ATTITUDE; NON-CONFORMISM
- SUPPORTIVE ENVIRONMENT
- STRONG SUPPORT NETWORK

EMOTIONAL
- ANXIETY, STRESS
- RELAXED PSYCHOLOGICAL STATE
- POSITIVE MOOD
- GOOD SELF-ESTEEM
- FEELING CONFIDENT IN OWN SEXUAL ROLE
- POSITIVE FEELINGS
- ABILITY TO EXPRESS OWN FEELINGS

COGNITIVE
- AWARENESS OF THE POSITIVE CONSEQUENCES OF A SEXUAL ACTIVITY (e.g. effect on the relationship; desired pregnancy)
- SEXUAL SELF-KNOWLEDGE
- POSITIVE ANTICIPATION
- POSITIVE ASSOCIATIONS ATTRIBUTED TO THE SEXUAL STIMULI

RELATIONAL
- RELATIONSHIP SATISFACTION
- GOOD RELATIONSHIP QUALITIES e.g. feelings of love, security, partner support, commitment, emotional closeness
- ROMANCE
- A TRUSTING SEXUAL PARTNER
- FEELING DESIRED AND ACCEPTED BY THE PARTNER
- PARTNER'S ACCEPTANCE OF THE WOMAN'S RESPONSES DURING SEXUAL ACTIVITY
- PARTNER'S ENTHUSIASM ABOUT THE WOMAN'S SEXUAL RESPONSE
- PARTNER FEELING COMFORTABLE WITH THE WOMAN'S SEXUAL PAST
- PARTNER ATTENTIVE TO THE WOMAN'S SEXUAL NEEDS
- RECIPROCITY OF GIVING & RECEIVING SEXUALLY
- FEELING ATTRACTED TO PARTNER
- PRESENCE OF CHEMISTRY & LUST

BEHAVIOURAL
- POSITIVE SEXUAL INTERPERSONAL EPISODES
- BEING 'SURPRISED' OR OVERPOWERED BY PARTNER
- SPENDING SUFFICIENT TIME ON FOREPLAY
- GIVING SUFFICIENT TIME TO THE WOMAN TO BECOME AROUSED, SLOWING DOWN
- PARTNER SKILL
- THE RIGHT TIME OF THE PARTNER'S SEXUAL INITIATING
- ADEQUATE EROTIC STIMULUS
- EXCITING SEXUAL FANTASY / IMAGERY
- ABILITY TO ACT ON OWN DESIRES

PHYSICAL
- POSITIVE BODY IMAGE
- THE PARTNER'S ACCEPTANCE OF THE WOMAN'S BODY
- POSSIBILITY OF BEING HEARD OR SEEN (LACK OF PRIVACY)
- GOOD ENERGY LEVELS
- GOOD GENERAL HEALTH
- HEALTHY HORMONAL BALANCE
- SEXUAL WELLBEING

Figure 4.7 Female sexual interest/arousal: enhancing factors

Factors that enhance female sexual arousal

Findings about factors that enhance or inhibit female sexual arousal from a qualitative research study, based on focus group discussions involving a diverse sample of 80 women, add to the understanding of the complexity and the multifaceted nature of this subject (Graham et al., 2004). These factors were classified into consistent themes which included: factors about one's body; consequences of a sexual activity (e.g. concerns about reputation, for example being seen 'as a whore' or 'a slut'; pregnancy); feeling desired and accepted by the sexual partner as opposed to feeling used, the partner's style of approach, and mood. It is interesting to note the individual variability of responses in that many of the factors were cited as inhibiting arousal for some, while enhancing it for others. In addition, the same factors could be experienced as inhibiting or enhancing by an individual, depending on specific circumstances. For example, stress and anxiety were reported to reduce sexual arousal for some women and to increase it for others. The possibility of being seen or heard while engaged in sexual activity was reported as inhibiting by some women while for others this enhanced excitement. Cultural constraints were also experienced as having variable effects; some women felt inhibited by the anticipation of their reputation being negatively affected as a consequence of sexual activity; others reported enjoying being 'bad' and choosing to make their own sexual decisions, not caring what others may be thinking of them and whether they would approve or not. Results of this research, specifically related to the question of what kinds of factors stimulate and enhance sexual arousal, are presented in Figure 4.7 in the form of a MOST map.

Genito-pelvic pain/penetration disorder (GPPPD)

Definitions and classification

Genito-pelvic pain/penetration disorder (GPPPD in further text) has been classified within the DSM-5 (APA, 2013) for the first time such that it combines what was previously diagnosed as separate disorders:

- *vulvodynia* or *vestibulodynia* (chronic discomfort inside the vulva, the entrance to the vagina and to the urethra), usually described as burning, itching, stinging, irritating, or a raw feeling; sexual intercourse, walking, sitting or exercise may make the pain worse; sometimes it affects clitoris, perineum and inner thighs; causes are often unidentifiable/difficult or impossible to detect (Kraft, 2014)
- *dyspareunia* (painful sex), and

- *vaginismus* (described in DSM-IV-TR, APA, 2000, as an involuntary contraction of the vaginal musculature that interferes with penetration, or makes penetration impossible).

The reasons for this merging of the diagnoses are described in sexology literature as a result of overlapping factors and the need to integrate physical and psychological aspects, emphasising the multidimensional nature of female genital pain (Lahaie et al., 2015). Exclusion of male dyspareunia from the DSM-5 categorisation of sexual disorders is a result of the paucity of research results and its likely primarily medical causes.

Diagnosis and assessment

GPPPD is a diagnosis pertinent to women only and is described in the DSM-5 (APA, 2013, pp.437–438) as involving a minimum of six months of at least one of the four persistent or recurrent symptoms and causing significant distress to the woman experiencing it:

1. *Difficulty with vaginal penetration*
   This difficulty can range from a complete inability to achieve vaginal penetration including intercourse, gynaecological examinations and tampon insertions, to the situational disorder which varies according to the context so that penetration difficulty is significantly more or less severe depending on the situation.
2. *Marked genital or pelvic pain during intercourse or during penetration attempts*
   The exact location of this pain may vary across the genito-pelvic area. Sexology typically distinguishes between superficial pain (such as vulvovaginal, the pain felt on the outside areas) and deep pain (felt on penetration deeply inside the vagina).
3. *Significant fear or anxiety about genito-pelvic pain in anticipation, during, or as a result of vaginal penetration*
   This fear is typically found in women who had experienced pain during vaginal penetration, which is reoccurring in relation to anticipated penetration. The intensity of this fear can be so high that it in some instances could be compared to a phobic reaction.
4. *Tensing or tightening of the pelvic floor muscles prior to or during attempted vaginal penetration.*
   This tensing can take the form of automatic spasm of the pelvic floor as a result of attempted or anticipated vaginal penetration. The experience

of the woman is lack of control over muscle tensing and against her will, often reported as involuntary and causing her significant distress.

All four groups of symptoms above should be explored in detail. The first step in assessment is to enable the woman to describe in as much detail as possible her experience of this pain, and questions to this end may include (Meana, Maykut and Fertel, 2015):

- Where exactly is the pain located, is it more on the outside of the genitals, i.e. vulva; how close is it to the vaginal entrance; is it felt inside the vaginal wall?
- Does it happen during penetration or during foreplay as well?
- Does it happen on every sexual occasion?
- How far into the sexual activity does it begin to be felt?
- What is the sensation; how could it be best described: burning, stinging, cutting, shooting, throbbing...?
- How could the intensity of the pain be rated, perhaps on a scale of 1–10?
- If the intensity of the pain varies, is there a pattern whereby there is an indication of what it may be related to?

Lifelong (primary) dysfunction relates to the presence of the symptoms described above since the first attempt of penetration (by an object such as a tampon, for example, or a finger, or the first intercourse attempt) and the acquired (secondary) dysfunction relates to the cases where the pain has developed after a period of non-painful experiences of penetration.

GPPPD can be further distinguished as:

- *generalised* (affecting the entire vulva) or localised (affecting certain areas), and
- *provoked/unprovoked,* depending whether it is experienced as a result of a trigger or it appears spontaneously without any obvious provocation (Lahaie et al., 2015).

While being aware of the changed diagnostic classification whereby vaginismus does not appear as a separate condition anymore, it may be of use to practitioners to still pay attention to the distinguishing features of vaginismus as reported symptomatology is usually distinctly different. Clinicians report that clients typically describe vaginismus as the difficulty or the impossibility of penetration. Pain does not necessarily feature in their description but the terms such as a 'strong spasm', 'tension', 'tightness', 'brick wall', and 'firm barrier' are used when describing how extremely difficult or impossible penetration is. The woman experiences pain only if the penetration attempts are prolonged and involve a level of pressure that then becomes hurtful. With genito-pelvic condition (or, previously, dyspareunia or vulvodynia), however, pain is the main complaint and the descriptors used are typically burning, itching, stinging and the like, in any part of the genito-pelvic area. For these reasons, one may argue that the diagnosis of vaginismus warrants a separate classification category, and indeed it still exists separately within the ICD-10 (WHO, 2010) diagnostic classification of sexual dysfunctions. In any case, if at any point a diagnosis of vaginismus seems helpful to communicate to a client, this therapeutic judgement seems more ethically relevant than a correct 'diagnosis' according to the dominant psychiatric discourse.

Prevalence

The prevalence of GPPPD is unknown, according to DSM-5, given that it is a new diagnosis. DSM-5 states that approximately 15% of women in North America report recurrent pain during intercourse. The difficulty of obtaining prevalence data is complicated by the fact that women do not seek help for fear of stigma and prejudice (Bond, Mpofu & Millington, 2015). According to a large US survey, 60% of women from the general population experiencing chronic lower genital tract pain sought treatment, and of these 40% remained undiagnosed (Harlow, Wise & Stewart, 2001). The results revealing a high proportion of women who do not seek help for this condition points at the importance of clinicians including standard questions about genital pain in their assessment (Lindau, Gavrilova & Anderson, 2007). A study reviewing research on prevalence of vaginismus in Denmark summarises that reported rates vary between 0.4% and 6.0% (Christensen et al., 2011). Research on the links between female genital pain and age has not produced consistent results. There is some evidence regarding links with cultural factors. In a European study, for example, vaginismus was rated as the second most frequently presented female problem in sexual clinics (Nobre & Pinto-Gouveia, 2008), while significantly higher prevalence was noted in more sexually conservative countries where women have restricted sexual rights with the tradition of arranged marriages without bridal consent (Amidu et al., 2010).

Factors contributing to GPPPD

Typical factors are presented in Figure 4.8 while having in mind, as with any disorder, that GPPPD may be a result of multifactorial influences. It is advisable that assessment, as with other disorders, covers as many areas as possible in order to get clear guidance for treatment. The map of contributing

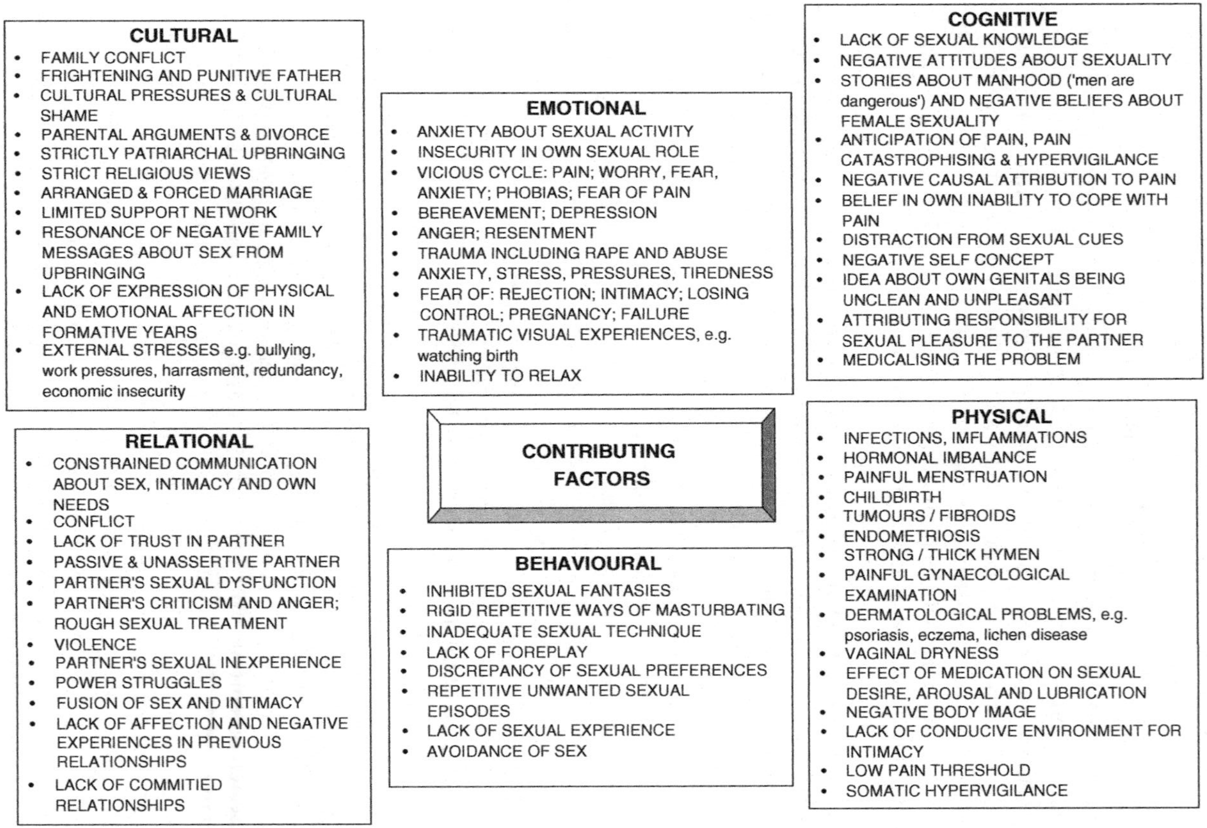

CULTURAL

- FAMILY CONFLICT
- FRIGHTENING AND PUNITIVE FATHER
- CULTURAL PRESSURES & CULTURAL SHAME
- PARENTAL ARGUMENTS & DIVORCE
- STRICTLY PATRIARCHAL UPBRINGING
- STRICT RELIGIOUS VIEWS
- ARRANGED & FORCED MARRIAGE
- LIMITED SUPPORT NETWORK
- RESONANCE OF NEGATIVE FAMILY MESSAGES ABOUT SEX FROM UPBRINGING
- LACK OF EXPRESSION OF PHYSICAL AND EMOTIONAL AFFECTION IN FORMATIVE YEARS
- EXTERNAL STRESSES e.g. bullying, work pressures, harrasment, redundancy, economic insecurity

EMOTIONAL

- ANXIETY ABOUT SEXUAL ACTIVITY
- INSECURITY IN OWN SEXUAL ROLE
- VICIOUS CYCLE: PAIN; WORRY, FEAR, ANXIETY; PHOBIAS; FEAR OF PAIN
- BEREAVEMENT; DEPRESSION
- ANGER; RESENTMENT
- TRAUMA INCLUDING RAPE AND ABUSE
- ANXIETY, STRESS, PRESSURES, TIREDNESS
- FEAR OF: REJECTION; INTIMACY; LOSING CONTROL; PREGNANCY; FAILURE
- TRAUMATIC VISUAL EXPERIENCES, e.g. watching birth
- INABILITY TO RELAX

COGNITIVE

- LACK OF SEXUAL KNOWLEDGE
- NEGATIVE ATTITUDES ABOUT SEXUALITY
- STORIES ABOUT MANHOOD ('men are dangerous') AND NEGATIVE BELIEFS ABOUT FEMALE SEXUALITY
- ANTICIPATION OF PAIN, PAIN CATASTROPHISING & HYPERVIGILANCE
- NEGATIVE CAUSAL ATTRIBUTION TO PAIN
- BELIEF IN OWN INABILITY TO COPE WITH PAIN
- DISTRACTION FROM SEXUAL CUES
- NEGATIVE SELF CONCEPT
- IDEA ABOUT OWN GENITALS BEING UNCLEAN AND UNPLEASANT
- ATTRIBUTING RESPONSIBILITY FOR SEXUAL PLEASURE TO THE PARTNER
- MEDICALISING THE PROBLEM

CONTRIBUTING FACTORS

RELATIONAL

- CONSTRAINED COMMUNICATION ABOUT SEX, INTIMACY AND OWN NEEDS
- CONFLICT
- LACK OF TRUST IN PARTNER
- PASSIVE & UNASSERTIVE PARTNER
- PARTNER'S SEXUAL DYSFUNCTION
- PARTNER'S CRITICISM AND ANGER; ROUGH SEXUAL TREATMENT
- VIOLENCE
- PARTNER'S SEXUAL INEXPERIENCE
- POWER STRUGGLES
- FUSION OF SEX AND INTIMACY
- LACK OF AFFECTION AND NEGATIVE EXPERIENCES IN PREVIOUS RELATIONSHIPS
- LACK OF COMMITIED RELATIONSHIPS

BEHAVIOURAL

- INHIBITED SEXUAL FANTASIES
- RIGID REPETITIVE WAYS OF MASTURBATING
- INADEQUATE SEXUAL TECHNIQUE
- LACK OF FOREPLAY
- DISCREPANCY OF SEXUAL PREFERENCES
- REPETITIVE UNWANTED SEXUAL EPISODES
- LACK OF SEXUAL EXPERIENCE
- AVOIDANCE OF SEX

PHYSICAL

- INFECTIONS, IMFLAMMATIONS
- HORMONAL IMBALANCE
- PAINFUL MENSTRUATION
- CHILDBIRTH
- TUMOURS / FIBROIDS
- ENDOMETRIOSIS
- STRONG / THICK HYMEN
- PAINFUL GYNAECOLOGICAL EXAMINATION
- DERMATOLOGICAL PROBLEMS, e.g. psoriasis, eczema, lichen disease
- VAGINAL DRYNESS
- EFFECT OF MEDICATION ON SEXUAL DESIRE, AROUSAL AND LUBRICATION
- NEGATIVE BODY IMAGE
- LACK OF CONDUCIVE ENVIRONMENT FOR INTIMACY
- LOW PAIN THRESHOLD
- SOMATIC HYPERVIGILANCE

Figure 4.8 Genito-pelvic pain/penetration disorder: contributing factors

factors for GPPPD can be a useful guideline for assessment facilitating explorations of the contextual influences on the presenting problem.

Emotional factors

Anxiety and fear seem to appear notably in the symptomatology of this disorder and are often major factors in its development and persistence. Worry, fear and anxiety can form a vicious circle whereby anxiety contributes to pain, which then increases anxiety and reinforces the problem. Typically, the woman and her partners would describe her emotional responses to all sorts of situations that she finds unpleasant as: becoming tense, stiff, 'going into her shell', withdrawing, and other ways of becoming inwardly oriented and detached from others. Partners report their frustration with failed attempts to engage them, or to reach through to them. One client described: 'When I am upset I go into my clam mode', to which her partner added: 'She is completely curled up'; both physically demonstrated her posture in these instances as forming a protective layer with her arms around her stomach and pelvic area.

Fear of pain, heightened anxiety and depression have been found in many research studies as significant influences in the development and persistence of genito-pelvic pain (ter Kulie & Reissing, 2014). A particular theory conceptualises vaginismus as vaginal phobia, based on catastrophic thinking about vaginal pain, leading to fear avoidance behaviour and avoidance of sex (ter Kuile & Reissing, 2014). Traumatic life experiences, including physical and sexual abuse, have been found in many studies as constituting factors in the development of this disorder (Landry & Bergeron, 2011).

Cognitive factors

A number of cognitive distortions seem to play a part in this disorder, in particular catastrophising and hypervigilance or attentional bias focused on pain (Payne et al., 2005). A model of fear avoidance developed within research on chronic pain and disability was applied to this disorder, whereby an initial pain experience leads to fear of pain and avoidance of threat to the pain reoccurring, which in turn can increase the focus on the risks and an over-focus on any pain sensations, as well as the perceived inability to cope, augmenting the symptomatology (Vlaeyen & Linton, 2000).

It is typical that a woman experiencing vaginismus holds distorted concepts about her genitals, believing that the size of her vagina would not allow comfortable entry of the penis. Some other cases reflect the woman's idea about her genitals being unclean or unpleasant (Hawton, 1985).

The usual questions related to learning about sex reveal layers of influences on beliefs about sex and the possible misconceptions, which might also bring forth feelings of fear, anxiety, insecurity and negative anticipation, interfering with sexual pleasure.

Physical factors

The nature of the disorder may be largely physical; stemming from infections, vaginal inflammatory conditions, endometriosis, post-delivery and episiotomy problems, or prolapsed ovaries (Fugl-Meyer et al., 2013). Hormonal factors are commonly associated with this disorder, such as declining oestrogen levels in post-menopausal women, causing vulvovaginal atrophy and lack of lubrication, and use of oral contraceptives from a young age (Weeks & Gambescia, 2015). Lower general touch and pain thresholds have also been found in women with genito-pelvic pain (van Lankveld et al., 2010). Given its strong physical symptomatology, it is of paramount importance that a thorough medical investigation is undertaken so the clients should be referred to medical professionals.

Behavioural factors

Certain behavioural factors can aggravate the situation, such as: lack of foreplay, inadequate sexual technique and discrepancy of sexual preferences between the partners. Repetitive unwanted sexual episodes involving genital pain can create an automatic response of further tensing of vaginal muscles, increasing the pain and aggravating the condition (Wincze & Weisberg, 2015). This can ultimately lead to avoidance of a sexual activity which can further contribute to increased anxiety and consolidate negative circumstances, as described above in the sections on emotional and cognitive factors. The fear avoidance model, developed within approaches exploring aetiology and management of pain, describes a pattern of pain avoidance that potentially exacerbates the situation: an initial pain response, possibly caused by a physical trigger, may be interpreted as threatening and create fear of pain and avoidant behaviours, which can then lead to hypervigilance and narrowing down of sexual options (Bergeron, Rosen & Pukall, 2014, p.163).

Relational factors

Vaginismus can be a body-protective response from unwanted sexual activity with a partner for whom there is a lack of attraction, or a feeling of distrust or resentment. Some cases of arranged marriages suggested this link where no other physical and health issues could be identified. GPPPD was also presented in cases of relational difficulties where at the behavioural level it seemed there was a discrepancy in the couple's approach to sex. For example, in one case, the woman was described as sensitive, soft, tender, overall more emotional and significantly slower-paced than the man. As a couple they experienced some difficulties in co-ordinating everyday activities; he would rush ahead of her, change the topic of the conversation while she would be still thinking of her response to the previous; decision making felt frustrating for both, given the different speeds at which they would consider various options. She also described her general body sensitivity to touch and the need for a careful and gentle approach in all physical contact. She seemed highly sensitive to a squeeze, tight holding, or anything that appeared, according to him, 'rough at the slightest'. Her genito-pelvic pain was described as burning and stinging at the point of vaginal entrance and although there was no physical obstacle to penetration, it would frequently cause her intense pain. These differences in the couple's physical sensitivity were very much on their minds and sometimes caused upset, but on most occasions as a couple they got on and showed high appreciation of each other. Through therapeutic conversations these links were made between their differences and the presenting problem of her genito-pelvic pain. A pattern was also identified whereby the couple's communication and other life worries and stresses seemed to be directly correlated to the genito-pelvic sensitivity whereby the anxiety would translate itself into a bodily response, affecting the sexual interaction.

On the other hand, a very different relationship constellation may be a factor contributing to the symptomatology of this disorder. For example, a woman described her partner as passive and insecure, a description with which he agreed and accepted as something given and unchangeable. Perhaps it was his insecurity in his masculine and sexual role that triggered her anxieties; or his passivity felt like abandonment, lack of care or even aggressive attack? Was he taking control by his passivity, thus eventually restricting her sexual experience? Was he expecting to be taken care of through appearing helpless and avoiding taking responsibility for the consequences of his action? The couple's anxieties seemed intertwined. Their communication was minimal at the beginning of therapy. Genito-pelvic pain was overly medicalised and their understanding of psychotherapy assessment was only in terms of a route towards the medical treatment. At the behavioural level, their sexual interaction was contrived.

There is a lack of research exploring the correlation between relationship factors and the development of genital pain. Some studies showed no connection between relationship satisfaction and dyspareunia (Desrochers et al., 2008); equally, no correlation between relationship and vaginismus was found (Reissing et al., 2003). However, a number of studies emphasised the importance of partners' reactions to the woman's genital pain and its ongoing presence. For example, a hostile or frustrated response (such as: 'It can't be hurting again'; 'You are just panicking') seems to worsen the symptoms; equally, solicitous attitudes (such as: 'Are you OK?'; 'Any pain?'; 'Are you sure?') can lead to greater catastrophising and increased pain, while facilitative response (such as: 'Let's try a sexual activity that doesn't hurt'), encouraging the woman's coping with pain in an emphatic and supportive way, were associated with the most positive outcomes resulting both in reduction of symptoms and increased relationship satisfaction (Bergeron, Rosen & Pukall, 2014, p.162).

Cultural factors

Therapeutic exploration of familial, religious and sociocultural contexts provides significant background information illuminating the predisposing factors as well as the ongoing influences that maintain a certain belief system and conceptualisation of sex, which contributes to sex-related apprehension and fear of intimacy. Strong emotional reactions such as fear or phobia related to sexual activity could have their origin in early negative messages about sex, intimacy, pregnancy and sexual relationships, coming from family, education, peers, wider culture, religion or social media. A survey of women with lifelong vaginismus found that these women developed a strong expectation that sex will be painful as a result of what they had heard in the media (Reissing, 2012). A clinical study in a psychosexual clinic in Dublin, for example, found that women with vaginismus tend to come from families with a fearful and threatening and/or violent father (O'Sullivan, 1979). Negative sexual beliefs could have been formed within a strictly patriarchal upbringing, disseminating messages about female sexuality being 'shameful', or about men being 'dangerous', creating early insecurity about their own sexual role and connecting sex and intimacy with danger, suffering, harm and pain. Punitive upbringing, negative sexual attitudes and childhood sexual abuse seem likely contributors to female sexual pain disorders; there is, however, no sufficient empirical data confirming this link. Conservative religious attitudes and religious orthodoxy were identified as possible factors (ter Kulie & Reissing, 2014). Given the women's cultural oppression and sociopolitical disempowerment, their sexuality remains central to their socioculturally defined sense of worth. Some studies refer to women's sense of inadequacy and the felt pressure to endure intercourse in spite of significant pain (Meana, Maykut & Fertel, 2015).

Male hypoactive sexual desire disorder (MHSDD)

Classifications of disorders of desire

Low sexual desire was first included in the *Diagnostic and Statistical Manual of Mental Disorders* in the third edition (APA, 1980), under the name 'inhibited sexual desire disorder'. In the revised version of DSM-III (APA, 1987) the name was changed to 'hypoactive sexual desire disorder' and in DSM-IV-TR (APA, 2000) the criterion that this disorder is causing marked distress was added to the diagnosis.

DSM-IV-TR classified desire disorders into two categories: hypoactive sexual desire disorder (HSDD) and sexual aversion disorder (SAD). According to the DSM-IV-TR, the criteria for a diagnosis of HSDD were: persistently deficient or absent sexual fantasy and desire for sexual activity causing marked distress, and for SAD, aversion to any genital contact causing marked distress (APA, 2000). Sexual aversion disorder is now classified in the DSM-5 within other specified sexual dysfunctions and not as a separate disorder any more, due to its rare occurrence (APA, 2013). DSM-5 merges sexual interest and arousal into one female disorder and leaves male hypoactive sexual desire disorder (MHSDD) as a separate category. The arguments for separation of female and male sexual desire disorders are in line with an 'increasing recognition that male and female sexuality could be quite different' (Sungur & Gunduz, 2014, p.365). Previously, DSM definitions 'assumed a linear cycle for both of the genders that consisted of successive stages of desire, arousal, and orgasm. This kind of classification was criticised for not taking into account the complexity of sexual experiences that are unique for each single person and especially for different genders' (p.365).

Gender differences in sexual desire

According to growing research evidence, amongst the main gender differences in relation to sexual desire is that men, more commonly than women, experience 'spontaneous sexual desire', therefore a less typical occurrence of spontaneous desire in women is normalised (Basson, 2002; Laan & Both, 2008). Additionally, if women engage in a sexual activity for reasons other than sexual desire, e.g. a wish to be close to the partner, pregnancy etc., possibly followed by increase of desire, this is named 'responsive sexual desire' (Basson, 2002) and is again normalised in women. A biological explanation for this relates to differences in hormonal processes such that, given that women's hormonal levels fluctuate in relation to menstrual cycle, pregnancy and perimenopause, it directly influences their varied levels of desire (Regan, 2013). Basson's research, on the other hand, explains this difference by psychological and relationship circumstances and past sexual experiences that influence women's sexual desire. Contextual factors, in particular lack of emotional intimacy and lack of adequate sexual stimulus, weaken women's sexual motivation (Basson, 2005).

Research has demonstrated some significant differences in how women and men experience and express sexual desire. Beck, Bozman and Qualtrough (1991) found that a high proportion of men experience sexual desire more frequently than women. Explorations on gender differences in desire found that men thought about sex more, and even had more unwanted and intrusive sexual thoughts. Men had more sexual fantasies and more spontaneous desire. Brotto (2010) refers to the research conducted in 2001 (Baumeister, Catanese & Vohs, 2001) whereby men reported a higher number of partners, more frequent masturbation, less willingness to forgo sex, an earlier emergence of sexual desire as an adolescent, and a greater likelihood of initiating sexual activity than women. The research concluded that men's desire is stronger than women's, both in frequency and in intensity, and that gender differences in sexual desire are likely due to both biological as well as sociocultural influences. Regan and Atkins (2006) found that men reported a significantly higher intensity of sexual desire compared to women, as well as a higher frequency of sexual desire overall. Significant gender differences in incidences of masturbation were found in some research studies, indicating that men masturbate more frequently (Hyde, 2007). One study (Nutter & Condron, 1985) found unexpected results that men with hypoactive desire disorder engaged in masturbation more than men without this disorder, leading the authors to conclude that masturbation may sometimes serve to reduce anxiety. Results of another study confirmed this hypothesis, suggesting that men did not experience masturbation as necessarily 'sexual' but described it as resorting to when 'bored', 'home alone without a partner', and did not integrate masturbation in their views of themselves as sexual beings (Janssen et al., 2008). Some studies suggest that relationship factors significantly influence sexual desire with both women and men (Conaglen & Conaglen, 2009), however other studies show that men's desire is less affected by relationship problems than is the case with women. Men and women also differed in describing their sexual 'peak': across three studies men associated their sexual peak with the times when they experienced the highest levels of sexual desire, whereas women defined their sexual peak according to the level of sexual satisfaction. Brotto (2010) concludes that, while studies suggest that men may experience more frequent and intense sexual desire, men and women may be quite similar in the ways they experience it.

'Moreover, differences in the experience of desire within genders are likely greater than the differences between genders' (p.2022).

The literature on the recent research findings and clinical practice experience suggest that, while appreciating the importance of a recognition of sexual gender differences, it is also important to recognise gender similarities, thus avoiding alpha bias (exaggerating gender differences) as well as beta bias (minimising gender differences) (Hare-Mustin & Marecek, 1988). Therefore assessment of the factors contributing to the development and maintenance of this disorder and treatment options should be attended to in each individual case.

Diagnosis and assessment

A diagnosis of male HSDD according to DSM-5 criteria requires a minimum of six months' persistent or recurrent deficient or absent sexual thoughts or fantasies and desire for sexual activity. In the case of the disturbance existing since the man became sexually active it is considered lifelong, and acquired if it began after a period of relatively normal sexual functioning. If the disturbance is not limited to a type of stimuli, situations or partners, it is considered generalised, and if it varies according to different contexts, it is regarded as situational (APA, 2013). It is important that assessment establishes whether it is a generalised or a situational disorder and, in the case of it being situational, to establish specifically how it varies in relation to different contexts. Therefore, the diagnosis should specify if there are any variations in the levels of sexual desire. Assessment should identify the determining factors to establish clarity about its manifestations, nature and specific characteristics, in order to focus the treatment on the problem areas that have caused and have been contributing to the development and persistence of the disorder. Assessment should carefully tease out the factors, and the MOST map can serve as a helpful guide to that end. It is best if the therapist is able to map out the factors through a conversation with clients in ways that helpfully link the different dimensions. Questions such as, 'When did you first notice the decrease in your sexual desire?' and 'What was happening in your life at that time or in the preceding weeks/months?' may be a good starting point and potentially highlight precipitating factors in cases of acquired hypoactive sexual desire. Precipitating factors could be stressful life events, such as: change of jobs, moving house and exams, which even with a good outcome can be a major contributor to the onset of the problem, causing fatigue, low mood and anxiety, affecting relationship tension and impacting the communication between partners. 'When low desire is acquired more recently, rather than being lifelong, it is important to assess changes in health status, life stressors, and relationship factors' (Wincze & Weisberg, 2015, p.65).

Prevalence

Lack of sexual desire in men is under-researched, particularly compared to the wealth of studies on female inhibited sexual desire (Brotto, 2010). This may be because low sexual desire in men is rarely presented (Wincze & Weisberg, 2015). Erectile functioning concerns sometimes reveal an underlying desire problem with men, whereas women are more likely than men to bring issues of sexual desire as the main concern (Kedde et al., 2011). Equally, a man can present with 'lack of interest in sex', while the main problem may be difficulties with arousal. Sexology and sex therapy treat MHSDD and ED as separate dysfunctions, therefore a careful assessment distinguishing 'arousal disorder' from a 'desire disorder' is relevant in order to establish a clear diagnosis and undertake appropriate treatment (Wincze & Carey, 2001).

The prevalence of low sexual desire in men has been a subject of a number of large-scale international quantitative studies reviewed by Brotto (2010). For example The National Health and Social Life Survey (NHSLS) on American men and women (Laumann et al., 2006) found a range from 14% to 17% depending on age. Men in the oldest category were three times more likely to experience low desire (Brotto, 2010, p.2016). The National Survey of Sexual Attitudes and Lifestyles (NATSAL) (Mercer et al., 2003) found that lack of interest in sex was the most prevalent problem in men. Najman et al. (2003) found that the prevalence of lack of sexual interest in Australian men lasting several months or more ranged from 16% to 19%. After premature ejaculation, low sexual interest became the second most common sexual problem reported by men. A nationally representative Swedish survey (Fugl-Meyer & Sjorgen, 1999) found that low sexual desire was the most frequent complaint, reported by 16% of the men, and 41% of men aged 66–74 reported decrease in sexual interest. A Danish study (Eplov et al., 2007) found that men had a significantly higher level of sexual desire than women. They measured the presence of factors increasing sexual desire and found the highest levels of desire with men who were younger, in a committed relationship, who had higher educational levels, higher economic status, who were not experiencing emotional problems, not anxious or depressed, who practised regular physical activity and were physically healthy. A map of factors enhancing sexual desire in men is presented in Figure 4.9 using the MOST model.

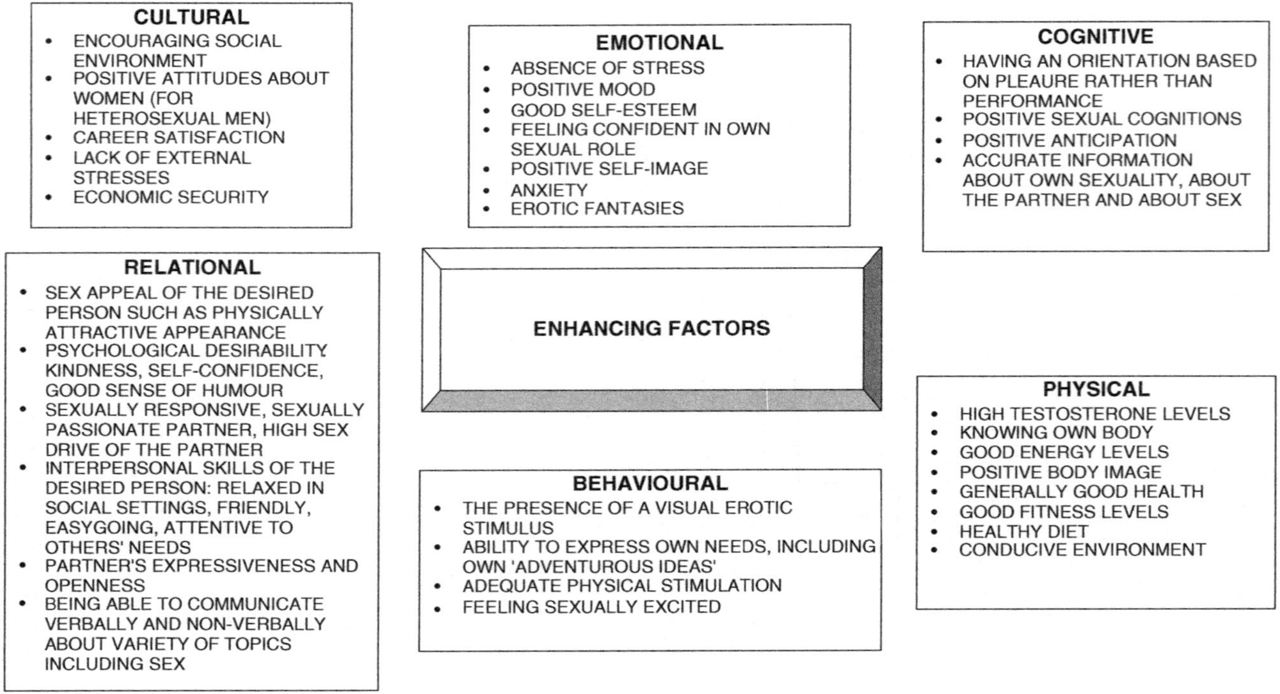

CULTURAL

- ENCOURAGING SOCIAL ENVIRONMENT
- POSITIVE ATTITUDES ABOUT WOMEN (FOR HETEROSEXUAL MEN)
- CAREER SATISFACTION
- LACK OF EXTERNAL STRESSES
- ECONOMIC SECURITY

EMOTIONAL

- ABSENCE OF STRESS
- POSITIVE MOOD
- GOOD SELF-ESTEEM
- FEELING CONFIDENT IN OWN SEXUAL ROLE
- POSITIVE SELF-IMAGE
- ANXIETY
- EROTIC FANTASIES

COGNITIVE

- HAVING AN ORIENTATION BASED ON PLEAURE RATHER THAN PERFORMANCE
- POSITIVE SEXUAL COGNITIONS
- POSITIVE ANTICIPATION
- ACCURATE INFORMATION ABOUT OWN SEXUALITY, ABOUT THE PARTNER AND ABOUT SEX

ENHANCING FACTORS

RELATIONAL

- SEX APPEAL OF THE DESIRED PERSON SUCH AS PHYSICALLY ATTRACTIVE APPEARANCE
- PSYCHOLOGICAL DESIRABILITY: KINDNESS, SELF-CONFIDENCE, GOOD SENSE OF HUMOUR
- SEXUALLY RESPONSIVE, SEXUALLY PASSIONATE PARTNER, HIGH SEX DRIVE OF THE PARTNER
- INTERPERSONAL SKILLS OF THE DESIRED PERSON: RELAXED IN SOCIAL SETTINGS, FRIENDLY, EASYGOING, ATTENTIVE TO OTHERS' NEEDS
- PARTNER'S EXPRESSIVENESS AND OPENNESS
- BEING ABLE TO COMMUNICATE VERBALLY AND NON-VERBALLY ABOUT VARIETY OF TOPICS INCLUDING SEX

BEHAVIOURAL

- THE PRESENCE OF A VISUAL EROTIC STIMULUS
- ABILITY TO EXPRESS OWN NEEDS, INCLUDING OWN 'ADVENTUROUS IDEAS'
- ADEQUATE PHYSICAL STIMULATION
- FEELING SEXUALLY EXCITED

PHYSICAL

- HIGH TESTOSTERONE LEVELS
- KNOWING OWN BODY
- GOOD ENERGY LEVELS
- POSITIVE BODY IMAGE
- GENERALLY GOOD HEALTH
- GOOD FITNESS LEVELS
- HEALTHY DIET
- CONDUCIVE ENVIRONMENT

Figure 4.9 Male sexual desire: enhancing factors

Factors contributing to MHSDD

A list of typical contributing factors is presented in Figure 4.10 using the MOST diagram. While it is important to recognise differences between female and male sexuality and the different genders' sexual responses, the symptoms and the map of contributing factors are strikingly similar (apart from the obvious physical factors influencing specifically female sexual interest, such as PMS, vaginal pain, miscarriage, abortion, menopause, menstrual cycle, contraceptive pills, pregnancy and childbirth; although these factors are also relevant to men's desire levels when their female partner is experiencing one or more of the above). Contrary to Brotto's (2010) suggestion that, given that a range of psychosocial factors contribute to both female sexual interest and MHSDD, these factors should be included in the DSM-5 coding of MHSDD, the DSM-5 document does not include the codes used for all other dysfunctions (partner factors/relationship factors/individual vulnerability/cultural and religious factors) in spite of the sexologists' recognition that: 'Men, it turns out, are influenced by many of the same factors as women: aging, hormones, relationship issues, stress, mood, and anxiety' (Wincze & Weisberg, 2015, p.64).

Emotional factors

A wide range of emotional experiences can underlie low sexual desire problem in men. Feelings of anger, guilt, shame, anxiety and fear can be common significant contributing factors and at times deeply ingrained and difficult to shift. Emotional stress and depression (McCabe & Connaughton, 2014) were reported as major factors in low sexual desire for men. Controversially, sexology research identified depression and anxiety as factors that can also increase sexual desire for men (Bancroft et al., 2003b; Lykins, Janssen & Graham, 2005). Bancroft et al. (2003b) explored the relationship between mood and sexual interest in heterosexual men and found that 51% reported a decrease of sexual desire when depressed, while 12% reported increased sexual desire when depressed, concluding that men may be using sex as a mood regulator, to feel validated, or as a stress release. A study of gay men found similar results in terms of using sex to regulate depressed or anxious mood (Bancroft et al., 2003a). Emotional distress is typically both a cause and an effect in low sexual desire, contributing to its development and maintaining its persistence as 'a person with low sexual desire reports that he or she is also experiencing negative affective states, including distress, sadness, disappointment, frustration, or embarrassment about having reduced desire' (Wincze & Carey, 2001, p.14).

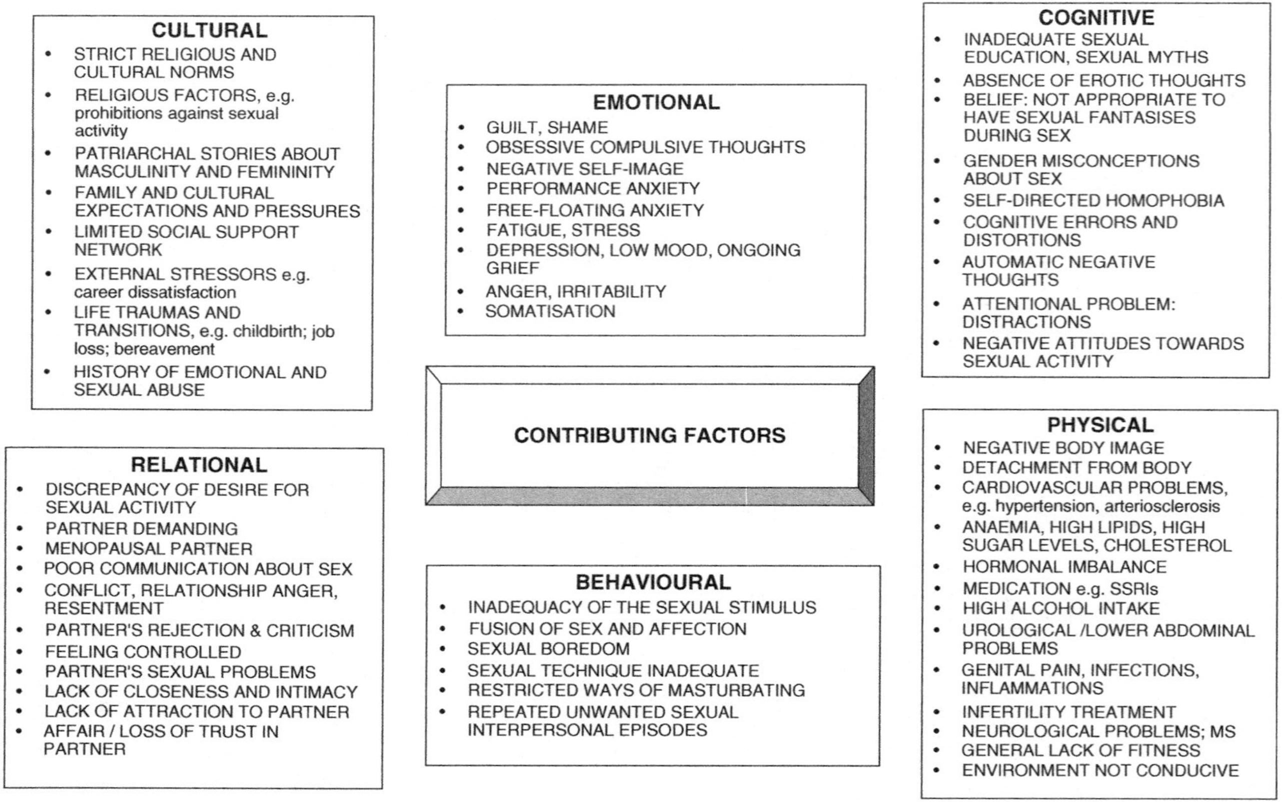

CULTURAL

- STRICT RELIGIOUS AND CULTURAL NORMS
- RELIGIOUS FACTORS, e.g. prohibitions against sexual activity
- PATRIARCHAL STORIES ABOUT MASCULINITY AND FEMININITY
- FAMILY AND CULTURAL EXPECTATIONS AND PRESSURES
- LIMITED SOCIAL SUPPORT NETWORK
- EXTERNAL STRESSORS e.g. career dissatisfaction
- LIFE TRAUMAS AND TRANSITIONS, e.g. childbirth; job loss; bereavement
- HISTORY OF EMOTIONAL AND SEXUAL ABUSE

EMOTIONAL

- GUILT, SHAME
- OBSESSIVE COMPULSIVE THOUGHTS
- NEGATIVE SELF-IMAGE
- PERFORMANCE ANXIETY
- FREE-FLOATING ANXIETY
- FATIGUE, STRESS
- DEPRESSION, LOW MOOD, ONGOING GRIEF
- ANGER, IRRITABILITY
- SOMATISATION

COGNITIVE

- INADEQUATE SEXUAL EDUCATION, SEXUAL MYTHS
- ABSENCE OF EROTIC THOUGHTS
- BELIEF: NOT APPROPRIATE TO HAVE SEXUAL FANTASISES DURING SEX
- GENDER MISCONCEPTIONS ABOUT SEX
- SELF-DIRECTED HOMOPHOBIA
- COGNITIVE ERRORS AND DISTORTIONS
- AUTOMATIC NEGATIVE THOUGHTS
- ATTENTIONAL PROBLEM: DISTRACTIONS
- NEGATIVE ATTITUDES TOWARDS SEXUAL ACTIVITY

CONTRIBUTING FACTORS

RELATIONAL

- DISCREPANCY OF DESIRE FOR SEXUAL ACTIVITY
- PARTNER DEMANDING
- MENOPAUSAL PARTNER
- POOR COMMUNICATION ABOUT SEX
- CONFLICT, RELATIONSHIP ANGER, RESENTMENT
- PARTNER'S REJECTION & CRITICISM
- FEELING CONTROLLED
- PARTNER'S SEXUAL PROBLEMS
- LACK OF CLOSENESS AND INTIMACY
- LACK OF ATTRACTION TO PARTNER
- AFFAIR / LOSS OF TRUST IN PARTNER

BEHAVIOURAL

- INADEQUACY OF THE SEXUAL STIMULUS
- FUSION OF SEX AND AFFECTION
- SEXUAL BOREDOM
- SEXUAL TECHNIQUE INADEQUATE
- RESTRICTED WAYS OF MASTURBATING
- REPEATED UNWANTED SEXUAL INTERPERSONAL EPISODES

PHYSICAL

- NEGATIVE BODY IMAGE
- DETACHMENT FROM BODY
- CARDIOVASCULAR PROBLEMS, e.g. hypertension, arteriosclerosis
- ANAEMIA, HIGH LIPIDS, HIGH SUGAR LEVELS, CHOLESTEROL
- HORMONAL IMBALANCE
- MEDICATION e.g. SSRIs
- HIGH ALCOHOL INTAKE
- UROLOGICAL /LOWER ABDOMINAL PROBLEMS
- GENITAL PAIN, INFECTIONS, INFLAMMATIONS
- INFERTILITY TREATMENT
- NEUROLOGICAL PROBLEMS; MS
- GENERAL LACK OF FITNESS
- ENVIRONMENT NOT CONDUCIVE

Figure 4.10 Male hypoactive sexual desire disorder: contributing factors

Cognitive factors

Inadequate sex education is an ever-present factor in sexual difficulties. A belief that *'it is not appropriate to have sexual fantasies during sexual activity with a partner'*, for example, may inhibit sexual desire by blocking sexual thoughts and erotic mental images that can be a significant enhancing factor in men's sexual desire (Carvalho & Nobre, 2011). The occurrence of such fantasies within this belief system leads to guilt and shame, subsequently contributing to MHSDD. Common myths such as: *'You can only initiate sex if you already feel desire'*; *'Men are responsible for initiating sex'*; *'Men are always ready for sex and only refuse an unattractive or undesirable partner'*; *'An erection is necessary sign of desire and the lack of erection means a lack of desire'* (Hall, 2015, p.65) are based on lack of sufficient sexual knowledge and can significantly impact the manifestations of desire. Negative attitudes towards sexual activity, such as *'sex is bad, wicked and sinful'* (Zilbergeld, 1999), coming from a familial, cultural and strict religious upbringing, can be deeply embedded and operating as both predisposing and maintaining factors. Strong negative beliefs about masturbation can also significantly interfere with sexual desire and induce guilt, shame and embarrassment as a result of masturbatory activity, thus blocking sexual desire (Zilbergeld, 1999). Patriarchal stories about gender roles, such as: *'In sex, like in dancing, the man must take the "lead" and the woman must follow'* (Sanders, 1994); *'Men are responsible for initiating sex'*; and *'Men are always ready for sex and only refuse an unattractive or undesirable partner'* (Hall, 2015, p.65) can all be equally oppressive to both women and men, imposing gender domination/submission, and potentially creating feelings of powerlessness in limiting one's sexual desires and inducing feelings of inadequacy.

Sometimes an attention problem creates difficulties with sexual desire by distracting the person's thinking and fantasy, inhibiting their initiation of a sexual activity and/or responsiveness to their partner's initiations. Usually, cognitive distortions related to negative views about sexuality interfere with sexual thoughts, blocking sexual material. The persons affected are not necessarily aware of this mental activity and often feel puzzled by their unresponsiveness to sex.

While there is a body of evidence that ageing influences sexual desire in both women and men, sometimes people exaggerate the effect of age. A man aged 50 came to therapy at the instigation of his wife who was distressed by his complete sexual withdrawal. Their relationship was otherwise harmonious and deeply committed. His explanation for the absence of any sexual instigations or responsiveness was completely age related. His belief that sex stops at 50 was apparently supported by a group of his peers, with whom he met regularly at the local pub. Reportedly they all stopped sexual activity with their partners because of reaching the age of 50, believing it to be the age limit for sex. For some reason this strong belief seems to have been constructed within this local culture and had impacted the couple's relationship in a major way. Similarly, a trainee therapist expressed surprise in supervision that a client aged 65 worried about his partner's lack of interest in sex. This was a major challenge to the trainee who reflected on his own firmly established belief that *'people over 60 do not have sex'*. Detachment between mind and body can occur whereby the mind is not registering the signals of desire, because of strictly moralistic attitudes, or sometimes as a protection in cases of past sexual trauma and/or sexual and emotional abuse. In such cases sex may become a threat and strongly associated with danger and hurt. Exploring previous sexual experiences so as to include possible unpleasant and abusive sexual episodes can determine the factors that may have created barriers to sexual desire in both men and women (Bancroft, 2009).

Physical factors

A range of medical conditions can cause loss of sexual desire in men. Cardiovascular problems, renal failure and HIV; neurological problems, e.g. multiple sclerosis (Lew-Starowicz & Rafal, 2014); hormonal imbalance, e.g. low testosterone; IBS including Crohn's disease (O'Toole, Winter & Friedman, 2014) can all be contributing factors. Antidepressants, anti-anxiety medication, sleeping pills and a range of other medications may have the side effect of inhibiting sexual desire. If the symptoms of the disturbance in sexual functioning are only side effects of a medical problem or of medical treatment, the diagnosis of sexual disorder is not appropriate. If administration or cessation of medical treatment results in alleviating the medical condition leading to improved levels of sexual desire, the diagnosis of sexual dysfunction would not be indicated and may even be counterproductive.

Ageing is a factor of a biological nature and it is useful to acknowledge that sexual functioning has a typical pattern over the lifespan with a tendency towards a reduction in the strength and vibrancy of sexual expression. These normal processes need to be taken into account and normalised in therapy.

Physical contributing factors can be either a single cause of the low desire levels or combined with others. A multifaceted combination is usually regarded as constituting a disorder, which can then be treated in psychosexual therapy.

Behavioural factors

Assessment should tease out behavioural aspects of the difficulty and aim to establish the level of adequacy of the sexual stimulus. Lack of sexual desire could be a response to unwanted repeated interpersonal sexual episodes involving lack of excitement, leading to sexual boredom. If the cause of the difficulty is identified as inadequacy of the sexual stimulus, and if the desire levels are improved with the introduction of a more adequate sexual and erotic stimulation, the diagnosis of the sexual desire disorder should not be made. Zilbergeld (1999, p.351) asks the question 'desire for what?', drawing attention to the relational and behavioural dimensions of sexual desire. When sex becomes identified with insufficiently exciting and unsatisfying sexual experience, the person may not desire to repeat such an experience; however, there may be a lot of scope for opening up different sexual opportunities.

It sometimes takes a while to discover what kind of sexual experience the person would potentially desire. Questions exploring unique outcomes (White, 2007), past successful sexual experiences and future hypothetical scenarios may facilitate that process.

A typical phenomenon of 'fusion of affection and sex' (Weeks & Gambescia, 2002, p.41) occurs in relationships where there is a discrepancy of desire. The person with the lower desire starts avoiding physical contact so as not to allow the partner to think that it means a prelude to a sexual activity. This can progress into relationship patterns over time becoming impoverished, void of physical affection and intimacy and ultimately may lead to relationship deterioration, creating a vicious circle between relational, behavioural and emotional factors, further aggravating lack of sexual desire.

Relational factors

Relational factors can significantly impact men's levels of sexual desire. Lack of satisfactory communication, anger between partners, lack of intimacy, hostility, dominance and control are typical factors influencing levels of desire (Meana and Steiner, 2014, p.48). Issues of power and control often feature concurrently with complaints of loss of desire. The only way of keeping a sense of control for the partner who feels over-controlled, overpowered by the other sometimes is to say 'no' to sex; typically this is not a conscious, deliberate decision. Schnarch (2009) posits that the partner with the lower desire always controls sex, a claim that may be problematic given that low sexual desire is an involuntary phenomenon, typically unwanted by the person experiencing it and often having a devastating impact.

The person experiencing loss of desire may be puzzled by it themselves and may, either because they may not want to (for fear of upsetting the partner, for example) or may not know how to communicate this to their partner, start avoiding physical closeness and withdrawing physically and emotionally in order to prevent the possibility of sex. They may invent excuses such as 'a headache', 'feeling unwell' and other temporary situational justifications. After a while these may raise suspicions or anger with the partner who then feels wounded, betrayed and rejected. Then, because of feeling hurt, or because it may raise anxieties for them and tap into their own insecurity in their sexual role, they may start being accusatory which increases distress in the couple and further reinforces the problem.

From time to time, it happens that a couple brings low sexual desire as a presenting problem; however, assessment may identify that the problem is relational, rather than individual, and in that case a formulation of 'discrepancy of sexual desire' would be indicated, whereby neither of the partners has the problem, but the problem is how their differing sexual desire levels are negotiated between them (Wincze & Carey, 2001). The discrepancy may also exist when one of the partners makes excessive demands, which in itself becomes a 'turn-off' for sexual desire (Wincze & Carey, 2001). Having a partner who has sexual problems has been identified as a significant factor contributing to low sexual desire in men (McCabe & Connaughton, 2014). The partner's anorgasmia, other sexual problems and menopausal symptoms were found to be significant factors in the relational component of men's desire (Corona et al., 2004). Schnarch (2000) names 'emotional fusion' as a relational contributing factor to low sexual desire in both women and men. Emotional fusion is a result of lack of differentiation between the partners, 'when couples are emotionally gridlocked', and so 'conflictual issues surface repeatedly' (p.29).

Cultural factors

Research studies have highlighted some important factors impacting sexual dysfunctions of both women and men: deterioration in economic position, poor quality of life, and work-related stress (Corona et al., 2004). Temporary withdrawal of sexual desire is a typical response to disturbing life events, bereavement, financial and other existential losses. When deep distress is caused by a major misfortune, loss of desire may be a normal reaction and should not be classified as a 'disorder'. Still, therapy assessment and treatment processes can help a person to make meaning of their loss of desire, enable their contextual understanding of this phenomenon and facilitate change through a combination of treatment approaches.

Sociocultural factors contributing to low sexual desire in men also operate through a cultural mythology that 'fuels many predominant beliefs about sex, particularly the notion that sex is something everyone should want' (Weeks & Gambescia, 2002, p.39). Peer culture, social media, popular magazines and pornography can impose unrealistic expectations about how sex should be, how men should perform, how they should be 'sexual supermen and conquerors' (Weeks & Gambescia, 2002, p.39), leaving men feeling ineffective in carrying their sexual identities, with a sense that they are failing to achieve externally prescribed standards of 'manly' sexual behaviour. Zilbergeld depicts this as 'the fantasy model of sex', summarising this gendered cultural myth about men's sexual performance as: *'It's two feet long, hard as steel and goes on all night'* (Zilbergeld, 1999, p.15).

Cultural stereotypes of masculinity and femininity have been the subject of social constructionist and feminist critique for decades. Feminist and gay/lesbian liberation movements criticised normative approaches to sexuality such as heterosexism, stereotyped gender roles and the dominance of the traditional institution of marriage, pointing towards the failures of sexual science to address sexual and gender politics (Irvine, 2005). Some of the sexual mythology constructed by social media is described in the section on cognitive factors. What follows in the quote below describes social and cultural sexual mythology impacting marginalised social groups, limiting possibilities of their sexual expression:

> Stereotypes and media representations that, for example, depict women as sexually undeveloped relative to men, the elderly as fundamentally asexual, and the physically different (e.g. obese, disabled) as sexually unappealing may conspire to teach individuals from those social groups (and their potential partners) that sexual desire they experience is 'abnormal' or 'wrong' and that they are undeserving of having their sexual needs met. This, in turn, may inhibit their opportunities to express, explore, and act on their desires (Hoffmann & Nordgren, 2015, p.361).

Sexual desire: what is 'normal'?

Criteria for diagnosing 'low' or 'excessive' sexual desire inevitably involve a level of judgement about what constitutes 'normal sexual desire', thus entering the realm of subjectivity, normative comparisons and potentially pathologising definitions:

> Disorders involving excessive sexual desire have enjoyed many names, including 'sexual addiction', 'sexual compulsion', 'nymphomania',

> 'satyriasis', or 'Don Juanism'. There is little agreement on the usage of these terms. The term 'sexual addiction', in particular, had been used to explain such varied practice as frequent masturbation, impersonal sex, emotional dependency, and extramarital affairs (Wincze & Carey, 2001, p.13).

On the other hand, 'asexuality', defined as the lifelong lack of sexual attraction (Scherrer, 2008), received strong opposition from Asexual Visibility and Education Network (AVEN), the largest online community of asexuals, which insisted that DSM should explicitly exclude asexual individuals from receiving a diagnosis of hypoactive sexual desire (AVEN, 2016), viewing asexuality as a chosen identity and a form of sexual orientation (Brotto, 2010). Feminist and queer perspectives on asexuality view asexuality as a complex, multifaceted phenomenon, not necessarily fixed in time or in the body. These views oppose the historical tendency of the medical models to pathologise and medicalise asexuality, overrelying on genitally focused paradigms and biological frameworks of desire. Zilbergeld (1999) posits: 'The question is not if it's "normal", but if it's a problem' (p.83), stating that ways of sex becoming a problem are: if it is illegal; if it's driven, compulsive, out of control; if it gets in your way; if it creates problems with the partner (p.84), thus providing space for normalisation of a range of different levels of sexual desire and sexual activity.

Therapists' self-reflexivity and relational reflexivity are crucial in working with sexual issues and in determining what is considered to be 'low', 'excessive', or indeed, 'normal' sexual desire. The need for reflection on the processes of deciding on criteria for establishing certain opinions through supervision, self-reflective practices, and personal and professional development activities is a highly relevant ethical responsibility of each professional in order to monitor bias, prejudice and narrow views in this delicate and complex domain of human existence.

Premature/early ejaculation (PE)

Definitions

'Premature ejaculation' was first classified in medical literature in the early 20th century as a condition whereby the man ejaculates just before vaginal penetration, and as 'rapid ejaculation' when ejaculation happens just after vaginal penetration (Huhner, 1917). The term 'premature ejaculation' was used consistently and sometimes interchangeably with 'rapid ejaculation' until the introduction of the term 'early' in addition to 'premature ejaculation' in DSM-5 (APA, 2013).

The reasons for this addition were based on the criticism that the term 'premature' could be understood as pejorative and therefore might be misleading. There is still a great deal of controversy surrounding the condition, spanning from attempts to classify it according to precise criteria to views that premature ejaculation should not be even considered a dysfunction. For example, Hong (1984) considered that unless ejaculation happens before penetration, it should not be classified as a dysfunction. Many research studies argue that the ejaculatory latency time (duration of penetration) is not a useful criterion, given its large variation, between one and ten minutes, may be a function of a variety of different circumstances (Metz et al., 1997).

DSM-5 defines premature/early ejaculation (PE in further text) as a pattern that has persisted for at least six months whereby a man ejaculates within approximately one minute following vaginal penetration, and this being contrary to his wishes. DSM-IV-TR did not state the precise timing and defined it more openly, as persistent and unwanted ejaculation with minimal sexual stimulation before, on, or shortly after penetration (DSM-IV-TR, 2000). The ICD-10 classification in 1992 (WHO, 1992, p.119) defined this disorder as 'occurrence of ejaculation ... before or within 15 seconds of the beginning of intercourse'; second edition (WHO, 2004) does not specify any precise timing and defines the disorder as 'the inability to control ejaculation sufficiently for both partners to enjoy sexual interaction' (code F52.4). American Urological Association Guidelines for management of PE (AUA, 2000) define the problem as ejaculation occurring 'sooner than desired either before or shortly after penetration, causing distress to either or both partners'.

Prevalence

A great variation in research findings about the prevalence of PE reflects the lack of a universally accepted definition of the condition. According to DSM-5 criteria, only 1%–3% of men would be diagnosed; whereas previously, estimates of premature/early ejaculation internationally suggested that 20%–30% of men suffered from this disorder (Wincze & Weisberg, 2015). Prior to the DSM-5 definition, sexology literature referred to PE as the most frequently presented sexual problem. Metz & McCarthy state that approximately 'three in ten adult males regularly experience PE' (Metz & McCarthy, 2003, p.3). Clearly, specifying the (narrow) time limit for the criteria of the disorder lowered the prevalence statistics.

Diagnosis and assessment

PE frequently leads to personal and relationship distress and is a typical presenting factor for seeking advice from medical and/or psychological services. The time factor is crucial in this diagnosis, as implied by the terms 'premature', 'early' and 'rapid'; and relates to the inability of the man to sufficiently control his ejaculatory mechanisms so as to allow for longer, mutually enjoyable sexual interaction. Many clients present to psychosexual and sexology services distressed by what they would describe as PE even though the diagnosis would not precisely fall within the criteria set out in DSM-5. However, clients' subjective experience of distress may constitute sufficient reason to undertake treatment, which typically combines sexology interventions aimed at improving ejaculatory control, with working towards enhancing psychological and interpersonal welfare.

PE, being time-determined by the individuals concerned, makes it a subjective problem. What is 'premature' for one person may not be so for another. DSM-5 sets a minimal objective duration of the sexual act before ejaculation in precise chronological terms in order for the diagnosis of PE to be given, but the practitioner needs to establish with their clients what specifically the difficulty is they wish to address in psychosexual work, and to draw a distinction between dysfunction and dissatisfaction (Wincze & Carey, 2001). If treatment is undertaken, it is important to agree on an appropriate basis for formulation. Even if the clients' description of the problem does not fit the definition as determined by sexology science, the individuals and/or their partners seeking help may, nonetheless, be dissatisfied with the duration of the sexual act and concerned about the impact of this on their satisfaction with their sexual relationship. In such cases, it is helpful to clarify that the treatment is not based on the diagnosis of a dysfunction but rather to increase sexual satisfaction (Waldinger, 2007).

Zilbergeld (1999) considered PE the most common male sexual problem, stating that the issue is not about the time factor but more about the man's feeling of lack of control over the ejaculatory process. Equally, it is important to acknowledge that there may be a 'misunderstanding or unreasonable expectations about sexuality' (Hawton, 1985, p.98). For this reason, clients are invited to provide detailed and specific factual information, in order for the assessment to determine the existence of any interfering sexual myths, particularly about the duration of a sexual activity. Psychosexual therapists sometimes advise clients to time their sexual activity, as it is not unusual that people under-or over-estimate the length of the sexual act. Recording factual information does not imply that 'objective facts' are more relevant than the subjective experience, but it enables a clearer understanding of the nature of the problem and of the factors contributing to it.

DSM-5 notes that this diagnosis may equally apply to 'individuals engaged in nonvaginal sexual activities, however for these activities, specific duration criteria have not been established' DSM-5 (APA, 2013, p.443). The phrase 'nonvaginal sexual activities' suggests the 'vaginal activities' as the norm with other sexual activities being sidetracked. Premature ejaculation is clinically reported in other forms of sexual activity whereby the man ejaculates too quickly after the onset of the sexual activity in his and/or his partner's estimate, sometimes even within seconds as a result of the partner's touch or stimulation. Sexual preferences may not necessarily include genital contact but rather involve oral sex, anal sex, hand stimulation of the genitals, or any of the numerous paraphilias. The primacy of vaginal penetration over any other forms of penetration and, indeed, other forms of sex, and the heteronormative approach, dominate the DSM-5 definition alongside the assumption that sex is an exclusively couple activity.

Factors contributing to PE

Sexology literature emphasises the multifactorial nature of PE aetiology (Metz & Pryor, 2000; Rowland, Cooper & Schneider, 2001). The likely contributing factors which are presented in Figure 4.11 within the six dimensions of the MOST model will be discussed below, while bearing in mind interconnectedness and mutual influences of the individual dimensions. As with other sexual dysfunctions, distinguishing lifelong from acquired, and generalised from situational symptomatology, is important in the understanding of PE. For example, in cases of acquired PE, assessment may tease out precipitating factors that may have triggered its onset, such as changes in health or medical treatment, various life stresses and relationship discord. In cases of situational as opposed to generalised dysfunction, when PE is not experienced during masturbation or if it only occurs with certain partners, the causes are likely to be psychological or relational, as opposed to potentially organic.

Emotional factors

Anxiety, depression and fear of intimacy have been found to feature in the symptomatology of PE (Assalian, 1994). Althof et al. (2010) identified a vicious circle between performance anxiety and PE. Performance anxiety distracts the man from focusing on his arousal, interfering with his ability to recognise the level of arousal and exert ejaculatory control. In addition, men suffering from PE tend to believe that focusing on their arousal levels

CONTRIBUTING FACTORS

CULTURAL

- PEER PRESSURE, BULLYING
- HARSH AND PUNITIVE EDUCATIONAL ENVIRONMENT
- EMOTIONAL CONFLICTS IN FAMILY OF ORIGIN
- RELIGIOUS RESTRICTIONS
- RIGID CULTURAL VIEWS ABOUT SEX
- RIGID CULTURAL STORIES ABOUT MASCULINITY AND FEMININITY
- LIMITED CULTURAL SUPPORT NETWORK

EMOTIONAL

- GUILT, SHAME, FEAR OF INTIMACY
- LOW SELF-CONFIDENCE
- PERFORMANCE ANXIETY
- FEAR OF COMMITMENT
- FEAR OF FAILURE
- STRESS, DEPRESSION
- TRAUMATIC LIFE EVENTS
- WORRIES ABOUT PLEASING THE PARTNER
- FEAR ABOUT PARTNER LEAVING

COGNITIVE

- LACK OF SEXUAL EDUCATION
- STRONG GENDER BELIEFS ABOUT SEX / MISCONCEPTIONS
- ANTICIPATION OF FAILURE
- COGNITIVE DISTORTIONS, e.g. catastrophlslng
- RESTRICTED SEXUAL KNOWLEDGE, MYTHS
- STRONG STORIES ABOUT MASCULINITY / FEMININITY
- NEGATIVE MESSAGES ABOUT SEX, INTIMACY AND AFFECTION
- COGNITIVE DISTRACTIONS

RELATIONAL

- RELATIONSHIP DISCORD
- PARTNER'S RESENTMENT
- POOR COMMUNICATION ABOUT SEX
- CONFLICT
- PARTNER TOO EXCITING NOVELTY
- PARTNER'S SEXUAL DYSFUNCTION e.g. arousal disorder
- PARTNER'S CRITICISM AND ANGER

BEHAVIOURAL

- INFREQUENT SEXUAL ACTIVITY
- HABITUAL & RIGID MASTURBATION PATTERNS (RUSHED)
- SEXUAL ACTIVITY RESTRICTED
- RESTRICTED FOREPLAY
- SEXUAL TECHNIQUE INADEQUATE
- REPETITIVE UNWANTED INTERPERSONAL EPISODES

PHYSICAL

- NEGATIVE BODY IMAGE
- CARDIOVASCULAR PROBLEMS
- DIABETES
- HIGH LIPIDS, CHOLESTEROL
- HORMONAL IMBALANCE
- OVERACTIVE THYROID
- INFLAMMATION AND INFECTION OF THE PROSTATE AND THE URETHRA
- HYPERSENSITIVITY OF PENIS
- UROLOGICAL /LOWER ABDOMINAL PROBLEMS
- NEUROLOGICAL PROBLEMS
- GENERAL LACK OF FITNESS

Figure 4.11 Premature/early ejaculation: contributing factors

would only worsen the problem and cause even more rapid ejaculation, leading them to deliberately detach from the arousal sensations (Althof, 2014, p.120). Performance anxiety may be connected with the fear of losing erections, particularly if there is a history of ED in the man's sexual experience. In these situations, men suffering from PE tend to get overly anxious, anticipating failure and predicting embarrassment about the lost erections (Hartmann, Schedlowski & Kruger, 2005).

The above factors, as presented on Figure 4.11, are connected and influence each other across the various dimensions; for example, feelings of guilt and shame may stem from strong stories about masculinity and femininity that have been promoted and enacted through the family, education and culture, predisposing feelings of sexual inadequacy. Some negative messages about sex, intimacy and affection from the client's early years coming from the family context may have had a powerful emotional impact creating fear of intimacy and commitment. These messages may not have been communicated directly in a conversational form 'on the topic of sex' but rather through a family atmosphere where being vulnerable felt unsafe, where emotional expression was suppressed, or where parents' or carers' conflict felt threatening.

A recent study (Rowland & Cooper, 2013) found that men suffering from PE exhibit symptoms of alexithymia, a condition characterised by an inability to identify, describe and interpret signs of emotional arousal in oneself and others.

Cognitive factors

Learning about sex may stem from a variety of contexts including: family messages, peer culture, religion, education, popular publications, media including the internet, pornography, magazines and films. The use of the internet and popular magazines as a source of sexual information has its disadvantages in promoting the idea that '*real men*' take the lead in heterosexual sexual encounters, and can stay erect before ejaculation for a very long time, as summarised in Zilbergeld's (1999, p.15) phrasing of 'the fantasy model of sex' that can have a terrifying effect on young persons, filling them with a sense of sexual inadequacy and performance anxiety which often contribute to the onset of PE.

Waldinger (2007) found that great personal distress related to the reported premature ejaculation is often due to unrealistic expectations that the normal length of intercourse exceeds 15 minutes. The typical sources of such information are internet pornography and sometimes friends' misrepresentations of their sexual 'successes'. Such distress can lead to performance anxiety and subsequent development of erectile dysfunction (Wincze & Weisberg, 2015). Metz and McCarthy list some typical false assumptions underlying PE complaints, such that, for example: *'most men engage in intercourse for twenty to thirty minutes'*, or that *'a good lover prolongs intercourse until his partner has an orgasm'*, that *'PE is caused by too much masturbation'*, or that *'thrusting alone is enough for most women to have orgasm during intercourse'* (Metz & McCarthy, 2003, p.3).

Strong gender beliefs about sex and various sexual misconceptions may not necessarily be obvious at the initial assessment. Clients may not be aware of their own sexual prejudices and may strongly believe in certain sexual misconceptions at an unconscious level. Sexual misconceptions tend to reveal themselves gradually over the course of treatment, indicating that assessment is a process that interlinks with treatment as new information emerges, allowing for problems and experiences to be deconstructed over time to provide a fuller picture.

Physical factors

Various medical problems can interfere with ejaculatory control in men, such as cardiovascular problems, diabetes mellitus, high cholesterol levels, urological, abdominal and neurological disorders. Metz et al.'s (1997) research findings suggest that PE results from biological factors. 'Hypersensitivity' to penile stimulation has been identified as a physical factor in the aetiology of PE (Athanasiadis, 1998).

Recent studies confirmed that hormones such as: testosterone, thyroid stimulating hormone and prolactine have significant impact on the male orgasmic control. High testosterone levels, for example, were associated with PE while low testosterone levels showed correlation with DE (Corona et al., 2011). Use of certain toxic substances showed correlation with PE. For example, Arachal and Benegal (2007) found that alcohol dependency, or withdrawal from certain drugs, particularly opiates, can lead to PE.

Behavioural factors

Sexology research has identified that certain rigid habits of masturbation, such as adolescents rushing it due to fear of discovery in cultural and religious contexts that strictly condemn and prohibit the practice, can lead to PE in later sexual relationships. Infrequent sexual activity, where the man is overly primed for orgasm, is a typical factor contributing to the development and persistence of PE. For this reason it is important to obtain a clear and precise picture of sexual frequency beyond vague descriptions, such as 'rare' or 'often'. Sometimes infrequent sexual activity can be both a cause and an effect of this difficulty; an unsatisfactory sexual relationship may reduce interest in sex, thus lowering frequency which then becomes a factor in maintaining PE. Abdo (2013) found that some men presenting lifelong PE demonstrate a lack of behavioural competence, such as dating and interpersonal skills.

To assess the behavioural dimension and its contribution to PE through exploring the sexual activity in detail, pertinent questions may include: How does the sexual activity begin? Who usually takes the initiative? In what way? What happens if the partner does not respond; in what way do they show this and how is it experienced by the person who initiated? Assessment can explore what happens at a process level without getting into the content too much, if it seems too intrusive, with questions such as: Are you pleased with how the sexual activity develops? What aspects of the sexual interaction do you enjoy most/least? What aspects of the sexual activity would you like to change, both in yours and in your partner's sexual response? How do you communicate your sexual needs to each other? How well do you believe your partner knows what you enjoy most/least in sex? Would you like to communicate differently with your partner about sex? How? What would you most want them to understand about you sexually? What would you most want to understand about them sexually? When something goes "wrong" in sex, what usually happens? How do you both react?

Relational factors

PE can be indicative of relationship issues. Power and control struggles, relationship discord, poor communication about sex, partners' resentment, criticism and anger, and pressure to perform can be major factors in this dysfunction (Metz & McCarthy, 2003). Research identified a correlation between PE and relationship dissatisfaction in heterosexual couples (Byers & Grenier, 2003). Partners reported distress about PE interrupting intimacy and feeling unheard, believing that the man is not trying hard enough to resolve the problem. Men, on the other hand, may be equally distressed, feeling misunderstood regarding their degree of frustration and humiliation they experience as a result of the sexual problem.

Men suffering with PE sometimes present with the feeling of being inferior to their partner, and/or with the idea that their partner is more sexually experienced, having had more sexually experienced partners, which can undermine the man's sense of his own capability. In a presenting case of PE, the partner was put on a pedestal in every possible way; he looked at her in the session with admiration and awe, while expressing this in words and accompanying gestures. He described her presence as equivalent to 'an untouchable aura', leaving him feeling so sexually aroused that his climax would happen seconds after physical intimacy commenced.

Sometimes the feeling that the woman is more decisive, competent, almost more 'manly' can further aggravate the man's feeling of gender inadequacy and intensify the sexual problem.

Partners' criticism and anger is a frequently encountered factor contributing to the development and persistence of a range of sexual dysfunctions through eroding sexual confidence, and creation of sexual inadequacy, worry, guilt, shame and anxiety. A client who had soft voice and a gentle mannerism, and had been heavily teased in both primary and secondary education for being 'girl-like', felt laughed at and self-conscious in social situations. He brought the presenting issue of PE to therapy with his partner, a strong, critical, feisty woman whose sexual pressure and expectations further undermined sense of his masculinity. The pattern of bullying seems to have been perpetuated within the couple relationship, reinforcing the earlier interpersonal scripts.

A male gay couple, Adam & Bill, presented with the issue of PE affecting Adam. Adam appeared a gentle, warm, soft and insecure person, a musician, 'a dreamer', as he described himself, 'a child in many ways'. Bill was a successful investment banker, a sharp, witty, quick, loud, vibrant person, often appearing to intimidate Adam. A pattern became evident whereby the more Bill tried to encourage Adam, the more Adam withdrew and the more Bill criticised him for being 'weak'. When a reframe was offered for this 'weakness' in terms of Adam being 'gentle, soft, kind...', Bill protested: 'This is so unattractive to me, as if he's a woman!' It seems that the couple's strong gender beliefs had a significant negative impact on their interactions, creating situations of communicational discord and sexual disappointment.

Sometimes one partner's presented sexual dysfunction masks the sexual dysfunction of the other. For example, one partner's PE may mask the other person's problems with sexual arousal. Equally, the problems with PE may affect the partner by inhibiting their sexual expression, thus interfering with sexual experience and feelings, and sometimes contributing to the development of secondary sexual performance problems.

Cultural factors

PE can be symptomatic of internalised emotional conflicts from the family of origin, or from negative messages about sex stemming from rigid cultural and religious beliefs. Early unpleasant sexual experiences may form a predisposition for sexual insecurity, or be a precipitating trigger for the problems related to sexual performance such as PE. Peer pressure, rigid religious values, and a punitive educational environment in childhood and puberty, often contribute to the development of sexual and gender insecurity, characteristic of PE.

A map of the effects of a sexual dysfunction could be created along the same lines as that for contributing factors and causes; such as with PE, the man's inability to control his ejaculation produces a cycle of effects that reinforces and maintains the existing problems. For instance, it brings the feelings of guilt, shame, low confidence and performance anxiety; it sets him up to anticipate failure and draw conclusions of him being inadequate sexually; it reinforces his negative body image, leads to further repetitive unwanted sexual and communicational patterns, and intensifies the relationship discord.

Persistent genital arousal disorder (PGAD)

Definitions

Cases of persistent sexual arousal disorder (PSAD) were first described in sexology literature by Leiblum and Nathan (2001). In 2007 Leiblum changed the original name to persistent genital arousal disorder (PGAD), as its manifestations are purely physical: genital swelling and sensitivity are felt in the areas of the clitoris, vagina, labia, or a combination of these locations. Less commonly it is felt around the anal area. Symptoms include wetness, feeling of congestion, fullness, tingling, and occasionally it involves throbbing pain sensations. PGAD is a rare condition, affecting women, characterised by 'spontaneous, intrusive and unwanted genital arousal (e.g. tingling, throbbing, pulsating) in the absence of sexual interest and desire' (Basson et al., 2004, p.45). This arousal usually persists for a prolonged period of time, such as hours or sometimes days, causing clinically significant distress and frustration. Some women, according to the limited sexology research that exists in this area, feel neutral about those symptoms (Leiblum & Chivers, 2007), and some welcome and enjoy the genital feelings and may or may not act on it by engaging in a sexual activity (Leiblum, Seehuus & Brown, 2007). These women should not be diagnosed with PGAD in the absence of any distress attached to it. The majority of presented cases, though, suggest high levels of stress and frustration, as a result of unsuccessful attempts to get rid of the sensation through masturbation and orgasm.

Diagnosis and assessment

Priapism was recognised as a medical condition in DSM-IV-TR (APA, 2000) and PGAD was added to the DSM for the first time in DSM-5 (APA, 2013) in the category 'other non-specified sexual disorders'. Many physicians are unaware of the condition, due to its rare presentation and the lack of empirically validated studies. Its prevalence may be under-reported, due to associated shame and, perhaps, misdiagnosis. It needs to be distinguished from 'hypersexuality' as clinicians might misinterpret the syndrome; the crucial difference lies in the intrusiveness of PGAD; while sexual desire typically accompanies 'hypersexuality', PGAD is experienced as unwanted and unrelated to sexual urges or fantasy, and lacks a subjective sense of sexual excitement.

Goldmeier, Sadeghi-Nejad and Facelle (2014, p.272) propose questions for assessment in order to establish the specificities of the experience:

1. Does sexual arousal of the woman's partner always trigger PGAD? In which situations does it happen? Does stimulating her partner trigger PGAD?
2. Are there certain places on her body where she can enjoy sexual stimulation or a sexual/sensual touch that does not trigger PGAD? Are there any sexual activities that do not trigger PGAD?

Although, according to the current state of sexology knowledge, its aetiology is purely physical (Komisaruk & Lee, 2012), the text that follows expands the possible contributing factors within the MOST dimensions (see Figure 4.12), based on the limited studies of the disorder, as described in the literature.

Emotional factors

Anxiety and psychological stress seem to contribute to this disorder. Leiblum et al. (Leiblum, Seehuus & Brown, 2007) found a high rate of psychological problems in women manifesting PGAD, such as: panic attacks, obsessive-compulsive illness and depression. Two-thirds of these women reported their anxiety predated PGAD symptoms by at least one year.

Cognitive factors

Leiblum and Chivers (2007) proposed that PGAD develops as a result of women's anxiety and hypervigilance in relation to their spontaneous genital arousal. Over-focusing on genital arousal then increases anxiety and brings about an elevated sympathetic tone, resulting in a vicious circle of mutual reinforcement of anxiety and genital arousal.

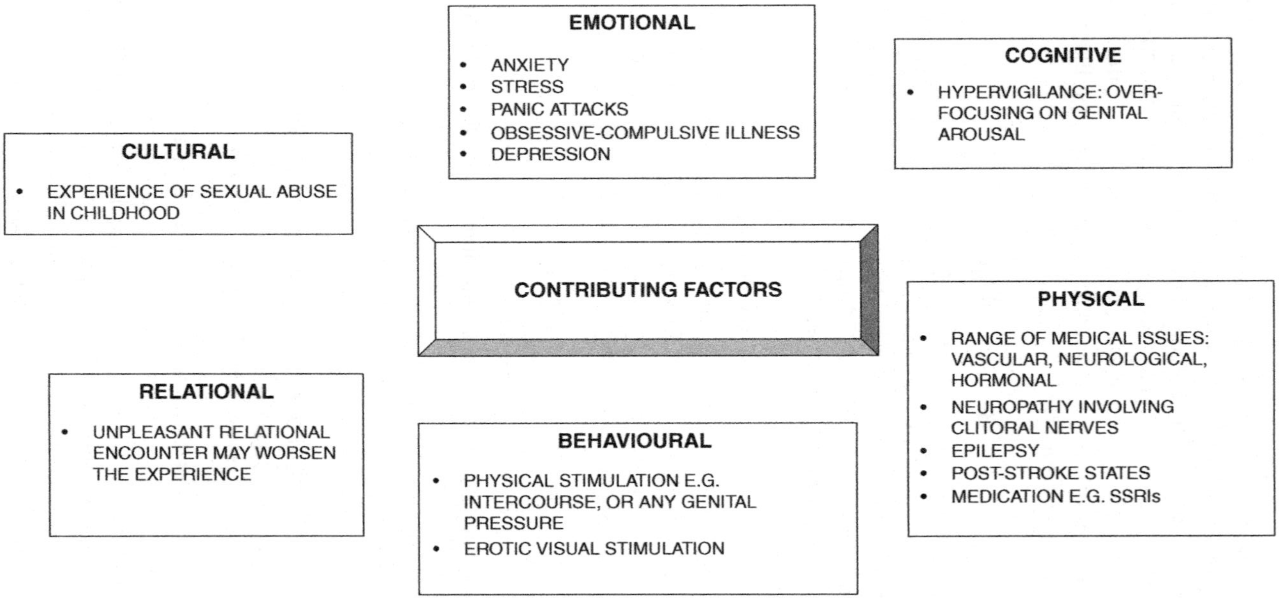

CONTRIBUTING FACTORS

CULTURAL

- EXPERIENCE OF SEXUAL ABUSE IN CHILDHOOD

EMOTIONAL

- ANXIETY
- STRESS
- PANIC ATTACKS
- OBSESSIVE-COMPULSIVE ILLNESS
- DEPRESSION

COGNITIVE

- HYPERVIGILANCE: OVER-FOCUSING ON GENITAL AROUSAL

RELATIONAL

- UNPLEASANT RELATIONAL ENCOUNTER MAY WORSEN THE EXPERIENCE

BEHAVIOURAL

- PHYSICAL STIMULATION E.G. INTERCOURSE, OR ANY GENITAL PRESSURE
- EROTIC VISUAL STIMULATION

PHYSICAL

- RANGE OF MEDICAL ISSUES: VASCULAR, NEUROLOGICAL, HORMONAL
- NEUROPATHY INVOLVING CLITORAL NERVES
- EPILEPSY
- POST-STROKE STATES
- MEDICATION E.G. SSRIs

Figure 4.12 Persistent *genital arousal* disorder: contributing factors

Physical factors

The condition may be associated with a range of biological pathologies, including vascular, neurologic, pharmacological and hormonal causes. Some medical research suggests that neuropathy, involving clitoral nerves, can produce PGAD or pain (Goldmeier, Sadeghi-Nejad & Facelle, 2014). Various other medical conditions, such as epilepsy and post-stroke states are also seen as possible contributors. Medication, such as SSRIs, are also likely factors in inducing the symptoms of PGAD.

Behavioural factors

PGAD can be triggered by physical stimulation during intercourse or masturbation. Erotic visual stimuli can be a contributor. In addition, slight physical touch when riding, wearing tight clothes, sitting in a moving vehicle, when experiencing any genital pressure of any kind, seems to have the power to trigger a PGAD response.

Relational factors

Some women report the importance of the context of the genital stimulus that triggers persistent arousal; if this is within a positive and pleasant relational encounter, it is likely to be experienced as more manageable and less distressing (Goldmeier, Sadeghi-Nejad & Facelle, 2014).

Cultural factors

Leiblum and Chivers' (2007) research findings suggested that 53% of women showing PGAD symptoms reported sexual abuse as children, leading to the researchers' speculation that such a history could be a factor contributing to anxiety and negative associations linked with genital arousal and thus trigger the cycle.

Sexual aversion disorder (SAD)

Definitions

Sexual aversion disorder (SAD in further text) is manifested by a strong repulsion to sexual contact. It bears similarity to lack of sexual interest, and is more commonly seen in women. The person avoids sexual interactions and only attends a sexual clinic at the instigation of the partner. Interpersonal distress is what prompts them to seek treatment, otherwise the person does not typically require treatment of SAD symptoms.

Diagnosis and assessment

SAD was first introduced in the sex therapy literature by Theresa Crenshaw, an American sex therapist, medical doctor and author (Crenshaw, 1985). Her description from 1985, joined by Kaplan's book in 1987 and followed by Carnes's book in 1997, remain the most comprehensive accounts of this disorder to date. Literature on SAD is scarce; it is hard to find a book or a chapter on the syndrome. Usually it is presented as part of other sexual dysfunctions such as low sexual desire, or sexual pain, or as part of anxiety and phobic disorders.

SAD was initially included in DSM-III-R (1987) and it was defined as 'persistent or recurrent extreme aversion to, and avoidance of all or almost all, genital sexual contact with a sexual partner' (p.293). According to this manual, the person exhibiting these symptoms does not completely lack interest in sex; they may engage in sexual fantasies and masturbation to release sexual tension. DSM-IV-TR (2000) extended the symptomatology of SAD to include feelings of fear, anxiety and disgust; these were related not only to a sexual activity, but also to other types of physical contact, including kissing, caressing and cuddling. DSM-5 (2013) removed SAD from the main diagnostic categories of sexual disorders and grouped SAD under the category of 'other specified sexual dysfunctions', due to lack of its clinical presence.

Identifying whether the aversion is primary or secondary is a pre-requisite for appropriate therapy as these different types of SAD are treated differently and have different prognoses (Crenshaw, 1985). Primary or lifelong disorder signifies that it has always been present, and secondary signifies an acquired type, triggered by certain events, such as traumatic experiences, losses, illnesses and major stresses. The situational type occurs with a specific partner or in a specific set of circumstances, and the generalised one occurs with any partner and in all situations. Kaplan (1987) described the enormous variability of situational forms of SAD, where certain aspects of sex would trigger the aversive reaction, such as: penetration, orgasm, oral sex, genital fluid, fantasies, etc. A person diagnosed with SAD may have sexual fantasies, or masturbate to release sexual tension but partnered sex causes anxiety, disgust and aversion (Borg, deJong & Elgersma, 2014). Barlow (2008) described a case of a woman who was comfortable with kissing and fondling, but very uncomfortable when hugging or holding hands with a partner (p.618). Symptoms can range from mild to severe; mild include lack of sexual interest, avoidance of sex and sex-related anxiety. Severe can include panic attacks, intense fear and disgust related to sex. Weeks, Gambescia and Hertlein (2016) recommend using a scale ranging from −10 to +10 to assess the strength of the aversion and the motivation for sex. Clients are asked to place themselves on the scale at various points in time: generally, in relation to sex; prior to initiation (theirs and/or partner's); during sexual activity; when the relationship is going well; when the relationship is not going well; and so on.

There has been a debate in sexology as to how to classify the disorder diagnostically. Some argue that it may be more appropriately placed within the specific phobic group as an anxiety disorder (Brotto, 2010). Others argue that SAD differs from specific phobias, as phobias do not include feelings of disgust and repulsion (Janata & Kingsberg, 2005). Tiefer (2001; Tiefer, Hall & Tavris, 2002) protests against placing a diagnosis of a disorder based on the 'sexology preoccupation with coitus and orgasm'. According to this perspective, the problem is contextual, and may be due to partner factors, such as discrepancy of desire and sexual preferences. Carnes, a counsellor and sex educator, who worked in the field of addiction for most of his career, uses the term 'sexual anorexia' to describe this condition (Carnes, 1997). He regards it as an obsessive state whereby the physical, mental, and emotional task of avoiding sex dominates one's life. He uses the addiction model (Carnes, 1998) to describe 'sexual anorexia' and 'sexual compulsivity' as different points on the same continuum. On one end he places 'sexual anorexia', or people who are preoccupied with the avoidance of sex, and on the other extreme he places 'sexual compulsivity' or 'hypersexuality', or people who had lost control of their sexual behaviour and use sex excessively. According to Carnes, the sufferer from sexual anorexia would typically experience the following (Carnes, 1997, pp.2–3):

- a dread of sexual pleasure
- morbid and persistent fear of sexual contact
- obsession and hypervigilance around sexual matters
- avoidance of anything connected to sex
- preoccupation with others being sexual
- distortions of body appearance
- extreme loathing of body functions
- obsessional self-doubt about sexual adequacy
- rigid, judgmental attitudes about sexual behavior
- excessive fear of and preoccupation with sexually transmitted diseases
- self-destructive behaviours to limit, stop, or avoid sex.

Carnes (1997, pp.64–69) identified six types of sexual anorexia:

1. *The Anorexia;* a total aversion to sexual thoughts, feelings and behaviours

2. *Binge and Purge;* sexually out of control behaviour is combined with rigid control of sexuality.
3. *The Addictive Switch;* the person stops acting out sexually but becomes addictive in other forms.
4. *The Anorexic Partner;* this person becomes anorexic as a result of feeling betrayed by their partner's sexual addiction.
5. *Simultaneous Anorexia;* both partners are anorexic.
6. *Simultaneous Binge and Purge;* both partners binge sexually outside their relationship while sexually anorexic with each other.

Prevalence

Prevalence of this disorder is unknown due to its low level of representation at sexual health clinics and the relative absence of research in this area. Some research suggests that it primarily affects women although the results are not necessarily reliable (Kingsberg & Janata, 2003). Two large internet-based studies in the Netherlands researching sexual health amongst adults suggested that the phenomenon may not be as rare as commonly thought. One study involving 4,147 participants within the age bracket of 16–69 revealed that 30% experienced sexual aversion at some point in their lives, and 4% met the diagnostic criteria (Bakker & Vanwezenbeek, 2006). Another study, involving 8,000 participants, suggested that 4.5% of women and 2.4% of men experienced regular symptoms of SAD (Kedde, 2012).

Mason and Richardson (2012) emphasise that the link between disgust and sex is currently an under-researched subject in sexology. More research studies on this link would contribute to a better understanding of the problem and would support specific treatment strategies.

Based on these studies, clinical psychology researchers and academics from the Netherlands (Borg, deJong & Elgersma, 2014) oppose the removal of SAD from DSM-5, arguing that its prevalence is masked by the low frequency of people seeking treatment for such a condition. The authors point out that the deletion of this disorder from DSM does not imply that it does not exist.

Factors contributing to SAD

A variety of factors may play a part in the development and the persistence of this disorder. The MOST map in Figure 4.13 summarises the likely contributing factors.

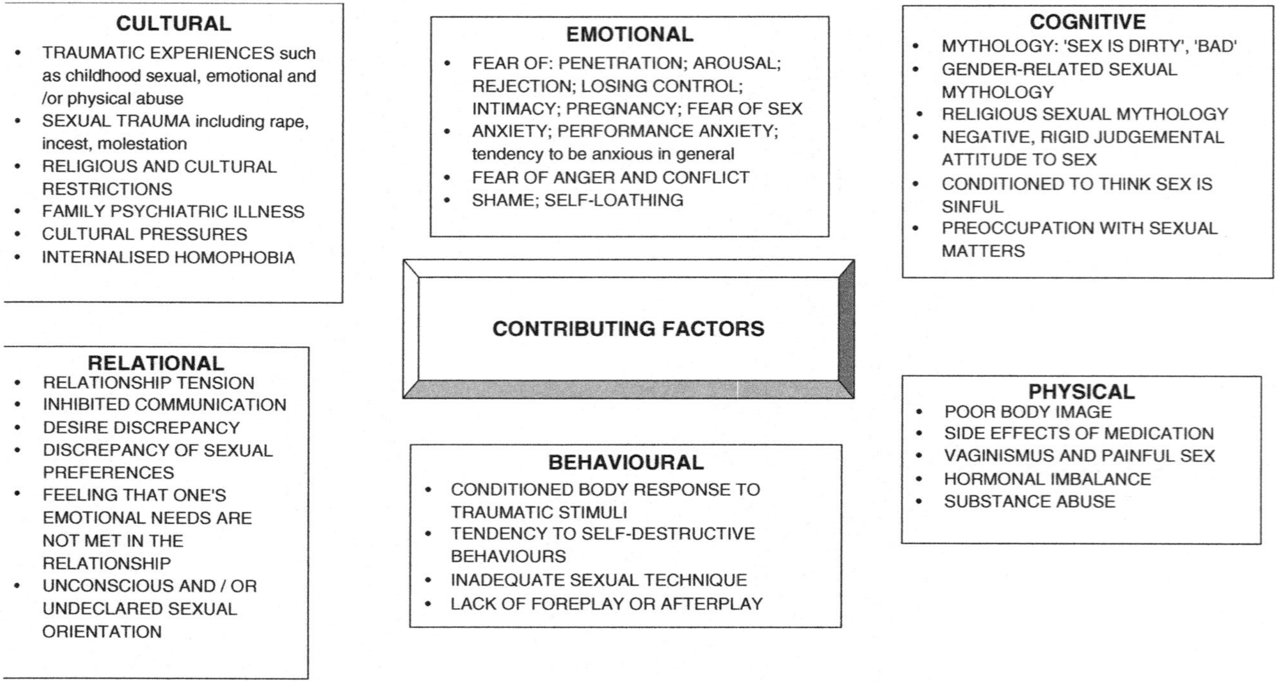

CONTRIBUTING FACTORS

CULTURAL

- TRAUMATIC EXPERIENCES such as childhood sexual, emotional and /or physical abuse
- SEXUAL TRAUMA including rape, incest, molestation
- RELIGIOUS AND CULTURAL RESTRICTIONS
- FAMILY PSYCHIATRIC ILLNESS
- CULTURAL PRESSURES
- INTERNALISED HOMOPHOBIA

EMOTIONAL

- FEAR OF: PENETRATION; AROUSAL; REJECTION; LOSING CONTROL; INTIMACY; PREGNANCY; FEAR OF SEX
- ANXIETY; PERFORMANCE ANXIETY; tendency to be anxious in general
- FEAR OF ANGER AND CONFLICT
- SHAME; SELF-LOATHING

COGNITIVE

- MYTHOLOGY: 'SEX IS DIRTY', 'BAD'
- GENDER-RELATED SEXUAL MYTHOLOGY
- RELIGIOUS SEXUAL MYTHOLOGY
- NEGATIVE, RIGID JUDGEMENTAL ATTITUDE TO SEX
- CONDITIONED TO THINK SEX IS SINFUL
- PREOCCUPATION WITH SEXUAL MATTERS

RELATIONAL

- RELATIONSHIP TENSION
- INHIBITED COMMUNICATION
- DESIRE DISCREPANCY
- DISCREPANCY OF SEXUAL PREFERENCES
- FEELING THAT ONE'S EMOTIONAL NEEDS ARE NOT MET IN THE RELATIONSHIP
- UNCONSCIOUS AND / OR UNDECLARED SEXUAL ORIENTATION

BEHAVIOURAL

- CONDITIONED BODY RESPONSE TO TRAUMATIC STIMULI
- TENDENCY TO SELF-DESTRUCTIVE BEHAVIOURS
- INADEQUATE SEXUAL TECHNIQUE
- LACK OF FOREPLAY OR AFTERPLAY

PHYSICAL

- POOR BODY IMAGE
- SIDE EFFECTS OF MEDICATION
- VAGINISMUS AND PAINFUL SEX
- HORMONAL IMBALANCE
- SUBSTANCE ABUSE

Figure 4.13 Sexual aversion disorder: contributing factors

Emotional factors

General anxiety as well as specific fears, such as fear of pregnancy, fear of losing control, fear of intimacy and fear of arousal are frequently associated with SAD. The phobic qualities involved in SAD have been emphasised by a number of sexology researchers and clinicians (e.g. Kaplan, 1987). Differentiating SAD from a panic disorder and from hypoactive sexual desire disorder may be difficult given the overlap of the symptoms.

Cognitive factors

Traumatic experiences can lead to associating sex with abuse, generating sexual aversion to prevent memories of trauma. Some argue that it fits more to classify this aversion as post-traumatic stress disorder than SAD (Coughtrey et al., 2013).

Strongly held moral beliefs, and a negative, rigid or judgemental attitude to sex may condition someone to think sex is sinful and produce feelings of repulsion and aversion regarding sexual matters (Borg, de Jong & Weijmar Schultz, 2011).

Physical factors

It is important to undertake a thorough medical examination before diagnosing SAD, as underlying physical causes can be numerous, e.g. hormonal imbalance, substance abuse and side effects of various medication. Vaginismus and painful sex have been identified as underlying factors in some cases of SAD (Borg, de Jong & Weijmar Schultz, 2011). Poor body image can be both a contributing factor and a symptom of SAD.

Behavioural factors

Carnes (1998) draws attention to the need to take this disorder seriously, considering it to be a destructive illness causing enormous pain and suffering to the person and often to their close relationships. He saw a pattern of a tendency to self-destructive behaviours as underlying this condition.

Traumatic experiences are often cited as a major cause of sexual aversion, and child sexual abuse in particular seems a high risk factor. Janata and Kingsberg (2005) viewed SAD as a conditioned aversion whereby the sexual stimulus is linked with painful or traumatic sexual stimuli, producing the aversive conditioned response.

In addition, unsatisfactory sexual experiences such as lack of foreplay or afterplay, or inadequacy of the sexual stimulus, lead to avoidance of sex. Resultant avoidance of sex then reinforces the symptoms in a vicious perpetuating circle (Brotto, 2010).

Relational factors

Interpersonal problems such as underlying tension or discontent with the relationship communicational problems can be significant factors in the development of SAD. Partner factors should be carefully assessed, as with other presenting sexual difficulties, and diagnosis of a sexual disorder should not be made if the problem is relational and can be treated in couple therapy. Similarly to inhibited sexual interest and arousal, relational factors contributing to SAD can be multiple, such as conflict, violence, feeling that one's emotional needs are not met in the relationship, and discrepancy of sexual preferences (Wylie, Markovic & Hallam-Jones, 2015). Unconscious and/or undeclared sexual orientation may be a root cause of gender-related sexual aversion. In such cases, the diagnosis of SAD should not be made.

Cultural factors

Traumatic experiences have been found to be connected with SAD; possible traumas include rape, incest, molestation and other forms of sexual abuse (Badour & Feldner, 2016). Carnes (1998) conducted research on 144 patients diagnosed with 'sexual anorexia' at his treatment clinic; 41% were male, 59% female, aged between 19 and 58 years, and all Caucasian. The main findings were: 67% reported a history of sexual abuse; 41% reported a history of physical abuse; 86% reported a history of emotional abuse; 65% reported that members of their immediate family suffered of some kind of addiction; 40% reported having a sex addict in the immediate family; 60% described their family as 'rigid' and 67% described their family as 'disengaged'.

Religious orthodoxy and strict religious teachings suggesting that sex is only for procreation and should be limited to married couples, prohibiting premarital, homosexual and extramarital sex, may be strong contributing factors for SAD. Crenshaw (1985) observed that clients presenting primary sexual aversion have been raised in strict religious communities. Kort, a psychotherapist and sexual and relationship therapist, describes the phenomenon of internalised homophobia in gay men and women who develop SAD as a means of fighting their natural homosexual urges, in order to avoid homosexual hatred and contempt held by wider contexts in which they live, such as familial, societal, cultural and religious. He reflects on his clinical practice with these men and women who choose self-identity as 'ex-gays', and become sexual anorexics: 'Preoccupied with any feelings towards the same gender, they're extremely judgmental towards those who do live out their homosexual orientation, sexually and romantically. They tell me they don't believe me when I say I'm happy in my life as a gay man' (Kort, 2004).

Sexual compulsivity, addiction or hypersexuality

Definitions

'Hypersexuality' as a term has been in use since the late 1800s when Krafft-Ebing described several cases of 'extreme sexual behaviours' in his book *Psychopathia Sexualis* (Krafft-Ebing, 1886/1965). 'Hypersexual' behaviours have been viewed by clinicians and researchers as: an addiction, a type of obsessive-compulsive disorder, or a disorder of impulsivity. Depending on theoretical perspectives, many labels have been used and are currently in use to refer to 'hypersexuality', such as: 'compulsive sexual behaviour', 'cybersex addiction', 'erotomania', 'excessive sexual drive', 'hypersexual disorder', 'sexual addiction', 'sexual compulsivity', 'sexual dependency', 'sexual impulsivity' and 'paraphilia-related disorder'. Historical names include 'Don Juanism', 'nymphomania' and 'satyriasis'. The clinical concept of 'sexual addiction' was popularised by the publication of the book *Out of the Shadows: Understanding Sexual Addiction* (Carnes, 1983). Carnes, a counsellor and sex educator in the field of addiction, saw 'sexual addiction' as based on certain distorted core beliefs and proposed that 'sex addicts' suffer extremely low self-esteem and experience themselves as worthless and unlovable. Carnes (1997, p.15) describes characteristics of 'sex addicts' as follows:

- They have a pattern of out of control sexual behavior
- They continue in that pattern even though it is destroying their lives
- They will often pursue dangerous or high-risk sex
- They are sexual even when they do not intend to be
- They have serious life consequences because of their sexual behavior
- Their sexual behavior affects their work, hobbies, friends, and families
- They use sex to help them control their moods and manage stress and anxiety
- They obsess about sexual things so much that it interferes with day-to-day living
- They may have periods when they extinguish all sexual behavior and become sex aversive.

Quadland, a sexuality researcher, introduced the term 'sexual compulsivity' (Quadland, 1985), conceptualising it as impairment of volition, and out-of-control behaviour related to a heightened sexual appetite, linked to both paraphilic and non-paraphilic disorders. The terms 'sexual addiction' and 'sexual compulsivity' have been a subject of debate resulting in a hybrid term 'sexual compulsivity/addiction' (Coleman, 1986). Kinsey Institute researchers have outlined a theoretical model, a dual-control theory explaining 'high risk sexual behaviours', linked to high sexual excitation levels, and low inhibitory reactions as having a tendency towards promiscuity and what could be called 'sexual addiction' (Bancroft et al., 2003b). Reid, Carpenter and Lloyd (2009) described 'excessive involvement in sex' as a behaviour with a high potential for damaging consequences in terms of individual physical and mental health, the relationship wellbeing, and financial stability. While the concepts of 'sexual addiction' and 'sexual compulsivity' have been widely accepted and popularised, many sexologists and psychosexual therapists oppose the use of this label and its implications for conceptualisation and treatment. Kafka, a psychiatrist and academic, suggested the term 'hypersexuality disorder' (Kafka, 2010, 2014), defining it as 'disinhibited or exaggerated expressions of human sexual arousal and appetites' (Kafka, 2014, p.281). Kafka proposed diagnostic criteria for 'hypersexuality disorder' as recurrent and intense sexual fantasies, urges and behaviours involving one or more of the following (p.283):

- Excessive time spent on sexual fantasies and planning of engagement in sexual behaviours
- Repetitive engagement in these in response to dysphoric mood states (such as anxiety, depression, boredom, irritability), or in response to various life stresses
- Disregarding the risks of such behaviours
- Repetitive but unsuccessful efforts to stop or reduce these behaviours.

The diagnosis of this disorder, according to Kafka, should only be made if there are signs of significant distress attached to these behaviours, or significant adverse consequences affecting the person's social life, work situation and relationships. He does not consider it as a sexual dysfunction or a paraphilic disorder, but as an impulsivity disorder, acknowledging that there is a significant lack of empirical data in this area (Kafka, 2014).

Kaplan and Kruger (2010) distinguish sub-types of 'hypersexual behaviour':

- *Compulsive masturbation sub-type:* compulsion to masturbate causing distress and/or social, occupational or psychological problems
- *Compulsive pornography use:* compulsion to watch pornography recordings or internet pornography sites resulting in distress

- *Compulsive sexual behaviour involving consenting adults:* excessive sexual behaviour appearing to be of compulsive nature and causing distress to the person
- *Telephone sex dependence:* usually associated with financial losses and patient distress related to the compulsive nature of the behaviour
- *Strip-clubs dependence:* no systematic research has been done in this area; however, clinical experience suggests that this type of dependency can cause concern and distress to the persons seeking treatment
- *Cybersex dependence:* compulsive online sexual talk for the purposes of sexual pleasure, causing distress.

There is some clinical evidence that cybersex has become one of the most frequently reported sexually addictive behaviours, write Delmonico, a researcher into internet psychology and Griffin, a family therapist (2015). These authors define 'cybersex' as including: 'both the viewing of pornography as well as sexual interactions with others using digital media. These sexual encounters with others online may either remain in the digital environment, or may be used to pursue sexual contact in the offline world' (Delmonico & Griffin, 2015, p.238). While the intersection between 'sex addiction' and cybersex requires further research, it is important to recognise that not all online sexual activity has a negative impact on its users (Delmonico & Griffin, 2015). An extensive research study (Cooper, Delmonico & Burg, 2000) found that 80% of cybersex users belong to the category of 'recreational users', and do not experience any problems related to their online activity. However, 20% report significant problems and within those, some experience devastating and long-lasting consequences.

Griffiths (2004) noted that the internet can be used for a number of different purposes related to sexual interest, such as: educational purposes; buying or selling sex-related products; seeking out sexual therapists; seeking out sexual partners for enduring relationships; seeking out sexual partners for sexual satisfaction; exploring gender and identity roles by assuming a different gender in online relationships, and using internet images for entertainment and/or masturbatory purposes. Griffiths concludes that very few of these behaviours are likely to be potentially excessive, addictive, obsessive or compulsive (p.192). Griffiths (2004) argues that 'internet sex addiction' can be relevant if the following characteristics are exhibited:

- *Salience* – when internet sex dominates the person's thinking (preoccupations), feelings (cravings) and behaviour (deterioration of socialised behaviour)

- *Mood modification* – engaging in internet sex creates a 'buzz', a 'high' or feeling of 'escape'
- *Tolerance* – use of the internet increases over time
- *Withdrawal symptoms* – moodiness and irritability, for example, result from reduced or discontinued use of internet for sex-related purposes
- *Conflict* – internet use conflicts with the person's relationships, work, and social life
- *Relapse* – the tendency to revert back to the same extreme patterns of internet use after a period of abstinence or control (Griffiths, 2004, p.194).

Fong, a psychiatrist and researcher from UCLA (University College Los Angeles), posits that the reasons for the lack of formalised criteria for diagnosing this phenomenon and the lack of a unified definition lie in the heterogeneous presentation of 'problematic sexual behaviour'; it presents itself in a variety of forms and degrees of severity: some clients present features that resemble an addictive disorder, i.e. they continue engagement with the problematic behaviour despite serious psychological, physical and potential legal consequences; sometimes the behaviours fit the picture of an impulse control disorder, featuring irresistible urges and impulses to act out sexually; some demonstrate sexual obsessions and compulsiveness that resemble obsessive compulsive disorders (Fong, 2006).

The debate around the use of the labels related to 'problematic/excessive sexual behaviour' continues, reflecting vast disagreements in the fields of sexual medicine, sexual therapy, psychiatry and psychology as to how to understand and relate to this complex phenomenon. The American Association of Sexuality Educators, Counselors and Therapists (AASECT) founded in 1967, a major US organisation devoted to the promotion of sexual health, published a position statement on 'sex addiction' in December 2016, recommending a non-pathologising approach to adult consensual sexual behaviours. The statement emphasises that in the absence of significant empirical evidence to support the classification of sexual addiction or pornography addiction as mental health disorders, linking problems related to sexual urges, thoughts and behaviours to 'sexual addiction' cannot be endorsed (AASECT, 2016). AASECT 'recognizes that people may experience significant physical, psychological, spiritual and sexual health consequences related to their sexual urges, thoughts or behaviors'. However, the organisation claims that 'sexual addiction training and treatment methods are not adequately informed by accurate human sexuality knowledge' and therefore 'advocates for a collaborative movement to establish standards of care supported by science, public health consensus and the rigorous protection of sexual rights for consumers seeking treatment for problems related to consensual sexual urges, thoughts or behaviors.' Proponents of anti-pathologising, anti-medicalisation views on sexuality (Tiefer, 2004; Kleinplatz, 2014; Davies, 2016) oppose any labelling of high levels of sexuality, advocating that it brings forth pathologising views imposed by social control and the practices of stigmatisation, constraining personal choice and freedom. Douglas Braun-Harvey, a sexual health author, sexuality educator and marriage and family therapist from the University of Minnesota, and Michael Vigorito, a sexual health psychotherapist and marriage and family therapist practising in Washington, offered an alternative model for considering the label of 'sexual addiction', based on a non-pathologising and empowering approach (Braun-Harvey & Vigorito, 2016). They contrast the addiction model to sex, which focuses on certain sexual activities such as paying for sex, using sexual entertainment sites and having multiple partners, to their sexual health model which focuses on basic principles of sexual communication. The six fundamental sexual agreements and principles, according to these authors, are: *consent*; engaging in *non-exploitative* sexual interaction; creating a *good plan* to avoid unwanted consequences such as pregnancy and sexually transmitted diseases; interacting with *honesty and transparency*; understanding *shared values* of a sexual activity; and acknowledging the *right to sexual pleasure* (Braun-Harvey & Vigorito, 2016). The authors state that these principles have been developed out of current research and from the World Health Organization definition of sexual health as: 'the state of physical, emotional, mental and social well-being related to sexuality', not purely the absence of pathology. Furthermore, it states:

> Sexual health requires a positive, respectful approach to sexuality and sexual relationships, as well as the possibility of having pleasurable and safe sexual experience free of sexual coercion, discrimination and violence. For sexual health to be attained and maintained, the sexual right of all persons must be respected, protected and fulfilled (World Health Organization, 2006, p.6).

In challenging the idea that sex can become an addictive process, Braun-Harvey and Vigorito draw attention that the sexual addiction model grew out of the fear of HIV and AIDS in the 1980s. They propose reconsidering the popular notions of addictive sex based on fear and pathologisation, stressing the importance of sexual rights of adult consenting sexual partners. They consider that there may be a small proportion of the population having a problem with regulating their sexual behaviour, which usually appears in conjunction with substance abuse and psychiatric issues; however, these situations do not justify the label of 'sexual addiction'. The sexual health model is based on the concept of 'out-of-control sexual behaviour' (OCSB), defined as: 'a sexual health problem in which an individual's consensual sexual urges, thoughts, or behaviors feel out of control' (Braun-Harvey & Vigorito, 2016, p.28). 'Feeling out of control' differs from 'being out of control' within this model, as the authors are interested in the clients' subjective experience of their out-of-control behaviour and unique set of vulnerability factors that hinder their motivation and ability to achieve a unique personal vision of their own sexual health. Braun-Harvey and Vigorito deliberately exclude the concept of 'personal distress' from the definition, given that personal distress can be caused by partner's distress, unreasonable expectations, or societal pressures and prejudices. 'These situations', the authors state, 'may cause a client distress, but may not motivate him towards sexual health' (p.31). They propose the concept of 'self-discrepancy' instead, meaning the discrepancy between one's sexual urges, thoughts and behaviours, and one's personal vision of sexual health.

The question of who decides on what is problematic and subversive behaviour and whether it should change remains a crucial challenge in this whole area, raising not only professional, theoretical and practical, but also ethical and political concerns. The normality criteria used in research are predominantly statistical and clinical (Tiefer, 2004) which, according to sexology research, assumes that what the majority does is 'normal'. Coleman (1995) cautioned: 'Overpathologizing this disorder is an ever-present danger. Professionals with conservative or restrictive attitudes about sexuality are likely to impose a pathological label on normative sexual behavior' (p.333). Lastly, research on female use of pornography and the internet for sexual purposes is probably amongst the most subjugated discourses currently in the sexology field.

A chart of theoretical perspectives on 'hypersexuality' is shown in Figure 4.14 to draw attention to the diversity and controversy surrounding the concept.

Diagnosis and assessment

DSM-III (APA, 1980) had sub-classified paraphilic disorders including 'Don Juanism' and 'nymphomania' as psychosexual disorders 'not otherwise specified'. DSM-IV-TR (2000) included in the same category a condition described as 'distress about a pattern of repeated sexual relationships involving a succession of lovers who are experienced by the individual only as a thing to be used' (APA, 2000, p.582). 'Sexual addiction/compulsivity' is excluded from DSM-5 (APA, 2013). However, many sexology researchers, educators, clinicians and therapists believe in the importance of this diagnosis so that the right treatment can be provided. Reid, Carpenter and

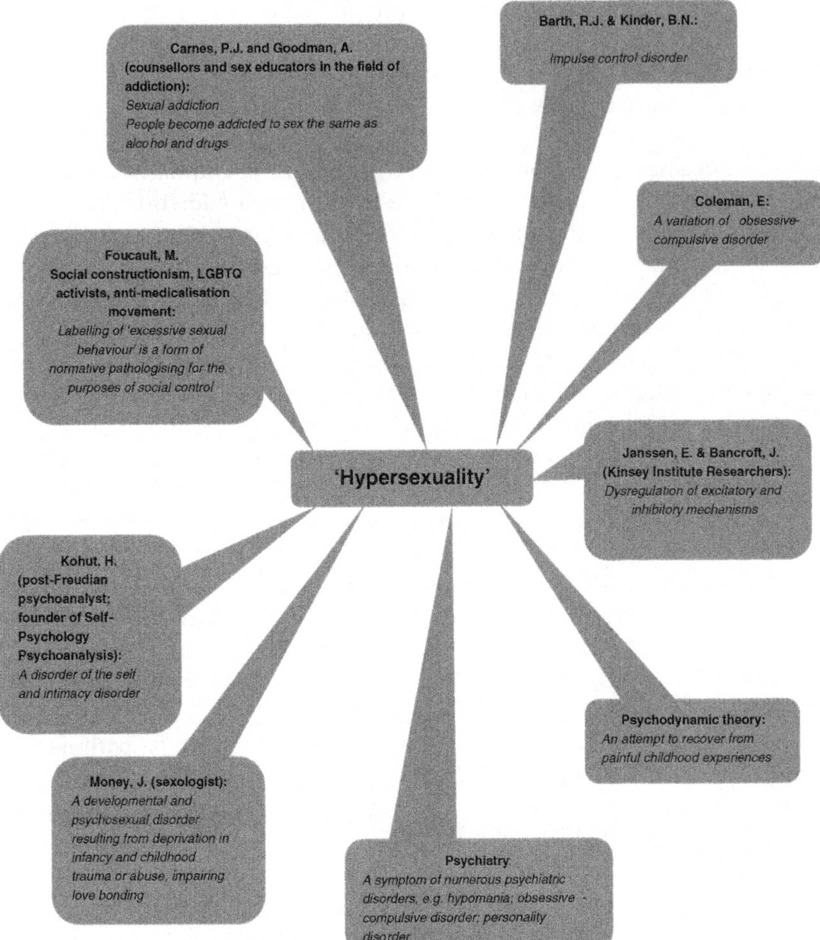

Figure 4.14 'Hypersexuality': theoretical perspectives

Lloyd (2009, pp.54–55), for example, emphasise the extremely damaging nature of this condition, bringing to the sufferers a series of losses at the level of relationships, employment and sometimes serious legal consequences. They propose that a careful assessment should include questions such as:

- Do you often find yourself preoccupied with sexual thoughts?
- Do you try unsuccessfully to manage your sexual behaviour?

- How much time do you spend thinking about sex or pursuing sexual encounters?
- Have you neglected important social, occupational, or recreational activities because you were thinking about or pursuing sex?

The importance of a thorough initial screening is emphasised by many sexology clinicians. Believers in the label of 'sexual addiction' claim that sexually addictive behaviours typically occur in conjunction with other difficulties, such as sexual dysfunction, other addictive habits, substance abuse and various mental health issues. Therefore, it is proposed that the assessment process uses a variety of tools and techniques, including medical examination, personality tests and sexual addiction tests, such as: the Sexual Addiction Screening Test, the Hypersexual Behavioural Inventory, and the Sexual Compulsivity Scale. These inventories could be used both as a diagnostic tool, and as a resource for therapeutic conversations, to inspire client's reflection. Clients are often encouraged to complete a structured written sexual history including detailed accounts of their sexual experiences since the onset of their sexual activity (Delmonico & Griffin, 2015). Such detailed assessment also serves the function of establishing a contextual understanding of the presenting concerns. 'It is important to remember', warn Delmonico and Griffin (2015), 'that sexual health and deviance are often culturally and individually defined' (p.242). Therefore, enquiring into the specific circumstances of the clients' sexual concerns may reveal the context which brought forth a pathological story. Sometimes clients present an overwhelming guilt about their sexual behaviours, constructing a self-diagnosis of 'sexual obsession' and similar, based on constricting, puritanical beliefs about sex. Equally, partners of the 'identified client' can instigate a deep concern triggered by the client's infidelity, masturbatory practice, use of pornography, or an expression of particular sexual interests to which the partners may attach strong negative feelings and judgements. Each case must be considered in the context of the information about the specific circumstances that surround it. Schneider (2000) advises that, in addition to enquiring about the frequency and the types of sexual behaviours, particular attention is paid to the consequences of 'sexual addiction':

- *physical* (e.g. rape, sexually transmitted diseases, physical injury)
- *psychological* (e.g. depression, shame, relationship problems)
- *and social* consequences, such as financial, legal or employment problems.

Hagedorn and Juhnke, from Florida International University, have developed the acronym WASTE Time to assist a structured interview with clients presenting the problem of 'sexual addiction'. The clinician would ask questions to address each of the acronym's letters which correspond to one or more diagnostic criteria for 'sexual addiction':

W- (*Withdrawal*): 'Have you experienced any withdrawal symptoms when you are unable to engage in sexual activities?' (e.g. anxiety, depression, anger, irritability and other negative mood states)

A- (*Adverse consequences*): 'Have you experienced any negative or adverse consequences as a result of your sexual behaviours?' (e.g. relationship breakdown, career and/or financial problems, physical injury or psychological trauma)

S- (*Inability to stop*): 'Have you attempted to cut back, control, or stop your sexual behaviours without success, even when you know that continuing will cause you harm?' (typical responses may include multiple attempts at stopping or controlling addictive behaviours without success)

T- (*Tolerance for intensity*): 'Have you found it necessary to increase the amount of intensity of your sexual behaviours to achieve the same effect?' (e.g. moving from compulsive use of internet pornography to sexual encounters with multiple anonymous partners, or from compulsive voyeurism or exhibitionism to compulsive stalking or rape)

E- (*Escape*): 'Do you use sexual activity as an escape from negative mood states, such as stress, anxiety, depression, sadness, loneliness, or anger?'

Time: 'Have you found yourself spending a lot of time preparing for, engaging in, or recovering from a sexual activity?' (e.g. ritualistic behaviours, such as cruising all evening in search of a sexual conquest, or use of addictive chemicals in preparation for sexual activities); 'Have you been spending more time and/or more resources on your sexual activities than you intended?' (e.g. hours spent on the internet, loss of sleep due to an entire weekend spent on voyeuristic activities) (Hagedorn & Juhnke, 2005, pp.76–77).

The authors hold that an affirmative answer to one of the above questions suggests a strong possibility of 'sexual addiction', while affirmative answers to two or more of the above questions suggests a high probability of 'sexual addiction', warranting immediate professional intervention, including counselling, self-help group support, or inpatient hospitalisation (Hagedorn & Juhnke, 2005, p.77).

Delmonico and Griffin (2015, p.242) advise using questions that can help distinguish between an overly concerned attitude and problematic sexual behaviours, for example:

- Have you made efforts to reduce the frequency of your sexual behavior?
- Have you experienced any consequences as a result of your sexual behaviors?
- Do you find yourself constantly thinking about and/or planning sexual behavior?

Davidson, Cheung and Jansen (2017) propose that the following questions are included in assessment: 'Did your parents have trouble with sexual behavior?' 'Do you often find yourself preoccupied with sexual thoughts?' (p.284). Clearly, the potential for pathologising perspectives is evident from many of the questions above in the absence of evidence-based diagnostic criteria.

Davies, a British psychotherapist and sex therapy educator, the founder of Pink Therapy, a service for working with LGBTQ clients, challenges the dominant discourse on sexual addiction as devaluing and excluding those who are: single; whose religious/moral beliefs are outside the Judeo/Christian tradition, who are polyamorous or in any other way non-monogamous, those who enjoy sex just for pleasure/recreation (without commitment), and those who are attracted to same-sex partners (particularly gay men) (Davies, 2016). Assessment questions aimed at identifying whether the criteria for the diagnosis of 'sexual addiction' have been met are vague and open to subjective interpretation, claims Davies. Moreover, they are based on socially and culturally induced negative beliefs about sex, assuming that giving into sexual desire/lust is a bad thing and that using sex to relieve anxiety or to help us feel better is abnormal. Due to the sex-negative society we live in, people often feel ashamed of their sexual fantasies and interests and feel guilty for their failed attempts to restrict their sexual desires (Davies, 2016).

Lack of consensus and a clash of perspectives in this context can lead to confusion amongst professionals and their clients alike. However, proposing set diagnostic criteria can be equally questioned, even if drawn from consensus and evidence-based practice, as these are also dependent on the subjectivity of the proposers and their chosen criteria. Plummer, a researcher into social psychology and the sociology of deviance, cautioned: 'the boundary between "being in control sexually" and "being out of control sexually" depends on the therapist's value orientation and purposes' (Plummer, 2002).

Prevalence

Prevalence is difficult to determine given the lack of consensus about the definition of the problem. Furthermore, it is not clear what is being measured and on the basis of which criteria. Some research studies estimate that 17 to 37 million Americans struggle with 'sexual addiction disorder' (Wolfe, 2000). Given the affordability, accessibility and anonymity of sexually explicit material available on the internet, the incidence of 'sexual addiction' is rising, claim psychology researchers and academics from the University of Florida (Hagedorn & Juhnke, 2005). A New Zealand study on 900 participants found that 13% of men and 7% of women reported 'out of control' sexual thoughts, fantasies and behaviours; however, only 4% of men and 2% of women thought this had a negative impact in their lives (Skegg et al., 2010). Kafka (2014) summarises research studies related to what he regards as 'hypersexual disorder'. For example, some studies suggest 'hypersexual disorder' may be common amongst men exhibiting paraphilic behaviours (Kafka & Hennen, 2003). Men and women with paraphilic behaviours describe their sexual behaviours as obligatory, repetitive and stereotyped, and sexually arousing fantasies, urges and behaviours as extremely time-consuming (Black et al., 1997). Carnes, Coleman and other sexology researchers describe pathological 'crushes', 'obsessional fixations' or 'love addictions' as predominant female experiences of sexual compulsivity, according to Kafka (2014). McCarthy and McCarthy (2012, p.55) claim the issue of 'sex addiction' and internet pornography is amongst the most controversial subjects in the field of human sexuality. They argue that the majority of men (over 80%) who occasionally use internet porn do not abuse it, and stress the importance of distinguishing the compulsive, addictive use of the internet from a non-abusive one.

Factors contributing to sexual compulsivity, addiction or hypersexuality

Factors discussed in sexology literature by the proponents of the need for the diagnostic classification of the phenomena related to 'hypersexuality'/'sexual addiction'/'sexual compulsivity' are presented in Figure 4.15 using the MOST model map as a way of providing information about existing views rather than a statement of agreement with the pathological emphasis.

Emotional factors

Certain individual characteristics have been associated with behaviours that may be grouped under the label of 'hypersexuality', such as: low self-esteem,

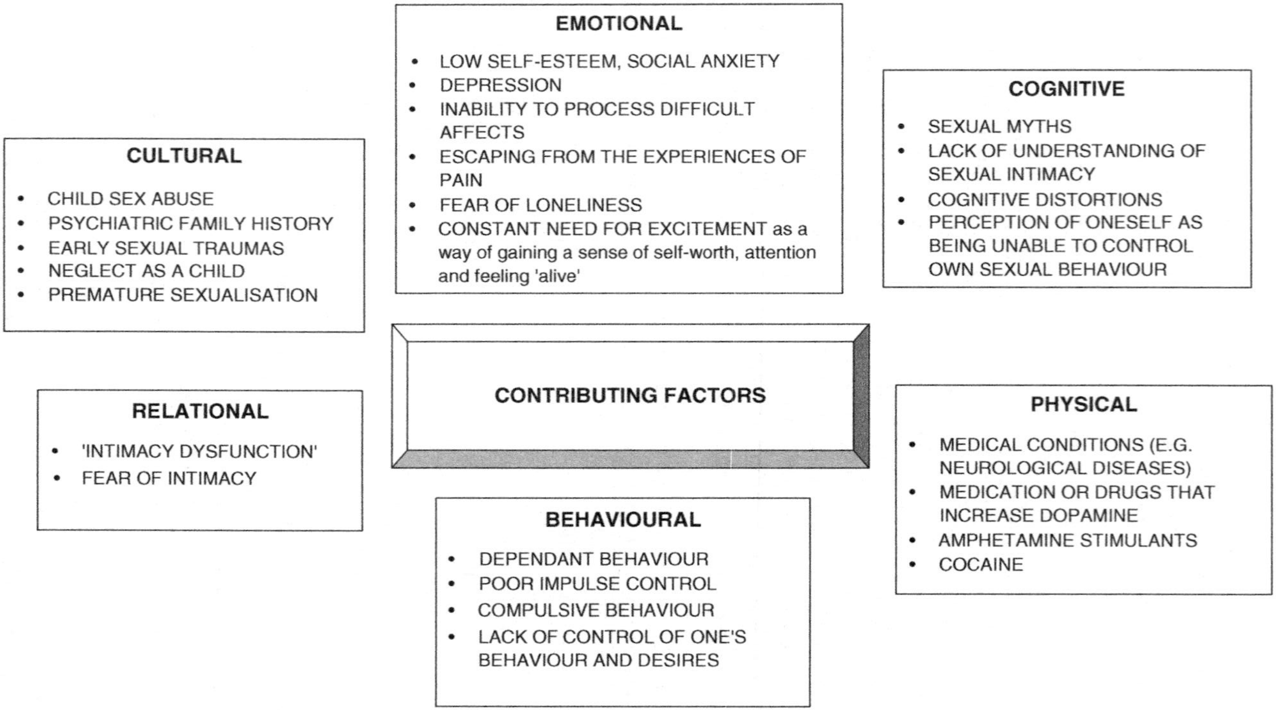

CONTRIBUTING FACTORS

EMOTIONAL

- LOW SELF-ESTEEM, SOCIAL ANXIETY
- DEPRESSION
- INABILITY TO PROCESS DIFFICULT AFFECTS
- ESCAPING FROM THE EXPERIENCES OF PAIN
- FEAR OF LONELINESS
- CONSTANT NEED FOR EXCITEMENT as a way of gaining a sense of self-worth, attention and feeling 'alive'

COGNITIVE

- SEXUAL MYTHS
- LACK OF UNDERSTANDING OF SEXUAL INTIMACY
- COGNITIVE DISTORTIONS
- PERCEPTION OF ONESELF AS BEING UNABLE TO CONTROL OWN SEXUAL BEHAVIOUR

CULTURAL

- CHILD SEX ABUSE
- PSYCHIATRIC FAMILY HISTORY
- EARLY SEXUAL TRAUMAS
- NEGLECT AS A CHILD
- PREMATURE SEXUALISATION

RELATIONAL

- 'INTIMACY DYSFUNCTION'
- FEAR OF INTIMACY

PHYSICAL

- MEDICAL CONDITIONS (E.G. NEUROLOGICAL DISEASES)
- MEDICATION OR DRUGS THAT INCREASE DOPAMINE
- AMPHETAMINE STIMULANTS
- COCAINE

BEHAVIOURAL

- DEPENDANT BEHAVIOUR
- POOR IMPULSE CONTROL
- COMPULSIVE BEHAVIOUR
- LACK OF CONTROL OF ONE'S BEHAVIOUR AND DESIRES

Figure 4.15 Sexual compulsivity, addiction or hypersexuality: contributing factors

low mood, high anxieties, obsessive thoughts and worries, and proneness to feeling ashamed of own sexual behaviour (Reid, Carpenter & Lloyd, 2009). Issues to do with loss and grief often surface when clients bringing 'hypersexuality' concerns begin to address their sexual behaviour, which can serve the purpose of escaping from the experience of emotional pain (Delmonico & Griffin, 2015). Fear of loneliness may underlie 'hypersexuality', manifesting itself as a constant search for excitement and a way of gaining a sense of worth, attention and feeling 'alive' (Kafka, 2014).

Cognitive factors

Clinical experience suggests that many clients have distorted views on what constitutes sexual intimacy and hold various sexual misconceptions. Delmonico and Griffin (2015) suggest a particular technique, 'concentric circles', that can be used to identify views on sexuality; clients draw three concentric circles and place the sexual behaviours they are avoiding in the centre; the sexual behaviours that may or may not be acceptable for them depending on their emotional state in the middle, and in the outer circle, the healthy sexual behaviours they may or may not be practising, which represent the desired behaviours towards which they strive.

Perception of oneself as being unable to control one's own sexual behaviour constitutes a significant factor in the construction of one's sexual 'self-schema' (Nobre & Pinto-Gouveia, 2009), undermining self-esteem and convincing the person that they lack the power to overcome their unwanted sexual activities. Sexology researcher John Money (1986) created the concept of 'lovemaps', a set of beliefs and cognitions that get imprinted into the brain at a very early age. In case of problematic sexuality, such 'lovemaps' usually stem from deprivation in infancy and childhood trauma and abuse, impacting a healthy development of sexuality and impairing love bonding.

Physical factors

Some sexology clinicians and researchers suggest a link between 'hypersexuality' and certain medical conditions, e.g. neurological diseases, brain injury and dementia. In such cases, the diagnosis of 'hypersexuality' should not be made, warns Kafka (2014). Sexology researchers are split in views regarding the role of neurochemistry in 'sexual addiction' and 'hypersexuality'. Some argue that 'sexual addiction' is an inherent neurobiological issue (Hilton & Watts, 2011). Some believe that neurobiological changes in the brain are a consequence of trauma, stress and other external pressures leading to 'hypersexual' behaviour (Money, 1986). Others support the neurochemistry argument based on pharmacological research: certain medications, such as drugs that increase dopamine in the brain and other medication used for the treatment of Parkinson's disease, and amphetamine stimulants, can be associated with sexual disinhibition (Kafka, 2014). On the other hand, many scientists emphasise the lack of clear evidence of the causal connection between neurochemistry and 'hypersexuality' (Ley, Prause & Finn, 2014).

Behavioural factors

Individual characteristics of the persons suffering from 'hypersexuality' have been linked with compulsive behavioural patterns and poor control of one's impulses, sexual behaviours and desires (Kafka, 2014). Some sexology studies linked excessive solitary use of pornography with sexual aggressiveness and increased difficulties in intimate relationships (Manning, 2006).

Relational factors

Fear of intimacy and social anxiety have been stated as significant factors in the aetiology of 'hypersexuality', leading individuals to resort to paid sex or cybersex in maintaining anonymity and preventing emotional closeness. These behaviours can then escalate into out-of-control, compulsive use (Kafka, 2014).

Some researchers consider that early attachment problems underlie 'sexual addiction', interfering with the development of adult, emotionally invested, both romantic and non-romantic relationships (Keane, 2004). Many sexologists have described 'hypersexuality' as an 'intimacy dysfunction' (e.g. Coleman, 1995).

Clinicians of various theoretical convictions issue advice to include the partner in the assessment and treatment wherever possible, both for diagnostic and therapeutic purposes.

Cultural factors

Child sexual abuse and early sexual traumas that remain unresolved in adulthood are seen in a high percentage of clinical presentations whereby sexually 'addictive' behaviour becomes a way to compensate for feelings of neglect, abuse and violation (Delmonico & Griffin, 2015).

Dyspareunia in men

Definitions and diagnosis

DSM-IV-TR diagnosed dyspareunia as recurrent or persistent genital pain associated with sexual intercourse in either a male or a female, causing a marked distress or interpersonal difficulty. The disorder was classified in the same sub-type categories as the other sexual dysfunctions, generalised (meaning occurring in all sexual situations) vs. situational (occurring only in certain sexual situations); lifelong (existing since the onset of the first sexual activity) vs. acquired (beginning after a period of pain-free sexual activities), and was graded in intensity as mild, moderate and severe (APA, 2000). Exclusion of male dyspareunia from DSM-5 (APA, 2013) is a consequence of its under-researched status and the high likelihood that the nature of the disorder is primarily medical (Bergeron, Rosen & Pukall, 2014). Given this situation, one is confined to investigating medical resources in search of an empirical definition. For example, Aviva Medical Dictionary (www.aviva.co.uk) describes two forms of presentations of this disorder:

- *Painful ejaculation,* a sudden pain in the penis, perineal region, testicular area or pelvis, which happens during or after ejaculation
- *Chronic prostatitis* or chronic pelvic pain that persists independently of a sexual activity and can be aggravated during sex.

A different term, urological chronic pelvic pain syndrome (UCPPS) is sometimes used to describe similar symptomatology such as chronic pelvic pain syndrome, or interstitial cystitis (Shoskes et al., 2009).

There are no specific diagnostic tests for identifying male dyspareunia. It is diagnosed on the basis of a thorough assessment involving a detailed sexual history and physical examination for the presence of physical factors that are seen as potentially causing the problem, such as Peyronie's disease, phimosis and infections of the uro-genital tract. If a medical condition is found to be the cause for dyspareunia, the diagnosis of a sexual dysfunction will not be made. If no organic cause can be established, it is considered that the condition is likely to be of a psychological nature; however, lack of research on the topic poses dilemmas as to how to diagnose and treat the problem.

Prevalence

Male dyspareunia has been far less researched than the female genital pain, therefore the prevalence of this disorder is unclear. In addition to the limited studies, the lack of an agreed definition of the disorder makes interpretation of data more difficult (Luzzi & Law, 2005). Limited research results suggest that it is much less prevalent than female sexual pain disorder; the rates being between 5 and 15% (Bergeron, Rosen & Pukall, 2014). Most long-term statistically significant studies focus on the specific medical conditions underlying sexual pain, such as prostatitis and

Peyronie's disease (Oommen & Hellstrom, 2010). In a US national survey of 58,955 outpatients' visits to physicians, 5% of complaints referred to genito-urinary tract symptoms; prostatitis was listed as a diagnosis in nearly 2 million encounters annually (Collins et al., 1999). The incidence of painful ejaculation among men of 50 years of age and above was found to be between 1 and 6.7% (Blanker et al., 2001). A study conducted on 4,000 men in Australia suggested that 5% of men suffer from pain associated with sexual activity (Pitts et al., 2008). Due to the social stigma surrounding male sexual pain, it is possible that under-reporting of the problem influences its official statistics of prevalence.

Factors contributing to dyspareunia in men

A big gap in literature and research exists on male dyspareunia. The MOST map in Figure 4.16 summarises contributing factors, factors that could aggravate the psychological wellbeing and the interpersonal functioning of the man, and the effects of this disorder on his psychological and relational functioning. These are derived from limited clinical experience and literature sources (Bergeron, Rosen & Pukall, 2014; Meana, Maykut & Fertel, 2015).

Emotional factors

Limited clinical experience shows that low self-esteem, anxiety (particularly performance anxiety), shame, fear, and guilt related to sex may be the underlying factors contributing to the development and persistence of male dyspareunia. A vicious cycle can get created whereby the existence of such emotions can contribute to further aggravation of the symptoms and in turn undermine the man's self-esteem, cause more fear and anxiety and intensify his insecurity in his sexual role. These then become risk factors for the development of sexual dysfunctions, such as premature ejaculation or erectile disorder. Equally, stress, worries, depression, low mood and tiredness can underlie the problem of painful sex and also further contribute to its persistence. Kaplan (1993) described post-ejaculatory pain syndrome resulting from the involuntary spasm of the muscles of male genitalia, which can be triggered by a variety of emotional difficulties and stresses. More recent research studies found an association between depression and chronic prostatitis causing genital pain (Wu et al., 2006).

Cognitive factors

Focus on pain and anticipation of pain will interfere with sexual activity and pleasure, aggravating the problem. As a result, the man can develop negative

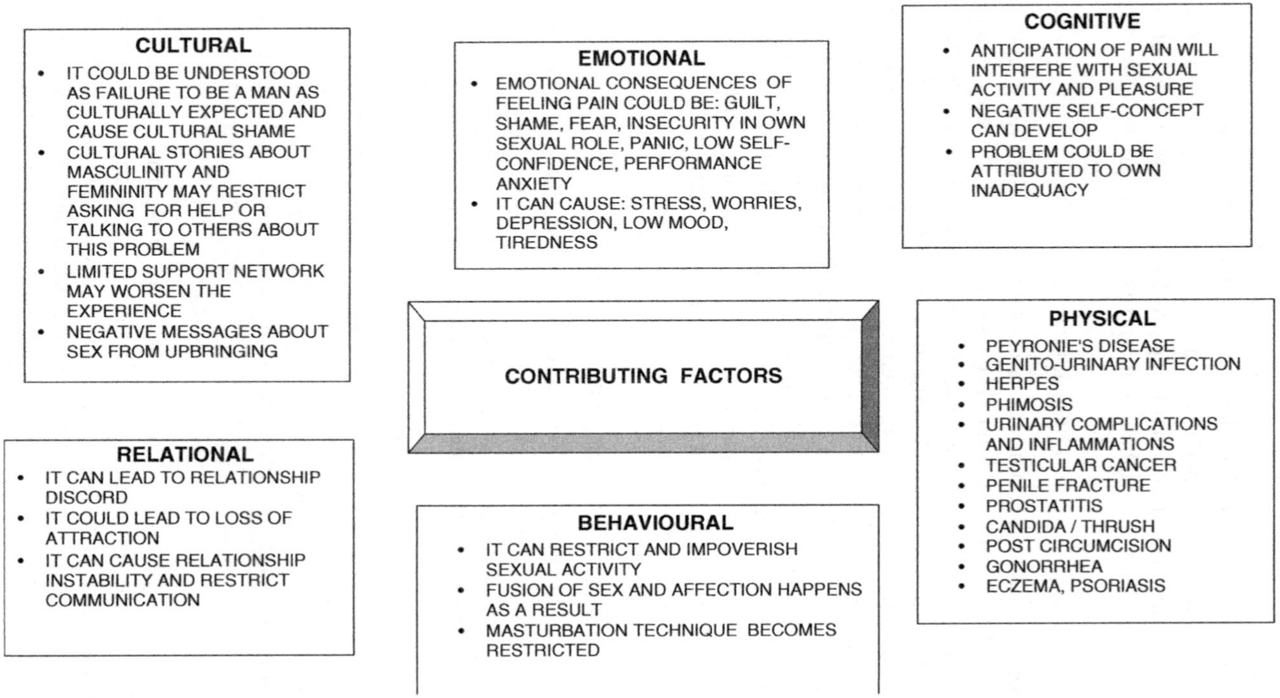

CULTURAL

- IT COULD BE UNDERSTOOD AS FAILURE TO BE A MAN AS CULTURALLY EXPECTED AND CAUSE CULTURAL SHAME
- CULTURAL STORIES ABOUT MASCULINITY AND FEMININITY MAY RESTRICT ASKING FOR HELP OR TALKING TO OTHERS ABOUT THIS PROBLEM
- LIMITED SUPPORT NETWORK MAY WORSEN THE EXPERIENCE
- NEGATIVE MESSAGES ABOUT SEX FROM UPBRINGING

EMOTIONAL

- EMOTIONAL CONSEQUENCES OF FEELING PAIN COULD BE: GUILT, SHAME, FEAR, INSECURITY IN OWN SEXUAL ROLE, PANIC, LOW SELF-CONFIDENCE, PERFORMANCE ANXIETY
- IT CAN CAUSE: STRESS, WORRIES, DEPRESSION, LOW MOOD, TIREDNESS

COGNITIVE

- ANTICIPATION OF PAIN WILL INTERFERE WITH SEXUAL ACTIVITY AND PLEASURE
- NEGATIVE SELF-CONCEPT CAN DEVELOP
- PROBLEM COULD BE ATTRIBUTED TO OWN INADEQUACY

CONTRIBUTING FACTORS

RELATIONAL

- IT CAN LEAD TO RELATIONSHIP DISCORD
- IT COULD LEAD TO LOSS OF ATTRACTION
- IT CAN CAUSE RELATIONSHIP INSTABILITY AND RESTRICT COMMUNICATION

BEHAVIOURAL

- IT CAN RESTRICT AND IMPOVERISH SEXUAL ACTIVITY
- FUSION OF SEX AND AFFECTION HAPPENS AS A RESULT
- MASTURBATION TECHNIQUE BECOMES RESTRICTED

PHYSICAL

- PEYRONIE'S DISEASE
- GENITO-URINARY INFECTION
- HERPES
- PHIMOSIS
- URINARY COMPLICATIONS AND INFLAMMATIONS
- TESTICULAR CANCER
- PENILE FRACTURE
- PROSTATITIS
- CANDIDA / THRUSH
- POST CIRCUMCISION
- GONORRHEA
- ECZEMA, PSORIASIS

Figure 4.16 Dyspareunia in men: contributing factors

self-concept or negative sexual self-schema (Nobre & Pinto-Gouveia, 2009). Given his low self-esteem in the situation and insecurity in his sexual role, he could attribute the problem to his own inadequacy, and develop a belief in his own lack of capability to deal with the pain. An area of future research with this condition might explore the potential impact of sexual misconceptions and negative beliefs about sex and sexual pleasure.

Physical factors

A number of medical conditions are commonly cited in literature as underlying dyspareunia in men, such as Peyronie's disease (where the penis becomes curved which might cause pain during erection and penetration), phimosis (tight foreskin), genito-urinary infections, urinary complications and inflammations, genital herpes, testicular cancer, penile fracture, prostatitis, candida, and other sexually transmitted diseases (Luzzi & Law, 2006). Medications such as antipsychotics and antidepressants are found to be associated with male dyspareunia as well. In some instances, discomfort during penetration results from skin irritation caused by an allergic reaction to a particular brand of condom or spermicide (www.aviva.co.uk). The experience of painful sex can both stem from and further contribute to negative body image.

Behavioural factors

Assessment should explore the sexual technique and establish where exactly the pain occurs and what the specific triggers are. According to the model of fear-avoidance developed within research of chronic pain and disability (Vlaeyen & Linton, 2000), painful sex may result in avoidance of sexual activity thus aggravating the problem, by the same pattern as described in the section on female genito-pelvic pain/penetration disorder in this chapter. Painful sex can also impair sexual activity, including masturbation (if pain occurs during masturbation as well). As a consequence of painful sex, fusion of sex and affection happens whereby any physical contact is avoided, further impoverishing the sufferer's physical, emotional and relational intimacy.

Relational factors

Anticipation of pain can seriously interfere with the sexual activity, potentially lead to relationship discord and cause relationship instability, exacerbating the problem. Incompatibility of partners' sexual preferences and desires might be an aggravating factor in the development and persistence of this condition. Some research studies strongly indicate that both men and women experiencing painful sex do not communicate this to their partners (Herbenick et al., 2015). Lack of communication, often combined with the avoidance of sex, can cause relationship conflict or distancing. The man might lose attraction to the partner by associating sex with a difficult and painful situation.

Cultural factors

Traumatic experiences from childhood including sexual and emotional abuse are often cited in relation to the aetiology of this disorder. Negative messages about sex from upbringing, stemming from family, education, religious orthodoxy and wider culture may contribute to the development of male dyspareunia. The experience of painful sex may be understood as a failure to meet the cultural expectations of being a man, and cause cultural shame. Prejudicial cultural stories about masculinity and femininity may inhibit asking for help or talking to others about this problem. Such a limited support network may worsen the experience.

Anodyspareunia-anal sex

The term 'anodyspareunia' was introduced by the researchers from the University of Minnesota (Rosser et al., 1998) to describe a sexual dysfunction associated with anal sex between men who have sex with men (MSM). They defined anodyspareunia as recurrent or persistent pain experienced by the receptive partner during anal intercourse, suggesting its inclusion in the DSM. Based on a sample of 197 homosexual men, painful anal intercourse was found to be a common, yet previously unacknowledged difficulty (Rosser et al., 1997). Damon and Rosser (2005) continued this work by researching the condition further, and focused on developing diagnostic criteria for it. They explored the experiences of 404 men who engaged or attempted to engage in receptive anal sex. Only 10% met clinical criteria for anodyspareunia; 14% met behavioural criteria but high levels of distress and interpersonal difficulty was reported by only 25% of those. The findings suggested that the four primary factors in experiences of anal pain were:

- *Psychological factors*; these were identified as: inability to relax; fear associated with the threat of pain, physical damage, acquiring an infection, or faecal accidents; and implications of being labelled as homosexual. Fear would sometimes reach the level of phobic reaction, interfering with sexual pleasure. Continued experiences of pain may lead to feelings of failure as a lover and may develop into deep guilt and shame.

- *Size of the penetrating penis*; this was another factor reported in the experience of painful receptive anal sex. Some other studies confirmed this physical factor as contributing to this condition (e.g. Underwood, 2003).
- *Lack of digito-anal foreplay and lack of lubrication* were the further factors reported in the aetiology of this condition; insufficient ano-receptive preparation such as digital stimulation, massage, lubrication and similar behavioural and physical factors were noted as important and often necessary preconditions for relaxation and successful anal intercourse.
- *Medical factors related to anal health problems* were reported with 19% of those who recounted experiences of anal pain; these include haemorrhoids, anal fissures and infections such as anogenital herpes, and perianal abscess.

The authors state that the pain caused by the last three factors should not be classified as a disorder; in this situation behavioural change, appropriate education and medical treatment could helpfully modify the practice of anal intercourse and enable positive change.

Damon and Rosser (2005) concluded that anodyspareunia has many parallel features to dyspareunia in women, in terms of prevalence, mental health consequences and participants' experiences that psychological factors are of primary importance. More recent research on male dyspareunia found similar patterns of sensitivity, pelvic floor muscle function and neural activation between men and women (Davis et al., 2011). Hollows, a specialist in sexual health medicine, however, argues that the issues of painful anal sex amongst gay men should not be measured by heterosexual standards. 'Differences', claims Hollows, 'can be discussed on almost every level, including anatomical, medical, behavioural, motivational, psychological and not least, gender-related aspects' (Hollows, 2007, p.437). Hollows goes on to critique DSM categorisation of sexual pain disorders being based on genital symptomatology, whilst, he stresses, depending on the sexual behaviour, pain can be experienced in other anatomical locations including the breasts, oral cavity or indeed, anal area. Furthermore, Hollows accentuates that anal sex does not equate exclusively to penile-anal penetration; various other parts of the anatomy may be used to stimulate and/or penetrate the anus, including the tongue (rimming), fingers, hands and forearm (fisting or handballing), as well as various objects and sex toys (e.g. vibrators, butt-plugs, etc.). Heterosexual women and gay men can experience orgasm as a result of anal penetration without any direct genital stimulation (Underwood, 2003). It is not known what proportion of heterosexual men receives pleasure during anal stimulation from a female partner (Hollows, 2007). Equally, anal sex and anodyspareunia in lesbian relationships does not seem to have been a subject of research studies.

Given that anal sex has been one of society's most persistent taboos, it is surrounded by common widespread myths, based on ignorance and homophobia. These myths include, for example, that: *'anal sex is dirty'*; *'perverted'*; *'unnatural'*; *'immoral'*; *'physically dangerous'*; that it *'always causes pain'*; that *'only gay men have anal sex'*; that *'all male receptive partners secretly want to be women, punished or humiliated'* (Hollows, 2007, p.430).

Few researchers have studied anodyspareunia and to date the phenomenon is lacking in empirical evidence on its prevalence, manifestations and subjective experiences. Anal sex has been associated with gay male sex; however, studies and clinical experience confirm that it is an increasingly practised heterosexual behaviour yet not much is known about female anodyspareunia. In the 2013 study by British National Survey of Sexual Attitudes (NATSAL), one of the largest scientific studies of sexual behaviour in the world, 13.4% of men and 10.5% of women reported having practised heterosexual anal sex (Mercer et al., 2013), compared to the respective figures of 7% and 6.5% in 1990 (Johnson et al., 2001). In a large survey in the USA, 40% of men and 35% of women reported anal sex with an opposite sex partner in their lifetime (Mosher et al., 2005). The UK Gay Men's Survey (Sigma Research, 2006) sampled 14,477 UK men; 70% reported having practised insertive and 65.5% receptive anal sex with a male partner. Although the percentage is high, it still highlights that a significant proportion of gay men do not engage in either insertive or receptive anal intercourse.

Assessment: discussion and conclusions

This chapter addressed definitions and diagnostic criteria for sexual disorders as described in sexology literature including DSM, recent research studies and sexology textbooks. It focused on the assessment of sexual dysfunctions emphasising certain factors that typically accompany various sexual difficulties. It is not possible to present an all-encompassing description of every factor that may contribute to each sexual problem and for all client situations, but hopefully this gives some ideas as to how to approach assessment of different sexual concerns and how to understand their development over time. The factors listed on the MOST model maps offer additional guidance in that direction, while further reading may be necessary in order to inform therapists in providing the most effective clinical service.

In debating the benefits and adverse effects of making a diagnosis, the medical and the psychotherapy fields seem split. From a social constructionist perspective, diagnoses are seen as dangerous, even harmful, while sexology science regards them as essential in order to ensure the right direction for treatment. The following pages will discuss both perspectives and outline their theoretical and practical integration within a 'both-and' framework.

Advantages and disadvantages of a diagnosis: towards a 'both-and' perspective

The importance of establishing a correct diagnosis when working with sexual issues in psychotherapy is proposed in sexology and sexual therapy, for the purpose of having a clear focus and helping clients and therapists to understand the nature and characteristics of the presenting difficulties, which, in itself, may contribute to the effectiveness of treatment. By contrast, from a social constructionist perspective, diagnoses provide narrow explanations and pathologise the person by fitting them into the pre-existing limiting and deficit-based categories, while suppressing the individual's uniqueness. The problem with diagnosis is that it can be seen as obscuring the contribution of economic life, media images, and social and cultural factors by over-focusing on a decontextualised individual (Gergen, Hoffman & Anderson, 1996, p.103). Furthermore, they assert the superior social authority of the oppressive hierarchical systems of dominance and power, taking away the client's voice and their subjective experience (Foucault, 1980). Diagnoses are seen as misleading people to believe that they are a true representation of reality whereas, from a social constructionist perspective, realities are multiple, multifaceted and open to a variety of different interpretations. 'Is it the diagnostic reality we should be treating in therapy?' asks Harlene Anderson (Gergen, Hoffman & Anderson, 1996, p.105), suggesting alternative questions, such as:

> What is the intent of a diagnosis? What questions are believed to be answered by a diagnosis? What information is thought to be gained? What do we want a diagnosis to communicate and to whom? If there are many ways to think about, to describe what may be the same thing (i.e. behaviours, feelings), how can we respect and work within these realities? Should we consider the possibility of multiple diagnoses? How can we bring the client in the process? How can, and is it possible for a diagnosis to be meaningful for all involved? How can it be collaborative, tailored to the individual, useful? (p.105)

Social constructionist therapists question the ethics of a diagnosis, for example Hoffman (in Gergen, Hoffman & Anderson, 1996) talks about the 'tyranny of diagnosis' and the harmfulness of labelling, whereby 'every move a person makes is dysfunctionalized' (p.106). Gergen (Gergen, Hoffman & Anderson, 1996) adds humans are 'too complex to slot into categories' and Anderson and Goolishian (1992) view diagnostic activities as concretising identities that limit people and form obstacles to more viable and liberating self-definitions. White (2007) sees diagnostic categories as objectifying the person, and reducing the person to the problem. A social constructionist favours a more mutual, personalised knowledge of the person, a jointly created description of the person via co-operative language that generates more possibilities than professional vocabularies based on pre-knowledge that produces lifeless, sterile look-a-likes (Anderson & Goolishian, 1992). Therapy is communication, a dialogue, not a monologue of a singular voice of diagnostic labelling practices, emphasises Gergen (Gergen, Hoffman & Anderson, 1996).

A 'both-and' approach of the MOST model used as a framework in this book brings together sexology and systemic social constructionist views, appreciating *both* the importance of establishing a correct diagnosis in terms of constructing a meaningful definition of the problem, *and* considering multiple contextual influences impacting a sexual problem. The model combines sexology perspectives to inform understanding of the nature and the characteristics of the clients' difficulties, while simultaneously embracing a perspective that diagnoses are social constructions and as such are relative, often approximate, and potentially stigmatising. Equally, it is important to consider that clinical experience suggests that diagnoses can also be normalising. On hearing the diagnosis of vaginismus, for example, many clients have felt reassured as a result of learning that their experience is shared by many other women, and is a condition known to clinicians, who have studied it and have a level of expertise in diagnosing and treating it. Female genital pain which had no evident organic cause was historically treated as 'all in the women's mind', indicating it was imagined, exaggerated, misinterpreted, all-in-all a non-existent issue. This brought forth aggravation of the symptoms and increased distress to the women suffering from it. The inclusion of this syndrome in the official classification of sexual disorders has reassured those women, respecting their subjective experience and acknowledging the pain as 'real' and to be taken seriously, not as a psychological illusion but as an actual physical, bodily felt sensation. A major question for this integrated approach becomes not *whether* to consider or discard a medical perspective and the relevance of a diagnostic system, but *how* to include it? How to make it relevant and useful to the client and communicate it within collaborative interaction with the client? The biological context is included in the MOST model amongst many other contexts within which a problem can be situated and understood. In this way, a medical perspective is utilised as part of a wider outlook on clients' presenting difficulties, ensuring that many perspectives are included and valued as potentially helpful contexts, enriching a comprehensive understanding of the multidimensional nature of sexual issues. To rephrase Tiefer's 'constructionist project', which she describes as: 'to define and locate sexuality in personal, relational, and cultural, rather than physical, terms' (2004, p.23), within the framework of the MOST model, it would be: 'to define and locate sexuality in personal, relational, cultural, *and* physical, terms'.

Maps of contributing factors are intended as a resource, informed by the extensive knowledge base from sexology informing clinicians as guidelines, rather than as a fixed norm. In their assessment, formulation and treatment of sexual difficulties, clinicians should be fully alert to clients' idiosyncrasies, differences and discrepancies from generalised lists. Clients must be included in the diagnostic process and their voice continually invited and their expertise on their lived experiences listened to with the utmost care. This does not exclude a respectful challenge, for instance, demystifying unhelpful mythology impeding clients' possibilities. The therapeutic relationship in this integrated model becomes a fusion of shared expertise and an 'interplay of prejudices' as Cecchin described it, acknowledging that any view has limitations and is based on privileging certain assumptions (Radovanovic, 1994). Such a therapeutic relationship, as Anderson states (Gergen, Hoffman & Anderson, 1996), challenges professional knowledge as well:

> It moves therapy from a relationship between a knower and one who is ignorant to a collaborative partnership in which the deciding of, the exploring of, and the 'solving' of problems is a process of shared inquiry, in which the diagnosis is not fixed and the problem may shift and dissolve over time (p.106).

The phrase 'therapeutic stories co-constructed' used in the diagrammatic depiction of the MOST model signifies this collaborative expertise and acknowledges the inevitability of prejudices. Gergen writes (Gergen, Hoffman & Anderson, 1996): 'I don't as a therapist observe dysfunctional behavior. I observe behavior that I label as dysfunctional given a set of values which I hold about what is functional' (p.107). It is within this perspective that the model is presented here and proposed to professionals as a resource to apply as and when they see it will benefit their clinical work. It is the ethical position of this integrated model that diagnostic manuals, while providing a helpful set of definitions, guidelines and parameters describing the particular characteristics of a disorder, its prevalence, likely causes and the most commonly presented features, are also social constructions of empirically based research and of the current interpretations of its findings. No therapy practitioner should use these guidelines rigidly as a true representation of objective reality.

The next section will offer further thoughts on how the information provided in this chapter could be used for constructing a formulation in systemic psychosexual therapy, informed by both the medical science and the discourse of social constructionism.

Formulation in systemic psychosexual therapy

In creating a formulation in systemic psychosexual therapy, sexology, sex therapy and systemic social constructionist perspectives and practices are integrated.

According to sexology and sex therapy practices:

- one of the goals of assessment is to develop a coherent case formulation i.e., a working hypothesis of the aetiology of the problem
- this formulation should relate to all aspects of clients' complaints and explain why the individual has developed the difficulties
- thus helping clients to understand their presenting problem in the context of their physiology, medical history, and life experiences
- which gives the clients hope and restores their optimism, building up their resources for change
- and provides a rationale for clinicians upon which to devise a therapeutic plan (Wincze & Weisberg, 2015, p.107).

The steps involved in presenting a formulation to clients described in sex therapy literature are the following:

1. Review the presenting problem, including normalising the problem and providing education where appropriate.
2. Review the clients' strengths in the biological, psychological and social domains.
3. Identify the factors that appear to be responsible for development and maintenance of the problem.

4. Invite clients' feedback including adding any other relevant information.
5. Outline the specific treatment components for addressing causal factors, especially the maintaining factors associated with the dysfunction (Wincze & Weisberg, 2015, p.107).

Step 3, identifying causes of the dysfunction, is seen as the core of the formulation. In presenting the causal factors as well as treatment plan, clinicians are advised not to encourage debate and keep their leading role consistent and clear, in order to give clients the confidence and reassurance of being in the hands of experts.

According to systemic social constructionist practices:

- a formulation would not be presented as 'objective reality' but as one possible view of which the therapist takes ownership. A formulation can be tentative and often includes questions that suggest areas for further exploration. Ideas incorporated in the formulation are not regarded as 'correct' and 'true' but are best viewed in terms of their usefulness for the client (Johnstone & Dallos, 2012); they are based on a provisional, good-enough-for-now hypothesis, held as temporary and subject to feedback and review as new information emerges through the interaction between the therapist and the clients (Vetere & Dallos, 2003)
- the language of 'difficulty', 'complaint' and 'concern' is generally preferred as opposed to the language of 'dysfunction' and 'disorder', considering that labels can be oppressive and lead to the further pathologising of the client's situations, and reinforce the initial problem (White, 1991)
- a formulation offers a multidimensional perspective considering clients' significant relationships such as: partners, immediate and extended family, social network of support, as well as their network of concern (McAdam, 1995). Gender, age, race, culture, religion, ability, employment, class, and other contexts of diversity and power may be included (Carter & McGoldrick, 1999). The therapist's task is seen as broadening the individualistic and linear causal definitions that clients and referring professionals often bring to therapy by encouraging a wider contextual understanding of the situation, going beyond blame and stigmatisation. Problem-saturated definitions, based on individually focused explanations, are seen as likely to perpetuate existing difficulties. A definition that respects the interpersonal level, considers wider contexts, and appreciates resources and resiliencies thus precluding a pathological focus can, in itself, be healing. It can invite clients to see how they may participate in unwanted repetitive patterns in their relationship (Pearce, 1994), therefore drawing attention to their power to change these dynamics. To enable a

shift from a problem-saturated couple identity to a more desired, preferred one (White, 1991) would be seen as a significant therapeutic aim.

Formulation in systemic psychosexual therapy: integrating sexology, sex therapy and systemic social constructionist perspectives

Formulation in systemic psychosexual therapy can be offered as a separate session in a structured therapy process involving specific stages: assessment, formulation, presentation of treatment options and goals, followed by a summary of the treatment process. Equally, formulation can be woven into sessions as an ongoing feature of the therapist's transparency (White, 1991), whereby the therapist's ideas and hypotheses about the clients' issues are shared with them openly and continuously throughout the therapeutic process.

Assessment information can be incorporated into a formulation under the following headings:

- *Definition of the problem*: from both sexology/sex therapy and systemic perspectives, it can be helpful for clients to hear a summary of their presenting problems from the therapist's point of view. This should be offered in a clear, concise and specific way, using language that has significance for the client. It is often useful for the clients to hear how their presenting concerns may be seen to fit or not fit in the existing diagnostic criteria. The therapist could briefly summarise the prevalence of the symptomatology according to relevant sexology research studies, both enhancing the client's understanding of their difficulties and potentially providing a context for normalisation. To enable a multidimensional perspective, the definition of the problem could be based on the MOST diagram, outlining factors contributing to the development and persistence of the presenting problem, incorporating the different dimensions of the client's lived experience. The diagram could be presented to clients in written form, to facilitate their engagement with the information presented, and enhance their understanding of the issues and, in particular, their comprehension of the multifaceted nature of the presented difficulty.
- *Resources and resiliencies:* resources and resiliencies, typically explored as part of assessment, should have a prominent place in a formulation. How do clients usually deal with difficulties in their lives? What helps? What are they good at? What are the best aspects of their relationship? What do they appreciate about each other? What motivates them? What do they enjoy? Responses to these questions could be used as a means of

enhancing therapeutic effects and supporting therapeutic interventions. The purpose of the formulation is both to establish a shared view on the problems brought to therapy, and to highlight clients' strengths and resiliencies. The therapeutic aim would be to utilise these resources and build on them while respecting clients' choices, preferences and priorities.

- *Expectations and aims of therapy:* in systemic psychosexual therapy, the therapist typically explores clients' expectations of successful therapeutic outcomes with questions such as: How do you see a successful outcome of therapy? What would you like to happen by the end of therapy? Sometimes clients are encouraged to look beyond the presenting problem, e.g.: Besides the presenting sexual problem, what else would you like to see being different in your relationship? They are encouraged to take a proactive, constructive part in therapy, taking active responsibility for therapy processes and outcomes: What would each of you be prepared to do in order to contribute to the positive change?, the intention being for clients to experience the empowering effects of therapy by actively involving them to participate in the creation of their therapeutic processes and aims (McNamee & Gergen, 1992). For some clients, the very act of starting therapy may, in their own minds, confirm their sense of failure, which, unless addressed, can adversely affect the outcome of the therapeutic process. Therefore it is useful to include in the formulation explicit appreciation of the clients' responsibility for taking the step to commence therapy as a means to overcoming their difficulties. Therapeutic aims, co-constructed between the therapist and the clients, are then summarised as part of the formulation.
- *Treatment options:* treatment options could be explained using the MOST diagram, particularly if the summary of the origins and the contributing factors have already been presented to clients in that format. Alternatively, they could be briefly summarised, outlining that the treatment would, for example, consist of a combination of physical exercises, medical interventions (administered by medical practitioners), couple communication enhancement techniques and individual reflections. Clients can then be offered the chance to comment, seek elaboration or clarification or add any suggestions from their point of view.

Ethical considerations in creating a formulation

The client's genuine involvement (Johnstone & Dallos, 2012) is of ultimate importance in communicating a formulation. To include the clients' voice, the therapist uses co-operative language, is open to being challenged and disagreed with and consults the clients on their views (Vetere & Dallos, 2003) in co-constructing a collaborative process whereby both the therapist and the clients are the experts (Markovic, 2010).

Within a social constructionist framework of systemic psychosexual therapy, the therapist's self-reflexive awareness of their own thoughts, feelings and reactions is regarded a crucial part of their professional ethical responsibility. The therapist would be reflecting internally on their own stories about sex, couples, relationships and intimacy, as well as their own power position in terms of professional status, gender, class, ethnicity, ability and other elements of social difference, and how these might impact the therapeutic process and the formulation. The therapist would be monitoring and exploring their own sexual myths, prejudices, gender expectations of sexual roles and beliefs about what is normal, what is pathological, what is acceptable or not in sex, and what their therapeutic role is supposed to be in this context. The types of questions listed below illustrate this self-reflexive enquiry: What hypothesis am I privileging? What informs me in my view about these clients? How do I feel about these clients? Which of my stories have their histories most touched on? Whose perspective do I believe in and how come I believe in it? How do I stay sensitive and attentive to the clients' needs as opposed being guided by my own views and stories about couples, sex and the desired ways of sexually relating?

Questions suggested by Harlene Anderson (Gergen, Hoffman & Anderson, 1996, p.115) related to the ethics of the diagnosis could be applied to the ethics of the formulation, and the meaning of it for the client that professionals should consider in the process of constructing and delivering a formulation: If there is a formulation process, towards what aim and who determines that aim? What meaning does the formulation have for each person involved? What meaning does it have for the client? Is it a useful meaning? Is it respectful? Does it allow for the opening of doors – the creating of potentials – or does it close the doors and restrict possibilities? Does it perpetuate the problem? Does it create new problems?

EXERCISES

- Make an outline of how you could create a formulation for an existing client, following the principles stated in the last section of this chapter.
- Discuss when a formulation can be helpful and necessary and when it may be irrelevant, unhelpful, or even harmful.

5

TREATMENT OPTIONS FOR SEXUAL DYSFUNCTIONS

Introduction

Treatment options are usually introduced as part of the formulation session. Clients are invited to contribute their comments and suggestions to the treatment plan and ask questions about issues they consider relevant. Specific treatment aims should be made clear to enable clients to mindfully engage with the therapeutic process. Working within this integrated frame, treatment is comprehensive and relates to all dimensions from the MOST model. Depending on the case, the emphasis placed on some dimensions may be greater than on others. This may change and shift over time as the process of therapy evolves and different issues get highlighted. If the problem is assessed as purely medical, psychosexual therapy may or may not be necessary, depending on the client's choice. A medical problem may bring about sexual and relationship issues, or adversely affect the client's self-image or emotional state, so psychotherapy may help with these while the medical treatment is separately undertaken.

Most typically, problems brought to psychotherapy are maintained by a multifaceted set of factors requiring a strategy that appreciates a multidimensional perspective. As in Chapter 4, each sexual 'disorder' will be discussed separately, in relation to various interventions that are typically used. Interventions comprehending sexology, sex therapy and systemic therapy will be outlined as relevant to particular presenting issues. Some of these apply to many or all sexual difficulties, while others are relevant only to particular ones. For example, sensate focus, a cornerstone of sex therapy, can be a helpful tool when working with a wide variety of presenting difficulties. Various techniques addressing the MOST dimensions that have been described and illustrated in Chapter 1 could be used effectively with a range of sexual difficulties. To avoid repetition, interventions that apply across different issues will be summarised, before focusing on specific sexual problems and types of treatment methods indicated for each. Specific methods and approaches are presented below within the structure of the MOST model, while keeping in mind that interventions can be relevant to and affect more than one dimension simultaneously.

The emotional dimension

Emotionally focused therapy (EFT)-based interventions

Because of its emphasis on a client's processing and reflection on emotional experiences, this approach is summarised within the emotional dimension; however, it also has significance for the relational, cultural and cognitive dimensions.

EFT (Johnson, 2004, 2013), an approach integrating attachment theory (Bowlby, 1969; Vetere & Dallos, 2008) and the systemic approach, focuses its interventions on helping individuals and couples to recognise the fears and attachment vulnerabilities underlying their repetitive patterns of anger and blame. Recognising the underlying emotion is followed by the therapist enabling the client to deepen their experience of the emotion in the present, and distil it, i.e. help the client own it and see its place in the repetitive cycles of their relationship interactions. The final part of the process is for the client to disclose their emotional experience to their partner, sharing their insights about the connection between their own vulnerability and repetitive interpersonal patterns. EFT sees unwanted repetitive patterns in couple communication as deeply rooted in attachment anxieties, seeking a secure base in their partners in ineffective ways that in turn only increase insecurities and extend the problematic interchanges. The therapist's task is seen as facilitating the couple's recognition of both the patterns they create in this way and the feelings that drive such repetitive cycles. By taking this 'meta-perspective' with respect to the patterns, the problem is shifted from being the fault of one or both partners to the 'repetitive negative cycle' being responsible for both partners' distress. Through this process, similar to the externalising conversations of narrative therapy (described later on in this section), the cycle becomes the problem, uniting the couple against a joint enemy.

Attachment narrative therapy (ANT)

ANT is an approach that integrates attachment theory, the systemic approach and narrative therapy, while emphasising the crucial importance of the therapeutic relationship. Creating a secure base within a trusting, non-judgemental and accepting therapeutic environment is seen as a context in which clients can feel safe to explore, express and reflect on their emotional experiences and where therapy can support emotional, cognitive and relational development (Vetere & Dallos, 2008).

The theoretical aspects of different approaches integrated within ANT are summarised below:

- Attachment theory's perspective that people need a secure base and a sense of safety and protection in relationships to enable them to form strong and satisfying emotional bonds is a fundamental premise of ANT. According to attachment theory, psychological problems develop from early experiences of separation and emotional deprivation, which can influence adult relationships. Secure attachment is manifested by a positive view of others as caring and of oneself as worthy of love and care; anxious, avoidant and ambivalent attachments are forms of insecure attachments manifesting themselves in relationship tension, conflict or distancing, leading to potential emotional dissatisfaction.
- Systemic aspects particularly relevant to ANT are a focus on patterns and processes in relationships over time, as well as the importance of the construction of meaning in understanding communication. The systemic link between meaning and context and the inclusion of wider social and cultural contexts of power and difference such as gender, race, religion, sexuality, class, age, ability, economy and employment are integrated within this view (Burnham, 2011). The systemic techniques that are considered as particularly relevant to 'dismissive attachment patterns' of growing up, replicated in adult relationships and manifested in emotional withdrawal and downplaying of the significance of emotions are: enactment, empathic questioning, a caring and comforting approach and de-escalating unsafe relational patterns. Systemic techniques seen as helpful in addressing 'preoccupied attachment patterns', whereby emotional expression is heightened, often leading to a symmetrical escalation of feelings including accusation and blame, are: use of genograms and timelines, tracking repetitive patterns, mapping relationships, circular and reflexive questions, and identification of individual, family and cultural beliefs.

- Drawing on certain aspects of the narrative approach, ANT explores how people story their experiences and live through narrative constructions, and within this, how it is that some stories become dominant and others remain marginalised. The ANT approach contends that early attachment experiences in families shape our capacity to reflect on emotions and our narrative ability to tell coherent stories about our lives (Vetere & Dallos, 2008).

ANT framework involves four stages:

1. The beginning involves creating a secure base in therapy whereby the therapist warmly, carefully and attentively listens to concerns, identifying unhelpful interpersonal patterns through a full exploration of the problematic emotional responses and needs, beliefs and behaviours as well as resources and resiliencies.
2. The second stage involves exploring narratives and attachments within a systemic framework, encouraging clients to move on from problem- and often blame-saturated narratives to a more reflective place. Any vulnerabilities, unfulfilled needs and emotional insecurities, which are brought to the surface, are then contextualised within trans-generational attachments, and cultural pressures and expectations.
3. De-escalating unhelpful patterns and considering alternatives evolves from building on suppressed stories of vulnerabilities and unmet needs; therapy encourages clients to take a different action, to soften and become less critical and engage in taking relational risks.
4. The ending stage, working towards the future, involves consolidating the changes achieved and supporting the development of the clients' shared narrative on how the change was brought about and what they have contributed to it.

This approach can be helpful in treating various sexual difficulties, and can be applicable to working both with individuals and couples. It stresses the importance of naming, understanding and reflecting on the process of clients' emotional responses as well as listening, feeling heard and understood, being present and attuned to the partner, being able to support, calm and comfort the partner and to receive their support. It is a process that can take time, as slowing down can prove crucial in some situations when working through difficult moments and helping clients to regulate their emotional reactivity. Dallos and Vetere (2014) offer possible questions to prompt the exploring of early attachment experiences, which can be used as a guideline both in assessment and treatment of sexual and relationship difficulties:

- When you were upset and frightened as a child, what happened? Who did you turn to?
- How did you get to feel better? Who helped you to feel better? How did they do this?
- What have you learnt from this for your own family? What else happened?
- What do you want to do the same? What do you want to do differently?
- How do people comfort each other in your own family/relationships? (Dallos & Vetere, 2014, p.500).

The cognitive dimension

Reframing

Reframing is a therapeutic technique used in different psychotherapy approaches and is particularly prominent in family therapy, solution focused brief therapy and narrative therapy. It involves re-description of a behaviour, feeling or experience, aimed at helping clients to see their situation in a new light, from a different perspective. It is based on the premise that the way in which people perceive an experience influences how they feel about it and ultimately what choices they see for themselves, and what action they take as a result. Milton H. Erickson based his approach to psychotherapy on the premise that: 'patients have problems because of learned limitations. They are caught in mental sets, frames of reference and belief systems that do not permit them to explore and utilize their own abilities to best advantage' (Erickson & Rossi, 1980, p.38). Child and family psychologist, sex therapist and academic, Gerald Weeks (1977) provided many examples of how negative labels could be turned into positive ones through the act of reframing, such as:

- 'passive' – ability to accept things as they are
- 'antisocial' – carefully selecting one's acquaintances
- 'controlling' – structuring one's environment
- 'impulsive' – ability to let go; spontaneous
- 'self-deprecating' – admitting one's faults, and so on (Weeks, 1977, p.286).

Reframing can be achieved by using different kinds of linguistic expressions, such as questions, stories, metaphors, tasks, suggestions, hypotheses, re-descriptions and wonderings. However, reframing is not simply re-labelling. It requires being in tune with the way the clients see the situation:

> Successful reframing must lift the problem out of the 'symptomatic' frame and into another frame that does not carry the implication of unchangeability. Of course, not any other frame would do, but only one that is congenial to the person's way of thinking and categorizing of reality (Watzlawick, Weakland & Fisch, pp.102–103).

Bandler and Grinder (1982) suggested a question for therapists as a guideline for using reframing; 'How else could I describe the same situation?' (Bandler & Grinder, 1982, p.15). The concept of 're-storying' from narrative therapy compares to reframing in that it evolves the developing of an 'alternative story or narrative' (White & Epston, 1989) of the client's life, leading to 're-authoring' of life experiences.

While using reframing, care ought to be taken so that it is not perceived as a way of minimising the problem or the pain and suffering the situation may have caused to clients. Instead, it should be put forward as a method of empathising and validating one's feelings, while proposing new language that may open up an alternative, non-blaming perspective that offers hope and engages clients in a more optimistic outlook.

Psycho-education

Clinical experience implies that elements of psycho-education play a significant part in psychosexual therapy. It can take the form of:

- Suggesting to clients to read specific texts, books or watch selected films, TV shows or theatre plays; or watch Internet-based material, such as YouTube videos or Ted Talks.
- Straightforward educational input by the therapist, sometimes supported by diagrams, photographs or drawings.

Psycho-education can be relevant to all sexual issues and can be a vital part of psychosexual therapy. The purpose of it is seen as:

- Helping dispel misinformation
- Reducing anxiety
- Providing accurate information
- Offering new perspectives
- Fostering attitudinal change

- Supporting use of new behaviours
- Suggesting new thoughts, ideas and viewpoints (Weeks, Gambescia & Hertlein, 2016, p.197).

The physical dimension

Improving body image

Looking after one's physical health and fitness contributes to feeling good about oneself, which in turn can increase sexual satisfaction. Encouraging a healthy lifestyle, regular exercise, maintaining good fitness levels, taking care of nutrition and avoiding toxic substances can be helpfully included in the treatment of all sexual concerns.

The following exercise, applied in sex therapy (Hallam-Jones, 2004), can be used for improving body image. The client draws a basic outline of their body and on a scale of 1–5 (with 5 being what they most like and 1 what they like the least) they score parts of the body and make a note of it on the actual drawing. The therapist should encourage a detailed list, to include eyebrows, eyelashes, fingernails, and so on, so that as many aspects as possible are included. The second part of the exercise involves devoting particular positive attention to those body parts, starting with the ones that are liked the most. This involves, for example, looking in the mirror noticing and appreciating the colour of one's eyes, or looking after one's body parts in more detail than usual, giving them special care and attention. The exercise then gradually progresses step-by-step, from the most-liked to the least-liked features. The therapist should normalise the fact that not all the parts are ever equally liked and that is probably unrealistic and unnecessary that one likes every bit of their body. However, a sense of ownership and positive acceptance can significantly improve by engaging in exercises such as this. Typically, with clients presenting sexual concerns, the genital areas are amongst the least liked. When these are included in the exercise, clients can treat them in the same way as with other parts of their body: paying close attention, gently stroking them, applying a nice lotion, caressing them with a foamy sponge in the bath, buying some pretty lingerie, looking at them more closely with curiosity, open-mindedness and kindness.

Exploring the conduciveness of the physical environment

The physical environment is always relevant to explore as it often has an impact on the sexual experience. Environmental factors are sometimes underestimated in terms of the effect they may have on sexual desire and sexual experience. At the same time, therapists should not assume what type of environment is more or less conducive for sex, as individual preferences vary in that respect; the noise next door, being likely to be overlooked from the building opposite, or heard from the street, may be oppressive for some and fantasy inspiring for others.

The behavioural dimension

Sensate focus

Given its prominent place in sex therapy, sensate focus will be described in some detail and further guidance can be found in various sexology and sex therapy literature (e.g. Weeks, Fife & Peterson, 2016). Originally developed by Masters and Johnson (1970), sensate focus exercises are particularly indicated when there is excessive focus on performance and the outcome of sex at the expense of enjoyment of the process in the moment (Wincze & Weisberg, 2015). The basic goal is to create sensual and sexual experience in a context that is free of anxiety. It is designed to produce a feeling of safety in an undemanding environment rather than a sense of pressure for the couple (Weeks & Gambescia, 2000, p.129). An outline of this exercise will be provided in the text that follows, while drawing attention to the importance of tailoring it to the couple's needs and adjusting the timing, pacing and specific instructions as relevant to the couple and their presenting sexual problem. In setting sensate focus, the therapist's task is to explain its purpose, which varies depending on the client situation, for example; enhancing sexual communication, equalising sexual participation, undoing of unsatisfactory habitual sexual patterns and developing new ways of sexually relating or increasing self- and mutual understanding. The therapist needs to explain that people react very differently to the sensate focus experience and normalise the variety of possible reactions. Therapy sessions are typically arranged at bi-weekly intervals with a certain amount of time devoted to reflect on the sensate focus experience. The couple is encouraged to seek clarification as and when it feels necessary to them, ensuring that they understand the purpose of this activity.

The exercise consists of a series of graduated steps that the couple is instructed to follow in the privacy of their own space and time, ideally two to three times a week and as previously agreed between them. The couple are required to abstain from any other form of sexual activity while engaged in this process and to adhere to the agreed structure and timing. The therapist determines when to move onto the next stage based on feedback from the clients. There is a degree of variety as to how different sex therapists take the couple through the various stages.

Step One

This consists of sensual touching of the whole body, avoiding only anogenital areas and breasts. The couple are advised to allocate one-and-a-half hours and ensure that the environment is conducive in terms of privacy and comfort. They may start the ritual by having a shower or a bath, together or separately. The lighting, temperature and other features in the room are jointly arranged. They may prefer to do this exercise completely or partially naked. The roles are clearly divided at this stage in that: one member of the couple first lies face down for ten minutes and then on their back for the same amount of time, while the other one touches them all over, everywhere from top of their head to the toes, avoiding anogenital areas and the woman's breasts. This touch is not a massage but may resemble one. There is no prescribed way of touching, this is an 'exploratory mission'. It may be stroking, caressing, tapping, slight pinching or a combination of all of these, going over the body with the hands in no particular order with no specific goal other than to explore what it feels like in the moment. The couple are advised that it is not a sexual activity and that there is no intention to get aroused or to arouse the other person, but if arousal happens, to ignore it and continue without acting on those feelings. Suggestions such as: 'Focus on what you are feeling, sensing, thinking...' emphasise that there is no right or wrong, and to tune into anything that happens. Firstly, the partners take turns in touching and being touched with no verbal communication during this phase. They then go on to the second part when they talk for 20 minutes about their experience of the exercise, verbalising both pleasurable and less pleasant sensations, feelings and thoughts. This communication is as important as the physical element and should happen after each sensate focus episode.

This step is sometimes extended and repeated with variations over time, whereby the couple is encouraged to experiment with using different materials whilst touching, such as: silk, rubber, feather, wooden spoons, ice cubes... anything that comes to mind and not necessarily materials that they may connect to sex. Use of lotions, or essential oils, may also be introduced. The environment can be enriched with candles, discrete music, scents, incense and anything else that the couples' creativity may introduce.

Step Two

This repeats step one in all aspects, except that the touching is extended to all areas of the body. This is again a non-sexual exercise, and the anogenital and breast touching is purely sensual and exploratory. The therapist gives more specific instructions at the beginning, and over time, relinquishes more decision making to the couple in terms of what 'ingredients' to add to creatively enrich the exercise. The couple are encouraged to be inventive and suggest what they would like to add to the experience. The therapist may invite them to take turns in surprising each other when coming up with ideas.

Step Three

There are some varieties in how sex therapists take the couple through step three. Sometimes the couple are advised to arouse each other respectively, sometimes they are advised to engage in mutual stroking, kissing and caressing. The choice depends on the therapist's assessment of the couple's needs and on their feedback during the previous stages. This stage is intended to be sexual and may be experienced as 'a session of foreplay'. The couple are advised that orgasm is not the goal, however it may occur for either or both partners. Time boundaries are equally respected as in the previous steps. The couple then, as with the previous steps, takes 20 minutes to talk about the experience in as much specific detail as possible.

Step Four

This evolves from the previous three steps and introduces penetration with no thrusting. After mutual stroking and caressing for at least ten minutes, penetration is performed into the vagina or anus, depending on the couple's gender, sexual preferences, or sexuality, for only a few seconds and without internal movement. This may happen in the same way once or twice during the exercise. After each penetration, the couple continues gentle stroking until the set time is up. Afterwards, the couple takes 20 minutes to talk about the experience.

Step Five

This builds on the previous exercises in that it slowly goes through the previous stages and incorporates elements of the previous exercises, allowing full penetration with thrusting as desired, and as it feels pleasurable for both partners.

Sexology and sex therapy literature (Weeks & Gambescia, 2016; Wincze & Weisberg, 2015) states multiple purposes of sensate focus:

- to help partners become more aware of their own sensations
- to help individuals become more in touch with their need for pleasure and worry less about the partner

- to build a physical and emotional connection
- to facilitate an awareness of each other's sensual and sexual needs
- to expand the repertoire of intimate, sensual and sexual behaviour
- to learn to appreciate sensuality and non-genitally-oriented sex more fully
- to communicate sensual and sexual needs, wishes and desires
- to create positive relational experiences
- to decrease sexual avoidance and enhance sexual desire
- to enhance a sense of cohesion, love, caring, commitment, intimacy, co-operation and sexual interest between the partners
- to enable a possible change in perception of their partners
- to learn new behaviours.

Additional benefits identified in clinical practice are stated below:

- the 'ban on sex' takes the pressure off, thereby reducing performance anxiety and making way for focusing on pleasurable sensations
- by equalising partners' participation, it takes pressure off who initiates sex and introduces reciprocity in the physical interaction
- the strict time boundary as well as clear agreement on the parameters of the activity creates a feeling of safety and enables clients to relax and tune into their experience without worrying about what comes next, thus preventing negative anticipation
- it has the potential to encourage couples to reach a series of agreements, on the conditions of the exercise, e.g. the environment, time boundaries and holding off from sex. It helps strengthen couples' bonds, increases mutual trust and enhances communication skills such as negotiating and joint planning; it also enhances their closeness in the context of working together towards a common goal
- verbal communication after the physical exercises supports expression of their own sexual needs and enhances mutual empathy and listening; as part of this, it allows for saying 'No' in terms of expressing what feels unpleasant or less desirable and creates the space in which the partner's 'No' would be heard without necessarily experiencing a sense of rejection
- it draws attention to the importance of afterplay
- the therapist's contextualising of the exercise in terms of 'listen openly and tune into your experience' helps create a non-judgemental atmosphere
- it enhances understanding of the clients' own sensations and emotional responses to physical stimulation in a sensual and sexual context by immersion in the experience of the 'here and now'

- it breaks old repetitive, sometimes deeply entrenched, patterns (deconstructing) and opens up space for development of new patterns of intimately relating (reconstructing)
- it encourages imagination, fun and playfulness in sex
- it can balance out different sensual and sexual preferences and increase closeness between partners by strengthening their negotiation skills
- for many couples it introduces sensuality as a novelty in their sexual interaction
- the slower pace of the interaction allows for deeper attunement to the pleasurable sensations, enjoyment of different kinds of touching and caressing without rushing to an end point, allowing for a fuller experience of the sexual act and expanding the meaning of sex, so as to add variety to sensually and sexually relating besides intercourse and penetration
- it creates a joint sexual history for the couple; sometimes the couple get together after having had very different prior sexual histories which can create imbalance and tension between them.

There are boundless variations and adjustments that can be created around this basic outline. The steps can be enriched thoughtfully and sensitively to the couple's context and preferences, with a light touch, encouraging the couple's inventiveness and supporting the use of their imagination and creativity. Treatment methods relevant for specific sexual problems can be incorporated within sensate focus, for example, the partner of the man experiencing erectile difficulties can be included in the 'wax and wane' exercise (explained in more detail in the section on treatment of erectile disorder in this chapter) as part of the sensate focus stages; women undertaking individual exercises with vaginal dilators as part of treatment for vaginismus can bring these individual exercises into the couple practice of sensate focus and show to their partners how gradual insertion of these dilators into the vagina can enhance their sense of safety and control; with premature/early ejaculation (PE), slowing down with sensate focus is particularly important and the specific individual masturbatory exercises suggested for treatment of this difficulty can be incorporated into the couple's sensate focus activity at stages four and five. Equally, the steps involving penetration may or may not be included depending on the couple's sexual preferences.

The method was originally created for heterosexual couples, and its descriptions in the literature appear to be biased towards heterosexism. In addition, it potentially implies that all sexual activity leads or should lead to intercourse. However, the components of this exercise can be used to the clients' advantage, leaving the therapist to decide how best to avoid the message of heterosexism, the primacy of intercourse and other narrow definitions of sex. Sexual varieties, for example, bondage/domination/sadism/masochism (BDSM) elements, can be incorporated as and when the couple wishes. They may use therapy sessions to discuss such options or decide to negotiate separately between themselves.

Some authors, such as Tiefer (2004), strongly oppose sensate focus, seeing it as a problematic, patriarchal tool that promotes biological reductionism by ignoring gender differences in privileging men's interests, such as sensory and physical experiences and performance, at the expense of women's interests, such as loving communication, eye contact and expression of feelings. However, it is worth noting that sensate focus is not only about tactile experience and physicality; intimacy, emotions and communication are equally valuable components. Gender and other differences between the couple should be attentively listened to by the therapist and addressed with care, sensitivity and appreciation. Iasenza (2010) proposed redesigning sensate focus as 'mindfulness meditation', describing how spectatoring in sex can be thought of as being reinforced by sensate focus. She writes:

> Instead of attempting to banish it [spectatoring], I welcome the 'observer' and frame it as an ally in helping each partner discover what distracts him/her during sexual engagement. I frame sensate focus as a sexual meditation practice whose goal is to increase sexual presence, comfort, and connection. Using meditation techniques, I ask clients to become aware of their thoughts, feelings, and bodily sensations, as well as their breathing, while touching (p.304).

A concept of 'interpersonal sexual mindfulness' may be created to emphasise a couple's tuning into each other's pace and responsiveness during this exercise.

When applying such ideas in practice, therapists should tailor the tasks for each step to the individual clients' situation as much as possible. For example, with clients who tend to 'rush through' sexual activity, which is often the case in premature ejaculation or erectile disorder, it may be crucial to significantly slow down the process. This can be achieved by keeping such clients on the early steps for a period of time, while inviting them to introduce changes and variations within each stage and enrich it with details of different kinds of touch, use of different materials, slight changes in the environment, and so on. With couples where sexual roles are unequally divided such that there is an imbalance and a rigidity of roles of the 'initiator' and the 'responder', or the 'leader' and the 'follower', it is helpful that these tasks are harmonised. Therapists can suggest that clients take turns in some aspects of their roles, such as who is taking charge; who creates a surprise, alternating these on a weekly basis. A female client once reported after sensate focus, 'this is the first time I am active whilst he is not doing anything; this is a totally new discovery to me'. Clients often make creative use of sensate focus and accommodate it to their own circumstances and preferences. A couple who completed the whole process reported that they had continued to make use of it after therapy had ended; they integrated different steps at different times; for example, sometimes they would only do the first part if they had some time in the morning, or equally, as a relaxing exercise before going to sleep; or sometimes they would play with mutual arousal and invent different ways of touching and caressing, different playful activities, teasing, seducing, restraining, without penetration or any genital or anal contact.

Sensate focus does not always go 'smoothly' in a straight line towards progress and positive outcome. It is a diagnostic as much as a healing tool, and any obstacles in the process highlight issues that need to be attended to and guide therapeutic conversations. Taking feedback from sensate focus is a significant therapeutic skill. Couples' reactions to sensate focus are often unpredictable and can be experienced as unpleasant by one or both individuals. It is of extreme importance that therapists listen attentively to the details of clients' feedback, clarifying any issues, acknowledging and normalising any difficulties and appreciating their efforts and successes. Sensate focus often highlights emotional, relational and cognitive blocks and sometimes triggers intense reactions. The 'graph' of the process can go in any direction, and the couple must be reassured that they are not doing anything 'wrong' when 'success' is not smooth and straightforward. Some couples embrace the opportunity and make the most of it with what seems like effortless progression; for others, the process is turbulent with many 'bumps' along the way. In some cases, however the couple tries, it does not make any positive difference, so is brought to an early closure. The range of couples' responses is vast, from those who say 'sensate focus is better than sex', to others not connecting at all and questioning many if not all aspects of it, and with a huge range of variations in between these two extremes.

Difficulties are to be expected and dealt with; sometimes it takes a great deal of explanation and listening in order to encourage clients to persist and benefit from it. However, like with any other therapeutic intervention, sensate focus simply does not work for everyone and it should not be insisted upon if the couple does not seem to be responding to it in a desired and useful way. Sensate focus can sometimes be the last straw that brings a relationship to an end, as through the process the couple realises the impossibility of generating a physical connection. For various reasons, including emotional distance, resentment or lack of physical attraction, a couple may decide to break up having attempted sensate focus. Usually, the ending of the relationship has been almost overdue in such situations, and the couple have just postponed the moment at which they have to face the situation, fearing to hurt the other or restart a single life.

Couples are sometimes just not ready, or the state of the relationship suggests that sensate focus would be impossible, such as if there was a great deal of conflict, anger, bitterness, hostility or deep upset. Sometimes the couple feel so emotionally and physically distant that a pre-sensate focus step can be suggested, involving spending time together, talking, looking at each other, holding hands, having a good night kiss and so on. This is often a necessary transition where the standard sensate focus exercises may feel too great of a leap for them to take.

There is currently a debate in the psychosexual field about whether one has to be a qualified sex therapist in order to utilise the sensate focus intervention. In the author's opinion, while specific training may certainly be beneficial, a wealth of already existing skills can be transferred to the area of sex and sexual relationships, including the use of sensate focus. Many couple therapists are accustomed to deconstructing interactional episodes or guiding clients through behavioural change. In addition, psychotherapists can enhance their expertise in this area through extensive reading combined with supervision by a therapist with psychosexual expertise.

Sex therapy has a well-established series of individual and couple exercises that are used for a variety of sexual dysfunctions. For example, individual self-focus, or individual sexual growth exercises for men and women are aimed at increasing knowledge and understanding of one's own bodily sensations and arousal preferences. This consists of a graduated series of individual exercises, repeated several times a week during therapy treatment, starting with observing one's own naked body, followed by first non-arousing, going onto arousing self-touching. Steps of this exercise are carefully paced and progress and any blocks are discussed with the therapist. In addition, Kegel exercises are suggested as part of the treatment for all sexual issues. The exercises consist of rhythmic alternating of contraction and relaxation of pelvic muscles which, if applied daily for a few minutes, can be beneficial in many aspects of sexual functioning such as intensifying orgasmic sensation, and increasing future desire and arousal. These exercises, regularly suggested to women during pregnancy as a means of recovery from urinary incontinence, are actually helpful to both women and men notwithstanding their sexual functioning, for healthy maintenance of the uro-genital tract.

The relational dimension

Appreciative inquiry

Appreciative inquiry, a method originally developed by Cooperrider & Srivastva (1987) in organisational consultancy, can be usefully applied to any relationship system and therefore can be a helpful resource in working with clients presenting sexuality and intimacy problems. It is based on the premise that focusing on positive aspects, both experienced and imagined, promotes growth and contributes to overcoming the difficulties. The authors (Ludema, Cooperrider & Barrett, 2000) propose a four-stage process of: Discovery (What do we do best? How are we good?), Dream (What might we be? What is our vision?), Design (How will we make it happen? What is our strategy?), and Destiny (How do we re-align our work and make our dream a reality?), which are summarised below. The appreciative inquiry method frames questions in such a way that leads to positive responses, emphasising strengths and successes.

1. Discovery consists of enquiring into the best of the past and the present. The sample questions guiding this enquiry are paraphrased below, adapted to the context of a couple relationship:
   - What do you most like about your relationship?
   - What first attracted you and what has most encouraged you to stay?
   - Can you recall a time when you felt most alive, most excited and satisfied about your relationship and your involvement in it?
   - What do you consider to be some of the most significant strengths of your relationship?
   - There are inevitably high points and low points in a relationship; enjoyments, excitements as well as frustrations. What stands out for you as a high point when you look back at any point in time in the relationship?
     - Please describe what happened; who did what?
     - Which of your strengths and talents were playing a part?
     - What contributed most to the good experience?
   - What do you especially value about your relationship now?
   - How are these aspects manifested?

2. Dream is about envisioning results and imagining how things may work in the future. Questions guiding this stage are, for example:
   - Imagine a time in the future where your relationship is as you would like it to be. How do you think it was made possible? What decisions and actions were made by whom to give the relationship such a positive direction?
   - What are your hopes for the relationship?
   - What would a successful outcome of therapy look like?
   - What do you imagine three accomplishments to be, so that your relationship achieves your hopes?
3. Design is about co-constructing, planning and prioritising what can be done to build the desired future. Sample questions include:
   - What do you think are the most promising areas of your relationship on which to expand its good qualities?
   - What communicational changes would need to be put in place to enable a positive move forward?
   - What motivates you to engage in working on the relationship and coming to therapy as part of it?
   - What do you consider to be the indicators that you are doing an excellent job?
   - What current aspects of the relationship give you most hope that positive movement will be possible and that your relationship will grow stronger?
   - What is contributing most to your willingness to make a difference in your relationship?
   - What are the most important factors likely to sustain your commitment to make a difference?
4. Destiny is about committing to and sustaining the change. The following questions can be helpful:
   - Imagine it is three years into the future and your relationship is just as you want it to be.
     - What is happening?
     - What makes it so vibrant and happy?
     - How have you contributed to this future?
     - What can you do to continue keeping it so good?
     - What can you begin to do to make it even better?
     - What can you stop doing, because it no longer serves you well, or gets in the way?
   - What specific ways would you like to contribute to realising your hopes and dreams about the relationship?

- What would you most look forward to contributing?
- What support and resources would you need to enable you to accomplish this?

Amongst many techniques that couple therapists of various different orientations apply, the ones summarised below, pertinent to the systemic way of thinking and practising, can be particularly useful when treating sexual difficulties.

Allocating regular talking times

The couple are advised to incorporate regular, time-boundaried communication sessions with each other. Certain 'rules' can be agreed during the therapy session, such as to use a gentle, soft tone without blaming, criticising or showing defensiveness; try be constructive and appreciative of the positives, focus on listening and sharing.

This technique can impact on everyday communication in that it ensures time to discuss difficult issues, bringing hope that things may be resolved while freeing daily communication from tension and interspersed criticism. It is sometimes referred to as 'the daily dialogue' (Carlson & Lorelle, 2016a), suggesting that the purpose is to maintain a continual connection between partners and build a safer and more co-operative relational system.

A technique named 'soft/hard/soft communication' (Papernow, 2016), based on John Gottman's research findings on the importance of a 'soft start-up' (Gottman, 2011), can be incorporated within this exercise, instructing the couple to talk in a way that is intended to enhance listening. The process consists of:

- Beginning communication in a soothing, soft, gentle, positive, empathic and appreciative way
- Expressing feelings and thinking about the difficulty to be addressed, while keeping the softness from the beginning
- Ending in the same soft mode, concluding with kindness and respect for the partner.

Taking ownership

This is suggested as a technique for guiding a couple towards enhancing their communication, while paying particular attention to taking responsibility for both the problems and the creation of positive change (Carlson & Lorelle, 2016b).

Using shared journalling

This technique can help couples who struggle with direct verbal exchanges, particularly when it quickly turns into a conflict and when negative emotions get triggered easily and overwhelmingly, blocking communication and increasing distress (Zimmerman & Haddock, 2016). The couple use a journal to communicate and resolve conflict, sometimes by simply sharing thoughts and feelings that arise for them during the day. Writing notes to each other can also be used for exchanging loving and sexy messages, or to communicate thoughts and feelings that are more difficult to say face-to-face.

Aspects of intimacy

Fife (2016), in keeping with the social constructionist perspective, expands the meaning and the possibilities of intimacy, stressing that it is a multidimensional phenomenon, and that a couple can experience closeness, connection and sharing in many different ways (Weeks & Fife, 2014). This technique involves giving a handout to clients that lists various types of intimacy, for them to think about and discuss in the context of their relationship. The list contains, for example:

- *'aesthetic intimacy'* (sharing experiences of beauty in music, nature, art, theatre or dance)
- *'communication intimacy'* (connection through talking)
- *'conflict intimacy'* (using resolution of conflict to grow closer together)
- *'crisis intimacy'* (developing closeness in dealing with problems and pain)
- *'financial intimacy'* (developing a unified financial plan of spending and saving)
- *'intellectual intimacy'* (connecting through sharing intellectual subjects)
- *'recreational intimacy'* (enjoying various recreational activities together)
- *'parenting intimacy'* (sharing the joys and the difficulties of bringing up children), and so on (Fife, 2016, p.145).

The usual confined meanings attached to the concept of 'intimacy' are significantly expanded and enriched, opening up possibilities for the strengthening of positive stories. Such an embracing, inclusive outlook can increase space for mutual positive regard; couples claiming there is 'no intimacy' between them may feel challenged and encouraged by this approach, as well as supported in their mutual appreciation of their existing relational bonds.

Clients can be invited to expand the list even more, so as to include their own, perhaps unique, ways of connecting. Couples tend to undermine the meaning of, for example, sometimes having pleasant relaxing times sitting on a sofa eating crisps and watching TV. A narrow description of intimacy is likely to bring forth pathology to such situations. If the only valid forms of intimacy are: deep emotional talk, eye contact, physical affection, or sexual activity, then what does not fall into these categories can be regarded as not valid, not 'proper' intimacy. In supporting broader, more embracing, diverse and varied definitions, this technique has great potential to de-pathologise stories and experiences of being in a relationship and increase opportunities for relationship satisfaction.

The cultural dimension

Externalising conversations

Externalising conversations is a method developed by Michael White in the 1980s within the postmodern social constructionist approach of narrative therapy (White, 1988, 1989, 2007). It is based on the premise that experience is shaped by the storied meaning attached to it, which derives from dominant societal, cultural and political discourses. These discourses often have a powerful oppressive impact on the person in forming their problem-saturated identity. Externalising conversations encourage individuals to objectify and personify the problem they find oppressive as if it is an external identity acting forcefully upon them. For example, referring to 'depression' rather than 'a depressed person'; or 'the orgasmic difficulty' rather than 'a disordered functioning of a person'; 'the anger', rather than 'an angry person'; 'the blame' rather than 'your blame' and so on, illustrates a particular way in which language is used in externalising conversations. These conversations are summarised by White as: 'it is not the person who is the problem. Rather, it is the problem that is the problem' (White, 1989, p.6), counteracting typical cultural practices that see problems as located within the individual. Narrative therapy posits that, by asking the persons to separate themselves from the problem, space is opened up for them to see alternative possibilities for self-description and understanding of the problem. Externalising conversations are led by therapists' questions in guiding clients through the steps of the externalising process. Once the problem is externalised, 'relative influence questioning' brings forth narratives about the impact of the problem on the many aspects of the person's life with questions such as:

- How long has this erectile difficulty been influencing you?
- When is the anxiety most likely to visit you?
- How does it manage to trick you?

Placing problems into storylines can begin to deconstruct the sociocultural and political influences contributing to problem formation through questions such as:

- What are some of your beliefs about how a black woman should behave sexually?
- How comfortable are you with these ideas that you inherited?
- Which of these ideas do you find helpful, and which do you see as having a negative impact on you?
- How do you see these ideas as having impacted your relationship? (adapted from Combs & Freedman, 2016).

The influence of broader political discourses and the implications of gender, race, culture, sexuality, class, ability and other relations of power in the life of the problem and the person's experience of themselves as the 'carriers of the problem' are deconstructed through such externalising explorations. This deconstruction allows space for the creation of alternative stories, which can be achieved through discovering the moments when the problem did not occur, when the client did not become dominated and disempowered by the problem. Questioning about what happened in these exceptional situations tracks these 'unique outcomes' in the life of the person in relation to the problem (which could be externalised as an 'intruder' or 'unwanted guest') while emphasising the person's strengths in standing up to the problem, such as:

- What did you do?
- How did you manage to close the door and not let the 'intruder' come into your life?

The building of a person's agency happens from this point, leading to affirmation of a new identity, a preferred view of themselves based on strengths and choices. Such conversations are seen within this approach as opening up more constructive possibilities for individuals and relationships than when problems are located within a person. Considering how social, cultural and political discourses are involved in constructing a person's identity can lead to new understanding of how lives are affected by broader cultural stories, creating the opportunity to 're-story' one's life and 're-author' one's identity.

Externalising conversations can be applied as a full process which can take the whole session or longer; alternatively, it can consist of a single question or a comment such as: 'It seems that anger tends to come upon you, making you say things you don't wish to say...' or, combined with metaphorical language: 'This jealousy seems to come into your life as a cloud over you, putting a shadow over the whole space around you...' It could be also used as part of playful questioning, inviting the clients' imagination: 'If you imagine this blame is a coat you can put on and take off as you wish, what would happen if today you decide to go home to your partner having left the coat behind you?'

The de-pathologising and collaborative nature of externalising conversations can engage clients more actively with the therapy process, leading to empowerment by bringing forth marginalised stories about their strengths, waking up their dormant skills, and energising them in taking constructive action towards creating positive change.

The sexual genogram

The sexual genogram, a method described in the Introduction to Chapter 4, can be used both as an assessment and a treatment tool. In expanding the focus of the presenting concerns to the wider context of systemic influences, the effect is often a reduction in criticism, blame and anger and de-pathologising of the individuals and their relationships. Allowing clients to reflect on the sexual topics through use of the sexual genogram method promotes communication about sexual themes in their lives, and has the potential to foster motivation, empathy and optimism (Gambescia, 2016).

This is just a selection of the many techniques and methods that are available to couple and relationship therapists in the treatment of emotional, relational and sexual difficulties. While appreciating the value of such diverse and imaginative techniques, it is worth noting that this list does not imply that treatment is all about using specific tools in problem solving. Sometimes the process of therapy requires staying with the difficulty, allowing thoughts and emotions to be experienced and processed in a way that is far less structured. Techniques are important and useful, often adding structure and focus to the therapy process and sometimes introducing elements of playfulness and experimentation. However, techniques can only be effective in the context of a safe, trusting, supportive and collaborative therapeutic relationship.

Delayed ejaculation (DE) treatment options

As stated previously, research on this disorder is limited due to its relatively rare clinical presentation. Treatment outcomes are therefore insufficiently evaluated (Althof, 2012). However, existing studies suggest a good success rate for resolution of this condition through sex therapy (Perelman & Rowland, 2006). The historical division between biological and psychogenic treatment of DE has proven less useful, suggesting that the most efficient treatment involves appreciation of the multidimensional nature of the problem and the need for a multidisciplinary approach (Perelman, 2014).

A thorough assessment is highly recommended in order to provide a focus for treatment. Differentiation between lifelong and acquired DE provides vital information as to the likely triggers and possible maintaining factors. It is helpful to explore life events and circumstances that may have contributed to the onset of the dysfunction, including illness and medical treatments, life transitions, losses, trauma, relationship distress, and other possible stresses. In addition, enquiring about the variability of ejaculatory control in terms of exploring the circumstances when the problem occurs to a greater or a lesser degree can be clinically helpful. If, for example, DE only occurs in situations where no contraception is applied, this may indicate that fear of pregnancy plays a part in the aetiology of this syndrome.

Sex therapy guidelines for treatment of this disorder suggest exploration of areas such as: relationship satisfaction, partner attractiveness, masturbatory patterns, use of fantasy, communication with the partner, adequacy of sexual stimulus and performance anxiety. Perelman (2014) suggests a series of straightforward questions to establish specific areas that need addressing in treatment, such as:

- How frequently do you masturbate?
- How do you masturbate?
- In what ways does the stimulation you provide yourself differ from your partner's stimulation style, in terms of speed, and pressure?
- Have you communicated your preference to your partner/s, and if so, what was their response? (p.144).

Psychotherapists may prefer to use questions more adjusted to their professional field, as the questions above typically reflect a medical approach.

While acknowledging the lack of empirical studies for the treatment of DE, the current state of treatment strategies suggests that integrating biological, relational, psychological, social, intergenerational and cultural factors seems the most useful approach (Foley & Gambescia, 2015).

A summary of treatment options for DE, including a range of dimensions, is presented in Figure 5.1 within the MOST map and discussed in the text that follows.

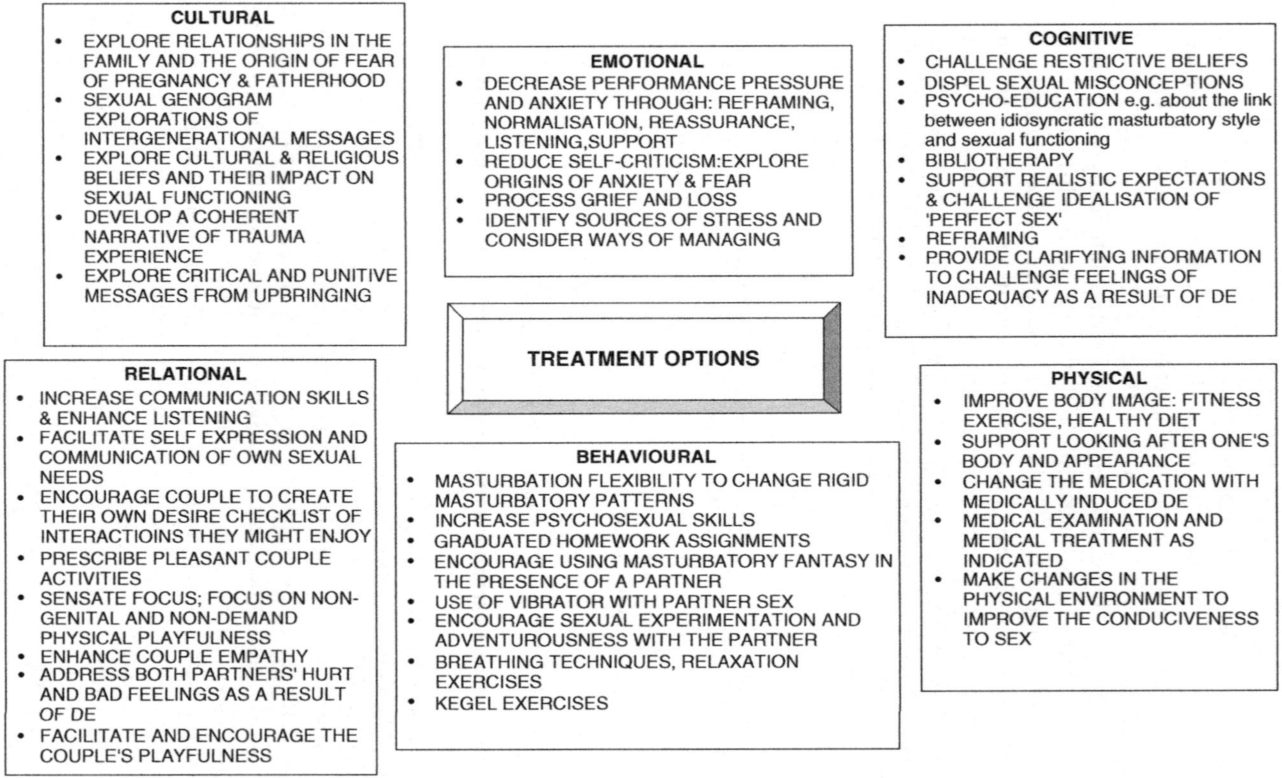

TREATMENT OPTIONS

CULTURAL

- EXPLORE RELATIONSHIPS IN THE FAMILY AND THE ORIGIN OF FEAR OF PREGNANCY & FATHERHOOD
- SEXUAL GENOGRAM EXPLORATIONS OF INTERGENERATIONAL MESSAGES
- EXPLORE CULTURAL & RELIGIOUS BELIEFS AND THEIR IMPACT ON SEXUAL FUNCTIONING
- DEVELOP A COHERENT NARRATIVE OF TRAUMA EXPERIENCE
- EXPLORE CRITICAL AND PUNITIVE MESSAGES FROM UPBRINGING

EMOTIONAL

- DECREASE PERFORMANCE PRESSURE AND ANXIETY THROUGH: REFRAMING, NORMALISATION, REASSURANCE, LISTENING,SUPPORT
- REDUCE SELF-CRITICISM:EXPLORE ORIGINS OF ANXIETY & FEAR
- PROCESS GRIEF AND LOSS
- IDENTIFY SOURCES OF STRESS AND CONSIDER WAYS OF MANAGING

COGNITIVE

- CHALLENGE RESTRICTIVE BELIEFS
- DISPEL SEXUAL MISCONCEPTIONS
- PSYCHO-EDUCATION e.g. about the link between idiosyncratic masturbatory style and sexual functioning
- BIBLIOTHERAPY
- SUPPORT REALISTIC EXPECTATIONS & CHALLENGE IDEALISATION OF 'PERFECT SEX'
- REFRAMING
- PROVIDE CLARIFYING INFORMATION TO CHALLENGE FEELINGS OF INADEQUACY AS A RESULT OF DE

RELATIONAL

- INCREASE COMMUNICATION SKILLS & ENHANCE LISTENING
- FACILITATE SELF EXPRESSION AND COMMUNICATION OF OWN SEXUAL NEEDS
- ENCOURAGE COUPLE TO CREATE THEIR OWN DESIRE CHECKLIST OF INTERACTIOINS THEY MIGHT ENJOY
- PRESCRIBE PLEASANT COUPLE ACTIVITIES
- SENSATE FOCUS; FOCUS ON NON-GENITAL AND NON-DEMAND PHYSICAL PLAYFULNESS
- ENHANCE COUPLE EMPATHY
- ADDRESS BOTH PARTNERS' HURT AND BAD FEELINGS AS A RESULT OF DE
- FACILITATE AND ENCOURAGE THE COUPLE'S PLAYFULNESS

BEHAVIOURAL

- MASTURBATION FLEXIBILITY TO CHANGE RIGID MASTURBATORY PATTERNS
- INCREASE PSYCHOSEXUAL SKILLS
- GRADUATED HOMEWORK ASSIGNMENTS
- ENCOURAGE USING MASTURBATORY FANTASY IN THE PRESENCE OF A PARTNER
- USE OF VIBRATOR WITH PARTNER SEX
- ENCOURAGE SEXUAL EXPERIMENTATION AND ADVENTUROUSNESS WITH THE PARTNER
- BREATHING TECHNIQUES, RELAXATION EXERCISES
- KEGEL EXERCISES

PHYSICAL

- IMPROVE BODY IMAGE: FITNESS EXERCISE, HEALTHY DIET
- SUPPORT LOOKING AFTER ONE'S BODY AND APPEARANCE
- CHANGE THE MEDICATION WITH MEDICALLY INDUCED DE
- MEDICAL EXAMINATION AND MEDICAL TREATMENT AS INDICATED
- MAKE CHANGES IN THE PHYSICAL ENVIRONMENT TO IMPROVE THE CONDUCIVENESS TO SEX

Figure 5.1 Delayed ejaculation: treatment options

Emotional dimension

Various psychotherapy techniques could be used to decrease performance pressure and anxiety related to sex, such as behavioural anxiety reduction, cognitive behavioural therapy (CBT), teaching mindfulness and breathing, and progressive relaxation (Metz & McCarthy, 2007).

Qualities of the therapeutic relationship pertinent to many psychotherapy approaches, particularly humanistic and systemic, such as listening, warmth, appreciation, supportive challenge, reassurance, encouragement and empathy are important when working with clients presenting DE as feelings of anxiety, guilt, shame and self-criticism often dominate their self-image.

Reframing, a widely used systemic and CBT technique, can challenge clients' exaggerated negative sexual self-image as a result of DE by emphasising the context of generosity and care for the partner that underlies this syndrome (Apfelbaum, 2000).

Exploring the origins of anxiety and fear related to sex and potentially fear of fatherhood/commitment can put the problem into perspective and provide reassurance, support and empathic understanding by the client's partner as well as self-understanding of the client and dissolve their self-blame. Sometimes such explorations normalise the situation: 'Of course you fear fatherhood, given your family history and the traumas you have experienced as a young man...'

Cognitive dimension

Reframing is also relevant to the cognitive dimension, allowing for different meanings to be generated, creating the possibility of different understanding of one's sexual functioning, thus altering the client's belief system as well as helping reduce anxiety caused by negative attributions (Weeks, 1994). Clients presenting a sexual dysfunction tend to develop a negative sexual self-construct and, in the case of DE, they typically consider themselves to be 'inadequate', 'withholding' or 'uncaring' sexual partners. Describing the psychological processes of this dysfunction whereby the man, contrary to his self-construct, is over-caring, overly responsive and attentive to his partner and trying 'too hard', provides a helpful educational reframe, challenging sometimes deeply rooted self-beliefs and associated guilt and shame that often exacerbates the problem. Hopefully, the client is enabled to understand how the context of performance pressure, the oppression of a negative belief system and the weight of worry can be affecting his sexual behaviour (Foley & Gambescia, 2015, p.119). The 'fantasy model of sex' described by Zilbergeld (1999), which exaggerates men's powerful role in sex and imposes a template of perfect functioning, is an orgasm-driven model of sex suggesting by implication that the absence of orgasm should have a highly problematic meaning.

Dispelling sexual myths, challenging idealisation of 'perfect sex' and supporting realistic expectations, as well as helping the man understand the link between his idiosyncratic masturbatory style and DE symptoms in partnered sex, are useful educational interventions. Psycho-educational interventions, however, rarely produce sufficient results on their own, but work best in combination with other forms of treatment (Perelman, 2014).

Physical dimension

Given that a range of medical reasons can underlie this dysfunction, it is of paramount importance to scrutinise the possible medical factors, including undertaking genito-urinary, neurological and endocrinological examination (Corona et al., 2012). In addition, possible side effects of medication and of medical treatments should be examined. Given the results of medical investigations, physical treatment advice should be followed as indicated.

Many studies have been undertaken to explore potential pharmacological treatments of DE; however, results are inconclusive. There is limited evidence that use of bupropion, an antidepressant sometimes applied for enhancement of sexual desire, may be helpful (Abdel-Hamid & Saleh, 2011).

DE can originate from negative body image affecting sexual experience and functioning, forming an escalating cycle of mutual reinforcement leading to further aggravation of the condition. As with other dysfunctions, supporting a healthy diet, regular exercise, reduction of smoking and alcohol intake and enhancing physical fitness and general state of health can all contribute to body image improvement and form a necessary part of comprehensive treatment.

Conduciveness of the environment where sex takes place can be explored with the man and his partner/s to identify any possible improvements to create a more relaxed and pleasant atmosphere for sex.

Behavioural dimension

'Masturbatory flexibility' is a technique described in sex therapy literature (e.g. Foley & Gambescia, 2015) aimed at altering rigid masturbatory patterns underlying this dysfunction. If assessment has identified that the man suffering DE has developed a highly ritualised rigid masturbatory style, it is essential to explain that this may well have conditioned his body to respond in a certain set way to sexual stimulation that is difficult to replicate in partnered sex. Such an explanation may provide a useful therapeutic intervention by minimising the stigma of this condition for the client and empower him with a sense of control and agency by pointing at the possible origins of the dysfunction and suggesting a clear way forward. Suggesting temporary masturbatory abstinence and alteration of masturbatory patterns can evoke clients' understandable resistance, which can be managed therapeutically by way of a supportive and encouraging attitude, while ensuring that the purpose and benefits of such an intervention are fully understood.

Sometimes therapists feel intrusive asking about the details of clients' masturbatory practice and, equally, clients may be shy and embarrassed to talk about this subject in specific terms. It is just as effective for the purposes of enabling clients' understanding of the link between their masturbatory style and DE to keep the conversation at a process level stating, for example: 'You don't have to tell me what exactly you do when you masturbate, but the important thing is if it is always in the same way, involving the same hand, the same type and level of pressure on the penis, the same place, the same fantasy and so on. If that is the case, gradually changing this pattern over time and developing a more flexible style can help in the treatment. If you use different positions and different intensities of touch, create different fantasies and use different visual prompts, you can expand on the variety of ways of masturbating, which can develop more receptivity of your sexual response in partnered sex.' Clearly, masturbatory style is only problematic in how it affects partnered sex; otherwise, there is nothing 'wrong' with a particular method of masturbation per se. It is important to convey it in such a way that is not going to be heard as 'yet another mistake' the man committed by developing this particular way of self-stimulation.

Lack of adequate stimulation can be a salient factor in inhibited orgasm and delayed ejaculation. It is helpful to identify the man's and their partner's arousal preferences, which requires relational interventions. Individual self-focus, or individual sexual growth exercises as described earlier, are helpful with increasing knowledge and understanding of own bodily reactions. The client's mindfulness while applying this technique is paramount in that he pays attention to arousal sensations and enhances his understanding of his sensual and sexual needs.

Relaxation techniques, mindfulness exercises, and guided meditation are useful techniques for reducing anxiety, increasing the ability to relax and manage stress, and strengthening one's resilience in coping with sexual difficulties.

Relational dimension

Typical widespread sexual mythology implies that men who 'last longer' are better performers and more likely to have satisfied sexual partners (Zilbergeld, 1999). The reality is, however, quite different. Partners are very often frustrated, sometimes experiencing soreness or even pain together with physical and emotional exhaustion and tend to feel rejected and unattractive to the man suffering from DE (Althof, 2012). Repetitive unsatisfactory interpersonal sexual episodes may lead to avoidance of sex, increasing a sense of rejection and failure. Couple treatment, wherever possible, encourages the man and his partner to communicate their emotional, physical and sexual needs to each other and work towards increased mutual empathy and a better understanding of both their sexual desires and frustrations. Sometimes, specific techniques are applied, such as: decentring, reflexive listening, sculpting and prescribing homework. These techniques are well described both in sex therapy and couple therapy literature (e.g. Weeks, Gambescia & Hertlein, 2016; Weeks, Fife & Peterson, 2016). The therapist as a facilitator of the couple's communication observes interaction, listening to their accounts of their relating to identify typical problematic patterns. Therapists' observations and hypotheses are shared using therapeutic transparency. In this way, the therapist recruits clients as active participants in the therapy process, inviting their comments on therapeutic ideas.

Exercises can be prescribed to encourage sexual experimentation and adventurousness between the partners. For example, the couple can create their own desire checklist of interactions they might appreciate, including pleasant activities such as walking, biking, hiking, playing various sports and games together, visiting places of interest and so on, expanding the scope for enjoyable joint outings. Particular emphasis may be placed on various sensual and sexual activities, increasing focus on non-genital and non-demand physical playfulness. Couples' physical and sexual playfulness can be facilitated by sensate focus, a fundamental technique of sex therapy, widely used as a treatment strategy in all sexual dysfunctions, described in the introduction to this chapter.

Apfelbaum (2000) places emphasis on the relational aspects in the treatment of DE and strongly recommends couple therapy wherever possible. The partner's reactions are considered crucial in the persistence and/or resolution of this difficulty as described in the section on contributing factors in Chapter 4 (McMahon et al., 2013). This, combined with the man's over-focusing on his partner's arousal with resultant lack of awareness of his own arousal processes, indicates the use of sensate focus in the treatment of this condition. Both partners often experience disempowerment as a result of the disorder; the man with DE feeling sexually inadequate and the partner feeling unattractive and unable to facilitate ejaculation. To avoid deterioration of feelings of failure, the couple may avoid sex. The man with DE sometimes fakes orgasm which reinforces the problem in that sex becomes mechanical and disconnected, performance oriented as opposed to pleasure led (Robbins-Cherry et al., 2011). Couple-focused strategies that promote intimacy and mutuality, including sensate focus, can support and enhance positive sexual interaction.

Cultural dimension

A sexual genogram could be used to explore intergenerational messages about sex, masculinity and femininity, affection and intimacy that may have impacted sexual expression and relationships in adult life (Hof & Berman, 1989). This helpful therapeutic tool can enhance contextual awareness of various presenting issues related to intimacy and sexuality, and enable contextual understanding of their origins, enhancing empathy and reducing stigma and blame.

Erectile disorder (ED): treatment options

Inability to gain or maintain an erection can be an immensely disturbing experience for a man, producing excruciating consequences for his psychological wellbeing, and undermining his self-esteem and his intimate relationships. The availability of Viagra in 1998 completely changed how ED was thought of and treated. It focused public attention on the physical and medical sides of the disorder, placing emphasis on the importance of performance and functioning, while ignoring the interpersonal, psychological and cultural factors so important for assessment and treatment. In more recent years, an integrative model of ED has emerged that incorporates both medical and psychological interventions. There is considerable research evidence that the most effective treatment strategy for ED takes a comprehensive view of aetiology; considers a range of biological, psychological, interpersonal and cultural factors; and combines treatment interventions to address all of the contributing factors (Carroll, 2011). Treatment options for ED are presented within the MOST model dimensions in Figure 5.2.

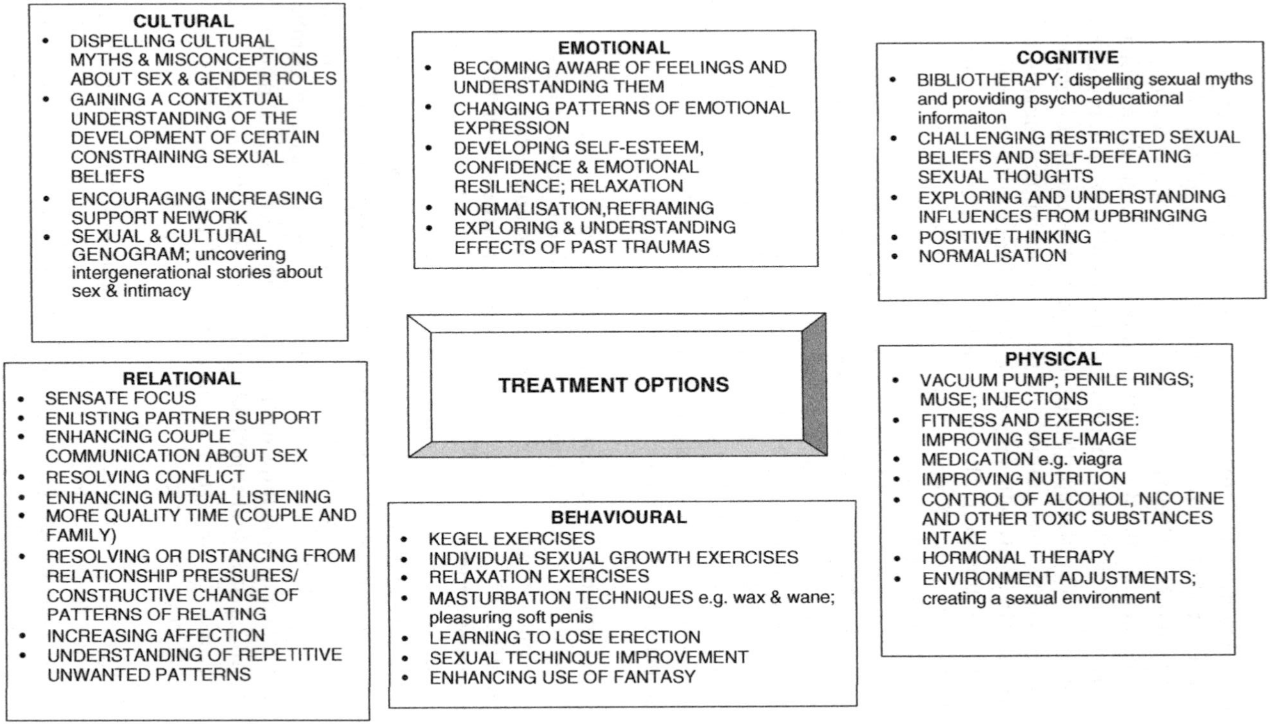

CULTURAL

- DISPELLING CULTURAL MYTHS & MISCONCEPTIONS ABOUT SEX & GENDER ROLES
- GAINING A CONTEXTUAL UNDERSTANDING OF THE DEVELOPMENT OF CERTAIN CONSTRAINING SEXUAL BELIEFS
- ENCOURAGING INCREASING SUPPORT NEIWORK
- SEXUAL & CULTURAL GENOGRAM; uncovering intergenerational stories about sex & intimacy

EMOTIONAL

- BECOMING AWARE OF FEELINGS AND UNDERSTANDING THEM
- CHANGING PATTERNS OF EMOTIONAL EXPRESSION
- DEVELOPING SELF-ESTEEM, CONFIDENCE & EMOTIONAL RESILIENCE; RELAXATION
- NORMALISATION,REFRAMING
- EXPLORING & UNDERSTANDING EFFECTS OF PAST TRAUMAS

COGNITIVE

- BIBLIOTHERAPY: dispelling sexual myths and providing psycho-educational informaiton
- CHALLENGING RESTRICTED SEXUAL BELIEFS AND SELF-DEFEATING SEXUAL THOUGHTS
- EXPLORING AND UNDERSTANDING INFLUENCES FROM UPBRINGING
- POSITIVE THINKING
- NORMALISATION

TREATMENT OPTIONS

RELATIONAL

- SENSATE FOCUS
- ENLISTING PARTNER SUPPORT
- ENHANCING COUPLE COMMUNICATION ABOUT SEX
- RESOLVING CONFLICT
- ENHANCING MUTUAL LISTENING
- MORE QUALITY TIME (COUPLE AND FAMILY)
- RESOLVING OR DISTANCING FROM RELATIONSHIP PRESSURES/ CONSTRUCTIVE CHANGE OF PATTERNS OF RELATING
- INCREASING AFFECTION
- UNDERSTANDING OF REPETITIVE UNWANTED PATTERNS

BEHAVIOURAL

- KEGEL EXERCISES
- INDIVIDUAL SEXUAL GROWTH EXERCISES
- RELAXATION EXERCISES
- MASTURBATION TECHNIQUES e.g. wax & wane; pleasuring soft penis
- LEARNING TO LOSE ERECTION
- SEXUAL TECHINQUE IMPROVEMENT
- ENHANCING USE OF FANTASY

PHYSICAL

- VACUUM PUMP; PENILE RINGS; MUSE; INJECTIONS
- FITNESS AND EXERCISE: IMPROVING SELF-IMAGE
- MEDICATION e.g. viagra
- IMPROVING NUTRITION
- CONTROL OF ALCOHOL, NICOTINE AND OTHER TOXIC SUBSTANCES INTAKE
- HORMONAL THERAPY
- ENVIRONMENT ADJUSTMENTS; creating a sexual environment

Figure 5.2 Erectile disorder: treatment options

Emotional dimension

A range of emotional factors that contribute to the development and maintenance of erectile problems needs to be addressed in treatment, in order to change patterns of restrained emotional expression, develop emotional resilience and strengthen confidence and self-esteem. Achieving these goals requires clients to develop an awareness and understanding of their feelings. The therapist's task is to help the client understand how performance anxiety, for example, and the often accompanying fear of failure and rejection, affect his self-confidence and contribute to the maintenance of the erectile dysfunction. The therapist helps the client to understand the various forms in which ED-related performance anxiety can manifest itself as:

- worry that an erection will not happen or will be lost
- worry about the partner's reaction and disappointment leading to eventual break up of the relationship
- feeling inadequate as a sexual partner, a failure as a man
- watching oneself during sexual activity focusing on erectile functioning ('spectatoring') (Carroll, 2011); the man focuses so intensely on getting an erection that for this very reason an erection is impossible as he is disconnected from the pleasurable sensations that create arousal.

Focusing on emotions, processing and reflecting on them in the safe and trusting context of the therapeutic relationship can enhance clients' awareness, and promote their sense of control and agency (Elliott & Greenberg, 2007). A man's obsessive focus on his partner's sexual satisfaction can also create performance anxiety and distract his attention from his own arousal needs and experiences, resulting in ED.

Sex therapy provides various behavioural suggestions, cognitive restructuring techniques and individual and/or couple exercises to tackle the performance anxiety attached to most sexual dysfunctions including ED, as described at the beginning of this chapter. Weeks and Gambescia (2000) recommend explaining to the client how destructive 'troublesome thoughts' can be to sexual functioning and how valuable it can be to stop these. The therapist's suggestion below could be given as part of instructions for individual or couple practice:

> You don't need to worry about what your penis is doing. It is going to do whatever it is going to do and you can't force it to do anything. You've learned that the harder you try to force an erection, the more likely you won't be able to get one or to keep it if you do get one. From now on,

> focus on the pleasurable physical and emotional sensations you feel when you are together with your partner. You might try asking yourself over and over again, 'What feels good at this moment?' and 'What would I like to do or have done to me to keep things feeling good?' (p.108).

Through the therapist's validation and normalisation, the clients' feelings can gradually be put into perspective. Men experiencing ED often feel isolated with their feelings, which reinforces the problem. Sometimes a clear, straightforward normalisation, affirming that it is typical to feel anxiety, worry, fear, apprehension, self-doubt and confusion with regards to a complex and sensitive area such as sex, can provide the necessary assurance. 'There's nothing abnormal or unusual about men being anxious about sex'; 'Sex problems are normal and typical', writes Zilbergeld in *The New Male Sexuality* (1999, p.74). Significant stressors in a person's or a couple's life, such as financial or legal problems, health worries, work pressures and career difficulties can become preoccupying, creating an often underestimated barrier to feeling sexual (Wincze & Weisberg, 2015). Men suffering from ED and their partners may not recognise the significant impact that life stresses can have on their sexual feelings and behaviour. In treating ED, the therapist may enquire about the conditions under which sex happens, and how the clients detect feeling 'in the mood'. These very questions can have a therapeutic effect in the assessment stages, allowing clients to understand how unfavourable circumstances such as feeling tired, stressed, exhausted or preoccupied with various acute life worries can block sexual arousal.

Cognitive dimension

Psycho-education, in which the therapist provides sexual information to clients, suggests relevant reading (bibliotherapy) and applies a variety of cognitive interventions in order to dispel misconceptions, combat negative thinking and challenge unrealistic expectations, is an essential element in the treatment of all sexual difficulties including erectile disorder (Wincze & Weisberg, 2015). Through this psycho-educational input, therapists provide up-to-date information about sexual matters that challenges clients' restrictive beliefs and dispels sexual myths that can adversely affect their sexual interaction. A helpful list of 'misconceptions about erections' is provided by Weeks and Gambescia (2000, pp.10–11), such as: '*An erection is necessary in order to have sex*'; '*An erection is an indication of sexual desire*'; '*An erection is necessary in order to ejaculate*'; '*Losing an erection one time must be a sign of impotence*'; and so on. Zilbergeld (1999) discusses misconceptions about erections based on a fantasy model of sex, assuming that men have ultimate responsibility for the sexual encounter and that firm erections are a pre-requisite for a satisfactory sexual experience. Loss of erection is, within this set of misconceptions, seen as loss of masculinity or a sign of a lack of interest in the partner.

Clinical work provides an opportunity for therapists to identify a wider spectrum of misconceptions than are cited in sexology literature. One couple initially brought forward the issue of the male partner's lack of sexual interest. The female partner appeared distressed about this, seeking help with understanding the origin of the problem and its resolution. After several sessions, a myth held by the male client emerged, whereby he believed that erections should pre-exist initiation of sexual contact. Given that his erections were not occurring as spontaneously as previously, he stopped initiating sexual encounters and, in the absence of an erection, stopped responding to his partner's initiations. In this case, straightforward educational input made a difference; the couple were reassured that there was variety and flexibility in how a sequence of a sexual interaction may develop, with no set order in which sexual responses should happen or at which point an erection should occur. Furthermore, it was explained that the penis can gain and lose its tumescence several times during any sexual encounter. This is a potentially significant therapeutic educational intervention as many couples, based on misconceptions about erections, stop the sexual activity once the erection is lost, often leaving them feeling frustrated and disappointed. The fact that frequency and strength of erections gradually reduces as part of the normal ageing processes was also explained, as was the fact that erectile capability, contrary to widespread mythology, is lifelong unless interfered with by ill health.

Conclusions drawn from episodes of erectile 'failure' combined with anticipation of future failure can lead to reinforcement of the sexual problem. Therapists can employ cognitive techniques of identifying and challenging a client's negative thoughts about their own performance with a view to enabling them to set more realistic expectations. In addition, by challenging the idea that sex is all about a hard erection, penetration and orgasm, clients are invited through therapeutic conversations and various behavioural exercises to explore and experiment with different sexual options. Bibliotherapy can be useful in providing specific ideas as to how non-penetrative sex can be enjoyable and fulfilling (Zilbergeld, 1999). A client mentioned in one session that her best sexual experience was with a man who had erectile dysfunction, as it allowed a lot of imaginative play; this account was then transformed into a therapeutic intervention to other clients to support therapeutic messages of the importance of going beyond erections and not allowing the whole experience to be dominated by this single aspect, at the expense of numerous alternative sexual possibilities.

Unusual sexual interests and fantasies can sometimes, through the cognitive processes of exaggeration and catastrophising, combined with typical myths and misconceptions, lead to extreme conclusions about one's abnormality. Therapy can explore the origin of such strong moral or even moralistic values and provide clarifying information, enabling clients to widen the spectrum of normality related to sexual interests and behaviour, initiating important de-pathologising processes.

Weeks and Gambescia (2000) developed a technique for the advancement of positive sexual thoughts and attitudes, which they termed the 'sexual bill of rights'. Clients are asked to write a statement about what they believe they are entitled to sexually. This may include how they perceive themselves and how they believe they are allowed to feel and behave. This technique can be conducted in the context of either an individual or a couple session. In any case, the couple can share their statements with each other and are encouraged to jointly decide how these can be incorporated into their sexual thinking and behaviour. Another technique used to encourage positive thinking involves suggesting that clients, either individually or collectively, make their best efforts to write down a comprehensive list of positive thoughts about themselves, their partner and the relationship. The couple is then encouraged to read their lists to each other and discuss them as a means of incorporating positive exchanges as part of their daily lives (Weeks & Gambescia, 2000, p.123).

Physical dimension

A range of physical treatments is available for ED: medication, vacuum constriction devices (a glass or plastic cylinder placed over the penis, combined with a pump creating a vacuum to help the penis become erect), vasoactive gels inserted into the urethra, intra-cavernosal injections and penile implant surgery.

PDE-5 inhibitors (such as Viagra, Levitra and Cialis) are being increasingly used, as opposed to other physical treatments. Perceived advantages of this type of treatment are: ease of use, availability through primary care practitioners, non-invasiveness and invisibility. Unfortunately, many men obtain this medication without having gone through a thorough medical check for any potentially rectifiable medical reasons for the problem. Medical examinations could also identify health conditions that may be contraindicated with such drugs. Specific medical risks associated with these medications include cardiovascular problems, sickle-cell disease, and ophthalmological disorders. Side effects may be experienced in the form of headaches, nasal congestion, facial flushing, blurred vision, upset stomach, dizziness, nausea and muscle aches (Rosen, Miner & Wincze, 2014, p.61).

While current sexology guidelines recommend psychological treatment in the form of sex therapy and/or couple therapy, many men opt for drug treatment, only resorting to therapy when oral medications fail, often trying to tackle the problem on their own without revealing its existence to their partner. It is worth noting that success rates with PDE-5 inhibitors are significantly lower in cases of relationship dissatisfaction, lack of desire of one or both partners (perhaps a function of the ED) or significant mental health issues (perhaps contributing to ED) (Perelman, 2005).

Behavioural dimension

A typical sexology behavioural intervention aimed at normalising the process of gaining and losing erections is termed 'wax and wane' (Zilbergeld, 1999). The man undertakes a regular masturbatory exercise stimulating his penis to the point of a firm erection, then stopping and observing the gradual loss of tumescence, then recommencing the stimulation of his flaccid penis until regaining a firm erection; this process is repeated several times in one session, providing the man with the lived experience of his ability to regain lost erections and helping him to strengthen a sense of control over his erectile functioning.

Similar exercises such as pleasuring the soft penis, learning to lose erections, self-stimulation focused on awareness of one's own sexual response, and stimulus control identifying conditions for a positive sexual encounter are further behavioural techniques effectively applied in sex therapy as part of the treatment of ED (Weeks & Gambescia, 2000).

Sexual technique improvement is sometimes indicated, if the clients are not aware of the kind of stimulus they require for sustained sexual excitement; through examination of the personal and interpersonal sexual script, such problems may be identified and treated in sex therapy (Carroll, 2011).

Guided fantasy is sometimes used to take clients through a fantasy exercise in the session (Weeks & Gambescia, 2000). Some clients feel worried that the act of fantasising and/or their specific fantasies are 'abnormal'. It is important to provide reassurance that the content of individual fantasies vary enormously and there are no fast and hard rules about the 'normality' as such judgements can block sexual desire and arousal. Couples sometimes share their fantasies but this should be an option rather than an expectation. If they decide to do so, a clear prior understanding should be established that fantasised activities do not necessarily represent a desire for their enactment in real life.

'Simmering', developed by Zilbergeld and Ellison (1980), is a technique aimed at enhancing fantasy and sexual desire and arousal. The client is advised to repeatedly imagine a sensual and sexual encounter with another person they feel attracted to and stay with those feelings for a few seconds a day, vividly picturing details of the physical interactions. They then let the images fade away, replacing them with those of their real partner in fantasy and subsequently in reality.

Relational dimension

The most common relationship problems seen in cases involving erectile dysfunction are couple conflict, unresolved anger and lack of communication (Weeks & Gambescia, 2000). Assessment can identify sources of couple conflict, which may relate to specific episodes of hurt such as infidelity, abuse or broken promises. Sometimes, a couple's ways of communicating lead to the creation and reinforcement of problems, which can potentially be resolved through facilitation of more effective communicational patterns. In some cases, however, couple conflict cannot be resolved easily if at all, such as when it is based on a discrepancy of core values or religious and/or cultural belief systems.

Enhancement of couple communication about sex as well as their general communicational effectiveness can be achieved through active therapeutic empathy, listening, facilitation of self-expression and therapeutic support in the form of respectful and appreciative interactions during the session. Equally, a variety of specific interventions are available, based on a combination of the cognitive, behavioural and systemic therapeutic techniques discussed in Chapter 1, as well as the wealth of interventions aimed at improving couple interaction, resolving conflict and enhancing mutual listening, which are typically applied in the course of couple therapy.

Enlisting the partner's support in the treatment of ED, if the client is currently in a committed relationship, is often crucial. The partner's response to the client's erectile difficulties often forms a part of the wider picture and further influences the sexual interaction. If the partner becomes angry, blameful or excessively distressed as a result of the problem, this typically raises anxiety and performance pressure on the man experiencing erectile difficulty, which exacerbates the problem. Partners can become very anxious and upset in such circumstances, emphasising that their previous partners have not displayed such difficulties, intensifying the man's fear of failure and rejection. This kind of situation can raise a therapeutic dilemma between challenging the response of the partner and employing therapeutic curiosity in understanding where such strong reactions may be coming from. For example, a couple reported that a female partner of a particular client displaying erectile difficulties would on occasions, when they were attempting having sexual intercourse unsuccessfully, show her anger and frustration through criticism, calling him 'incapable', and 'lazy', and once even slapping him. This situation presented a challenge to the therapeutic relationship when the therapist made a firm statement that such behaviour constituted verbal, emotional and physical abuse, and that the only way in which therapy could proceed was if a contract was made such that this should immediately cease, at least for the duration of treatment. A strong challenge such as this one, when conveyed in a supportive way, and with the therapeutic purpose well explained, is an important therapeutic skill as it may be required in such situations to prevent further damage to clients and their relationship.

Frequently an issue arises whereby the partners experience arousal problems, which in turn can decrease the level of arousal of the man suffering with ED themselves. It may be that the partner suffers arousal difficulty or another sexual dysfunction themselves, or that their own sexual experience is limited by the erectile difficulty. In any case, inclusion of the partner in the treatment programme often increases the likelihood of its success. Poor couple communication and sexual difficulties are often intertwined and mutually reinforcing. Communication problems can be a contributing factor in the development of ED, which may then increase anxiety and upset, further deteriorating the couple's communication and leading to avoidance of sex and intimacy. Sensate focus is indicated in such situations, whereby sensuality and affection may be restored and communication about sex, emotions and intimacy opened up.

Cultural dimension

Negative attitudes about sex can stem from cultural or societal norms, familial messages, education, the media or religion. Sexual genograms can uncover such issues, enhancing contextual understanding of rigid beliefs and associated shame and guilt. Sometimes, anxiety and fear are deeply embedded, stemming from past traumatic and abusive experiences. The therapeutic space allows for exploration of these experiences and their possible effects on the person's emotional, physical, relational and sexual wellbeing.

A male gay client shared with significant distress how his father used to talk about gay men in a harsh, aggressive way using derogatory terms.

The client didn't disclose his sexual orientation during his father's lifetime, only coming out in his late adolescence after his death. Still, years later, the father continued to represent a fear-inducing figure to the client and his voice remained persistently present in his mind, dominating his intimate sphere, creating lasting anxiety about not being manly enough and behaving inappropriately. Therapy was mainly focused on the paternal relationship, with the effect of culturally and societally induced homongeativity and homophobia that his father represented. As a result of the harsh treatment by the father, who bullied him for being too soft, too emotional and refusing to physically fight, the client experienced fear, shame, anger, anxiety, resentment, rage and a deep sadness that he grew up with and carried through life. Initially, ED was presented as the problem but, in response to the client's lead, the focus of therapeutic conversations shifted to reflection on this relationship and the profound effect it had on him. This alone, without any specific interventions addressing sexual behaviour, led to the gradual resolution of the erectile problem as the client reflected on the meaning of his experiences and developed an understanding and a sense of healthy distance from them, leading him to gain a sense of greater control over his life choices and his sexual rights.

Female orgasmic disorder (FOD): treatment options

When a woman presents with FOD, in establishing whether the problem is primarily orgasmic, it should be identified whether arousal has occurred, which requires assessment of the adequacy of sexual stimuli and a detailed exploration of sexual relationship practices (Graham, 2014). In cases where the problem is mainly due to a lack of adequate stimuli, a diagnosis of dysfunction would not be made (McCabe, 2015). Sometimes, a woman reporting orgasmic difficulty undertakes treatment solely to please her partner and does not consider her sexual experience unsatisfactory otherwise. Such motivation for treatment is best addressed in couple therapy and while it is possible to apply effective strategies for facilitating orgasm as part of the couple sexual activity, it is vital that the context for such treatment is explained and de-pathologised. Educational input normalises the variety and flexibility of female sexual response, explaining that many women can experience sexual desire, arousal and sexual satisfaction without necessarily achieving orgasm.

Treatment effectiveness of FOD lacks systematic research methodology, therefore results are not necessarily reliable. Such weaknesses include: the definition of the problem lacks clarity; the programmes are not described in sufficient detail; outcome measures are not clearly defined; and the samples are too small (McCabe, 2015). As a result, sexology lacks precise data on the best forms of treatment of FOD. Current understanding in sexology suggests that cognitive behavioural approaches offer the leading treatment choice for FOD, perhaps simply resulting from the fact that there is most empirical research evidence for this treatment approach (Komisaruk & Whipple, 2011).

The International Society for Sexual Medicine recommends a procedure whereby directed masturbation in combination with sex education, anxiety reduction techniques and CBT are the main therapeutic tools in the treatment of FOD (Laan, Rellini & Barnes, 2013). Figure 5.3 summarises treatment options for FOD within the dimensions of the MOST model.

Emotional dimension

As discussed in the previous chapter, a range of emotional factors potentially contribute to the development and maintenance of female orgasmic difficulties. Through therapeutic conversations, emotions attached to sexual activity and orgasm are explored with a view to facilitating a process of self-reflexive change. The origins of these feelings can lie in the distant or more recent past revealing, in CBT terms, predisposing, precipitating and maintaining factors contributing to the problem. Performance anxiety, an emotional factor playing a part in all sexual dysfunctions to a greater or a lesser extent, often features in associated female orgasmic difficulties. There is range of therapeutic interventions that can be effectively employed to address this issue, including normalisation, reframing, behavioural relaxation exercises and a variety of couple communication exercises. Anxieties frequently encountered in the aetiology of this dysfunction include fear of rejection, of losing control and of 'letting go'. A normalising intervention, acknowledging that these fears are commonly experienced by women presenting sexual difficulties, provides reassurance and places the problem in perspective, potentially encouraging self-acceptance. Mindfulness techniques, designed to enhance non-judgemental present moment awareness, are currently used for tackling a range of emotional difficulties, and are increasingly applied in the treatment of sexual difficulties, including FOD.

Fear of rejection and feelings of obligation towards the partner can be addressed both in individual and in couple therapy. Assertiveness training may helpfully contribute to the development of emotional resilience and enhancement of self-esteem. Equally, a therapeutic relationship based on listening, reassurance, respect, warmth and appreciation can be a part of the healing process leading to clients' greater self-confidence and self-appreciation.

TREATMENT OPTIONS

CULTURAL

- RELIGIOUS SEXUAL PROHIBITIONS
- EXPLORING CULTURAL ISSUES OF PRIDE AND SHAME
- STRONG CULTURAL STORIES ABOUT MASCULINITY AND FEMININITY / GENDER ROLE EXPECTATIONS
- LIMITED CULTURAL SUPPORT NETWORK
- TRAUMATIC LIFE EVENTS e.g. abuse, rape, job loss
- DISTURBED FAMILY RELATIONSHIPS
- ECONOMIC PRESSURES, e.g. unemployment

EMOTIONAL

- ASSERTIVENESS TRAINING
- CHANGING PATTERNS OF EMOTIONAL EXPRESSION
- DEVELOPING EMOTIONAL RESILIENCE
- NORMALISATION
- ENHACING EMOTIONAL EMPATHY
- EXPLORING PAST TRAUMAS AND THEIR EFFECTS
- MINDFULNESS: to increase non-judgemental, present-moment awareness

COGNITIVE

- EDUCATIONAL INPUT
- UNDERSTANDING BLOCKS TO SEXUAL EXPERIENCE
- ADVISING CLIENTS OF THE CYCLE OF PERFORMANCE ANXIETY: FEAR OF FAILURE- NEGATIVE ANTICIPATION
- EXPANDING THE MEANING OF SEX BEYOND INTERCOURSE AND ORGASM
- CHALLENGING GENITAL FOCUS AND GOAL-DIRECTED CONCEPT OF SEX

RELATIONAL

- IMPROVING COUPLE COMMUNICATION, e.g. facilitate opening up and sharing feelings and expressing own desires, blocks and inhibitions
- ENLISTING PARTNER SUPPORT
- ENHANCING COUPLE COMMUNICATION ABOUT SEX
- RESOLVING CONFLICT
- ENHANCING MUTUAL LISTENING
- MORE QUALITY TIME (COUPLE AND FAMILY)
- RESOLVING OR DISTANCING FROM RELATIONSHIP PRESSURES/ CONSTRUCTIVE CHANGE OF PATTERNS OF RELATING
- SENSATE FOCUS
- COUPLE THERAPY

BEHAVIOURAL

- SYSTEMATIC DESENSITISATION
- TEACHING EFFECTIVE TECHNIQUES OF SELF-STIMULATION; DIRECTED MASTURBATION
- TRANSFER ABILITY TO REACH ORGASM THROUGH MASTURBATION TO REACHING ORGASM IN INTERCOURSE
- SELF-FOCUS; INDIVIDUAL SEXUAL GROWTH EXERCISES; USING MIRROR TO EXAMINE OWN GENITALS
- ENCOURAGING USE OF FANTASY IN MASTURBATION AND SEX
- SEXUAL SKILLS TRAINING
- KEGEL EXERCISES

PHYSICAL

- FITNESS AND EXERCISE
- PHARMACOTHERAPY e.g. bupropion, sildenafil
- HORMONAL THERAPY e.g. oestrogen, testosterone
- NUTRITIONAL SUPPLEMENTS e.g. gingko biloba, ginseng
- EROS CLITORAL THERAPY DEVICE
- STOP / CHANGE MEDICATION CAUSING SEXUAL PROBLEMS SIDE EFFECTS
- ENVIRONMENT ADJUSTMENT

Figure 5.3 Female orgasmic disorder: treatment options

Contextualising emotional responses within past experiences, such as criticism and trauma, can enhance self-empathy and facilitate de-pathologising of the client's emotional reactions while reframing of such responses, e.g. as self-protection in the context of past emotional and sexual trauma, provides a different and potentially helpful outlook on the situation.

Cognitive dimension

Many clinical studies have found a positive correlation between FOD and negative attitudes towards sex, often grounded in myths and misconceptions concerning the female orgasm, which could be usefully addressed in treatment through exploration of their origin and dispelled through providing correct information. Extensive research into female sexuality suggests that orgasm is not always essential to sexual satisfaction and that the inability to experience orgasm during intercourse is not abnormal (Komisaruk & Whipple, 2011). Case examples from sexology literature describe cognitive interventions where clients are encouraged to broaden their view of sexual satisfaction whereby 'orgasm is a possible by-product of a sexual exchange but not a necessity' (Wincze & Weisberg, 2015, p.37).

Through an educational, supportive, encouraging and empowering attitude, therapists convey the message that each individual is responsible for their own sexual pleasure and satisfaction and communicate to the women that 'they can *have* an orgasm but no one else can *give* them an orgasm' (Komisaruk & Whipple, 2011, p.73).

Challenging expectations that a woman (and her partner) may have about female orgasm is a vital part of treatment in cases where rigid, narrow and exaggerated views are firmly held, negatively impacting sexual experience. For example, misconceptions that '*orgasm is essential for a woman's sexual satisfaction*' or that '*the absence of female orgasm from a partnered sexual activity necessarily implies abnormality*' and that '*orgasm should happen via intercourse and occur during each partnered sexual activity*' are some examples of oppressive sexual beliefs. Wincze and Weisberg (2015) write: 'in describing female orgasmic disorder it must be emphasized that an orgasm is an orgasm and it does not matter how an orgasm is produced' (p.35).

Past episodes of 'orgasmic failure' can cause anxiety and trigger self-defeating and distracting thoughts, leading to negative anticipation (McCabe, 2015). Drawing the woman's attention to such patterns whereby performance anxiety and negative cognitions reinforce each other in a repetitive cycle of thoughts, feelings and behaviours, can enable a fuller understanding of factors contributing to and exacerbating the condition, potentially enhancing her sense of self-control and personal agency.

Physical dimension

At present, no approved pharmacological treatment for FOD exists (Graham, 2014). There is limited evidence of the effectiveness of bupropion and sildenafil (Viagra) and of hormonal replacement therapy such as testosterone and oestrogen (pills, cream and patches) (Davis et al., 2008). Given that female orgasmic functioning can be adversely affected by certain medications such as antidepressants or oral contraceptives, diminishing their use significantly contributes to effective treatment. Some studies have investigated the effect of herbal remedies such as ginkgo biloba and ginseng, noting positive effects on sexual functioning, including orgasmic response; however, such results are of limited reliability. Eros clitoral stimulation therapy is a device, approved by the US Food and Drug Administration (FDA) agency, which purports to improve clitoral blood flow, thus increasing sexual arousal; however, there is no clear evidence to support this claim (Graham, 2014).

Body image and general state of fitness and health usually improve as a result of healthy nutrition, regular exercise and moderation or cessation of intake of alcohol, nicotine and other toxic substances.

Lack of privacy and comfort can impede the ability to relax and enjoy a sexual encounter and it seems that women are generally more sensitive to such environmental factors than men. These factors should be explored with clients so as to ensure the most conducive context for sexual activity.

Behavioural dimension

During the 1970s, a small group format of teaching women masturbation techniques developed and became increasingly popular (Dodson, 1976). Books and videos were created to 'give women permission to experience orgasm' (1970s expression) (Komisaruk & Whipple, 2011, p.72). The masturbation training programme comprised educational input on effective ways to achieve orgasm, combined with practical guidelines starting with exploration of own body followed by use of self-pleasuring techniques (directed masturbation). In a popular and widely used book, *Becoming Orgasmic* (Heiman & LoPiccolo, 1988/2010), the authors describe a treatment programme applicable to lifelong generalised FOD. The process of self-exploration enables the woman to learn what is sexually arousing for her, as well as what feels pleasant and unpleasant, firstly through non-genital touching and then gradually progressing to genital stimulation, sometimes incorporating a vibrator. The subsequent stages of the programme involve guiding the woman to incorporate this experience into her relationship, by transferring the methods of achieving orgasm through masturbation to her sexual interaction with her partner, whose co-operation here is crucial for success of the process.

Heiman (2007) states that there is sufficient evidence to support the idea that directed masturbation is an effective treatment for lifelong generalised FOD but less so for secondary FOD, a more common variation, that seems to be more difficult to treat (Heiman, 2007). While masturbation is such an 'important learning mechanism' (Chalker, 2000, p.60) in the treatment of most sexual dysfunctions, clinicians should carefully examine cultural, religious, and personal attitudes and beliefs towards the practice. There seems to be consistent evidence that women engage in masturbation less frequently than men (Petersen & Hyde, 2011), which may reflect cultural attitudes to women's sexuality.

Heiman (2007) applied a 'coital alignment technique' whereby the woman's clitoris is stimulated during intercourse by positioning the man's pelvis in alignment with the woman's.

Kegel exercises, which are aimed at strengthening pelvic floor muscles seem to be particularly effective in regulating orgasmic response. Research studies have found a significant correlation between the women's pelvic muscle strength and the intensity of her orgasmic response (Ladas, Whipple & Perry, 2005).

Encouraging development and use of sexual fantasy has proven helpful in the treatment of many sexual dysfunctions. Clinical studies have shown that sexual fantasy seems to have different meanings for men and women. For example, McCabe (2015) describes that therapeutic guidance for use of fantasy helps women to achieve greater self-acceptance as a sexual person. Sexual fantasies also serve the purpose of distraction from performance anxiety.

Relational dimension

Empirical studies have consistently evidenced that communication with the partner plays a major role in women's sexual satisfaction and that relationship factors appear directly related to female orgasmic functioning (McCabe & Giles, 2012). Communication exercises developed in sex therapy and couple therapy aim to enhance general couple communication, as well as that which is specifically sex-related, through facilitation of opening up and sharing feelings, expressing one's own sexual desires, and revealing sexual blocks and inhibitions. Planning pleasant joint activities and increasing the variety of ways of spending enjoyable times together is incorporated as a regular part of sex therapy (Wincze &

Weisberg, 2015) aimed at improving the quality of the relationship and increasing relationship satisfaction. In the context of sex therapy, these exercises would tend to be more structured, in the style of a CBT goal-oriented approach. Systemically, the use of exercises is incorporated within a range of different therapeutic possibilities. For example, McCabe (2015) proposes a series of instructions to couples within a structured therapeutic communication exercise, starting with specific questions for clients to consider, such as: 'What do I like about us as partners and how does that make me feel?', and 'How do I feel about differences between us in desire for sexual contact?' (p.180). Systemic interventions most typically include various types of questions aimed at facilitating communication and encouraging reflective processes and self-healing (Tomm, 2016) and could be used as a means of enhancing intimacy between partners. The MOST model proposes an integration of a variety of therapeutic approaches, including both more and less structured, as well as more and less directive therapeutic attitudes, so as to tailor the approach to specific client needs.

Sensate focus exercises, originally developed to reduce performance anxiety, can be usefully applied to FOD; however, there are insufficient research findings to confirm their effectiveness in producing a substantial improvement in orgasmic response (Meston et al., 2004). Sensate focus still represents a great therapeutic resource in reducing performance anxiety and co-ordinating couple sexual responses and it has many benefits for the couple interaction, being most effective, it seems, when used in conjunction with other techniques.

Cultural dimension

Dispelling cultural myths about sex and gender roles is a major therapeutic task in the treatment of female sexual dysfunction. Cultural stereotypes about gender roles and female sexuality can be helpfully reflected upon in therapy, supported by an educational approach, bibliotherapy and sharing of research data. Particular cultural pressures on women in terms of their physical appearance and age are summarised in *Becoming Orgasmic* (Heiman & LoPiccolo, 1988/2010), an excellent resource for both professionals and clients: 'If you are over eighteen you may be a victim of our cultural stereotype that only very young, very thin, and very beautiful women qualify as truly sexy' (1988, p.228).

Therapeutic conversations can enable the woman and her partners to gain a contextual understanding of the development of certain narrow sexual beliefs, stemming from familial, educational, religious and cultural influences. Sexual and cultural genogram explorations are particularly helpful in deconstructing intergenerational stories about sex and intimacy that may have impacted the woman's understanding of sex and her sexual rights, choices and restrictions.

Research studies suggest that there are no differences in femininity, sexual adjustment, maturity or psychological health between women who have orgasms during intercourse and those who have their orgasms in other ways; sharing such findings can be an important normalising intervention, tackling a frequent tendency of women to self-pathologise, or their partners to hold pathologising attitudes as illustrated by the case below: a woman aged 50 sought sex therapy treatment for 'anorgasmia' (the referring GP's diagnosis). Her male partners' comments that *'it takes her too long to orgasm'* and that all their previous partners *'took a lot less time to reach orgasm'* led her to believe that her sexual response was abnormal. She was able to reach orgasm via oral sex quite easily and sometimes via intercourse if it involved clitoral stimulation, not through penetration alone. This, quite typical, female sexual response was constructed by her partners as abnormality, a view unfortunately supported by the referring professional. Educational input was provided, based on a wealth of information, literature, DVDs and clinical examples; however, it still took several months of therapy sessions, bibliotherapy, behavioural exercises and genogram analysis before the client felt she could engage with a different perspective and accept a non-pathologising viewpoint. After so many years of receiving consistent messages that there was something wrong with her, educational input alone was not sufficient and it required time to process the emotional impact of such denigrating communications.

The example above also illustrates the social constructionist idea about the meaning of orgasm deriving from social and cultural contexts and the current prevalent masculine meanings given to it (Wincze & Weisberg, 2015). Heiman and LoPiccolo (1988) suggest an important question for a couple presenting for treatment for FOD: 'Why do you want to have an orgasm during intercourse?' (p.277). In this way, a possible set of cultural and gender myths may be revealed such that vaginal orgasm, particularly through intercourse, is a more mature sexual response than clitoral orgasm. While offering a wealth of therapeutic interventions, a combination of cognitive, behavioural and physical techniques, the authors also warn that orgasm through intercourse is not an universally desired goal. In some cases, pressure to achieve orgasm in certain ways during partnered sex can make the situation worse. They present a client example whereby such interventions diminished pleasure previously experienced through a combination of masturbation and partner touch. Therefore, therapists' contextual understanding of clients' motivation and goals for therapy is equally important and should always inform their approach to treatment.

Female sexual interest/arousal disorder (FSI/AD): treatment options

As described in the previous chapter, female sexual interest/arousal disorder is a multifactorial condition, requiring detailed assessment and distinguishing subjective sexual arousal disorder from genital sexual arousal disorder. As with other sexual dysfunctions, it is important to establish whether the problem is primary (lifelong) or secondary (acquired). In the case of a primary problem, the predisposing factors would have predated first sexual experience, and in the case of a secondary problem assessment establishes the length of time that it has been experienced, any variations in its manifestations, such as whether there are any contextual differences in how it presents, and any precipitating factors, such as life transitions, ill health, stresses, and relationship distress. The treatment options for FSI/AD are summarised in Figure 5.4 using the MOST model.

Emotional dimension

One of the most widespread precipitants in all sexual dysfunctions, performance anxiety, significantly contributes to FSI/AD as well. Various anxiety reduction techniques, such as normalisation of anxiety and fear; clarification of their effect on sexual functioning; contextualising emotional responses within past experiences such as criticism, trauma and abuse, are applicable in the treatment of this disorder.

Sex therapists typically apply various cognitive and behavioural techniques in anxiety reduction. For example, Weeks and Gambescia (2002) describe the following techniques to lower sexual response anxiety:

- *Education about the response anxiety*: providing clients with information about how sexual response anxiety works, followed by the suggestion to notice when this happens
- *Thought stopping*: a cognitive technique whereby clients are advised to say to themselves, for example: 'Stop trying to force feeling turned-on'
- *Paradoxical intention* (a technique developed by Frankl in 1952 (Frankl, 1985), and subsequently used as part of early family therapy) whereby the therapist prescribes the symptom usually using some humour, for

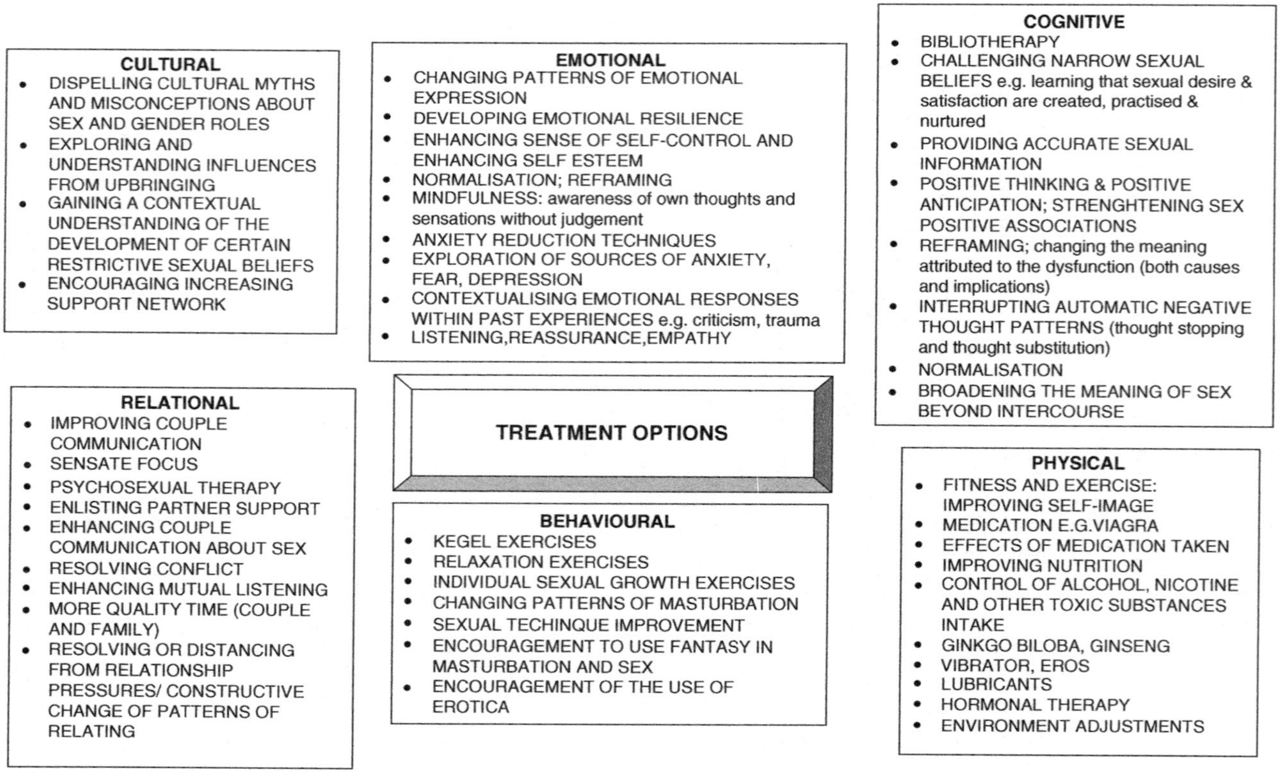

TREATMENT OPTIONS

CULTURAL
- DISPELLING CULTURAL MYTHS AND MISCONCEPTIONS ABOUT SEX AND GENDER ROLES
- EXPLORING AND UNDERSTANDING INFLUENCES FROM UPBRINGING
- GAINING A CONTEXTUAL UNDERSTANDING OF THE DEVELOPMENT OF CERTAIN RESTRICTIVE SEXUAL BELIEFS
- ENCOURAGING INCREASING SUPPORT NETWORK

EMOTIONAL
- CHANGING PATTERNS OF EMOTIONAL EXPRESSION
- DEVELOPING EMOTIONAL RESILIENCE
- ENHANCING SENSE OF SELF-CONTROL AND ENHANCING SELF ESTEEM
- NORMALISATION; REFRAMING
- MINDFULNESS: awareness of own thoughts and sensations without judgement
- ANXIETY REDUCTION TECHNIQUES
- EXPLORATION OF SOURCES OF ANXIETY, FEAR, DEPRESSION
- CONTEXTUALISING EMOTIONAL RESPONSES WITHIN PAST EXPERIENCES e.g. criticism, trauma
- LISTENING,REASSURANCE,EMPATHY

COGNITIVE
- BIBLIOTHERAPY
- CHALLENGING NARROW SEXUAL BELIEFS e.g. learning that sexual desire & satisfaction are created, practised & nurtured
- PROVIDING ACCURATE SEXUAL INFORMATION
- POSITIVE THINKING & POSITIVE ANTICIPATION; STRENGHTENING SEX POSITIVE ASSOCIATIONS
- REFRAMING; changing the meaning attributed to the dysfunction (both causes and implications)
- INTERRUPTING AUTOMATIC NEGATIVE THOUGHT PATTERNS (thought stopping and thought substitution)
- NORMALISATION
- BROADENING THE MEANING OF SEX BEYOND INTERCOURSE

RELATIONAL
- IMPROVING COUPLE COMMUNICATION
- SENSATE FOCUS
- PSYCHOSEXUAL THERAPY
- ENLISTING PARTNER SUPPORT
- ENHANCING COUPLE COMMUNICATION ABOUT SEX
- RESOLVING CONFLICT
- ENHANCING MUTUAL LISTENING
- MORE QUALITY TIME (COUPLE AND FAMILY)
- RESOLVING OR DISTANCING FROM RELATIONSHIP PRESSURES/ CONSTRUCTIVE CHANGE OF PATTERNS OF RELATING

BEHAVIOURAL
- KEGEL EXERCISES
- RELAXATION EXERCISES
- INDIVIDUAL SEXUAL GROWTH EXERCISES
- CHANGING PATTERNS OF MASTURBATION
- SEXUAL TECHINQUE IMPROVEMENT
- ENCOURAGEMENT TO USE FANTASY IN MASTURBATION AND SEX
- ENCOURAGEMENT OF THE USE OF EROTICA

PHYSICAL
- FITNESS AND EXERCISE: IMPROVING SELF-IMAGE
- MEDICATION E.G.VIAGRA
- EFFECTS OF MEDICATION TAKEN
- IMPROVING NUTRITION
- CONTROL OF ALCOHOL, NICOTINE AND OTHER TOXIC SUBSTANCES INTAKE
- GINKGO BILOBA, GINSENG
- VIBRATOR, EROS
- LUBRICANTS
- HORMONAL THERAPY
- ENVIRONMENT ADJUSTMENTS

Figure 5.4 Female sexual interest/arousal disorder: treatment options

example: 'Try to force yourself as hard as possible to feel turned on', where the opposite effect is intended
- *Eliminating ideas that foster response anxiety*: one way of accomplishing this goal may be to broaden the definition of the meaning of sex; typically, sex is equated with intercourse and this cognitive technique aims at moving beyond such a narrow definition, often combined with behavioural prescriptions for couples to enjoy an extensive range of sexual interactions that do not include coital activity
- *Manipulating the environment*: educating the couple about how to create a sexual environment (Weeks & Gambescia, 2000, pp.134–135).

Sexual therapy literature offers guidelines for treating intimacy fears (e.g. Wincze & Weisberg, 2015). Firstly, it recommends identifying the fear, after which cognitive therapy may be used to neutralise negative thoughts associated with this fear and then replace these thoughts with more flexible ones. Fear of intimacy can be dealt with by using cognitive and behavioural techniques in individual and in couple therapy by addressing interpersonal patterns and each partner's cognitions and behaviours that maintain it. In couple therapy, exploration of each partner's genogram can unveil the origins of fear of intimacy and commitment in their upbringing (Weeks & Fife, 2014).

Mindfulness-based interventions are positively indicated in the treatment of FSI/AD, as women presenting with these issues frequently describe a disconnection between their mind and their body; this form of therapy, based on an ancient Eastern practice that embodies present-moment non-judgemental awareness, gives the woman permission to feel whatever she is feeling and listen to and observe her feelings without judgement or trying to force the feeling (Sipe & Eisendrath, 2012). Mindfulness exercises can be first practised in the therapy session, before incorporating them into the client's daily routine. Clinical studies have shown the effectiveness of this practice in increasing an active awareness of the body and sexual feelings in an accepting and compassionate manner (Brotto & Heiman, 2007).

It is possible that fear of pregnancy can be so intense that it can interfere with the sexual experience by negatively affecting arousal. As a result of this fear, the woman may tense up her bodily muscles and not relax which, together with the thoughts of getting pregnant, can inhibit the enjoyment of sex and prevent arousal. This example does not constitute a 'disorder', but rather an understandable, protective bodily reaction to a perceived threat. Sometimes fear of pregnancy dominates the woman's/both partners' mind to the extent that it is almost impossible to engage in a sexual activity.

It can be helpful to advise the use of multiple contraceptive measures, for example combining the 'rhythm method' (monitoring of the safest timing in the menstrual cycle to avoid sex during ovulation), with the use of condoms, spermicides and the withdrawal technique. The knowledge of the fact that none of the measures individually secure 100% protection against pregnancy, exaggerated by the extreme fear of pregnancy, may bring about a need to maximise the contraceptive effect by using several types of precaution simultaneously.

Cognitive dimension

Through providing psycho-educational input and challenging restrictive sexual beliefs, the therapist dispels misinformation about sexual desire, including perfectionistic expectations about sex and intimacy often underlying the belief system in women presenting symptoms of FSI/AD.

Negative cognitions about sex, intimacy, affection and the partner frequently underlie lack of sexual interest and arousal difficulties. For example, a belief that sex is more an obligation than a pleasure can contribute to the maintenance of these symptoms by blocking the emergence of enjoyable sexual thoughts, feelings and fantasies. As part of this automatic thinking process, when sexual thoughts occur, they are almost reflexively rejected because of underlying negative beliefs. A powerful self-perpetuating cycle of mutual influence between anxiety and such beliefs can be formed. Anxiety, brought about by negative thoughts, then creates further cognitive interference in the form of thoughts such as: *'I will never be able to get aroused'*, *'I must feel desire but am unable to'*, and so on, leading to more anxiety and sometimes associated shame and embarrassment, a sense of failure and low sexual self-esteem. Clinicians often find such cognitive catastrophising and negative anticipation patterns in women presenting with sexual response concerns (Brotto & Luria, 2014). These self-critical sexual self-schemas, based on a sense of one's own sexual incompetence, trigger negative automatic thoughts and create cognitive distractions during sexual activity, preventing the woman from responding to sexual stimuli, eliciting negative affect and blocking her sexual response. CBT techniques, such as challenging problematic thoughts, shifting attentional focus, and strengthening sex-positive associations (Brauer et al., 2012), have been used effectively in sex therapy in combination with behavioural exercises and couple therapy wherever possible.

Sometimes women erroneously believe that they are suffering a sexual desire disorder because they do not feel sexual desire at the onset of sexual activity even if it subsequently emerges as the sexual encounter evolves. Psycho-education on this specific aspect of sexual response can be an immensely helpful intervention, enabling greater self-understanding, and de-pathologising of their own sexual experience (Hall, 2010).

Bibliotherapy reinforces therapeutic educational interventions. A plethora of DVDs and self-help books are available on the market. It is useful if therapists are able to recommend specific readings to avoid clients being further misinformed by choosing inappropriate resources.

Physical dimension

'The search for a pharmacological means to cure women's low desire has been fierce', write Brotto and Luria (2014, p.32). Findings on the use of medications for treatment of FSI/AD have not been conclusive. There is limited evidence for the beneficial effects of sildenafil (Viagra) and bupropion; however, no consistent conclusions have been reached. Use of testosterone for the problems of female sexual desire and arousal has been controversial, not only in terms of its dubious benefits, but also in terms of its androgenic side effects and the risk of breast cancer.

Negative body image often has a significant impact on sexual functioning. Dissatisfaction with body shape, physical appearance or negative feelings about genital areas are factors that contribute powerfully to female sexual interest and arousal responses. Usual health and fitness advice, in terms of regular exercise, improvement in nutrition and reduction of the intake of alcohol, nicotine, caffeine and other toxic substances, can greatly contribute to enhancement of body image and overall sense of power, control and self-confidence. Individual sexual growth exercises are often prescribed to this end, encouraging the woman to own her body emotionally and mentally, in an accepting and appreciative way. Various mechanical tools such as vibrators and the Eros clitoral stimulation device are sometimes incorporated in directed masturbation and partnered sexual activities.

Adjustments in environment are sometimes necessary and immensely important. Research and clinical experience suggest that women are more easily distracted in a sexual situation than men (Leiblum, 2010) and so environmental circumstances such as proximity of children and the possibility of them coming into the bedroom, or displeasing room conditions in terms of temperature or untidiness, uncomfortable clothing or outside noise can all impact the woman's experience of a sexual situation and interfere with her readiness to feel attuned to it.

Behavioural dimension

Kegel exercises (strengthening of pelvic floor muscles) are a recommended technique for enabling the woman's greater control over her genital functioning and also as part of her physical uro-genital tract fitness.

Relaxation exercises, sometimes demonstrated in the therapy session, are advised to be regularly undertaken to release stress and alleviate anxiety, fear, worry and distracting negative thoughts. These exercises can either take the form of creative visualisation, mindfulness breathing exercises, self-hypnosis and meditation or are incorporated as part of traditional yoga, Pilates and other gentle holistic practices integrating body and mind.

Various masturbation exercises can be prescribed enabling the woman to learn about her sensual and sexual reactions and the pattern of her arousal, as well as encouraging her to expand the repertoire of sexually responding. Rigid habitual masturbation patterns established in a set way over time can get in the way of partnered sexual activity inhibiting the woman's sexual arousal. Sometimes women report lack of arousal during masturbation and the resultant abandonment of masturbatory practice. Directed masturbation in these cases can be beneficial, combined with psycho-educational input, focused on sexual response information and the dispelling of any sexual misconceptions.

Weeks and Gambescia (2015) recommend a series of homework exercises including guided imagery, graduated exposure to sexual material, directed masturbation and exposure to fantasy through bibliotherapy. Wincze and Weisberg (2015) suggest use of erotica for the purpose of encouragement of fantasy both during masturbation and partnered sex.

Relational dimension

Partnerships where the woman presents lack of sexual interest and arousal can suffer from 'poor regulation of intimacy needs' (Weeks & Gambescia, 2015, p.135) in that too much attention is given to career, children, family members' needs, hobbies, social commitments and so on, at the expense of focusing on the relationship. At times, this is linked to loss of romance and de-eroticisation of the relationship following marriage, creation of the family and the series of roles and responsibilities attached to these. Women often bring feelings that sex has become a chore or an obligation in the context of overfamiliarity of partner roles and over-availability and predictability of sex (Sims & Meana, 2010).

In these situations, creating more quality time for the partners, with or without sensate focus exercises, can enhance mutual empathy and increase emotional and physical intimacy. A lesbian couple came to therapy after a year of not having sex, worried about intimacy and affection disappearing from their relationship. They both brought 'loss of desire' but, respectively, seemed to be more aware of the lack of sexual interest of the other person. By the time they reached therapy, the situation had become chronic and they both felt stuck, unloved and unattractive, devoid of sexual desire, angry with each other and worried about the future prospects of further distancing. They were both very busy women, running between household chores, career tasks, familial and social duties, trying to please and fulfil others' expectations of their socially constructed female roles. At the end of each day, they were tired and stressed, desperate for some sleep and 'peace and quiet'. They both missed the sexual intimacy they had experienced earlier on in the relationship. A pattern emerged whereby they interpreted each other's lack of initiation of sex as disinterest in it, which then became a reason for their respective decline in sexual desire. This situation is better defined as a 'responsive lack of desire' rather than a disorder. In this case, it brought about a pattern of mutual blame, whereby they both had many examples to illustrate the other partner's avoidance of sex. These were described vividly, in rich detail and with some humour. The therapist asked them to use their imagination and create individual lists of what they would like to do together to rekindle romance. They both came up with many ideas, from walking in the park, to massage sessions, weekends away, laughing together. Interestingly, the first thing on their respective lists was 'talk more'. It felt as if they were both bursting with a need for closeness and desire for intimate communication. Therapy provided a nudge in the right direction and the clients were able to make resourceful use of the sessions and of their imagination to rekindle desire and learned to protect and prioritise couple time, while revising some of the innumerable responsibilities they both had assumed over time.

Couples sometimes seem to hold the misconception that if a relationship does not work by itself, if sex does not happen spontaneously and if partners need to put effort into the relationship, there is something fundamentally wrong. It seems too frequently forgotten and under-appreciated that relationships need nurturing, care and ongoing attention.

It is important to consider whether the problem lies in the discrepancy of sexual desire between partners, rather than within the individual with lower desire. Most frequently, individuals and couples attend clinics presenting the partner with the lower desire as the one who has the problem and needs treatment. A mismatch of sexual interest does not necessarily constitute a disorder, and when taking such clients into treatment it is of ultimate importance to define the problem as a discrepancy of desire rather than defining either 'low' or 'high' desire as the problem.

Treating disorders of desire involves a range of individual and relationship interventions, depending on the specificities of the situation. It is not uncommon that assessment of couples presenting issues of sexual desire reveals general relationship and communication problems (Wincze & Weisberg, 2015). Many treatment strategies and models of relational intervention have been developed within couple therapy. For example, Schnarch (2000) has developed 'crucible therapy' an approach based on Bowenian differentiation theory (Bowen, 1978), applied to intimacy and emotional relationships. According to Schnarch, poorly differentiated partners rely on other-validated intimacy, and their sense of self depends on others' acceptance and validation. Crucible therapy approaches desire as a relational phenomenon rather than an individual problem, rejecting the diagnostic framework of 'hypoactive', 'inhibited' or 'low sexual desire'. It focuses on differentiation in the relationship, achieving a balance between attachment, self-direction and self-regulation.

Cognitive therapy can be usefully applied in treating couples with the presenting problem of FSI/AD. Partners' irrational beliefs, fears and anxieties may evolve into interlocking sets that maintain the ongoing presence of this sexual problem. A woman experiencing lack of sexual desire might think: '*Sex is just not for me*' and her partner might think: '*She is obviously not finding me sexually attractive*'; an example of two interlocking thoughts enabling sexual avoidance to continue. Cognitive couple therapy enables partners to recognise these interlocking beliefs and to develop more positive, affirmative and enabling sexual thoughts, feelings and fantasies, creating a state of positive anticipation for the sexual encounter (Weeks & Gambescia, 2015, p.139).

A genogram can be used in couple sexual therapy to identify fears stemming from family and cultural contexts. Therapy provides a learning context for couples to understand more about the many reasons for them to fear intimacy that have developed over time (Weeks & Fife, 2014).

The fear of losing control or being controlled, often linked to the fear of loss of identity and autonomy, is sometimes manifested in relationships where power imbalance is experienced and where the woman presenting with FSI/AD, often unconsciously, feels the only way for her to keep in control is to turn off sexually (Weeks & Gambescia, 2002). It is vital that the therapist explores in couple sessions the contribution of each partner to the relationship patterns through active exploratory curiosity and empathic listening. In this way, it is hoped that both partners will take responsibility for their own behaviour and their sexual pleasure, owning and communicating their needs, while attending to their partner's through listening and responding within the context of ongoing active dialogue.

Cultural dimension

Therapy can usefully dispel cultural mythology and unrealistic expectations through use of a sexual genogram, and processing and reflecting in therapeutic conversations on the layers of internalised messages about sexuality, frequently distorted through culture, religion, racism and sexism (McGoldrick, Loonan & Wohlsifer, 2007). Being raised in an extremely religious context where sex is regarded as exclusively for procreation and not for personal enjoyment; being molested as a child or raped as an adult; being taught that to be a woman means subjugating oneself to the insatiable and unstoppable force of the male sexual drive; are all examples illustrating the potential for these messages to be reactivated when engaging in sex, which is then linked to unpleasant and traumatic experiences. Sometimes, unrealistic expectations of love, sex, intimacy and relationships communicated via the media perpetuate the feeling of failure to be feminine and perform to the standards of a desirable and sexually fulfilled woman. Pervasive societal messages are reminders of the importance of sex and sexual desire: films, magazines, shop displays, the internet, messages in advertisements, alongside the ever-growing industry of sex toys and medication for enhancement of sexual desire and arousal and various devices to boost sexual performance. The pressure to conform to these messages influences many individuals and couples who feel low or no sexual desire to become worried that there is something wrong with them rather than 'the society's (and the medics) ever-constant preoccupation with sex' (Leiblum, 2010, p.2). A client presenting with FSI/AD was relieved to hear the therapist's description of 'The hurried woman syndrome' (Bost, 2005), consisting of: fatigue or low mood, weight gain and low libido. The 'hurried woman' juggles many burdensome responsibilities within her family, career, relationships and various chores and tasks, is always running and either frequently late or is in absolute dread of being late and suffers from high levels of stress. It is estimated, according to this particular source, that about 30 million women worldwide suffer from these symptoms. The client was fascinated to hear about this and readily accepted the 'diagnosis': 'I am the hurried woman!' This intervention provided her with a contextual perspective on her situation, normalised her feelings and her sexual responses and supportively acknowledged the pressures of expectations of her that she has been constantly struggling with. It enabled her to feel part of a large community of women experiencing the same struggles, as opposed to feeling isolated and lonely in her recurring pursuit of ever-existing duties.

Sometimes, the highest context affecting the layers of the sexual spectrum (see Chapter 2) comprises a number of severely restraining beliefs and misconceptions about sex not always visible or easily accessible to the conscious mind. Therapeutic explorations focusing on learning about sex and its meaning can lead to the origins of these myths. When enquiring about such beliefs, it is important to work within a framework that allows for a variety of values and stories to be held, however constraining the therapist might consider them to be. The task of the therapist is to allow for these to emerge and to assist clients in making connections between their beliefs and their sexual experiences, and to support them in making changes if they wish to, while respecting their choices. A heterosexual couple came to therapy because the woman did not enjoy sex, and this was causing relationship distress. They both seemed satisfied with other aspects of their relationship. The woman reported absence of sexual arousal as well as a lack of pleasure and enjoyment from sex. Therapeutic conversations revealed deeply embedded negative sexual beliefs stemming from her childhood linked to her familial, cultural and religious upbringing to which she felt deeply loyal. The main reason for undertaking therapy was the couple's desire to have children and, given the infrequent sexual activity, they felt their chances were significantly reduced. Therapeutic intentionality was initially directed towards enabling the couple's fuller expression of sexuality, strengthening their deeper connection with the pleasure of sex and a more embracing approach to the meaning of sex and sexual rights. However, this therapeutic approach seemed to evoke some negative effects in that the woman appeared more worried and unhappy. When the therapist decided to change her stance and normalise the woman's right to hold onto her framework of beliefs and values, which essentially considered women's sexual pleasure as negative, this seemed to allow her to engage in sex for the reasons she chose for herself, namely to be close to her husband, to provide him with sexual pleasure, and to become pregnant, rather than for 'enjoying sex'. Once freed up from the pressure that sex has to be sexy, enjoyable, exciting, arousing, orgasmic, and so on, she was confirmed in her right to hold onto her beliefs and continue participating in the sexual activity that provided her emotional satisfaction and that was coherent with her cultural, religious, familial and gender loyalties, dissolving both the internal and couple conflict.

Basson (2001) provided normalisation for the reasons why people may choose to have sex other than for sexual pleasure, including closeness with a partner, physical affection and intimacy, calming down conflict, pleasing the partner, and procreation. If the woman's reasons for having sex and her experience of sex are coherent and cause no problem for her, part of the complex therapeutic task is to determine what kind of change, for what purpose, for whose benefit and from whose perspective it is indicated. A research study conducted by psychologists from the University of Texas, involving around 2,000 participants, identified 237 distinct reasons for having sex, thus extending this normalising message (Meston & Buss, 2007). The most frequently given reasons were divided into four categories:

- *Physicality* (stress reduction, pleasure, physical desirability, experience seeking).
- *Goal attainment* (utilitarian reasons, social status, gaining popularity, revenge).
- *Emotions* (love, wanting to express a positive feeling) and
- *Insecurity* (self-esteem boost, feeling obligated, attempts to keep the partner interested).

The less frequently given reasons may not be less important, claim the researchers. For example, manipulative motives can lead to long-lasting damaging consequences for personal health, safety or the relationship. Men exceeded women in endorsing factors related to pure physical pleasure, and women exceeded men in endorsing certain emotional motivations; however, it emerged that desire for intimacy and emotional connectedness from sexual activity were frequently endorsed by both women and men, and in equal measure. The findings provided an expanded understanding of the complexities and the wide range of reasons that people believe motivate them to have sex.

Genito-pelvic pain/penetration disorder (GPPPD): treatment options

GPPPD can be immensely distressing for both the woman suffering from this disorder and her partner/s. This syndrome has a long history of being treated by medical professions as a somatic representation of individual and/or relational issues, negating the reality of the physical experience. Many women may have been told 'it's all in their head' which may have reinforced the emotional aspects of the issues in terms of feeling unsupported and unheard. However, over the last 20 years, a tremendous amount of research has been conducted in the field of sexology to examine the various aspects of this syndrome, that attempts to identify and understand its multidimensional nature, a development that has proven validating for those women affected by the disorder.

Currently, GPPPD is recognised primarily as a pain disorder impacting sexual activity; however, its classification within sexual dysfunctions still remains. Whether its categorisation stays within sexual dysfunctions in the future or shifts to pain disorders, further understanding of this phenomenon will continue to be highly relevant for clinicians given its impact on sexual functioning and sexual and relationship satisfaction. It seems vital to recognise that this disorder, as with any disorder involving sexuality, is likely to be impacted by psychological, relational and sociocultural factors, as well as to maintain a systemic perspective with regard to this multifaceted spectrum of contexts.

Sexology and sex therapy literature indicates that, given that physical pain is the primary presenting complaint, it should be assessed first (Meana, Maykut & Fertel, 2015). To this end, preliminary assessment should begin with the detailed enquiry including:

- The exact location of the pain (is the pain located closer to the opening of the vagina or deeper in the pelvis?)
- A description of the duration and intensity of the pain.
- What are the trigger points (does the pain start before, during or after penetration)?
- Does finger or tampon insertion, oral sex, or gynaecological examination also activate the pain?
- Does the pain happen spontaneously, without any obvious provocation?
- Are any patterns observed in relation to what makes the pain more or less intense (fatigue, menstrual cycle, level of arousal, relationship factors)?
- Partners' reaction and the effect of the pain on the sexual relationship (such as avoidance of sex).
- Whether the pain occurs only in sexual activity or perhaps also during non-sexual activities such as urinating, tampon use, walking, riding a bike.
- It is important to establish, as with other dysfunctions, whether the symptoms have been lifelong, or acquired after a period of painless sexual activity.

Taking the experience of the client's pain seriously can be validating for the woman and form the basis for a trusting and empathic therapeutic relationship. It is important to explain to the client that the purpose of exploring wider issues, such as her psychological wellbeing and the status of her relationship(s), is trying to establish their possible connection to the pain rather than to imply that the pain is 'not real'.

If the client has yet to consult a medical professional regarding GPPPD, it may be helpful that her psychosexual therapist conducts such an assessment as a basis for a gynaecological referral. Ideally, psychotherapy would continue in parallel with physical examinations and treatment, with professionals from each field consulting with each other and exchanging any information that may be relevant for co-ordinated holistic treatment.

Further psychotherapy assessment focuses on the impact of the pain on the client and her partner, in order to determine how the partner/s respond/s to the pain both emotionally and behaviourally. Specifically, whether they interrupt and abandon sexual activity or whether they try to find ways of engaging in a form of sexual interaction that does not induce pain. Systemic exploratory questions enquiring about explanations and meanings attributed to the pain, both in the assessment stages and as part of treatment, can open up important therapeutic reflective space. For example:

- How do you understand this pain and where it comes from?
- What do you believe brings it about?
- What explanation, if any, do you have for why this happens?
- How would you describe the effects of it on you individually and as partners?
- What worries you most about it?
- What concerns do you have?
- What do you think your partner is most worried about?
- What kind of communication have you had about it?
- What kind of communication was most/least productive?
- What kind of communication would you like to have?

It is not possible to assess all factors and their impact within the initial assessment, but the therapist can obtain an outline of the main aspects of the presenting problem within the context of the six dimensions, as delineated in the MOST model (see Figure 5.5 and the text that follows). Assessment should be continuous and intertwined with therapeutic work. While hope is integral to treatment, it is also essential to set realistic goals. Clinical experience suggests that it may not be possible to attain a complete resolution of genital pain, so it is important to try to modify the client's expectations in line with achievable outcomes.

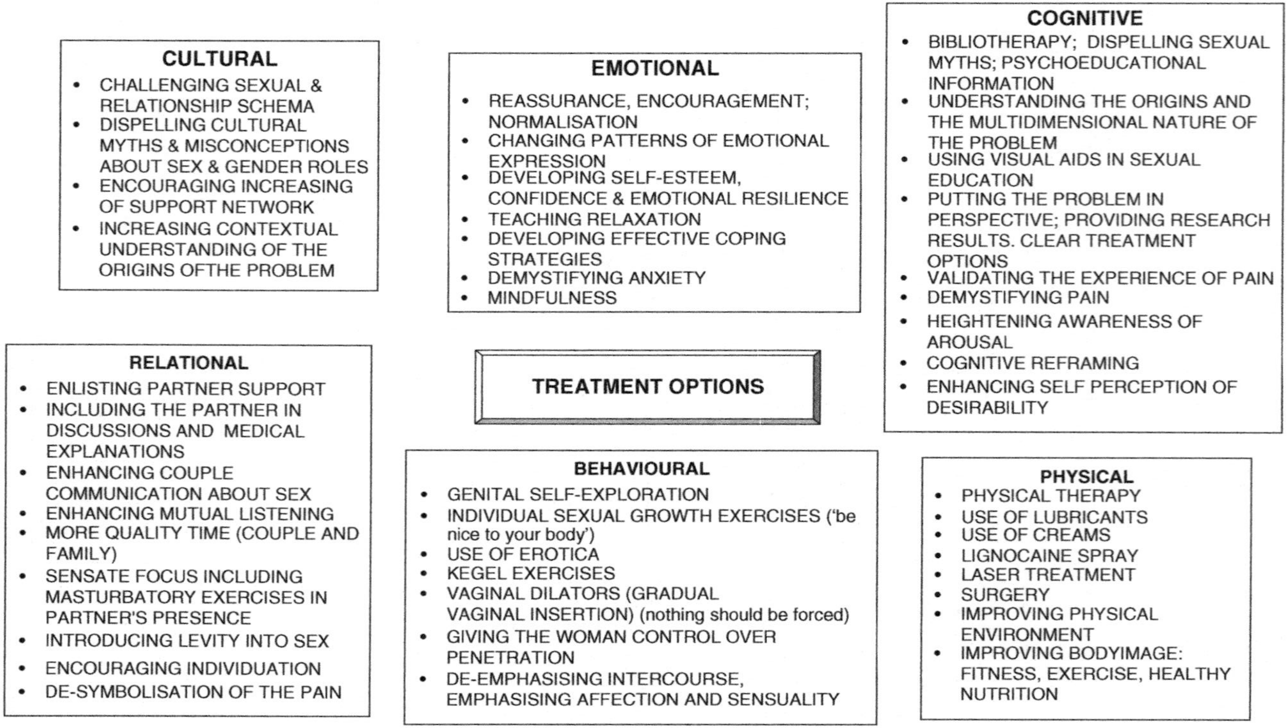

TREATMENT OPTIONS

CULTURAL

- CHALLENGING SEXUAL & RELATIONSHIP SCHEMA
- DISPELLING CULTURAL MYTHS & MISCONCEPTIONS ABOUT SEX & GENDER ROLES
- ENCOURAGING INCREASING OF SUPPORT NETWORK
- INCREASING CONTEXTUAL UNDERSTANDING OF THE ORIGINS OFTHE PROBLEM

EMOTIONAL

- REASSURANCE, ENCOURAGEMENT; NORMALISATION
- CHANGING PATTERNS OF EMOTIONAL EXPRESSION
- DEVELOPING SELF-ESTEEM, CONFIDENCE & EMOTIONAL RESILIENCE
- TEACHING RELAXATION
- DEVELOPING EFFECTIVE COPING STRATEGIES
- DEMYSTIFYING ANXIETY
- MINDFULNESS

COGNITIVE

- BIBLIOTHERAPY; DISPELLING SEXUAL MYTHS; PSYCHOEDUCATIONAL INFORMATION
- UNDERSTANDING THE ORIGINS AND THE MULTIDIMENSIONAL NATURE OF THE PROBLEM
- USING VISUAL AIDS IN SEXUAL EDUCATION
- PUTTING THE PROBLEM IN PERSPECTIVE; PROVIDING RESEARCH RESULTS. CLEAR TREATMENT OPTIONS
- VALIDATING THE EXPERIENCE OF PAIN
- DEMYSTIFYING PAIN
- HEIGHTENING AWARENESS OF AROUSAL
- COGNITIVE REFRAMING
- ENHANCING SELF PERCEPTION OF DESIRABILITY

RELATIONAL

- ENLISTING PARTNER SUPPORT
- INCLUDING THE PARTNER IN DISCUSSIONS AND MEDICAL EXPLANATIONS
- ENHANCING COUPLE COMMUNICATION ABOUT SEX
- ENHANCING MUTUAL LISTENING
- MORE QUALITY TIME (COUPLE AND FAMILY)
- SENSATE FOCUS INCLUDING MASTURBATORY EXERCISES IN PARTNER'S PRESENCE
- INTRODUCING LEVITY INTO SEX
- ENCOURAGING INDIVIDUATION
- DE-SYMBOLISATION OF THE PAIN

BEHAVIOURAL

- GENITAL SELF-EXPLORATION
- INDIVIDUAL SEXUAL GROWTH EXERCISES ('be nice to your body')
- USE OF EROTICA
- KEGEL EXERCISES
- VAGINAL DILATORS (GRADUAL VAGINAL INSERTION) (nothing should be forced)
- GIVING THE WOMAN CONTROL OVER PENETRATION
- DE-EMPHASISING INTERCOURSE, EMPHASISING AFFECTION AND SENSUALITY

PHYSICAL

- PHYSICAL THERAPY
- USE OF LUBRICANTS
- USE OF CREAMS
- LIGNOCAINE SPRAY
- LASER TREATMENT
- SURGERY
- IMPROVING PHYSICAL ENVIRONMENT
- IMPROVING BODYIMAGE: FITNESS, EXERCISE, HEALTHY NUTRITION

Figure 5.5 Genito-pelvic pain/penetration disorder: treatment options

Emotional dimension

Enabling clients to develop effective coping strategies in order to regulate emotions and change patterns of emotional expression can be a significant therapeutic task. Through therapeutic reassurance, encouragement and normalisation, clients may experience enhanced self-esteem and greater emotional resilience. Sex therapy practice typically employs behavioural and cognitive techniques for emotional regulation. Teaching clients relaxation techniques may be invaluable in providing therapeutic input for managing high tension and stress levels that may be contributing to the pain and worsening the experience. Through educational input, clients learn that emotional reactions are more in their control than previously envisaged, that one can decide to submit to a feeling or not, and that there are opportunities to respond to feelings in constructive ways (Meana, Maykut & Fertel, 2015).

Anxiety is effectively managed and reduced via relaxation, mindfulness, breathing exercises and use of imagination. Mindfulness, i.e. a meditative technique that encourages focusing on present moment without judgement, can alleviate anxiety and the negative thoughts attached to it. For sufferers of GPPPD, anxiety typically increases during sexual activity in anticipation of pain with the consequent tensing of body muscles, which can inhibit arousal and build on negative images related to sexual activity. Practising mindfulness techniques helps the woman to focus on the pleasant sensations in the moment without the interfering negative thoughts and feelings (Rosenbaum, 2013).

Cognitive dimension

Educational input is particularly important at the beginning stages of therapy. Most clients will not be aware of the definition of the disorder what it involves, and its multidimensional nature. Providing accurate information on its characteristics and its typical negative impact on the person's wellbeing and on their relationship is essential to treatment, dispelling any misconceptions and assuring that the origins and the complex nature of the problem are understood. Visual aids often used in sex therapy, such as drawings, diagrams and pictures for the purposes of sexual education, serve to normalise the painful experiences and put problems into perspective so long as the information is detailed, accurate and well explained.

Various cognitive techniques are used in the treatment of GPPPD, such as:

- *Demystifying pain*; close examination of pain patterns leading to a greater understanding of the circumstances contributing to its occurrence which can increase the client's sense of control and agency over its management.

- *Enhancing self-perception of desirability*; building on the woman's sense of her own attractiveness using cognitive restructuring.
- *Heightening awareness of arousal*; enabling the woman to pay attention to her arousal indicators may help her to refocus from over-attentiveness to pain cues.
- *Cognitive reframing*; challenging catastrophising that envisages the worst case and magnifies its consequences; this is achieved through education, reality testing and paying attention to the evidence that supports or does not support such catastrophic thoughts (Meana, Maykut & Fertel, 2015).

Physical dimension

Gynaecological examination may be followed by a referral to a physiotherapist who specialises in pelvic floor dysfunction. Research indicates that physical therapy leads to pain reduction and improved sexual functioning (Reissing, Armstrong & Allen, 2013). Pelvic floor physical therapy involves education about the pelvic floor musculature and its impact on pain and sexual functioning, as well as techniques to develop and strengthen control of these muscles. Research shows that clients prefer a combination of treatment strategies including physical therapy as opposed to psychotherapy alone (Meana, Maykut & Fertel, 2015).

Medical options include: topical application such as creams, lubricants and lidocaine, a local anaesthetic; oral medication and, as a last resort, surgery, if medically assessed as appropriate (Bergeron, Rosen & Pukall, 2014).

Therapeutic conversations address the conduciveness of the physical environment, aiming to identify any environmental factors that could be adversely impacting the sexual experience.

Body image usually improves through encouraging the client to enhance their general state of health and fitness through regular exercise, healthy nutrition and reducing their intake of toxic substances.

Behavioural dimension

A number of behavioural techniques are regularly used in the treatment of GPPPD, such as:

- *Genital self-exploration*; encouraging the woman to explore her genitalia and locate painful areas using a mirror can help her to get in touch with her body and overcome related blocks and avoidance.
- *Individual sexual growth exercises and directed solitary masturbation* can be useful in encouraging the woman to be 'nicer to her body', facilitating desire and arousal.

- *Use of erotica*; erotic books and videos can be used either by the woman privately or with her partner or both as part of 'getting in the mood' strategies and for educational purposes; it is vital that the woman exercises her own choice regarding the materials that she would like to use.
- *Vaginal dilatation*; a form of systematic desensitisation whereby the woman is instructed to insert vaginal dilators of increasing size through a series of carefully guided exercises over time.
- *Giving the woman control over penetration*; partners are instructed that the woman is in charge of whether and how penetration happens and of its pacing. This intervention crucially shifts the position of the woman from one who is subjected to penetration to one who decides on it.
- *De-emphasising intercourse*; this can be done as part of sensate focus or through educational input and behavioural suggestions for partners to explore a range of ways of engaging in sexual intimacy without penetration.
- *Emphasising affection and sensuality*; in relationships where the woman suffers genital pain, the couple often falls into a loop of avoiding sex and sometimes even any physical contact, impoverishing their relationship; by encouraging them to re-introduce and increase non-sexual demonstrations of physical affection, they may take an important step towards re-building their emotional intimacy and relationship satisfaction, paving the way for overcoming the pain issue (Meana, Maykut & Fertel, 2015, p.198).

Relational dimension

Enlisting the partner's support is an important factor in the success of relational therapy with this disorder. Managing the partner's reaction to the pain is a crucial element as anger, hostility, frustration or disappointment can be damaging. Equally, solicitous reactions may be ineffective, even counterproductive. Partners in relational therapy should be guided to employ facilitative responses and to understand the delicate line between encouragement and forcing of an activity that is too painful for the woman to enjoy.

Enhancing couple communication is essential, and various interventions can be effective in this regard. Typical destructive communicational patterns particularly pertinent to GPPPD involve mind-reading i.e. forming unchecked assumptions, expressing upset in a critical way or withholding emotional expression for fear of hurting the partner. These patterns may be usefully highlighted in therapy, resulting in more effective communication. Making more quality time for pleasant interactions can facilitate intimacy and ensure the couple's needs for emotional connection are met. This can be done as a prelude to sensate focus exercises or in parallel, depending on the therapist's assessment of the specific situation. Through sensate focus exercises, the couple not only develops skills to physically relate to each other with more sensitivity and attention, but also learns to communicate about sex more openly and directly.

Introducing levity into sex, in the form of a healthy sense of lightness and some humour, often takes the pressure off and can be liberating. It is common that partners dealing with problems of painful sex develop intense mutual worry and protective behaviours, which may make them feel they are 'walking on eggshells'; encouraging individuation may be very relevant and helpful in enmeshed (Minuchin, Rosman & Baker, 1978) couple dynamics. De-symbolisation of the pain is an important component of therapy in stressing that the pain is no more than the pain; it does not represent any negative implications on the woman, on the partner, or on the relationship.

Cultural dimension

Given that this pain disorder typically occurs in the context of intercourse, a gendered and socioculturally valued activity, the diagnosis, treatment and meaning of this pain will inevitably be impacted by the context of gender and social politics, feminist ideology and cultural discourses (Curtin et al., 2011).

Clients' beliefs about pain, sex and relationships, sometimes referred to as a 'sexual and relationship schema' may have their origins in personal experiences, familial upbringing, education, culture, religion, or wider societal messages about gender and sexuality (Meana, Maykut & Fertel, 2015). Sometimes, this schema consists of negative and prohibitory beliefs and may also contain beliefs about painful intercourse, 'rooted in sexist notions of femininity and intrinsically linked to receptivity' (Meana, Maykut & Fertel, 2015, p.202). There is a fine line between therapeutic sensitivity and respect for clients' cultural belief systems, and appropriately challenging this sexual and relationship schema.

Male hypoactive sexual desire disorder (MHSDD): treatment options

There is no universal definition of 'normal' and 'disordered' levels of desire, which on the one hand is an advantage of the diagnostic system, as it allows for wide individual variations of the levels of desire and its accompanied contextual relativity; on the other hand, it means that diagnostic conclusions are based on the clinical judgement of individual clinicians, leaving scope for professional bias. This is one of the reasons why assessment of the problem of hypoactive sexual desire requires a thorough investigation into medical, personal, interpersonal and cultural factors. It is strongly advised in sexology literature that a medical evaluation is routinely recommended, even if clients report no physical symptoms or medical concerns.

The issue of MHSDD may also relate to the man's perception of his partner's sexual functioning. If the man perceives that his partner has arousal or orgasmic difficulties, this is likely to influence his desire to instigate sexual activity and/or his enjoyment and pleasure in being sexual with his partner. Locating the problem is a major task in assessment and a complex undertaking, that requires detailed enquiry and ongoing attentiveness of the clinician throughout treatment.

Some diagnostic dilemmas associated with MHSDD are listed below:

- *Distinguishing between sexual desire and sexual arousal.* Some men may complain of a lack of desire, whereas the primary problem may be the inability to achieve and/or maintain an erection. Some believe that an erection should happen prior to initiating a sexual activity, and this needs to be taken into account when MHSDD is presented. On the other hand, the problem of ED (erectile disorder) may be a manifestation of an underlying sexual desire problem. Sexual dysfunctions are sometimes difficult to distinguish, and clients often present with what they believe is a main difficulty. Research studies show that men are more likely to present with erectile difficulties, while women more typically present with desire concerns (Kedde et al., 2011).
- *Distinguishing between sexual desire and sexual motivation.* Asexuality and lifelong and generalised MHSDD may present in very similar ways. The main point of difference is the absence of distress in the case of asexuality. It is likely that asexuality would be reported as a chosen path, and such individuals would only refer themselves to a clinical setting at the instigation of their distressed partners. It is important that clinicians are able to distinguish between the two presenting situations and not pathologise asexuality or lack of motivation for sex.
- *Desire discrepancy* is a frequent occurrence in sexual therapy and, indeed, does not necessarily mean that either of the partners individually has a problem. Careful attention should be paid to avoid pathologising the person with the lower level of desire. The aim of couple therapy in these situations is to enable more mutually satisfying sexual lives and, in this respect, it is important to formulate the problem at an interactional level rather than to problematise either person's levels of

desire. The issue may relate to the couple's communicational patterns or the way in which they manage difference; alternatively, it may be that the underlying issue is within the realms of sexual mythology such that *'real men want sex all the time'*, or that either or both of the partners have unrealistic expectations. Sometimes, tensions in what appear to be differing levels of partners' desire can be symptomatic of underlying emotional conflict, lack of trust, hurt and betrayal. A myriad of possible reasons might be contributing to the situation, and assessing the factors from the six dimensions as suggested by the MOST model (see Figure 5.6 and the text that follows) is a tool both for providing clarity as to the definition of the problem and determining relevant treatment options. Equally, there may not be a 'problem' if neither partner is experiencing distress, and the couple's desire discrepancy may simply be a feature of their individual ways of functioning and responding sexually. Such a 'non-diagnosis' may be reassuring and affirming for the clients.

- *Sexual secrets.* Individual assessment interviews may reveal sexual secrets such as affairs, internet/pornography addiction; same gender preferences; gender identity conflict; hidden interest in paraphilic activities or loss of attraction to the partner. These issues may pose a dilemma for the clinician as to how best to handle them.

Emotional dimension

Given the high level of distress often associated with clients presenting with MHSDD, therapists may find it helpful to attend to these emotional issues first, as they can affect the ongoing persistence of the problem. While some clients are open about their distress, others suppress their feelings, and it is up to the clinician to distinguish and manage these different positions as each can equally contribute to the maintenance and worsening of the problem.

Emotionally focused coping can result in a combination of anger, hostility, resentment, disappointment and low mood. Through empathic therapeutic listening and the creation of a safe context where distress is heard and understood, clients can begin to reflect on their emotional response to the problem, appreciate the extent of the difficulty and move on toward resolving the difficult feelings.

Stress reduction strategies such as relaxation techniques and mindfulness can be immensely helpful in managing affective expression and modulation of emotional reactivity. At the same time, these techniques help clients to accept and adjust their expectations and understand the factors that are

TREATMENT OPTIONS

CULTURAL

- DISPELLING CULTURAL MYTHS AND MISCONCEPTIONS ABOUT SEX AND GENDER ROLES
- EXPLORING AND UNDERSTANDING INFLUENCES FROM UPBRINGING
- GAINING A CONTEXTUAL UNDERSTANDING OF THE DEVELOPMENT OF CERTAIN RESTRICTIVE BELIEFS
- ENCOURAGING INCREASING OF SUPPORT NETWORK

EMOTIONAL

- DEVELOPING AFFECTIVE AWARENESS
- MODULATION OF EMOTIONAL REACTIVITY
- ACCEPTANCE STRATEGIES such as mindfulness, relaxation
- REDUCING STRESS
- NORMALISATIONe.g. HSDD is not uncommon in men

COGNITIVE

- EDUCATION
- STRENGHTENING SEXUAL SELF-CONCEPT
- POSITIVE ANTICIPATION
- COGNITIVE REFOCUSING
- IDENTIFYING AND CHALLENGING MALADAPTIVE THOUGHTS AND RESTRICTIVE SEXUAL SCRIPTS
- EXPLAINING THE CIRCULAR MODEL OF SEXUAL DESIRE
- PROVIDING INFORMATION TO REGULATE UNREALISTIC
- EXPECTATIONS; establish reasonable expectations; learning to accept certain realities
- BRINGING BACK THE MEMORY OF 'UNIQUE OUTCOMES' OR 'EXCEPTIONS' to the dominant story of a sexually inadequate self

RELATIONAL

- REDUCING COUPLE DISTRESS
- CONFLICT RESOLUTION STRATEGIES; e.g.t aking responsibility rather than blaming
- DISTURBING THE DEMAND/ WITHDRAWAL PATTERN OF RELATING
- REACTIVATING ROMANTIC WAYS OF RELATING
- MOTIVATIONAL INTERVIEWING; increasing readiness to change
- SENSATE FOCUS AND BAN ON SEX
- ENCOURAGING COUPLE TO EXPLORE AND DEVELOP THEIR SEXUAL INTERESTS
- ENCOURAGING COUPLE TO HAVE SEX WITHOUT DESIRE
- SHARE EROTICA
- ENCOURAGE EXPANSION OF SEXUAL REPERTOIRE

BEHAVIOURAL

- IMPROVE AND EXPAND SEXUAL REPERTOIRE
- INDIVIDUAL SEXUAL GROWTH ('individual sensate focus')
- SIMMERING
- USE OF IMAGERY AND FANTASY
- JUMP START DESIRE BY BYPASSING IT

LIFESTYLE

- TESTOSTERONE REPLACEMENT THERAPY
- MEDICAL TREATMENT OF ILLNESSES AFFECTING DESIRE
- CHANGE OF MEDICATION WHICH HAS SIDE EFFECTS OF LOWERING SEXUAL DESIRE
- HEALTHY LIFESTYLE e.g. increasing exercise, smoking cessation, decreasing alcohol and other toxic substances intake
- HEALTHY NUTRITION
- HERBAL REMEDIES, e.g. gingko biloba, ginseng

Figure 5.6 Male hypoactive sexual desire disorder: treatment options

beyond their control. Sometimes, a straightforward intervention emphasising that levels of sexual desire are involuntary and not easily consciously controlled, takes the pressure off the man suffering the condition and reassures his partner who may be attributing conscious intent to them.

Normalisation, such as providing information on the prevalence of MHSDD, offers reassurance to distressed men and their partners, which removes stigma often associated with low sexual desire in men and enables a de-pathologising focus.

Cognitive dimension

Men and/or their partners often lack understanding of the complex ways in which sexual desire can be influenced by the interplay of physiological, psychological, interpersonal and cultural factors. Providing clear and accurate information usually enhances understanding of sexual functioning and of the contextual and multidimensional disposition of sexual desire, as well as normalises its many variations and sometimes unpredictable fluctuations. Educational input also regulates unrealistic expectations and enables clients to accept the limitations of what is possible to achieve.

Identifying and challenging maladaptive thoughts and sexual scripts forms an integral part of sexual therapy with MHSDD. For example, typical myths and misperceptions that form sexual scripts which limit sexual needs and pleasure, taking the enjoyment out of sex include beliefs that:

- *Real men are always interested and ready to perform sexually*
- *All men are potential rapists*
- *Perfect sexual performance is the most important factor in satisfying your partner*
- *What men most want and need in a relationship is sex*
- *It is the man's responsibility to give his partner an orgasm each time*
- *Men can't control their sex drives*

(McCarthy & Metz, 2008, pp.1–20)

Zilbergeld (1999, p.351) asks 'desire for what?', emphasising the importance of the need for a contextual outlook on sexual desire. In therapeutic conversations clients sometimes become aware of their own beliefs for the first time. Prompting reflection on their origin and impact might create a significant shift in their belief system. Bibliotherapy further supports this new learning and opens up different perspectives on male sexual desire. Sex therapy sometimes includes coaching advice as, for example, how when his partner expresses a need for sexual intimacy, the man might initiate sex in the absence of his own sexual desire.

Directly challenging irrational thoughts is a further cognitive restructuring technique for addressing situations where negative anticipation, catastrophising and cognitive distractions interfere with sexual desire and enjoyment of sex. Men suffering from low desire often become distracted during sex by non-erotic thoughts (Nobre & Pinto-Gouveia, 2008). The use of sexual imagery and fantasy are commonly applied cognitive strategies encouraging refocusing on sexual stimuli and pleasurable sensations as opposed to worrisome, sexually unrelated thoughts. Mindfulness and meditation can both be usefully applied in sex therapy either in the form of a basic suggestion to 'focus on current awareness of the experience without judgement', or in more complex ways requiring further guidance from a qualified practitioner.

Sexual self-concept is a cognitive schema influenced by one's sexual experiences and perception of oneself in the context of cultural and gender stories about sex and sexuality. With clients suffering distress associated with MHSDD, the therapist aims to strengthen the client's sexual self-concept through identifying 'unique outcomes' (White, 2007) of the established script of inadequate sexual functioning so as to begin the process of empowerment through restoring his sexual confidence.

Physical dimension

Hormonal therapy, such as testosterone replacement therapy, generally increases sexual desire; it can also contribute to mood enhancement and improved energy levels (Khera et al., 2011). Other hormones, such as cortisol, oestradiol, and other androgens are currently the subject of research as potential enhancers of sexual desire in men (Hall, 2015). However, the possible side effects of such treatment should be carefully considered and clients should seek appropriate medical advice before resorting to such measures. Extensive pharmaceutical research into effective medication for the treatment of MHSDD has, as yet, failed to produce any effective results and the search for a magic pill continues.

Where sexual desire problems relate to medical conditions or side effects from the use of certain medications, undertaking the indicated medical treatment or changing or ceasing the use of medication may either partially or completely resolve the problem, depending on the presence of other contributing factors. Most commonly associated with low desire are various anti-anxiety drugs and anti-depressants. Unfortunately, such medications may exacerbate the loss of sexual desire that those suffering from these conditions already experience.

Changes in lifestyle, such as regular exercise, healthy nutrition and regulation of sleep patterns and other life habits can be a healthy substitute for medication, contributing to the improvement of both the physical and psychological dimensions of one's body image and fitness. Natural supplements, vitamins, minerals, and herbal remedies, such as gingko biloba and ginseng, if taken on a GP's and/or nutritionist's advice, may serve as an effective holistic alternative to medical treatment of MHSDD.

Behavioural dimension

A man's sexual desire can be rekindled by encouraging him to explore and develop his sexual interests. If he is currently in a relationship, the therapist can facilitate playful and creative ways for the couple to generate ideas as to what kind of sexual, seductive, erotic and sensual interaction they would like to try out. An exercise whereby the clients can create and share their individual lists, followed by deciding what they might like to try and making plans for how they might go about it, could begin in the therapy session and continue between appointments. In order to provide inspiration for such new ideas, the therapist could suggest that the couple might like to visit erotic websites, sex shops, erotic lingerie shops, or read erotic literature. Therapists prompt clients to approach these activities with curiosity and humour, supporting each other, and being attentive to any inhibitions that may be experienced. Within this frame, such activities can lead to an expansion of the sexual repertoire and an improvement of the sexual experience, which in turn can enhance sexual desire for couples whose sexual lives may have become stagnant or mechanistic, thus leading to a reduction in interest and motivation for sex (Meana & Steiner, 2014).

The technique of simmering, first described by Zilbergeld and Ellison (1980), is a helpful tool in treating MHSDD. The man is advised to pay attention to any sexual thoughts and feelings that occur during the day and to develop them into a sexual fantasy, in essence to 'run his own X-rated movie' through his mind (p.312), then, after a few minutes, let the fantasy fade. He is encouraged to repeatedly engage in this process of fantasising and letting go several times a day and, after a while, to include his partner in his fantasy and eventually, if agreed consensually, to enact some of the scenarios.

Another technique, 'jump start desire by bypassing it' (Hall, 2015) is based on encouraging the couple to start to have sex unprompted by desire. It may be useful to explain the circular model of sexual response (Basson, 2001), as it might apply to men's sexual functioning as well, and the potential value of the use of erotica, fantasy and the simmering technique.

Relational dimension

A variation of simmering involves encouraging the couple to reactivate romantic ways of relating by being flirtatious with each other, keeping in contact during the day, exchanging sexy messages, and inventing surprises for one another.

Sensate focus exercises, designed to assess and remedy problems of communication about sex, imbalance in sexual participation, a limited repertoire of sexually relating and performance anxiety, can likewise rekindle sexual desire and open up more satisfying sexual possibilities. A ban on sex takes the pressure off expectations at the same time as fuelling desire for the 'forbidden fruit'. Feedback is taken at each stage of these exercises alongside discussion about the couple's experiences to enhance effective communication patterns. Sensate focus exercises are contraindicated for couples experiencing a high level of conflict; they would unlikely be accepted even if offered. In such situations, priority should be placed on applying conflict resolution strategies. Such strategies revolve around encouraging clients to take responsibility for their own behaviour and anxieties and empathically tune into their partner's experience rather than to direct blame towards them (Schnarch, 2003).

Disturbing the frequently developed demand/withdrawal interactional pattern can significantly modify sexual communication and feelings. Typically, when one withdraws, the partner's demands increase as a consequence of feeling worried and abandoned, which in turn leads to the first partner's further withdrawal and so on, in an escalating pattern.

Sometimes, due to a range of circumstances, it is simply not achievable to change the desire levels in a relationship. In cases of loss of affection or sexual attraction, attempts at improving the situation often end up with increased disappointment and frustration. Where loss of attraction has become definitive, such attempts are even hurtful and detrimental, so the therapist needs to be sensitive to the narrow line between enthusiastic encouragement and enforcement of interventions, always ensuring that both partners fully subscribe to the treatment options without feeling pressurised.

Cultural dimension

Cultural norms make it difficult for men to admit problems with sexual desire and to seek help. Research and clinical studies consistently reveal that men's shame and embarrassment about such problems are often the result of cultural assumptions that real men should always feel desire and at all times be ready for sex, highly sexually functioning and exert their sexual desires proactively. These cultural assumptions form cumbersome pressures both on men and their partners, contributing to their feelings of lacking in masculinity when experiencing levels of sexual desire not matching their partners' or perceived societal expectations.

In addition, media and pornography-propagated prototypes, for example that sex should be spontaneous, or that absence of sexual desire in men signifies something seriously abnormal, can make some men feel extremely worried about their gender and sexual inadequacy, further interfering with their sexual desire.

Enhancing clients' awareness of these cultural stories, which are often determined by patriarchal values, can contribute to their contextual understanding of the origins of pressures on men to fulfil culturally imposed standards and ideals. Exploring and understanding childhood influences, such as strict religious norms or patriarchal stories about gender, can put these issues into perspective, enable a widening of horizons and support development of the clients' freedom to exercise their own sexual choices. Contrary to widespread mythology, a growing body of research in sexology as well as clinical studies demonstrate that men's sexual desire is far more complex and multifaceted than previously thought and is influenced by many of the same factors influencing women's sexual interest such as ageing, hormones, relationship issues, stress, mood and anxiety (Wincze & Weisberg, 2015).

Premature/early ejaculation (PE): treatment options

PE can be hugely troublesome, causing relationship discord and eroding a man's self-confidence. Treatment was based on psychological therapies and behavioural exercises, until the mid-1990s and the discovery of drugs, such as certain SSRIs to delay ejaculatory latency. Currently, treatments are split mainly between a purely medical or a purely psychological approach, while a growing number of studies are showing that a combination of both produces the most effective results (Althof, 2014).

Distinguishing lifelong from acquired PE throws light on the precise nature of the problem and the factors contributing to its development and persistence. Equally, differentiating between generalised and situational types of the difficulty will further clarify the intricacies of its manifestations.

It is relevant to establish, for example, how the ejaculatory latency differs between partnered sexual activity and masturbation; a shorter latency with partnered sex indicates psychological and relational factors. In assessing the presenting problem of PE and delivering a diagnosis and a formulation to clients, distinguishing between dissatisfaction with ejaculatory latency and the sexology diagnostic definition is highly recommended. If the ejaculatory latency does not meet criteria for the official diagnostic classification, it is then important to convey to clients that this does not mean the clinician is not taking their concerns seriously; acknowledgment of it, nonetheless, being a problem for the man and/or his partner needs to be made explicit. The MOST map in Figure 5.7 summarises treatment options for PE.

Emotional dimension

Performance anxiety is considered one of the most powerful contributing factors to the development and maintenance of PE. Numerous anxiety and stress reduction techniques, many of which have been described in the previous sections relating to different sexual dysfunctions, can equally be applied in the treatment of PE. Explanation of performance anxiety and how it can affect a sexual relationship may helpfully enlighten the clients' understanding of this problem and its emotional underpinnings. Significant therapeutic work can be done on building the man's self-esteem and addressing any feelings of humiliation, shame and embarrassment this problem can often cause. Individual and couple therapists regularly address problems of low self-esteem and anxiety with clients, aimed at developing emotional resilience and changing patterns of emotional expression. Sexual issues need to be addressed specifically as the client's emotional reactions may be largely based on their and/or their partners' misconceptions and idealistic expectations of sexual activity.

Cognitive dimension

A frequent misconception includes unrealistic expectations about the duration of intercourse. Clinical examples cited in the literature refer to expectations varying from 40 minutes to one hour or longer. Educational input in sex therapy may dispel some of the mythology and provide clarifying information. Exploring the meaning attributed to the sexual difficulty as experienced by the man and by his partner can reveal and

TREATMENT OPTIONS

CULTURAL

- EXPLORATION OF FAMILY OF ORIGIN ATTITUDES AND RULES ABOUT SEXUALITY
- SEXUAL GENOGRAM
- DISPELLING CULTURAL MISCONCEPTIONS ABOUT SEX AND GENDER ROLES
- GAINING A CONTEXTUAL UNDERSTANDING OF THE DEVELOPMENT OF CERTAIN RESTRICTIVE SEXUAL BELIEFS
- ENCOURAGING INCREASING OF SUPPORT NETWORK

EMOTIONAL

- CHANGING PATTERNS OF EMOTIONAL EXPRESSION
- DEVELOPING EMOTIONAL RESILIENCE
- DECREASING ANXIETY
- DEEP BREATHING, RELAXATION
- MINDFULNESS, MEDITATION
- NORMALISATION
- ENHACING EMOTIONAL EMPATHY UNDERSTANDING PAST TRAUMAS AND EXPLORING THEIR EFFECTS

COGNITIVE

- BIBLIOTHERAPY
- SEXUAL EDUCATION re sexual anatomy and sexual response
- CHALLENGING OPPRESSIVE SEXUAL BELIEFS
- EXPLORING AND CHALLENGING THE MEANING AND THE REASONS ATTRIBUTED TO PE
- COGNITIVE RESTRUCTURING; addressing negative beliefs about sex
- EXPLORING AND UNDERSTANDING INFLUENCES FROM UPBRINGING
- POSITIVE THINKING, enhancing optimism
- FOCUSING ON PLEASURE OF SENSATIONS RATHER THAN PERFORMANCE

RELATIONAL

- IMPROVING COUPLE COMMUNICATION
- ELIMINATING BLAME AND CORRECTING
- MISUNDERSTANDINGS & MISINTERPRETATIONS
- SENSATE FOCUS
- ENLISTING PARTNER SUPPORT
- ENHANCING COUPLE COMMUNICATION ABOUT SEX
- RESOLVING CONFLICT
- ENHANCING MUTUAL LISTENING
- MORE QUALITY TIME
- RESOLVING OR DISTANCING FROM RELATIONSHIP PRESSURES
- CONSTRUCTIVE CHANGE OF PATTERNS OF RELATING

BEHAVIOURAL

- INDIVIDUAL SEXUAL GROWTH EXERCISES
- CHANGING PATTERNS OF MASTURBATION
- STOP AND START TECHNIQUE
- TEACHING TO RECOGNISE THE POINT OF EJACULATORY INEVITABILITY
- KEGEL EXERCISES
- SIMMERING
- SYSTEMATIC DESENSITISATION
- EXPANDING NON-INTERCOURSE OPTIONS
- JUMP START DESIRE BY BYPASSING IT
- POSITIVE IMAGERY TRAINING
- CONTINUE HAVING SEX AFTER EJACULATION

PHYSICAL

- MEDICATION E.G. SSRI
- NEUROLEPTICS
- LIDOCAINE SPRAY
- PROLONG
- VIAGRA
- IMPROVING NUTRITION
- CONTROL OF ALCOHOL, CAFFEINE, NICOTINE AND OTHER TOXIC SUBSTANCES INTAKE
- PHYSICAL EXERCISES TO IMPROVE BODY IMAGE AND FITNESS
- CHANGE IN SEXUAL ENVIRONMENT IF NOT CONDUCIVE

Figure 5.7 Premature/early ejaculation: treatment options

challenge some of the cognitive distortions and thinking processes which may cause severe disturbance. For example:

- All-or-nothing thinking (e.g. *'My sex life is a complete disaster'*; or *'I am worthless'*; *'My whole life is a failure'*)
- Over-generalisation (e.g. *'I will never be able to control my ejaculation'*)
- Disqualifying the positive (e.g. *'My partner says s/he loves me but I know deep down s/he must resent me for being so bad at sex'*)
- Mind-reading (e.g. *'My partner will not tell me how s/he really feels but I know s/he is angry'*)
- Negative predictions (e.g. *'I will come quickly again'*)
- Exaggerating the negative (e.g. *'My partner must be disgusted by my sexual performance'*)
- Catastrophising (e.g. *'If I keep failing we will both feel awful and s/he will leave me'*) (Althof, 2014, p.127).

Partners also often draw negative and exaggerated conclusions about the reasons for PE (e.g. *'He doesn't really care about me'*; or *'He's not attracted to me if he is rushing through sex'*; or *'He could easily control his ejaculation if he just put in a little effort, but he's obviously not bothered'*) (Wincze & Weisberg, 2015, p.46).

Psycho-education is crucial in these situations and therapists should at all stages of work be attentive to such assumptions, as they tend to undermine progress in sexual therapy. Identifying a range of contributing factors to the sexual problem significantly expands the clients' understanding of the multifactorial origins of the difficulties, which may enable them to reduce blame of self and others and create more constructive attitudes.

Physical dimension

Thorough medical investigations should be undertaken, preferably by a urologist experienced in working with sexual difficulties. If specific medical conditions are causing PE, treatment of these might significantly improve the man's sexual functioning. Hormonal imbalance can be treated with hormonal therapy, such as testosterone replacement therapy or drugs to correct an underactive thyroid. There is no universally approved pharmacological treatment for PE; however, antidepressants and anti-anxiety medication are often prescribed and have proven to be effective. Other forms of medication used for pain relief are sometimes prescribed (e.g. Tramadol). PE is sometimes comorbid with ED, either as a cause or a result of it (Linton & Wylie, 2010), so Viagra can be helpful in such situations. Pharmacological treatment alone is recommended in lifelong, generalised PE in the absence of major psychological, relational or physical factors.

Anaesthetising spray, which is available to buy over the counter, or local anaesthetic cream could be applied about 30 minutes before intercourse and washed off before sexual activity starts. Side effects of these measures include: pain and burning, erectile difficulties and delayed ejaculation. Natural treatments with unknown side effects and insufficient evidence of efficacy include herbal remedies and certain foods.

Healthy nutrition will improve fitness and general state of health and body image, and for that reason is generally advised. Warning should be given regarding toxic substances, such as nicotine, caffeine, alcohol and drugs as these are known to have adverse effects on sexual functioning and often increase anxiety, a major contributing factor to all sexual dysfunctions.

Finally, changes in the physical environment, if not conducive to sex, should be considered as discomfort, distractions and lack of privacy often have a major impact on sexual experience.

Behavioural dimension

In attempting to regulate PE, men frequently resort to a range of counter-productive practices limiting their excitement, believing it to be the major cause for their sexual problem, such as: wearing multiple condoms, repeatedly masturbating prior to intercourse, limiting foreplay, not allowing their partners to stimulate them, detaching physically or emotionally, and distracting themselves from pleasurable sensations by focusing on non-sexual thoughts during sexual activity (Althof, 2014, p.127). These measures, however creative, are usually not successful and, moreover, can worsen the situation by diminishing sexual pleasure and turning sex into a mechanistic and dispassionate activity.

Graduated behavioural exercises described in the sexology literature and frequently applied in sex therapy can be taught, in order for clients to become familiar with the varying levels of their sexual excitement, and to eventually gain control of their orgasmic functioning. In addition to individual sexual growth exercises, and Kegel exercises, both recommended in the treatment of all sexual difficulties, a particular technique called 'stop-start' based on the general principle of systematic desensitisation (Wolpe & Wolpe, 1981) has been developed specifically for the treatment of PE (Betchen, 2015). Stop-start exercises are gradually introduced as part of changing masturbatory patterns, and sometimes then transferred into partnered sexual activity. The man is advised to stimulate his penis gently and slowly, paying attention to the pleasurable sensations and noticing his increasing levels of arousal. When he feels orgasm is approaching but not inevitable, he stops the stimulation and allows for the penis to become flaccid whilst his erotic feelings dissipate. After a few minutes, he repeats the same cycle over again. At the third or fourth cycle, he stimulates himself to ejaculation. The exercise is done a few times a week, and after the man has consolidated this practice, gaining sufficient ejaculatory control, he brings the exercise to the partnered sexual act, instructing his partner to stroke his penis in the same way. It is important that clients understand the instructions clearly and feel comfortable with the graduated steps. In some literature (Althof, 2014), this type of exercise is described as the man's learning to recognise the different levels of arousal and to rehearse lingering in the midrange of excitement, enjoying the sensation. Sometimes, clinicians suggest to clients to imagine their arousal on a scale of 0–10, and when they reach 6 during genital stimulation, to stop and allow the arousal to decline to a 3 or 4 before continuing. In a case described in recent sexology literature (Althof, 2014) clients were advised to engage in the exercise as a couple after the man had practised it on his own. The partner was told to manually and/or orally stimulate the man until he asked them to stop. The client's task was to concentrate on his level of arousal and ask his partner to stop when he reached point 6 on the scale. This was repeated several times before progressing to orgasm.

Another behavioural intervention frequently applied to alter unhelpful repetitive patterns and to open a more intimate space for sexual activity consists of advising the couple to continue having sex after ejaculation. The man suffering from PE is specifically advised not to apologise to his partner (Althof, 2014) (which often happens) but to continue holding and caressing them and continue being emotionally intimate. Couples are taught that men can sometimes reach more than one orgasm during an episode of sexual activity and to allow for this possibility in their sexual interactions.

Relational dimension

Effective communication is facilitated by, for example, enhancing mutual listening, eliminating blame, correcting misunderstanding and learning to compromise. It is helpful for couples to learn how to communicate the problem of PE and their sexual needs in a non-defensive and constructive manner (Mrdjenovic, Bischof & Menichello, 2004). Partners are often encouraged to allocate regular, mutually agreed protected times to talk with each other, discussing their day-to-day activities, thoughts and feelings with emphasis on listening, sharing and empathy. Different therapeutic interventions, aimed at improving couple communication, increasing intimacy and strengthening conflict resolution can helpfully contribute to a constructive change in the previous unwanted repetitive patterns of relating and bring forth enhancement of personal agency both of the man suffering PE and his partner.

Cultural dimension

Negative sexual messages during upbringing can lead to internalised sexual conflict, guilt and shame related to sexual activity. Using the sexual genogram, both with individual clients and in couple sessions, aims to elucidate internalised misconceptions and oppressive messages about sexuality received throughout childhood and young adulthood from the wider contexts of family, culture, education and religion. Clients are asked to remember any negative messages about sex, intimacy, affection and relationships from their family and other systems when growing up and are encouraged over time to differentiate themselves from these messages. One of the techniques supporting this differentiation, the 'sexual bill of rights' developed by Weeks and Gambescia (2015) consists of asking clients to write a list of statements about what they are entitled to sexually, thus supporting their autonomy and ownership of their sexuality.

Persistent genital arousal disorder (PGAD): treatment options

Leiblum and Chivers (2007) reported success with a client using self-monitoring, massage and stretching exercises. Goldmeier, Sadeghi-Nejad and Facelle (2014) suggest a combination of approaches, including mindfulness-based CBT, medication and pelvic floor physical therapy. Figure 5.8 and the next section will classify treatment strategies in relation to the six dimensions of the MOST model.

Emotional dimension

Mindfulness is strongly recommended for PGAD as it decreases anxiety and alleviates depression. Anxiety reduction methods and interventions are highly relevant, as not only is anxiety seen as a contributing factor, but also because the condition itself aggravates anxiety. Stress reduction techniques can also alleviate the experience and make it more manageable. The accompanied feelings of shame and guilt can be also alleviated through a supportive therapeutic relationship and acknowledgment that the frustration and distress is normal and warranted. Explaining to the woman that there

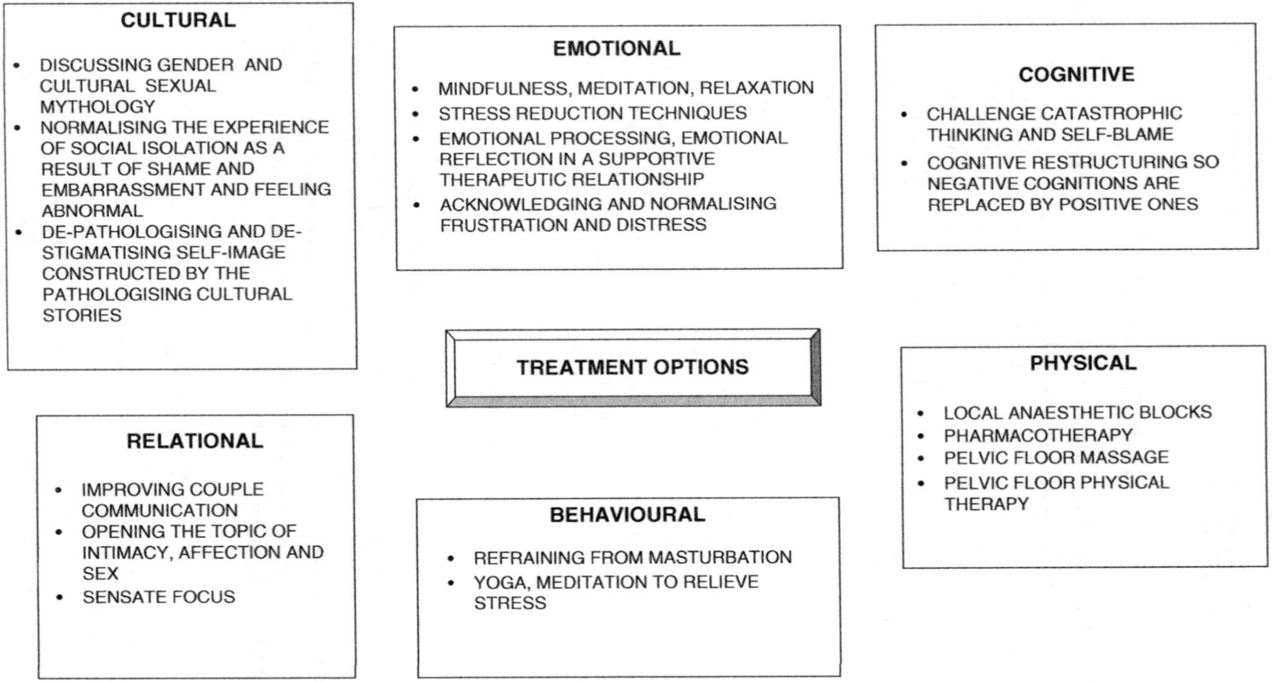

CULTURAL

- DISCUSSING GENDER AND CULTURAL SEXUAL MYTHOLOGY
- NORMALISING THE EXPERIENCE OF SOCIAL ISOLATION AS A RESULT OF SHAME AND EMBARRASSMENT AND FEELING ABNORMAL
- DE-PATHOLOGISING AND DE-STIGMATISING SELF-IMAGE CONSTRUCTED BY THE PATHOLOGISING CULTURAL STORIES

EMOTIONAL

- MINDFULNESS, MEDITATION, RELAXATION
- STRESS REDUCTION TECHNIQUES
- EMOTIONAL PROCESSING, EMOTIONAL REFLECTION IN A SUPPORTIVE THERAPEUTIC RELATIONSHIP
- ACKNOWLEDGING AND NORMALISING FRUSTRATION AND DISTRESS

COGNITIVE

- CHALLENGE CATASTROPHIC THINKING AND SELF-BLAME
- COGNITIVE RESTRUCTURING SO NEGATIVE COGNITIONS ARE REPLACED BY POSITIVE ONES

TREATMENT OPTIONS

RELATIONAL

- IMPROVING COUPLE COMMUNICATION
- OPENING THE TOPIC OF INTIMACY, AFFECTION AND SEX
- SENSATE FOCUS

BEHAVIOURAL

- REFRAINING FROM MASTURBATION
- YOGA, MEDITATION TO RELIEVE STRESS

PHYSICAL

- LOCAL ANAESTHETIC BLOCKS
- PHARMACOTHERAPY
- PELVIC FLOOR MASSAGE
- PELVIC FLOOR PHYSICAL THERAPY

Figure 5.8 Persistent genital arousal disorder: treatment options

is nothing wrong or abnormal in terms of what she is doing to cause th symptoms produces significant relief of her stress (Goldmeier, Sagedhi-Nejad & Facelle, 2014, pp.270–271).

Cognitive dimension

Researchers have identified that women exhibiting these symptoms ar prone to catastrophic thinking and self-blame, such as: *'This problem rule my whole life'*; *'My genitals must be grossly abnormal'*; *'This must be due t me masturbating too much as a teenager'*. Such thinking can be challenge through cognitive restructuring, so that negative cognitions are replaced b more positive ones, such as: *'I can have a productive and enjoyable life in spit of having PGAD'* (Goldmeier, Sadeghi-Nejad & Facelle, 2014, p.270).

Physical dimension

Local anaesthetic blocks can produce temporary relief of the symptom. Pharmacotherapy is reported as effective in some cases of both femal (Goldmeier, Sadeghi-Nejad & Facelle, 2014) and male (Kamatchi & Ashley Smith, 2013) symptomatology; however, the opposite sexual problem can develop as side effects, such as inhibited interest, arousal and orgasm Pelvic floor massage and pelvic floor physical therapy have been reported a effective in combination with other treatments.

Behavioural dimension

Some women compulsively masturbate in order to stop the sensation which in some cases can aggravate symptoms. Refraining from masturbatio has been shown to lead to a lessening of the symptoms for some client In addition, yoga, mindfulness, meditation and other techniques successfu in managing anxiety and stress can help by supporting the woman to b more accepting of her PGAD symptoms, leading to improvement of he quality of life (Goldmeier, Sagedhi-Nejad & Facelle, 2014, p.271).

Relational dimension

If the woman is in a relationship, her partner's input and support can b vital (Goldmeier, Sagedhi-Nejad & Facelle, 2014, p.271). The disorder ca create relationship tension and conflict, and so the therapists' explanatio of the disorder and the ways of managing it can support the couple i creating more constructive relational dynamics. Therapeutic options sometimes involve detailed discussions on ways of relating physically, identifying practices that seem more enjoyable and less likely to trigger a PGAD response.

Cultural dimension

How women experience PGAD relates to cultural shame and embarrassment, intensified by strong gender mythology that interprets women's high levels of sexuality as a sign of abnormality or inappropriateness. This may lead to social isolation, which worsens the experience. Reflecting on these issues in the safe context of a therapeutic relationship can alleviate some of the tensions and stresses caused by the condition and de-pathologise and de-stigmatise the woman's sexual self-image.

Sexual aversion disorder (SAD): treatment options

In treating the presenting issue of SAD, a thorough assessment is indicated in order to establish the nature, severity and extent of the problem. Information about whether the problem is lifelong or acquired may provide helpful insights into its origin and development and identify precipitating factors that may be relevant for treatment. Many possibilities of working with such presenting problems exist within the psychotherapy and sex therapy fields, including the interventions used in the treatment of FSI/AD and MHSDD. Equally, as Tiefer (2001) suggested, this diagnosis may not be appropriate in situations where there is a major discrepancy between sexual partners and pressure on the person experiencing sexual aversion to perform sexually in a certain way. Treatment is most effective and ethical if takes into account contextual influences, relieving pressure from the individual who already may feel blamed and abnormal. To diagnose a disorder may not be helpful as it may contribute to harmful pathologising. Still, the experience can be explored and reflected upon in therapy, resulting in a more positive sense of self and increasing options for understanding and dealing with the problem.

The map in Figure 5.9 briefly summarises interventions as indicated within the different dimensions of the MOST model; clinicians should be sensitive to their own sexual assumptions and values when engaging with this provocative, controversial and insufficiently explored topic.

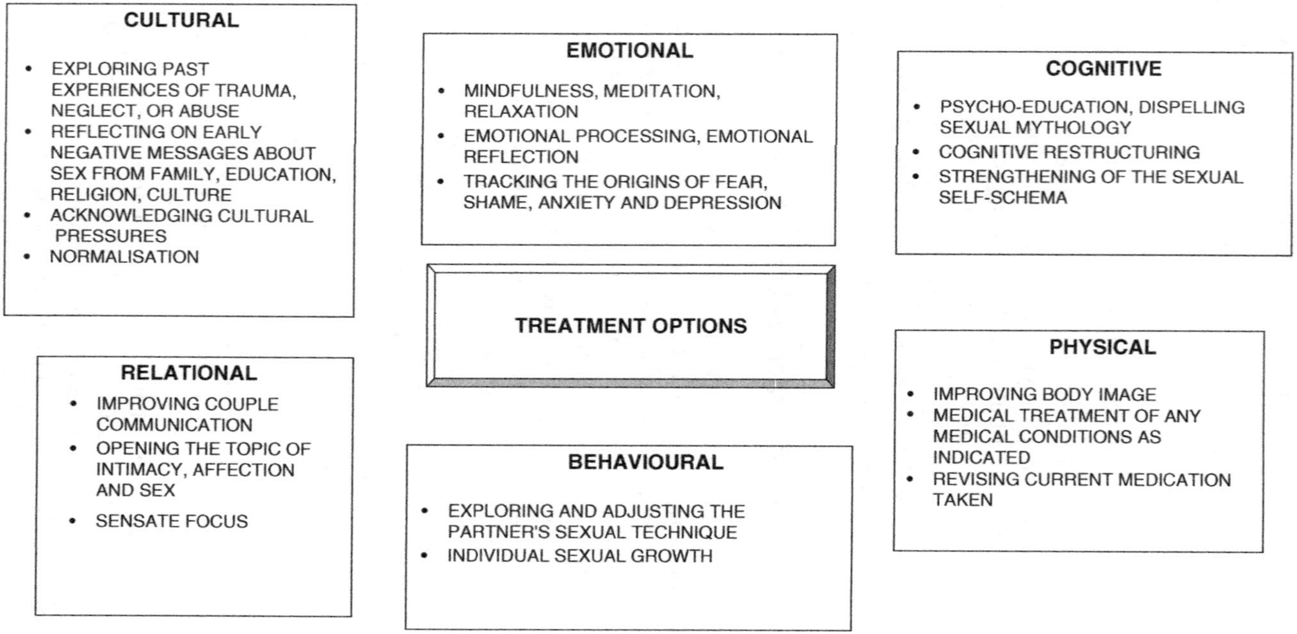

TREATMENT OPTIONS

CULTURAL

- EXPLORING PAST EXPERIENCES OF TRAUMA, NEGLECT, OR ABUSE
- REFLECTING ON EARLY NEGATIVE MESSAGES ABOUT SEX FROM FAMILY, EDUCATION, RELIGION, CULTURE
- ACKNOWLEDGING CULTURAL PRESSURES
- NORMALISATION

EMOTIONAL

- MINDFULNESS, MEDITATION, RELAXATION
- EMOTIONAL PROCESSING, EMOTIONAL REFLECTION
- TRACKING THE ORIGINS OF FEAR, SHAME, ANXIETY AND DEPRESSION

COGNITIVE

- PSYCHO-EDUCATION, DISPELLING SEXUAL MYTHOLOGY
- COGNITIVE RESTRUCTURING
- STRENGTHENING OF THE SEXUAL SELF-SCHEMA

RELATIONAL

- IMPROVING COUPLE COMMUNICATION
- OPENING THE TOPIC OF INTIMACY, AFFECTION AND SEX
- SENSATE FOCUS

BEHAVIOURAL

- EXPLORING AND ADJUSTING THE PARTNER'S SEXUAL TECHNIQUE
- INDIVIDUAL SEXUAL GROWTH

PHYSICAL

- IMPROVING BODY IMAGE
- MEDICAL TREATMENT OF ANY MEDICAL CONDITIONS AS INDICATED
- REVISING CURRENT MEDICATION TAKEN

Figure 5.9 Sexual aversion disorder: treatment options

Emotional dimension

Mindfulness, meditation, yoga and relaxation exercises are all recommended in cases of underlying fear, anxiety and phobic avoidance of sex. Tracing the origins of fear, shame and anxiety related to sex and encouragement of emotional processing and reflection can help reduce these feelings and support positive outcomes.

An interesting finding by Basson (2010) suggests that women who feel unable to say 'no' to sexual invitations, or to set the pace and the frequency of their sexual encounters, often speak of being 'aversive to sex' (p.171). This indicates the need for increasing the woman's self-confidence and assertiveness with the view of empowering her voice and ability to respond in sexual situations in ways that are consistent with her own feelings and desires.

Cognitive dimension

The scarce literature on treatment of sexual aversion describes the effectiveness of CBT (Janata & Kingsberg, 2005). Underlying sexual mythology could be usefully dispelled through psycho-education and cognitive restructuring, leading to strengthening of the sexual self-schema.

Physical dimension

The usefulness of pharmacotherapy in the treatment of SAD has not been adequately explored. SSRIs have been effective in treating panic and may therefore have a role in the treatment of SAD as well (Janata & Kingsberg, 2005).

Other interventions within the physical dimension, such as improving body image, medical treatment and revising current medication taken are all potentially helpful in situations where an indication for such treatment is identified.

Behavioural dimension

Behavioural techniques of systematic desensitisation have been identified in literature as potentially improving SAD (Finch, 2001). The idea is that gradual exposure to increased sexual stimuli over time, in a safe environment where the client can feel in control of the situation, could increase familiarity with sexual situations and enable a positive experience thus combating fear, anxiety and sometimes disgust related to sex. Janata and Kingsberg (2005) describe a case of a client whose treatment consisted firstly of utilising the hierarchy of aversion-and anxiety-provoking images, ranging from masturbation, which evoked the least anxiety, to intercourse, which evoked the greatest anxiety. In addition, she was taught deep breathing and a relaxation technique. Sexual situations were designed to remain fully in her control. The anxiety was modulated over time and the aversion response was gradually desensitised (Janata & Kingsberg, 2005, p.118).

Different activities could be suggested to clients as part of the systematic desensitisation programme, such as:

- Reading educational material on sex and sexual relationships
- Reading erotic and romantic novels that describe enjoyable sexual experiences explicitly
- Talking about sex and intimate matters with others, to whom the client feels close
- Visualising pleasant sexual encounters and developing positive sexual fantasy.

In addition, typical behavioural techniques relevant to different sexual dysfunctions could be applied here, such as individual sexual growth and deconstruction of the sexual activity, in order to identify the adequacy of sexual stimuli, together with suggested adjustments of the sexual technique of the client and/or their partner/s so as to improve the efficacy of sexual stimulation (Basson, 2010).

Relational dimension

As stated in the literature, it is interpersonal distress that tends to bring the sufferers of SAD to sexual clinics (Weeks, Gambescia & Hertlein, 2016). The person experiencing sexual aversion usually avoids sex and conversations about it, which leads to relationship strain and sometimes conflict. Psychotherapy can help provide a safe space to talk about intimacy, affection and sex and improve couple communication.

Carnes (1997) believes that 'it is possible to learn how to love better' stating that 'learning how to better show one's love can dramatically affect the success couples have in improving and remaining satisfied with their sexual relationships' (p.293). The 'love behaviors' one can learn include: showing appreciation to the partner; expressing love non-verbally through voice, gestures, postures, and facial expressions; verbalising love; being open and vulnerable; showing acceptance of the less-pleasant aspects of the other;

and demonstrating physical affection. These only work, states Carnes, alongside reciprocal action of noticing, appreciating and commenting on the expression of love from the partner.

Sensate focus can be helpful in restoring intimacy and creating a safe context where sensual and sexual needs can be expressed, negotiated and co-ordinated between the partners.

Cultural dimension

Sexology literature advises a gentle approach in the handling of SAD, given strong evidence of the underlying traumatic experiences that may have contributed to the development of this condition. Studies have repeatedly linked traumatic experiences, such as childhood abuse, neglect and rape to SAD. Exploring these experiences in a safe therapeutic environment can enhance self-understanding and normalise the aversive reaction to sex in the context of such difficulties (Weeks, Gambescia & Hertlein, 2016, p.53).

Reflecting on early negative messages about sex stemming from family, education, culture and religion enables deconstruction of such messages and their impact on the person over time. 'Sexual anorexia', claims Carnes, 'gathers strength from a culture that makes sexual satisfaction both an unreachable goal and a nonnegotiable demand' (Carnes 1997, p.4). Acknowledging cultural pressures and contradictions related to sexual behaviour can be a useful intervention leading to enhanced contextual understanding of the sexual problem and an increased sense of choice and individual sexual rights.

Sexual compulsivity, addiction or hypersexuality: treatment options

The absence of a universal definition for these conditions makes it harder to determine helpful treatment parameters. Given this lack of consensus and the risk of over-pathologising 'sexual compulsivity', 'sexual addictions' or 'hypersexuality', it is vital that two aspects of working with these phenomena are considered:

- *Undertaking a thorough assessment*; exploring the particular details of what is being presented as the 'addictive' sexual behaviour, as well as its meaning for the client and their significant others. Sometimes assessment reveals that the origin of the distress brought to therapy may

be social stigma or the partner's construction of watching pornography as infidelity; or cybersex and internet pornography use may be a way for clients to explore their interest in same-sex relationships which may be an area they find difficult to be open about. Personal sexual insecurity and/or a lack of sexual experience may prompt people to search for answers and guidance from the internet; online sex education may be a safer way for those who feel too shy to openly express their sexual curiosity or admit their sexual inexperience. Working with couples where internet pornography is seen as problematic by one of the partners can involve mediating a compromise on this issue. Enabling them to find new ways of sexually relating through expanding their sexual options can lead to fulfilment of their sexual needs that had previously been met through the internet. Equally, internet and pornography use can feel out of control to the person and this is where clinicians need to pay close attention when undertaking assessment. A wide variety of client situations and histories may be revealed in assessment and therapy under the presenting problem of 'sexual addictions'; the therapist's task is to create a contextual understanding of the issue and its impact on the person's life and relationships.
- *Employing therapists' self-reflexivity and relational reflexivity*; as the phenomena of 'sexual addictions', 'sexual compulsivity' and similar labels seem to be prone to evoking personal judgements, even moralistic and punitive attitudes, or an over-medicalised approach based on normative models of health and pathology, self-monitoring, supervisory consultations and ongoing further education in the field are highly advisable. Within this, it may be enlightening and enriching for professionals to step out of their usual zone of expertise and investigate further methods of practising. It is vital for professionals to engage with the complexities and obscurities of this phenomenon and the controversies and perplexities that surround it, while considering the wide span of possibilities for enhancing its understanding and treatment.

Typical treatment approaches in sexology and sex therapy for 'sexual compulsivity', 'sexual addiction', 'hypersexuality' and similar labels are summarised below:

- *12-step groups:* This model, originally developed for alcohol and drug dependency, has been adapted for use with sexual addictions (Carnes, 1992; Salmon, 1995). Multiple groups for 12-step recovery from 'sexual addiction' exist worldwide, such as: Sexaholics Anonymous (SA); Sex

Addicts Anonymous (SAA); Sexual Recovery Anonymous (SRA); Sexual Compulsives Anonymous (SCA); and Sex and Love Addicts Anonymous (SLAA). The availability of these groups span the world, with many residing in North America, Canada, Central America, South America, Australia, New Zealand, Europe, Asia and Africa. However, there is hardly any evaluation data on the effectiveness of these groups. Their popularity is explained by them being an easily available and complimentary service, providing a strong support network, promoting solidarity and companionship (Fong, 2006). The method remains controversial, mainly with regard to the issue of abstinence and whether it can be usefully applied to sexual behaviour in the same way in which it is used in the treatment of substance abuse.

- *Pharmacology:* Several studies have confirmed a reduction in 'hypersexual behaviour' as a result of medication and hormonal treatments; however, a long list of severe physical side effects can pose serious health risks; unfortunately, these are not always made clear to patients.
- *CBT:* Relapse prevention therapy is a self-control programme that uses skills training, cognitive restructuring and lifestyle change to help identify and avoid high-risk situations, and learn ways of coping with highly stressful life events.
- *Psychodynamic therapy:* An insight-oriented approach is aimed at resolving the effects of painful childhood experiences and past trauma through analysis of unconscious motivations and ineffective defence mechanisms. The goal is to facilitate strengthening of impulse control through an increased awareness of one's own psychological processes, and to work towards learning alternative and more suitable ways for sexual fulfilment.
- *Holistic treatments:* Methods involving the integration of various approaches are increasingly being applied in the area of 'sexual addiction'. For example, the BERSC model of addiction, created by a UK-based sexual and relationship therapist (Hall, 2013) comprehends five dimensions:
    - *Biological*; based on the latest neuroscience research Hall claims that there is a biological disposition towards addiction, related to the dopamine (a chemical associated with motivation and drive) levels in the brain
    - *Emotional*; Hall states that compulsive sexual behaviour is used as a primary mechanism for emotional regulation
    - *Relational*; this concerns early attachment wounds, manifesting themselves in adult relationships as difficulties with commitment and intimacy

- *Social* issues relate to a lack of responsibility as well as confusion as to how to manage multiple tasks and the greater sexual freedom afforded in the current social climate
- *Cultural* influences may include: gender identity, sexual orientation, race, faith, peer influences, family, friends and the workplace (Hall, 2013).

The BERSC model provides a comprehensive treatment framework for addressing the significant influences coming from these five dimensions of the clients' experience. Treatment is a combination of theoretical perspectives including psychodynamic, cognitive-behavioural, systemic, and transactional analysis. This therapeutic approach addresses sexually problematic behaviour by helping clients to cope with difficult feelings, leading to increased options for managing anger and challenging their acting-out behaviour when feeling frustrated and powerless; and helping clients understand the neurobiology of addiction and the social and cultural influences that create pressures and challenges.

- *Sexual health model:* An alternative model challenging the concept of 'sexual addiction' provides treatment for 'out-of-control sexual behaviours' (as defined in Chapter 4) for individual men and gay male couples (Braun-Harvey & Vigorito, 2016). This model is aimed at empowerment, based on the principles of sexual health rather than promoting out-of-control sexual behaviour as necessarily a 'disorder'. The authors acknowledge that some clients have a problem with regulating sexual behaviour, accompanied by a subjective experience of feeling out of control. However, it rarely deserves the label of a 'disorder' but is rather viewed on a spectrum of sexual worries, problems and disorders. A non-pathologising emphasis is crucial: treatment is based on defining and building a personal vision of sexual health. In contrast to the addiction model which focuses on specific sexual activities, the sexual health model focuses on six fundamental agreements and principles of sexual health. The principles, as follows, provide the treatment frame for clients to define and enact their own personal vision of sexual health: sex has to be based on *consent*; it has to be *non-exploitative*; there has to be a degree of *honesty*, of understanding *sexual values*, and there need to be *sexual rights* in the pursuit of *sexual pleasure*.

  Individual clients are encouraged to reflect on: How do I ensure consent? How do I ensure non-exploitation? How am I meeting a level of honesty in my sexual relationships? Questions for partners in couple therapy are along the lines of: How do you engage with each other and what are the principles that guide you? How transparent are you with your partner? Are your wants and desires expressed? Do you keep to your agreements? Is the sexual experience on balance satisfactory for you both? Explorations of these principles are designed to address each man's vulnerability factors and competing motivations that impede his ability to achieve his vision of sexual health. Emphasis is on clients' motivation for change and learning to live by agreements and principles of sexual health that ensures sexual safety and pleasure.

The authors stress the importance of therapists providing a compassionate and accepting stance. In order for this to be achieved, therapists need to examine their own values, in addition to completing specific training about the diversity of sexuality and ways of facilitating effective, person-centred conversations about sexual health (Braun-Harvey & Vigorito, 2016).

The following pages, including Figure 5.10, summarise treatment options in relation to the presenting issues regarding 'sexual compulsivity', 'sexual addiction', 'hypersexuality', or 'out-of-control sexual behaviour', and similar labels, in relation to the six dimensions of the MOST model. Application of this model to the treatment of this complex and controversial phenomenon allows for drawing on experiences and knowledges deriving from various perspectives, while calling for:

- a broad outlook, appreciating the multidimensional nature of sexuality and sexual behaviour
- consideration that sexual behaviours are socially and culturally constructed categories to which value judgements and normative assumptions are attached as part of prevalent social and cultural practices
- a non-pathologising approach allowing for embracing a wide variety of sexual expressions as part of the human sexuality spectrum; while acknowledging the difficulties that some individuals and sexual partners experience with the regulation of sexual behaviours
- a mindful, self and relationally reflexive empowering approach to clients presenting worries about their regulation of their sexual behaviours
- consideration of the importance of language and its influence on the meaning attributed to certain behaviours; the choice of how to name the issue may have a major impact on its treatment process and outcome. 'Labels such as sexual addiction, sexual compulsion, sexual impulsivity or hypersexuality can affect how and what treatments are provided. The terms also influence both the client's perception of the problem and his or her partner's perception of the problem' (Weeks, Gambescia & Hertlein, 2016, p.27).

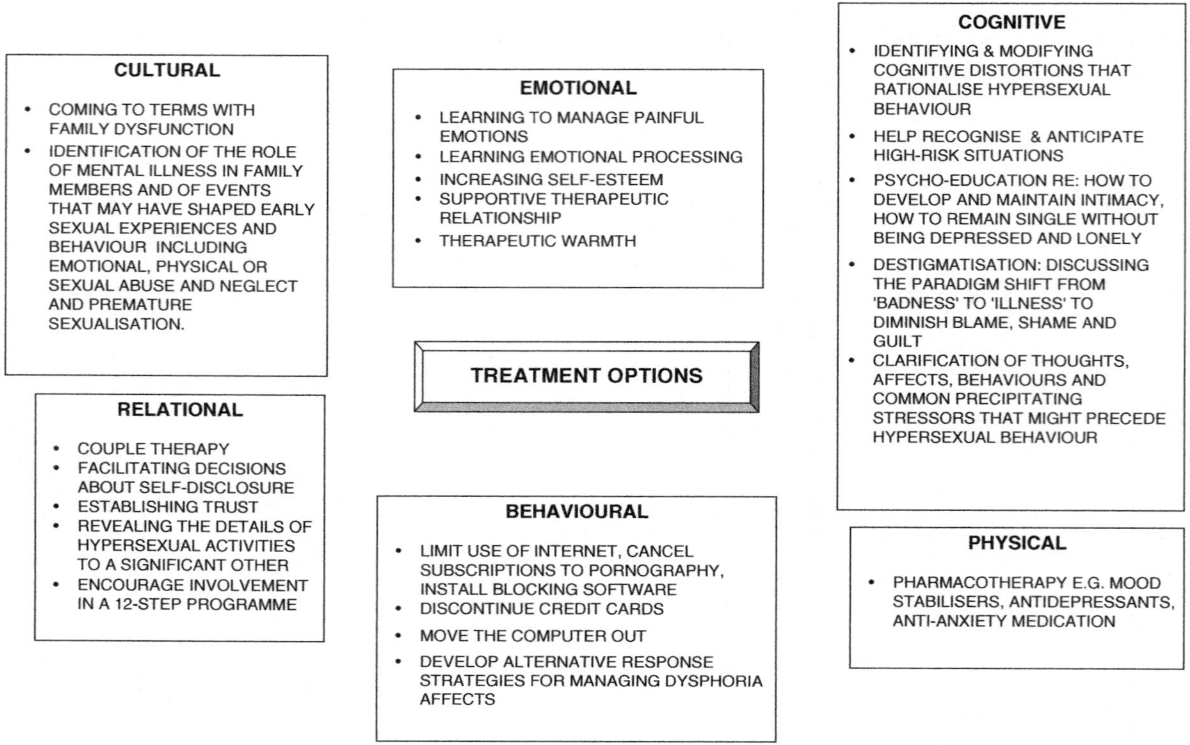

TREATMENT OPTIONS

CULTURAL

- COMING TO TERMS WITH FAMILY DYSFUNCTION
- IDENTIFICATION OF THE ROLE OF MENTAL ILLNESS IN FAMILY MEMBERS AND OF EVENTS THAT MAY HAVE SHAPED EARLY SEXUAL EXPERIENCES AND BEHAVIOUR INCLUDING EMOTIONAL, PHYSICAL OR SEXUAL ABUSE AND NEGLECT AND PREMATURE SEXUALISATION.

EMOTIONAL

- LEARNING TO MANAGE PAINFUL EMOTIONS
- LEARNING EMOTIONAL PROCESSING
- INCREASING SELF-ESTEEM
- SUPPORTIVE THERAPEUTIC RELATIONSHIP
- THERAPEUTIC WARMTH

COGNITIVE

- IDENTIFYING & MODIFYING COGNITIVE DISTORTIONS THAT RATIONALISE HYPERSEXUAL BEHAVIOUR
- HELP RECOGNISE & ANTICIPATE HIGH-RISK SITUATIONS
- PSYCHO-EDUCATION RE: HOW TO DEVELOP AND MAINTAIN INTIMACY, HOW TO REMAIN SINGLE WITHOUT BEING DEPRESSED AND LONELY
- DESTIGMATISATION: DISCUSSING THE PARADIGM SHIFT FROM 'BADNESS' TO 'ILLNESS' TO DIMINISH BLAME, SHAME AND GUILT
- CLARIFICATION OF THOUGHTS, AFFECTS, BEHAVIOURS AND COMMON PRECIPITATING STRESSORS THAT MIGHT PRECEDE HYPERSEXUAL BEHAVIOUR

RELATIONAL

- COUPLE THERAPY
- FACILITATING DECISIONS ABOUT SELF-DISCLOSURE
- ESTABLISHING TRUST
- REVEALING THE DETAILS OF HYPERSEXUAL ACTIVITIES TO A SIGNIFICANT OTHER
- ENCOURAGE INVOLVEMENT IN A 12-STEP PROGRAMME

BEHAVIOURAL

- LIMIT USE OF INTERNET, CANCEL SUBSCRIPTIONS TO PORNOGRAPHY, INSTALL BLOCKING SOFTWARE
- DISCONTINUE CREDIT CARDS
- MOVE THE COMPUTER OUT
- DEVELOP ALTERNATIVE RESPONSE STRATEGIES FOR MANAGING DYSPHORIA AFFECTS

PHYSICAL

- PHARMACOTHERAPY E.G. MOOD STABILISERS, ANTIDEPRESSANTS, ANTI-ANXIETY MEDICATION

Figure 5.10 Sexual compulsivity, addiction or hypersexuality: treatment options

Emotional dimension

Clinicians and researchers supporting the label of 'sexual addiction', and 'sexual compulsivity' view anxiety, stress and depression as the most frequent precipitating factors triggering addictive behaviours. According to this perspective, clients presenting such problems suffer from 'emotional dysregulation', i.e. an inability to appropriately manage their own emotions (Adams & Robinson, 2001; Reid, Bramen, Anderson & Cohen, 2014). Such clients may benefit from developing coping skills often gained through practising yoga, meditation, mindfulness and guided imagery, learning strategies to manage stress and anxiety levels, and enhancing social skills.

Themes of shame, avoidance, anger, grief, loss and impaired self-esteem are viewed as common in 'sexual compulsivity' (Fong, 2006). Learning to manage painful emotions, and learning emotional processing instead of escaping painful affect is seen as a path to recovery. An empowering approach provided within a warm and supportive therapeutic relationship is likely to enhance clients' self-esteem and reduce feelings of shame and embarrassment often underlying such issues (Kafka, 2014; Braun-Harvey & Vigorito, 2016).

Some view 'sexual addiction'/'hypersexuality' patterns as associated with past trauma that may have adversely impacted the client's ability to form adult attachments, creating difficulties with establishing committed relationships. It is believed that in these situations, it is paramount that therapists address and help to resolve trauma issues when treating this type of problem (Flores, 2004).

Cognitive dimension

Identifying and modifying cognitive distortions that rationalise 'hypersexual' behaviour is suggested as an important therapeutic task (Kafka, 2014, p.295); e.g.: *'I am not really cheating on my spouse if I go to a massage parlor'* (Fong, 2006, p.56). Psycho-educational input enabling clients to learn about addictive and compulsive behaviour and the nature of 'sexual addiction disorder', as well as the impact of past abuse issues on their sexual health, supports clients in gaining control over their 'hypersexual' symptomatology (Weiss, 2004; Delmonico & Griffin, 2015). In addition, psycho-education on what constitutes healthy sexuality and a healthy sexual relationship, how to develop and maintain intimacy and how to remain single without being depressed and lonely, can help prevent further out-of-control sexual behaviours (Kafka, 2014).

Assisting clients to recognise and anticipate high-risk situations and identify the usual triggers for their 'hypersexual' behaviour can help with the prevention of such behaviour and support the development of healthier choices (Fong, 2006). Clarification of thoughts, affects, behaviours and common precipitating stressors that precede 'hypersexual' behaviour supports the same aim (Kafka, 2014). 'Like with any addictive behaviour, it is important that the client understands their addiction cycle, the triggers and rituals leading up to the addictive behaviour, and steps that can be taken to interrupt the cycle' (Delmonico & Griffin, 2015, p.245).

Destigmatisation, i.e. discussing the paradigm shift from 'badness' to 'illness', similarly to 'externalisation of the problem' (White, 2007), serves to diminish blame, shame and guilt associated with 'hypersexual' behaviour (Kafka, 2014).

Physical dimension

When clients presenting 'hypersexual behaviour' suffer from certain medical conditions, these should be treated as indicated. Administering medication in the treatment of 'hypersexuality' is sometimes justified by the psychiatric comorbidity in certain cases. For example, the use of mood stabilisers, antidepressants, neuroleptics, anti-anxiety medication and antipsychotics can have a profound effect in ameliorating 'hypersexual' behaviours (Kafka, 2014). These clearly suggest that the rationale for the use of such medication sits with the primary psychiatric diagnosis, whereby 'hypersexual' behaviour seems to be one of the accompanying symptoms. Medication used for substance abuse and obsessive compulsive disorder has been also tried in treatment of 'hypersexuality'. Limited clinical evidence suggests that for example SSRIs decrease the craving and preoccupation associated with 'sexual addiction' (Fong, 2006).

While some clinicians and researchers strongly believe in the importance of psychopharmacological treatment of 'hypersexuality' (e.g. Kafka, 2014), it is also worth noting that there are no officially approved medications for these conditions and no systematic evidence on their effectiveness (Fong, 2006).

Behavioural dimension

Various strategies are typically applied in stopping unwanted sexual behaviours, such as:

> negotiating the use of phone blocks; discarding paraphernalia such as pornography; cancelling subscriptions for pornography; installing password

> protection pornography blocking software; holding or discontinuing credit cards; using an Internet censor with password controlled by partner, family member, or therapist; moving a computer out of a private setting; consider eliminating Internet access completely... (Kafka, 2014, pp.289–290).

Kafka (2014) talks about 'collaborative limit setting' in establishing effective behavioural strategies together with clients, while working co-operatively towards achieving agreed therapeutic goals.

Stopping unwanted behaviours is the first step in the treatment strategy followed by working on developing alternative response strategies for managing stressful situations and responding to the usual triggers that lead to problematic sexual behaviours (Kafka, 2014).

Relational dimension

Discovery of the partner's 'hypersexual' behaviour can have a devastating effect on a relationship. Treating both partners in couple therapy is often helpful, enabling restoration of trust and re-establishment of the couple bond. Facilitating decisions about self-disclosure in revealing the details of 'hypersexual' activities to the significant other is one of the crucial initial therapeutic tasks that needs to be carefully thought through and sensitively carried out (Kafka, 2014). Some believe that the timing of introducing couple therapy is crucial; often it proves useful if it follows individual sessions with each partner, allowing for processing of the discovery of 'hypersexual' behaviour, and accompanied feelings of shock, betrayal, often compared to the experience of a traumatic event. The trauma of the discovery of the partner's 'hypersexual behaviour' may impact the person's self-esteem and bring forth anxiety and depression, calling for individual therapy support in processing traumatic thoughts and feelings (Schneider, 2000).

In certain situations, the client is unwilling to include the partner if the perceived risk of disclosure to the stability or the existence of the relationship is too high. Research evidence, however, suggests that full disclosure most likely leads to positive relationship outcomes, although re-establishment of trust may take a long time (Corley & Schneider, 2012).

Cultural dimension

Literature points to the predisposing factors in the development of 'hypersexual behaviour' as family dysfunction and childhood abuse. Invaluable therapeutic effects can be achieved in situations where one is coming to terms with disturbed family relationships and recognising the impact of psychiatric illness in family members. In addition, therapy can enlighten one's understanding of early experiences including emotional, physical and sexual abuse or neglect that may have led to premature sexualisation in relationships (Kafka, 2014).

When considering the cultural dimension, it seems highly relevant to acknowledge the social and cultural construction of 'hypersexuality', 'sexual addiction' and so on, and the meaning of these terms as expressed in communication and language. These labels are culturally bound and determined by the dominant cultural discourses often embedded in normative assumptions about sexual desire, sexual expression and sexual rights.

Dyspareunia in men: treatment options

There is no uniformly accepted treatment protocol for male dyspareunia, due to its heterogeneous presentation and the lack of research studies that might throw some light on this complex phenomenon. Unlike with female GPPPD (genito-pelvic pain/penetration disorder), which has been the subject of extensive research interest and where a wealth of support is offered including charities, self-help groups and specialised clinics, there is limited treatment available for male dyspareunia and an absence of forums where it is discussed.

The MOST map in Figure 5.11 summarises approaches to treatment of both organically caused and non-specific male dyspareunia (where no medical reasons are found). Certain interventions relevant to GPPPD could be applied to this condition, depending on clinical assessment and the client's response to proposed treatment choices.

Treatment is typically directed at the underlying causes; if an organic cause is detected, medical remedy is undertaken accordingly; in the absence of an identified medical condition, treatment modalities vary from medical to behavioural and psychological interventions (Oommen & Hellstrom, 2010). A recent systematic review of articles on chronic pelvic pain syndrome in men concluded that this is an enigmatic condition that requires a multimodal approach, and that inclusion of alternative therapies supports successful treatment. Effective strategies seem to be a combination of CBT, dietary and lifestyle modification, acupuncture, phytotherapy and myofascial physical therapy (Herati & Moldwin, 2013).

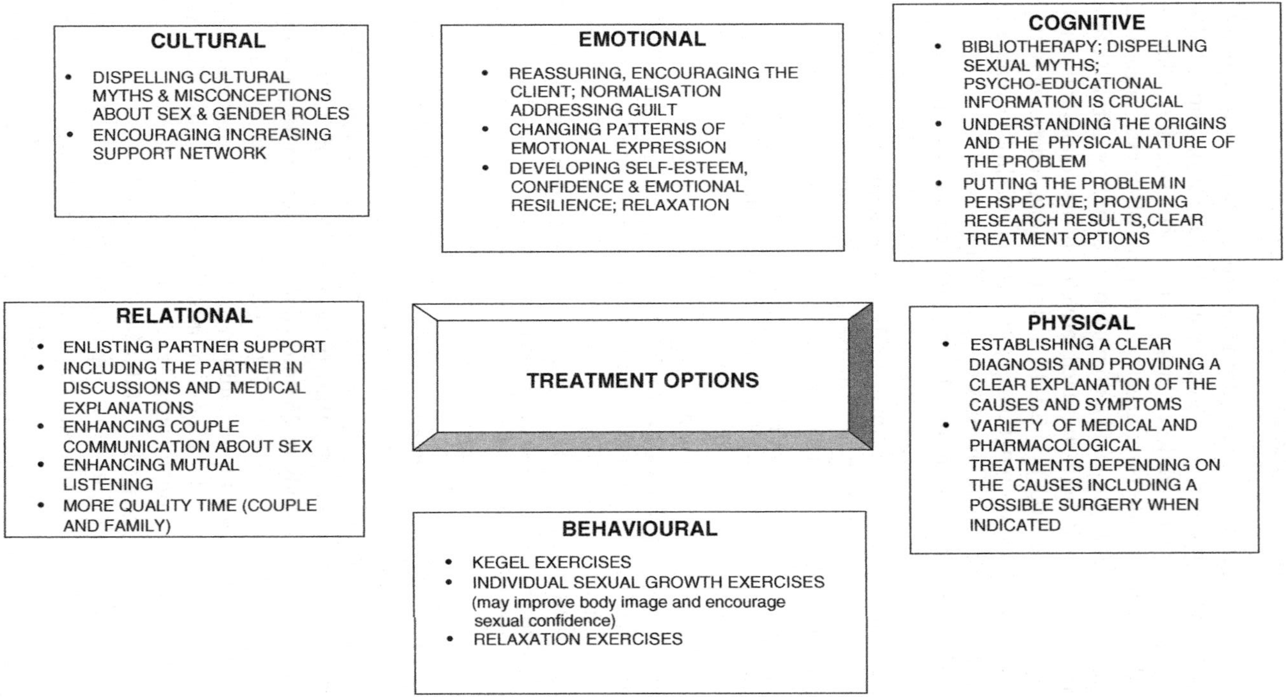

TREATMENT OPTIONS

CULTURAL

- DISPELLING CULTURAL MYTHS & MISCONCEPTIONS ABOUT SEX & GENDER ROLES
- ENCOURAGING INCREASING SUPPORT NETWORK

EMOTIONAL

- REASSURING, ENCOURAGING THE CLIENT; NORMALISATION ADDRESSING GUILT
- CHANGING PATTERNS OF EMOTIONAL EXPRESSION
- DEVELOPING SELF-ESTEEM, CONFIDENCE & EMOTIONAL RESILIENCE; RELAXATION

COGNITIVE

- BIBLIOTHERAPY; DISPELLING SEXUAL MYTHS; PSYCHO-EDUCATIONAL INFORMATION IS CRUCIAL
- UNDERSTANDING THE ORIGINS AND THE PHYSICAL NATURE OF THE PROBLEM
- PUTTING THE PROBLEM IN PERSPECTIVE; PROVIDING RESEARCH RESULTS,CLEAR TREATMENT OPTIONS

RELATIONAL

- ENLISTING PARTNER SUPPORT
- INCLUDING THE PARTNER IN DISCUSSIONS AND MEDICAL EXPLANATIONS
- ENHANCING COUPLE COMMUNICATION ABOUT SEX
- ENHANCING MUTUAL LISTENING
- MORE QUALITY TIME (COUPLE AND FAMILY)

PHYSICAL

- ESTABLISHING A CLEAR DIAGNOSIS AND PROVIDING A CLEAR EXPLANATION OF THE CAUSES AND SYMPTOMS
- VARIETY OF MEDICAL AND PHARMACOLOGICAL TREATMENTS DEPENDING ON THE CAUSES INCLUDING A POSSIBLE SURGERY WHEN INDICATED

BEHAVIOURAL

- KEGEL EXERCISES
- INDIVIDUAL SEXUAL GROWTH EXERCISES (may improve body image and encourage sexual confidence)
- RELAXATION EXERCISES

Figure 5.11 Dyspareunia in men: treatment options

Emotional dimension

Research and clinical evidence suggests that emotional factors can both underlie and aggravate symptoms of male dyspareunia. A reassuring and encouraging approach can assist clients in developing stronger self-esteem, confidence and emotional resilience. Addressing negative emotions often associated with this condition, such as shame, fear and guilt related to sex utilises normalisation and emotionally focused methods that facilitate clients' reflection and emotional processing (Greenberg, 2008). This is likely to encourage changing patterns of emotional expression and strengthen emotional adjustability, flexibility as well as one's ability to cope with life stresses, worries and anxieties.

Certain case studies link deeply situated emotional memories and repressed feelings of rejection, betrayal, humiliation, helplessness and unexpressed resentment and anger with psychogenic male dyspareunia. In one such study, clients were offered 'journey therapy', an alternative emotionally based therapy developed by Brandon Bays, a UK mind-body healing psychotherapist. This approach is influenced by alternative health interventions, including neuro-linguistic programming (NLP), meditation, relaxation and guided imagery, and informed by scientific research on emotional suppression resulting in bodily changes. It encourages individuals to locate repressed memories in the body 'where old hurts are held' and release negative emotions, leading to accessing under-used resources and the creation of a new memory (Bays, www.thejourney.com). For the majority of clients in this study, this type of approach seemed more effective than previously undertaken medical interventions (Naim & Ende, 2011).

Cognitive dimension

The prominent cognitive therapy techniques and methods applied to a range of sexual difficulties, such as bibliotherapy, cognitive restructuring and challenging narrow beliefs about sex, intimacy, masculinity and relationships, can also helpfully support the treatment of male dyspareunia. Findings of a recent North American study of 253 men diagnosed with chronic prostatitis support the effectiveness of a CBT programme, specifically designed to improve both symptoms of the condition and the quality of life of patients. Data suggest that psycho-educational information is crucial; dispelling sexual myths and providing patient educational materials significantly supported overall treatment success (Nickel, Mullins & Tripp, 2008).

Hollows (2007) highlights the importance of sex education for male dyspareunia and anodyspareunia; including understanding of the origins and physical nature of the problem and putting it into perspective by providing reliable research results and clear treatment options.

Physical dimension

Establishing a clear diagnosis and providing a cogent explanation of the causes of the symptoms for clients forms an essential standpoint from which to base medical interventions. A variety of medical and pharmacological treatments can be applied, including possible surgical intervention when indicated, depending on the medical diagnosis.

The choice of treatment varies based on aetiology and specific symptoms; e.g. alpha-blockers are typically used for pain symptoms such as painful ejaculation; antibiotics for infections; finasteride and other anti-inflammatory medications for inflammatory diseases underlying the problem; and for dyspareunia associated with dermatological conditions, treatment may include steroids and other medication appropriate to the diagnosis. Pharmacological treatment for Peyronie's disease has not been shown to be consistently effective; minimally invasive surgical procedures are offered as a treatment of choice (Oommen & Hellstrom, 2010). For phimosis and frenulum brave (short frenulum), circumcision is suggested as an effective treatment option. Contrary to widespread beliefs about the adverse effects of circumcision, a recent systematic review of 2,675 scientific publications conducted by researchers from the University of Sydney, concluded that medical male circumcision has no adverse effects on men's sexual functioning and satisfaction (Morris & Krieger, 2013).

Behavioural dimension

Behavioural exercises such as pelvic floor (Kegel) exercises and individual sexual growth, as with other sexual difficulties, may contribute to treatment by improving body image and encouraging sexual confidence. Relaxation exercises, yoga, meditation and a healthy lifestyle equally combat anxiety related to sex, support sexual self-care and a general state of wellbeing, often easing the symptoms. In discussing treatment options for male dyspareunia and anodyspareunia, Hollows (2007) stresses the importance of relaxation and communication, acknowledging anatomical differences between anal and vaginal intercourse, and adapting behaviours accordingly.

Relational dimension

Relational aspects of treatment of male dyspareunia are often crucial. Including the partner in discussions and medical explanations and enlisting the partner's support significantly enhances couple intimacy and their relationship satisfaction. Couple communication about sex is often constrained by the experience of pain and related worry, stress and feelings of inadequacy of the man suffering from the condition. Enhancing mutual listening and encouraging the couple to spend more quality time together can ease tension and reduce the couple distancing that sometimes results from the difficulties relating to the symptomatology.

Clinical experience suggests that men can develop secondary sexual dysfunction as a result of suffering pain during or after intercourse. In such situations, involving partners in medical and psychological treatment can be essential for a successful outcome and the enhancement of intimacy. Clinical studies highlight the need to consider relationship factors in this condition, and indicate that involving both partners and addressing a wider psychosocial context in the treatment of prostatitis may be worthwhile (Smith et al., 2007).

Cultural dimension

Men suffering from pain associated with sexual intercourse and ejaculation are sometimes victims of sexual abuse or come from familial, cultural and religious backgrounds that view sexual enjoyment as inappropriate (Oomman & Hellstrop, 2010). Working with the trauma of abuse with patients exhibiting male dyspareunia symptoms may involve similar therapeutic processes to those for post-traumatic stress disorder; various therapeutic options are open in such situations depending on the clients' situation.

Shame associated with sexual activity and/or with the experience of sexual pain often presents a barrier to talking even with close family or friends. Clinicians can encourage clients to increase their support network by opening up the subject of intimacy, sex and their sensitive condition with others from their family and social circles. The condition sometimes raises feelings of inadequacy leading to disengagement from the social environment and, in this regard, therapeutic input can helpfully encourage rebuilding of the social network in order to combat social isolation.

EXERCISES

- Complete a MOST map of treatment options, combining sexology and systemic social constructionist perspectives, for a client presenting, for example, erectile difficulties.
- What do therapists need to pay attention to in each of the MOST model dimensions, when working with sexual minority clients? Discuss.
- Create a treatment plan for a lesbian couple presenting FSI/AD.

6

CLIENT VIGNETTES

Introduction

The illustrations in this chapter relate to a variety of presenting sexual difficulties encompassing several therapy session summaries, and transcripts of a formulation session and a supervision session. Each case is presented in a different format, for example a chronological sequence of the therapy session, or a thematic summary, illustrating the variety of ways in which psychotherapeutic interactions can be described, discussed and reflected upon. These examples from clinical practice elucidate the combined use of sexology, sex therapy and systemic therapy resources and elaborate ideas from previous chapters, in particular the value of an integrated approach.

To protect clients' and therapists' confidentiality and anonymity, various means were employed: combining different client situations as part of one client case; altering background details; and fictionalising some aspects of the presented scenarios.

Melanie: 'anorgasmia'

The following vignette illustrates working with a female client who had been given the diagnosis of anorgasmia by a medical professional. The therapeutic process focused on de-pathologising the client's socially constructed identity as a sexually inadequate person who needed mental health treatment for her 'disorder'.

Referral and psychosocial background

Melanie, a 50-year-old white British heterosexual woman, was referred to a psychosexual service by her GP for her presenting concern of 'anorgasmia'. She was a factory worker, divorced ten years prior to coming to therapy.

The first two sessions mainly consisted of assessment: understanding the client's presenting problems, tracking relevant psychosexual history and other background information while engaging the client with the therapeutic process. The client's main concerns were to do with what she described as her inability to reach orgasm during penetrative sex with her partners. On many occasions she experienced orgasm through oral sex after what she perceived as a 'very long time', about 20 minutes. She was also concerned about her lack of sexual arousal which she described as 'going numb' subsequent to the initial feeling of being turned on during foreplay. She wanted to know why she was losing sensation so early in sexual activity and how she could become orgasmic during penetrative sex. Melanie attributed these difficulties to her own personal and sexual inadequacy, blaming herself for the divorce and for her subsequent unsuccessful relationships. For eight years following her divorce she was on Prozac as she had been diagnosed with depression by her GP.

History of sexual learning and sexual relationships

Melanie's parents divorced 20 years ago after 35 years of marriage. She shared memories of parental conflict, an unaffectionate marital relationship and a family atmosphere where sex and intimacy were taboo. She described her mother, who had a history of depression and stress, as 'affectionate to some extent' and her father as a much-feared figure, who used physical punishment such as beating her with a dog lead. Melanie grew up with family messages that sex was bad and dirty. A lack of sexual education, negative messages and the absence of perceived parental affection contributed to her feeling sexually apprehensive, frightened and inadequate as a young woman.

Her first sexual relationship was at the age of 18, with a man who she had been courting since she was 17 and whom she then married at the age of 19. They had two, now adult, children who were living away from home and with whom she had a good relationship. Melanie left her husband ten years ago, after 20 years of marriage, having found it increasingly difficult, lacking in love and intimacy at all levels. Ten years prior to the divorce her husband had started drinking heavily and had become aggressive towards her to the point that she described him as having a 'changed personality'. The relationship had been sexless for the final six years. She had never enjoyed sex with her husband but 'felt bad to be with someone else'. A year after the divorce she had a brief sexual encounter with a colleague, which left her feeling 'dirty'. Subsequently she had had a series of sexual relationships with men who were still part of her life either as friends or occasional lovers. Since the divorce Melanie had been living on her own which she was finding difficult; she felt stressed about her monotonous, physically demanding and poorly paid job. Her mother had died two years ago and her father lived on his own as a widower from his second marriage.

The therapist's initial ideas

The therapist perceived the problem as 'sexual dissatisfaction' rather than 'sexual dysfunction'. However, based on the client's description, the problem would in DSM-5 terms be defined as primary female arousal and orgasmic disorder. The client's own portrayal of her condition fitted a situation described in the literature where frequent lack of arousal and orgasm was interpreted 'as a statement of gender inadequacy; because she could not reach orgasm, she did not feel like a woman' (Wincze & Carey 2001, p.175). The therapist saw the sexual difficulties described by the client as largely due to anxiety, self-blame and performance fears; the client's initial description of the problem was seen by the therapist as the major part of the problem such that reframing of the difficulties in terms of lack of sexual confidence became the main therapeutic challenge.

Assessment and formulation: sexology and systemic resources

Sexology resources used for the initial assessment helped bring clarity to the definition, based on a detailed account of the problem, and the diagnosis of sexual dysfunctions. Melanie's description of her sexual experiences led to her communicating certain relevant information, including regularly experiencing orgasm during masturbation and in partner sex when receiving clitoral stimulation orally. She reported high levels of personal distress; however, a systemic exploration brought further understanding of the presenting problem, highlighting the importance of viewing the problem through the relational perspective. Questions such as:

- How did it become a concern in the first place?
- Who is it a problem for?
- Who is most distressed?
- What stresses you most?

engaged the client from the onset of assessment in reflecting and making contextual connections. She described how her various partners and ex-boyfriends thought that it was not normal that she failed to have orgasms during vaginal penetration and all expressed grave concerns about her sexual functioning because of that issue. She shared that her greatest worry was frustrating her partners. Furthermore, her distress seemed to have been supported by sexual misconceptions; she thought her experiences of orgasm and pleasure were not valid given her strongly held sexual myths, such as: '*sex equals penetration*', '*oral sex is not proper*', and '*a clitoral orgasm is not a real one*'.

Systemic explorations of the client's explanation and meaning given to her problems suggested that these seemed to constitute a crucial part of the problem. Melanie's self-belief system operated such that her 'abnormality' was held responsible for the problems she brought to therapy. Assumptions that she was abnormal and that there was something sexually seriously wrong with her seemed to have become deeply rooted at the level of her sexual self-schema. The therapist considered that a crucial element of therapy was to create a context for empowerment, whereby the client would be encouraged to reflect on the impact of the punitive relational, cultural and gender stories on her self-construct. Over the course of several sessions, the problem was jointly redefined as a 'lack of sexual confidence', having been first introduced by the client in the formulation session. This definition took away the premise that there was something inherently wrong with her and opened up possibilities for different contextual understanding.

The map in Table 6.1 summarises both CBT and Most model factors contributing to the presenting problem.

Treatment process and therapeutic interventions

Educational input played a significant part in the further process of treatment. It enabled the client to redefine the problem, broaden her understanding of sexual normality and to see her concerns in a different light. The therapist explained research findings and evidence-based facts about orgasmic functioning and the variety of ways in which women experience orgasm. The sexology treatment resources offered to the client included educational DVDs and selected literature on women's sexual response such as Betty Dodson's DVD on 'Self-Loving'; a diagram representing the female sexual response model developed by Rosemary Basson; and a list of typical sexual misconceptions from the therapist's own notes collected from various sources including literature, clinical experience, conferences and other professional contexts.

Table 6.1 Formulation: from 'anorgasmia' to 'lack of sexual confidence'

Factors	Emotional	Cognitive	Physical	Behavioural	Relational	Cultural
PREDISPOSING	Family history of depression Early insecurity in own sexual role	Sexual myths (lack of sexual education) Beliefs / stories about manhood and womanhood	Hormonal imbalance/ fibroids	Restricted ways of masturbating	Previous relationship: Lack of affection Previous partner's aggression and alcohol abuse	Strictly patriarchal upbringing Restricted upbringing Negative messages re: sex, intimacy, affection Dysfunctional family Lack of warmth and affection Frightening and punitive father
PRECIPITATING	Depression Emotional distress/guilt following divorce/low self- esteem	Sexual myths Negative sexual self-schema	Childbirth Vaginal pain/lack of arousal and lubrication Contraceptive pills Antidepress-ants	Inadequate sexual technique of partners Restricted foreplay	Relationship conflict in marriage Divorce/loss of trust Lack of committed partner relationships Partners' rejection and criticism	Pressures at work/stressful events Parental arguments and divorce Assuming blame for own divorce/ doubting her femaleness
MAINTAINING	Low self-esteem Performance anxiety Stress Fear of failure and rejection Insecurity in sexual role	Resonance of negative family messages	Negative body image Irritable bowel syndrome Genital pain	Inadequate sexual technique of partners Fusion of affection and sex Restricted foreplay	Poor communication	External stresses Job dissatisfaction Tiredness Patriarchal stories/gender submission Powerless: gender, education, employment, class

The use of systemic techniques such as: interventive questioning, reframing, deconstruction of stories told and stories lived (Pearce, 1994), logical connotation, positive connotation, together with educational and behavioural tasks from sex therapy including self-focus and bibliotherapy, enabled her to feel affirmed as a sexually normally functioning person, exhibiting healthy sexual patterns, whose sexual responses had been linked to longstanding unhelpful relational patterns and pathologising cultural myths.

Exploration of the client's sexual genogram mapped out a network of concern, which revealed how her individual physical and emotional needs were met in her environment. A long history of deprecation, starting from the very hostile attitude of her father and a generally punitive upbringing, through her marriage where she suffered her husband's physical and emotional abuse, all linked into the identity of a woman who felt inadequate sexually, emotionally and in her capacity to maintain successful relationships with men. Therapeutic conversations provided space for reflecting on cultural taboos and societal pressures on women and their sexuality which, combined with sex therapy input on female sexuality, helped her to place herself in a large community of women sharing similar experiences and reactions rather than in a lonely, isolated place. The therapist used the systemically pertinent technique of 'bringing in a community of views'; by calling upon numerous other people's views, ideas, articles and research, bringing in voices of other experts, other clients and other women. By doing so, the therapist provided a challenge to the community of views that the client had been exposed to throughout her life, on the basis of which she had classified herself as abnormal.

Sessions encouraged her to broaden her system of support. For example, as the therapist and client were drawing a chart of her relationships she mentioned a 'sexual friend' to whom she had started expressing her sexual needs differently, leading her to experience a more satisfying intimate connection.

The therapist offered specific sexual knowledge, while asking the client regularly throughout their work together:

- What does this mean to you?
- How does it sound?
- How is this relevant?
- Do you see it the same or differently?

The client was also constantly invited to use her own expertise to comment on the therapeutic process using relational reflexivity (Burnham, 2005):

- How do you think we are doing?
- Should we change anything in our approach?
- How is it all making sense?

The experience of therapy as a co-constructed process became an empowering intervention in itself.

Systemic work in detecting hidden strengths and bringing forth the underutilised, suppressed skills and positive aspects, combined with acknowledging the client's worries, stressful experiences and oppressive stories from her upbringing, contributed to the changes that she demonstrated.

Through reframing, what had been originally seen as a problem by the client she now saw as her strength, which became a significant healing force in the treatment. The concerns she brought to therapy evolved into her resources:

- instead of thinking *'oral sex was improper'*, it became her *'particular sensitivity'*
- instead of thinking that she was *'unable to orgasm'*, orgasm was an option for her that she could choose under the enabling circumstances
- instead of resorting to masturbation to prove her *'sexual inadequacy'*, it was a healthy sexual activity.
- instead of the time it took her to orgasm during intercourse being *'too long'*, the length of time became an indicator of her healthy bodily response.

Having a systemic interest in the meaning of therapy for clients in mind, the therapist hypothesised that the client might see coming to therapy as a failure, considering the multiple domains of powerlessness in which she lived. The therapist was aware of the client's socially underprivileged position, and that she was likely to have been marginalised throughout her life due to the social and cultural contexts that defined her identity: gender, age, class, education, employment, economic status, marital status, geographical origin, ability and sexuality. The therapist was mindful of the likely links between these contexts and her lack of awareness of her sexual rights.

Therapeutic outcomes

Combining a wide variety of methods from sexology and the systemic approach, the outcome of this integrated systemic psychosexual therapy enabled an identity shift from a marginalised, depressed, deprived and deficient person to an able, competent one, who was creating options for herself and assuming the right to her individuality. She made resourceful use of the therapeutic context, embracing therapeutic opportunities thoughtfully and creatively. For example, she invited a girlfriend to watch a recorded programme on female sexuality that the therapist had lent her, which inspired her first open and important conversation about sex with anyone in her personal network.

A map of Melanie's resources and resiliencies (Figure 6.1) was used to bring forth stories of competence and strengths that had been subjugated by her dominant experiences of oppression, marginalisation and pathologisation. The map was used throughout the work as a tool for reflection, enriched by examples that brought back the client's memory through therapeutic conversations, and broadening her understanding of certain life situations by emphasising the positive and the resourceful aspects of her personality and relationships.

EXERCISES

- Think of an example illustrating female social and cultural oppression from your personal experience.
- Think of a client example and discuss, in light of the social and cultural oppression of women, its impact on female sexuality.
- How might you apply the ideas from this discussion to working with the client concerned?

Formulation session with Melanie

An excerpt from the formulation session with Melanie is presented below, with the therapist's commentary (in italics). The aims for the session were to offer a formulation of the presented problem and introduce treatment possibilities, while actively engaging the client throughout, specifically:

- To reframe the presenting problem as a couple communicational issue
- To move towards recognising the issue of sexual confidence
- To provide educational input on sexual issues
- To present the origins of the experienced sexual difficulties in the context of the cultural, societal, familial influential factors, thus normalising her responses
- To outline treatment and suggest sex therapy tasks, as part of the wider goal of improving the client's self-image.

This excerpt illustrates some of the therapeutic interventions as well as the combined use of sexology and systemic therapy. It highlights how

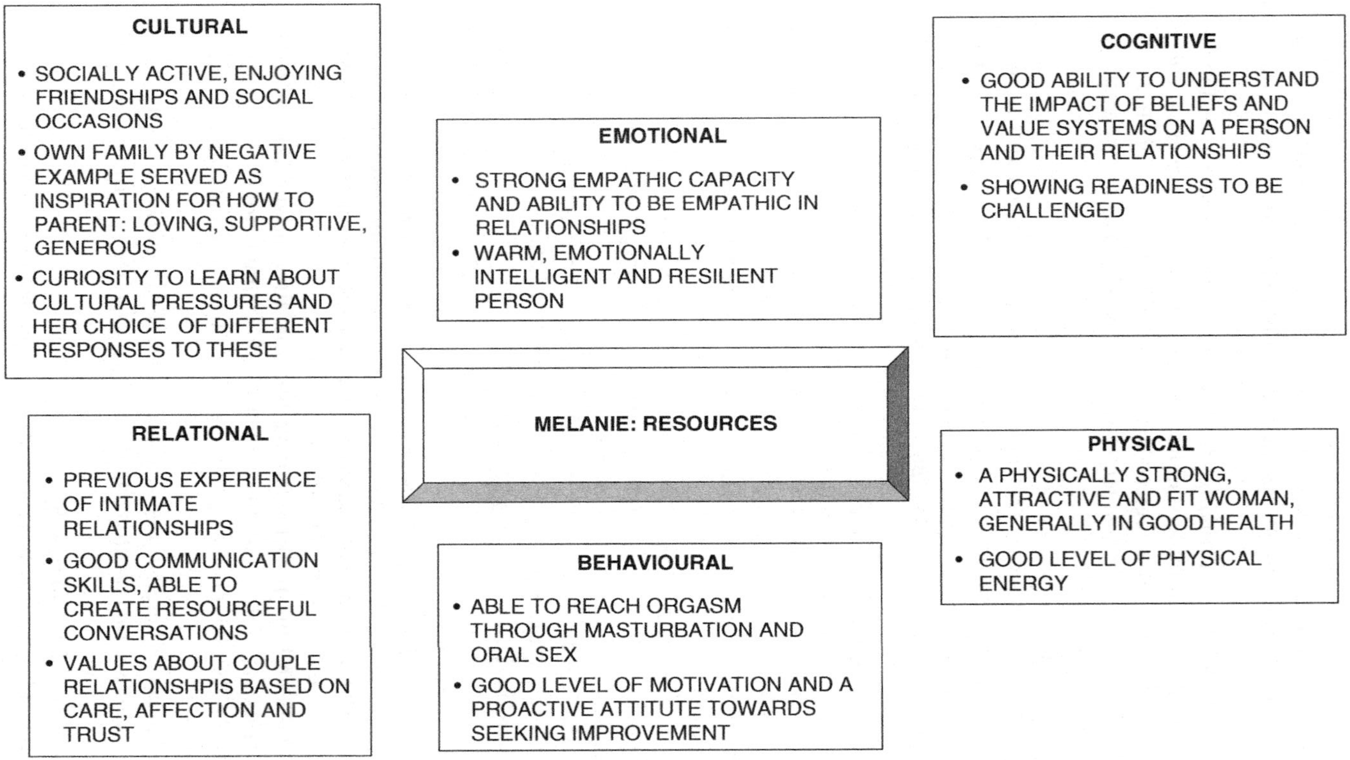

Figure 6.1 Melanie: resources

systemic and sex therapy can work in conjunction and how the therapeutic relationship can encompass the expertise of both the therapist and the client.

THERAPIST: I was thinking, Melanie, in the previous two sessions we talked about your understanding of the problems you are experiencing sexually, and we then agreed that today I will give you my view...
Co-constructing the agenda for the session. Checking the client's expectations of the session.
CLIENT: Yes please!
THERAPIST: But please do let me know what you think and ask me, if you wish, anything that feels important and whether or not you agree...
Ensuring the client is fully engaged, encouraging her active involvement; intending to emphasise the importance for the client to communicate her thoughts about the therapists' ideas. Hoping to empower the client's right to voice her views and question the therapist's.
CLIENT: (nods, smiles somewhat nervously)
THERAPIST: So let me see if I understood well what you told me about your worries. First, you think that you can't orgasm through vaginal penetration, and that because of this you are frustrating your sexual partners.
As a starting point for the formulation, the therapist summarises the definition of the problem as understood to have been presented by the client, while taking ownership for her understanding.
CLIENT: It has ruined all my relationships, I am very worried...and keen to fix this problem. I will do whatever it takes...
THERAPIST: It is great you have such determination. I understand you are very worried, you think your sexual problem is ruining your relationships.
Showing appreciation of the client's proactive, determined attitude and her expression of willingness to be actively engaged in contributing to the treatment, while communicating an empathic understanding and warmth in relation to the client's concerns.
CLIENT: All my boyfriends have told me, they all said they've never ever had anything like this with their girlfriends before.
THERAPIST: And you also told me that you can orgasm easily with oral sex...
Continues with establishing a clear definition of the main issues, incorporating the client's sexual abilities and pleasures, such as that she can reach orgasm with oral sex.
CLIENT: I can come orally but not with sex.
THERAPIST: And you can come when you stimulate yourself.

Switching to the client's language, the therapist replaces her previous use of the term 'orgasm' to 'come', in continuing to stress the client's resources such as that she can come on self-stimulation.

CLIENT: I can, I can do it better myself...

THERAPIST: Well, I'm thinking of... this is very important information for our understanding of what you're experiencing as a difficulty, what you see as a difficulty. That you are able to come, whatever way, whether with a partner or yourself, there is a way, so we know you have that capacity; and when you give yourself pleasure you can come, so you know how your body works...

The therapist elaborates on the client's sexual strengths and competencies. Given the client's strong self-pathologising focus, and her myths that 'oral sex is not proper', that 'masturbation is a result of sexual frustration', and that 'orgasm in masturbation is not proper', the therapist uses therapeutic intensity to convey the message reframing what the client brings as her inadequacy into her competency, such as: 'you know how your body works'.

CLIENT: Sometimes.

THERAPIST: Sometimes.

CLIENT: Sometimes when we were having sex and my ex-boyfriend was gone I would do it myself... because he'd be impatient with me and back then I just didn't even like sex.

THERAPIST: Of course you didn't. So, when he was impatient, I understood he was criticising you? Because this criticism can make you switch off from sex.

Provides a logical connotation, acknowledging that of course, one wouldn't like sex in the context of the partner's impatience. Following this, the therapist enquires into how he showed his impatience, sharing her hypothesis that the criticism was explicitly communicated and, explaining in an educative manner, that it is normal that criticism can make one switch off from sex.

CLIENT: He was never critical, he just didn't understand why I never come with sex, as all women do; he was never critical but he mentioned it a lot: 'Why don't you'... I said to him: 'I told you, I never have done...' but he would still go on about it.

THERAPIST: I am interested by what you told him; that you have never come with sex, however with oral sex you always come, is that right?

The client disagreed with the description of 'criticism' and the therapist backed off. Challenging the client's description that she never comes with sex, intending to dispel the client's myth that 'oral sex is not really sex'.

CLIENT: Not so easily, no, it takes me really long.

THERAPIST: Two hours? Three hours?

(both laugh)

The client insists on her negative explanations and the therapist uses humour as a way of introducing some lightness to the atmosphere as the client seemed nervous and tense.

CLIENT: It sometimes takes me twenty minutes or bit longer.

THERAPIST: Aha. You see, from my perspective and my experience of working with clients, that wouldn't be a problem in itself. It would actually be seen as perfectly healthy sexual response.

A straightforward educational intervention intending to teach, dispel sexual mythology and to normalise the client's sexual response. At the same time, a contextual perspective is taken; rather than conveying the 'truth', the ideas are attributed to certain perspectives.

CLIENT: OK...? Because this is not normal to me.

THERAPIST: Individual times vary; people take longer, shorter... twenty minutes I would say is a brilliant record!

Reinforcing the educational intervention in the form of individual differences, in response to the client's expressed views about her sexual abnormality.

CLIENT: Aha... but also, all my boyfriends told me it never happened to them, their girlfriends always came with sex and it took them much less time...

THERAPIST: I know, this is what they said, you told me. That wouldn't be something that anyone who is an expert in this field would call a dysfunction or a disorder though.

'Filling the room with people' (Cecchin, 1992), in order to offer an alternative frame of reference to counteract the community of views comprising the client's point of reference, i.e. her sexual partners implying her abnormality.

CLIENT: Right... (looks puzzled)

THERAPIST: I am happy to explain. Please let me know what you think. When working with couples, we can often see how problems can arise when there is a difference in experience and ideas between people, so... you know, if your partners weren't thinking 'this is too long', maybe you wouldn't...?

Reframing the presenting problem from an individual to a relational issue.

CLIENT: I don't know... maybe I wouldn't...

THERAPIST: Maybe it's hard to tell because it is hypothetical... You have to imagine...

The client seemed uncertain and at this point the therapist wasn't sure whether she might be perturbed and challenged in a helpful way, or confused, not connecting with the therapeutic reframe.

CLIENT: Mmmm....

THERAPIST: I'm asking the same question, but do you think you can imagine, just try to imagine for a second, if your partners weren't saying this is not normal, would you be worried?
A past hypothetical question intending to facilitate the client's reflection. Imagining, hypothetically, the absence of a certain context (i.e. the partners' messages about abnormality), exploring how the meaning of the issue might be different; in other words, enabling the client to make the link between the context of the partners' messages and the effect of those on her conceptualisation of the problem.
CLIENT: I don't think so! (laughter)
THERAPIST: Right. So, from that point of view it is a relational thing, a couple thing, and how couples negotiate their intimacy, how they give each other pleasure and communicate about that.
Continuing to elaborate on the importance of the relational context.
CLIENT: (nodding)
THERAPIST: So I think it is something that you felt, in my understanding, through experience and contact with your partners, that it is their frustration, they felt it was too long, and that it wasn't normal not to come during penetration; and some were more impatient than others... Is that fair to say?
The therapist perceives the client as beginning to connect with this point of view, and checks her perception with the client.
CLIENT: X used to make me orgasm orally because he used to persevere, then he'd moan about how long it took...
THERAPIST: So then this idea is built within you that there is something wrong with you. That you are not doing something right or, there is something wrong with your body...
Psycho-educational intervention explaining the process of how 'stories told' became 'stories lived'.
CLIENT: Mmmm... I suppose so...
THERAPIST: And then you don't go into the next sexual encounter with enthusiasm, looking forward or... you're not relaxed, you're more thinking: 'What's going to happen?' 'Am I going to come?' 'Will my partner be frustrated?'... The more these thoughts are there, the more you're disconnected from sex. Anxiety, worry... these are the usual things that stop arousal and orgasm.
Explaining the phenomenon of 'spectatoring' linked to performance anxiety, and normalising these as typical factors having a negative impact on sexual arousal.
CLIENT: Yeah, I don't want to keep him that long, all that time...

THERAPIST: Yes. I'm thinking, if your partner was doing what you do to yourself, to keep you aroused... if the criticism, anxiety, all of these were out of the way... which I suppose when you're on your own, you don't have...
Future hypothetical question, inviting the client to imagine a different, more satisfactory sexual stimulus in terms of both the technique of a sexual partner and the type of communicational exchange between them. Creating, hypothetically, a more favourable sexual context for sexual intimacy, inviting the client to engage with what difference this might make for her in terms of her sexual experience.
CLIENT: ... obliged...
THERAPIST: ... obliged, anxious... there is no worry about the partner, how they are experiencing it, and whether they're frustrated... so you are more relaxed and focused, that's what helps you.
The client joins in the creation of this future scenario, adding the word 'obliged', which the therapist incorporates as part of the description of a sexual pattern.
CLIENT: Yeah I feel better when I do it myself but I would really like... to feel like that with a boyfriend... if I ever have one again! (laughs)
THERAPIST: I know you feel you won't! (laughs). If you were with a boyfriend at the moment, it would help if we talked here together, because it's really important how you communicate... it does matter how two people say to each other what they like and don't like. Do you agree? What do you think of that?
Encouraging the client to voice her views, allowing her more space to express any thoughts about the new perspective that has just been introduced.
CLIENT: I've just never been able to say what I liked. I don't know why... maybe I'm not sure myself. Or I don't know what to say.
THERAPIST: Well, for example, what you told me was that something that particularly gives you pleasure is receiving oral sex isn't it? Something you are particularly sensitive to, able to enjoy, your sensuality is engaged...
While the client emphasises what she 'didn't know', the therapist reminds her of what she had said previously, implying that she did actually know what she enjoyed in sex.
CLIENT: Yeah I can come with playing about but not with sex.
THERAPIST: It's slightly more complicated with women than for men. It's kind of... working out where the sensitive area is. It's unusual for women to have sufficient sexual pleasure to reach orgasm through

penetration only. So, vaginal stimulation is just not enough. It happens, but the majority of women need clitoral stimulation and many women only come in that way.

An educational intervention intending to normalise the client's sexual functioning in the context of gender sexual differences. Gently challenging the myth that 'oral sex is not sex' and that clitoral stimulation is 'playing about' and not sex.

CLIENT: I thought my situation was very rare, that all women come through penetration or when there is a medical problem or something, maybe something psychological...

THERAPIST: Many research studies on hundreds and thousands of women across the different countries showed that women come in different ways, and no one way is better than the other...

Normalising female orgasmic diversity. An educational intervention based on sexology research.

CLIENT: I never heard that. I never knew that. I also read some books, don't remember now... it says sex therapists can teach you to come with sex. 'How to orgasm in sex' or something...

THERAPIST: I know, there are many different books out there. Some can be more useful than others so it can be confusing. Have you talked to any of your girlfriends? Because from boyfriends you don't necessarily know what exactly the woman is experiencing.

Normalising the client's confusion in the context of the enormous amount of available texts, of differing qualities, on sexual issues. Introduces the idea that a female perspective would, in all likelihood, be different.

CLIENT: I never have done, I think I'm too shy and... how to talk about sex... But I can try! I can ask my friend Alison, she is quite open, she's not in a relationship now but... we talked about boyfriends and stuff. I might ask her. Not sure what I'm going to say... (laughs)

THERAPIST: So let me ask you, if you imagine, if your future partner gave you oral sex combined with stimulation with his hands still in that outer vaginal area, do you imagine that that, combined with a kind and sensitive approach, with no criticism, no pressure, would enable you to come?

Careful questioning asking a hypothetical question to ensure as much space as possible for the client's view to be heard.

CLIENT: Yeah...

THERAPIST: Sounds like... you think so?

CLIENT: I think so...

THERAPIST: Yes?

CLIENT: (nods)
THERAPIST: So ... from that point of view, there is no disorder. I would like you to understand that certainly, the medical books, a sexology diagnosis would say: 'there is no disorder there'. That is the first thing in my view.
Ensuring there is a shared definition of the presenting problem which does not fall into the category of sexual disorders. De-pathologising through referring to sexology knowledge.
CLIENT: If it is not a disorder ... there is still something.
THERAPIST: There are still things you and I can work on. Because I think, part of what we are talking about here is psychological; it's to do with how you feel, that there's something 'wrong' with you, you are embarrassed, you think you are frustrating your partners...
Beginning to introduce treatment possibilities, and clarifying the client's implied question 'if there is no disorder, how can there be treatment?'
CLIENT: That's true, very much so. I'm always thinking he's going to lose patience with me, or say something ... like 'come on', or 'what's wrong?'... and all of that.
THERAPIST: What if you say 'Nothing is wrong, I'm having a great time'? (both laugh)
Hypothetical embedded suggestion introduced in a light-hearted manner.
CLIENT: I couldn't say that, I'm not that confident.
THERAPIST: Aha. So it's the confidence problem...?
The therapist highlights the word 'confidence' used by the client intending to build the definition of the problem based on this new emphasis.
CLIENT: Yeah I think so, my confidence in sex is not that great...
THERAPIST: Aha.
CLIENT: I wish I was more confident! Maybe then I would be able to enjoy sex more!
THERAPIST: It looks very much like confidence to me as well.
CLIENT: I know...
THERAPIST: Another thing is about what you learned about sex over many, many years since you were very young; sometimes ideas when we were very young influence us for a long time ... Some of it is to do with maybe understanding even better how one's body works ... and we can make progress on all of these. Towards improving your sexual confidence. I wonder ... have you ever looked at your genitals?
The therapist goes along with the client's own formulation, that the problem lies in her lack of sexual confidence. At the same time, puts this 'lack of confidence' in wider contexts such as early sexual learning, lack of sexual education, and reassures that therapy will address the problem as it has just

been redefined by the client. Begins to introduce a behavioural intervention aimed at improving the client's body image.

CLIENT: I have done yes.

THERAPIST: Have you? Aha.

CLIENT: I don't like them.

THERAPIST: You don't like them?

(both laughing)

THERAPIST: Why not?

CLIENT: (laughs)

THERAPIST: You don't like the look of them or you don't like looking...?

CLIENT: I just don't like it.

THERAPIST: What in particular don't you like?

CLIENT: I just think they're ugly.

THERAPIST: Aha.

CLIENT: Yeah.

THERAPIST: What do you think about male genitals, are they ugly?

CLIENT: I don't mind! (laughs)

THERAPIST: You don't mind because it's not yours... (laughs)

This line of questioning aims to ensure the client is not prescribed a task that she finds too uncomfortable. The client communicates further negative body image thoughts. She seems nervous and the therapist goes along with her slight laughter, to keep the atmosphere warm, light-hearted and gentle.

THERAPIST: What made you decide to take the mirror and look?

CLIENT: It was because I felt sore sometimes after sex. But I couldn't see anything. I didn't look again.

THERAPIST: A lot of women don't ever look... there's something about culture and society... women are... more... their sexuality is more suppressed; male sexuality is much talked about and if women are explicitly and openly sexual it's criticised, if men are it's supported, so... there are different criteria for men and women. That influences how women often withdraw and take the guilt on themselves, if something goes wrong it's up to them... But also biologically, men whether they want to or not, look at their penis each time they pee; it's outside and women's genitals are hidden, so you have to make a special effort to look there and you can avoid it... for shyness, embarrassment, you are taught to be like that sexually, so... If I suggest that you...

The therapist made a mental note about 'feeling sore after sex' as a biological context for further exploration at a later stage. Decides not to enquire there and then but rather focuses on introducing an exercise so the client goes home with something to do, as a marker that the treatment has begun. While introducing it, the therapist normalises the client's apprehension in the context of gender and culture.

CLIENT: OK...! (laughter)

THERAPIST: I'd like to suggest few things to you...

CLIENT: As I said, I'm here and will do anything...

THERAPIST: The things I'd like to suggest to you today are the first step of a kind of programme that we'll be following here if you agree. And I wouldn't insist on anything that you feel is totally unacceptable; sometimes you may think 'I don't like it, but maybe I'll try...' then you see what you can do and come back and tell me. If things didn't quite work out, we can talk about it. What do you think? Shall I tell you want I had in mind...? And then you can tell me if you have some ideas about what you would like to focus on in this treatment.

Reassures the client that her views will be respected at all times and no treatment intervention will be forced. At the same time, exerts a slight positive pressure to provide the client with a nudge in the direction of embracing hope and the possibility that treatment might make a positive difference. Reinforces the message that the client will be 'held' in a safe environment of a trusting therapeutic relationship while being engaged in the process of working towards making the desired changes.

EXERCISES

- Make an outline of how you could create a formulation for an existing client following the principles stated in this section.

David and Janet: presenting problem of male hypoactive sexual desire disorder

The following client example illustrates working with the presenting problem of 'male hypoactive sexual desire disorder' (MHSDD). The work is presented in chronological order, highlighting some aspects of the shifting couple dynamics over the course of therapy. The emerging changes, challenges and dilemmas are reflected upon, based on the therapist's observations of the therapeutic process.

The importance of the clients' interpretation of the loss of desire is also highlighted, with the aim of drawing the readers' attention to the need to devote time to deconstructing meanings with clients and to facilitate their understanding of the multifactorial nature of desire. Certain strong gender and cultural stories about sex seem to have had a powerful impact on the clients and it proved particularly helpful to explore these through use of the sexual genogram.

Presenting problem

David and Janet were referred to psychosexual and relationship therapy by their GP due to David's loss of sexual drive over a period of two years. At the point of referral their sexual relationship was almost non-existent. This was highly upsetting for Janet who had initiated the search for professional help.

The couple history and psychosocial background

David and Janet had been married for 23 years and had three adult children, all of them married and living with their families. The couple were both White British, born and raised in a coastal area of southern England where they and their close family members were still living. Janet, a teacher in her late 40s, described her job as highly stressful. David, in his early 50s, was a self-employed property developer. The working patterns of both partners were described as contributing to their stress levels on an ongoing basis. Janet was actively involved in charity work at her local church and David was a keen fisherman. They both came from intact nuclear families, but their experiences had in many aspects been contrasting: in Janet's family, parental conflict had been intense and upsetting for her throughout her childhood; David's experience had been a complete absence of conflict, but along with this an absence of explicit emotional expression, including affection.

Medical history

Janet had been diagnosed by the GP with 'depressive anxiety' four years previously. Extreme work pressures were seen as the major reason for this problem and she was off work for several months, treated by medication and individual counselling sessions. Neither had any other medical or psychiatric history of note. They did not smoke and their alcohol intake was moderate. Blood test results undertaken by David through his GP suggested normal hormonal levels and no issues of concern from the medical perspective. The couple both felt that their general health was good and had no specific physical complaints.

The initial sessions

The couple remained apprehensive throughout the whole of the first session. Janet spoke of her upset related to the absence of the sex in the relationship and her worries about the causes of David's lack of sexual interest. Her main concerns were whether David was finding her unattractive as he was demonstrating neither physical affection nor any signs of wishing to resolve the sexual problem and re-create their sexual intimacy. Indeed, David expressed that the absence of sex 'did not bother him at all'. He stated that the only reason why he had come to therapy was 'because Janet was upset'. He reported the absence of any sexual thoughts or fantasies and stated that he did not practise masturbation. For the last seven years his sexual feelings arose exclusively when they were on holiday, which was the only time they had sex over that period. He has been the sole initiator of sex over the last 12 years. Janet stopped initiating as she was unsure whether he wanted sex or not and did not want to pressurise him. She had not mentioned worries about the absence of sex, not wanting to cause friction.

The couple seemed apprehensive to talk about sex in the second session as well. Janet showed a great need for reassurance that it was 'normal' to have a sex drive at her age. David commented that he had spoken to a few of his male friends of a similar age who all felt equally uninterested in sex. They both described their relationship as completely committed, caring and friendly; they saw each other as 'best mates'. Quite a few of the couple's mutual worries emerged through this conversation: about their jobs, about each other's wellbeing, and about their elderly parents' health.

The formulation and the treatment plan

Presented below is the first of two formulations the therapist drafted in preparation for the formulation session with the clients:

Diagnosis: an acquired and situational/'environment-specific' hypoactive sexual desire disorder, accompanied by a deficiency of sexual fantasies, unlikely to be a result of medical factors. Distress for the female partner in the relationship resulted from a lack of sexual intimacy.

Factors contributing to the sexual problem in relation to both partners could be summarised as:

Predisposing factors: restrictive upbringing; disturbed family relationships; inadequate sexual information; early insecurity in psychosexual role; lack of affection in the family and between the parents.

Precipitating factors: ageing; mild depression; anxiety; stress; fusion of sex and affection; beliefs about sex and age (*'when you get to 50 sex naturally stops'*).

Maintaining factors: negative body image; fear of intimacy; fear of conflict; high stress levels, anxiety, fatigue; inadequate sexual information/ sexual myths.

The factors above cover all dimensions from the MOST model, which could alternatively be used for presenting the formulation based on the same information.

In addition, the following relational hypothesis could be proposed: as a function of perceiving personal rejection, Janet withdrew sexually which may have influenced David to become more detached, in turn making communication between the couple more difficult and further contributing to the presenting problem.

The treatment plan to be offered based on this formulation would be a combination of an exploration of the couple's beliefs and stories about gender, age, sexuality and intimacy with some psycho-educational input and encouragement towards more open couple communication and exercises, such as sensate focus, to improve the couple's intimacy.

The second version of the formulation was as follows:

Definition of the problem: discrepancy of sexual desire. In this formulation the concept of a perpetuating cycle of withdrawal/detachment was still considered valid. In addition, further aspects that may have contributed to the lessening of sexual interest over time could be tentatively proposed, in an attempt to normalise their differences, including aspects of their family histories and different meanings attached to sex, as well as the impact of various life stresses on the couple's sexual life.

Resources and resiliencies: the couple's resiliencies and resources would be presented early on, putting an emphasis on their care and respect for each other; coming to therapy as a proactive effort to improve certain aspects of the relationship; their many strengths as a couple, including being 'best mates', being proud parents and grandparents, being responsible and attentive to their work duties and to the financial care of the family, and being warm and considerate carers for their elderly parents.

Through reflection in self-supervision, the therapist decided to bypass the first formulation, even though it fitted perfectly well with the 'books'; a case of MHSDD was, according to official sexology, DSM and CBT perspectives, clear and evident. It was not discarded but instead formed a basis upon which the second version was constructed. Indeed, this second version was only possible once the case for MHSDD had first been formulated. However, it did not seem appropriate to deliver it to the clients in a form stating the presence of a 'disorder'; instead, it was elevated to a contextual level, de-pathologising the husband and the couple, and bringing many of their strengths to the fore. Given that the couple had already felt depressed by their situation, overwhelmed by their many worries and guilty about not doing things well, the therapist hypothesised that it could only aggravate the situation if more negativity was brought in and the work became pathology oriented.

Session three: formulation session

The session evolved as a discussion without any strictly formal structure, firm definitions or strategies. 'Discrepancy of desire' was the working definition of the problem that was thoughtfully considered by the couple. At the same time, there were many questions about how it had reached the stage it had. Janet particularly seemed preoccupied with the question 'why'; adding that sex used to be an important release for both of them. It seemed she was intrigued by the meaning of David's sexual withdrawal; more than the sex itself, she desperately wanted to know the reasons why the sex had stopped. The negative attributions given to the absence of sex seemed to really upset her and the therapist saw it as an important therapeutic task to facilitate a wider contextual understanding of the absence of sex, and to engage the couple in reflection on the meaning of sex for them.

Session four: Aspects of Intimacy

A defining point in the following session was brought forth when the couple were introduced to an exercise based on the handout 'aspects of intimacy' (Fife, 2016) to indicate which of the listed aspects they felt they had in their relationship, which ones they would wish to develop further, and which ones they would add to the list as already existing in their relationship. The exercise was first done individually, and then they shared thoughts with each other. Their views were very similar in most areas; they both identified many aspects of their intimacy, such as: 'aesthetic intimacy':

enjoying the same movies and TV programmes; 'financial intimacy': sharing a financial plan for the family, having common goals regarding saving and spending; 'friendship intimacy': being best mates, sharing companionship and enjoying each other's company; 'parenting intimacy': sharing the responsibilities of bringing up children and grandchildren, caring and worrying about them, supporting them, having fun with them; 'work intimacy': sharing common tasks such as looking after the household, raising a family, earning a living, participating in community affairs. Both noted a wish to improve their 'physical intimacy'. Janet was surprised that David chose this, saying: 'I thought you didn't care about physical intimacy', to which he replied: 'Of course I care. I care about you!' 'Emotional' and 'communicational' intimacy were the other aspects Janet wanted to improve on and, while David disagreed that there was any need for improvement in these areas, he was open to discussing the subject further. 'We don't really talk', Janet said, to which David replied: 'We do talk', 'We get on really well', 'We are close'. Janet emphasised that their conversations would evolve around the weather, the practical needs of family members, as well as 'kitchen talk'. This area of disagreement was seen as something to work on in therapy, to explore and understand further, while appreciating the many aspects of the existing intimate connections between them. In this way, the starting point for treatment was on strong ground. Rather than coming to therapy with a sense of failure, with the identity of a problem-saturated couple, or the assumption that 'there is no intimacy in the relationship', they started from the position of their many strengths, many intimacies, many connections enjoyed as a couple and with others. They also established a commonly defined goal, and an agreed path forward.

The therapist's self-reflection

In supervision and personal reflection, the therapist thought about her anger towards the husband who appeared to hold control over their sexual life; and feelings of frustration with the wife who assumed a submissive role, enabling the same repetitive patterns to continue. The therapist further reflected on her own family experiences, particularly in respect of her frustrated wish that her mother had stood up more independently and firmly to her father, the male dominant influence in her family. She became aware that the 'aspects of intimacy' exercise had had a therapeutic effect on herself as well; in this regard, she was able to view the couple relationship in a different way, appreciating its many positive sides.

The treatment did not proceed without difficulty; it was a turbulent journey presenting challenges both to the couple and the therapist. However, overall, the progress continued and evolved in a direction where the couple felt more united and connected. The text that follows summarises the therapy sessions, continuing in a chronological sequence.

Sessions five and six: sensate focus

Sensate focus was suggested as a possibility for improving physical intimacy. David immediately communicated that 'it would be difficult to find the time to do it', but Janet seemed enthusiastic and David, somewhat reluctantly, expressed his willingness 'to try'. When the couple came back after having attempted the first session, they reported that 'it did not go well at all'. Janet liked some parts of her body being touched and some not; David commented: 'I don't like massage.' When they tried to talk about it afterwards, there was tension and awkward silences.

The focus of the therapy session moved onto an exploration of the initial stages of their relationship and their decision to marry. Janet described an attraction to David and his family, in contrast to hers. However, she viewed him differently now; what she used to see as calmness she now experienced as coldness and detachment. She was concerned that he was 'set in his ways' with no intimate relationships or friendships whatsoever. David agreed with Janet's views, but he was 'not bothered' by how he was. He had never felt particularly sexy during his life, indeed had rarely felt much passion or excitement about anything, apart from work and fishing, activities requiring not much communication with others.

The therapist explored the couple's expectations of the therapeutic process, explaining what therapy might entail. When the clients agreed to have another attempt at sensate focus, the therapist encouraged them to do so in a way that would suit them and to adjust the exercise to their preferences, not to force anything, not to aim for any particular outcome, to be open and go on 'an exploratory mission' with no expectations.

The next time around sensate focus did not go well either; just at the thought of it Janet 'felt a deep gloom'; she mentioned ageing, her not so slim body, wrinkles... David felt similarly, emphasising the word 'artificial' when describing the experience. Further exploration of the stresses in their lives revealed that their family relationships were high on the list of influential factors. The therapist pointed out the circular relationship pattern between stress and the absence of sex, whereby stresses inhibit sexual desire leading to sexual frustration, which, in turn, contributed to higher overall stress levels... In this way a spiralling 'more of the same' pattern evolved where the two aspects involved reinforced each other creating an escalating picture. The couple were then encouraged to create their own exercise that would be pleasurable for both.

Session seven: 'I feel like a slut!'

Janet cried apologetically for most of the session, showing anger with David: *'I feel like a slut, wanting sex!'* while he seemed timid and helpless. The therapist conveyed that 'everybody moves at a different pace', which seemed to reassure them. At the end of the session it was agreed to look at their family trees next time.

Sessions eight and nine: the sexual genogram

David started by drawing the map himself. Janet added lots of information and vivid descriptions to his basic, extremely brief version. A complex four-generation genogram began to emerge revealing many important influences. The themes of losses, shame, guilt and secrets came out strongly from his family script, as well as of men carrying a lot of pain (emotional, physical illness, financial burdens) and women looking after them. Similarities between David and his father were drawn and between his parents' marital relationship and his own marriage. Sex was not talked about in the family and not much amongst his friends either, throughout his youth. They both described his parents as 'people whom you would not imagine ever having sex'.

Janet's genogram revealed upsetting issues for her: her father's longstanding physical and emotional violence towards her mother, his alcoholism, and Janet's feeling of responsibility for her mother as well as for her three siblings. Janet felt she had mothered them all, as well as having had responsibility for being the major source of comfort and support to her mother, and that her parents pulled her into their conflict, using her as a messenger between them. There was significant early insecurity in the psychosexual role of both partners; Janet had no sexual experience prior to David and his was very limited. He described himself as never feeling very 'sexy' in his life, never considering sex as particularly important. The genograms revealed both contrasts and similarities. In David's family the relationships between children and parents lacked warmth and affection; his difficulties in establishing intimate relationships in childhood and adulthood were discussed in this context. In Janet's family the relationship between her parents was characterised by friction and lack of affection, especially physical affection, which presented a poor initial model for intimate relationships. Being brought up to feel bad about feeling sexual may have led Janet to seek out a non-responsive partner. Janet's religious beliefs may have influenced her developing sexuality as a young woman and caused confusion, particularly when strong sexual urges conflicted with her religious ideals. The therapist shared her hypothesis that Janet's depression was a way of protecting her partner from his depression and perhaps other powerful feelings.

The work on the sexual genograms provided a wider framework from which to understand the couple's issues and significantly contributed to their engagement with the therapeutic process. At the end of the session an agreement was reinstated in terms of adding practical/behavioural tasks alongside discussion. The couple decided to allocate regular weekly times to be together without distractions with the aim of talking more intimately.

Session ten: self-created physical intimacy

In the following meeting Janet and David reported significant mutual satisfaction with the time they had spent together since the last session. They even managed to have their phones switched off for five hours and cuddled on the sofa, which they both found very enjoyable. It appeared to be more difficult for Janet to do so than for David; he explained that Janet found it difficult to let go of her worries about her family members. Before going to bed she listened to their messages, of which there were quite a few, some sounding frustrated by their lack of response. This highlighted the demands on the couple and how the family systems around them had adjusted over time to them being always approachable, always available and at their disposal.

When the question of the sexual desire was raised, David's belief about it became apparent when he said: '*You have to want it first in order to have it*'. The therapist took a psycho-educational stance, gently challenging this obstructive belief. The session ended with the couple agreeing to continue with their protected intimate time in any way that they wished.

Session eleven: David's upset

The next session had an unusual start: David showed a proactive stance for the first time during therapy and initiated comments about it in a rather emotionally charged way. He expressed his frustration that he had not obtained sufficient understanding about why he had become '*impotent*' and he wanted to know where the treatment was going. Janet responded that she was pleased that he 'finally became upset'; she reported feeling bad about being the only one who was upset all the time. 'You have got your own upset now' she said, 'and it feels much fairer.'

The therapist acknowledged the shift in the couple's dynamics and devoted the session to discussing these changing relationship patterns. The reframe was communicated that the couple had developed two more aspects of intimacy, a 'conflict intimacy', which enables couples to learn and grow from their conflictual communication; and a 'crisis intimacy' whereby there is a shared experience of being in a crisis situation and coping with it together.

The couple were encouraged to co-construct their own treatment plan for further therapy sessions. This was guided by the following therapeutic questions:

- What aspects of intimacy would you like to continue nurturing and enjoying?
- Which aspects would you want to increase? How would you like to do that?
- Out of all the activities you have done since you started therapy, which ones would you most like to continue with?
- Is there anything else you would like to add in terms of talking about, or doing together?

They both wrote separately and then shared their ideas with each other. In the end they decided to continue with switching their phones off and spending time together talking, cuddling, holding hands, being 'light-hearted' and 'cosy'.

Sessions twelve and thirteen: ending

The work with the couple continued over two more sessions during which they reported an increased sense of satisfaction and contentment in their togetherness. Janet now felt David cared and was pleased to see how much he enjoyed the physical closeness with her, which challenged her previously constructed negative meanings. David reported enjoying the physical intimacy in the absence of pressure to be sexual. He felt invited and welcomed into the joint physical space. Previously, he said, it was all surrounded by tears, upset and angry silences, which for him wasn't inviting. They were both open to being sexual again but there was no exclusive emphasis on that aspect; the many aspects of their intimacy were mutually appreciated and the many layers of the spectrum of sex provided them with great enjoyment.

EXERCISES

- Discuss the therapeutic approach that you consider was applied in the work with these clients. Which of the interventions do you see were particularly effective? What other therapeutic possibilities do you think could have also been applied in working with this case?
- Identify the sexual mythology underlying the clients' belief system.
- Identify therapeutic interventions based on the sexology science and the ones deriving from the systemic approach.

Supervision session with Emily

Introduction

The transcript presented here is an illustration of a supervisory conversation that may take place in the context of discussing working with sex and sexual relationships in psychotherapy practice. The supervision session evolves through a peer-level exchange between two experienced systemic therapists, while the supervisor, who is also a qualified psychosexual therapist, offers specific sexual knowledge as and when necessary.

The supervisory interventions include a range of systemic questions, practical suggestions, advice and educational sexology input, personal disclosure, inviting the therapist's self-reflexivity, and the sharing of hypotheses. The supervisor welcomes learning from the supervisee, inviting the supervisee to teach her about the 'basket exercise'. Near the end of the session the supervisee brings an example of the clients' 'unique outcomes', an episode where they used their imagination to create a different interpersonal context, overcoming their communicational problem in that situation. The supervisor encourages the supervisee to build on the clients' resourcefulness emerging from that example. The transcript includes a commentary on supervisory interventions shown in italics.

The supervision session (Clients: Raf and Sofia)

THERAPIST: I've been seeing this couple for just over eight months who are in their 30s. Sofia is a medical doctor, Raf a property developer. She is a European immigrant, he's of Asian origin. She comes from a large, emotionally articulate family, in which talking about feelings and relationships features in the majority of their conversations. He has an older brother with whom he hardly has any contact, his father suffered some form of mental illness and the mother was seriously depressed. He saw his father being violent to his mother in his early years. He is a workaholic and finds it difficult to keep his girlfriend in mind. He admits openly that he feels her issues are lesser than his. He knows this is not fair and not right, he just can't help it. He has traits of what may be described as being on the autistic spectrum. He is quite literal, obsessive about things he wants to achieve, but when it comes to her he forgets to pay the attention she needs. He definitely wants to learn to be a better partner, he wants her to be happy with him and that includes their sex life, but their sex life has dwindled to almost nothing. They also remember episodes extremely differently... I think they want to focus more on sex in our sessions. So I need your help!

SUPERVISOR: OK. Sure. You will tell me what kind of help you need and what questions you have for me.

Making sure that the session is supervisee focused and led by what she wants to gain from the session.

THERAPIST: I'll just give some background.

SUPERVISOR: Sure.

THERAPIST: He hadn't had an extensive sex life before as he was always so shy. He got used to solitary sex, using porn... and he got used to holding himself in a particular way, masturbating in a particular way.

SUPERVISOR: Do you know how frequently he masturbates?

A linear question, aimed at gaining more information about the clients. The information shared about the client so far indicates a possibility of a rigid masturbatory pattern that may have become a part of the sexual problem.

THERAPIST: According to her, he masturbates 4–5 times a day. He doesn't hide it from her. She told me this in an individual session, he didn't specifically mention it. When they have sex, very rarely, it has to be in the morning and very quick.

SUPERVISOR: Has to be?

THERAPIST: He dictates it. He says he's very tired in the evenings. And he responds to his body telling him when he is ready to have sex. In the morning he has an erection and then he lets her know it's time for sex. He always likes the same position. When I saw her on her own she talked about sex, but when I saw him individually he didn't talk about it at all.

SUPERVISOR: What are their reasons to come to therapy?

An orienting question; clients' meaning of therapy and reasons for coming to therapy are crucial in orienting therapists as to how to approach the treatment.

THERAPIST: For him, how to keep her in mind; how to manage work/life balance; how not to argue. They argue a lot. I know all relationships are unique but look at the difference between them...! She experiences everything deeply and emotionally... He's emotionally quite unaware. Although he is becoming more aware now, particularly when he's angry and upset. In the beginning of the relationship he did much more to arouse her and engage her sexually. She said if we are going to be a couple, we have to go to therapy. He admits everything revolves around him. At the same time he conveys an air of humour about it. They aren't arguing nearly so much anymore. They also have a better relationship with his family and he is reconciled with his father. The biggest bone of contention for her is that she feels pushed out, that he is over-focused on work... I wonder what keeps them going!

SUPERVISOR: What did she say she wanted from therapy?

THERAPIST: She wants intimacy, it's not so much about sex, it's more about feeling loved which is very difficult for him to understand. He doesn't want a relationship without sex, he thinks it's all part of love, they're getting married in a year. He planned several amazing holidays, it was all a surprise and wonderful... They really want it to work...

SUPERVISOR: Do you understand why?

Inviting the therapist's reflection on how she understands the clients' issues.

THERAPIST: She says he can be very amusing. They can have fun together. It's one of those situations when you fall in love with somebody for certain traits and those are the very ones that irritate you after some time and you want them changed. She is aware she needs a lot of looking after. She liked the fact that he is fascinated by his work. He finds her very beautiful, energetic, and loves that she's part of a close family.

SUPERVISOR: What keeps them in therapy?

An orienting question for the supervisor, whilst also intending to engage the therapist in thinking about the meaning of therapy for clients.

THERAPIST: He says 'I've got so much to learn...' He says openly he's on the autistic spectrum. He's willing to accept that.

SUPERVISOR: What does he say that he's noticing to make him think he's on the autistic spectrum apart from what other people are saying...?

A reflexive observer-perspective question.

THERAPIST: He's noticing that things don't go right for him sometimes and he is continually learning, there is so much to learn, he always says that... He knows he's very bright, recognises he doesn't do certain things well... He's thinking therapy can help him learn emotional intelligence.

SUPERVISOR: Do you believe that it can?
Inviting the therapist's self-reflexivity.
THERAPIST: I don't know if I'd call it that myself but I think he's a learner. She is happy with that, that he is attentive...When he is, he does it for a little while and then he forgets. He engages with quite a lot of things we've done, then it disappears in pursuit of his business. I'm learning a lot! I would never be able to say whether this is more his lack of recognisable nurturing traits or more his nature, because he had quite brutal upbringing. There are moments when he panics about this. He is beginning to recognise that there are links between his emotions and his father being violent to his mother. I don't know if he's neurologically unable to do certain things or if he closed down certain feelings and I'm working with that all the time, we don't know, maybe we can't know what the outcome of what we do will be.
SUPERVISOR: How would she like him to change?
A circular question addressing the interpersonal level and tracking relational patterns.
THERAPIST: To be more attentive to her...so that she feels more valued. That he listens to her. He doesn't have to sort out the problem. He doesn't listen to her or talk to her if she says she's upset about a problem, he just tells her it's not a problem, or goes for a solution without any consideration...
SUPERVISOR: Does he understand that process now?
THERAPIST: Yes, but he forgets...
SUPERVISOR: So it's learning but also retaining the learning.
THERAPIST: Yes, there is no consistency, over time it is very difficult.
SUPERVISOR: I wonder what effect it has on you as well, you get somewhere then he forgets it all...
Inviting the therapist's self-reflexivity.
THERAPIST: Yes, we have to start all over again! (laughter) But I'm fascinated by them. I want the situation to be good for them as a couple. But we did also talk about what if things don't change that much. At the moment she says she knows she has to do most of the adapting and compromising, but really she just doesn't want to lose him.
SUPERVISOR: What do you think about the way they have sex? It feels a bit sad to me...
Inviting the therapist's reflection on her feelings about the way clients have sex, while making a personal disclosure type of comment, sharing how it feels to her.

THERAPIST: Very! He used to give her oral sex but hasn't done so in a long time. He said to me 'I know what she likes, so I go down on her.' He can be quite concrete and literal. Then she will jump in and say 'You haven't done it in ages', he then says 'I don't like it when you push me away', to which she replies 'But I don't', and he responds 'Yes in the mornings you say...' and so on.

SUPERVISOR: There's something about how they communicate who wants what when and how... There's something quite frozen in the communication.

Sharing a hypothesis, a bit tentatively, leaving space for the supervisee to add her views.

THERAPIST: Yes, she says she wants to be treated as desirable, and told him this in the work-up to potentially having sex. He'll say let's have dinner tonight. It will be a lovely dinner, quite romantic, then they go home and either he won't mention it or he'd say 'I'm desperately tired', and go to sleep.

SUPERVISOR: Sounds like he's developed an autoerotic and very restricted pattern of arousal. Almost killing desire by masturbating so frequently. It's like you have four meals and then at the end of the day you go out for dinner with your partner.

A straightforward educational input informed by sexology.

THERAPIST: Yes, it's how you keep your appetite... They only have sex in the morning, but when they have it it feels like he's not focusing on her.

SUPERVISOR: Right. So you feel sex is becoming more of a topic in your sessions?

Keeping the focus of the session on what the supervisee asked for, making sure the supervisee addresses the questions she may have for the supervisor.

THERAPIST: Yes, it may have been that all we discussed before has been leading up to it. Coming from a family where they talked so much about feelings, she's looking at him to produce something all the time and he is expecting her to understand it all but is not giving back. A more satisfactory intimate sex life may make them more of a couple.

SUPERVISOR: What does she want from sex?

Inviting the supervisee's tuning into the client's perspective.

THERAPIST: She wants intimacy.

SUPERVISOR: How would she describe the sex they've been having in terms of intimacy?

THERAPIST: I haven't asked. I know what she'd say but I think it would be a useful question. She might say it only takes five minutes, so it doesn't feel intimate.

SUPERVISOR: Because it's not long enough or because of what happens? What would intimacy in sex look like?

A type of reflexive, distinction clarifying question for the therapist while suggesting questions that could be useful to ask of clients.

THERAPIST: To a certain extent she said it's about focusing on each other and knowing he's paying attention to her.

SUPERVISOR: Given how concrete and literal he is, it would be helpful if she gave specific examples.

A practical suggestion.

THERAPIST: I don't know why I feel there's fragility about this whole process. I feel I could do the wrong thing. He talks a lot about right and wrong and we talk a lot about maybe there's more to things than rightness and wrongness and he finds those things difficult to think about, but he really wants to. He can understand the concept but in practice finds it really difficult. He agrees with the concepts too.

SUPERVISOR: There seems to be so much about him needing to change although she feels she has to adapt.

THERAPIST: This is absolutely so, we did a certain amount of work around that to equalize their roles in the relationship.

SUPERVISOR: I wonder if he has a dilemma of change...for another person he may be perfect. His forgetting may have to do with '...well why should I have to change so much...'?

Sharing a hypothesis.

THERAPIST: He wants to be as she wants him to be. However, he keeps falling back quite naturally and unrepentantly to how he has always been. There was a time when he was really feeling he was getting it all wrong for her. That has improved because that was making him unable to do anything. Then it was more about what she needs to do differently. I did the basket exercise for her, rather than focusing on how everything needs to change...

SUPERVISOR: What is the basket exercise?

Showing an openness to learning from the supervisee. The supervisee's expertise is explicitly appreciated.

THERAPIST: You have three sizes of baskets and you have all the things you want changed, you look at them and then begin to sort them into 1: those that don't really upset you; 2: 'it would be nice if these could change but it is not a priority', and a maximum of three in the smallest basket, 'these have to change'. That went really well, her criticism lessened quite a lot as she was focusing on the most important aspects. But still, she has to prompt him all the time and that's tiring.

SUPERVISOR: Could he have some reminders like on his phone, for example, so it's not her who reminds him and then he feels criticised? Maybe when it's her job he doesn't take responsibility to remember, he's just relying on her.
A practical suggestion.
THERAPIST: We talked about her putting up a red card, for example, so she doesn't say things that sound critical.
SUPERVISOR: How about if she doesn't do anything?
THERAPIST: He relies on her around emotional things, it's a difficult one.
SUPERVISOR: But he's not taking responsibility, when it doesn't happen, 'this is how I am', when it does, 'she's nagging me'...
Challenging the supervisee who seems insistent that the situation is difficult to change.
THERAPIST: That's true. I am also thinking, right now they want to address something more directly sexual... to start on a route of a more sexual life...
SUPERVISOR: The idea of reminders can apply to anything.
THERAPIST: True, it can be romance, flirtatiousness...
SUPERVISOR: I have clients who bring their own notes to the session. I take notes and they do ... so, because he has this problem remembering, in the end of the session you can ask them both 'So what are the three things you want to take away with you from today?' or something like that...
THERAPIST: (nodding).
SUPERVISOR: I like the idea of three baskets. Could you do three baskets with positive things?
The supervisor recognises she has become insistent herself and changes the focus. Proposes an exercise, building on from the therapist's previous interventions which seemed to have had a positive effect.
THERAPIST: Oh that's good.
SUPERVISOR: With the same principle.
THERAPIST: So the greatest positive things go to the biggest basket?
SUPERVISOR: What do you think, they should go to the biggest?
Appreciating the therapist's expertise in using this exercise.
THERAPIST: Lovely.
SUPERVISOR: And it could be about the other person or it could be about the relationship, which I guess would be a separate exercise.
THERAPIST: Yes, the relationship could be about a completely different set of values and qualities.

SUPERVISOR: There's something about reflecting on interventions that made a difference, you've worked with them for over eight months, can you think of what they respond well to?
A practical suggestion, at the same time a general point, a reminder about using clients' resources.
THERAPIST: Oh I just remembered they did something brilliant! On the way back from holiday they talked on the train and made a story book, like where one would start and the other adds, only using the third person, so she'd start using her name, 'Sofia was one day at home waiting for Raf to come back home'... and they went through the whole sequence of events. It became quite a negative story in the end, they both got angry and shouted at each other... Then they sat down a few days later and wrote another story book about the 'Good Life'. It was about how they would have liked it to have happened. What they wanted from one another. Then she would say 'He came home and gave her a hug.' The rule is you have to keep it sequential. 'He was so happy to see her and she asked him how his business deal had gone that day.' They completely made it up, and they said they had such fun. They've got to that point where they could actually do it; they haven't analysed it to get to that point.
SUPERVISOR: Maybe it's better not to analyse? Analysis brings forth negativity...
Advice, put through as a question, tentatively.
THERAPIST: I said to them, 'Thank you, I will be inviting clients to engage in that sort of activity'. They were having fun and talking about their relationship without actually analysing it.
SUPERVISOR: Amazing.
THERAPIST: But how do I get to talk about sex with them?
SUPERVISOR: Well I was just thinking you could use the same thing, 'Raf goes to bed and does what...?'
A practical advice, as a direct response to the therapist's request for 'help' from the supervisor.
THERAPIST: (laughing) Yes, a sex story book... they are bringing their own solutions in a way... I still can't believe they've done it.
SUPERVISOR: They surprised you. Now you can use their resources.
Confirming the therapist's experience, joining in with the therapist's excitement about the clients' resourcefulness.
THERAPIST: And then I can get into more sexual subjects through this kind of play...

SUPERVISOR: We can continue talking about them when you start talking about sex more specifically, it may be that specific knowledge is helpful. It's almost like they need to start from scratch.

THERAPIST: He doesn't know anything about women, about engaging them intimately. She's partly worried about being heard as a nag so she hasn't done any nagging for a while. She keeps it all in but can become resentful over time. I can hear it; sex is more on the agenda in a more formal way in therapy now, so I'm wondering what the first steps might be as they're not having sex at the moment. It usually starts, in the morning he says something like, 'get on top of me'... It doesn't do anything for her but she is frightened to tell him.

SUPERVISOR: To me it seems more effective to work from the perspective that neither one of them knows anything. Like, it's not working how it is, nobody is satisfied with it, you want to do things differently, you both have things to learn...

Giving advice, while owning her perspective.

THERAPIST: I know he would be happy with that otherwise, he would hear it as if he has no experience and she knows it all...

EXERCISES

- What are the qualities of the supervisory relationship that you can perceive in this session?
- Can you recall a helpful supervision session you have experienced? What made it so helpful?
- What are the important qualities of a supervisor and the supervisory relationship when discussing issues of sex and sexuality?

Dan and Eric: obsession with visiting sex workers

The theme of the following two case vignettes is working with men who came to therapy individually, wanting to resolve their longstanding obsession with visiting sex workers, behaviour which they saw as intruding on their lives. A combination of sex therapy and systemic therapy approaches worked productively in both cases. Brief examples summarise therapeutic interventions, emphasising the deconstruction of encounters with sex workers. This method brought forth interesting and crucial insights to both individuals, which led to reframed meanings for each of the clients concerned.

Dan

Dan, a single man in his 40s, a successful professional, who described his relationships with his work colleagues, his social life, and familial relationships as satisfying, came to therapy in order to resolve his obsession with visiting sex workers, both women and men, since his early 20s. This practice had been taking a significant amount of time, distracting him from his work and getting in the way of his intimate relationships. On average he would be doing this five to six times a week, but sometimes it could be double that. He described 'finding himself' at his desk at work, suddenly slipping into searching websites, and looking for sex workers' details without remembering how he had begun to think about it. As his career progressed, he felt his behaviour had become more and more inconsistent with his professional identity and he was keen to put a stop to it, but felt unable to do so by himself. In the past his relationships, both with women and men, had tended to reduce but not completely eliminate this behaviour. He currently felt inhibited from having relationships, as he couldn't be honest with his future partner about his past and felt in a bind, either to withhold the information and be dishonest or to potentially face rejection if he admitted the truth. He frequently experienced DE (delayed ejaculation) with his sexual partners with whom he had a personal relationship, with the incidence not varying with the gender of the partner. However, he had never suffered such performance difficulties in his encounters with sex workers.

In the initial sessions the therapist explored issues to do with his bisexuality and the complex challenges that accompany this sexual orientation, including social exclusion. Was this behaviour a form of self-punishment for the feelings of guilt and shame? Was he torn between the sexual possibilities and choices, feeling constrained by the prevalent social norms in expressing his sexuality more freely and openly, resulting in him turning to the hidden and anonymous sexual practices to satisfy his sexual desires? These were some of the hypotheses that focused on his sexuality and his sense of his sexual rights and choices. During therapeutic conversations about what he thought had enabled him to function less problematically with sex workers, it transpired that for him it was about the lack of expectation and pressure to perform.

Treatment addressed the problem of DE combining the use of relaxation, psycho-education and a suggestion to vary his masturbatory technique which, up until then, had been to grip his penis very tightly, a sensation that is not easy to replicate during partnered sex. The client engaged in various therapeutic exercises and reflections, but what seemed to make the greatest difference was the process of deconstructing each of his encounters with sex workers. The therapist led him sequentially, step-by-step over the whole process in slow-motion mode, encouraging him to connect with the experience of the moment at each step. The details about how he felt and what was going on in his mind were reflected on, while tracking the level of excitement at each stage of the journey, from the moment he started the search, then finding the number to contact, making the appointment, getting ready to leave, walking towards the destination, pressing the door bell, meeting the person, to having sex with them. Ranking the level of excitement identified that the highest levels were at the initial stages; his pulse was racing as he started to look at the sites, choosing who to call, and dialling the number. He described feeling a mixture of excitement and anxiety as he was approaching the door. Having reviewed such activities in this way he reported he had achieved most of his enjoyment by the time the person opened the door. It seemed that he found this a revelatory, challenging, and a most surprising insight.

Dan found it helpful to take some practical steps to support his progress in the desired direction: he blocked himself from adult sites, and made a diary of each of his subsequent sex worker visits while ranking the level of satisfaction it gave him out of ten. He gradually reduced the frequency over time until, eventually, he stopped them completely. A follow-up after six months, and again after one year, confirmed the absence of relapse. He was still single, having a vibrant sex life and was open to meeting a long-term partner at some point, without feeling any urgency to do so. He sometimes struggled with desire and performance, particularly with 'ultra-vanilla sex', but was overall much happier in his life, and his career continued to blossom.

Eric

Eric, a married man in his mid-50s, a father of three children, presented at a psychotherapy practice asking for help with his obsessional visits to sex workers. This obsession had started several years previously, evolving from what had initially begun as having an innocent massage, but, over time had included all sorts of sexual 'extras' and eventually evolved to engaging in the full sexual act. These experiences excited him enormously. At that time he was having deep doubts about the durability of his marriage, as frequent marital conflicts had become draining, both emotionally and to his sexual desire for his wife. He felt helpless to do anything about the situation and started, somewhat shyly, visiting massage parlours, bars and other places where the likelihood of meeting a sex worker existed without the explicit outlining that such services were provided. It evolved from a sporadic 'slip' into a regular, seven-day-a-week practice, taking an enormous amount of time, energy and money, followed by lies and manoeuvres to cover his tracks. The thrill of succeeding in this 'other life' was exhilarating. The elation seems to have come from a sense of success as if he 'passed the test', being skilful enough to accurately assess the sexual opportunity and 'seduce' a woman into offering the sexual pleasure that he craved. He enjoyed being able to feel sexual desire as well as feeling desired and attractive to another person.

In addition to the actual time spent on these activities, he increasingly fantasised about such encounters, which filled him with a sense of achievement, joy and pleasure, and provided relief from the stresses of his marriage. However, the quality of his work started to suffer and his marital relationship deteriorated further. Eric expressed a measure of guilt about these behaviours but at the same time a certain sense of righteousness, particularly when he felt angry and blameful of his wife who he felt treated him too harshly.

Tracking his self-esteem issues in therapy led back to his early experiences of being bullied at secondary school. Frequent verbal, emotional and occasional physical abuse aimed at his body weight and his propensity for social withdrawal seemed to have had a powerful adverse impact on his self-esteem. His educational performance suffered as a result, his social life became impoverished, and he had no intimate relationships until the age of 25. When talking about his marital situation, he seemed to have attributed similar bullying behaviour to his wife, while his position in their conflictual exchanges he experienced as being the innocent victim. Therapeutic conversations, with an emphasis on tracking the unwanted repetitive episodes in some detail, highlighted his own part in the marital interpersonal patterns, which at the same time brought forth a sense of his own power and strength to bring about the changes he wanted to make in the relationship.

Deconstructing the episodes of sexual encounters with sex workers demystified the process and challenged the meaning of his desirability that he had ascribed to them. Rather than being a process that was helping build his self-esteem, he recognised that he was heading towards losing what he had achieved over the past decades. As a result of taking charge of his life in his early 20s, he had managed to create a thriving professional identity, formed a partnership with a woman with many special qualities, successfully raised three children with her, and built a wide social circle of friends and acquaintances within which he felt liked, respected and cared for. In all these obsessional cycles of searching, fantasising, covering up, and looking for justifications, he had lost sight of the many positive aspects of his life.

A simple psycho-educational intervention regarding sexual health brought reality further into focus. The fact that wearing a condom does not constitute foolproof protection from sexually transmitted diseases was news to him, and he took the first practical steps towards moderating his behaviour by having a sexual health screening test.

Once his attention had been redirected to constructively focusing on resolving the marital conflict, he ended with his individual therapist and agreed with his wife to start addressing their relationship difficulties through couple therapy.

EXERCISES

- Discuss and practise the method of deconstruction in a role play exercise using your client material.
- How do you view situations when men become obsessed with visiting sex workers? Discuss your views and beliefs about such situations.
- How do you see that therapists' judgements on men visiting sex workers can impede psychotherapy?

Ben and Roy; Alma and Jay: use of sensate focus

These two clinical vignettes present different client situations; in the first example male gay clients presented with PE (premature/early ejaculation), while in the second, an elderly heterosexual couple brought the issues of relationship discord, lack of sexual intimacy and occasional erectile difficulties. A common feature in these vignettes is the successful outcome of the sensate focus method which, alongside other therapeutic interventions, contributed to the enhancement of clients' satisfaction and psychological wellbeing.

Ben and Roy

Ben, a white man in his late 20s, suffering from dystonia, came to therapy with his partner Roy, a black man in his late 30s, presenting the problem of Ben's PE. Ben had suffered from dystonia since early childhood, affecting most of his body and often causing pain in his arms and legs. This was his first sexual relationship, while Roy himself had quite extensive prior sexual experience. Differences between the couple immediately caught the therapist's attention, namely: race, age, ability and contrasting sexual experience. They had been together for a year, felt deeply committed and happy with their relationship, apart from, at least according to their initial accounts, the sexual aspects. PE was distressing for both partners; it would occur seconds after Ben penetrated Roy, and often just before penetration. Oral sex produced the same outcome. Ben was overwhelmed with guilt, shame and worry that Roy would leave him. In his keenness to support and encourage Ben, Roy appeared forceful and impatient which, in turn, contributed to Ben feeling more anxious and stressed.

The map presented in Table 6.2 sets out the MOST model dimensions in relation to three groups of factors typically explored within the CBT approach: predisposing, precipitating and maintaining. This map allows for further contextual understanding of PE, dividing it within the particular time frame in terms of predisposing factors from the distant past and formative years; precipitating episodes that trigger the onset of a problem, and factors still operating that maintain the problem and explain its ongoing persistence. The map was presented to clients as part of the formulation session.

Treatment

The couple readily accepted to start sensate focus, and Ben agreed to individual masturbatory exercises in the form of the 'stop-start' technique. Both responded well to the exercises, commenting that sensate focus opened up a level of sensuality and close communication about physical affection that they had never experienced previously and which they both enjoyed very much. Through this positive experience, Ben's confidence rapidly grew and, with this, his performance anxiety decreased. He was able to maintain erections and hold off from ejaculating for increasingly longer periods during the sensate focus stages. Mastering the 'stop-start' technique gave him a sense of control over his sexual functioning, which was then successfully brought into the couple's joint sexual activity. Therapeutic conversations went smoothly and co-operatively as the couple progressed with building on the sensate focus stages and creating a more satisfactory joint sexual experience.

At the start of the process the therapist had enquired directly about the symptoms of dystonia, and how it was affecting Ben physically and mentally, with a view to understanding not only the limits of what he might be able to do physically but also his emotional experience of living with such a serious illness. This was the first time in his life that Ben had talked about his illness openly. He reflected on the early stages of it, through its development and the pattern of intensifying symptoms over time, and talked about the shock he suffered due to the severity of the pain on certain occasions. His illness had been a taboo subject in his family throughout his life and equally, at present, between the couple. Acting as if it didn't exist felt as if it was too shameful to mention. As a result of being left to draw his own conclusions,

Table 6.2 Premature/early ejaculation: MOST and CBT factors combined

MOST dimensions → CBT factors ↓	Emotional	Cognitive	Physical	Behavioural	Relational	Cultural
Predisposing	Guilt Shame Fear of intimacy Fear of failure	Negative sexual self-schema Strong beliefs about gender sexual roles	Ill health Negative body image	Rigid masturbation patterns	Experiences of rejection in attempted relationships	Homophobic cultural context Cultural issues of pride and shame Cultural pressures re: masculinity and femininity
Precipitating	Emotionally difficult coming-out process	Episodes of sexual 'failure' leading to anticipation of failure	Medication side effects	Repetitive unwanted interpersonal episodes in the current relationship	Partner's keenness to help experienced as impatience and pressure	Shame attached to own sexuality and disability
Maintaining	Stress Depression Performance anxiety Low self-confidence; lack of trust in own sexual ability	Anticipation of failure Restricted sexual knowledge; myths Unrealistic sexual expectations Construction of illness as insurmountable factor	Negative body image General lack of fitness Persisting health problems	Spectatoring Infrequent sexual activity Lack of sexual experience	Limited communication about sex Partner too exciting Worry about the partner's frustration	Limited cultural support network as a result of being disabled and being sexual minority

Ben constructed fantasises about his illness, attributing a list of unrealistic adverse consequences to it, including the idea that he was 'sexually disabled'. The realisation that he'd been blaming the illness for his sexual problem was a revelation to him: 'This belief has been holding me back all my life', he said, 'but it is not true.'

The couple continued therapy long after the sexual problem was resolved. Conversations evolved around certain past events from their lives including certain traumatic experiences, the management of their differences, living as sexual minorities in a largely homophobic society, living with the disability, and the impact of racial difference. At other times they talked about the good experiences that gave them their greatest pleasure, such as listening to jazz, spending time in nature, or with friends. Therapy became a context that provided opportunities for reflection and for strengthening their connection, without a specific problem in focus or a particular issue to resolve.

Alma and Jay

Alma initiated couple therapy as she wanted to separate from her husband Jay. At this time they were both in their mid-70s. Initial sessions focused on the clients' early histories as this seemed relevant to them as a means of setting the scene for discussing their differences and, in many ways, contrasting experiences. Alma's upbringing had had many restrictions. There were psychiatric issues within the close family, her parents divorced when she was a teenager, and her educational experience was dominated by memories of religious repression and punitive messages. She felt isolated, lonely, repressed and frightened for most of her youth. Jay came from a different culture, where closeness in the family was encouraged and his family members had regular contact and group gatherings. He grew up in a hot climate and had a big house at the seaside, which to Alma looked like 'heaven' when she first visited. She was extremely attracted by this environment which she experienced as warm, welcoming and liberating. However, over time she felt as if she was losing her identity; in order to be accepted and fit into the family and the cultural expectations, she felt obliged to exhibit certain behaviours and learn particular forms of emotional expression to be a 'legitimate' member of that community. After many years of marriage and after their five children had left home, she began to suffer from 'empty nest syndrome', felt disconnected from her husband, her children, herself and the world around her. Jay was shocked to hear all this as he had been under the impression she was happy and content. He felt guilty and deeply regretful that he had been unaware of what Alma communicated as her buried feelings of many years. At times they both felt angry and blameful of the other and shared these feelings quite openly. They spent many hours crying in the therapy sessions. He admitted he had never cried before in his life, not even when his most beloved family members had died.

The therapist experienced them as deeply connected in grief and loss, and admired their capacity to accept their responsibility for the interactional patterns that, although without any intentionality to hurt or punish, had misled, distanced and wounded the other person. There was no formal or informal assessment or formulation in the therapy process. Instead, the therapist's transparency throughout the sessions meant the ideas, observations and hypotheses were openly shared with the couple. After several months, conversations started addressing sex directly. It was understood early on that the couple stopped having sex several years prior to coming to therapy as their relationship became more distant in its many aspects. What is sometimes referred to as 'pre-sensate focus' spontaneously evolved alongside therapeutic conversations, in that the couple started spending more time together, communicating more openly and through this, building on their emotional intimacy. The topic of sex then started to slowly emerge more explicitly. They talked about the premature ending of their sexual lives. Some shy signals were given that they were potentially interested in rekindling their sexual intimacy, but the therapist's impression was that neither would make this explicit so she took a more interventive role in this regard. It transpired that the last few years of being sexual were frequently interspersed with erectile difficulties for Jay, while Alma confessed that she had lost her sexual desire long before these first signs of ED. The therapist hypothesised that these were interlinked, and diagnosed the problem as relational and emotional, given that the results of their physical examinations were satisfactory.

A sensate focus programme was suggested and the couple continued therapy for another year, progressing gradually through the stages. They had to grapple with many obstacles such as: shyness and embarrassment about their ageing body appearance; performance anxiety; beliefs about sex in old age; and the challenge of being sexual again after many years of living an asexual life. Sometimes they would come to sessions exhilarated, sometimes edging on despair. There were some blocks in the process, meaning the need to revert back to the first steps or, on occasions, going back to the pre-beginning stage. Through the therapeutic context of appreciation, listening, normalisation, calmness and patience, the couple persisted and progressed in building on their emotional and physical intimacy. They were in their late 70s when they completed therapy, having gone through a complete sensate focus cycle. Penetration would sometimes work with the help of Viagra, and at other times it did not seem necessary as the couple had developed a wide spectrum of ways of intimately connecting. They experienced a level of mutual satisfaction that gave them joy and pleasure of togetherness, and, despite all the rough patches that went with it, the conflict, the tears, the frustration and the impatience, there was still a sense of ongoing movement and hope, without necessarily looking either to the past or to the future, but with an ability to enjoy the moment.

EXERCISES

- Discuss applications of sensate focus; what are the potential client situations where it may be more/less indicated as a treatment option?
- Practise introducing sensate focus to clients.
- Practise taking feedback from clients from a sensate focus exercise.
- Discuss your own beliefs about sex and ageing.

Karl and Dalia: presenting problem of delayed ejaculation

This client example illustrates a method of working with a couple presenting with the problem of DE. This vignette demonstrates the use of MOST maps, one in relation to couple resources, and the other in relation to restraints contributing to the development and the maintenance of the sexual problem. These maps formed the basis for the formulation which was delivered to clients in a conversational manner.

Clients' background

Karl, a white British man in his early 40s was referred to psychosexual therapy by his psychiatrist for the problem of delayed ejaculation, being unable to reach orgasm intra-vaginally with his partner. Referral information stated that Karl had been undergoing psychiatric treatment for depression over the last two years, following a very distressing divorce. A year previously he had begun a relationship Dalia, a 35-year-old woman with whom he had been experiencing sexual problems in that he could only reach orgasm if he manually self-stimulated. He had recently stopped taking antidepressants but his incessant worry about the impact of the sexual problem on his relationship caused him low mood, so the psychiatrist considered reinstating medication. Karl, a self-employed computer programmer, was successful in his career and was currently developing his own business. His general state of health and his physical fitness were good, which was confirmed by a recent thorough medical examination.

Initial assessment

Karl and Dalia attended the first appointment which focused on:

- *Description and history of the sexual problem*, including any patterns and changes over time
- *The history of the relationship* and the effect of the sexual problem on it
- *Prior attempts to reach a solution* to the sexual problem
- *Conversations* they had about the problem as a couple and with others
- *Expectations of therapy*.

Description of the relationship

The couple appeared distressed and somewhat inhibited in expressing their feelings and giving details of their sexual life. They hadn't been sexual in any way with each other (or anyone else) for the previous four months and were very concerned about the future of their relationship. Both conveyed feelings of love, enjoyment, fun, mutual attraction and a deep commitment to each other. Their sole concern about the relationship was this particular sexual aspect. Since the beginning of their relationship they had felt sexually attracted to each other and very much enjoyed their sexual interaction, however Karl was never able to come inside her. Sex would last between one and two and sometimes close to three hours. Apart from vaginal penetration, they practised oral sex, anal sex, use of sex toys, wearing sexy lingerie, 'dirty talk', threesome fantasies, and role-play enactment of various fantasies. They enjoyed visits to sex clubs, and participated in swinging and group sex. In the end, still, the only way in which Karl could orgasm would be if he masturbated. They would both end up exhausted after every sexual activity, which gradually led to reduced frequency of sex, and eventually to total sexual avoidance. They remained physically affectionate with each other and enjoyed spending time together but the absence of sex made them sad and worried. They never spoke about this with anyone else in any specific terms, the only exception being Karl's psychiatrist. They both felt awkward, believing that no one else around them had similar problems.

Therapeutic plan

The clients agreed with the therapist's suggestion that the assessment process would consist of one additional couple session, followed by a single individual session with each of them.

In agreement with the couple, the second couple assessment session focused on:

- *Cultural and family background*; description of upbringing environment/ family of origin; cultural influences in formative years; emotional atmosphere in the household; any history of abuse of trauma; family/ carer relationship
- *Social interests/network of support*; career satisfaction
- *Relationship characteristics*; typical communicational patterns; ways of handling disagreement and difference; division of roles and responsibilities in the relationship; priorities between work and couple time.

The following details emerged:

Karl grew up in a town in Northern England as the eldest of two brothers of parents who divorced when he was 13. He remembered frequent fights between his parents and described being angry with his father who he suspected of having affairs. Following the divorce, his mother fell into a deep depression and he was left with the responsibility of caring for his brother. He remembers the feeling of never being able to please either his mother or his brother, who seemed to have a strong bond, leaving him feeling left out. His father maintained only sporadic contact in the meantime and after several years left for Australia, at which point contact was completely lost. There was speculation that he had a new family but, as there has been no communication over the last 20 years, this was not confirmed. Karl left home to study computer science at university where he met his future wife. This relationship 'never felt right' but he didn't want to admit this to himself; he feels he worked hard on the relationship but the differences between him and his wife and their frequent conflict led them to grow apart over time.

Dalia was born in Eastern Europe and was raised in a strictly religious household consisting of two parents, an older brother and a younger sister. She remembers her family as loving and protective; however, she always feared 'doing something wrong' as there seemed to have been 'rules about everything'. Sometimes she would be punished, such as sent to her room without dinner or not allowed to go out with friends; however, a lot of the time she didn't know what the punishment was for. She came to England to study art and music and had several jobs after qualifying at different colleges. She felt happy and fulfilled at work, although it was hard financially. She had several brief, and one long-term, sexual relationships with men. Karl was the first man she had a relationship with who was not from her culture of origin. Previous partners bore some similarity with the way she experienced being treated at home: patriarchal, rather dominant men to whom she surrendered in a passive role, feeling ambivalent about being controlled, yet safe with the familiarity of that feeling and the position of low responsibility which 'in a funny way', as she described, allowed her a sense of freedom. Dalia was attracted to Karl's gentle and warm approach. She found him charming, attentive and caring, all the qualities of a close relationship she always longed for but had never experienced before. Karl was eager to please her, to cheer her up and felt extremely excited to be in her company as, for the first time in his life, his generosity of mind and spirit were appreciated and reciprocated. Falling in love with Dalia was a major factor in lifting his depression and he was delighted to feel loved and experience hope and the joy of life again.

As a couple, they feel they communicate well and have great respect for each other. They hardly ever have conflict and any disagreements are easily resolved. They both feel a little stressed about their work for different reasons, Karl for working too long hours not allowing him enough sleep and rest, and Dalia for feeling underappreciated by being paid a salary that kept her hardly able to afford to pay the basic bills. They both wish they had more time as a couple but they could not see how that was possible in the foreseeable future, given that Karl was developing a new business.

Individual assessment

The individual assessment sessions focused on:

Physical dimension: health issues and fitness; sleeping patterns; medication; alcohol and other toxic substance use; nutrition; body image

Emotional dimension: mood and typical feelings; anxiety, stress, fears and other difficult feelings; sense of self, self-esteem

Cognitive and cultural dimensions: learning about sex; messages from childhood and youth: the family's attitudes to sex and sexuality; emotional expression in the family; the dominant cultural and religious beliefs; any experiences of sexual mistreatment, abuse, bullying and traumas.

Behavioural dimension: previous sexual experiences; masturbation patterns; current sexual relationship patters; current sexual experience: what is most/least enjoyable?

Both reported good health and healthy eating habits. They appeared fit and energetic. Karl seemed a bit obsessive about keeping fit and slim, insisting on frequent exercising and noticing many signs of ageing with some despair. He worried about being exhausted for much of the time and was concerned with how to juggle his many responsibilities, including looking after his now very fragile mother.

MOST model: formulation

The various dimensions as presented in the MOST model were explored with both clients in their individual sessions, after which a joint session was arranged to communicate feedback from the initial assessment. The MOST diagram was used in the delivery of this feedback in a conversational rather than a didactic way. A map of 'resources' was first offered (Table 6.3), which seemed to enthuse them as it summarised what, in the therapist's view, were the couple's strengths and abilities across the different dimensions.

Table 6.4 illustrates the contributing factors to Karl's sexual difficulties. These were presented as related to influences from various life experiences over time and the relational and behavioural dimensions included Dalia and her part in the couple's sexual and general relationship interactions. The factors were explained as having varied degrees of contribution to the sexual functioning and the session was spent exploring each one of them.

Treatment options

Treatment options were then explained, and a programme of sensate focus was introduced, to which the couple responded enthusiastically. The behavioural technique of directed masturbation was used to teach Karl how to alter his habitual masturbatory patterns and encourage development of masturbatory variety.

Treatment process and outcome

Sensate focus exercises enabled the couple to reconnect without performance pressure, and facilitated their communication about their sexual interests and fantasies. It also inspired a more playful approach to physical intimacy. The couple used humour and imagination in designing their own version of the exercises. For example, once they began by Karl pretending to be a neighbour ringing the bell to borrow some sugar and she answered the door wearing a transparent negligée. Or, after the exercise they would occasionally spend time drawing each other in 'sexy' poses. They included

Table 6.3 Delayed ejaculation: couple resources

CULTURAL	EMOTIONAL	COGNITIVE
• Rich life experience • High sense of responsibility and ethics in work and relationships • Successful career, important professional achievements; recognition and fulfilment • Supportive network of family, friends and colleagues • Good relationship with the partner's family • Highly sociable, well respected and liked socially	• Warm, caring personalities, capable of deep love • Devotion to the partner, highly empathic abilities, loving and attentive • Able to show emotional resilience in some difficult life situations such as bereavement and loss • Capable of processing complex emotions and reflecting on them • Emotional adaptability • In tune with own emotions • A wide spectrum of emotional experiences and emotional expression	• High intellectual functioning • Well educated, broad-minded in many ways and areas of life • Sexually curious, open to further explorations • Able to recognise sexual mythology and oppressive beliefs and their negative effects
RELATIONAL	**BEHAVIOURAL**	**PHYSICAL**
• Good quality relationship, communication important; emotional closeness, valuing physical affection and intimacy • Strong mutual support • Committed, loving connection • Compatibility of sexual interests and openness to further explorations • Compatibility of expectations of the relationship • Respectful communication, with no conflict or tension, genuine understanding and interest in each other • Mutual sexual attraction	• Open to broadening their sexual repertoire • Rich fantasy life • Open to experimenting with sex and taking graduated risks • Motivated for behavioural change • Proactive attitude in different contexts, able to take challenge and risks	• Physically fit and healthy • Understand importance of good nutrition and exercise • Take health issues seriously

Table 6.4 Acquired and situational delayed ejaculation: restraints

CULTURAL	EMOTIONAL	COGNITIVE
• Hostility/abandonment by the father • Protectiveness of the mother/feeling underappreciated • Inferiority to his brother • Resentment re: suspicion of father's affairs • High achiever; pressure of expectations • Bullied at school (always studying) • Concerns about the mother's deteriorating health • Stress; working hard, pleasing people	• Unresolved anger towards the father • Feeling underappreciated by the mother • Low self-esteem • Stress of divorce leaving guilt, feeling failure • Performance anxiety; desperate to please; fear of fatherhood • Fear of commitment, intimacy, abandonment • Insecurity in own sexual and masculine role • Fear of violence • Fear of selfishness leading to compulsive giving	• Exaggerated expectations of 'perfect', 'ideal sex' • Performance-oriented, goal-oriented sex: genital, orgasmic focused • Rigid expectations of the masculine role in sex • Fantasy model: myths: men lead; men should know what women want; men are responsible for the woman's pleasure • Catastrophising, negative anticipation • Cognitive distractions • Obsessive rumination about sexual functioning • Pathologising of sexual fantasies
RELATIONAL	**BEHAVIOURAL**	**PHYSICAL**
• Resentment about previous relationship • Previous partner's rejection • Protectiveness of the couple restricting sexual communication • Partner's sexual insecurity • Compulsion to satisfy the partner • Worrying about the partner being shocked by his sexual needs • Power differential (gender/ethnicity/financial resources)	• Idiosyncratic masturbatory style, strong pressure on the penis • Autoerotic orientation • Feeling of 'betrayal' about sexual fantasies not involving the partner • Restricted sexual patterns • Insufficient erotic stimuli prior to sex • Avoidance of sex reinforcing the problem	• Obsession with being fit and healthy, dreading ageing • Alcohol intake • Tiredness, physical exhaustion • Environment not always conducive • Concerns about body image • Antidepressants taken in the past

certain kinky activities, including bondage, restraint and some playful humiliation games.

Sexual mythology was discussed in depth, revealing the layers of cultural influences affecting each of them, including cultural paradigms of 'perfectly functioning sex', and the men's powerful leading role in sex. These beliefs were deconstructed and reflected upon, enabling Karl to feel less under pressure to perform and less obligated to please Dalia who, in turn, took more responsibility for her own sexual pleasure. The couple's sexual life became more fun, enriched with variety and less predictable; they both looked forward to sex. Karl became less orgasm focused and was more able to tune into the pleasurable sensations of the moment.

The therapeutic process did not go smoothly at all times and at certain points felt stuck to both the therapist and the clients. On several occasions the clients expressed doubts that the treatment was right for them. A huge conflict between them opened up as a result of Karl's revelation about his secret habit of frequently masturbating over pornography. At the same time, this sincerity gave him a sense of relief bringing forth more openness in couple communication. By the end of treatment he still had a strong habitual autoerotic preference and was still able to reach orgasm more easily when masturbating. He learned over time to allow Dalia to masturbate him and took a significantly shorter time to reach orgasm. Soon after he managed to ejaculate with her intra-vaginally, they decided that they were ready to end therapy. Even though their sexual relationship was 'not perfect', they felt happier sexually, less goal focused and more intimately connected.

EXERCISES

- Discuss how use of the MOST resources and restraints maps might contribute to the clients' experience of empowerment.
- Practise a formulation session using these MOST maps.
- Create a map of resources for one of your current clients.

Gary: presenting problem of erectile disorder

This client example illustrates a way of approaching working with the problem of acquired 'erectile disorder' of psychosocial origin and demonstrates how the MOST model can be applied at various stages of the work. Assessment and formulation sessions are summarised using the theoretical lens of CBT, combined with the MOST dimensions, incorporating both sexology and systemic perspectives. This client summary also demonstrates the possibility of working on a couple relationship with just one of the partners. The treatment comprised a multidimensional framework, including psycho-education, behavioural and physical exercises, and processing and reflecting on certain salient emotional experiences. Over the course of therapy, through the process of therapeutic normalisation and utilisation, the client started to recognise his 'weaknesses' as his resources; such as his 'emotionality', that he had been ashamed of and criticised and bullied for, now became his strength in the context of his developing interest in mindfulness as his future career path. His erectile 'failure' was normalised through recognition that the situation in which this occurred had not been conducive for an arousing and sexually inviting context for him.

Client background

Gary, a mixed race gay man in his mid-30s presented in a sexual and relationship therapy clinic with a 'longstanding erectile disorder', having been referred by his GP. He was seen by an experienced white female heterosexual therapist.

Assessment

In the first session Gary appeared shy, rather nervous and worried. He had never been in therapy before although he had thought about it on many occasions. He repeated several times 'I should have done this years ago'. The erectile problem, according to his description, had affected around 80% of his sexual encounters over the last 6–7 years. He described the erectile difficulty as complete inability to obtain an erection during sexual activity with a partner, causing him and his partner a great deal of distress. This difficulty was acquired, in the form of sudden onset at the age of 30, after having had previous satisfactory sexual activities since the age of 16. The first episode of erectile failure involved a combination of factors such as tiredness, high alcohol intake and pressure to perform. Further assessment explored the following dimensions:

Emotional: Gary presented as highly anxious and worried about his 'sexual failures'. Fear of further failures seemed to preoccupy him, connected to the worry that his partner would leave him for that reason. He appeared to feel guilty, shaken, and ashamed that he could not preform sexually to satisfactory levels and blamed himself for being ineffective in resolving the problem. The therapist had the impression that the client was emotionally fragile, while also experiencing him as a gentle, warm, kind and quiet man, whose emotional expression was subtle and somewhat subdued.

Physical: Gary's general health was good and no signs of any medical issues of concern were identified. He regularly experienced morning erections, and had no erectile problems when masturbating (2–3 times a week). His alcohol intake was moderate to high; he consumed alcohol on most days in the week and sometimes the equivalent of two bottles of wine at the weekends. He smoked marijuana occasionally. He was not very satisfied with his state of fitness and exercised rarely. He was not on any medication of any sort.

Behavioural: His masturbatory practice followed the same pattern each time: it would happen usually in the evenings (which 'helped to go to sleep'), it would be very quick, always in bed, in the same positon, and mainly using the same fantasy (he dominated a man, penetrating him vigorously and both reaching ecstasy within seconds). Episodes of erectile failure happened only with men for whom he had feelings and he believed this was the reason for relationship endings. He had no problems of erectile functioning with men whom he didn't know very well, strangers he met in bars or over the internet. Impersonal sex was functioning well but left him feeling emotionally frustrated.

Relational: Gary met his current partner, Mark, several months prior to the appointment at the clinic. Mark, a white man in early 30s, seemed caring, loving and supportive of Gary, and showed tremendous understanding about Gary's frequent erectile failures. Gary was worried that this kind of warm, loving and patient support would not be sustainable and that Mark would eventually leave him when he realised that sex was not getting any better. Gary did not want Mark to join the therapy sessions. This was his problem, he insisted, and he could not bear to put Mark 'through the procedure as if he was doing something wrong'.

Cultural: Gary grew up in a family where conflict between his parents was almost a daily occurrence, sometimes involving physical fights. He remembers being scared and hiding in his room for fear and shame. As a result, his social network was limited as he avoided developing friendships. He experienced extensive verbal and emotional bullying based on homophobic and racial discrimination, from primary to higher education and in many other contexts throughout life. He had not come out to his parents although he believed they must know he was gay however, they were constantly asking questions, such as whether he had a girlfriend and when he was going to get married.

Cognitive: Gary had become obsessed with his sexual performance since he met Mark. He seemed to be constantly thinking about it and was finding it more and more difficult to concentrate at work. He felt 'weighed down' by these constant thoughts about the sexual situation and his predictions that it would end up badly for him and for the relationship.

Evolution of the problem

The following session revealed further details of the first episode of erectile failure. Gary spoke of the partner with whom this has happened, and the circumstances that had led to it. He had had feelings for this man for quite some time but he was unavailable as he used to be a partner of Gary's friend. He admired the man's confidence, intelligence and his physical appearance. On the night when they had sex, Gary drank far too much 'to calm his nerves', which obviously did not help. They ended up in a hotel room; Gary describes 'the whole thing was wrong, foolish, too rushed and unpleasant'. He felt ridiculed by the man, who as Gary vividly remembers, just packed his things and left saying that Gary was 'a waste of time'. He felt not only 'not like a man' but also a 'non-person', almost justifying the aggressive reaction towards him and blaming himself for being 'so stupid'.

Even though this first erectile failure occurred after having had regular satisfactory experiences for 14 years prior to this episode, it had a major impact on his sexual confidence. The strong influence of factors such as tiredness, excessive alcohol intake and the pressure of high performance expectations together contributed to the sexual performance failure. His own, as well as the partner's disappointment, criticism and harsh rejection impacted on Gary's feelings strongly, evoking guilt, shame and worry, creating ongoing anticipation of failure with consequent anxiety and leading to performance spiralling downwards. He began to develop a negative sexual self-concept which increased his insecurity in his sexual role and further interfered with his ability to experience sexual arousal.

The impact of this episode can be summarised in the context of predisposing factors such as: restrictive upbringing, growing up amongst disturbed family relationships, lack of affection in the family and between the parents, and inadequate sexual information. A single episode of erectile failure (precipitating factor) can produce such dramatic effects in the context of predisposing factors in all or most of the dimensions, which reinforced his lack of confidence, fear of failure and negative body image. The client engaged in the practice of 'spectatoring' (maintaining factor), a typical mental activity linked to sexual performance anxiety, whereby the person observes themselves during the sexual activity from the perspective of an outsider observing in judgement the 'success' of his own sexual performance and, specifically the hardness, or otherwise, of his penis. This is typically linked to high levels of anxiety and worry, anticipating the reoccurrence of previous problems, thus perpetuating the problem itself.

Formulation

The formulation, presented to Gary using the chart in Table 6.5, was designed to explain the multifactorial influences leading to his sexual difficulty. This example illustrates how combining CBT factors with the MOST dimensions can be relevant for both assessment and treatment purposes.

Gary was also presented with a map which showed the evolution of the problem over time. He spent some time looking at both diagrams and commented that it all made sense now, but until it had been explained he could not see the link between many of the factors and the erectile difficulty. 'I understand it rationally but I just need some time to digest it'; he asked for a copy of the map which he took away with him.

Agreeing the treatment plan

The treatment plan suggested by the therapist included:

- Reading literature specifically selected by the therapist about male sexuality and erections
- Practising different ways of masturbating
- Practising a 'wax and wane' masturbatory technique, first individually, and then potentially incorporating into partnered sex
- Undertaking regular physical exercise, improving nutrition and reducing alcohol, caffeine and quitting smoking
- Opening up communication with his partner about intimacy, sexual needs and fantasies
- Introducing inventive ways of engaging in sexually arousing activities using imagination, playfulness and experimentation with different erotic possibilities
- Focusing on relaxation in the form of mindfulness, yoga or meditation

The therapist offered various couple sensate focus exercises, to be adapted such that Gary could use the therapist's instructions to conduct them at home with Mark. Gary listened attentively and then proposed to think about the treatment plan and bring his comments to the next session. Having considered the proposed treatment plan between sessions, Gary tentatively

Table 6.5 Erectile disorder: an integrated analysis using MOST and CBT factors

MOST dimensions → **CBT factors ↓**	**Emotional**	**Cognitive**	**Physical**	**Behavioural**	**Relational**	**Cultural**
Predisposing	Low self-confidence Lack of affection in the family and between parents	Restricted sexual knowledge Myths about erections and sexuality Idealising male sexuality	Lack of fitness	Lack of exercise	Previous relationship problems, conflict and anger	Disturbed family relationships Cultural pressures re: masculinity and femininity Cultural shame about own inadequate gender role
Precipitating	Guilt and shame in response to erectile failure	Negative conclusions on own sexual adequacy on the basis of one episode of 'failure'	Alcohol Tiredness	Erectile 'failure'	Partner's criticism and abusive reaction	Homophobic experiences Racial discrimination
Maintaining	Fear of failure Worry Performance anxiety	Repetitive cycle of negative thoughts, e.g. catastrophising, generalising, anticipation of failure Negative sexual self-concept	Negative body image Alcohol Smoking	Spectatoring Repetitive unwanted interpersonal episodes Rigid masturbatory patterns	Worry about the partner's rejection Lack of openness about sexual needs and intimacy Fear of conflict Partner's solicitous responses	Gender myths about erection and sex Limited support network Restricted ways of expressing own sexuality in homophobic environment

accepted the ideas in the next session, saying 'Can I see how it goes...?'. The therapist confirmed that there was no pressure to commit beyond the next step and that treatment options could be adjusted and shaped as therapy continued. The therapist then asked Gary to decide how he wanted to go ahead, what he wanted to do first. Gary took some time to organise the treatment options in the form of a list of priorities. During this process he sought clarification on certain issues and remained adamant about his reluctance to directly involve Mark.

Individual sessions addressing the couple relationship

As treatment progressed, Mark became very much part of the process. Despite never attending a therapy session 'in body' he was included and thought of continually. Gary and Mark read the literature on sexual myths together and discussed them, and Gary brought some of their ideas to therapy. It became evident just how strong an emphasis he had been placing on erections and how sexual activity without an erection, for him, was almost unimaginable. A suggested couple exercise aimed at broadening sexual options, which involved engaging in sexual activity whilst ignoring erections, proved to be one of the greatest challenges for the couple. Although he struggled initially, Gary did his individual masturbatory exercises patiently, eventually benefiting from them by changing his masturbatory patterns in ways that allowed more flexibility during couple sex. These new ways of experiencing sex influenced his thinking patterns and altered certain negative automatic thought processes. Gary encouraged Mark to be more proactive and less comforting when erectile difficulties emerged; he explained that, while he understood that Mark wanted to reassure him by trying to smooth things over, he said it felt like 'you were giving up on me'. This helped Mark realise, despite his best intentions, such support was not producing the desired effects.

Focusing on past experiences, mindfulness and ending therapy

Quite a few sessions were spent without even mentioning sex. Some memories had been stirred by the therapeutic conversations and Gary wanted space to process them and make sense of their meaning in his current life. He talked about his struggles to 'fit in' as a young person, his desperation to belong, coupled with a fear of emotional closeness, which had led to a state of constant turmoil for him. He worried about talking to Mark about these experiences and at the same time felt as if he was betraying him by not telling. It was a new idea to him that in a close relationship one still has a choice as to whether one discloses painful past experiences or not. It seemed that Gary was worried about Mark's possible rejection as, being a sensitive, gentle and emotional person, he thought he might be perceived as 'not manly enough'. Keeping Mark separate from therapy was his choice, which the therapist fully respected. The therapist decided to focus on the advantages of individual sessions, such that it allowed Gary space to think more freely. He reflected on his emotional withholding that may have contributed to keeping a level of relationship distance, which in turn worried him. Such tendency to withhold affect was reflected on in the context of Gary's difficult experiences with his father, from whom he had received critical messages throughout his youth about being too 'feminine', 'soft', and 'weak'.

He took a great deal from practising mindfulness. The therapist suggested some reading and guided him in one mindful exercise to focus on deep and slow breathing and the present, non-judgemental awareness of body and mind. Gary seemed fascinated by this approach, and, after undertaking a wealth of further reading, eventually signed up for a short course in mindfulness. This enthused him tremendously and he started contemplating undertaking further training and possibly developing a new career in this field. Therapy came to an end at this point as he started refocusing his intellectual energies into this new interest. His sexual functioning became less of a worry as a result of these positive, optimistic emotions. While it seemed that his sexual life had greatly improved, he felt there was still more progress to be made, but he was happy to continue on his own having been 'pointed in the right direction'.

EXERCISES

- Create a paragraph summarising the qualities of the therapeutic relationship that you can identify from this client vignette.
- Create a map of resources and restraints for a couple you are working with in your clinical practice.

REFERENCES

Introduction

American Psychiatric Association (APA) (2013). *Diagnostic and Statistical Manual of Mental Disorders* (*DSM*) (5th ed.). Washington DC.

Gorrell-Barnes, G., Down, G. and McCann, D. (2000). *Systemic Supervision: A Portable Guide for Supervision Training.* London: Jessica Kingsley Publishers.

Iasenza, S. (2010). What is queer about sex? Expanding sexual frames in theory and practice. *Family Process,* 49: 291–308.

Kantor, D. and Okun, B. (Eds) (1989). *Intimate Environments. Sex, Intimacy and Gender in Families.* New York: The Guilford Press.

Madanes, C. (1990). *Sex, Love, and Violence: Strategies for Transformation.* New York: W.W. Norton.

Markovic, D. (2013). Multidimensional sex therapy: A model of integration between sexology and systemic therapy. *Sexual and Relationship Therapy,* 28(4): 311–323.

Mason, M.J. (1991). Family therapy as the emerging context for sex therapy. In A.S. Gurman and D.P. Kniskern (Eds). *Handbook of Family Therapy* Vol. 2. New York: Brunner/Mazel, Inc.

Maturana, H.R. and Varela, F.J. (1980). *Autopoiesis and Cognition.* Boston, MA: Reidel.

McNamee, S. and Gergen, K.J. (Eds). (1992). *Therapy as Social Construction.* Sage.

Pascoe, W. (1994a). Integrating sexuality in family therapy: 1. *Context* 17: 26–28.

Pascoe, W. (1994b). Integrating sexuality in family therapy: 2. *Context* 18: 14–16.

Pearce, W.B. (1989). *Communication and the Human Condition.* Southern Illinois Univ.

Pearce, W.B. (1994). *Interpersonal Communication: Making Social Worlds.* New York: Harper Collins.

Sanders, G.L. (1988). Of cybernetics and sexuality. Applying systems thinking to sex therapy. *Family Therapy Networker Special Issue: The Great Cover Up: Sexuality,* 39.

Selvini-Palazzoli, M., Boscolo, L., Cecchin, G. and Prata, G. (1980). Hypothesising - Circularity – Neutrality; Three Guidelines for the Conductor of the Session. *Family Process,* 19(1): 3–12.

Weeks, G.R. (2005). The emergence of a new paradigm in sex therapy: integration. *Sexual and Relationship Therapy,* 20(1): 89–103.

Whiteley, R. (2006). *Getting the Most of Psychosexual Therapy. Information for Users of Our Service.* Porterbrook Clinic, Sheffield Care Trust.

Wylie, K.R., DeColomby, P., and Giami, A.J. (2004). Sexology as a profession in the United Kingdom. *International Journal of Clinical Practice*, 58(8), 764–768.

Chapter 1: Multidimensional open-minded sex therapy (MOST)

American Psychiatric Association (APA) (2013). *Diagnostic and Statistical Manual of Mental Disorders (DSM)* (5th ed.). Washington DC.

Andersen, B. L. and Cyranowski, J. M. (1994). Women's sexual self-schema. *Journal of Personality and Social Psychology*, 67, 1079–1100.

Anderson, H. (2000). Becoming a postmodern collaborative therapist: A clinical and theoretical journey. *Journal of the Texas Association for Marriage and Family Therapy*, 5(1) 5–12.

Bancroft, J. (2009). *Human Sexuality and Its problems* (3rd ed.). Oxford: Elsevier.

Barrett, F.J. and Fry, R.E. (2005). *Appreciative Inquiry: A Positive Approach to Building Cooperative Capacity*. Chagrin Falls, OH: Taos Institute.

Basson, R. (2000). The female sexual response: A different model. *Journal of Sex & Marital Therapy*, 26(1), 51–65.

Bateson, G. (1972). *Steps to an Ecology of Mind; Mind and Nature*. New York: Jason Aronson.

Beck, A., Emery, G. and Greenberg, R. (2005). *Anxiety Disorders and Phobias: A Cognitive Perspective*. Basic Books.

Berne, E. (1964). *Games People Play: The Psychology of Human Relationships*. Grove Press USA.

Brotto, L.A. and Barker, M. (2014). *Mindfulness in Sexual and Relationship Therapy*. New York, Oxon: Routledge.

Burnham, J. (2005). Relational reflexivity: a tool for socially constructing therapeutic relationships. In C. Flaskas, B. Mason, and A. Perlesz (Eds). *The Space Between: Experience, Context, and Process in the Therapeutic Relationship*. Karnac.

Chalker, R. (2000). *The Clitoral Truth: The World at Your Fingertips*. New York: Seven Stories Press.

Cecchin, G., Lane, G. and Ray, W.A. (1992). *Irreverence: A Strategy for Therapists' Survival*. London: Karnac Books.

Cecchin, G., Lane, G. and Ray, W.A. (1994). *The Cybernetics of Prejudices in the Practice of Psychotherapy*. London: Karnac Books.

Clifton, D., Doan, R. and Mitchell, D. (1990). The reauthoring of therapist's stories: taking doses of our own medicine. *Journal of Strategic and Systemic Therapies*, 9(4) 61–66.

Cooperrider, D. L. and Srivastva, S. (1987). Appreciative inquiry in organizational life. In R.W. Woodman and W.A. Pasmore. *Research in Organizational Change and Development*. Vol. 1. Stamford, CT: JAI Press.

Crowe, M. and Ridley, J. (1990). *Therapy with Couples. A Behavioural – Systems Approach to Couple Relationship and Sexual Problems*. Blackwell Science.

Dallos, R. (1997). *Interacting Stories. Narratives, Family Beliefs, and Therapy.* Karnac Books.

Dallos, R. and Draper, R. (2000). *An Introduction to Family Therapy: Systemic Theory and Practice.* Open University Press.

Dallos, S. and Dallos, R. (1997). *Couples, Sex and Power. The Politics of Desire.* Open University Press.

deShazer, S. (1991). *Putting Difference to Work.* W.W. Norton.

Dodson, B. (2010). *My Romantic Love Wars. A Sexual Memoir.* Self-published e-book. http://dodsonandross.com/product/my-romantic-love-wars-sexual-memoir-ebook-edition-memoir-dl.

Erickson, M.H. (2009). Further clinical techniques of hypnosis: Utilization techniques. *American Journal of Clinical Hypnosis,* 51(4), 341–362.

Flaskas, C. and Perlesz, A. (Eds) (1996). *The Therapeutic Relationship in Systemic Therapy.* Karnac Books.

Foreman, S. and Dallos, R. (1992). Inequalities of power and sexual problems. *Journal of Family Therapy,* 14, 349–369.

Foucault, M. (1980). *Power / Knowledge.* New York: Pantheon Books.

Fruggeri, L. (1989). *Videotape.* Kensington Consultation Centre Oxford summer school.

Gabb, J., Klett-Davies, M., Fink, J. and Thomae, M. (2013). *Enduring Love? Couple Relationships in the 21st Century.* Milton Keynes: The Open University Survey Findings Report. http://www.open.ac.uk/researchprojects/enduringlove/files/enduringlove/file/ecms/web-content/Final-Enduring-Love-Survey-Report.pdf. (accessed 1 January 2014).

Gergen, K.J. (1999). *An Invitation to Social Construction.* Sage Publications.

Goldner, V. (2004). When love hurts: Treating abusive relationships. *Psychoanalytic Inquiry,* 24, *346–372.*

Greenberger, D. and Padesky, C.A. (2014). *Mind Over Mood: Change How You Feel by Changing the Way You Think.* (2nd ed.). Guilford Press.

Hare-Mustin, R.T. (1991). Sex, lies and headaches: the problem is power. Chapter 4 in T.J. Goodrich (Ed.) *Women and Power. Perspectives for Family Therapy.* W.W. Norton.

Hare-Mustin, R.T. (1994). Discourses in the mirrored room: A postmodern analysis of therapy. *Family Process,* 33(1), 19–35.

Heiman, J. and LoPiccolo, J. (1988). *Becoming Orgasmic: A Sexual and Personal Growth Program for Women.* New York: Prentice Hall.

Heschel, A.J. (author), Heschel, S. (Ed.) (1996). *Moral Grandeur and Spiritual Audacity.* Farrar, Straus and Giroux.

Hoffman, L. (2007). The art of 'withness': A new bright edge. In H. Anderson and D. Gehart (Eds), *Collaborative Therapy: Relationships and Conversations That Make a Difference.* New York, NY: Taylor & Francis Group.

Hollway, W. (1983). Heterosexual sex. Power and desire for the other. In S. Cartledge and J. Ryan (Eds), *Sex and Love: New Thoughts on Old Contradictions.* London: The Women's Press.

Hollway, W. (1989). *Subjectivity and Method in Psychology.* London: Sage.

Hornstrup, C., Tomm, K. and Johansen, T. (2009). Questioning expanded and revisited. *Journal of Work Psychology.*

Iasenza, S. (2004). Multicontextual sex therapy with lesbian couples. Chapter Two in S. Green and D. Flemons (Eds): *Quickies. The Handbook of Brief Sex Therapy*. New York and London: W. W. Norton.

Johnson, S.M. (2008). Emotionally focused couple therapy. In A. S. Gurman (Ed.) *Clinical Handbook of Couple Therapy* (4th ed.). New York: Guilford Press.

Lankton, S. and Lankton, C. (2007). *Enchantment and Intervention in Family Therapy: Using Metaphor in Family Therapy*. Crown House Publishers.

Leiblum, S.R. and Rosen, R.C. (Eds) (2000). *Principles and Practice of Sex Therapy*. (3rd ed.). New York: Guilford Press.

Ludema, J.D., Cooperrider, D.L. and Barrett, F.J. (2000). Appreciative inquiry: The power of the unconditional positive question. In P. Reason and H. Bradbury (Eds) *Handbook of Action Research*. Thousand Oaks, CA: Sage.

Lyotard, J. (1984). *The Postmodern Condition*. University of Minnesota Press.

Madigan, S.P. (1993). Questions about questions: Situating the therapist's curiosity in front of the family. In S. Gilligan and R. Price (Eds), *Therapeutic Conversations*. New York: W.W. Norton.

Markovic, D. (2010). A case of enhancing sexual confidence: Both the client and the therapist are the experts. *Australian and New Zealand Journal of Family Therapy*, 31(1), 13–24.

Markovic, D. (2011). Systemic and psychosexual therapy integration. Regent's University London lecture.

Markovic, D. (2013). Multidimensional sex therapy: A model of integration between sexology and systemic therapy. *Sexual and Relationship Therapy*, 28(4), 311–323.

McAdam, E. (1995). Tuning into the voice of influence: the social construction of therapy with children. *Human Systems: The Journal of Systemic Consultation & Management*, 6(3–4), 171–188.

McCarthy, B. and McCarthy, E. (2012). *Sexual Awareness: Your Guide to Healthy Couple Sexuality* (5th ed.). Routledge.

McCarthy, B. and Thestrup, M. (2008). Integrating sex therapy interventions with couple therapy. *Journal of Contemporary Psychotherapy*, 38, 139–149.

McTaggart, L. (2005). *What Doctors Don't Tell You: The Truth About the Dangers of Modern Medicine*. Thorsons.

Minuchin, S. and Fishman, H.C. (1981). *Family Therapy Techniques*. Harvard University Press.

Morawski, J.G. (1990). Toward the unimagined: Feminism and epistemology in psychology. In R.T. Hare-Mustin and J. Marecek (Eds), *Making a Difference: Psychology and the Construction of Gender*. Yale University Press.

Nevis, E. (Ed.) (2000). *Gestalt Therapy: Perspectives and Applications*. Cambridge, MA: Gestalt Press.

Nobre, P.D. and Pinto-Gouveia, P. (2009). Cognitive schemas associated with negative sexual events: A comparison of men and women with and without sexual dysfunction. *Archives of Sexual Behavior*, 38(5), 842–851.

Pearce, W.B. (2007). *Making Social Worlds: A Communicational Perspective*. USA and UK: Blackwell Publishing.

Pearce, W.B. and Cronen, V. (1980). *Communication, Action and Meaning: The Creation of Social Realities.* New York: Praeger.

Penn, P. (1985). Feed-Forward: Future questions, future maps. *Family Process*, 24(3), 299–310.

Rorty, R. (1979). *Philosophy and the Mirror of Nature.* Princeton NJ: Princeton University Press.

Sanders, G.L. (1986). The interview as intervention in sexual therapy. *Journal of Strategic and Systemic Therapies*, 5(1–2), 50–63A.

Scaife, J. (2010). *Supervising the Reflective Practitioner: An Essential Guide to Theory and Practice.* Routledge.

Schnarch, D. (1991). *Constructing Sexual Crucible: An Integration of Sexual and Marital Therapy.* New York and London: W.W. Norton.

Staunton, T. (Ed.). (2002). *Body Psychotherapy.* Brunner-Routledge.

Tiefer, L. (2001). A new view of women's sexual problems: Why new? Why now? *The Journal of Sex Research*, 38(2), 89–96.

Tomm, K. (1987). Interventive interviewing: Part II. Questioning as a means to enable self-healing. *Family Process*, 26, 167–183.

Tomm, K. (1991). *Ethical Postures in Therapy. Facilitating Clients' Empowerment.* Workshop held in London under the auspices of Kensington Consultation Centre.

Tomm, K. (2011). Workshop in London under the auspices of the Institute of Family Therapy.

Varah, C. (1973). *The Samaritans in the 70's. To Befriend the Suicidal and the Despairing.* (2nd ed.). Constable.

Vetere, A. and Dallos, R. (2008). *Systemic Therapy and Attachment Narratives.* London. New York: Routledge.

Watzlawick, P., Weakland, J. and Fisch, R. (1974). *Change.* New York: Norton.

Weeks, G.R. (2005). The emergence of a new paradigm in sex therapy: Integration. *Sexual and Relationship Therapy*, 20(1), 89–103.

Weeks, G.R. and Hof, L. (Eds) (1995). *Integrative Solutions: Treating Common Problems in Couples Therapy.* New York: Brunner/Mazel.

Weeks, G.R. and Gambescia, N. (2000). *Erectile Dysfunction: Integrating Couple Therapy, Sex Therapy, and Medical Treatment.* W.W. Norton.

White, M. (1991). Deconstruction and therapy. *Dulwich Centre Newsletter*, 3, 21–40.

White, M. (1995). *Re-authoring Lives: Interviews and Essays.* Adelaide, South Australia: Dulwich Centre Publications.

White, M. (2007). *Maps of Narrative Practice.* New York: W. W. Norton.

White, M. and Epston, D. (1989). *Literate Means to Therapeutic Ends.* Adelaide, South Australia: Dulwich Centre Publications.

White, M. and Epston, D. (1990). *Narrative Means to Therapeutic Ends.* New York: W. W. Norton.

Wincze, J.P. and Carey, M.P. (2001). *Sexual Dysfunction: A Guide to Assessment and Treatment.* (2nd ed.). New York, London: The Guilford Press.

Wincze, J.P. and Weisberg, R.B. (2015). *Sexual Dysfunction: A Guide to Assessment and Treatment.* (3rd ed.). New York: The Guilford Press.

Wittgenstein, L. (2009). *Philosophical Investigations.* (4th ed.). Blackwell Publishing.

World Association of Sexual Health (WAS) (2014). *Declaration of Sexual Rights.* WAS Advisory Council.

World Health Organization (WHO) (2010). *ICD-10 Classification of Mental and Behavioural Disorders. Clinical Descriptions and Diagnostic Guidelines.* Geneva: World Health Organisation.

Zilbergeld, B. (1999). *The New Male Sexuality.* (revised version). Bantam Books. USA.

Chapter 2: Definitions of sex and sexual response

Aggrawal, A. (2009). *Forensic and Medico-legal Aspects of Sexual Crimes and Unusual Sexual Practices.* Boca Raton: CRC Press. London and New York: Taylor and Francis Group.

Ahlers, C.J., Schaefer, G.A., Mundt, I.A., Roll, S., Englert, H., Willich, S.N. and Beier, K.M. (2011). How unusual are the contents of paraphilias? Paraphilia-associated sexual arousal patterns in a community-based sample of men. *Journal of Sexual Medicine,* 8(5), 1362–1370.

American Psychiatric Association (APA) (2000). *Diagnostic and Statistical Manual of Mental Disorders (DSM-IV-TR)* (4th ed.). Washington DC.

American Psychiatric Association (APA) (2013). *Diagnostic and Statistical Manual of Mental Disorders (DSM)* (5th ed.). Washington DC.

Anderson, S. C. and Holliday, M. (2007). How heterosexism plagues practitioners in services for lesbians and their families: An exploratory study. *Journal of Gay & Lesbian Social Services,* 19(2), 81–100.

AVEN (Asexual Visibility and Education Network) (n.d.). www.asexuality.org (accessed 16 May 2017).

Barker, M. (2013). Gender and BDSM revisited. Reflections on a decade of researching kink communities. *Psychology of Women Section Review,* 15(2), 20–28.

Barker, M. and Langdridge, D. (2010). *Understanding Non-Monogamies.* New York, London: Routledge.

Barker, M., Iantaffi, A. and Gupta, C. (2007). Kinky clients, kinky counselling? The challenges and potentials of BDSM. In L. Moon (Ed.), *Feeling Queer or Queer Feelings: Radical Approaches to Counselling Sex, Sexualities and Genders.* London: Routledge.

Basson, R. (2000). The female sexual response: A different model. *Journal of Sex & Marital Therapy,* 26(1), 51–65.

Basson, R. (2001). Using a different model for female sex response to address women's problematic low sexual desire. *Journal of Sex & Marital Therapy,* 27, 395–403.

Beaber, T. (2008). *Well-being Among Bisexual Females: The Roles of Internalized Biphobia, Stigma Consciousness, Social Support, and Self-disclosure.* Unpublished doctoral dissertation, The California School of Professional Psychology, Alliant International University, San Francisco, CA.

Bhugra, D., Popelyuk, D. and McMullen, I. (2010). Paraphilias across cultures: contexts and controversies. *Journal of Sexual Research*, 47(2), 242–256.

Bishop, C.J. (2014). A mystery wrapped in an enigma – asexuality: A virtual discussion. In M. Carrigan, K. Gupta and T.G. Morrison (Eds), *Asexuality and Sexual Normativity. An Anthology*. London and New York: Routledge.

Blair, K. and Pukall, C. (2014). Can less be more? Comparing the duration vs. frequency of sexual encounters in same-sex and mixed-sex relationships. *Canadian Journal of Human Sexuality*, 23(2), 123–136.

Bockting, W., Benner, A. and Coleman, E. (2009). Gay and bisexual identity development among female-to-male transsexuals in North America: Emergence of a transgender sexuality. *Archives of Sexual Behavior*, 38, 688–701.

Bogaert, A. (2012). *Understanding Asexuality*. Toronto, ON: Rowman & Littlefield.

Brooks, V.R. (1977). *Minority Stress and Adaptation Among Lesbian Women*. University of California, Berkeley.

Brooks, V.R. (Ed.) (1981). *Minority Stress and Lesbian Women*. Lexington Massachusetts.

Brotto, L.A. and Yule, M. (2017). Asexuality: Sexual orientation, paraphilia, sexual dysfunction, or none of the above? *Archives of Sexual Behavior*, 46(3), 619–627.

Brotto, L., Knudson, G., Inskip, J., Rhodes, K. and Ereskine, Y. (2010). Asexuality: A mixed method approach. *Archives of Sexual Behavior*, 39, 622–623.

Burnham, J. (2005). Relational reflexivity. A tool for socially constructing therapeutic relationships. Chapter 1 in C. Flaskas, B. Mason and A. Perlesz (Eds), *The Space Between: Experience, Context and Process in the Therapeutic Relationship*. Karnac Books.

Burr, V. (2003). *Social Constructionism*. (2nd ed.). Routledge.

Carrigan, M., in Bishop, C.J. (2014). A mystery wrapped in an enigma – asexuality: a virtual discussion. In M. Carrigan, K. Gupta, T.G. Morrison (Eds), *Asexuality and Sexual Normativity. An Anthology*. London and New York: Routledge.

Carrigan, M., Gupta, K., Morrison, T.G. (Eds.) (2014). *Asexuality and Sexual Normativity. An Anthology*. London and New York: Routledge.

Clifton, D., Doan, R. and Mitchell, D. (1990). The reauthoring of therapist's stories: Taking doses of our own medicine. *Journal of Strategic and Systemic Therapies*, 9(4), 61–66.

Cobin, M. and Angello, M. (2012). Sex therapy with lesbian couples. In J.J. Bigner and J.L. Wetchler (Eds), *Handbook of LGBT-Affirmative Couple and Family Therapy*. New York. Hove: Routledge.

Coleman, E. (Ed.) (1988). Assessment of sexual orientation. In *Psychotherapy With Homosexual Men and Women*. New York: Haworth.

Connolly, C.M. (2014). Lesbian couples and marriage counselling. In S. H. Dworkin and M. Pope. (Eds), *Casebook for Counseling Lesbian, Gay, Bisexual, and Transgender Persons and Their Families*. John Wiley & Sons.

Cormier-Otaño, O. and Davies, D. (2012). Gender and sexual diversity therapy (GSDT). Pink Therapy. www.pinktherapy.com/Portals/Downloadables/Translations/GB_GSD, (accessed 30 November 2016).

Curra, J. (2011). *The Relativity of Deviance*. (4th ed.). Thousand Oaks, CA: Sage Publications.

Diamond, L. M. (2008). *Sexual Fluidity*. Harvard University Press.

Dodge, B. and Sandfort, T.G.M. (2007). A review of mental health research on bisexual individuals when compared to homosexual and heterosexual individuals. In B. A. Firestein (Ed.), *Becoming Visible: Counseling Bisexuals Across the Lifespan*. New York: Columbia University Press.

Easton, D. and Hardy, J.W. (2009). *The Ethical Slut: A Practical Guide to Polyamory, Open Relationships & Other Adventures*. Berkeley California: Celestial Arts.

Easton, D. and Liszt, C.A. (1997). *The Ethical Slut: A Guide to Infinite Sexual Possibilities*. Greenery Press.

Everyday Feminism (n.d.). www.everydayfeminism.com (accessed 26 April 2016).

Fausto-Sterling, A. (2000). *Sexing the Body: Gender Politics and the Construction of Sexuality*. New York: Basic Books.

Foucault, M. (1980). *Power/knowledge*. New York: Pantheon Books.

Frank, K. and DeLamater, J. (2010). Deconstructing monogamy. Boundaries, identities, and fluidities across relationships. In M. Barker and D. Langdridge, *Understanding Non-Monogamies*. New York and London: Routledge.

Gabb, J., Klett-Davies, M., Fink, J. and Thomae, M. (2013). *Enduring Love? Couple Relationships in the 21st Century*. Milton Keynes: The Open University Survey Findings Report. http://www.open.ac.uk/researchprojects/enduringlove/files/enduringlove/file/ecms/web-content/Final-Enduring-Love-Survey-Report.pdf. (accessed 1 January 2014).

Gender Diversity (n.d.) www.genderdiversity.org (accessed 14 August 2016).

Giammattei, S. and Green, R.J. (2012). LGBTQ Couple and family therapy: History and future directions. In J.J. Bigner and J.L. Wetchler (Eds) (2012), *Handbook of LGBT-Affirmative Couple and Family Therapy*. New York. Hove: Routledge.

Gilligan, C. (1982). *In a Different Voice*. Harvard University Press.

Gressgard, R. (2014). Asexuality: from pathology to identity and beyond. In M. Carrigan, K. Gupta, T.G. Morrison (Eds), *Asexuality and Sexual Normativity. An Anthology*. London and New York: Routledge.

Gupta, K. in Bishop, C.J. (2014). A mystery wrapped in an enigma – asexuality: a virtual discussion. In M. Carrigan, K. Gupta, T.G. Morrison (Eds): *Asexuality and Sexual Normativity. An Anthology*. London and New York: Routledge.

Haffner, D.W. and Stayton, W.R. (1998). Sexuality and reproductive health. In P.A. Hatcher et al. (Eds), *Contraceptive Technology*, (7th revised ed.) New York: Ardent Media.

Halstead, K. (2003). Over the rainbow: The lesbian family. In L.B. Silverstein and J.T. Goodrich (Eds), *Feminist Family Therapy: Empowerment in Social Context*. Washington, DC: American Psychological Association.

Hinderliter, A. (2009). Methodological issues for studying asexuality. *Archives of Sexual Behavior*, 38, 619–621.

Hinderliter, A. (2014). How is asexuality different from hypoactive sexual desire disorder? In M. Carrigan, K. Gupta and T.G. Morrison (Eds), *Asexuality and Sexual Normativity. An Anthology*. London and New York: Routledge.

Hite, S. (2004). *The Hite Report: A Nationwide Study of Female Sexuality*. Seven Stories Press.

Hudson-Allez, G. (2005). *Sex and Sexuality: Questions and Answers for Counsellors and Therapists*. London: Whurr Publishers.

Iasenza, S. (2002). Beyond 'lesbian bed death': The passion and play in lesbian relationships. *Journal of Lesbian Studies*, 6, 111–120.

Iasenza, S. (2004). Multicontextual sex therapy with lesbian couples. In S. Green and D. Flemons (Eds): *Quickies: The Handbook of Brief Sex Therapy* (revised. ed.). New York, NY: WW Norton.

Iasenza, S. (2010). What is queer about sex? Expanding sexual frames in theory and practice. *Family Process*, 49, 291–308.

Kaplan, H.S. (1979). *Disorders of Sexual Desire*. New York: Brunner / Mazel.

Kaschak, E. and Tiefer, L. (2014). *A New View of Women's Sexual Problems*. Routledge.

Kinsey, A.C., Pomeroy, W.B. and Martin, C.E. (1948). *Sexual Behavior in the Human Male*. Philadelphia: W.B. Saunders Co.

Kinsey, A.C, Pomeroy, W.B., Martin, C.E and Gebhard, P. (1953). *Sexual Behavior in the Human Female*. Philadelphia: W.B. Saunders Co.

Kleinplatz, P.J. (2014). The paraphilias. An experiential approach to 'dangerous' desires. In Y.M. Binik and S.K. Hall (Eds), *Principles and Practice of Sex Therapy* (5th ed.). New York: Guilford Press.

Knudson, G. A., Brotto, L. A. and Inskip, J. (2008). Understanding asexuality: sexual characteristics and personality profiles of asexual men and women. *Journal of Sex Research*, 45(2), 95–95.

Kolmes, K., and Weitzman, G. (2010). A guide to choosing a kink-aware therapist [Fact sheet]. https://ncsfreedom.org/images/stories/pdfs/KAP/kap_white_paper%20final.pdf (accessed August 24, 2013).

Langstrom, N. and Seto, M.C. (2006). Exhibitionistic and voyeuristic behavior in a Swedish national population survey. *Archives of Sexual Behavior*, 35(4), 427–435.

LaSala, M. (2004). Monogamy of the heart: Extradyadic sex and gay male couples. *Journal of Gay and Lesbian Social Services*, 17(3), 1–24.

Lev, A. I. (2004). *Transgender Emergence: Therapeutic Guidelines for Working With Gender-variant People and Their Families*. Binghamton, NY: Haworth Clinical Practice Press.

Lev, A.I. and Nichols, M. (2015). Sex therapy with lesbian and gay male couples. In K.M. Hertlein, G.R. Weeks and N. Gambescia (Eds), *Systemic Sex Therapy*. (2nd ed.). New York and East Sussex: Routledge.

Lewis, R.J., Derlega, V.J., Brown, D. and Rose, S. (2009). Sexual minority stress, depressive symptoms, and sexual orientation conflict: Focus on the experiences of bisexuals. *Journal of Social and Clinical Psychology*, 28(8), 971–992.

Lloyd, E. A. (2009). *The Case of the Female Orgasm: Bias in the Science of Evolution*. Harvard University Press.

Lottes, I.L. and Grollman, E.A. (2010). Conceptualization and assessment of homonegativity. *International Journal of Sexual Health*, 22, 219–233.

Masters, W.H. and Johnson, V.E. (1966). *Human Sexual Response*. Boston: Little Brown.

Martin, J.I. (2006). Transcendence among gay men: Implications for HIV prevention. *Sexualities*, 9(2), 214–235.

Matthews, A.K., Hughes, T.L. and Tartaro, J. (2006). Sexual behavior and sexual dysfunction in a community sample of lesbian and heterosexual women. In A.M.

Omoto and H.S. Kurtzman (Eds), *Sexual Orientation and Mental Health: Examining Identity and Development in Lesbian, Gay, and Bisexual People*. Washington, DC: American Psychological Association.

McCann, D. and Delmonte, H. (2005). Lesbian and gay parenting: babes in arms or babes in the woods? *Sexual and Relationship Therapy*, 20(3), 333–347.

McManus, M.A., Hargreaves, P., Rainbow, L. and Alison, L.J. (2013). Paraphilias: definition, diagnosis and treatment. *F1000 Prime Reports*, 5(36). (doi:10.12703/P5-36).

Meyer, I.H. (2003). Prejudices, social stress and mental health in lesbian, gay, and bisexual populations: Conceptual issues and research evidence. *Psychological Bulletin*, 129, 674–697.

Moon, D. (1995). Insult and inclusion: The term fag hag and gay male 'community'. *Social Forces*, 74, 487–510.

Moser, C. and Kleinplatz, P. J. (2005). DSM-IV-TR and the paraphilias: An argument for removal. *Journal of Psychology and Human Sexuality*, 17(3/4), 91–109.

Nichols, M. (2006). Psychotherapeutic issues with "kinky" clients: Clinical problems, yours and theirs. *Journal of Homosexuality*, 50(2/3), 281–300.

Nichols, M. (2011). Variations on gender and orientation in a first interview. In C. Silverstein (Ed.), *The Initial Psychotherapy Interview: A Gay Man Seeks Treatment*. New York: Elsevier.

Nichols, M. (2014). Therapy with LGBTQ clients. Working with sex and gender variance from a queer theory model. In Y.M. Binik and S.K. Hall (Eds), *Principles and Practice of Sex Therapy* (5th ed.). New York: Guilford Press.

Oswald, R.F., Blume, L.B. and Marks, S.R. (2005). Decentering heteronormativity: A model for family studies. In: V.L. Bengston, A.C. Acock, K.R. Allen, P. Dilworth Anderson and D.M. Klein (Eds), *Sourcebook of Family Theory and Research*. Thousand Oaks, CA: Sage Publications.

Oxford English Dictionary (n.d). www.oed.com, (accessed 14 August 2016).

Parsons, J.T., Starks, T.J., DuBois, S., Grov, C. and Golub, S.A. (2011). Alternatives to monogamy among gay male couples in a community survey: Implications for mental health and sexual risk. *Archives of Sexual Behavior*, 42(2), 303–312.

Perlesz, A., Brown, R., Lindsay, J., McNair, R., deVans, D. and Pitts, M. (2006). Family in transition: Parents, children and grandparents in lesbian families give meaning to 'doing family'. *Journal of Family Therapy*, 28 (2), 175–199.

Pillai-Friedman, S., Pollitt, J.L. and Castaldo, A. (2015). Becoming kink-aware: A necessity for sexuality professionals. *Sexual and Relationship Therapy*, 30(2), 196–210.

Pink Therapy (n.d.). www.pinktherapy.com (accessed 14 August 2016).

Popovic, M. (2006). Psychosexual diversity as the best representation of human normality across cultures. *Sexual and Relationship Therapy*, 21(2), 171–186.

Przybylo, E. (2014). Afterword: some thoughts on asexuality as an interdisciplinary method. In M. Carrigan, K. Gupta, T.G. Morrison (Eds), *Asexuality and Sexual Normativity. An Anthology*. London and New York: Routledge.

Quincey, V.L. (2012). Pragmatic and Darwinian views on the paraphilias. *Archives of Sexual Behaviour*, 41, 217–220.

Ritchie, A. (2017). Consensual non-monogamy and polyamory: psychological and relational well-being. European Society for Sexual Medicine Congress, Nice, France.

Sanders, G.L. (1992). Kensington Consultation Centre Workshop, London.

Sandfort, R. and deKeizer, M. (2001). Sexual problems in gay men: An overview of empirical research. *Annual Review of Sex Research*, 12, 93–120.

Savin-Williams, R.C. (2005). *The New Gay Teenager*. Cambridge, MA: Harvard University Press.

Seidman, S. (2014). *The Social Construction of Sexuality*. (3rd ed.). W.W. Norton.

Shaw, E. (2010). Introduction. In: C. Butler, A. Donovan and E. Shaw (Eds), *Sex, Sexuality and Therapeutic Practice. A Manual for Therapists and Trainers*. West Sussex UK, USA and Canada: Routledge.

Slater, S. (1995). *The Lesbian Family Life Cycle*. New York, NY: Free Press.

Tiefer, L. (Ed.) (2004). *Sex is Not a Natural Act and Other Essays*. (2nd ed.) Boulder: Westview Press.

Tomm, K. (1987). Interventive interviewing: Part II. Questioning as a means to enable self-healing. *Family Process*, 26, 167–183.

Tunnell, G. (2012). Gay male couple therapy. An attachment based model. In J.J. Bigner and J.L. Wetchler (Eds), *Handbook of LGBT-Affirmative Couple and Family Therapy*. New York. Hove: Routledge.

UK Intersex Association (n.d.). www.ukia.co.uk (accessed 15 May 2017).

Van Den Wijngaard, M. (1997). *Reinventing the Sexes: The Biomedical Construction of Femininity and Masculinity*. Indiana University Press.

Veaux, F. and Rickert, E. (2014). *More Than Two: A Practical Guide to Ethical Polyamory*. Portland, OR: Thorntree Press.

Weeks, G.R. and Gambescia, N. (2002). *Hypoactive Sexual Desire. Integrating Sex and Couple Therapy*. W.W. Norton.

Weeks, G.R., Gambescia, N. and Hertlein, K.M. (2015). Sex therapy: A panoramic view. In: K.M. Hertlein, G.R. Weeks and N. Gambescia (Eds), *Systemic Sex Therapy* (2nd ed.), New York: Routledge.

West, C. and Zimmerman, D.H. (2000). Doing gender. In M. Kimmel (Ed.) with A. Aronson, *The Gendered Society Reader*. New York: Oxford University Press.

Whipple. B. and Brash-McGreer, K. (1997). Management of female sexual dysfunction. In M.L. Sipski and C. Alexander (Eds), *Sexual Function in People with Disability and Chronic Illness: A Health Professionals' Guide*. Gaithersburg, M.D.: Aspen Publishers.

Whitaker, B. (2013). An interview with Dominic Davies. *Sheffield Central Counselling*. www.sheffieldcentralcounselling.co.uk/blog/dominic-davies-lgbt-therapist-interview (accessed 16 May 2017).

Williams, C.J. and Weinberg, M.S. (2003). Zoophilia in men: A study of sexual interest in animals. *Archives of Sexual Behavior*, 32(6), 523–535.

Wincze, J.P. and Carey, M.P. (2001). *Sexual Dysfunction: A Guide to Assessment and Treatment*. (2nd ed.) New York, London: The Guilford Press.

World Health Organization (WHO) (2010). *ICD-10 Classification of Mental and Behavioural Disorders. Clinical Descriptions and Diagnostic Guidelines*. Geneva: World Health Organisation.

Wylie, K.R., Ng, E.M.L., Chambers, L., Ward-Davies, L. and Hickey, F. (2008). Sexual disorders, paraphilias, and gender dysphoria. *International Journal of Sexual Health,* 20(1-2), 109–129.

Zilbergeld, B. (1999). *The New Male Sexuality* (revised version). USA: Bantam Books.

Zucker, K.J. and Brown, N. (2014). Gender dysphoria. In Y.M. Binik and S.K. Hall (Eds), *Principles and Practice of Sex Therapy* (5th edition). New York: Guilford Press.

Chapter 3: Sexual misconceptions and prejudice

Barker, M. (2013). Reflections: Towards a mindful sexual and relationship therapy. *Sexual and Relationship Therapy,* 28(1–2), 148–152.

Burnham, J. (2005). Relational reflexivity. A tool for socially constructing therapeutic relationships. Chapter 1 in C. Flaskas, B. Mason and A. Perlesz (Eds), *The Space Between: Experience, Context and Process in the Therapeutic Relationship.* Karnac Books.

Clement, U. (2002). Sex in long-term relationships: A systemic approach to sexual desire problems. *Archives of Sexual Behaviour,* 31(3), 241–246. June.

Dallos, R. (1997). *Interacting Stories. Narratives, Family Beliefs, and Therapy.* Karnac Books.

Dallos, S. and Dallos, R. (1997). *Couples, Sex and Power. The Politics of Desire.* Open University Press.

Foreman, S. and Dallos, R. (1992). Inequalities of power and sexual problems. *Journal of Family Therapy,*14, 349–369.

Hare-Mustin, R.T. (1991). Sex, lies and headaches: The problem is power. Chapter 4 in T.J. Goodrich (Ed.) (1991), *Women and Power. Perspectives for Family Therapy.* W.W. Norton.

Hare-Mustin, R.T. (1994). Discourses in the mirrored room: A postmodern analysis of therapy. *Family Process,* 33(1), 19–35. March.

Hawton, K. (1985). *Sex Therapy. A Practical Guide.* Oxford University Press.

Heiman, J. and LoPiccolo, J. (1988). *Becoming Orgasmic: A Sexual and Personal Growth Program for Women.* New York: Prentice Hall.

Larson, J.H. (2016). Myths about marriage. In G.R. Weeks, S.T. Fife and C.M. Peterson (Eds), *Techniques for the Couple Therapist. Essential Interventions From the Experts.* New York, Oxon: Routledge.

Markovic, D. (2013). Multidimensional sex therapy: A model of integration between sexology and systemic therapy. *Sexual and Relationship Therapy,* 28(4), 311–323.

Mason, M. J. (1993). Shame: Reservoir of family secrets. Chapter 2 in E. I. Black (Ed.) *Secrets in Families and Family Therapy.* W.W. Norton.

Masters, W. and Johnson, V.E. (1966). *Human Sexual Response.* Boston: Little, Brown and Company.

McCarthy, B. and McCarthy, E. (2012). *Sexual Awareness.* (5th ed.). New York. Hove: Routledge. Taylor and Francis.

McCarthy, B. and Metz, M. (2008). *Men's Sexual Health Fitness for Satisfying Sex.* New York, London: Routledge. Taylor and Francis Group.

Metz, M. E. and McCarthy, B. W. (2004). *Coping with Erectile Dysfunction: How to Regain Confidence and Enjoy Great Sex.* Oakland, CA: New Harbinger Publications Inc.

Sanders, G.L. (1994). Kensington Consultation Centre Workshop, London.

Schnarch, D. M. (2000). Sexual desire: A systemic perspective. In S.R. Leiblum and R. C. Rosen (Eds), *Principles and Practice of Sex Therapy* (3rd ed.). New York: Guilford Press.

Tiefer, L. (Ed.) (2004). *Sex is Not a Natural Act and Other Essays.* (2nd ed.) Boulder: Westview Press.

Watzlawick, P. (1993). *The Situation Is Hopeless, but Not Serious: The Pursuit of Unhappiness.* W.W. Norton & Co: New York. London.

Weeks, G.R. and Gambescia, N. (2000). *Erectile Dysfunction: Integrating Couple Therapy, Sex Therapy, and Medical Treatment.* W.W. Norton.

Weingarten, K. (1991). The discourses of intimacy: Adding a social constructionist and feminist view. *Family Process*, 30(3), 285–305.

Winter, D. A. (1988). Reconstructing an erection and elaborating ejaculation: Personal construct theory perspectives on sex therapy. *International Journal of Personal Construct Psychology*, 1(1), 81–99.

Zilbergeld, B. (1999). *The New Male Sexuality* (revised version). *USA:* Bantam Books.

Chapter 4: Classification and assessment of sexual disorders

Introduction

American Psychiatric Association (APA) (2013). *Diagnostic and Statistical Manual of Mental Disorders (DSM)* (5th ed.). Washington DC.

Anderson, H., Goolishian, H. and Windermand, L. (1986). Problem determined systems: Towards transformation in family therapy. *Journal of Strategic and Systemic Therapies*, 5(4), 1–14.

Bancroft, J., Graham, C.A., Janssen, E. and Sanders, S.A. (2009). The dual control model: Current status and future directions. *Journal of Sex Research*, 46(2-3), 121–142.

Bateson, G. (1972). *Steps to an Ecology of Mind; Mind and Nature.* New York: Jason Aronson.

Belous, C.R., Timm, T.A., Chee, G. and Whitehead, M.R. (2012). Revisiting the sexual genogram. *American Journal of Family Therapy*, 40(4), 281–296.

Cecchin, G. (1987). Hypothesizing, circularity, and neutrality revisited: An invitation to curiosity. *Family Process*, 26, 405–413.

Cecchin, G., Lane, G. and Ray, W. A. (1992). *Irreverence: A Strategy for Therapists' Survival.* Karnac Books.

Cornwell, M. (1989). Falling in love with ideas. An interview with Luigi Boscolo. *Australian and New Zealand Journal of Family Therapy,* 10(2), 97–103.

Dallos, R. and Draper, R. (2000). *An Introduction to Family Therapy: Systemic Theory and Practice.* Open University Press.

Gambescia, N. (2016). The use of the sexual genogram. In G.R. Weeks, S.T. Fife and C.M. Peterson (Eds), *Techniques for the Couple Therapist. Essential Interventions From the Experts.* New York and London: Routledge.

Gergen, K. J., Hoffman, L. and Anderson, H. (1996). Is diagnosis a disaster? A constructionist trialogue. In F. W. Kaslow (Ed.), *Handbook of Relational Diagnosis and Dysfunctional Family Patterns*. Oxford: John Wiley.

Hof, L. and Berman, E. (1989). The sexual genogram: Assessing family-of-origin factors in the treatment of sexual dysfunction. Chapter 11 in D. Kantor and B. Okun (Eds), *Intimate Environments. Sex, Intimacy and Gender in Families*. The Guilford Press.

McGoldrick, M., Gerson, R. and Shellenberger, S. (1999). *Genograms: Assessment and Intervention*. (2nd ed.). New York. London: W.W. Norton.

Mendez, C.L., Coddou, F. and Maturana, H.R. (1988). The bringing forth of pathology. *The Irish Journal of Psychology*, 9(1), 144–172.

Pearce, W. B. (2007). *Making Social Worlds: A Communicational Perspective*. London: Blackwell Publishing.

Tomm, K. (1991). Beginning of a HIPs and PIPs approach to psychiatric assessment. *The Calgary Participator*, 1, 21–24.

Vetere, A. and Dallos, R. (2003). *Working Systemically with Families: Formulation, Intervention and Evaluation*. London: Karnac Books.

White, M. (1991). Deconstruction and therapy. *Dulwich Centre Newsletter*, No.3, 21–40.

White, M. (2007). *Maps of Narrative Practice*. New York, NY: W. W. Norton.

Wincze, J.P. and Carey, M.P. (2001). *Sexual Dysfunction: A Guide to Assessment and Treatment* (2nd ed.). New York, London: The Guilford Press.

Wincze, J.P. and Weisberg, R.B. (2015). *Sexual Dysfunction: A Guide to Assessment and Treatment* (3rd ed.). New York: The Guilford Press.

Delayed ejaculation

Abdel-Hamid, I. and Saleh, E. (2011). Primary lifelong delayed ejaculation: Characteristics and response to bupropion. *Journal of Sexual Medicine*, 8, 1772–1779.

Althof, S. (2012). Psychological interventions for delayed ejaculation/orgasm. *International Journal of Impotence Research*, 24(4), 131–136.

American Psychiatric Association (APA) (2013). *Diagnostic and Statistical Manual of Mental Disorders (DSM)* (5th ed.). Washington DC.

Apfelbaum, B. (2000). Retarded ejaculation: A much-misunderstood syndrome. In S.R. Leiblum and R.C. Rosen (Eds), *Principles and Practice of Sex Therapy* (2nd ed.). New York: Guilford Press.

Christensen, B.S., Gronbaek, M., Osler, M., Pedersen, B.V., Graugaard, C. and Frisch, M. (2011). Sexual dysfunctions and difficulties in Denmark: Prevalence and associated sociodemographic factors. *Archives of Sexual Behaviour*, 40, 121–132.

Foley, S. and Gambescia, N. (2015). The complex etiology of delayed ejaculation: Assessment and treatment implications. In K.M. Hertlein, G.R. Weeks and N. Gambescia (Eds), *Systemic Sex Therapy* (2nd ed.). New York: Routledge.

Gagliardi, F.A. (1976). Ejaculation retardata. *American Journal of Psychotherapy*, 30, 85–94.

Hartmann, U. and Waldinger, M. (2007). Treatment of delayed ejaculation. In S. R. Leiblum and R.C. Rosen (Eds), *Principles and Practice of Sex Therapy* (4th ed.). New York: Guilford Press.

Kaplan, H.S. (1974). Retarded ejaculation. In H.S. Kaplan (Ed.), *The New Sex Therapy*. New York: Brunner/Mazel.

Komisaruk, B., Beyer-Flores, C. and Whipple, B. (2006). *The Science of Orgasm*. Baltimore: The Johns Hopkins University Press.

Lew, M. (2004). *Victims No Longer: The Classic Guide for Men Recovering From Sexual Child Abuse* (2nd ed.), New York: Quill.

Lincoln, R. and Thexton, R. (1983). Retarded ejaculation. *Practice of Psychosexual Medicine*, 151–155.

Lue, T.F., Basson, R., Rosen, R., Giuliano, F., Khoury, S. and Montorsi, F. (2004). *Sexual Medicine: Sexual Dysfunctions in Men and Women*. Paris: Health Publications.

Masters, W.H. and Johnson, V.E. (1970). *Human Sexual Inadequacy*. Boston: Little, Brown.

Metz, M.E. and McCarthy, B.W. (2007). The 'good-enough sex' model for couple sexual satisfaction. *Sexual and Relationship Therapy*, 22(3), 351–362.

Perelman, M.A. (2004). Retarded ejaculation. *Current Sexual Health Reports*, 1, 95–101.

Perelman, M.A. (2005). Idiosyncratic masturbation patterns: A key unexplored variable in the treatment of retarded ejaculation by the practicing urologist. *Journal of Urology*, 173(430), Abstract 1337.

Perelman, M.A. (2014). Delayed ejaculation. In Y.M. Binik and S.K. Hall (Eds), *Principles and Practice of Sex Therapy* (5th ed.). New York: Guilford Press.

Perelman, M.A. and Rowland, D.L. (2006). Retarded ejaculation. *World Journal of Urology*, 24, 645–652.

Preda, A. and Bienenfeld, D. (2013). Delayed ejaculation. http://emedicine.medscape.com/article/2184956-overview, (accessed 24 April 2017).

Robbins-Cherry, S., Hayter, M., Wylie, K. and Goldmeier, D. (2011). The experience of men living with inhibited ejaculation. *Sexual and Relationship Therapy*, 26(3), 242–253.

Segraves, R.T. (2010). Considerations for diagnostic criteria for erectile dysfunction in DSM V. *Journal of Sexual Medicine*, 7, 654–671.

Shull, D.R. and Sprenkle, D.H. (1980). Retarded ejaculation reconceptualization and implications for treatment. *Journal of Sex & Marital Therapy*, 6(4), 234–246.

Waldinger, M.D. and Schweitzer, D.H. (2005). Retarded ejaculation in men: An overview of psychological and neurobiological insights. *World Journal of Urology*, 23, 76–81.

Wincze, J.P. and Weisberg, R.B. (2015). *Sexual Dysfunction: A Guide to Assessment and Treatment* (3rd ed.). New York: The Guilford Press.

Erectile disorder

American Psychiatric Association (APA) (1954). *Diagnostic and Statistical Manual of Mental Disorders (DSM-I)* (1st ed.). Washington DC.

American Psychiatric Association (APA) (1980). *Diagnostic and Statistical Manual of Mental Disorders (DSM-III)* (3rd ed.). Washington DC.

American Psychiatric Association (APA) (1994). *Diagnostic and Statistical Manual of Mental Disorders IV (DSM)* (4th ed.). Washington DC.

REFERENCES

American Psychiatric Association (APA) (2013). *Diagnostic and Statistical Manual of Mental Disorders (DSM)* (5th ed.). Washington DC.

Crenshaw, T.L. and Goldberg, J.P. (1996). *Sexual Pharmacology: Drugs That Affect Sexual Function*. Norton Professional Books.

Davidson, J.M. and Rosen, R.C. (1992). Hormonal determinants of erectile function. In R.C. Rosen and S.R. Leiblum (Eds), *Erectile Disorders: Assessment and Treatment*. New York: Guilford Press.

Feldman, H.A., Goldstein, I., Hatzichristou, D.G., Krane, R.J. and McKinlay, J.B. (1994). Impotence and its medical and psychosocial correlates: Results of the Massachusetts male aging study. *Journal of Urology*, 151(1), 54–61.

Gottman, J. M. (1994). An agenda for marital therapy. In S. M. Johnson and L. S. Greenberg (Eds), *The Heart of the Matter: Perspectives on Emotion in Marital Therapy*. New York: Brunner/Mazel.

Hare-Mustin, R.T. (1994). Discourses in the mirrored room: A postmodern analysis of therapy. *Family Process*, 33(1), 19–35.

Hawton, K. (1985). *Sex Therapy. A Practical Guide*. Oxford University Press.

Kaplan, H.S. (1974). *The New Sex Therapy: Active Treatment of Sexual Dysfunctions*. New York: Bruner/Mazel.

Leiblum, S.R. and Rosen, R. C. (Eds) (2000). *Principles and Practice of Sex Therapy*. (3rd ed.). New York: Guilford Press.

Lue, T.F., Basson, R., Rosen, R.C., Giuliano, F., Khoury, S. and Montorsi, F. (2004). *Sexual Medicine: Sexual Dysfunctions in Men and Women*. Paris: Health Publications.

Masters, W. H. and Johnson, V. E. (1970). *Human Sexual Inadequacy*. USA: Ishi Press International.

Metz, M. E. and McCarthy, B. W. (2004). *Coping with Erectile Dysfunction: How to Regain Confidence and Enjoy Great Sex*. Oakland, CA: New Harbinger Publications Inc.

Minuchin, S. (1974). *Families and Family Therapy*. Cambridge, Massachusetts: Harvard University Press.

Nobre, P.D. and Pinto-Gouveia, J. (2009). Cognitive schemas associated with negative sexual events: A comparison of men and women with and without sexual dysfunction. *Archives of Sexual Behavior*, 38(5), 842–851.

Rakic, Z., Starcevic, V., Starcevic, V.P. and Marinkovic, J. (1997). Testosterone treatment in men with erectile disorder and low levels of total testosterone in serum. *Archives of Sexual Behavior*, 26, 495.

Rosen, R.C., Miner, M.M. and Wincze, J.P. (2014). Erectile dysfunction: Integration of medical and psychological approaches. In Y.M. Binik and K. Hall (Eds) (2014). *Principles and Practice of Sex Therapy* (5th ed.). New York: The Guilford Press.

Weeks, G.R. and Gambescia, N. (2000). *Erectile Dysfunction: Integrating Couple Therapy, Sex Therapy, and Medical Treatment*. W.W. Norton.

Weisberg, R.B., Brown, T.A., Wincze, J.P. and Barlow, D.H. (2001). Causal attributions and male sexual arousal: The impact of attributions for a bogus erectile difficulty on sexual arousal, cognitions, and affect, *Journal of Abnormal Psychology*, 110, 324–334.

Wincze, J.P. and Carey, M.P. (2001). *Sexual Dysfunction: A Guide to Assessment and Treatment* (2nd ed.). New York, London: The Guilford Press.

Wincze, J.P. and Weisberg, R.B. (2015). *Sexual Dysfunction: A Guide to Assessment and Treatment* (3rd ed.). New York: The Guilford Press.

Wylie, K.R., Hallam-Jones, R. and Perrett, A. (1999). Some of the potential implications of integrated assessment for male erectile disorder. *Journal of Sex & Marital Therapy,* 14, 359–369.

Zilbergeld, B. (1999). *The New Male Sexuality* (revised version). USA: Bantam Books.

Female orgasmic disorder

American Psychiatric Association (APA) (1980). *Diagnostic and Statistical Manual of Mental Disorders (DSM-III)* (3rd ed.). Washington DC.

American Psychiatric Association (APA) (1994). *Diagnostic and Statistical Manual of Mental Disorders IV (DSM)* (4th ed.). Washington DC.

American Psychiatric Association (2000). *Diagnostic and Statistical Manual of Mental Disorders (DSM-IV-TR)* (4th ed.). Washington DC.

American Psychiatric Association (APA) (2013). *Diagnostic and Statistical Manual of Mental Disorders (DSM)* (5th ed.). Washington DC.

Avis, N.E., Stellato, R., Crawford, S., Johannes, C. and Longcope, C. (2000). Is there an association between menopause status and sexual functioning? *Menopause,* 7, 297–309.

Bancroft, J., Long, J.S. and McCabe, J. (2011). Distress about sex: A national survey of women in heterosexual relationships. *Archives of Sexual Behavior,* 32, 193–208.

Bancroft, J., Graham, C.A., Janssen, E. and Sanders, S.A. (2009). The dual control model: Current status and future directions. *Journal of Sex Research,* 46(2–3), 121–142.

Basson, R. (2002). Are our definitions of women's desire, arousal, and sexual pain disorders too broad and our definition of orgasmic disorder too narrow? *Journal of Sex and Marital Therapy,* 28, 289–300.

Brotto, L.A., Bitzer, J., Laan, E., Leiblum, S. and Luria, M. (2010). Women's sexual desire and arousal disorders. *Journal of Sexual Medicine,* 7, 586–614.

Chalker, R. (2000). *The Clitoral Truth: The World at Your Fingertips.* New York: Seven Stories Press.

Curra, J. (2016). *The Relativity of Deviance.* (4th ed.). Sage Publications.

Freud, S. (1953). *Three Essays on the Theory of Sexuality.* Standard Edition, 7, London: Hogarth Press.

Graham, C.A. (2010). The DSM diagnostic criteria for female orgasmic disorder. *Archives of Sexual Behavior,* 39, 256–270.

Graham, C.A. (2014). Orgasm Disorders in Women. Chapter 4 in Y.M. Binik and S.K. Hall (Eds), *Principles and Practice of Sex Therapy* (5th ed.). New York. London: The Guilford Press.

Graham, C.A. and Bancroft, J. (2006). Assessing the prevalence of female sexual dysfunction with surveys: What is feasible? In I. Goldstein, C.M. Meston, S.R. Davis and A.M. Traish (Eds), *Women's Sexual Function and Dysfunction: Study, Diagnosis and Treatment.* Abingdon, Oxon, UK: Taylor & Francis.

Heiman, J. and LoPiccolo, J. (1988). *Becoming Orgasmic: A Sexual and Personal Growth Program for Women.* New York: Prentice Hall.

Heiman, J.R. (2007). Orgasmic disorders in women. In S.R. Leiblum (Ed.), *Principles and Practice of Sex Therapy* (4th ed.). New York: Guilford Press.

Hite, S. (1976). *The Hite Report*. New York: Dell.

Hobbs, K., Symonds, T., Abraham, L., May, K. and Morris, M.F. (2008). Sexual dysfunction in partners of men with premature ejaculation. *International Journal of Impotence Research*, 20, 512–517.

King, M., Holt, V. and Nazareth, I. (2007). Women's views of their sexual difficulties: Agreement and disagreement with clinical diagnoses. *Archives of Sexual Behavior*, 36, 281–288.

King, R., Belsky, J., Mah, K. and Binik, Y. (2011). Are there different types of female orgasm? *Archives of Sexual Behavior*, 40, 865–875.

Komisaruk, B.R. and Whipple, B. (2011). Non-genital orgasms. *Sexual and Relationship Therapy*, 26, 356–372.

Laan, E. and Rellini, A.H. (2011). Can we treat anorgasmia in women? The challenge to experiencing pleasure. *Sexual and Relationship Therapy*, 26, 329–341.

Laumann, E.O., Nicolosi, A., Glasser, D.B., Paik, A., Gingell, C., Moreira, E., et al. (2005). Sexual problems among women and men aged 40–80 years: Prevalence and correlates identified in the Global Study of Sexual Attitudes and Behaviors. *International Journal of Impotence Research*, 17, 39–57.

Mercer, C.H., Fenton, K.A., Johnson, A.M., Wellings, K., Macdowall, W., McManus, S., et al. (2003). Sexual function problems and help seeking behaviour in Britain: National probability sample survey. *British Medical Journal*, 327, 426–427.

Meston, C.M., Levin, R.J., Sipski, M.L., Hull, E.M. and Heiman, J.R. (2004). Women's orgasm. *Annual Review of Sex Research*, 15, 173–257.

Muehlenhard, C.L. and Shippee, S.K. (2010). Men's and women's reports of pretending orgasms. *Journal of Sex Research*, 47, 552–567.

Nobre, P.J. and Pinto-Gouveia, J. (2006). Dysfunctional sexual beliefs as vulnerability factors for sexual dysfunction. *Journal of Sex Research*, 43, 68–75.

Purnine, D.M. and Carey, M.P. (1997). Interpersonal communication and sexual adjustment: The roles of understanding and agreement. *Consulting and Clinical Psychology*, 65, 1017–1025.

Ramage, M. (2004). Female sexual dysfunction. *Women's Health Medicine*, 3(2), 84–88.

Richters, J., Grulich, A.E., de Visser, R.O., Smith, A.M.A. and Rissel, C.E. (2003). Sexual difficulties in a representative sample of adults. *Australian and New Zealand Journal of Public Health*, 27, 164–170.

Robinson, B.E., Munns, R.A., Weber-Main, A.M., Lowe, M.A. and Raymond, N.C. (2011). Application of the sexual health model in the long-term treatment of hypoactive sexual desire and female orgasmic disorder. *Archives of Sexual Behavior*, 40, 469–478.

Shifren, J.L., Monz, B.U., Russo, P.A., Segreti, A. and Johannes, C.B. (2008). Sexual problems and distress in United States women. *Obstetrics and Gynaecology*, 112, 970–978.

Staples, J., Rellini, A.H. and Roberts, S.P. (2012). Avoiding experiences: Sexual dysfunction in women with a history of sexual abuse in childhood and adolescence. *Archives of Sexual Behavior*, 41, 341–350.

Whipple, B. (2003). Opening Plenary, World Association of Sexology, Havana, Cuba.

Wincze, J.P. and Carey, M.P. (2001). *Sexual Dysfunction: A Guide to Assessment and Treatment* (2nd ed.). New York, London: The Guilford Press.

Wincze, J.P. and Weisberg, R.B. (2015). *Sexual Dysfunction: A Guide to Assessment and Treatment* (3rd ed.). New York: The Guilford Press.

Zietsch, B.P., Miller, G.F., Bailey, M. and Martin, M.G. (2011). Female orgasm rates are largely independent of other traits: Implications for 'Female Orgasmic Disorder' and evolutionary theories of orgasm. *Journal of Sexual Medicine*, 8, 2305–2316.

Female sexual interest/arousal disorder

American Psychiatric Association (APA) (2000). *Diagnostic and Statistical Manual of Mental Disorders (DSM-IV-TR)* (4th ed.). Washington DC.

American Psychiatric Association (APA) (2013). *Diagnostic and Statistical Manual of Mental Disorders (DSM)* (5th ed.). Washington DC.

Azadzoi, K.M. and Siroky, M.B. (2006). Neurogenic sexual dysfunction in men and women. In J.J. Mulcahy (Ed.), *Male Sexual Function. A Guide to Clinical Management.* (2nd ed.). Totowa, New Jersey: Humana Press Inc.

Bartlik, B. and Goldberg, J. (2000). Female sexual arousal disorder. In S. R. Leiblum and R. C. Rosen (Eds), *Principles and Practice of Sex Therapy* (3rd ed.). New York: Guilford Press.

Brotto, L.A. (2010). The DSM diagnostic criteria for hypoactive sexual desire disorder in women. *Archives of Sexual Behavior*, 39(2), 221–239.

Brotto, L.A. and Luria, M. (2014). Sexual interest / arousal disorder in women. In Y.M. Binik and K. Hall. (Eds) (2014), *Principles and Practice of Sex Therapy* (5th ed.). New York: The Guilford Press.

Boul, L., Hallam-Jones, R. and Wylie, K.R. (2009). Sexual pleasure and motivation. *Journal of Sex & Marital Therapy*, 35(1), 25–39.

Brezsnyak, M. and Whisman, M.A. (2004). Sexual desire and relationship functioning: The effects of marital satisfaction and power. *Journal of Sex & Marital Therapy*, 30(3), 199–217.

Carvalheira, A.A., Brotto, L.A. and Leal, I. (2010). Women's motivations for sex: Exploring the diagnostic and statistical manual (4th ed.). Text Revision criteria for hypoactive sexual desire and female sexual arousal disorders. *Journal of Sexual Medicine*, 9, 1134–1148.

Chalker, R. (2000). *The Clitoral Truth: The World at Your Fingertips*. New York: Seven Stories Press.

Chivers, M.L., Seto, M.C., Lalumiere, M.L., Laan, E. and Grimbos, T. (2010). Agreement of self-reported and genital measures of sexual arousal in men and women: A meta-analysis. *Archives of Sexual Behaviour*, 39(1), 5–56.

Frankl, V.E. (1985). Logos, paradox, and the search for meaning. In M. J. Mahoney and A. Freeman (Eds), *Cognition and Psychotherapy*. New York: Plenum Press.

Frost, R. N. and Donovan, C. L. (2015). Low sexual desire in women: Amongst the confusion, could distress hold the key? *Sexual and Relationship Therapy*, 30(3), 338–350.

Geonet, M., De Sutter, P.Y. and Zech, E. (2013). Cognitive factors in women hypoactive sexual desire. *Sexologies*, 22(1), 9–15.

Graham, C.A., Sanders, S.A., Milhausen, R.R. and McBride, K.R. (2004). Turning on and turning off. A focus group study of the factors that affect women's sexual arousal. *Archives of Sexual Behavior*, 33(6), December, 527–538.

Greenwald, E., Leitenberg, H., Cado, S. and Tarran, M.J. (1990). Childhood sexual abuse: Long-term effects on psychological and sexual functioning in a nonclinical and nonstudent sample of adult women. *Child Abuse and Neglect*, 14(4), 503–513.

Hawton, K. (1985). *Sex Therapy. A Practical Guide*. Oxford University Press.

Hayes, R.D., Dennerstein, L., Bennett, C.M. and Fairley, C.K. (2008). What is the 'true' prevalence of female sexual dysfunctions and does the way we assess these conditions have an impact? *Journal of Sexual Medicine*, 5(4), 777–787.

Kaplan, H.S. (1974). *The New Sex Therapy: Active Treatment of Sexual Dysfunctions*. New York: Bruner/Mazel.

Komisaruk, B., Beyer-Flores, C. and Whipple, B. (2006). *The Science of Orgasm*. Baltimore: The Johns Hopkins University Press.

Laumann, E.O., Paik, A. and Rosen, R.C. (1999). Sexual dysfunction in the United States: Prevalence and predictors. *Journal of the American Medical Association*, 281(6), 537–544.

Laumann, E.O., Nicolosi, A., Glasser, D.B., Paik, A., Gingell, C., Moreira, E. and Wang, T. (2005). Sexual problems among women and men aged 40–80 y: Prevalence and correlates identified in the global study of sexual attitudes and behaviors. *International Journal of Impotence Research*, 17(1), 39–57.

Leiblum, S.R. (2009). Sexual pleasure. Royal Society of Medicine London seminar.

Leiblum, S.R., Koochaki, P.E., Rodenberg, C.A., Barton, I.P. and Rosen, R.C. (2006). Hypoactive sexual desire disorder in postmenopausal women: U.S. results from the Women's International Study of Health and Sexuality (WISHeS). *Menopause*, 13, 46–56.

Masters, W.H. and Johnson, V.E. (1970). *Human Sexual Inadequacy*. Boston: Little, Brown.

McCabe, M. and Goldhammer, D.L. (2012). Demographic and psychological factors related to sexual desire among heterosexual women in a relationship. *Journal of Sexual Research*, 49(1), 78–87.

Mercer, C.H., Fenton, K.A., Johnson, A.M., Wellings, K., Macdowall, W., McManus, S., et al. (2003). Sexual function problems and help seeking behaviour in Britain: National probability sample survey. *British Medical Journal*, 327, 426–427.

Nobre, P.J., Pinto-Gouveia, J. (2008). Cognitive and emotional predictors of female sexual dysfunctions: Preliminary findings. *Journal of Sex & Marital Therapy*, 34(4), 325–342.

Oberg, K., Fugl-Meyer, A.R. and Fugl-Meyer, K.S. (2002). On sexual well-being in sexually abused Swedish women: Epidemiological aspects. *Sexual and Relationship Therapy*, 17, 329–341.

Richters, J., Grulich, A.E., Visser, R.O., Smith, A.M.A. and Rissel, C.E. (2003). Sex in Australia: Sexual difficulties in a representative sample of adults. *Australian and New Zealand Journal of Public Health*, 27(2), 164–170.

Sanders, G.L. (1988). An invitation to escape sexual tyranny. *Journal of Strategic and Systemic Therapies*, 7(3), Fall, 23–35.

Santoro, N., Torrens, J., Crawford, S., Allsworth, J.E., Finkelstein, J.S., Gold, E.B., et al. (2005). Correlates of circulating androgens in mid-life women: The study of women's health across the nation. *Journal of Clinical Endocrinology and Metabolism*, 90(8), 4836–4845.

Smith, N.K., Jozkowski, K.N. and Sanders, S.A. (2014). Hormonal contraception and female pain, orgasm, and sexual pleasure. *Journal of Sexual Medicine*, 11, 462–470.

Sungur, M.Z. and Gunduz, A. (2014). A Comparison of DSM-IV-TR and DSM-5 Definitions for Sexual Dysfunctions: Critiques and Challenges. *Journal of Sexual Medicine*, 11(3), 364–373.

Tiefer, L. (2001). A new view of women's sexual problems: Why new? Why now? *Journal of Sex Research*, 38(2), 89–96.

Tiefer, L., Hall M. and Tavris, C. (2002). Beyond dysfunction: A new view of women's sexual problems. *Journal of Sex & Marital Therapy*, 28(Suppl.1), 225–232.

Weeks, G.R. and Gambescia, N. (2002). *Hypoactive Sexual Desire. Integrating Sex and Couple Therapy*. W.W. Norton.

Weeks, G.R. and Gambescia, N. (2015). Definition, etiology, and treatment of absent/low desire in women. In K.M. Hertlein, G.R. Weeks and N. Gambescia (Eds) (2015). *Systemic Sex Therapy* (2nd ed.). New York: Routledge.

West, S.L., D'Aloisio, A.A., Agans, R.P., Kalsbeek, W.D., Borisov, N.N. and Thorp, J.M. (2008). Prevalence of low sexual desire and hypoactive sexual desire disorder in a nationally representative sample of U.S. women. *Archives of Internal Medicine*, 168, 1441–1449.

Wincze, J.P. and Weisberg, R.B. (2015). *Sexual Dysfunction: A Guide to Assessment and Treatment* (3rd ed.). New York: The Guilford Press.

Witting, K., Santtila, P., Alanko, K., Harlaar, N., Jern, P., Johansson, A., . . . Sandnabba, N.K. (2008). Female sexual function and its associations with number of children, pregnancy, and relationship satisfaction. *Journal of Sex & Marital Therapy*, 34(2), 89–106.

Woo, J.S., Brotto, L.A. and Gorzalka, B.B. (2012) The relationship between sex guilt and sexual desire in a community sample of Chinese and Euro-Canadian women. *Journal of Sex Research*, 49, 290–298.

Zilbergeld, B. (1999). *The New Male Sexuality* (revised version). USA: Bantam Books.

Genito-pelvic pain/penetration disorder

American Psychiatric Association (APA) (2000). *Diagnostic and Statistical Manual of Mental Disorders (DSM-IV-TR)* (4th ed.). Washington DC.

American Psychiatric Association (APA) (2013). *Diagnostic and Statistical Manual of Mental Disorders (DSM)* (5th ed.). Washington DC.

Amidu, N., Owiredu, W.K., Woode, E., Addai-Mensah, O., Quaye, L., Alhassan, A., et al. (2010). Incidence of sexual dysfunction: A prospective survey in Ghanian females. *Reproductive Biology and Endocrinology*, 8, 1–6.

Bergeron, S., Rosen, N.O. and Pukall, C.F. (2014). Genital pain in women and men: It can hurt more than your sex life. In Y.M. Binik and K. Hall. (Eds) (2014). *Principles and Practice of Sex Therapy* (5th ed.). New York: The Guilford Press.

Binik, Y.M. and Hall, K. (Eds) (2014). *Principles and Practice of Sex Therapy* (5th ed.). New York: The Guilford Press.

Bond, K.S., Mpofu, E. and Millington, M. (2015). Treating women with genito-pelvic pain / penetration disorder: Influence on patient agendas on help seeking. *Journal of Family Medicine*, 2(4), 1033, 1–8.

Christensen, B.S., Gronbaek, M., Osler, M., Pedersen, B.V., Graugaard, C. and Frisch, M. (2011). Sexual dysfunctions and difficulties in Denmark: Prevalence and associated sociodemographic factors. *Archives of Sexual Behavior*, 40, 121–132.

Desrochers, G., Bergeron, S., Landry, T. and Jodoin, M. (2008). Do psychosexual factors play a role in the etiology of provoked vestibulodynia? A critical review. *Journal of Sex & Marital Therapy*, 34, 198–226.

Fugl-Meyer, K.S., Bohm-Starke, N., Damsted Petersen, C., Fugl-Meyer, A., Parish, S. and Giraldi, A. (2013). Standard operating procedures for female genital sexual pain. *Journal of Sexual Medicine*, 10, 83–93.

Harlow, B.L., Wise, L.A. and Stewart, E.G. (2001). Prevalence and predictors of chronic lower genital tract discomfort. *American Journal of Obstetrics and Gynecology*, 185, 545–550.

Hawton, K. (1985). *Sex Therapy. A Practical Guide.* Oxford University Press.

Kraft, S. (2014). What is vulvodynia? What causes vulvodynia? http://www.medicalnewstoday.com/articles/189076.php, (accessed 8 November 2016).

Lahaie, M.A., Amsel, R., Khalifé, S., Boyer, S., Faaborg-Andersen, M. and Binik, Y.M. (2015). Can fear, pain, and muscle tension discriminate vaginismus from dyspareunia/provoked vestibulodynia? Implications for the new DSM-5 diagnosis of genito-pelvic pain/penetration disorder. *Archives of Sexual Behavior*, 44(6), 1537–1550.

Landry, T. and Bergeron, S. (2011). Biopsychosocial factors associated with dyspareunia in a community sample of adolescent girls. *Archives of Sexual Behavior*, 40, 877–889.

Lindau, S.T., Gavrilova, N. and Anderson, D. (2007). Sexual morbidity in very long-term survivors of vaginal and cervical cancer: A comparison to national norms. *Gynecologic Oncology*, 106, 413–416.

Meana, M., Maykut, C and, Fertel, I. (2015). Painful intercourse: Genito-pelvic pain/ penetration disorder. In K. M. Hertlein, G.R. Weeks and N. Gambescia (Eds), *Systemic Sex Therapy* (2nd ed). New York and London: Routledge.

Nobre, P.J. and Pinto-Gouveia, J. (2008). Cognitive and emotional predictors of female sexual dysfunctions: preliminary findings. *Journal of Sex & Marital Therapy*, 34(4), 325–342.

O'Sullivan, K. (1979). Observations on vaginismus in Irish women. *Archives of Genetic Psychiatry*, 36(7), 824–826.

Payne, K.A., Binik, Y.M., Amsel, R. and Khalife, S. (2005). When sex hurts, anxiety and fear orient attention towards pain. *European Journal of Pain*, 9, 427–436.

Reissing, E.D. (2012). Consultation and treatment history and causal attributions in an online sample of women with lifelong and acquired vaginismus. *Journal of Sexual Medicine*, 9, 251–258.

Reissing, E.D., Binik, Y.M., Khalife, S., Cohen, D. and Amsel, R. (2003). Etiological correlates of vaginismus: Sexual and physical abuse, sexual knowledge, sexual self-schema and relationship adjustment. *Journal of Sex & Marital Therapy*, 29, 47–59.

ter Kulie, M.M. and Reissing, E.D. (2014). Lifelong vaginismus. In Y.M. Binik and K. Hall. (Eds) (2014), *Principles and Practice of Sex Therapy* (5th ed.). New York: The Guilford Press.

Van Lankveld, J.J., Granot, M., Weijmar Schulz, W.C., Binik, Y.M., Wessleman, U., Pukall, C.F., et al. (2010). Women's sexual pain disorders. *Journal of Sexual Medicine*, 7, 615–631.

Vlaeyen, J.W. and Linton, S.J. (2000). Fear-avoidance and its consequences in chronic muscosceletal pain: A state of the art. *Pain*, 85, 317–332.

Weeks, G.R., Gambescia, N. (2015). Definition, etiology, and treatment of absent / low desire in women. In K.M. Hertlein, G.R. Weeks and N. Gambescia (Eds), *Systemic Sex Therapy*. New York and London: Routledge.

Wincze, J.P. and Weisberg, R.B. (2015). *Sexual Dysfunction: A Guide to Assessment and Treatment*. (3rd ed.). New York: The Guilford Press.

World Health Organization (WHO) (2010). ICD-10 Classification of Mental and Behavioural Disorders. Clinical Descriptions and Diagnostic Guidelines. Geneva. World Health Organisation.

Male hypoactive sexual desire disorder

American Psychiatric Association (APA) (1980). *Diagnostic and Statistical Manual of Mental Disorders (DSM-III)* (3rd ed.). Washington DC.

American Psychiatric Association (APA) (1987). *Diagnostic and Statistical Manual of Mental Disorders (DSM-III)* (3rd ed.). Washington DC.

American Psychiatric Association (APA) (2000). *Diagnostic and Statistical Manual of Mental Disorders (DSM-IV-TR)* (4th ed.). Washington DC.

American Psychiatric Association (APA) (2013). *Diagnostic and Statistical Manual of Mental Disorders (DSM)* (5th ed.). Washington DC.

Asexuality Visibility and Education Network (AVEN; http://www.asexuality.org).

Bancroft, J. (2009). *Human Sexuality and Its Problems* (3rd ed.). Oxford: Elsevier.

Bancroft, J., Janssen, E., Strong, D. and Vukadinovic, Z. (2003a). The relation between mood and sexuality in gay men. *Archives of Sexual Behavior*, 32, 231–242.

Bancroft, J., Janssen, E., Strong, D., Carnes, L., Vukadinovic, Z. and Long, J.S. (2003b). The relation between mood and sexuality in heterosexual men. *Archives of Sexual Behavior*, 32, 217–30.

Basson, R. (2002). Rethinking low sexual desire in women. *International Journal of Obstetrics and Gynaecology*, 109(4), 357–363.

Basson, R. (2005). Women sexual dysfunctions: revised and expanded definitions. *Canadian Medical Association Journal*, 172(10), doi: 10.1503/cmaj.1020174.

Baumeister, R.F., Catanese, K.R and Vohs, K.D. (2001). Is there a gender difference in strength of sex drive? Theoretical views, conceptual distinctions, and a review of relevant evidence. *Personality and Social Psychology Review*, 5, 242–273.

Beck, J.G., Bozman, A.W. and Qualtrough, T. (1991). The experience of sexual desire: Psychological correlates in a college sample. *Journal of Sex Research*, 28, 443–456.

Brotto, L.A. (2010). The DSM diagnostic criteria for hypoactive desire disorder in men. *Journal of Sexual Medicine*, 7, 2015–2030.

Carvalho, J. and Nobre, P. (2011). Predictors of men's sexual desire: The role of psychological, cognitive-emotional, relational, and medical factors. *Journal of Sex Research*, 48(2–3), 254–262.

Conaglen, J.V. and Conaglen, H.M. (2009). The effects of treating male hypogonadism on couples' sexual desire and function. *Journal of Sexual Medicine* 6, 456–463.

Corona, G., Mannucci, E., Petrone, L., Giomni, R., Mansani, R., Fei, L, et al. (2004). Psycho-biological correlates of hypoactive sexual desire in patients with erectile dysfunction. *International Journal of Impotence Research*, 16, 275–281.

Eplov L, Giraldi A, Davidsen M, Garde K and Kamper-Jørgensen, F. (2007). Sexual desire in a nationally representative Danish population. *Journal of Sexual Medicine*, 4, 47–56.

Fugl-Meyer, A. and Sjorgen, K. (1999). Sexual disabilities, problems and satisfaction in 18–74 year old Swedes. *Scandinavian Journal of Sexology*, 2, 79–105.

Hall, K. (2015). Male hypoactive sexual desire disorder. In Y.M. Binik and S.K. Hall (Eds), *Principles and Practice of Sex Therapy* (5th ed.). New York: Guilford Press.

Hare-Mustin, R.T. and Marecek, J. (1988). The meaning of difference: Gender theory, postmodernism, and psychology. *American Psychologist*, 43(6), 455–464.

Hertlein, K.M, Weeks, G.R. and Gambescia, N. (Eds) (2015). *Systemic Sex Therapy* (2nd ed.) New York: Routledge.

Hoffmann, W. and Nordgren, L. (2015). *The Psychology of Desire*. New York: Guilford Press.

Hyde, J.S. (2007). New directions in the study of gender similarities and differences. *Current Directions in Psychological Science*, 16, 259–263.

Irvine, J. (2005). *Disorders of Desire: Sexuality and Gender in Modern American Sexology*. Philadelphia: Temple University Press.

Janssen, E., McBride, K., Yarber, W., Hill, B. and Butler, S. (2008). Factors that influence sexual arousal in men: A focus group study. *Archives of Sexual Behavior*, 37, 252–265.

Kedde, H., Donker, G., Leusink, P.and Kruijer, H. (2011). The incidence of sexual dysfunction in patients attending Dutch general practitioners. *International Journal of Sexual Health*, 23(4), 269–277.

Laan, E. and Both, S. (2008). What makes women experience desire? *Feminism Psychology*, 18(4), 505–514.

Laumann, E.O., Paik, A., Glasser, D.B., Kang, J-H., Wang, T., Levinson, B., Moreira Jr, E.D., Nicolosi, A. and Gingell, C. (2006). A cross-national study of subjective sexual well-being among older women and men: Findings from the global study of sexual attitudes and behaviors. *Archives of Sexual Behavior*, 35(2), 143–159.

Lew-Starowicz, M. and Rafal, R. (2014). Sexual dysfunctions and sexual quality of life in men with multiple sclerosis. *Journal of Sexual Medicine*, 11(5), 1294–1301.

Lykins, A.D., Janssen, E. and Graham, C.A. (2005). The relationship between negative mood and sexuality in heterosexual college women and men. *The Journal of Sex Research*, 43(2), 136–143.

McCabe, M. and Connaughton, C. (2014). Psychosocial factors associated with male sexual difficulties. *Journal of Sex Research*, 51(1), 31–42.

Meana, M. and Steiner, E.T. (2014). Hidden disorder/hidden desire. Presentations of low sexual desire in men. In Y.M. Binik and S.K. Hall (Eds), *Principles and Practice of Sex Therapy* (5th ed.). New York: Guilford Press.

Mercer, C.H., Fenton, K.A., Johnson, A.M., Wellings, K., Macdowall, W., McManus, S., Nanchahal, K. and Erens, B. (2003). Sexual function problems and help seeking behaviour in Britain: National probability sample survey. *British Medical Journal*, 327, 426–427.

Najman, J.M., Dunne, M.P., Boyle, F.M., Cook, M.D. and Purdie, D.M. (2003). Sexual dysfunction in the Australian population. *Australian Family Physician*, 32, 951–954.

Nutter, D.E. and Condron, M.K. (1985). Sexual fantasy and activity patterns of males with inhibited sexual desire and males with erectile dysfunction versus normal controls. *Journal of Sex & Marital Therapy*, 11, 91–98.

O'Toole, A., Winter, D. and Friedman, S. (2014). The psychosexual impact of inflammatory bowel disease in male patients. *Alimentary Pharmacology & Therapeutics*, 39(10), 1085–1094.

Regan, P.C. (2013). Sexual desire in women. In D. Castañeda (Ed.), *The Essential Handbook of Women's Sexuality* (Vol. 1). Santa Barbara, CA: Praeger.

Regan, P.C. and Atkins, L. (2006). Sex differences and similarities in frequency and intensity of sexual desire. *Journal of Social Behavior and Personality*, 34, 95–102.

Sanders, G.L. (1994). Kensington Consultation Centre Workshop, London.

Scherrer, K.S. (2008). Coming to an asexual identity: Negotiating identity, negotiating desire. *Sexualities*, 11, 621–641.

Schnarch, D. (2009). *Intimacy & Desire. Awaken the Passion in Your Relationship*. New York: Beaufort Books. Sterling Productions.

Schnarch, D.M. (2000). Sexual desire: A systemic perspective. In S.R. Leiblum and R. C. Rosen (Eds), *Principles and Practice of Sex Therapy* (3rd ed.). New York: Guilford Press.

Sungur, M.Z. and Gunduz, A. (2014). A comparison of DSM-IV-TR and DSM-5 definitions for sexual dysfunctions: Critiques and challenges. *Journal of Sexual Medicine*, 11(2), 364–373.

Weeks, G.R. and Gambescia, N. (2002). *Hypoactive Sexual Desire. Integrating Sex and Couple Therapy*. W.W. Norton.

White, M. (2007). *Maps of Narrative Practice*. WW Norton & Company.

Wincze, J.P. and Carey, M.P. (2001). *Sexual Dysfunction: A Guide to Assessment and Treatment* (2nd ed.). New York, London: The Guilford Press.

Wincze, J.P. and Weisberg, R.B. (2015). *Sexual Dysfunction: A Guide to Assessment and Treatment* (3rd ed.). New York: The Guilford Press.

Zilbergeld, B. (1999). *The New Male Sexuality* (revised version). USA: Bantam Books.

Premature/early ejaculation

Abdo, C.H.N. (2013). Treatment of premature ejaculation with cognitive therapy. In E. Jannini, C. McMahon and M. Waldinger (Eds), *Premature Ejaculation: From Etiology to Diagnosis and Treatment*. Italy: Springer-Verlag.

Althof, S., Abdo, C., Dean, J., Hackett, G., McCabe, M., McMahon, C, et al. (2010). International Society for Sexual Medicine guidelines for the diagnosis and treatment of PE. *Journal of Sexual Medicine, 7*, 2847–2969.

Althof, S.E. (2014). Treatment of premature ejaculation. Psychotherapy, pharmacotherapy, and combined therapy. In Y.M. Binik and S.K. Hall (Eds), *Principles and Practice of Sex therapy* (5th ed.). New York: Guilford Press.

American Psychiatric Association (APA) (2000). *Diagnostic and Statistical Manual of Mental Disorders (DSM-IV-TR)* (4th ed.). Washington DC.

American Psychiatric Association (APA) (2013). *Diagnostic and Statistical Manual of Mental Disorders (DSM)* (5th ed.). Washington DC.

American Urological Association (AUA) (n.d.). www.auanet.org, accessed 13 April 2017.

Arachal, B.S. and Benegal, V. (2007). Prevalence in sexual dysfunction in male subjects with alcohol dependence. *Indian Journal of Psychiatry*, 49, 109–112.

Assalian P. (1994). Premature ejaculation: is it psychogenic? *Journal of Sexual Medicine*, 20, 1–4.

Athanasiadis, L. (1998). Premature ejaculation: Is it a biogenic or a psychogenic disorder? *Journal of Sex & Marital Therapy*, 13, 241–255.

Byers, E.S. and Grenier, G. (2003). Premature or rapid ejaculation: Heterosexual couples' perceptions of men's ejaculatory behavior. *Archives of Sexual Behavior*, 32(3), 261–270.

Corona, G., Jannini, E.A., Lotti, F., Boddi, V., De Vita, G., Forti, G., et al. (2011). Premature and delayed ejaculation: Two ends of a single continuum influenced by hormonal milieu. *International Journal of Andrology*, 34(1), 41–48.

Hartmann, U., Schedlowski, M. and Kruger, T.H. (2005). Cognitive and partner-related factors in rapid ejaculation: Differences between dysfunctional and functional men. *World Journal of Urology*, 23(2), 93–101.

Hawton, K. (1985). *Sex Therapy. A Practical Guide*. Oxford University Press.

Hong, L.K. (1984). Survival of the fastest: On the origin of premature ejaculation. *Journal of Sex Research*, 20, 109–122.

Huhner, M. (1917). *A Practical Treatise on Disorders of the Sexual Function in the Male and Female*. Philadelphia: F.A. Davis.

Metz, M. and McCarthy, B. (2003). *Coping With Premature Ejaculation: How to Overcome PE, Please Your Partner and Have Great Sex*. Oakland, CA: New Harbinger Publications.

Metz, M.E. and Pryor, J.L. (2000). Premature ejaculation: A psychophysiological approach for assessment and management. *Journal of Sex & Marital Therapy*, 26(4), 293–320.

Metz, M.E., Pryor, J.L., Nesvacil, L.J., Abuzzahab, F., Sr and Koznar, J. (1997). Premature ejaculation: A psychophysiological review. *Journal of Sex & Marital Therapy*, 23, 3–23.

Rowland, D., Cooper, S. (2013). Risk factors for premature ejaculation: The intrapsychic risk factor. In E. Jannini, C. McMahon and M. Waldinger (Eds), *Premature Ejaculation: From Etiology to Diagnosis and Treatment*. Italy: Springer-Verlag.

Rowland, D.L., Cooper, S.E. and Schneider M. (2001). Defining premature ejaculation for experimental and clinical investigations. *Archives of Sexual Behavior*, 30(3), 235–253.

Waldinger, M.D. (2007). Premature ejaculation: Definition and drug treatment. *Drugs*, 67(4), 547–568.

Wincze, J.P. and Carey, M.P. (2001). *Sexual Dysfunction: A Guide to Assessment and Treatment* (2nd ed.). New York, London: The Guilford Press.

Wincze, J.P. and Weisberg, R.B. (2015). *Sexual Dysfunction: A Guide to Assessment and Treatment* (3rd ed.). New York: The Guilford Press.

World Health Organization (WHO) (1992). *The ICD-10 Classification of Mental and Behavioural Disorders: Clinical Descriptors and Diagnostic Guidelines*. Geneva: World Health Organization.

World Health Organization (WHO) (2004). *International Statistical Classification of Diseases and Health Related Problems: ICD-10* (2nd ed.). Geneva: World Health Organization.

Zilbergeld, B. (1999). *The New Male Sexuality* (revised version). USA: Bantam Books.

Persistent genital arousal disorder

American Psychiatric Association (APA) (2000). *Diagnostic and Statistical Manual of Mental Disorders (DSM-IV-TR)* (4th ed.). Washington DC.

American Psychiatric Association (APA) (2013). *Diagnostic and Statistical Manual of Mental Disorders (DSM)* (5th ed.). Washington DC.

Basson, R., Leiblum, S., Brotto, L., Derogatis, L., Fourcroy, J., Fugl-Meyer, K., Graziotin, A., Heiman, J., Laan, E., Meston, C., van Lankveld, J., Schover, L. and Weijmar Schultz, W. (2004). Revised definitions of women's sexual dysfunction. *The Journal of Sexual Medicine*, 1(1), 40–48.

Goldmeier, D., Sadeghi-Nejad, H. and Facelle, T.M. (2014). Persistent genital arousal disorder. In Y.M. Binik and S.K. Hall (Eds), *Principles and Practice of Sex Therapy* (5th ed.). New York: Guilford Press.

Komisaruk, B.R. and Lee, H.J. (2012). Prevalence of sacral spinal (Tarlov) cysts in persistent genital arousal disorder. *The Journal of Sexual Medicine*, 9(8), 2047–2056.

Leiblum, S.R and Chivers, M.L. (2007). Normal and persistent genital arousal in women: New perspectives. *Journal of Sex & Marital Therapy*, 33(4), 357–373.

Leiblum, S.R. and Nathan, S.G. (2001). Persistent sexual arousal syndrome: A newly discovered pattern of female sexuality. *Journal of Sex & Marital Therapy*, 27(4), 365–380.

Leiblum, S.R, Seehuus, M. and Brown, C. (2007). Persistent genital arousal: Disordered or normative aspect of female sexual response? *Journal of Sexual Medicine*, 4(3), 680–689.

Sexual aversion disorder

American Psychiatric Association (APA) (1987). *Diagnostic and Statistical Manual of Mental Disorders (DSM-III)* (3rd ed.). Washington DC.

American Psychiatric Association (APA) (2000). *Diagnostic and Statistical Manual of Mental Disorders (DSM-IV-TR)* (4th ed.). Washington DC.

American Psychiatric Association (APA) (2013). *Diagnostic and Statistical Manual of Mental Disorders (DSM)* (5th ed.). Washington DC.

Badour, C.L. and Feldner, M.T. (2016). Disgust and imaginal exposure to memories of sexual trauma: Implications for the treatment of posttraumatic stress. *Psychological Trauma: Theory, Research, Practice, and Policy*, 8, 267–275.

Bakker, F. and Vanwezenbeek, I. (2006). *Seksuele gezondheid in Nederland 2006 [RNG-studies nr. 9]*. Delft: Eburon.

Barlow, D.H. (Ed.) (2008). *Clinical Handbook of Psychological Disorders. A Step-by-step Treatment Manual* (4th ed.). New York, London: The Guilford Press.

Borg, C., de Jong, P.J. and Elgersma, H. (2014). Sexual aversion and the DSM-5: An excluded disorder with unabated relevance as a trans-diagnostic symptom, *Archives of Sexual Behavior*, 43(7), 1219–1223.

Borg, C., de Jong, P.J. and Weijmar Schultz, W. (2011). Vaginismus and dyspareunia: Relationship with general and sex-related moral standards. *Journal of Sexual Medicine*, 8, 223–231.

Brotto, L.A. (2010). The DSM diagnostic criteria for sexual aversion disorder. *Archives of Sexual Behavior*, 39, 271–277.

Carnes, P.J. (1997). The case for sexual anorexia: An interim report on 144 patients with sexual disorders. *Sexual Addiction & Compulsivity: The Journal of Treatment and Prevention*, 5(4), 293–309.

Carnes, P.J. (1997). *Sexual Anorexia: Overcoming Sexual Self-Hatred.* Hazelden Publishing.

Coughtrey, A.E., Shafran, R., Lee, M. and Rachman, S. (2013). The treatment of mental contamination: A case series. *Cognitive and Behavioral Practice*, 20, 221–231.

Crenshaw, T. (1985). The sexual aversion syndrome. *Journal of Sex & Marital Therapy* 11(4), 285–292.

Janata, J.W. and Kingsberg, S.A. (2005). Sexual aversion disorder. In R. Balon and R.T. Segraves (Eds), *Handbook of Sexual Dysfunction*. Boca Raton: Taylor and Francis Group.

Kaplan, H.S. (1987). *Sexual Aversion, Sexual Phobias, and Panic Disorders.* New York: Brunner/Mazel.

Kingsberg, S.A. and Janata, J.W. (2003). The sexual aversions. In S. B. Levine, C. B. Risen and S. E. Althof (Eds), *Handbook of Clinical Sexuality for Mental Health Professionals*. New York: Brunner-Routledge.

Kedde, H. (2012). Seksuele disfuncties in Nederland: Prevalentie en samenhangende factoren. *Tijdschrift voor Seksuologie*, 36, 98–108.

Kort, J. (2004). Kort's corner no. 24. www.korts_korner_sexual_anorexia.pdf (accessed 22 December 2016).

Mason, E.C. and Richardson, R. (2012). Treating disgust in anxiety disorders. *Clinical Psychology Science and Practice*, 19(2), 180–194.

Tiefer, L. (2001). A new view of women's sexual problems: Why new? Why now? *Journal of Sex Research*, 38(2), 89–96.

Tiefer, L., Hall M. and Tavris, C. (2002). Beyond dysfunction: A new view of women's sexual problems. *Journal of Sex & Marital Therapy*, 28(Suppl.1), 225–232.

Weeks, G.R., Gambescia, N. and Hertlein, K.M. (Eds) (2016). *A Clinician's Guide to Systemic Sex Therapy*. (2nd ed.). New York and London: Routledge.

Wylie, K., Markovic, D. and Hallam-Jones, R. (2015). Inhibited arousal in women Chapter 9. In K.M. Hertlein, G.R. Weeks and N. Gambescia (Eds), *Systemic Sex Therapy* (2nd ed.). New York: Routledge.

Sexual compulsivity, addiction or hypersexuality

AASECT (2016). AASECT position on sex addiction. https://www.aasect.org/position-sex-addiction (accessed 16 May 2017).

American Psychiatric Association (APA) (1980). *Diagnostic and Statistical Manual of Mental Disorders (DSM-III)* (3rd ed.). Washington DC.

American Psychiatric Association (APA) (2000). *Diagnostic and Statistical Manual of Mental Disorders (DSM-IV-TR)* (4th ed.). Washington DC.

American Psychiatric Association (APA) (2013). *Diagnostic and Statistical Manual of Mental Disorders (DSM)* (5th ed.). Washington DC.

Bancroft, J. (2008). Sexual behavior that is 'out of control': A theoretical conceptual approach. *Psychiatric Clinics of North America*, 31(4), 593–601.

Bancroft, J., Janssen, E., Strong, D. and Vukadinovic, Z. (2003a). The relation between mood and sexuality in gay men. *Archives of Sexual Behavior, 32*, 231–242.

Bancroft, J., Janssen, E., Strong, D., Carnes, L., Vukadinovic, Z. and Long, J.S. (2003b). The relation between mood and sexuality in heterosexual men. *Archives of Sexual Behavior, 32*, 217–230.

Barth, R.J. and Kinder, B.N. (1987). The mislabeling of sexual impulsivity. *Journal of Sex & Marital Therapy*, 13(1), 15–23.

Black, D.W., Kehrberg, L.L.D., Flumerfelt, D.L. and Schlosser, S.S. (1997). Characteristics of 36 subjects reporting compulsive sexual behaviour. *American Journal of Psychiatry*, 154, 243–249.

Braun-Harvey, D. and Vigorito, M.A. (2016). *Treating Out of Control Sexual Behavior. Rethinking Sex Addiction.* New York: Springer Publishing Company.

Carnes, P.J. (1983). *Out of the Shadows.* Minneapolis: Compcare.

Carnes, P.J. (1992). *Don't Call it Love: Recovery from Sexual Addiction.* New York: Bantam.

Carnes, P.J. (1997) *Sexual Anorexia. Overcoming Sexual Self-Hatred.* Minnesota: Hazelden Publishing.

Coleman, E. (1986). Sexual compulsion vs. sexual addiction: The debate continues. *SIECUS Report*, 14(6), 7–11.

Coleman, E. (1995). Treatment of compulsive sexual behaviour. In R.C. Rosen and S.R. Leiblum (Eds), *Case Studies in Sex Therapy.* New York: Guilford Press.

Cooper, A., Delmonico, D. and Burg, R. (2000). Cybersex users, abusers, and compulsives: New findings and implications. In A. Cooper (Ed.), *Cybersex: The Dark Side of the Force.* Philadelphia: Brunner: Routledge.

Davidson, C.K.D., Cheung, G. and Jansen, K. (2017). Hypersexuality in psychiatric conditions observer-rated scale (HIPCORS): Evaluation of reliability and validity. *Journal of Sex & Marital Therapy*, 43(3), 277–287.

Davies, D. (2016). I'm too sexy: Reconsidering sexual addiction as a valid concept for gay and bi men who feel out of control. www.pinktherapy.com/portals/0/Courseresources/cardiff_sa_presentation.pdf, accessed 12 December 2016.

Delmonico, D.L. and Griffin, E.J. (2015). Sexual compulsivity: Diagnosis, assessment and treatment. In K.M. Hertlein, G.R. Weeks and N. Gambescia, *Systemic Sex Therapy* (2nd ed.). New York and East Sussex: Routledge.

Fong, T.W. (2006). Understanding and managing compulsive sexual behaviors. *Psychiatry (Edgmont)*, 3(11), 51–58.

Foucault, M. (1998). *The History of Sexuality: The Will to Knowledge*. London: Penguin.

Goodman, A. (1990). Addiction: Definition and implications. *British Journal of Psychiatry*, 85, 1403–1408.

Goodman, A. (2001). What's in a name? Terminology for designating a syndrome of driven sexual behavior. *Sexual Addiction and Compulsivity*, 8(3–4), 191–213.

Griffiths, M. (2004). Sex addiction on the Internet. *Janus Head*, 7(1), 188–217.

Hagedorn, W.B., Juhnke, G.A. (2005). Treating the sexually addicted client: Establishing a need for increased counselor awareness. *Journal of Addictions & Offender Counseling*, 25, 66–86.

Hilton, D. and Watts, C. (2011). Pornography addiction: A neuroscience perspective. *Surgical Neurology International*, 2,(19), 1–4.

Janssen, E. and Bancroft, J. (2007). The dual control model: The role of sexual inhibition & excitation in sexual arousal and behaviour. In E. Janssen (Ed.). (2007), *The Psychophysiology of Sex*. Bloomington: Indiana University Press.

Kafka, M. (2010). Hypersexual disorder: A proposed diagnosis for DSM-V. *Archives of Sexual Behavior*, 39(2), 377–400.

Kafka, M.P. (2014). Nonparaphilic hypersexuality disorders. In Y.M. Binik and S.K. Hall (Eds), *Principles and Practice of Sex Therapy* (5th ed.). New York: Guilford Press.

Kafka, M.P. and Hennen, J. (2003). Hypersexual desire in males: Are males with paraphilias different from males with paraphilia-related disorders? *Sexual Abuse*, 15, 307–321.

Kaplan, M.S. and Krueger, R.B. (2010). Diagnosis, assessment, and treatment of hypersexuality. *Journal of Sex Research*, 47, 181–198.

Keane, H. (2004). Disorders of desire: Addiction and problems of intimacy. *Journal of Medical Humanities, 25*, 189–204.

Kleinplatz, P. (2014). The paraphilias: An experiential approach to 'dangerous' desires. In Y.M. Binik and K. Hall (Eds) (2014), *Principles and Practice of Sex Therapy* (5th ed.). New York: The Guilford Press.

Kohut, H. (1977). *The Restoration of the Self.* New York: International University Press.

Krafft-Ebing, R. (1965). *Psychopathia Sexualis*. New York: Putnam. (Original work published 1886).

Ley, D., Prause, N. and Finn, P. (2014). The emperor has no clothes: A review of the 'pornography addiction' model. *Current Sexual Health Reports*, 6(2), 94–105.

Manning, J.C. (2006). The impact of Internet pornography on marriage and the family: A review of the research. *Sexual Addiction & Compulsivity*, 13, 131–165.

McCarthy, B. and McCarthy, E. (2012). *Sexual Awareness: Your Guide to Healthy Couple Sexuality* (5th ed.). Routledge.

Money, J. (1986). *Lovemaps*. Amherst, New York: Prometheus Books.

Nobre, P.D. and Pinto-Gouveia, J. (2009). Cognitive schemas associated with negative sexual events: A comparison of men and women with and without sexual dysfunction. *Archives of Sexual Behavior*, 38(5), 842–851.

Plummer, K. (Ed.). (2002). *Sexualities: Critical Assessments*. Four Volumes. London: Routledge.

Quadland, M.C. (1985). Compulsive sexual behaviour: Definition of a problem and an approach to treatment. *Journal of Sex & Marital Therapy*, 11, 121–132.

Reid, R.C., Carpenter, B.N. and Lloyd, Q. (2009). Assessing psychological symptom patterns of patients seeking help for hypersexual behaviour. *Sexual and Relationship Therapy*, 24(1), 47–63.

Schneider, J.P. (2000). Effects of cybersex addiction on the family: Results of a survey. In A. Cooper (Ed.), *Cybersex: The Dark Side of the Force*. Philadelphia: Brunner: Routledge.

Skegg, K., Nada-Raja, S., Dickson, N. and Paul, C. (2010). Perceived 'out of control' sexual behavior in a cohort of young adults from the Dunedin Multidisciplinary Health and Development Study. *Archives of Sexual Behavior*, 39(4), 968–978.

Tiefer, L. (2004). *Sex is Not a Natural Act & Other Essays* (2nd ed.). Boulder, CO: Westview Press.

Wolfe, J.L. (2000). Assessment and treatment of compulsive sex/love behavior. *Journal of Rational-emotive and Cognitive-behavior Therapy*, 18(4), 235–246.

World Health Organization (WHO) (2006). *Defining Sexual Health: Report of a Technical Consultation on Sexual Health 28–31 January 2002*. Geneva, Switzerland: Author.

Dyspareunia in men

American Psychiatric Association (APA) (2000). *Diagnostic and Statistical Manual of Mental Disorders (DSM-IV-TR)* (4th ed.). Washington DC.

American Psychiatric Association (APA) (2013). *Diagnostic and Statistical Manual of Mental Disorders (DSM)* (5th ed.). Washington DC.

Aviva Medical Dictionary. www.aviva.co.uk/medicalencyclopedia/painfulinter courseinmen (accessed 21 January 2017).

Bergeron, S., Rosen, N.O. and Pukall, C.F. (2014). Genital pain in women and men: It can hurt more than your sex life. In Y.M. Binik and S.K. Hall (Eds), *Principles and Practice of Sex Therapy* (5th ed.). New York: Guilford Press.

Blanker, M.H., Ruud Bosch, J.L.H., Groenveld, F.P.M.J., Bohnen, A.M., Prins, A., Thomas, S. and Hop, W.C.J. (2001). Erectile and ejaculatory dysfunction in a community-based sample of 50 to 78 years old: Prevalence, concern, and relation to sexual activity. *Urology*, 57(4), 763–768.

Collins, M.M., Stafford, R.S., O'Leary, M.P. and Barry, M.J. (1999). Distinguishing chronic prostatitis and benign prostatic hyperplasia symptoms: Results of a national survey of physician visits. *Urology*, 53(5), 921–925.

Damon, W. and Rosser, B.R. (2005). Anodyspareunia in men who have sex with men: Prevalence, predictors, consequences and the development of DSM criteria. *Journal of Sex & Marital Therapy*, 31, 129–141.

Davis, S.N.P., Morin, M., Binik, Y.M., Khalife, S. and Carrier, S. (2011). Use of pelvic floor ultrasound to assess pelvic floor muscle function in urological chronic pelvic pain syndrome in men. *Journal of Sexual Medicine*, 8, 3173–3180.

Herbenick, D., Schick, V., Sandres, S.A., Reece, M. and Fortenberry, J.D. (2015). Pain experienced during vaginal and anal intercourse with other-sex partners: findings from a nationally representative probability study in the United States. *Journal of Sexual Medicine*, 12(4), 1040–1051.

Hollows, K. (2007). Anodyspareunia: a novel sexual dysfunction? An exploration into anal sexuality. *Sexual and Relationship Therapy*, 22(4), 429–443.

Johnson, A.M., Mercer, C.H., Erens, B., Copas, A.J., McManus, S., Wellings, K., Fenton, K.A., Korovessis, C., Macdowall, W., Nanchahal, K., Purdon, S. and Field, J. (2001). Sexual behaviour in Britain: Partnerships, practices, and HIV risk behaviours: Findings from the *National Surveys of Sexual Attitudes and Lifestyles (Natsal). The Lancet*, 358, 1835–1842.

Kaplan, H.S. (1993). Post-ejaculatory pain syndrome. *Journal of Sex & Marital Therapy*, 19(2), 91–103.

Luzzi, G. and Law, L. (2005). A guide to sexual pain in men. *The Practitioner*, 249(1667), 73–75.

Luzzi, G.A. and Law, L.A. (2006). The male sexual pain syndromes. *International Journal of STD & AIDS*, 17(11), 720–726.

Meana, M., Maykut, C. and Fertel, I. (2015). Painful intercourse: Genito-pelvic pain/penetration disorder. In K.M. Hertlein, G.R. Weeks and N. Gambescia (Eds), *Systemic Sex Therapy* (2nd ed.). New York and London: Routledge.

Mercer, C.H., Tanton, C., Prah, P., Erens, B., Sonnenberg, P., Clifton, S., Macdowall, W., Lewis, R., Field, N., Datta, J., Copas, A.J., Phelps, A., Wellings, K. and Johnson, A.M. (2013). Changes in sexual attitudes and lifestyles in Britain through the life course and over time: Findings from the *National Surveys of Sexual Attitudes and Lifestyles (Natsal). Lancet*, 382(9907), 1757–1856.

Mosher, W.D., Chandra, A. and Jones, J. (2005). Sexual behavior and selected health measures: Men and women 15–44 years of age, United States, 2002. *Advance Data from Vital and Health Statistics*, 362, 1–55.

Nobre, P.D. and Pinto-Gouveia, J. (2009). Cognitive schemas associated with negative sexual events: A comparison of men and women with and without sexual dysfunction. *Archives of Sexual Behavior*, 38(5), 842–851.

Oommen, M. and Hellstrom, W.J.G. (2010). Male Dyspareunia. www.uptodate.com/contents/male-dyspareunia (accessed 27 April 2017).

Pitts, M.K., Ferris, J.A., Smith, A.M., Shelley, J.M., and Richters, J. (2008). Prevalence and correlates of three types of pelvic pain in a nationally representative sample of Australian women. *Journal of Sexual Medicine*, 5(5), 1223–1229.

Rosser, B.R.S., Metz, M.E., Bockting, W.O. and Buroker, T. (1997). Sexual difficulties, concerns, and satisfaction in homosexual men: An empirical study with implications for HIV prevention. *Journal of Sex & Marital Therapy*, 23, 61–73.

Rosser, B.R.S., Short, B.J., Thurmes, P.J. and Coleman, E. (1998). Anodyspareunia, the unacknowledged sexual dysfunction: A validation study of painful receptive anal intercourse and its psychosexual concomitants in homosexual men. *Journal of Sex & Marital Therapy*, 24, 281–292.

Shoskes, D.A., Nickel, J.C., Rackley, R.R. and Pontari, M.A. (2009). Clinical phenotyping in chronic prostatitis/chronic pelvic pain syndrome and interstial cystitis: A management strategy for urologic chronic pelvic pain syndromes. *Prostate Cancer and Prostatic Diseases*, 12, 177–183.

Sigma Research (2006). Vital statistics 2005 – the UK gay men's sex survey: England Strategic Health Authorities data report (online). UK: Sigma Research. www.sigmaresearch.org.uk/gmss/year/yr2006 (accessed 21 January 2017).

Underwood, S.G. (2003). *Gay Men and Anal Eroticism: Tops, Bottoms and Versatiles*. New York: The Haworth Press Inc.

Vlaeyen, J.W. and Linton, S.J. (2000). Fear-avoidance and its consequences in chronic musculoskeletal pain: A state of the art. *Pain*, 85, 317–332.

Wu, L.X., Liang, C.Z., Hao, Z.Y., Guo, Q.K., Liu, C., and Tang, Z.G. (2006). Epidemiological study of chronic prostatitis patients with depression symptoms. *Zhonghua nan ke xue= National journal of andrology*, 12(7), 583–586.

Assessment: discussion and conclusions

Anderson, H. and Goolishian, H.A. (1992). The client is the expert: A not-knowing approach to therapy. In S. McNamee and K. J. Gergen (Eds), *Therapy as Social Construction*. Newbury Park, CA: Sage Publications, Inc.

Foucault, M. (1980) *Power / Knowledge*. New York: Pantheon Books.

Gergen, K.J., Hoffman, L. and Anderson, H. (1996). Is diagnosis a disaster? A constructionist trialogue. In F. W. Kaslow (Ed.), *Handbook of Relational Diagnosis and Dysfunctional Family Patterns*. Oxford: John Wiley.

Radovanovic (now Markovic), D. (1994). Prisoners of identity: Interview with Dr Gianfranco Cecchin: *Human Systems, The Journal of Systemic Consultation and Management*, 4, 3–18.

Tiefer, L. (Ed.) (2004). *Sex Is Not a Natural Act and Other Essays*. (2nd ed.) Boulder: Westview Press.

White, M. (2007). *Maps of Narrative Practice*. New York, NY: W. W. Norton.

Formulation in systemic psychosexual therapy

Carter, B. and McGoldrick, M. (Eds) (1999). *The Expanded Family Life Cycle. Individual, Family, and Social Perspectives*. (3rd ed.) Allyn & Bacon.

Gergen, K.J., Hoffman, L. and Anderson, H. (1996). Is diagnosis a disaster? A constructionist trialogue. In F.W. Kaslow (Ed.), *Handbook of Relational Diagnosis and Dysfunctional Family Patterns*. Oxford: John Wiley.

Johnstone, L. and Dallos, R. (Eds) (2012). *Formulation in Psychology and Psychotherapy* (2nd ed.). London: Routledge.

McAdam,E. (1995). Tuning into the voice of influence: the social construction of therapy with children. *Human systems: The Journal of Systemic Consultation & Management*, 6(3–4), 171–188.

Markovic, D. (2010). A case of enhancing sexual confidence: Both the client and the therapist are the experts. *Australian and New Zealand Journal of Family Therapy*, 31(1), 13–24.

McNamee, S. and Gergen, K.J. (Eds) (1992). *Therapy as Social Construction.* Sage: London.

Pearce, W.B. (1994). *Interpersonal Communication: Making Social Worlds*. New York: Harper Collins.

Vetere, A. and Dallos, R. (2003). *Working Systemically with Families: Formulation, Intervention and Evaluation*. London: Karnac Books.

White, M. (1991). Deconstruction and therapy. *Dulwich Centre Newsletter*, 3, 21–40.

Wincze, J.P. and Weisberg, R.B. (2015). *Sexual Dysfunction: A Guide to Assessment and Treatment* (3rd ed.). New York: The Guilford Press.

Chapter 5: Treatment options for sexual dysfunctions

Introduction

Bandler, R. and Grinder, J. (1982). *ReFraming - NLP and the Transformation of Meaning*. Real People Press.

Bowlby, J. (1969). *Attachment and Loss: Volume I: Attachment*. The International Psycho-Analytic Library, 79, 1–401. London: The Hogarth Press and the Institute of Psychoanalysis.

Burnham, J. (2011). Development in Social GRRRAAACCEEESSS: Visible-invisible and voiced-unvoiced. In I.B. Krause (Ed.), *Culture and Reflexivity in Systemic Psychotherapy: Mutual Perspectives*. London: Karnac.

Carlson, J. and Lorelle, S. (2016a). The daily dialogue. In G.R. Weeks, S.T. Fife and C.M. Peterson (Eds), *Techniques for the Couple Therapist. Essential Interventions From the Experts*. New York, Oxford: Routledge.

Carlson, J. and Lorelle, S. (2016b). Taking ownership. In G.R. Weeks, S.T. Fife and C.M. Peterson (Eds), *Techniques for the Couple Therapist. Essential Interventions From the Experts*. New York, Oxon: Routledge.

Combs, G. and Freedman, J. (2016). Externalizing Conversations. In G.R. Weeks, S.T. Fife and C.M. Peterson (Eds): *Techniques for the Couple Therapist. Essential Interventions From the Experts*. New York, Oxon: Routledge.

Cooperrider, D.L., Srivastva, S. (1987). Appreciative inquiry in organizational life. In R.W. Woodman and W.A. Pasmore (Eds), *Research in Organizational Change and Development*, Vol. 1. Stamford, CT: JAI Press.

Dallos, R. and Vetere, A. (2014). Systemic therapy and attachment narratives: Attachment Narrative Therapy. *Clinical Child Psychology and Psychiatry*, 19(4), 494–502.

Erickson, M.H. (author) and E.L. Rossi (editor) (1980). *The Collected Papers of Milton H. Erickson*. Irvington Publishers Inc.

Fife, S.T. (2016). Aspects of intimacy. In G.R. Weeks, S.T. Fife and C.M. Peterson (Eds), *Techniques for the Couple Therapist. Essential Interventions From the Experts*. New York, Oxon: Routledge.

Gambescia, N. (2016). The use of the sexual genogram. In G.R. Weeks, S.T. Fife and C.M. Peterson (Eds), *Techniques for the Couple Therapist. Essential Interventions From the Experts*. New York. Oxon: Routledge.

Gottman, J.M. (2011). *The Science of Trust*. New York: Norton.

Hallam-Jones, R. (2004). MA in Sexual and Relationship Therapy, Porterbrook Clinic, Sheffield, training session.

Iasenza, S. (2010). What is queer about sex? Expanding sexual frames in theory and practice. *Family Process*, 49(3), 291–308.

Johnson, S.M. (2004). *The Practice of Emotionally Focused Couple Therapy* (2nd ed.) New York and East Sussex: Brunner-Routledge.

Johnson, S.M. (2013). *Love Sense: The Revolutionary Science of Romantic Relationships*. New York: Little Brown.

Ludema, J.D., Cooperrider, D.L. and Barrett, F.J. (2000). Appreciative inquiry: The power of the unconditional positive question. In P. Reason and H. Bradbury (Eds) *Handbook of Action Research*. Thousand Oaks, CA: Sage.

Masters, W.H. and Johnson, V.E. (1970). *Human Sexual Inadequacy*. USA: Ishi Press International.

Papernow, P.L. (2016). Soft/hard/soft communication. In G.R. Weeks, S.T. Fife and C.M. Peterson (Eds), *Techniques for the Couple Therapist. Essential Interventions From the Experts*. New York. Oxon: Routledge.

Tiefer, L. (2004). *Sex is Not a Natural Act & Other Essays* (2nd ed.). Boulder, CO: Westview Press.

Vetere, A. and Dallos, R. (2008). Systemic therapy and attachment narratives. *Journal of Family Therapy*, 30(4), 374–385.

Watzlawick, P., Weakland, J. and Fisch, R. (1974). *Change*. New York: Norton.

Weeks, G. R. (1977). Toward a dialectical approach to intervention. *Human Development*, *20*(5), 277–292.

Weeks, G.R. and Fife, S.T. (2014). *Couples in Treatment: Techniques and Approaches for Effective Practice*. New York: Routledge.

Weeks, G.R. and Gambescia, N. (2000). *Erectile Dysfunction: Integrating Couple Therapy, Sex Therapy, and Medical Treatment*. W.W. Norton.

Weeks, G.R. and Gambescia, N. (2016). Expanding levels of communication, In G.R. Weeks, S.T. Fife and C.M. Peterson (Eds), *Techniques for the Couple Therapist. Essential Interventions From the Experts*. New York, Oxon: Routledge.

Weeks, G.R., Fife, S.T. and Peterson, C.M. (Eds) (2016). *Techniques for the Couple Therapist. Essential Interventions From the Experts*. New York, Oxon: Routledge.

Weeks, G.R., Gambescia, N. and Hertlein, K.M. (Eds) (2016). *A Clinician's Guide to Systemic Sex Therapy* (2nd ed.). New York and London: Routledge.

White, M. (1988). The externalizing of the problem and the re-authoring of lives and relationships. *Dulwich Centre Newsletter*, Summer.

White, M. (1989). *Selected Papers*. Adelaide, Australia: Dulwich Centre Publications.
White, M. (1995). *Re-authoring Lives: Interviews and Essays*. Adelaide, South Australia: Dulwich Centre Publications.
White, M. (2007). *Maps of Narrative Practice*. New York: W. W. Norton.
White, M. and Epston, D. (1989). *Literate Means to Therapeutic Ends*. Adelaide, South Australia: Dulwich Centre Publications.
White, M. and Epston, D. (1990). *Narrative Means to Therapeutic Ends*. New York: W. W. Norton.
Wincze, J.P. and Weisberg, R.B. (2015). *Sexual Dysfunction: A Guide to Assessment and Treatment* (3rd ed.). New York: The Guilford Press.
Zimmerman, T.S. and Haddock, S.A. (2016). Using shared journaling to practice communication skills with couples. In G.R. Weeks, S.T. Fife and C.M. Peterson (Eds): *Techniques for the Couple Therapist. Essential Interventions From the Experts*. New York, Oxon: Routledge.

Delayed ejaculation (DE): treatment options

Abdel-Hamid, I. and Saleh, E. (2011). Primary lifelong delayed ejaculation: Characteristics and response to bupropion. *Journal of Sexual Medicine*, 8, 1772–1779.
Althof, S. (2012). Psychological interventions for delayed ejaculation/orgasm. *International Journal of Impotence Research*, 24(4), 131–136.
Apfelbaum, B. (2000). Retarded ejaculation: A much-misunderstood syndrome. In S.R. Leiblum and R.C. Rosen (Eds), *Principles and Practice of Sex Therapy* (2nd ed.). New York: Guilford Press.
Corona, G., Jannini, E.A., Vignozzi, L., Rastrelli, G. and Maggi, M. (2012). The hormonal control of ejaculation. *Nature Reviews Urology*, 9, 508–519.
Foley, S. and Gambescia, N. (2015). The complex etiology of delayed ejaculation: Assessment and treatment implications. In K.M. Hertlein, G.R. Weeks and N. Gambescia (Eds), *Systemic Sex Therapy* (2nd ed.). New York: Routledge.
Hof, L. and Berman, E. (1989). The sexual genogram: Assessing family-of-origin factors in the treatment of sexual dysfunction. Chapter 11 in D. Kantor and B. Okun (Eds), *Intimate Environments. Sex, Intimacy and Gender in Families*. The Guilford Press.
McMahon, C.G., Jannini, E.A., Waldinger, M. and Rowland, D. (2013). Standard operating procedures in the disorders of orgasm and ejaculation, *Journal of Sexual Medicine*, 10(1), 204–29.
Metz, M.E. and McCarthy, B.W. (2007). The 'good-enough sex' model for couple sexual satisfaction. *Sexual and Relationship Therapy*, 22(3), 351–362.
Perelman, M.A. (2014). Delayed ejaculation. In Y.M. Binik and S.K. Hall (Eds), *Principles and Practice of Sex Therapy* (5th ed.). New York: Guilford Press.
Perelman, M.A. and Rowland, D.L. (2006). Retarded ejaculation. *World Journal of Urology*, 24, 645–652.
Robbins-Cherry, S., Hayter, M., Wylie, K. and Goldmeier, D. (2011). The experience of men living with inhibited ejaculation. *Sexual and Relationship Therapy*, 26(3), 242–253.

Weeks, G.R., Fife, S.T. and Peterson, C.M. (Eds) (2016). *Techniques for the Couple Therapist. Essential Interventions From the Experts.* New York, Oxon: Routledge.

Weeks, G.R., Gambescia, N. and Hertlein, K.M. (Eds) (2016). *A Clinician's Guide to Systemic Sex Therapy* (2nd ed.). New York and London: Routledge.

Zilbergeld, B. (1999). *The New Male Sexuality* (revised version). USA: Bantam Books.

Erectile disorder (ED): treatment options

Carroll, R.A. (2011). Psychological aspects of erectile dysfunction. In K.T. McVary (Ed.), *Contemporary Treatment of Erectile Dysfunction. A Clinical Guide.* Springer International Publishing.

Elliott, R., and L.S. Greenberg. (2007). The essence of process-experiential /emotion-focused therapy. *American Journal of Psychotherapy*, 61, 241–254.

Hof, L. and Berman, E. (1989). The sexual genogram: Assessing family-of-origin factors in the treatment of sexual dysfunction. Chapter 11 in D. Kantor and B. Okun (Eds), *Intimate Environments. Sex, Intimacy and Gender in Families.* The Guilford Press.

McVary, K.T. (2011). *Contemporary Treatment of Erectile Dysfunction. A Clinical Guide.* Springer International Publishing.

Perelman, M.A. (2005). Combination therapy for sexual dysfunction: Integrating sex therapy and pharmacotherapy. In R. Balon and R.T. Segraves (Eds), *Handbook of Sexual Dysfunction.* Boca Raton: Taylor & Francis.

Rosen, R.C., Miner, M.M. and Wincze, J.P. (2014). Erectile dysfunction. integration of medical and psychological approaches. In Y.M. Binik and K.S.K. Hall (Eds), *Principles and Practice of Sex Therapy* (5th ed.). New York, London: The Guilford Press.

Weeks, G.R. and Gambescia, N. (2000). *Erectile Dysfunction: Integrating Couple Therapy, Sex Therapy, and Medical Treatment.* W.W. Norton.

Wincze, J.P. and Weisberg, R.B. (2015). *Sexual Dysfunction: A Guide to Assessment and Treatment* (3rd ed.). New York: The Guilford Press.

Zilbergeld, B. (1999). *The New Male Sexuality* (revised version). USA: Bantam Books.

Zilbergeld, B. and Ellison, C.R. (1980). Desire discrepancies and arousal problems in sex therapy. In S.R. Leiblum and L.A. Pervin (Eds), *Principles and Practice or Sex Therapy.* New York: Guilford.

Female orgasmic disorder (FOD): treatment options

Chalker, R. (2000). *The Clitoral Truth: The World at Your Fingertips.* New York: Seven Stories Press.

Davis, S.R., Moreau, M., Kroll. R., et al. (2008). Testosterone for low libido in postmenopausal women not taking estrogen. *New England Journal of Medicine,* 359(19), 2005–2017.

Dodson, B. (1976). *Liberating Masturbation: A Meditation on Self Love.* New York: Betty Dodson.

Graham, C.A. (2014). Orgasm disorders in women. Chapter 4 in Y.M. Binik and K.S.K. Hall (Eds), *Principles and Practice of Sex Therapy* (5th ed.). New York. London: Guilford Press.

Heiman, J.R. (2007). Orgasmic disorders in women. In S.R. Leiblum (Ed.), *Principles and Practice of Sex Therapy* (4th ed.). New York: Guilford Press.

Heiman, J.R. and LoPiccolo, J. (1988). *Becoming Orgasmic: A Sexual and Personal Growth Programme for Women*. Prentice Hall Press.

Komisaruk, B.R. and Whipple, B. (2011). Non-genital orgasms. *Sexual and Relationship Therapy*, 26, 356–372.

Laan, E., Rellini, A.H. and Barnes, T. (2013). Standard operating procedure for female orgasmic disorder: Consensus of the International Society for Sexual Medicine. *Journal of Sexual Medicine*, 10, 74–82.

Ladas, A., Whipple, B. and Perry, J. (2005). *The G Spot: And Other Discoveries About Human Sexuality*. New York: Holt.

McCabe, M. (2015). Female Orgasmic Disorder. In K.M. Hertlein, G.R. Weeks and N. Gambescia (Eds), *Systemic Sex Therapy* (2nd ed.). New York and East Sussex: Routledge.

McCabe, M. and Giles, K. (2012). Differences between sexually functional and dysfunctional women in psychological and relationship domains. *International Journal of Sexual Health*, 24, 181–194.

Meston, C.M., Levin, R.J., Sipski, M.L., Hull, E.M. and Heiman, J.R. (2004). Women's orgasm. *Annual Review of Sex Research*, 15, 173–257.

Petersen, J.L. and Hyde, J.S. (2011). Gender differences in sexual attitudes and behaviour: A review of meta-analytic results and large datasets. *Journal of Sex Research*, 48, 149–165.

Tomm, K. (2016). Reflexive Questioning as a Means to Enable Intimacy with Couples. Institute of Family Therapy London workshop.

Wincze, J.P. and Weisberg, R.B. (2015). *Sexual Dysfunction: A Guide to Assessment and Treatment* (3rd ed.). New York: Guilford Press.

Female sexual interest/arousal disorder (FSI/AD): treatment options

Basson, R. (2001). Are the complexities of women's sexual function reflected in the new consensus definitions of dysfunction? *Journal of Sex & Marital Therapy*, 27(2), 105–112.

Bost, B.W. (2005). *The Hurried Woman Syndrome: A Seven-Step Program to Conquer Fatigue, Control Weight and Restore passion to Your Relationship*. McGraw Hill Professional.

Bowen, M. (1978). *Family Therapy in Clinical Practice*. Jason Aronson USA.

Brauer, M., van Leeuwen, M., Janssen, E., Newhouse, S.K., Heiman, J.R. and Laan, E. (2012). Attentional and affective processing of sexual stimuli in women with hypoactive sexual desire disorder. *Archives of Sexual Behavior*, 41(4), 891–905.

Brotto, L.A. and Heiman, J.R. (2007). Mindfulness in sex therapy: Applications for women with sexual difficulties following gynecologic cancer. *Sexual and Relationship Therapy*, 22(1), 3–11.

Brotto, L.A. and Luria, M. (2014). Sexual interest / arousal disorder in women. In Y.M. Binik and K. Hall. (Eds) (2014). *Principles and Practice of Sex Therapy* (5th ed.). New York: Guilford Press.

Frankl, V.E. (1985). Logos, paradox, and the search for meaning. In M.J. Mahoney and A. Freeman (Eds), *Cognition and Psychotherapy*. New York: Plenum Press.

Hall, K. (2010). The canary in the coal mine: Reviving sexual desire in long-term relationships. In S.R. Leiblum (Ed.), *Treating Sexual Desire Disorders. A Clinical Casebook*. New York: Guilford Press.

Leiblum, S.R. (Ed.) (2010). *Treating Sexual Desire Disorders. A Clinical Casebook*. New York: Guilford Press.

McGoldrick, M., Loonan, R. and Wohlsifer, D. (2007). Sexuality and culture. In S. Leiblum (Ed.), *Principles and Practice of Sex Therapy* (4th ed.). New York: Guilford Press.

Meston, C.M. and Buss, D.M. (2007). Why humans have sex. *Archives of Sexual Behavior*, 36(4), 477–507.

Schnarch, D. (2000). Desire problems: A systemic perspective. Chapter 2 in S. Leiblum, and R. C. Rosen (Eds), *Principles and Practice of Sex Therapy* (3rd ed.). New York: The Guilford Press.

Sims, K.E.and Meana, M. (2010). Why did passion wane? A qualitative study of married women's attributions for declines in sexual desire. *Journal of Sex & Marital Therapy*, 36(4), 360–380.

Sipe, W. and Eisendrath, S. (2012). Mindfulness-based cognitive therapy: Theory and practice. *Canadian Journal of Psychiatry*, 57(2), 63–69.

Weeks, G.R. and Fife, S. (2014). *Couples in Treatment*. New York: Routledge.

Weeks, G.R. and Gambescia, N. (2002). *Hypoactive Sexual Desire. Integrating Sex and Couple Therapy*. W.W. Norton.

Weeks, G.R. and Gambescia, N. (2015). Definition, etiology, and treatment of absent/ low desire in women. In K.M. Hertlein, G.R. Weeks and N. Gambescia (Eds) (2015), *Systemic Sex Therapy* (2nd ed.) New York: Routledge.

Wincze, J.P. and Weisberg, R.B. (2015). *Sexual Dysfunction: A Guide to Assessment and Treatment* (3rd ed.). New York: Guilford Press.

Genito-pelvic pain/penetration disorder (GPPPD): treatment options

Bergeron, S., Rosen, N.O. and Pukall, C.F. (2014). Genital pain in women and men: It can hurt more than your sex life. In Y.M. Binik and K. Hall. (Eds) (2014), *Principles and Practice of Sex Therapy* (5th ed.). New York: Guilford Press.

Binik, Y.M. and Hall, K. (Eds) (2014). *Principles and Practice of Sex Therapy* (5th ed.). New York: Guilford Press.

Curtin, N., Ward, L.M., Merriwether, A. and Allison, C. (2011). Femininity ideology and sexual health in young women: A focus on sexual knowledge, embodiment, and agency. *International Journal of Sexual Health*, 23, 48–62.

Meana, M., Maykut, C. and Fertel, I. (2015). Painful intercourse: Genito-pelvic pain/ penetration disorder. In K. M. Hertlein, G.R. Weeks and N. Gambescia (Eds), *Systemic Sex Therapy* (2nd ed.). New York and London: Routledge.

Minuchin, S., Rosman, B. and Baker, L. (1978). *Psychosomatic Families: Anorexia Nervosa in Context*. Cambridge, MA: Harvard University Press.

Reissing, E.D., Armstrong, H.L. and Allen, C. (2013). Pelvic floor physical therapy for lifelong vaginismus: A retrospective chart review and interview study. *Journal of Sex & Marital Therapy*, 39, 306–320.

Rosenbaum, T.Y. (2013). An integrated mindfulness-based approach to the treatment of women with sexual pain and anxiety: Promoting autonomy and mind/body connection. *Sexual and Relationship Therapy*, 28(1–2), 20–28.

Male hypoactive sexual desire disorder (MHSDD): treatment options

Kedde, H., Donker, G., Leusink, P. and Kruijer, H. (2011). The incidence of sexual dysfunction in patients attending Dutch general practitioners. *International Journal of Sexual Health*, 23(4), 269–277.

Khera, M., Bhattacharya, R.K., Blick, G., Kushner, H., Nguyen, D. and Miner, M.M. (2011). Improved sexual function with testosterone replacement therapy in hypogonadal men: real-world data from the Testim Registry in the United States (TRiUS). *Journal of Sexual Medicine*, 8, 3204–3213.

Hall, K. (2015). Male hypoactive Sexual Desire Disorder. In K.M. Hertlein, G.R. Weeks and N. Gambescia (Eds), *Systemic Sex Therapy* (2nd ed.). New York and East Sussex: Routledge.

McCarthy, B.W. and Metz, M.E. (2008). *Men's Sexual Health. Fitness for Satisfying Sex*. New York and Oxon: Routledge.

Meana, M. and Steiner, E.T. (2014). Hidden disorder/hidden desire. Presentations of low sexual desire in men. In Y.M. Binik and S.K. Hall (Eds), *Principles and Practice of Sex Therapy* (5th ed.). New York: Guilford Press.

Nobre, P.J. and Pinto-Gouveia, J. (2008). Differences in automatic thoughts presented during sexual activity between sexually functional and dysfunctional men and women. *Cognitive Therapy and Research*, 32(1), 37–49.

Schnarch, D. (2003). *Resurrecting Sex: Solving Sexual Problems and Revolutionizing Your Relationship*. New York: Harper Paperbacks.

White, M. (2007). *Maps of Narrative Practice*. New York: W. W. Norton.

Wincze, J.P. and Weisberg, R.B. (2015). *Sexual Dysfunction: A Guide to Assessment and Treatment* (3rd ed.). New York: Guilford Press.

Zilbergeld, B. (1999). *The New Male Sexuality* (revised version). USA: Bantam Books.

Zilbergeld, B. and Ellison, C.R. (1980). Desire discrepancies and arousal problems in sex therapy. In S.R. Leiblum and L.A. Pervin (Eds), *Principles and Practice of Sex Therapy*. New York: Guilford Press.

Premature/early ejaculation (PE): treatment

Althof, S.E. (2014). Treatment of premature ejaculation. psychotherapy, pharmacotherapy, and combined therapy. In Y.M. Binik and S.K. Hall (Eds), *Principles and Practice of Sex Therapy* (5th ed.). New York: Guilford Press.

Betchen, S.J. (2015). Premature ejaculation: An integrative, intersystems approach for couples. In K.M. Hertlein, G.R. Weeks and N. Gambescia: *Systemic Sex Therapy.* (2nd ed.). New York and East Sussex: Routledge.

Linton, K. and Wylie, K.R. (2010). Recent advances in the treatment of premature ejaculation. *Drug Design, Development and Therapy*, 4, 1–6.

Mrdjenovic, A.J., Bischof, G.H. and Menichello, J.L. (2004). A biopsychosocial systems approach to premature ejaculation. *Canadian Journal of Human Sexuality*, 13(1), Spring. The Sex Information and Education Council of Canada.

Weeks, G.R. and Gambescia, N. (2015). Definition, etiology, and treatment of absent/low desire in women. In K.M. Hertlein, G.R. Weeks and N. Gambescia (Eds) (2015), *Systemic Sex Therapy* (2nd ed.). New York: Routledge.

Wolpe, J. and Wolpe, D. (1981). *Our Useless Fears*. Boston: Houghton Mifflin Company.

Persistent genital arousal disorder (PGAD): treatment options

Goldmeier, D., Sadeghi-Nejad, H. and Facelle, T.M. (2014). Persistent genital arousal disorder. In Y.M. Binik and S.K. Hall (Eds), *Principles and Practice of Sex Therapy* (5th ed.). New York: Guilford Press.

Kamatchi, R. and Ashley-Smith, A. (2013). Persistent genital arousal disorder in a male: A case report and analysis of the cause. *British Journal of Medical Practitioners*, 6(1).

Leiblum, S.R. and Chivers, M.L. (2007). Normal and persistent genital arousal in women: New perspectives. *Journal of Sex & Marital Therapy*, 33(4), 357–373.

Sexual aversion disorder (SAD): treatment options

Basson, R. (2010). Women's difficulties with low sexual desire, sexual avoidance, and sexual aversion. *Handbook of clinical sexuality for mental health professionals*, 159–179.

Carnes, P.J. (1997). *Sexual Anorexia: Overcoming Sexual Self-hatred.* Hazelden Publishing.

Finch, S. (2001). Sexual aversion disorder treated with behavioural desensitization. *Canadian Journal of Psychiatry*, 46(6), 563–564.

Janata, J.W. and Kingsberg, S.A. (2005). Sexual aversion disorder. In R. Balon and R.T. Segraves (Eds), *Handbook of Sexual Dysfunction.* Boca Raton: Taylor and Francis Group.

Tiefer, L. (2001). A new view of women's sexual problems: Why new? Why now? *Journal of Sex Research*, 38(2), 89–96.

Weeks, G.R., Gambescia, N. and, Hertlein, K.M. (Eds) (2016). *A Clinician's Guide to Systemic Sex Therapy* (2nd ed.). New York and London: Routledge.

Sexual compulsivity, addictions or hypersexuality: treatment options

Adams, K.M. and Robinson, D.W. (2001). Shame reduction, affect regulation, and sexual boundary development: Essential building blocks of sexual addiction. *Sexual Addiction & Compulsivity*, 8(1), 23–44.

Braun-Harvey, D. and Vigorito, M.A. (2016). *Treating Out of Control Sexual Behavior. Rethinking Sex Addiction.* New York: Springer Publishing Company.

Carnes P. J. (1992). *Don't Call It Love: Recovery From Sexual Addiction.* New York: Bantam.

Corley, M.D. and Schneider, J.P. (2012). *Disclosing Secrets: An Addicts Guide for When, to Whom, and How Much to Reveal.* Seattle, WA: CreateSpace Independent Publishing.

Delmonico, D.L. and Griffin, E.J. (2015). Sexual compulsivity: diagnosis, assessment and treatment. In K.M. Hertlein, G.R. Weeks and N. Gambescia: *Systemic Sex Therapy* (2nd ed.). New York and East Sussex: Routledge.

Flores, P.J. (2004). *Addiction as an Attachment Disorder.* New York: Jason Aronson Publishing.

Fong, T.W. (2006). Understanding and managing compulsive sexual behaviors. *Psychiatry (Edgmont)*, 3(11), 51–58.

Hall, P. (2013). *Understanding and Treating Sex Addiction. A Comprehensive Guide for People Who Struggle With Sexual Addiction and Those Who Want to Help Them.* UK, USA and Canada: Routledge.

Kafka, M.P. (2014). Nonparaphilic hypersexuality disorders. In Y.M. Binik and S.K. Hall (Eds), *Principles and Practice of Sex Therapy* (5th ed.). New York: Guilford Press.

Reid, R.C., Bramen, J.E., Anderson, A. and Cohen, M.S. (2014). Mindfulness, emotional dysregulation, impulsivity, and stress proneness among hypersexual patients. *Journal of Clinical Psychology*, 70(4), 313–321.

Salmon, R.F. (1995). Therapist's guide to 12-step meetings for sexual dependencies. *Sexual Addiction & Compulsivity* 2, 193–213.

Schneider, J.P. (2000). Effects of cybersex addiction on the family: Results of a survey. *Sexual Addiction & Compulsivity*, 7, 31–58.

Weeks, G.R., Gambescia, N. and Hertlein, K.M. (Eds) (2016). *A Clinician's Guide to Systemic Sex Therapy* (2nd ed.). New York and London: Routledge.

Weiss, R. (2004). Treating sex addiction. In R.H. Coombs (Ed.), *Handbook of Addictive Disorders: A Practical Guide to Diagnosis and Treatment.* Hoboken, NJ: John Wiley & Sons Inc.

White, M. (2007). *Maps of Narrative Practice.* New York: W. W. Norton.

Dyspareunia in men: treatment options

Bays, B. (n.d.) www.thejourney.com (accessed 2 November 2016).

Greenberg, L. S. (2008). Emotion and cognition in psychotherapy: The transforming power of affect. *Canadian Psychology*, 49(1): 49–59.

Herati, A.S. and Moldwin, R.M. (2013). Alternative therapies in the management of chronic prostatitis/chronic pelvic pain syndrome. *World Journal of Urology*, 31(4), 761–766.

Hollows, K. (2007). Anodyspareunia: A novel sexual dysfunction? An exploration into anal sexuality. *Sexual and Relationship Therapy*, 22(4), 429–443.

Morris, B.J. and Krieger, J.N., (2013). Does male circumcision affect sexual function, sensitivity, or satisfaction?—a systematic review. *The Journal of Sexual Medicine*, 10(11), 2644–2657.

Naim, M. and Ende, D. (2011). A new approach to the treatment of non-specific male genital pain. *British Journal of Urology international*, 107(s3), 34–37.

Nickel, J.C., Mullins, C. and Tripp, D.A. (2008). Development of an evidence-based cognitive behavioral treatment program for men with chronic prostatitis/chronic pain syndrome. *World Journal of Urology*, 26, 167.

Oommen, M. and Hellstrom, W.J.G. (2010). Male Dyspareunia. http://www.uptodate.com/contents/male-dyspareunia (accessed 27 April 2017).

Smith, K.B., Pukall, C.F., Tripp, D.A. and Nickel, J.C. (2007). Sexual and relationship functioning in men with chronic prostatitis/chronic pelvic pain syndrome and their partners. *Archives of Sexual Behavior*, 36(2), 301–311.

Chapter 6: Client vignettes

Cecchin, G. (1992). Personal communication.

Burnham, J. (2005). Relational reflexivity: A tool for socially constructing therapeutic relationships. In C. Flaskas, B. Mason, and A. Perlesz. (Eds), *The Space Between: Experience, Context, and Process in the Therapeutic Relationship*. Karnac.

Fife, S.T. (2016). Aspects of intimacy. In G.R. Weeks, S.T. Fife and C.M. Peterson (Eds), *Techniques for the Couple Therapist. Essential Interventions From the Experts*. New York. Oxon: Routledge.

Pearce, W.B. (1994). *Interpersonal Communication: Making Social Worlds*. New York: Harper Collins.

Wincze, J.P. and Carey, M.P. (2001). *Sexual Dysfunction: A Guide to Assessment and Treatment* (2nd ed.). New York, London: The Guilford Press.

AUTHOR INDEX

A
Abdo, C.H.N., 171
Aggrawal, A., 72
Allen, W., 17
Althof, S.E., 167
American Association of Sexuality Educators, Counselors and Therapists (AASECT), 186
American Psychiatric Association (APA), 53
American Urological Association (AUA), 165
Anderson, H., 94, 204, 205, 206, 211
Apfelbaum, B., 108, 109, 112, 113, 239
Arachal, B.S., 170
Asexual Visibility and Education Network (AVEN), 63, 164
Atkins, L., 153
Aviva Medical Dictionary, 197

B
Bancroft, J., 96, 127, 157
Bandler, R., 217
Barker, M., 73, 75, 87
Barlow, D.H., 177
Basson, R., 17, 40, 41, 153, 266, 293
Bays, B., 306
Beck, J.G., 153
Benegal, V., 170
Berman, E., 101
Beyer-Flores, C., 133
Blume, L.B., 57
Bogaert, A., 63
Bozman, A.W., 153
Brash-McGreer, K., 40
Braun-Harvey, D., 187, 188
Brooks, V.R., 61
Brotto, L.A., 64, 136, 153, 155, 157, 261
Burnham, J., 32
Burr, V., 52

C
Carnes, P.J., 177, 178, 181, 182, 183, 193, 294, 295
Carpenter, B.N., 184, 188
Castaldo, A., 74
Cecchin, G., 206
Chalker, R., 132
Cheung, G., 192
Chivers, M.L., 134, 174, 176, 288
Clement, U., 86
Clifton, D., 31
Coleman, E., 188, 193
Cooperrider, D.L., 25, 227
Crenshaw, T.
Curra, J., 52, 82

D
Dallos, R., 23, 28, 82, 215
Dallos, S., 82
Damon, W., 201, 202
Davidson, C.K.D., 192
Davidson, J.M., 120
Davies, D., 67, 192
Delmonico, D.I., 185, 190, 192, 195
Delmonte, H., 58
Diamond, L.M., 56

Doan, R., 31
Dodson, B., 312
Donovan, C.L., 136
Down, G., xii
Draper, R., 23

E
Easton, D., 48, 55
Ellison, C.RE., 247, 289
Erickson, M., 13, 216

F
Facelle, T.M., 174, 288
Fausto-Sterling, A., 52
Fong, T.W., 186
Foreman, S., 28, 82
Foucault, M., 72
Frankl, V.A., 140, 257
Freud, S., 128
Frost, R.N., 136
Fruggeri, L., 11

G
Gambescia, N., 9, 27, 79, 117, 119, 120, 122, 123, 177, 242, 243, 245, 257, 262, 288
Gavey, 28
Gergen, K.J., 205, 206
Giammattei, S., 57
Goldmeier, D., 174, 288
Goolishian, H., 94, 205
Gorrell-Barnes, G., xii
Gottman, J.M., 122, 229
Green, R.J., 57
Griffin, E.J., 185, 190, 192, 195
Griffiths, M., 185
Grinder, J., 217
Gupta, C., 73, 75
Gupta, K., 64

H
Hagedorn, W.B., 191
Hall, P., 297
Hardy, J.W., 48, 55
Hare-Mustin, R.T., 28, 82, 124
Hayes, R.D., 136
Heiman, J.R., 81, 126, 132, 254, 256
Hertlein, K.M., 177
Heschel, A.J., 26
Hinderliter, A., 63, 64
Hof, L., 101
Hoffman, L., 205
Hollows, K., 202, 306, 307
Hong, L.K., 165

I
Iantaffi, A., 73, 75
Iasenza, S., xii, 59, 60, 74, 224

J
Janata, J.W., 181, 293
Jansen, K., 192
Johnson, V.E., 37, 38, 39, 40, 86, 114, 115, 117, 140, 219
Juhnke, G.A., 191

K
Kafka, M.P., 184, 193, 195, 303
Kantor, D., xii
Kaplan, H.S., 40, 116, 117, 134, 177, 198
Kaplan, M.S., 184
Kingsberg, S.A., 181, 293
Kinsey, A.C., 52, 71
Kinsey Institute, 184
Kleinplatz, P.J., 69, 72
Kolmes, K., 74
Komisaruk, B.R., 133
Kort, J., 182
Krafft-Ebing, R., 183
Kruger, R.B., 184

L
Larson, J.H., 80
Leiblum, S.R., 2, 173, 174, 176, 288
Lev, A.I, 52, 63
Lloyd, Q., 184, 189

LoPiccolo, J., 81, 132, 256
Luria, M., 261

M
Madanes, C., xiii
Marks, S.R., 57
Mason, E.C., 179
Mason, M.J., xii
Masters, W.H., 37, 38, 39, 40, 86, 114, 115, 117, 140, 219
Maturana, H.R., 94
McCabe, M., 254, 255
McCann, D., xii, 58
McCarthy, B.W., 80, 82, 86, 119, 165, 170, 193
McCarthy, E., 80, 193
Metz, M., 82, 86, 119, 165, 170
Metz, M.E., 170
Meyer, I.H., 62
Miner, M.M., 121, 122
Mitchell, D., 31
Money, J., 195
Moser, C., 69

N
Najman, J.M., 155
Nathan, S.G., 173
National Survey of Sexual Attitudes and Lifestyles (NATSAL), 127, 155, 203
New view on women's sexual problems, 39, 141
Nichols, M., 57, 58, 60, 63

O
Okun, B., xii
Oswald, R.F., 57

P
Pascoe, W., xii
Perelman, M.A., 113, 234
Pillai-Friedman, S., 74
Pink Therapy, 192
Plummer, K., 192
Pollitt, J.L., 74

Q
Quadland, M.C., 183
Qualtrough, T., 153
Quincey, V.L., 69

R
Reed, D., 40
Regan, P.C., 153
Reid, R.C., 184, 188
Richardson, R., 179
Ritchie, A., 58
Rosen, R.C., 2, 120, 121, 122
Rosser, B.R., 201, 202

S
Sadeghi-Nejad, H., 174, 288
Sanders, G.L., xii, 52, 82
Savin-Williams, R.C., 56
Schnarch, D.M., 86, 161, 162, 264
Schneider, J.P., 190
Seidman, S., 53
Shull, D.R., 110, 113
Sprenkle, D.H., 110, 113
Srivastva, S., 25, 227

T
Tiefer, L., 39, 41, 42, 84, 85, 178, 206, 224, 291
Tomm, K., 31, 33, 95
Tunnell, G., 59

V
Varah, C., 12
Ve Ard, C., 66
Veaux, F., 66, 67
Vetere, A., 215
Vigorito, M.A., 187, 188

W
Waldinger, M.D., 169
Weeks, G.R., xii, 9, 27, 79, 117, 119, 120, 122, 123, 177, 216, 242, 243, 245, 257, 262, 288
Weingarten, K., 82

Weisberg, R.B., 25, 113, 114, 120, 252, 262
Weitzman, G., 74
Whipple, B., 40, 126, 133
White, M., 95, 205, 231
Wincze, J.P., 25, 113, 114, 121, 122, 252, 262
Windermand, L., 94
Winter, D.A., 78
Wittgenstein, L., 26
World Association of Sexology (WAS), 126
World Health Organization (WHO), 187

Y
Yule, M., 64

Z
Zilbergeld, B., 24, 34, 84, 161, 163, 164, 166, 169, 237, 243, 247, 278, 280

SUBJECT INDEX

A

acquired, *see also* secondary, sexual difficulty
  client vignettes and, 328, 360, 361
  definition, 93
  distinguishing from primary / lifelong, 108, 114, 116, 117, 126, 127, 135, 145, 154, 167, 177, 197, 234, 257, 268, 282, 291
afterplay
  part of sexual activity, as, 99
  lack of, 129, 181
ageing
  client examples 159–60, 329, 332, 352, 353, 357
  lack of testosterone and, 112
  myths about sex and, 87, 159
  normal processes and, 160, 244
  sexual difficulties and, 117, 120, 160, 282
agency
  enhancement of, 5, 8, 232, 238, 242, 252, 271, 288
  questions, 13
agender, definition, 54
AIDS *see* sexually transmitted diseases, *see also* HIV; STI's
alcohol consumption
  abusive, client vignette, 333
  reducing of, 237, 253, 261, 284, 364
  sexual difficulties, and, 98, 121, 170, 286, 361, 362, 363
alexithymia, and PE, 169
allocating regular talking times technique, 229
anal sex
  DSM and, 167
  myths about, 203
  pain, *see anodyspareunia*
  research studies, 203
anger
  client vignettes, 333
  emotionally focused coping, as, 276
  emotionally focused therapy, and, 213
  reduction / management of, 233, 273, 298, 306
  sexual difficulties, and, 4,19, 20, 48, 49, 94, 97, 113, 117, 122, 123, 137, 157, 161, 162, 171, 172, 191, 226, 301
  therapist's, 331
anodyspareunia
  definitions, 201
  factors in experiencing, 201–2
  similarities / differences between male and female dyspareunia, 202
  treatment, 306, 307
anorgasmia
  client vignette, 256, 309–16
  coital, 107
  masturbatory, 108
  partner, 109
  partner's, 162
anticipation
  failure, of, 118, 139, 244, 363
  negative, 22, 119, 149, 222, 252, 260, 279
  pain, of, 144, 198, 200, 271
  positive, 27, 264

anxiety
client vignettes, 321, 322, 329, 346, 356, 364
enhancement of sexual interest and, 143
myths and, 74, 192
sexual difficulties and, 4, 5, 6, 7, 11, 12, 29, 33, 34, 42, 97, 112, 114, 117, 119, 121, 123, 128, 137, 143, 144, 148, 150, 149, 154, 157, 167, 172, 174, 176, 177, 178, 181, 183, 191, 192, 196, 198, 247, 248, 249, 252, 260, 282, 301, 303, 311
sexual minorities and, 57, 62
treatment of sexual difficulties and, 153, 217, 219, 236, 238, 243, 250, 257, 259, 262, 271, 283, 286, 288, 290, 293, 294, 301, 307
appreciative inquiry
four steps, 227–9
method, 25
questions, 227–9
unconditional positive question, 25–6
aspects of intimacy
client vignette, 330–1, 335
fusion of sex and intimacy and, 44
technique, 230–1
attachment
anxieties and emotionally focused therapy, 213
in crucible therapy, 264
impaired, adult, 301
injuries, gay men, 59
myths and sexual minorities and, 59
patterns, 214
sexual genogram and, 102
sexual problems and, 42, 196
theory, 4, 214
therapy, 35
vulnerabilities and emotionally focused therapy, 213
wounds, 297, 301
attachment narrative therapy
approach and stages, 214–6
attitudes
negative, towards sex 78
pathologising, 256, 296
positive, towards one's body, 130
positive, towards one's sexual rights, 245, 285
sexual difficulties and negative, towards sex, 130, 159, 160, 178, 181, 188, 248, 252
sexual minorities and celebratory, 75
sexual minorities and negative, 57, 62
sexual myths and negative, towards sex, 87
attitudes, partners
conciliatory, 122
facilitative, 151, 273
hostile, 151, 273
solicitous, 151, 273
asexuality
couple example, 352
definitions, 63–4, 164, 275
feminist views, 164
myths, 64–5
sexual diversity and, 67
atypical sexual interests, *see* BDSM; *see also* kink; paraphilias; unusual sexual practices; unusual sexual preferences
autoerotic
autoerotic focus, 113
autoeroticism, 108
client vignettes, 340, 360
avoidance
attachment and, 214
behaviours, 6, 148, 195
conflict, of, 109
decrease of / overcoming of, in treatment of sexual difficulties, 222, 239, 240, 263, 264, 268, 272, 273, 293, 294, 310, 325
fear, of, 148, 149, 200
homosexual hatred, of, 182
pattern, 149

physical contact of, 44, 161, 162, 200
relationships, of, 128
sex, of, and sexual difficulties, 113, 148, 149, 176, 177, 178, 181–2, 200, 201, 354

B

BDSM (bondage / domination / sadism / masochism), *see also* atypical sexual interests; kink; paraphilias; unusual sexual practices; unusual sexual preferences
client examples, 47, 360
definitions, 68
misconceptions, 74
resolving in therapy, 71
sensate focus and, 224
sexual diversity and, 67, 72
sexual minorities and, 55, 58, 60, 62
stigma, 7
therapists' self-reflexivity and relational reflexivity, 73–76
behavioural dimension
factors contributing to sexual difficulties and, 113, 121, 131, 137, 140, 149, 161, 170, 176, 181, 196, 200
MOST model, 6
questions in assessment, 99
resources and resiliencies, 18–9
behavioural-systems model
model, 2
technique of, (reflective listening), 24
behavioural techniques
behavioural therapy, 16
treatment, MOST model and, 14, 16–7, 19
treatment, sexual disorders and, 219, 237, 242, 246, 253, 257, 259, 262, 272–3, 280, 286–7, 290, 293–4, 302–3, 307
sexual fantasy and, 45
bereavement *see* loss
BERSC model
treatment of sexual addiction, 297–8
bibliotherapy, *see* education, *see also* psycho-education
bigender, definition, 54
binary definitions
asexuality, of, 64
gender, of, 53, 54, 62
gender identity, of, 54
sex, of, 53
sexual orientation, of, 56
sexual practices, of, 68
bisexuality
biphobia, 62
client vignette, 345
continuum of sexual orientation and, 52
myths and prejudices, 62, 123
sexual diversity and, 67
sexual minorities and, 55–6, 58
blame
attachment narrative therapy and, 215
emotionally focused therapy and, 213
overcoming of, 128, 233, 240, 285, 287
self-blame, 5, 13, 83, 236, 290, 311
sexual difficulties and, 122, 247, 263
body image, 14–5
factor in sexual difficulties as, 98–9
improving of, 218, 237, 253, 272, 280, 286
negative, 112, 130, 139, 173, 181, 200, 261
positive, and female orgasm, 130
body psychotherapy, 14
boredom
masturbation and, 153
relationship, 94, 100
sexual, 161
sexual difficulties and, 113, 123, 184

C

catastrophising
challenging of, 272, 279, 285
sexual difficulties and, 148, 151, 260, 290
unusual sexual practices and, 245

CBT, *see* cognitive-behavioural therapy
child sexual abuse
  sexual disorders and, 128, 151, 176, 181–2, 195, 196, 201, 265, 295
  understanding of, 303–4, 308
chronic pelvic pain, *see* dyspareunia in men, *see also* painful ejaculation; painful sex; prostatitis
cisgender, definition, 54
clitoris
  biological features and, 52
  enlargement, sexual response, 37
  myths, 81, 128, 256, 312
  orgasm and, 133
  presence of ignored, 132
  size, client example, 11
  stimulation, 128, 253, 261
  undermining importance of, and FSI/AD, 140
CMM theory, *see* co-ordinated management of meaning theory
co-construction
  appreciative inquiry and, 26, 228
  client examples, 12, 318, 335
  therapeutic relationship and, 11, 32, 33, 89, 102, 107, 206, 210–11, 315
cognitive-behavioural therapy, 6, *see also* CBT
  effectiveness, 293, 306
  techniques, 12, 260
  treatment of sexual difficulties, 297
cognitive dimension
  factors contributing to sexual difficulties and, 112, 119, 130, 139, 148, 159, 169, 174, 181, 195, 198
  MOST model and, 9–14
  questions to explore, 97–8
  resources and resiliencies and, 12–14
  treatment of sexual difficulties and, 216, 236, 242, 243, 252, 257, 259, 260, 271–2
cognitive distortions, 12
  challenging of, 244, 285, 301
  sexual difficulties and, 119, 148, 159
cognitive restructuring
  treatment of sexual difficulties and, 279, 306
cognitive therapy
  treatment of sexual difficulties and, 264
collaboration
  diagnosis and, 204, 206
  limit setting and, 303
  therapeutic relationship and, 11, 33, 107, 211, 233
collaborative assessment, 107
collaborative competence, 26
communication
  cultural discourses on sex and, 28, 29, 31, 94
  importance of, sexual response and, 41, 316, 329, 331, 357
  improvement of, in treatment of sexual difficulties, 19, 105, 219, 228, 247, 254, 255, 256, 273, 276, 281, 287
  problems and attachment narrative therapy, 214
  problems and emotionally focused therapy, 213
  sexual difficulties and poor, 20, 21, 25, 96, 100, 122–3, 131, 137, 141, 150, 154, 161, 171, 172, 173, 201
  spectrum of sex and, 42, 48–50, 51
  techniques to improve, 220–234, 239
compersion, definition, 66
conflict
  contribution to sexual difficulties, 20, 21, 24, 26, 42, 58, 100, 113, 121, 122, 141, 162, 201
  fear of, client vignette, 329
  resolution techniques, 247, 281
  tools for dealing with, 24–5
control
  dual, model, 184
  fear of losing, 117, 181, 264
  lack of, 145, 178, 196, 285

need to gain, treatment of sexual difficulties, 271, 272, 273, 286–7, 293, 294, 298, 301
need to maintain, 49, 113, 128
out of, behaviour, 179, 183–4, 188
power and, 161, 171
social, 85, 187
co-ordinated management of meaning, *see also* CMM; theory
description and example, 17
unwanted repetitive patterns and, 20, 95
creating own desire checklist
couple technique, 239
cultural dimension
exploring in assessment, 100–1
exploring in treatment of sexual difficulties, 214, 215, 231–2, 248, 255, 256, 274, 282, 288, 291, 295, 314–6
factors contributing to sexual difficulties, 117, 121, 123, 131–2, 136, 137, 141, 143, 146, 151, 153, 159, 160, 162, 163, 169, 170, 172, 192, 201, 304, 351
MOST model and, 27–31
myths and misconceptions, 132
criticism
addressing of, in treatment of sexual difficulties, 6, 21–2, 229, 319
sexual difficulties and, 5, 12, 14, 171–2, 248
crucible therapy
treatment of sexual desire problems, 264
culture
assumptions, masculinity, 282
norms, female sexuality and, 42
oppression, women, 34, 41, 151
pressures, acknowledgment of, 295
shame and embarrassment, 291
stereotypes, 163

D

deconstruction
client example, 33
couple interaction of, 49, 95, 223
discourses on sex of, 85, 139
externalising conversations, in, 232
intergenerational stories of, 256, 295, 314
questions, 89, 232
sexual episodes, of, 18, 44, 294, 346–7
delayed ejaculation (DE)
client vignettes, 345, 353–60
definitions, 107
diagnosis & assessment, 108–9
factors contributing to, 110–14
prevalence, 110
treatment guidelines, 234
treatment options, 235–240, 286
depression
alleviating of, treatment of sexual difficulties, 288, 301
client example, 33–4
sexual difficulties and, 4, 12, 42, 119, 122, 137, 139, 148, 157, 167, 174, 184, 198, 334, 353
sexual minorities and, 62
desire, *see* sexual desire
diagnosis
advantages and disadvantages of, 204–6
normalisation and, 15–6
sexology and, 91, 93, 96
social construction, as, 91, 207
disappointment
emotionally focused coping, as, 276
sexual difficulties and, 42, 157, 172, 242, 244, 273, 281, 363
distress, *see* stress
discourse
analysis, 28
deconstructing of, 33, 47, 85
deficiency, 47
definition, 28
dominant, 146, 231, 232
gender, 29, 124
intimacy, 28–9
political, 28
psychiatric, 146
questions addressing cultural, 30

discourse (*continued*)
scientific, 92
sex addiction, 192, 304
sexuality, 9, 28–9, 47–8, 76, 82, 85, 274, 304
shifting, 19
subjugated, 188
dyspareunia
female, 143, 150
dyspareunia in men *see also* chronic pelvic pain; painful ejaculation; painful sex; prostatitis
definitions and diagnosis, 196–7
factors contributing to, 198–201
prevalence, 197–8
treatment, 304–8

E

education *see also* psycho-education
bibliotherapy, and, 243, 244, 255, 256, 261, 262, 278, 306, 314
encourage reading, 11
environment, restrictive, 173, 274, 288, 310
formulation and, 207, 316
inadequate, about sex, 42, 159, 169, 201
input, treatment of sexual difficulties, 29, 202, 217–8, 236, 237, 243, 244, 249, 250, 252, 255, 257, 260, 261, 262, 271, 272, 273, 278, 283, 285, 293, 294, 301, 306, 312
lack of sexual, and sexual difficulties, 12, 112, 139, 141
need for therapists', 74, 296
social difference and, 315
ejaculation
delayed, *see* delayed ejaculation
myths, 112
premature, *see* premature ejaculation
emotional dimension
attachment narrative therapy and, 214–6
closeness, importance of, female sexuality, 131
factors contributing to sexual difficulties and, 97, 110, 117, 124, 128, 148, 157, 162, 169, 172, 178, 182, 195, 196
MOST model and, 4–7
questions to explore, 97
resources and resiliencies and, 7–8
spectrum of sex and, 43, 44, 48
suppression of, 59
treatment of sexual difficulties and, 222, 242, 250, 271, 273, 276, 283, 293, 306
emotional dysregulation
sexual difficulties and, 301
emotional fidelity, definition, 66
emotionally focused therapy approach, 213
empty chair technique, 7
emotional fusion, 162
emotional processing
treatment of sexual difficulties, 306
empty chair technique, 7
enmeshed
couples, 274
families, 123
environment
adjustment of, 261
conduciveness for sex: 17, 121, 140
creating conducive, in treatment of sexual difficulties, 220, 237, 253, 259, 261, 272, 286
exploring the conduciveness of, 99, 218–9
non-conduciveness of, and sexual difficulties, 121, 140
erection
myths about, *see* myths about erections
erectile disorder (ED)
client vignette, 360–7
definitions, 114
diagnosis & assessment, 115–6
factors contributing to, 117–124
prevalence, 61, 116
treatment options, 241–9

erotica
myths about, 81
use of, in treatment of sexual difficulties, 262, 273, 281, 294
ethical slut, definition, 66
exhibitionism, definition, (DSM-IV-TR), 69
externalisation of the problem, 21, 302
externalising interventions, 22, 232
externalising conversations
facilitating development of new patterns, 95, 213
method, description of, 231, 233

F

fantasy
encouraging use of, 234, 246, 254, 262, 279, 280, 294
guilt and shame about, 159
limited, and sexual difficulties, 152, 362
myths about, 159
sexual desire, women and, 135
spectrum of sex, and, 43, 45
fear
arousal, of, 117, 137, 181
bisexuality, of, 62
commitment, of, 137, 169
exposure, of, 117
expressing feelings, of, 117
failure, of, 117, 363
father, of, 151, 249
homosexuality, of, 57
intimacy, closeness and commitment, of, 21, 83, 117, 123, 128, 137, 139, 151, 167, 169, 181, 196, 329, 366
letting go, 128
losing control, of, 117, 181, 264
losing erections, of, 169
losing the partner, of, 121
loss of identity and autonomy, of, 264
pain, of, 144, 148
pregnancy, of, 117, 137, 181, 234, 259–60
rejection, of, 250
sexual activity, of, 151, 177, 178
sexually transmitted diseases, of, 178, 187
treatment of, in treatment of sexual difficulties, 236, 242, 243, 250, 257, 259, 262, 264, 273, 293
upsetting the partner, of, 162, 273
fear avoidance model
sexual difficulties and, 148–9, 200
female genital mutilation
cultural beliefs and, 132
female orgasmic disorder (FOD)
definitions, 124–5
diagnosis and assessment, 126
factors contributing to, 128–133
prevalence, 127–8
treatment options, 249–57
female sexual interest / arousal
enhancing factors, 143–4
female sexual interest/arousal disorder (FSI/AD)
definitions and classification, 133–5
diagnosis and assessment, 135
factors contributing to, 137–141
prevalence, 136–7
treatment options, 257–67
feminism
critique of cultural stereotypes of masculinity / femininity, 163
view on gender, 53
feminist approach
gender inequalities, and, 28
lesbian couples, 59
fetishism, definition, (DSM-IV-TR), 69
fetishistic disorder
classification, (DSM-5), 70
foreplay
exploring adequacy of, 44, 99, 122
insufficient, 131
lack of, 140, 149, 181, 202

formulation
ethical considerations, and, 206, 210–11
client vignette, session, 316–26, 328–30
sexology and sex therapy, in, 207–8
systemic social constructionist therapy, in, 208–9
systemic psychosexual therapy, 209–10
frotteurism, definition, (DSM-IV-TR), 69
frotteuristic disorder, definition (DSM-5), 70
fusion of affection and sex
in sexual disorders, 161, 200, 329

G

gender
bullying and discrimination, 53
comfort with one's, 53
continuum of, 52
definitions, 52–3
differences, 39, 41, 154
discourses, 29, 33
diversity, 54, 58, 62
doing, 51–3, 57
dysphoria, 53–4, 63
expression, 54, 55, 57
fluidity, 56
identity, 53–4, 57, 62
inequalities, 23, 28, 32, 52
insensitivity, 39
neutral, 54
normative, 54
oppression, 41
roles, 29, 57, 59, 60
stereotypes, 53
variance, 61
genderblank, definition, 54
genderfree, definition, 54
genderless, definition, 54
genderqueer, definition, 54
questioning, definition, 54
generalised sexual difficulty
definition, 93
distinguishing from situational, and, 114–5, 116, 127, 135, 145, 154, 167, 177, 197
questions to explore, 95
treatment of, 253–4, 282–4, 286
genito-pelvic pain/ penetration disorder (GPPPD)
definitions and classification, 143
diagnosis and assessment, 144–5
factors contributing to, 146–51
preliminary assessment of, 268–9
prevalence, 146
treatment options, 267–74
genogram
benefits of, 101
cultural, 255
description of, 101, 102
relationship map and, 102, 103, 104
sexual, 101, 102, 233, 240, 248, 255, 265, 289
use of, in treatment of sexual difficulties, 214, 256, 259, 264, 313, 327, 333–4
gestalt psychotherapy, 7, 35
grief
sexual difficulties, and, 195, 301
group marriage, definition, 66
guilt
female sexual functioning, and, 132
sex, about, 4
sexual difficulties, and, 137, 157, 169, 192, 201
treatment of sexual difficulties, and, 236, 288, 306

H

heteronormativity
definition, 57
DSM-5, and, 167
heterosexism
cultural stereotypes, and, 163
definition, 57
media promotion of, 34
myths, based on, 82

questions to explore, 30
sensate focus and, 223
Hite report
orgasm problems, 128
HIV, *see* sexually transmitted diseases, *see also* AIDS; STI's
homonegativity, definition, 57
homophobia
definition, 57
internalised, 58, 123, 182, 249
hostility
emotionally focused coping, as, 276
sexual difficulties, and, 113, 161, 226
treatment of sexual difficulties, and, 273
hypersexuality, *see* sexual compulsivity, addiction, and hypersexuality
hypervigilance
sexual difficulties and, 148, 149, 174, 178
hyperreflection, *see* spectatoring
hypothesising
formulation and, 207, 208
general, 92
relational, 329
sharing of, 319, 340, 341
specific, 92
systemic stance, as, 92
hurried woman syndrome
sexual difficulties, and, 265

I

identity management (coming out), 59
incompatibility of sexual needs, preferences and fantasies *see* sexual preferences
individual sexual growth, *see also* self-focus; self-exploration
description of, 226–7
technique, 17–8
treatment of sexual difficulties, 261, 272, 286, 294, 307,
intercourse
anal, 201
duration of, unrealistic expectations, 170, 283
gendered and socio-culturally valid activity, as, 274
misconceptions and, 80, 87, 109, 119, 128
primacy of, heterosexual, 132, 224
sexual minorities and, 58, 70
spectrum of sex and, 42, 48, 76
intergender, definition, 54
internet
different purposes of, 185, 296
pervasive messages about sex and, 265
sexual difficulties, and, 169, 184, 185, 186, 191
intersex
definition, 52
exclusion of, 56, 67
intimacy
enhancement of, 222, 240, 255, 259, 263, 273, 287, 288, 308, 335
fear of, *see* fear of intimacy, closeness and commitment
genogram and exploring, 102, 105, 256
importance of, female sexual response, 41
lack of, and sexual difficulties, and, 154, 161
meaning of, as a multidimensional phenomenon, 230–1
misconceptions about, 80, 119, 265
negative messages about, 169
poor regulation of needs, 262
social construct as, 27, 82
spectrum of sex and, 43

J

journey therapy
method, 306
jump start desire by bypassing it
treatment of sexual difficulties, 280–1

K
Kegel exercises
  treatment of sexual difficulties, 226, 254, 262, 286, 307
kink, *see* BDSM, *see also* atypical sexual interests; paraphilias; unusual sexual practices; unusual sexual preferences

L
lesbian and gay parenting
  challenges of, 58–9
  myths, about, 59
lesbian couples
  dual minority status, 59
lesbian and gay couples
  similarities with heterosexual, 60–1
  differences from heterosexual, 60–1
LGBTQ communities
  BDCSM and, 60
  definitions, 55, 67
  discrimination of and, 56, 61
  discrimination of, 56
  minority stress and, 61–2
  myths about, 57–8
  therapists' views and, 61
lifelong, *see also* primary, sexual difficulty
  diagnosis and assessment, 93, 126, 151
  distinguishing from secondary / acquired, 108, 116, 117, 154, 167, 171, 177, 182, 197, 234, 254, 257, 268, 275, 282, 291
love
  addiction, 193
  behaviours, 294–5
  enhancing of, sensate focus, 222
  myths about, 80, 81
  reasons for sex and, 267
  unrealistic expectations of. 265
lovemaps
  concept as, 195
loss, *see also* bereavement
  attraction to the partner, of, 276, 281
  desire, of, *see* sexual desire
  erections, of, myths, 87, 244
  female sexual problems and, 42
  romance, of, 262
  sexual difficulties, and, 94, 137, 162, 195, 234, 280, 301, 326

M
male hypoactive sexual desire disorder (MHSDD)
  client vignette, 326–35
  contributing factors, 157–63
  diagnosis & assessment, 152, 154–5
  diagnostic dilemmas, 275–6
  prevalence, 155
  treatment options, 274–82
masochism
  definition, (DSM-IV-TR), 69
  disorder, DSM-5, 70
masturbation
  compulsive, 184, 290
  directed, 250, 262
  frequency, high, 113
  guilt and, 7, 159, 290
  idiosyncratic style, 113
  gender differences and, 153
  myths about, 80, 84, 170, 319
  negative beliefs about, 34, 78, 114, 130, 141, 159
  refraining from, 290
  rigid habitual patterns, 99, 108, 109, 121, 170, 262
  technique, treatment of sexual difficulties, 223, 238, 246, 253, 254, 261–2, 272, 286
masturbatory flexibility
  treatment of DE, 237–8
media
  construction of sexual mythology, 151, 163, 169, 248
  propagation of prototypes of sex, 282
  unrealistic expectations of sex, and, 265
medical conditions
  assessment of, 98, 116, 275

sexual difficulties and, 108, 110, 112, 120, 130, 133, 149, 160, 170, 174, 176, 181, 195–6, 197, 200, 202
medical perspective
assessment and, 107, 234
diagnosis and, 204, 205, 206
formulation and, 207
MOST model and, 35
pathologising and, 95
medical treatment
sexual difficulties, of, 15, 237, 240, 245–6, 253, 261, 272, 279–80, 285–6, 290, 293, 302, 304, 307
medicalisation
asexuality, of, 164
new view of female sexual problems, and 42, 141
sex, of, 16
sexual addictions, of, 296
sexual problems, of, 49, 150
Milan systemic family therapy, xiv, 92
mindfulness
treatment of sexual dysfunctions, and, 236, 238, 250, 259, 262, 271, 276, 288, 290, 293, 301
minority stress
LGBTQ communities, and, 61–2
misconceptions about sex, *see* myths
models of human sexual response
circular, 40, 41
Kaplan, three-stage, 40
Master's & Johnson's, four stage, 37–8
spectrum of sex, 42–77
monogamish relationships, definition, 61
monogamy
stereotyping, 67
boundaries, 67–8
multiple realities, xiii, 31
myths, *see also* misconceptions about sex
anal sex, about, 203
couple's sexual lives, about, 80
deconstruction of, 85, 98, 139
dispelling of, 206, 237, 239, 243, 255, 265, 266, 283, 293, 360
erections, about, 79–80, 119, 244
fantasy model of sex, 34, 169, 237–8
female orgasm, about, 252, 312
gender-related, 81–2, 120, 123, 128, 278, 291
happiness, of, 83–4
honesty, 21
lesbian and gay parenting about, 59
marriage, about, 80–1
normality, of, 84
polyamory, about, 66–7
power, based on (heterosexism and patriarchy), 82, 159
professional sexual, 86–7
romantic relationships about, 87
self-reflexivity and relational reflexivity, and, 87–9, 211
sexual intimacy, masculinity and femininity, 119

N

narrative approach, 8, 31, 95
narrative therapy
attachment narrative therapy, and, 214–7
externalising conversations, and, 231
strengthening agency, and, 7–8
neutrality
gender, 52
systemic stance, as, 92
therapists, sexual minorities, 75
new view of women's sexual problems, 141
nicotine intake, *see* smoking
non-gendered, definition, 54
non-monogamy
myths about, 57
pathologising views on, 61, 67, 192
setting boundaries and, 68
sexual minority, as, 55
variety, of, 68

normalisation
  ageing, of, 160
  asexuality, of, 64
  aversion to sex of, 295
  formulation, and, 207, 209, 316
  interventive questions, 5, 10,
  medical diagnosis, as, 15, 205
  psychoeducation, as, 12, 29, 34, 278
  reasons for sex, of, 266–7
  sexual response, of, 94, 135, 152, 164, 249
  therapy, as, 7, 33
  treatment of sexual disorders, 236, 243, 246, 250, 256, 257, 265, 266, 267, 271, 278, 306
normality
  difficulty defining of, 70
  meanings of, 47, 84–5
  myth of, 84
  theory, paraphilias, 72
  widening the spectrum of, 245, 246
null gender, definition, 54

O

orgasm
  ageing and, 130
  anal, 202
  clitoral, as less desirable, 128, 132
  clitoral stimulation and, 128
  control of, 287
  ejaculation, difference, 107–8
  enhancement of, functioning, 130, 131, 253, 254
  intercourse, in, women, 256
  faking of, men, 109, 240
  faking of, women, 29, 83
  gender differences, 125–6
  human sexual response models, and, 38–9, 40, 41
  lesbian sex, and, 60
  meaning of, as social construction, 256
  myths about, 79, 80, 81, 87, 130, 170, 252
  option, as, spectrum of sex, 48
  pressure to achieve, 132
  vaginal, myth of superiority, 132
  variability of, 113, 126, 127, 128, 132, 249
orgasmic disorders
  classification, 124–5
out-of-control sexual behaviour, *see* sexual health model

P

painful ejaculation, *see* dyspareunia in men; *see also* chronic pelvic pain; painful sex; prostatitis
painful sex, *see* dyspareunia in men, *see also* chronic pelvic pain; painful ejaculation; prostatitis
pangender, definition, 54
pansexual, definition, 54
paraphilias, *see also* BDSM; atypical sexual interests; kink; unusual sexual practices; unusual sexual preferences
  definitions, 68–9
  prevalence, 72–1
  theoretical perspectives, 73
paraphilic disorders
  definitions, 70
  listed in DSM-5, 70
  sexual compulsivity, addictions, or hypersexuality, and, 188, 193
partner's responses
  facilitative, 151, 273
  frustrated / hostile, 151, 247–8, 273
  negative, angry, 122
  solicitous, 151, 273
  unhelpful, motherly / conciliatory, 122
patriarchy
  oppression of, 28, 29, 82
  sensate focus, and, 224
  sexual difficulties, and, 141, 151
  stories about gender roles, and, 159
  values, and men's sexual desire, 282
patterns
  attachment, 214
  circular, anger & withdrawal, 20

competitive, 51
conflictual, 100
cultural, 31
demand/withdrawal, modifying, 172, 281
destructive relational, 122, 273
development of new, 219, 223, 247, 273
family, damaging, 123
genogram exploration of, 102, 105
masturbation, 121, 237, 238, 262, 286
mental, 12, 119, 120, 252, 260
more of the same, 332
out of control behaviour, 183, 186, 196
pain avoidance, 149
pain, female genital, of, 145, 268
pathological interpersonal, 95
positive, 100
power and, 23
repetitive interpersonal, 22, 25, 44, 213, 215, 239, 263
rigid, 82
sexual activity of, 99
symmetrical, 11
that connect, 95
unwanted repetitive, 20, 95, 208, 213
performance
over-emphasising, sexual, 79, 82, 87, 114, 119, 120, 163, 169, 240, 265, 278, 363
performance anxiety, 4
reducing of, in treatment of sexual difficulties, 219, 222, 236, 242, 244, 250, 254, 257, 283, 349, 357
sexual difficulties and, 4, 5, 83, 110, 115, 117, 137, 140, 167, 173, 198
persistent genital arousal disorder (PGAD)
definitions, 134, 173
diagnosis and assessment, 174
factors contributing to, 174–6
prevalence, 174
treatment options, 288–91
physical dimension
factors contributing to sexual difficulties, and, 112, 120, 130, 139, 149, 160, 170, 176, 181, 190, 191, 195, 200, 202, 205
MOST model and, 14–6
questions to explore, 98–9
resources and resiliencies, and, 16
spectrum of sex and, 43, 44, 50
treatment of sexual difficulties, and, 218, 222, 224, 237, 239, 245, 253, 261, 267, 272, 279, 285, 288, 290, 293, 302, 304, 307, 334
pleasure
compersion and, 66
human sexual response and, 40, 41
increasing sexual, 221, 252
inhibition of sexual, 119, 133, 135, 149, 198, 200, 201, 240, 256, 260, 266, 275, 286, 312
lesbian sex and, 60
myths about sexual, 80, 82, 83, 123, 130, 132, 192, 278
orgasm and physical, 107, 124
right to sexual, 187, 298, 299
sexual preferences and, 47, 70, 72–3, 322
social construct, as, 27
polyamory
definitions, 54, 68
diversity and, 58, 291
myths, 66–7
structural forms, 65
therapists' effectiveness, and, 61
polygender, definition, 54
pornography
addiction, 186, 193, 276
client example, 48
compulsive use of, 184, 185, 191
excessive use of, 196, 360
female use of, 188
negotiated use of, 67, 302
relational conflict and, 296

pornography (*continued*)
source of learning about sex, as, 169, 185, 296
supporting sexual mythology, 124, 163, 282
postmodernism
constructivism, and, 94
externalising conversations, and, 231
social constructionism, and, 94
systemic philosophy and, xiii
power
balanced, 60, 71
control and, 161, 171
couples, barriers to sex, 22–3
destructive, 122
gender and, 28, 29, 41, 59
negative, 23
positive, 23
social, difference and, 72, 78, 82, 83, 204, 232
therapist and client, xvi, 211
premature / early ejaculation (PE)
definitions, 164–5
diagnosis and assessment, 166–7
factors contributing to, 167–73
prevalence, 165
treatment options, 282–8
priapism
definition, 109–10, 174
primary, *see* lifelong, sexual difficulty
prostatitis *see* dyspareunia in men, *see also* chronic pelvic pain; painful ejaculation; painful sex
psycho-education *see* education, *see also* bibliotherapy
psychosexual therapy, definition, *see* sex therapy

Q

questions
affirm existing sexuality, 49 (spectrum of sex)
alternative questions, diagnosis, 204
appreciative inquiry, 227–9
assessment, 145, 154, 171, 174, 189–91, 192
attachment narrative therapy, 216
audience, 30
circular, 339
collaborative assessment, 107
co-constructing treatment plan, 335
construct collaborative conversations, 33
contextual, 34
contextual perspective, 10
contextual situation, 30
creating a positive anticipation, 27
deconstructing sexual episodes, 44
deconstructing sociocultural and political influences (externalising conversations), 232
describe 'ideal sexual scenario', 19
describe desired future possibilities, 22
discourage generalisations and challenge assumptions, 10
distinction clarifying, 341
embedded suggestion reflexive, 10
emphasise connectedness of spectrum areas, 50 (spectrum of sex)
encourage agency, 13
encourage making of connections, 13
encourage self-reflexivity, 9, 18
expand meaning of sex, 51 (spectrum of sex)
expectations of therapy, 210
explore communication about sex, 45 (spectrum of sex)
explore sexual fantasy, 45 (spectrum of sex)
explore sexual options, 46–7 (spectrum of sex)
facilitate understanding of sexual preferences, 18–19
hypothetical, 5,6, 321, 322, 323
linear, 337, 338
normative comparison, 10
observer perspective, 21, 26, 50
orienting, 337

prompt exploring of early attachment, 216 (attachment narrative therapy)
reflect on own strengths, 50 (spectrum of sex)
reflect on a relationship, 51 (spectrum of sex)
relationally reflexive, 32–3, 75–6, 89
relative influence (externalising conversations), 231
resources and resiliencies, 209
semi-open, 97–8, 100–1
sexology, assessment, 94, 95, 234
sexual health model, 298–9
support thinking about change and options for future, 50 (spectrum of sex)
systemic exploratory, 269
therapist's self-reflexive, 23, 31–2, 87–8, 90, 211
two rooms, 30
unexpected context change, 13, 26
unique outcomes (externalising conversations), 232
queer, definition, 54

R

reframing
description and examples, 8, 10, 216–7
treatment of sexual difficulties, 236, 252, 272, 311, 315, 319, 320
relational dimension
factors contributing to sexual difficulties, and, 113–4, 122–3, 131, 141, 149–51, 161–2, 171–2, 176, 182, 196, 200–1
MOST model, and, 19–25
questions to explore, 100
resources and resiliencies, 25–7
spectrum of sex, and, 48–9
treatment of sexual difficulties, and, 227–31, 239–40, 247–8, 254–5, 262–5, 273–4, 281, 287–8, 290–1, 294–5, 303, 307–8, 320, 329
relational reflexivity
BDSM, and, 75–6
definitions, 32
sexual desire and, 164
questions, 32–3, 50, 88–9
treatment of sexual difficulties, 296, 314
relaxation
technique, in treatment of sexual difficulties, 236, 238, 250, 262, 271, 276, 293, 294, 306, 307, 345, 369
religious beliefs
discrepancy of, 247
exploring of, 105–6, 282, 254, 255, 265, 266, 274, 282, 288, 295
negative, about sex, and sexual problems, 34, 72, 114, 121, 141, 248, 308
orthodox, 151, 182, 201
restrictive, 123, 159, 170, 192, 265, 334, 351, 355
rigid, 172–3
resentment
barrier to sex, as, 4, 48
emotionally focused coping, as, 276
sexual difficulties, and, 83, 94, 122, 123, 137, 149, 171, 249, 306
resources and resiliencies
attachment narrative therapy and, 215
client vignette, map of, 317
couple examples, 47, 51
couple, map of, 358
formulation, and, 208, 209, 329
utilisation of clients', 343

S

sadism
client example, 47
definition, (DSM-IV-TR), 69
disorder, sexual, 70 (DSM-5)
myths about, 74
sensate focus and, 224
stigma and, 7, 62–3

secondary, *see* acquired, sexual difficulty
self-concept, *see* sexual self-schema
self-esteem,
  building on, 99, 242, 250, 271, 283, 301, 306, 347
  low, and sexual difficulties, 4, 117, 119, 120, 137, 183, 193, 195, 198, 200, 240, 260, 347
  reason for sex, boost of, 267
self-exploration, *see* individual sexual growth, *see also* self-focus
self-focus, *see* individual sexual growth, *see also* self-exploration
self-reflexivity
  BDSM, and, 73, 74
  definitions, 11, 31, 32, 93
  formulation, and, 211
  MOST model and, 35
  treatment of sexual difficulties, 296
  questions to facilitate, 10, 23, 31–32, 46–7, 50, 87–8
  sexual compulsivity, addictions, or hypersexuality, and, 296
  sexual desire, and, 164
  sexual minorities, and, 55
  spectrum of sex, and, 76
sensate focus
  additional benefits, 222–3
  applicability, 212–3
  client vignette, 332, 348–53
  contraindications, 281
  difficulties with, 225–6
  opposing views on, 224
  purposes of, 221–222
  steps of, 219–21
  taking feedback from, 225
  treatment of sexual difficulties, 239, 240, 248, 255, 262–3, 273, 274, 281, 295, 329
  variations in, 223–4
sex
  biological dimorphism, as binary categorisation, 56
  definition, as a biological category, 52–3
  obligation, as, 262
  reasons for, 267
sex therapy, definition, xiii-xiv, *see also* psychosexual therapy
sexology
  definition of term, xiv, 2
  compared to systemic social constructionist therapy, 1–2
sexual anorexia, *see* sexual aversion disorder
  SAD, and, 178–9
sexual addiction, *see* sexual compulsivity, addiction, or hypersexuality
sexual arousal
  gender differences, 134
  factors that enhance, female, 142–3
sexual aversion disorder (SAD) *see also* sexual anorexia
  definitions, 176
  diagnosis and assessment, 177–9
  factors contributing to, 179–83
  prevalence, 179
  sexual desire and, 152
  treatment options, 291–5
sexual bill of rights
  technique, 245
  treatment of sexual difficulties, 288
sexual compulsivity, addiction, or hypersexuality, *see also* sexual addiction hypersexuality
  definitions, 183–8
  diagnosis and assessment, 188–93
  factors that contribute to, 193–6
  theoretical perspectives, 189
  treatment options, 295–304
sexual confidence
  client vignette, 312, 316, 324
sexual desire
  discrepancy, 122–3, 131, 275–6
  disorders, classification, 152
  for what? 161, 278
  gender differences, 152–4

lack of, client example, 263
male, enhancing factors, 155–6
self-reflexivity and relational reflexivity, 164
what is normal, 163–4
sexual diversity
asexuality and, 63, 64
BDSM, and, 299
definitions, xv, 67
female orgasmic, 323
MOST model, and, 3, 31
non-monogamies, 68
paraphilias, and, 70, 72
sexual genogram and, 102
sexual fluidity
concept, 56
sexual genogram
application, 101–6
client vignettes, 314, 327, 333–4
treatment option, as, 233; 240, 248, 256, 259, 264, 265, 288
sexual health model
assessing and treating out of control sexual behaviour, 187–8
treatment of out of control sexual behaviour, 298–9
sexual identity
asexuality, and, 65
label, as, 56, 58
meaning of, 78
transgender people, and, 62
sexual knowledge
evolution of, 86
increasing of, in treatment of sexual difficulties, 226, 238, 299, 314, 324
limited, and sexual difficulties, 114, 130, 159
relevance of, for clients, 9, 98
relevance of, for therapists, 55, 75
sexology, and, 91, 92, 186, 206
social constructionism, and, 205
sexually transmitted diseases
consequence as, sexual 'addiction', 190
contributing factor to sexual difficulties, as, 160, 200
fear of (HIV/AIDS), 187
lower incidence of, lesbians, 61
myths about, and bisexuals, 62
myths about, and polyamory, 67
plan to avoid, 187
protection from, 348
preoccupation with, 178
sexual genogram and exploring of, 105
sexual problems classification, and, 42
sexual minorities
client vignette, 351
clinical implications, and, 57–60
definition, 55
discrimination of, 56, 62, 65
therapists' stance, and, 74
sexual orientation
asexuality, and, 63, 64, 164
biases, and, 57
bisexuality, and, 62, 345
concept, as, 56
confusion about, and sexual difficulties, 119
continuum, as, 52
homosexual, judgmental attitudes, 183
questioning, 54
sexual diversity, and, 67
sexual genogram, and, 102
transgender, and, 56
unconscious / undeclared, 182, 249
sexual preferences
checking clients', 58
concept, xv, 67
condemnation, of, 123
discrepancy of, 149, 178, 182
heteronormativity in DSM-5, and, 167
incompatibility of, 27, 99, 121, 123, 140, 141, 200
openness about, 121–2
questions to facilitate understanding and expression of, 18–9, 44, 45, 46–7, 48
sensate focus, and, 221, 223

sexual preferences (*continued*)
unusual, example, 113
unusual, repressed, 68
sexual response
adaptive /protective inhibition of, 96, 127, 160
anxiety about, lowering, 257, 259
awareness of one's own, 246
education about, in treatment of sexual difficulties, 261, 262, 280–1, 312
exploration of, relational, 171
female, 17, 40, 41, 134, 135, 140, 249
gender differences in, 134, 157
human, models, 37–8, 38–9, 40, 86, 124
inhibited, and relational conflict, 141
myths about, 256
pathologisation of, 256, 260
subjective experience of, 126
synchronised / co-ordinated between partners, 131, 255
therapist's endorsement of, 74
undesired, normalisation of, 15, 94, 265
variations in, 244
sexual self-schema, *see also* self-concept
concept of, 9
negative, and sexual difficulties, 120, 195, 200, 279, 363
questions about, 13
strengthening of, 279
sexual technique
adjustment of / improvement of, 131, 246, 294
exploring of, 17, 44–5, 99, 200, 322
inadequacy of, 149
incompatibility of partners', 131
myths about, 80
sexual stimulus
inadequate, 140, 181
sex workers
obsession with, client vignettes, 344–8
shame, 4
cultural, about sex, 31, 33, 78, 137, 141, 151, 201, 282
exploring of, 97, 105
fantasy, sexual, and, 192
female sexual functioning and, 83, 132
men's emotions, and, 59
sexual difficulties, and, 4, 5, 7, 114, 123, 132, 137, 157, 159, 169, 172, 173, 174, 195, 198, 249, 260, 301, 349, 361–3
sexual preferences, about, 47, 113
therapeutic sensitivity to; exploring of, in treatment, 236, 248, 283, 288, 291, 293, 302, 306, 333
transgender people, and, 62
simmering
technique, 247
treatment of sexual difficulties, 280, 281
situational sexual difficulty
definition, 93
questions to explore, 95
distinguishing from generalised, and, 114–5, 116, 127, 132, 134, 135, 140, 144, 154, 167, 177, 197
treatment of, 282–4, 328
skoliosexual, definition, 55
smoking, *see also* nicotine intake
reduction of, 237, 261, 286, 364
sexual difficulties, and, 98, 121, 261, 253
social constructionism
appreciative inquiry and, 25
asexuality and, 63, 64
CMM and, 20, 95
culture and, 27–8, 31, 131, 256
diagnoses and, xvi, 1, 91, 94, 204, 205, 207
discourse and, 27–8
externalising conversations and, 231
formulation and, 207, 208, 209, 211
gender and, 28, 51, 52, 53, 54, 56, 82, 163
intimacy and, 230

narrative approach and, 8
paraphilias and, 72
power and, 28
practice framework as, 2, 27, 35
premise, realities, xiii
sexual response models and, 39, 41, 42
therapeutic relationship and, 11, 107
solution focused therapy, 7, 216
spectatoring, *see also* hyperreflection
definition, 140
sexual difficulties, and, 242, 363
treatment of sexual difficulties, and, 224, 321
spectrum of sex, *see also* models of human sexual response, 42–77
STI's, *see* sexually transmitted diseases, *see also* AIDS, HIV
stop-start technique
treatment of PE, 286–7, 349
stress, *see also* distress
managing of, in treatment of sexual difficulties, 176, 230, 234, 239, 243, 247–8, 257, 262, 265, 271, 276, 279, 283, 288, 290, 291, 297, 302, 303, 306, 308, 315
minority, *see* minority stress
reduction, as reason for sex, 267
sexual difficulties, and, 4, 51, 61, 93, 94, 96, 108, 110, 112, 114, 117, 119, 123, 124, 126, 135, 136, 137, 140, 141, 143, 144, 145, 150, 152, 154, 155, 157, 159, 162, 165, 166, 167, 171, 173, 174, 177, 181, 183, 184, 185, 188, 191, 195, 197, 198, 201, 205, 213, 267, 294, 295–6, 301, 311, 312, 329, 332
structural family therapy
and enactment, 20
suicide
lack of sexual education, and, 12
sexual minorities, and, 62
supervision
importance of, xiii, 74, 164, 226
questions to guide self-reflexivity in, 87–8
relationship map, use of in, 103, 104
session, transcript, 336–42
systemic approach
definition, 1
compared to sexology, 1–2
in attachment narrative therapy, 214
systemic mind, xvi, 91

T

taking ownership
couple technique, 229
therapeutic relationship
agent of change, as, 21, 75, 288
attachment narrative therapy, and, 214
challenge to, 240
collaborative, 233, 318
empathic listening, and, 268, 276
empowering, 301
healing, as, 250
qualities of, 236
reassuring and encouraging, 306
safety and trust, 242, 291
systemic, xvi, 205, 236
warm and supportive, 301
therapeutic stories co-constructed
diagnosis, and, 206
MOST model diagram, and, 3
transgender people
definition, 55
sexual orientation, and, 56, 58, 64
social ostracism, 62
therapeutic work with, 63
transitioning, definition, 55
transparency
sexual health principle, as, 187, 298
therapeutic, 11, 107, 209, 239, 352
transsexual, definition, 55
transvestite, definition, 55
traumatic experiences, *see also* child sexual abuse
dealing with, in treatment of sexual difficulties, 234, 252, 297, 301, 308

traumatic experiences (*continued*)
lovemaps, and, 195
sexual abuse, and, 160
sexual, and sexual difficulties, 181, 190, 191, 195, 295

U

unique outcomes
exploring, 232, 279
treatment of sexual difficulties, identifying of, 279, 336
unusual sexual practices, *see* BDSM, *see also* atypical sexual interests; kink; paraphilias; unusual sexual preferences
utilisation
client examples, 13–4, 27, 315, 361
definition, 13
formulation and, 210
using shared journaling
couple technique, 230

V

vaginismus
body-protective, as. 149
client examples, 145-6
cultural oppression, and, 34, 151
diagnosis, 205
distorted concept about own genitals, and, 148
definitions (DSM-IV-TR), 144, 145
factor in sexual aversion, as, 181
prevalence, 146
treatment of, 18, 223
vaginal phobia, as, 148
vestibulodynia, *see also* vulvodynia, 143
violence
asexuals and, 65
emotional, 333
exploration of, sexual (genogram), 102, 105
inhibited sexual interest and, 182
marital, 28
power of, 23
sexual health and, 187
transgender people towards, 62
voyeurism, definition, (DSM-IV-TR), 69
vulvodynia, *see* vestibulodynia

W

wax and wane
technique, 223, 246, 364
What Doctors Don't Tell You, 15
'words create worlds', 26
worry
myths and, 79, 84
exploring of / reducing, treatment of sexual difficulties, 221, 222, 236, 242, 243, 246, 262, 274, 279, 281, 282, 299, 306, 308, 315, 318, 321, 322, 328, 331, 334
sexual difficulties, and, 4, 94, 97, 1119, 148, 150, 172, 195, 198, 265, 362

CPSIA information can be obtained
at www.ICGtesting.com
Printed in the USA
BVOW06s0216210917
495500BV00011B/140/P